# Dix on
# Contracts of
# Employment

# Dix on Contracts of Employment

## Fifth Edition

## D. W. Crump
*LL.B., LL.M., Solicitor*

London
Butterworths
1976

| England | **Butterworth & Co (Publishers) Ltd** |
| London | 88 Kingsway WC2B 6AB |

| Australia | **Butterworths Pty Ltd** |
| Sydney | 586 Pacific Highway, Chatswood, NSW 2067 |
| | Also at Melbourne, Brisbane, Adelaide and Perth |

| Canada | **Butterworth & Co (Canada) Ltd** |
| Toronto | 2265 Midland Avenue, Scarborough M1P 4S1 |

| New Zealand | **Butterworths of New Zealand Ltd** |
| Wellington | 26/28 Waring Taylor Street, 1 |

| South Africa | **Butterworth & Co (South Africa) (Pty) Ltd** |
| Durban | 152/154 Gale Street |

| USA | **Butterworth & Co (Publishers) Inc** |
| Boston | 19 Cummings Park, Woburn, Mass 01801 |

| | | | | | | |
|---|---|---|---|---|---|---|
| *First Published* | .. | .. | .. | .. | .. | *November 1963* |
| *Second Impression* | | .. | .. | .. | .. | *March 1964* |
| *Third Impression* | .. | .. | .. | .. | .. | *June 1964* |
| *Second Edition* | .. | .. | .. | .. | .. | *January 1966* |
| *Second Impression* | | .. | .. | .. | .. | *October 1966* |
| *Third Edition* | .. | .. | .. | .. | .. | *September 1968* |
| *Fourth Edition* | .. | .. | .. | .. | .. | *September 1972* |
| *Fifth Edition* | .. | .. | .. | .. | .. | *November 1976* |

© Butterworth & Co (Publishers) Ltd 1976

ISBN 0 406 17803 8

# PREFACE

In its fifth edition Dix has undergone a major change in presentation. Employment law has continued to be the subject of rapid and far reaching statutory intervention and the continued piecemeal approach adopted by the legislature has meant that a volume dependent upon annotated statute could be no longer a ready source of reference. Practically the whole of the text has been rewritten so that contracts of employment are approached chronologically from formation to determination and beyond, bringing together the common law and relevant statutory provisions. As in the past the work does not purport to be exhaustive in its coverage of contracts of employment as a whole, or even of particular statutes, but I hope that it continues to provide in an accessible form the law applicable in the majority of situations encountered in practice. The opportunity has also been taken to expand the model forms and check lists in the Appendices.

A glance at the following pages will show that labour law is far too complex to serve its purpose effectively, and Parliament which has produced these complications should now exert its energies towards its simplification. Unfortunately little inclination has been shown in this direction. The Remuneration Grants and Charges Act 1975 (see p. 47, below) has been continued in operation until 31st July 1977 and the White Paper *The Attack On Inflation The Second Year* has been added to Cmnd. 6151 for the purposes of that Act. The present Race Relations Bill (discussed in Appendix 11) if enacted will alter the law affecting racial discrimination in an employment context and Chapter VI of the White Paper on Patent Law Reform (Cmnd. 6000) envisages changes relating to ownership of inventions made by employees.

A large number of decisions relating to the statutes covered are mentioned and the creation of the Employment Appeal Tribunal has resulted in yet another source of authority in the field. The new Tribunal regards itself as bound by decisions of the Court of Appeal and House of Lords on matters of Law of England, and by the Court of Session Inner House and House of Lords on matters of the Law of Scotland. The pronouncements of the National Industrial Relations Court, the High Court in England and the Court of Session Outer House in Scotland are considered by it as of great persuasive authority only. Industrial tribunals are bound by

the decisions of appellate bodies and regard their own pronouncements as being persuasive. However there is a danger in being too
legalistic and technical in approaching precedents. They may be of
great significance in matters of statutory interpretation, but in
areas in which of their nature factual situations are likely to vary
greatly, their value is limited. When questions of reasonableness
and justice and equity fall to be considered each case is looked at
on its own merits and they alone determine the outcome. In
such circumstances whenever examples are given in the text they
sould be treated as such and no more. Detailed analysis of these
cases is more likely to do harm than good.

The law is stated on the basis of all sources available to me on
1st August 1976. Those parts of the Employment Protection Act
1975 of particular revelance to individual employment relationships which are not in force on that date and for which a
commencement date has not yet been specified (in general those
relating to time off work, guarantee payments and the qualification
of part-time employees for certain statutory rights), are discussed,
as are those which are not in force but for which the date of
operation has been set.

The pressures of practice and of time have left me unable to
take advantage of several kind offers to read parts of the text to
assist in eliminating gremlins and I will be particularly pleased to
receive comment and criticism. The Publishers have provided case
references and tables and have produced the book notwithstanding
an indolent editor constantly in a rush. My wife has typed,
retyped and typed again. To her the greatest thanks are due, both
for hard work and never-ending patience.

*August 1976*                                                    D. W. C.
5 Newton Square
Great Barr
Birmingham B43 6DY

# CONTENTS

## Contents

# Contents

# Contents

# TABLE OF STATUTES

References in this Table to *"Statutes"* are to Halsbury's Statutes of England (Third Edition) showing the volume and page at which the annotated text of the Act will be found.

# Table of Statutes

## Table of Statutes

# Table of Statutes

# TABLE OF CASES

**In the following Table references are given to the English and Empire Digest where a digest of the case will be found**

# Table of Cases

# Table of Cases

# Table of Cases

# Table of Cases

xxvi

# Table of Cases

# Chapter 1

# DEFINITION AND FORMATION OF CONTRACTS OF EMPLOYMENT

## EMPLOYMENT RELATIONSHIPS

### Introduction

At common law the relationship between employer and employee is one of contract, but today statute places numerous restrictions on the freedom of the parties to negotiate terms of employment and grants to employees' rights of a non-contractual nature. The employer and employee are bound by contract, but Parliament has created new incidents which arise from the relationship or even before it comes into existence, and can continue after its determination. Recent legislative developments do not in any sense govern the whole contract of employment, but superimpose new provisions on the existing law. These developments are so far-reaching and are of such importance that, although knowledge of the common law and early statutory regulation is still an essential requirement for understanding their effects, the statutory provisions themselves are tending to distort the contractual basis of the relationship between employer and employee upon which they are founded.

### The contract

The formation of the contract of employment depends on the general law of contract with regard to offer and acceptance. Either or both of these may be by words, or conduct, and the rule that the response to the offer must be an absolute and unqualified acceptance of it for a contract to come into existence, may give rise to difficulties.

> "Questions of this sort are constantly arising. Where a contract is to be made out by an offer on one side and an acceptance on the other, if the answer is equivocal or anything is left to be done, the two do not constitute a binding contract."[1]

[1] Per GROVE, J., in *Appleby* v. *Johnson* (1874), L.R. 9 C.P. 158, at p. 163.

I

It is not necessary, although it is usually wise, to set out every term of the contract.[1] Frequently, as with other agreements, the relationship comes into being informally, when few terms are expressed, perhaps only those relating to salary and hours of work. In such cases the courts may imply those terms as are reasonably necessary to give effect to the contract. The rule was expressed by Lord ESHER, M.R., as follows:[2]

> "... A large number of cases have been cited, in some of which the Court implied a stipulation, and in others refused to do so. In my opinion, it is useless to cite such cases, so far as they merely show that in the particular case an implication was or was not made. The only use of citing such cases is where they lay down the rules as to such implications, upon which the Court will act in dealing with the particular case before it. I have for a long time understood that rule to be that the Court has no right to imply in a written contract any such stipulation, unless, on considering the terms of the contract in a reasonable and business manner, an implication necessarily arises that the parties must have intended that the suggested stipulation should exist. It is not enough to say that it would be a reasonable thing to make such an implication. It must be a necessary implication in the sense that I have mentioned."

[1] But see the requirements of Contracts of Employment Act 1972, s.4; Chapter 3, below.
[2] In *Hamlyn & Co.* v. *Wood & Co.*, [1891] 2 Q.B. 488, at p. 491, C.A.

Unless the contract of employment is under seal it must be supported by consideration, i.e., there must be obligations which bind both parties. The normal case will be the payment of remuneration by the employer and the provision of his labour or other services by the employee. Whether the consideration is adequate or not is immaterial provided that the *quid pro quo* exists.

## Contracts of service

Not every contract to provide service creates the relationship of employer and employee. This only arises where the contract is a "contract of service", and not when it is a "contract for services". The distinction is a fine one and may be difficult to apply in borderline cases. It is necessary to differentiate between the two both at common law and in applying numerous statutory provisions.

Whether or not the correct test has been applied is a matter of law but the test itself is a question of fact.[1]

Traditionally, the existence of a contract of service was dependent in part on the amount of control exercised by the employer,[2] but the test of control is not an absolute one.[3]

> "The nature of the control which is required in order to bring the employment within the scope of a contract of service flows almost infinitely with the general nature of the duties involved. If, therefore, for example, one finds that the contract, whether a written contract or an oral contract, has laid down in considerable detail what the duties are which are to be performed, and that the employer has the right to dispense with the services of the employee if not satisfied with the manner in which he carries out that duty, the actual absence of any expressed provision as to the right of the employer to control the manner of carrying out the work may be of much less importance than it would be in other cases."[4]

[1] *Global Plant, Ltd.* v. *Secretary of State for Health and Social Security*, [1972] 1 Q.B. 139; [1971] 3 All E.R. 385.

[2] *Simmons* v. *Heath Laundry Co.*, [1910] 1 K.B. 543, C.A.; *Amalgamated Engineering Union* v. *Minister of Pensions and National Insurance*, [1963] 1 All E.R. 864; [1963] 1 W.L.R. 441; *Morren* v. *Swinton and Pendlebury Borough Council*, [1965] 2 All E.R. 349; [1965] 1 W.L.R. 576: *Ready Mixed Concrete (South East), Ltd.* v. *Minister of Pensions and National Insurance*, [1968] 2 Q.B. 497; [1968] 1 All E.R. 433.

[3] *Global Plant, Ltd.* v. *Secretary of State for Health and Social Security*, [1972] 1 Q.B. 139; [1971] 3 All E.R. 385.

[4] Per MEGAW, J., *Amalgamated Engineering Union* v. *Minister of Pensions and National Insurance*, [1963] 1 All E.R. 864, at p. 871; [1963] 1 W.L.R. 441, at p. 453.

In *Stevenson Jordan and Harrison, Ltd.* v. *Macdonald and Evans*[1], DENNING, L. J. (as he then was), pointed out that the test usually applied is whether the employer has the right to control the manner of doing the work, but that in *Cassidy* v. *Ministry of Health*[2] SOMERVELL, L. J., said that this test is not universally correct, and there are many contracts of service where the employer cannot control the manner of doing the work. The passage from the judgment of DENNING, L. J., is as follows:

> "... This case ... raises the troublesome question of the distinction between a contract of service and a contract for services.

The test usually applied is whether the employer has the right to control the manner of doing the work.... In *Cassidy* v. *Ministry of Health*, SOMERVELL, L.J., pointed out that that test is not universally correct. There are many contracts of service where the master cannot control the manner in which the work is to be done, as in the case of a captain of a ship. SOMERVELL, L.J., went on to say: 'One perhaps cannot get much beyond this: "Was the contract a contract of service within the meaning which an ordinary person would give under the words?"' I respectfully agree. As my Lord has said, it is almost impossible to give a precise definition of the distinction. It is often easy to recognise a contract of service when you see it, but difficult to say wherein the difference lies. A ship's master, a chauffeur, and a reporter on the staff of a newspaper are all employed under a contract of service; but a ship's pilot, a taxi-man, and a newspaper contributor are employed under a contract for services. One feature which seems to run through the instances is that, under a contract of service, a man is employed as part of the business, and his work is done as an integral part of the business. Whereas, under a contract for services, his work, although done for the business, is not integrated into it but is only accessory to it."

[1] [1952] 1 T.L.R. 101, at 111.
[2] [1951] 2 K.B. 343; [1951] 1 All E.R. 574.

*Whittaker* v. *Minister of Pensions and National Insurance*[1] concerned a trapeze artist engaged by a circus, but in addition to performing her act she agreed to help in moving the circus from place to place and to perform the duties of an usherette. MOCATTA, J., held that the contract was one of service, having regard to the hybrid character of the duties required. With regard to the test of control MOCATTA, J., said: "It seems clear, therefore, from the more recent cases that persons possessed of a high degree of professional skill and expertise, such as surgeons and civil engineers, may nevertheless be employed as servants under contracts of service, notwithstanding that their employers can, in the nature of things, exercise extremely little, if any, control over the way in which the skill is used. The test of control is, therefore, not as determinative as used to be thought to be the case, though no doubt it is still of value in that the greater the degree of control exercisable by the employer, the more likely it is that the contract is one of service."

[1] [1967] 1 Q.B. 156; [1966] 3 All E.R. 531 distinguishing *Gould* v. *Minister of National Insurance*, [1951] 1 K.B. 731; [1951] 1 All E.R. 368. See also *Zuijs* v. *Wirth Brothers Proprietary Ltd.* (1955), 93 C.L.R. 561. For a recent summary of the law see per MacKENNA, J., in *Ready Mixed Concrete (South East) Ltd.* v. *Minister of Pensions and National Insurance*, [1968] 1 All E.R. 433; [1968] 2 W.L.R. 775 which was followed in *Ferguson* v. *Dawson & Partners (Contractors), Ltd.*, [1976] 1 Lloyds Rep. 143, Crn. Ct., upheld, (1976) *Times*, 23rd July, C.A.

In the *Ready Mixed Concrete*[1] case MACKENNA, J., said:

"A contract of service exists if the following three conditions are fulfilled: (i) The servant agrees that in consideration of a wage or other remuneration he will provide his own work and skill in the performance of some service for his master. (ii) He agrees, expressly or impliedly, that in the performance of that service he will be subject to the other's control in a sufficient degree to make that other master. (iii) The other provisions of the contract are consistent with its being a contract of service."

In applying the judge's third condition matters other than control are taken into account. The terms of the contract and surrounding circumstances are looked at to see whether factors which categorise it as either one of service, or for services, are present. There is no exhaustive list of these characteristics,[2] but items such as the provision of large capital assets, the right to delegate the work, methods of payment, the form of contractual documents and many others have been considered. It is only when all these have been examined that a decision can be reached.

[1] *Ready Mixed Concrete (South East), Ltd.* v. *Minister of Pensions and National Insurance*, [1968] 1 All E.R. 433, at p. 439.
[2] *Construction Industry Training Board* v. *Labour Force, Ltd.*, [1970] 3 All E.R. 220.

Since the Second World War the distinction between contracts of service and contracts for service has assumed an increased significance for the purposes of social and fiscal legislation, as is evidenced by several of the above decisions. Various economic factors have led, particularly in the building industry, to the employment of gang labour.[1] In such cases often the men have a contract of service with the gang leader, and a contract for services exists between the gang leader and the contractor who is responsible for erecting the building. Thus the contractor has no contract of service with the men working on the site. The employment of self-employed labourers is distinct from the employment of gang labourers who do in fact have a contract of employment with someone, i.e. the gang leader.[2] The Industrial Court (a predecessor of the Central Arbitration Committee),[3] has held that a contract whereby roofing and tiling contractors paid an agreed amount for every completed 100 square feet to men who were employed at piece-work rates, remuneration being paid to one man in a group of two or three tilers who in turn shared it out, amounted to a contract of service.

In *Re C. W. and A. L. Hughes Ltd.*,[4] the legal position of a "labour only" contract was considered in relation to the question of priority under section 319 (4) of the Companies Act 1948, in a voluntary winding up, and the relationship was held not to be one of master and servant, i.e. not to amount to a contract of service.

An employee may be under a contract of service with his original employer while the use and benefit of his services are transferred to a temporary employer.[5]

[1] See *Construction Industry Training Board* v. *Labour Force, Ltd.*, [1970] 3 All E.R. 220.

[2] See *Guest* v. *Construction Industry Training Board* (1966), 1 I.T.R. 354.

[3] *Re W. Creighton & Co., Ltd.* (1966), Decision of the Industrial Court No. 3107.

[4] [1966] 2 All E.R. 702; [1966] 1 W.L.R. 1369.

[5] *Denham* v. *Midland Employers' Mutual Assurance, Ltd.*, [1955] 2 Q.B. 437, C.A.; [1955] 2 All E.R. 561.

## Form of contracts of employment

Apart from the provisions of the Contracts of Employment Act 1972 (which provides that a written statement is to be given to the employee specifying certain particulars of the contract of employment), there are no formal requirements for a contract of service and it may even be inferred from conduct.

Since the Corporate Bodies Contracts Act 1960, corporate bodies (not being companies within the meaning of the Companies Act 1948) need not contract under seal and may enter into contracts with no more formality than is required in the case of an individual. Section 1 of the Corporate Bodies Contracts Act overrules the decision in *A.R. Wright & Son, Ltd.* v. *Romford Borough Council.*[1] By the Companies Act 1948, section 32, the position of companies is approximated to that of individuals.

[1] [1957] 1 Q.B. 431; [1956] 3 All E.R. 785.

Certain contracts of employment, by virtue of specific Acts of Parliament, must be in writing. These include the following categories:

(1) *Apprentices*

A contract of apprenticeship need not be by deed although it frequently is. It must be in writing,[1] and an oral contract of apprenticeship is not enforceable.[2]

[1] Apprentices Act 1814, s. 2; *McDonald* v. *John Twiname, Ltd.*, [1953] 2 Q.B. 304, at p. 313; [1953] 2 All E.R. 589, at p. 592, C.A.
[2] *Kirkby* v. *Taylor*, [1910] 1 K.B. 529.

(2) *Seamen on sea fishing boats*

The form of agreement for seamen is governed by the Merchant Shipping Act 1970, section 95 and Schedule 2.[1]

[1] See also the Merchant Shipping (Crew Agreement, Lists of Crews and Discharge of Seamen) (Fishing Vessels) Regulations 1972, S.I. 1972 No. 919.

(3) *Crews of merchant ships*

By the Merchant Shipping Act 1970, sections 1 and 2, agreements with the crew of a merchant ship are required to be in writing.[1]

[1] See also the Merchant Shipping (Crew Agreements, Lists of Crews and Discharge of Seamen) Regulations 1972, S.I. 1972 No. 918.

(4) *Contracts between drivers of hackney carriages and the proprietors of the carriages*

Under the London Hackney Carriage Act 1843, section 23, claims against drivers or conductors of hackney carriages relating to earnings cannot be enforced unless they are in writing.

(5) *Specified stoppages and deductions under the Truck Acts* 1831–1940[1]

Certain contracts of employment are governed by the Truck Acts.[2] The object of the Acts is to ensure that the employees to whom the Acts apply receive the full amount of their wages without deductions other than the permitted ones. Where the articles, money, or services are permissible deductions, the employee must sign a written agreement covering the stoppage or deduction.[3]

[1] "Truck" *cf.* French "*troquer*" = to barter or exchange.
[2] For the modification of the Truck Acts and other legislation requiring

wages to be paid by cash, see Payment of Wages Act 1960, which allows payment by cheque.

[3] Truck Act 1831, s. 23; *Pillar* v. *Llynvi Coal and Iron Co., Ltd.* (1869), L.R. 4 C.P. 752; *cf. Lamb* v. *Great Northern Rail. Co.,* [1891] 2 Q.B. 281. For requisites as to contract or notice see Truck Act 1896, ss. 1, 2 and 3.

In *Williams* v. *Butlers, Ltd.*[1] an employee authorised his employers to deduct his union subscriptions due to the Transport and General Workers Union. After a time by written notice he requested the employers to stop doing this. They continued to deduct the contributions saying that they would carry on doing so until they received a notice to stop, through the union. The Divisional Court held that there was no breach of section 3 of the Truck Act 1831, since the employee had agreed that the procedure for withdrawal required receipt of a notice through the trade union. The magistrate had found that the agreement to deduct between the union and the employer formed part of the contract between the employer and the employee and so was not severable, or separate from the employment contract. The "clock-off agreement" was not itself void under section 2 of the Truck Act.

[1] [1975] 2 All E.R. 889; [1975] 1 W.L.R. 946.

The Truck Act, 1940, section 1 (2) provides as follows:

"For the removal of doubt it is hereby declared that in determining for any purpose other than the purpose of the Truck Acts, 1831 to 1896, whether a person is or was before the commencement of this Act employed under a contract of service, the person shall not be deemed not to be or not to have been so employed by reason only of the contract being or having been illegal, null, or void under the said Acts."

The phrase "in determining for any purpose other than" covers the purposes of employment legislation, and therefore the mere fact that a contract of service may be void under the Truck Acts, does not make it void for the purposes of the statutes considered in this volume.

**Stamp duty**

There is no longer any requirement for the payment of stamp duty on contracts of employment, whether under hand or under seal. Section 23 of the Finance Act 1964, provides as follows:

"(1) No stamp duty shall be chargeable on, or on any memorandum of, a contract of service in any office or employment or a contract varying or terminating such a contract.

(2) This section shall have effect as from 6th July, 1964, and if before the passing of this Act any duty has been paid which by virtue of this section is not chargeable, the Commissioners shall, on application made to them within two years after the date of the payment, cancel the relevant stamps and repay this duty.

(3) This section shall be construed as one with the Stamp Act, 1891."

## PARTIES TO THE CONTRACT

In general at common law any individual who was *sui juris* could enter into an employment contract and the limitations as to the bargains struck by the parties were small. Recent developments have meant that in addition to imposing significant limitations on the freedom of the employer and the employee as to the terms of the contract, factors as to the personality of the contracting parties have also been the subject of Parliamentary intervention. A prospective employer has to consider in addition to the abilities and other attributes of the candidate for employment, legislation relating to sex, race and disability. The importance of such matters arises not only when the contract has been entered into, but beforehand. Those situations most frequently encountered where personal factors are of legal effect are set out below but others beyond the scope of this work, for instance the operation of a closed shop, may be of overriding significance.

### Minors

Minors[1] (i.e., people under 18 years) are protected by the law of contract against disadvantageous bargains.[2] This aspect of the law in its detailed exposition belongs more properly to the law of contract as a whole, and reference should be made to works on that subject. In certain circumstances the question may have to be considered in relation to a minor employer or a minor employee. Broadly speaking, the position is that a contract to serve, or a contract to be bound as an apprentice, is voidable at the option of the minor if the contract as a whole is not for the minor's benefit. In *Clements* v. *London and North Western Rail. Co.*, KAY, L.J., said[3]:

"...It has been clearly held that contracts of apprenticeship and with regard to labour are not contracts to an action on which the plea of infancy is a complete defence, and the question has always been, both at law and in equity, whether the contract, when carefully examined in all its terms, is for the benefit of the infant. If it is so, the Court before which the question comes will not allow the infant to repudiate it. I will take only one or two of the cases that illustrate this. In *R.* v. *Hindringham (Inhabitants)*,[4] LORD KENYON said: 'I desire it may not be taken for granted that an infant who binds himself apprentice, a contract so notoriously for his own benefit, may put an end to that contract at any time during his minority.' He did not decide the question, but he clearly expressed his opinion that an infant was not able to put an end to a contract that was for his benefit. I will only take one more of the cases, that of *Leslie* v. *Fitzpatrick*.[5] There an apprenticeship agreement was pronounced to be not necessarily unfair because of certain unilateral provisions which made against the infant. That was the case of an apprenticeship deed, giving the master power to terminate the agreement in certain events; and LUSH, J., in giving the judgment of the Court, said: 'If such a provision were at the time common to labour contracts, or were in the then condition of trade such as the master was reasonably justified in imposing as a just measure of protection to himself, and if the wages were a fair compensation for the services of the youth, the contract is binding, inasmuch as it was beneficial to him by securing to him permanent employment, and the means of maintaining himself.'"

[1] Also called infants and so referred to in the older authorities. There are very few modern authorities relating to the employment of minors.
[2] Infants Relief Act 1874.
[3] [1894] 2 Q.B. 482, at p. 491, C.A.
[4] (1796), 6 Term Rep. 557.
[5] (1877), 3 Q.B.D. 229.

In *Young* v. *Hoffmann Manufacturing Co., Ltd.* COZENS-HARDY, M.R., said[1]:

"... A contract of service is regarded as beneficial to an infant; and it is no objection that the contract contains stipulations and provisions usual in the particular trade, and such as a master may reasonably impose as a protection to himself: *Leslie* v. *Fitzpatrick*.[2] There can be no legal difficulty in implying as one of the terms of the contract a stipulation which, if the contract were expressed in writing, would be free from objection. In other words, an infant can enter into a contract of service upon the usual reasonable terms upon which alone the master will employ him."

If a minor enters into a contract which he can subsequently avoid on the plea of his minority, the transaction will be valid and binding until he chooses to repudiate it, and any payment made by the minor of which he has obtained the benefit cannot be recovered by him after he has avoided the contract.[3]

In a contract of service or apprenticeship the master, as well as the servant, may be a minor, and the same principles apply.[4]

[1] [1907] 2 K.B. 646, at p. 650, C.A.
[2] (1877), 3 Q.B.D. 229.
[3] *Valentini* v. *Canali* (1889), 24 Q.B.D. 166.
[4] *R.* v. *St. Petrox (Inhabitants)* (1791), 4 Term Rep. 196; *Thomas* v. *Waldo* (1858), 1 F. & F. 173 (successful claim by servant against master who, at the time of making the contract, was a minor, for wages accruing due after majority).

## Apprentices

At common law an apprentice is someone who by contract is to be taught a trade or calling, in contradistinction from a person who engages to serve another person generally.[1]

In some trades and vocations apprenticeship is still a vital part of training, but in others its role is on the decline. The State is now taking a more active part in the education of future employees as is evidenced by the Industrial Training Act 1964 and the Employment and Training Act 1973. The organs created pursuant to these statutes play a significant role in an area which was formerly left to the individual employers. However, the importance of apprenticeship can be understated since the effect of some of the statutory provisions has been to reinforce apprenticeship training schemes.

Much of the case law on apprenticeship dates from the 19th century and so must be used with caution. Teaching and learning must be the principal object of the contracting parties and service is incidental.[2]

[1] *R. v. Lairdon Inhabitants* (1799), 8 Term Rep. 379.
[2] *R. v. Crediton (Inhabitants)* (1831), 2 B & Ad. 493

The Family Allowances Act 1965, section 19, gave the following definition:

" 'Apprentice' means a person undergoing full-time training for any trade, business, profession, office, employment or vocation, and not in receipt of earnings exceeding two pounds a week..."

At common law the payment of a premium is strong, though not conclusive, evidence of a contract of apprenticeship rather than of service.[1] In some modern statutes premiums are prohibited, for example, section 16 of the Wages Councils Act 1959, provides:

"(1) **Where a worker to whom a wages regulation order** applies is an apprentice or learner, it shall not be lawful for his employer to receive directly or indirectly from him, or on his behalf or on his account, any payment by way of premium:
Provided that nothing in this section shall apply to any such payment duly made in pursuance of any instrument of apprenticeship not later than four weeks after the commencement of the apprenticeship or to any such payment made at any time if duly made in pursuance of any instrument of apprenticeship approved for the purposes of this proviso by a wages council.
(2) **If any employer acts in contravention of this section,** he shall be liable on summary conviction in respect of each offence to a fine not exceeding [one hundred] pounds, and the court may, in addition to imposing a fine, order him to repay to the worker or other person by whom the payment was made the sum improperly received by way of premium."[2]

By section 24 of the same Act "worker" includes "apprentice".

[1] *R. v. St. Margaret's, Kings Lynn (Inhabitants)* (1826), 6 B. & C. 97, at p. 98, per BAYLEY, J.
[2] The words in brackets have effect in place of the word "twenty"; Employment Protection Act 1975, Sch. 7, para. 6.

Similar provisions relating to an apprentice or learner will be found in section 6 of the Agricultural Wages Act 1948, the relevant sub-sections of which are as follows:

"(5) It shall not be lawful for the employer of a worker, being an apprentice or learner, who is employed in agriculture in a county for which an agricultural wages committee is established under this Act to receive directly or indirectly from the worker, or on his behalf or on his account, a payment by way of premium unless the payment is duly made in pursuance of an agreement approved for the purposes of this sub-section by the agricultural wages committee, and the amount of a payment received in contravention of this sub-section shall be recoverable by the person by whom the payment was made.

"(6) If an employer acts in contravention of the last preceding sub-section he shall be liable on summary conviction in respect of each offence to a fine not exceeding [one hundred] pounds, and in any proceedings against an employer under this sub-section the court shall, whether there is a conviction or not, order the employer to repay any sum which the court finds to have been received by way of premium in contravention of the last preceding sub-section.

(7) Nothing in the last preceding sub-section shall be taken to exclude the bringing otherwise than in accordance with that sub-section of proceedings for the recovery of an amount due under sub-section (5) of this section."[1]

---

[1] The words in brackets have effect in place of the word "twenty"; Employment Protection Act 1975, Sch. 9, para. 5.

In *Horan* v. *Hayhoe*,[1] for the narrow purpose of a taxing statute, the relationship created by apprenticeship was held not to be one of master and servant; but in a case involving the interpretation of a will JENKINS, J., said:[2]

"I was referred to *Horan* v. *Hayhoe*.[3] That case was a decision to the effect that an apprentice is not a servant for the purposes of the Revenue Act, 1869; though he is employed by the master, and it seems that he could be regarded as an employee. The case, arising as it did under a taxing Act, was, however, one in which a strict and narrow construction of the word 'servant' was appropriate. I was also referred to some passages concerning apprenticeship in a summary in *Halsbury's Laws of England*, 2nd Edn., vol. 34, at p. 482, para. 560, where the expression 'contract of service or apprenticeship' appears; both forms of contract are included in the term employee with the designation 'workman' at p. 803, para. 1138, where it is stated that every employee within the Workmen's Compensation Act, 1925, is a 'workman'. There, again, one finds apprentices regarded as employees within the designation 'workmen'. I was referred to one workman's compensation case: *Pomphrey* v. *Southwark Press*,[3] the facts of which are far removed from those of the present case, but which does, I think, bear out the conception of an apprentice as being employed by and working for an employer, although, as was pointed out in the course of the argument, the relation of master and apprentice is different from that of master and servant."

[1] [1904] 1 K.B. 288.
[2] *Re Marryat, Westminster Bank, Ltd.* v. *Hobcroft*, [1948] 1 Ch. 298, at p. 311; [1948] 1 All E.R. 796, at p. 802.
[3] [1901] 1 K.B. 86. C.A.

In the past almost all apprentices were minors but with the reduction of the age of majority and increase in the school leaving age, this is less likely to be the case in future.

## Holders of offices

At first sight some holders of offices, such as ministers of religion and policemen, may appear to fall within the category of employees. However, they are not the subjects of an employment relationship[1] and, save in uncommon instances, the law relating to contracts of employment does not apply to them.

[1] *Re National Insurance Act*, 1911, *Re Church of England Curates*, [1912] 2 Ch. 563 (curate); *Fisher* v. *Oldham Corporation*, [1930] 2 K.B. 364 (police not servants or agents of corporation); *A.-G. for New South Wales* v. *Perpetual Trustee Co., Ltd.*, [1955] A.C. 457, [1955] 1 All E.R. 846, P.C. (police); *Ridge* v. *Baldwin*, [1964] A.C. 40; [1963] 2 All E.R. 66, H.L. (chief constable).

## Crown servants

There is some doubt whether or not the Crown servant is bound by an employment contract, but the modern view is that a contractual relationship does exist.[1] What is clear is that the Crown has an absolute right of dismissal which is unfettered unless it is expressly restricted by statute.[2] Anything falling short of a statute which purports to take away this right is void as contrary to public policy and, unless there is a statutory provision to the contrary, employment of a Crown servant is at the pleasure of the Crown and may be terminated without notice.[3]

[1] *Kodeeswaran* v. *A.-G. for Ceylon*, [1970] A.C. 1111.
[2] Per DIPLOCK, J., *Riordan* v. *The War Office*, [1959] 3 All E.R. 552, at p. 557 quoting Stuart Robertson, *Civil Proceedings by and against the Crown*, (1908 Edition), at p. 357; affirmed, [1960] 3 All E.R. 774, C.A.
[3] The position of Crown servants, so far as the statutes considered in this book, is explained in each relevant chapter.

In practice established Crown servants have considerable security and appear to have suffered little as a result of the possible weakness in their legal position. The rules governing such employment appear in the Estacode. The immunity which the Crown enjoyed at common law has significance so far as Crown servants are concerned since some statutes in the field of employment are not expressed to apply to civil servants.[1] In *Wood* v. *Leeds Area Health Authority (Training)*[2] a technical assistant (building) employed by the respondents applied to an industrial tribunal (*inter alia*) under section 4 of the Contracts of Employment Act 1972. On appeal, the National Industrial Relations Court upheld the tribunal's decision that it did not have jurisdiction to hear a case since the Contracts of Employment Act 1972 was silent as to the position of Crown servants.

[1] The position of Crown servants so far as the statutes considered in this book is explained in each relevant chapter.
[2] [1974] I.C.R. 535.

## Directors

The position of company directors is somewhat anomalous. The director holds an office with the company but may in addition be an employee of it. If he performs services for the company in circumstances where, but for his directorship he would be an employee, then he has a dual relationship with the company being both an office-holder and an employee. This dichotomy of roles affects the rules applicable to the director employee. He may be removed from his directorship in accordance with the Articles of Association of the employing company or the Companies Act 1948 but the relationship of employer and employee is governed by the usual employment law rules, and the removal may well be in breach of contract as well as giving rise to the possibility of a claim under the unfair dismissal provisions.[1] A director who is not a shareholder, or holds only a small percentage of the company's capital, and who serves under a contract of employment is clearly an employee. Difficulties sometimes arise when the working director holds a substantial amount of the equity, or is able to exercise a large degree of control over the company's activities. It was held in 1944 that a managing director was not an employee[2] but this decision must be treated as of doubtful authority today, and each case has to be judged on its merits. What is applicable for the purpose of one scheme of legislation is not necessarily so for another.[3]

[1] See Chapter 7, below. *Stanbury* v. *Overmass and Chapple, Ltd.* (1976), 11 I.T.R. 7.

[2] *Sputz* v. *Broadway Engineering, Ltd.* (1944), 171 L.T. 50; *Normandy* v. *Inde Coope & Co., Ltd.,* [1908] 1 Ch. 84.

[3] *Robinson* v. *George Sorby, Ltd.* (1967), 2 I.T.R. 148.

Although under Table A of the Companies Act 1948 the board of directors has power to dismiss employees (including director employees), it does not have power to remove directors from that office. Thus the board can terminate the employment relationship of a director but not the directorship. Unless there is specific provision to this effect in the company's Articles of Association a director may be removed from his office only by retirement, removal under the terms of the Articles of Association, resignation, a requirement of the Companies Act or a resolution at a general meeting of the company.[1]

[1] When drawing service agreements for directors of quoted companies and subsidiaries the requirements of the Stock Exchange have to be taken into account. A service agreement for ten years or more must be approved by the company in general meeting.

## Partners

A partner cannot be employed by the partnership, even though he is paid so-called wages for working in the partnership business. It is legally impossible to be under a contract of service with oneself and others as joint masters. In a case under the Workmen's Compensation Act 1897,[1] MATHEW, L.J., said:

"The deceased man in this case was a partner; and the arrangement made between him and his co-partners as to payment of wages to him was really an agreement with regard to the mode in which accounts were to be taken between the partners, and to the share of profits to be received by him in excess of that received by the other partners in consideration of the work done by him. The Workmen's Compensation Act, 1897, cannot in my opinion apply to such a case."

Although the act of 1897 no longer applies, this is a correct statement of the present law.

[1] *Ellis* v. *Joseph Ellis & Co.,* [1905] 1 K.B. 324, at p. 329, C.A. Contrast *Easdown* v. *Cobb,* [1940] 1 All E.R. 49, H.L. (workmen's compensation, partners executed a deed of assignment, former partner as manager).

## Independent contractors

An independent contractor, e.g., a plumber, or a tailor, is one who undertakes to produce a given result, but for the actual execution of the work he is not under the order or control of the person for whom he does it[1]; he thus enters into a contract for services rather than one of service. Many outworkers come within this category. A definition of outworker may be found in the Workmen's Compensation Act 1925, section 48 (1), where "outworker" is defined as:

> "a person to whom articles or materials are given out to be made up, cleaned, washed, altered, ornamented, finished, or repaired, or adapted for sale, in his own home or on other premises not under the control or management of the person who give out the materials or articles".

[1] *Performing Rights Society, Ltd.* v. *Mitchell and Booker (Palais de Danse), Ltd.,* [1924] 1 K.B. 762, at p. 766 *et seq.*; also *Honeywill and Stein, Ltd.* v. *Larkin Brothers (London's Commercial Photographers), Ltd.,* [1934] 1 K.B. 191, at p. 196, C.A.

## Agents

So-called "representatives" of commercial houses and traders are employed under so many varieties of contracts that it is often difficult to describe their exact legal position, and in each case the facts must be carefully studied. A number of decided cases will be found arising, for instance, out of actions for wrongful dismissal, claims by commercial travellers for commission, and cases on the law of principal and agent in addition to claims for redundancy payments, unfair dismissal and under the other employment legislation.

Agents *per se* are not the subject of contracts of service, or contracts for services. In so far as any person has authority to act on behalf of another, he is that other person's agent. All employees are in some matters agents of their employers. Many agents, however, are under no contract of employment.[1]

[1] *Sellers* v. *London Counties Newspapers*, [1951] 1 K.B. 784, [1951] 1 All E.R. 544, C.A. (commercial traveller, remuneration by salary and commissions). *Levy* v. *Goldhill & Co.*, [1917] 2 Ch. 297 (not "employment", not contract of service, merely an agreement to remunerate in respect of orders accepted).

## Aliens

During peacetime aliens are not under any contractual disability but at times of war contracts, including contracts of employment, with enemy aliens are void and so not enforceable. The only exception to this is where the contract is entered into with the licence of the Crown. Non-patrials[1] as defined by the Immigration Act 1971 are subject to restrictions on entry into the United Kingdom and conditions of entry may be imposed when they arrive here. With certain exceptions, for instance doctors or dentists coming to follow their professions, a non-patrial will be allowed to enter to take up employment only if he holds a current work permit. Work permits are issued by the Department of Employment and are for specific jobs only.

Appeals against refusal of entry and imposition of restrictions forbidding employment on entry lie to an adjudicator and subject to certain requirements on to the Immigration Appeal Tribunal.

Employment restrictions of this type do not affect nationals of states which are members of the European Economic Community who are generally free to take up employment in the United Kingdom.[2]

[1] "Patrial" is a purely artificial concept. It is used of a person having the right of abode within the meaning of the Immigration Act 1971, Part 1.

[2] Immigration (Revocation of Employment Restrictions) Order 1972, S.I. 1972 No. 1647.

## Disabled persons

The Disabled Persons (Employment) Act 1944 was a wartime measure introduced to assist the employment of disabled persons. The Act was amended by the Disabled Persons (Employment) Act 1958 and together the two statutes are referred to as the Disabled Persons (Employment) Acts 1944 and 1958. A "disabled person" means a person who, on account of injury, disease, or congenital deformity, is substantially handicapped in obtaining or keeping employment, or in undertaking work on his own account, of a kind which apart from that injury, disease or deformity would be suited to his age, experience and qualifications.[1]

[1] Disabled Persons (Employment) Act 1944, s. 1.

The Secretary of State for Employment maintains a register[1] in which he records details of disabled persons in accordance with the Disabled Persons (Registration) Regulations 1945.[2] Save in cases of 1914–18 disablement pensioners[3] a person who wishes to be registered makes application to the Secretary of State on the prescribed form and if the Secretary of State is satisfied that the applicant is a disabled person, that his disablement is likely to continue for 12 months or more and that the conditions laid down in the regulations are complied with, the applicant will be registered as a disabled person. He is then issued with a certificate to that effect ("the green card"). The period of registration is that specified by the Secretary of State with a minimum of one year and a maximum of ten years.

[1] Disabled Persons (Employment) Act 1944, s. 6.
[2] S. R. & O. 1945 No. 938, as amended by S. R. & O. 1946 No. 262 and S.I. 1959 No. 510.
[3] Defined in Disabled Persons (Employment) Act 1944, s. 7.

No longer than two months before the expiry of the registration period a disabled person may apply for his registration to be renewed. A name may be removed from the register if the person ceases to fulfill the conditions for registration or becomes disqualified from registration. However, before removal the Secretary of State has to refer to a district advisory committee for their recommendation and only after considering this, if he is satisfied that a prescribed condition is not complied with, or that the person is disqualified from registration, the name will be removed from the register.[1]

[1] Disabled Persons (Employment) Act 1944, s. 8 (3).

Unless an employer is authorised by permit he should not employ any person other than a registered disabled person as a passenger lift (except a lift installed in a ship) attendant or a car park attendant (which occupations are called "designated employment").[1]

[1] Disabled Persons (Employment) Act 1944, s. 12 and the Disabled Persons (Designated Employments) Order 1946, S. R. & O. 1946 No. 1257. This is not the case when an employer is required to employ a person pursuant to statute, for instance under the provisions of the Reinstatement in Civil Employment Acts 1944 and 1950 and the National Service Act 1948.

It is the duty of every employer who has a substantial number of employees to employ his quota of registered disabled persons.[1] An employer to whom the requirement applies is a person who for the time being has, or in accordance with his normal practice and apart from transitory circumstances would have, in his employment 20 or more persons.[1] Other than in cases where there is a statutory requirement to the contrary, or a permit has been issued by the Secretary of State for Employment, an employer should not at any time take, or offer to take, into his employment any person other than a registered disabled person, if immediately after taking that person into employment the number of registered disabled persons employed by him would be less than the applicable quota.[2] The references to employment are construed as references to employment in Great Britain,[3] which includes employment in the capacity of master or a member of the crew of a British ship (other than a ship employed exclusively outside Great Britain) if the owner or managing owner or person having the management of the ship is resident or has his principal place of business in Great Britain.[4]

[1] Disabled Persons (Employment) Act 1944, s. 9 (1).
[2] *Ibid.*, s. 9 (2). The number can be reduced by order of the Secretary of State for Employment.
[3] *Ibid.*, s. 21 (1).
[4] *Ibid.*, s. 21 (2).

The standard quota has been fixed at $3\%$ but this may be varied, either up or down, by ministerial order for particular trades or industries, or branches of trades or industries. At present only one special percentage has been laid down, that by the Disabled Persons (Special Percentage) (No. 1) Order 1946[1] which relates to employment as a master or crew member of a British ship. In these circumstances the percentage is $0.1\%$. In calculating the number of employees, those employed in designated employment are excluded and a person whose employment ordinarily involves less than ten hours employment has also to be disregarded, a person whose employment usually involves less than ten but no more than 30 hours per week is counted as one half unit, and a person whose employment ordinarily involves more than 30 hours per week is a whole unit.[2] The percentage of the quota is applied to the number of employees calculated in this way. If the number produced is a fraction less than one-half, it is rounded down, in other cases it is rounded up.[3] An employer who wishes to do so may apply to the Secretary of State to determine his quota for a period not exceeding 12 months. The Secretary of State issues the appropriate certificate and if the employer employs that number of registered disabled persons during the period (excluding those in designated employment) then he is deemed to satisfy the quota requirements.

[1] S. R. & O. 1946 No. 236.
[2] Disabled Persons (General) Regulations 1945, S. R. & O. 1945 No. 1558, para. 5 (1).
[3] Disabled Persons (Employment) Act 1944, s. 10 (4).

An employer should not, without reasonable cause, discontinue the employment of a registered disabled person if immediately after the discontinuance the number of such persons employed would be less than his quota.[1] If an employee's name is removed from the register he continues to count as a registered disabled person whilst he remains in the employment of the employer in whose employment he was at the date when he ceased to be so registered, but on leaving that employment he no longer counts as a registered disabled person.

[1] Disabled Persons (Employment) Act 1944, s. 9 (5).

An employer may apply to the Secretary of State for Employment for permits to allow him to employ persons other than disabled persons for designated employment and to employ less than the quota applicable to him. The applicant has to persuade the Secretary of State that it is expedient to grant the permit having regard to the nature of the work for which the applicant desires to employ persons and the qualifications and suitability for the work of any registered disabled person who is available, or he must satisfy the Secretary of State that there is no such person or an insufficient number of such persons available for the work.[1] The permit may be unconditional, or subject to conditions, and may be granted in respect of either one or more specified persons, or of a specified number of persons.[1]

[1] Disabled Persons (Employment) Act 1944, s. 11.

All employers to whom the quota requirements apply are under a duty to maintain records showing the total number of employees employed by them and the number of registered disabled persons who they employ together with other information relating to the quota obligation.[1] These records should be kept for a period of two years from the date to which they relate.[2]

[1] Disabled Persons (Employment) Act 1944, s. 14.
[2] Disabled Persons (General) Regulations 1945, S. R. & O. 1945 No. 1558, para. 9.

The provisions of the Disabled Persons (Employment) Act 1944 are enforced by criminal proceedings and an employer commits an offence if he takes, or offers to take, into employment someone other than a registered disabled person, or dismisses a registered disabled person without reasonable cause, in contravention of the quota requirements, or takes, or offers to take, a person into designated employment who is not a registered disabled person. In addition it is a crime to fail to maintain and keep the required records. For the first mentioned offences, the employer, if a body corporate, is liable on summary conviction to a fine not exceeding £500[1] (£100 if not), or the offender may be liable to imprisonment for a term not exceeding three months, or to both a fine and imprisonment.[2] A person who fails to keep the necessary records is liable on summary conviction to a fine not exceeding £20, and if a failure to produce records in respect of which persons have already been convicted continues after conviction they may be liable on summary conviction to a fine not exceeding £5 for each day on which the failure continued. For some of these offences it is necessary for the matter to have been referred to the district advisory committee before prosecution is instituted.

[1] Disabled Persons (Employment) Act 1944, s. 19 (3).
[2] *Ibid.*, s. 9 (6).

The arrangements established by the Disabled Persons (Employment) Acts as to retraining and rehabilitation have been replaced by a more modern regime.

# ANTI-DISCRIMINATION LEGISLATION[1]

## Equality of terms and conditions of employment

The Equal Pay Act 1970 came fully into force on 29th December 1975. In general terms its purpose is to eliminate discrimination between the sexes as regards terms and conditions of employment. Section 1 (1) to (6)[2] is as follows:

"1.—(1) If the terms of a contract under which a woman is employed at an establishment in Great Britain do not include (directly or by reference to a collective agreement or otherwise) an equality clause they shall be deemed to include one.

(2) An equality clause is a provision which relates to terms (whether concerned with pay or not) of a contract under which a woman is employed (the 'woman's contract'), and has the effect that—

(a) where the woman is employed on like work with a man in the same employment—

    (i) if (apart from the equality clause) any term of the woman's contract is or becomes less favourable to the woman than a term of a similar kind in the contract under which that man is employed, that term of the woman's contract shall be treated as so modified as not to be less favourable, and

    (ii) if (apart from the equality clause) at any time the woman's contract does not include a term corresponding to a term benefiting that man included in the contract under which he is employed, the woman's contract shall be treated as including such a term;

(b) where the woman is employed on work rated as equivalent with that of a man in the same employment—

    (i) if (apart from the equality clause) any term of the woman's contract determined by the rating of the work is or becomes less favourable to the woman than a term of a similar kind in the contract under which that man is employed, that term of the woman's contract shall be treated as so modified as not to be less favourable, and

(ii) if (apart from the equality clause) at any time the woman's contract does not include a term corresponding to a term benefiting that man included in the contract under which he is employed and determined by the rating of the work, the woman's contract shall be treated as including such a term.

(3) An equality clause shall not operate in relation to a variation between the woman's contract and the man's contract if the employer proves that the variation is genuinely due to a material difference (other than the difference of sex) between her case and his.

(4) A woman is to be regarded as employed on like work with men if, but only if, her work and theirs is of the same or a broadly similar nature, and the differences (if any) between the things she does and the things they do are not of practical importance in relation to terms and conditions of employment; and accordingly in comparing her work with theirs regard shall be had to the frequency or otherwise with which any such differences occur in practice as well as to the nature and extent of the differences.

(5) A woman is to be regarded as employed on work rated as equivalent with that of any men if, but only if, her job and their job have been given an equal value, in terms of the demand made on a worker under various headings (for instance effort, skill, decision), on a study undertaken with a view to evaluating in those terms the jobs to be done by all or any of the employees in an undertaking or group of undertakings, or would have been given an equal value but for the evaluation being made on a system setting different values for men and women on the same demand under any heading.

(6) Subject to the following sub-sections, for purposes of this section:

(a) 'employed' means employed under a contract of service or of apprenticeship or a contract personally to execute any work or labour, and related expressions shall be construed accordingly;

(c) two employers are to be treated as associated if one is a company of which the other (directly or indirectly) has control or if both are companies of which a third person (directly or indirectly) has control,

and men shall be treated as in the same employment with a woman if they are men employed by her employer or any associated employer at the same establishment or at establishments in Great Britain which include that one at which common terms and conditions of employment are observed either generally or for employees of the relevant classes."

[1] Discrimination on the grounds of race, etc. will be dealt with in Appendix 11.

[2] The sub-sections are shown as amended by the Sex Discrimination Act 1975. Since the Act was in this form when it came into force no indication of the alterations is given. It is to be noted that the Act relates to more than just pay. The provisions of s. 6 (1A), as substituted by the Sex Discrimination Act 1975, do not come into force until 6th April 1978; Sex Discrimination Act 1975 (Commencement) Order 1975, S.I. 1975 No. 1845. For restrictions on contracting out of the Equal Pay Act 1970 see Sex Discrimination Act 1975, s. 77 at p. 38, below.

Thus the Act seeks to effect its objectives by the incorporation of the contractual term as to equality into the individual employment contract. Although the provisions of the Equal Pay Act 1970 are framed with reference to women and their treatment relative to men, they apply equally in a converse case to men and their treatment in relation to women.[1] The equality clause does not operate in relation to terms affected by compliance with the laws relating to the employment of women[2] (for instance those provisions of the Factories Act 1961 which relate to women's employment), or affording special treatment to women in connection with pregnancy and childbirth.[2] The operation of the equality clause is limited in connection with occupational pension schemes.[3]

[1] Equal Pay Act 1970, s. 1 (13).

[2] *Ibid.*, s. 6 (1).

[3] *Ibid.*, s. 6 (1A). From 6th April 1978 access to most occupational pension schemes must be on equal terms. Sex Discrimination Act 1975 (Commencement) Order 1975, S.I. 1975 No. 1845.

Difficulties arise in deciding whether women are employed on like work with men, and whether the woman is employed on work rated as equivalent with that of a man. Comparisons are not always easy to make and one has to be careful when making them.[1] There is no obligation placed on the employer by the Act to carry out job evaluation studies.[2]

[1] For early decisions on this point see *Piper* v. *Southern Electronic Services, Ltd.*, [1976] I.R.L.R. 102, *Brodie* v. *Startrite Engineering Co., Ltd.*, [1976] I.R.L.R. 101, *Dugdale* v. *Kraft Foods, Ltd.*, [1976] I.R.L.R. 204, *Dorman* v. *Hadrian Plastics, Ltd.*, [1976] I.R.L.R. 207, and *Harper* v. *Redland Roof Tiles, Ltd.*, [1976] I.R.L.R. 208. It must be possible to make a comparison, see *Meeks* v. *National Union of Agricultural and Allied Workers*, [1976] I.R.L.R. 198.

[2] For a case where a job evaluation exercise had been carried out see *Bedwell* v. *Hellerman Deutsch, Ltd.*, [1976] I.R.L.R. 98.

If an employee has a complaint in respect of a contravention of a term which is modified, or included, by virtue of the equality clause she may present the complaint to an industrial tribunal.[1] An employer can apply to an industrial tribunal for an order declaring the right of the employer and employee when a dispute arises in relation to the effect of an equality clause.[2] The Secretary of State for Employment can refer a question to an industrial tribunal when it appears to him that there may be a question whether an employer of any women is, or has been, contravening a term modified, or included, by virtue of their equality clauses but it was not reasonable to expect them to take steps to have the question determined. Such a reference may be in respect of all the cases, or an individual case, and is dealt with as if the reference was by the women or woman against the employer.[3]

[1] Equal Pay Act 1970, s. 2 (1). In addition the woman can seek the assistance of a conciliation officer. See Chapter 9, below.

[2] *Ibid.*, s. 2 (1A).

[3] *Ibid.*, s. 2 (2).

Claims may be made during and after termination of the employment, but must be referred to the industrial tribunal within six months of the woman ceasing to be in the employment in respect of which the reference is made. If the claim succeeds, the employee is entitled to be awarded any payment by way of arrears of remuneration, or damages, for her loss but these cannot be recovered in respect of a time earlier than two years before the date on which the proceedings were instituted.[1] If in proceedings before the courts, it appears to the court seized of the case that a claim or counter-claim in respect of the operation of an equality clause could be more conveniently disposed of separately by an industrial tribunal, there is a procedure for striking out the appropriate claim and refering, or directing reference of the question to an industrial tribunal and the proceedings may be stayed in the meantime.[2] The time limit for reference to the industrial tribunal does not apply in these cases.[3]

[1] Equal Pay Act 1970, s. 2 (5). But not in respect of the period before 29th December 1975.

[2] *Ibid.*, s. 2 (3).

[3] The Equal Opportunities Commission may advise or assist an employee in connection with proceedings, see p. 42, below. It also can conduct formal investigations, issue non-discrimination notices and obtain injunctions in relation to the Equal Pay Act 1970 as well as under the Sex Discrimination Act 1975 itself.

The Act also contains detailed provisions for references to be made to the Central Arbitration Committee relating to collective agreements and wages orders made pursuant to the Wages Council's Act 1959 and the Agricultural Wages Act 1948 when the agreement, or wages orders, contain provisions which apply specifically to men only or women only following which amendments to the collective agreement or wages order may result.[1]

[1] Equal Pay Act 1970, ss. 3, 4, 5 and 10; s. 3 also applies to "pay structures".

As has been seen the Act applies to employees[1] (i.e., those employed under a contract of services) and not office-holders or persons performing services under contracts for services. It does not cover the Armed Forces or women's services administered by the Defence Council,[2] but does apply to Crown servants. It also applies to those in employment regarded as being at an establishment in Great Britain (including such of the territorial waters of the United Kingdom as are adjacent to Great Britain) unless the employee does his work wholly or mainly outside Great Britain. It does, however, cover employment on board a ship registered in Great Britain or on an aircraft or hovercraft registered in the United Kingdom and operated by a person who has his principal place of business, or is ordinarily resident in Great Britain, unless the employee does his work wholly outside Great Britain.[3] There is provision for employment concerned with the exploration of the seabed and its natural resources to be added by order.[4] There are no requirements as to the number of hours worked or length of service for an employee to be entitled to benefit from the Equal Pay Act 1970.

[1] Equal Pay Act 1970, s. 1 (6).

[2] *Ibid.*, s. 1 (9), but see s. 7.

[3] Sex Discrimination Act 1975, s. 10 (2).

[4] *Ibid.*, s. 10 (5).

## Sex discrimination

(1) *Discrimination*

The majority of the provisions of the Sex Discrimination Act 1975[1] dealing with discrimination on the grounds of sex came into force by 29th December 1975.[2] The Act applies equally to men[3] as women, and insofar as employment is concerned makes unlawful discrimination on the ground of married status[4] as well as on the grounds of sex.

[1] The provisions of the Act are referred to only insofar as they are relevant for the purpose of this work. The object is to give an outline of the Act and not to make a detailed examination of the statute.

[2] All the provisions discussed are in force at the date of going to press.

[3] Sex Discrimination Act 1975, s. 2. Although discussed in the context of discrimination against women it applies equally in respect of discrimination against men save that no account is taken of special treatment afforded to women in connection with pregnancy and childbirth.

[4] Sex Discrimination Act 1975, s. 3. Discrimination is defined in a similar way to discrimination on the grounds of sex with appropriate modifications as follows:

"3.—(1) A person discriminates against a married person of either sex in any circumstances relevant for the purposes of any provision of Part II if—
  (a) on the ground of his or her marital status he treats that person less favourably than he treats or would treat an unmarried person of the same sex, or
  (b) he applies to that person a requirement or condition which he applies or would apply equally to an unmarried person but—
    (i) which is such that the proportion of married persons who can comply with it is considerably smaller than the proportion of unmarried persons of the same sex who can comply with it, and
    (ii) which is such that the proportion of married persons who can comply with it is considerably smaller than the proportion of unmarried persons of the same sex who can comply with it, and
    (ii) which he cannot show to be justifiable irrespective of the marital status of the person to whom it is applied, and
    (iii) which is to that person's detriment because he cannot comply with it.

(2) For the purposes of sub-section (1), a provision of Part II framed with reference to discrimination against women shall be treated as applying equally to the treatment of men, and for that purpose shall have effect with such modifications as are requisite.
Part II of the Act relates to discrimination in the employment field."

But what about a person about to be married? Contrast *Bick* v. *Royal School for the Deaf*, [1976] C.L.92, and *McLean* v. *Paris Travel Services, Ltd.*, [1976] I.R.L.R. 202.

Sex discrimination is defined by section 1 of the Act as follows:

"1.—(1) A person discriminates against a woman[1] in any circumstances relevant for the purposes of any provision of this Act if:

(*a*) on the ground of her sex he treats her less favourably that he treats or would treat a man, or

(*b*) he applies to her a requirement on condition which he applies or would apply equally to a man but:

   (i) which is such that the proportion of women who comply with it is considerably smaller than the proportion of men who can comply with it[2] and

   (ii) which he cannot show to be justifiable irrespective of the sex of the person to whom it is applied, and

   (iii) which is to her detriment because she cannot comply with it.

(2) If a person treats or would treat a man differently according to the man's marital status, his treatment of a woman is for the purposes of sub-section (1) (*a*) to be compared to his treatment of a man having the like marital status."

[1] "Woman" includes a female of any age, Sex Discrimination Act 1975, s. 82 (1).

[2] For an example of a situation falling within this sub-section see *Meeks* v. *National Union of Agricultural and Allied Workers*, [1976] I.R.L.R. 198.

Discrimination is known as victimisation if a person treats another ("the person victimised") in circumstances relevant for any provision of the Sex Discrimination Act 1975, less favourably than in those circumstances he treats, or would treat, other persons and does so by reason that the person victimised has brought proceedings against the discriminator or any other person under the Sex Discrimination Act 1975 or the Equal Pay Act 1970, or has given evidence or information in connection with proceedings brought by any person under those Acts, or has done anything otherwise under or by reference to those Acts in relation to the discriminator or any other person, or has alleged that the discriminator, or any other person, has committed an act which would amount to a contravention of either of those statutes, or by reason that the discriminator knows the person victimised intends to do any of those things, or suspects that the person victimised has done or intends to do any of them,[1] unless the allegation was false and not made in good faith.[2]

[1] Sex Discrimination Act 1975, s. 4 (1).
[2] *Ibid.*, s. 4 (2).

Part II of the Act sets out situations of discrimination in the employment field. Employment is defined widely as "employment under a contract of service or of apprenticeship or a contract personally to execute any work or labour".[1] It is unlawful for a person in relation to employment by him in an establishment in Great Britain, to discriminate against a woman, in arrangements he makes for the purpose of determining who should be offered that employment, or in the terms in which he offers her that employment, or by refusing or deliberately omitting to offer her that employment.[2] So far as an existing employee is concerned, it is unlawful for the employer to discriminate against her in the way he affords her access to opportunities for promotion, transfer, or training, or to any other benefits, facilities or services, or by refusing, or deliberately omitting to afford her access to them, or by dismissing her or subjecting her to any other detriment.[3] This provision does not apply to benefits, facilities, or services of any description, if the employer is concerned with the provision of such matters to the public, or a section of the public, comprising the women in question, unless the provision differs in a material respect from the provision of such matters by the employer to his employees, or the provision of benefits, facilities or services of the women in question is regulated by her contract of employment, or they relate to training.[4]

[1] Sex Discrimination Act 1975, s. 82.
[2] *Ibid.*, s. 6 (1).
[3] *Ibid.*, s. 6 (2). See *Meeks* v. *National Union of Agricultural and Allied Workers*, [1976] I.R.L.R. 198, where differential rates of pay were *held* not to be such benefits.
[4] *Ibid.*, s. 6 (7). Complaints in respect of such discrimination are made to the county court and not industrial tribunal. See *ibid.*, s. 29.

(2) *Exceptions*

There are a number of exceptions which are as follows:

1. Genuine occupational qualifications.[1] It is not unlawful for the employer to discriminate against a woman when recruiting personnel, or providing opportunities for promotion, or training if

the essential nature of the job calls for a man by reason of physiology (excluding physical strength or stamina), or in dramatic performances, or other entertainment, for reasons of authenticity, so that the essential nature of the job would be materially different if carried out by a woman.[2] A good example of this would be a male model. It is also a genuine occupational qualification if the job needs to be held by a man to preserve decency, or privacy, because it is likely to involve physical contact with men in circumstances where they might reasonably object to it being carried out by a woman[3] or the holder of the job is likely to do his work in circumstances where men might reasonably object to the presence of women because they are in a state of undress, or using sanitary facilities.[4] Another type of genuine occupational qualification is where the nature or location of the employer's establishment makes it impracticable for the holder of the job to live elsewhere than in the premises provided by the employer, and the only such premises available are lived in, or normally lived in, by men and are not equipped with separate sleeping accommodation and sanitary facilities for women, and it is not reasonable to expect the employer to equip those premises with such accommodation and facilities or to provide other premises for women.[5] Yet another type of genuine occupational qualification occurs when the nature of the employer's establishment, or the part in which the work is done, requires the job to be done by a man because it is part of a hospital, prison, or other establishment, requiring special care, supervision or attention and those persons are all men, save in exceptional cases, and it is reasonable having regard to the essential character of the establishment that the job should not be held by a woman.[6] When the holder of a job provides individuals with personal services promoting their welfare or education or similar personal services and those services can be most effectively performed by a man that again can be a genuine occupational qualification,[7] as is the case where a job which needs to be held by a man because of the restrictions imposed by laws regulating the employment of women.[8] Also if a job needs to be held by a man because it is likely to involve the performance of duties outside the United Kingdom in a country whose laws and/or customs are such that the duties could not, or could not effectively be performed by a woman, that is also a genuine occupational qualification.[9] The final exclusion of this type is where the job is one of two which are to be held by a married couple.[10]

[1] Sex Discrimination Act 1975, s. 7 (1).
[2] *Ibid.*, s. 7 (2) (*a*).
[3] *Ibid.*, s. 7 (2) (*b*) (i).
[4] *Ibid.*, s. 7 (2) (*b*) (ii).
[5] *Ibid.*, s. 7 (2) (*c*).
[6] *Ibid.*, s. 7 (2) (*d*), and it should be reasonable that the job should not be done by a woman.
[7] *Ibid.*, s. 7 (2) (*e*).
[8] *Ibid.*, s. 7 (2) (*f*).
[9] *Ibid.*, s. 7 (2) (*g*).
[10] *Ibid.*, s. 7 (2) (*h*).

The job is still one for which sex is a genuine occupational qualification where some only of the duties fall within the above heads,[1] but with the exception of the exclusion relating to two related jobs held by a married couple, the genuine occupational qualification exclusion does not apply to the filling of a vacancy when the employer already has male employees capable of carrying out the duties, whom it would be reasonable to employ on those duties, and whose numbers are sufficient to meet the employer's likely requirement in respect of them without undue inconvenience. There is a similar exclusion where the employee would be caused to share communal accommodation being residential accommodation which includes dormitories or other shared sleeping accommodation which for reasons of privacy should be used by one sex only.[2]

[1] Sex Discrimination Act 1975, s. 7 (3).
[2] *Ibid.*, s. 46 which sets out the extent of this exclusion. It can only be relied on if such arrangements as are reasonably practicable are made to compensate for the detriment caused by the discrimination, s. 46 (6).

2. The office of police constable is treated as employment for the purposes of the Sex Discrimination Act 1975 and subject to certain minor amendments the Act applies to it.[1]

[1] Sex Discrimination Act 1975, s. 17.

3. The Act also applies to prison officers but it does not render unlawful any discrimination between male and female prison officers as to requirements relating to their height.[1]

[1] Sex Discrimination Act 1975, s. 18.

4. The Act does not apply to employment for purposes of an organised religion where the employment is limited to one sex so

as to comply with the doctrines of the religion, or to avoid offending the religious susceptibilities of a significant number of its followers.[1]

[1] Sex Discrimination Act 1975, s. 19 (1).

5. Although the Act amends the Midwives Act 1951 to allow men to become midwives it is not unlawful to discriminate against them on recruitment, promotion, or training.[1]

[1] Sex Discrimination Act 1975, s. 20.

6. The provisions of the Mines and Quarries Act 1954 are amended to allow women to go underground in certain circumstances.[1]

[1] Sex Discrimination Act 1975, s. 21.

7. It is not unlawful to do any act necessary to comply with a statutory requirement[1] or for the purpose of safeguarding national security.[2]

[1] Sex Discrimination Act 1975, s. 51.
[2] *Ibid.*, s. 52. The usual rules as to Ministerial certificates apply, s. 52 (2) and (3).

8. Employers who together with any associated employers do not employ more than five employees are excluded, as is employment for the purposes of a private household,[1] but not if the discrimination is by victimisation.

[1] Sex Discrimination Act 1975, s. 6 (3). For victimisation, see p. 29, above.

9. It is not unlawful to differentiate as to terms of benefits of death or retirement of the employee or prospective employee.[1]

[1] Sex Discrimination Act 1975, s. 6 (4). But from 6th April 1978 there should be equal access to most occupational pension schemes; Equal Pay Act 1970, s. 6 (1A).

10. It is not unlawful to discriminate by affording special treatment to women in connection with pregnancy or childbirth.[1]

[1] Sex Discrimination Act 1975, s. 2 (2).

The employment provisions of the Sex Discrimination Act 1975 are limited to employment by the employer at an establishment in Great Britain,[1] which is defined as including such of the territorial waters of the United Kingdom as are adjacent to Great Britain.[2] By virtue of section 10 (1) employment is regarded as being at an establishment in Great Britain unless the employee does his work wholly or mainly outside Great Britain. Employment on a ship registered in Great Britain, or on a United Kingdom registered aircraft or hovercraft operated by a person whose principal place of business, or who is ordinarily resident in Great Britain, is treated as a Great Britain establishment unless the employment is wholly outside Great Britain.[3] With appropriate amendments the provisions relating to discrimination on the basis of sex apply to the Crown,[4] except in the case of the armed forces or a woman's service administered by the Defence Council.[5]

[1] Sex Discrimination Act 1975, s. 6.
[2] *Ibid.*, s. 82 (1).
[3] *Ibid.*, s. 82 (1). The area of operation may be extended by Order in Council. See p. 27, above.
[4] *Ibid.*, s. 85 (1).
[5] *Ibid.*, s. 85 (4).

(3) *Miscellaneous*

There are special provisions relating to discrimination against contract workers.[1] This covers the case of work for a person ("the principal") which is done by individuals (the "contract workers") who are not employed by the principal himself, but by another person who supplies them under a contract made with the principal.[2] It is unlawful for the principal to discriminate against a woman who is a contract worker in the terms on which he allows her to do that work, or by not allowing her to do it, or continue to do it, or in the way in which he affords her access to benefits, facilities or services or by refusing or deliberately omitting to afford her access to them,[3] or by subjecting her to any other detriment.[4] However, when being a man would be a genuine occupational qualification for the job if directly employed, it is not unlawful discrimination for the principal not to allow a woman to do the job or continue to do it.[5] It is unlawful for an employment agency[6] to discriminate against a woman either in the terms on which the agency offers to provide any of its services, or by refusing or deliberately omitting to provide any services, or in the way it provides any of its services.[7] The reference to services includes guidance on careers and other services related to employment, but it is not unlawful for the agency to carry out such acts if the discrimination only concerns employment which the employer could reasonably refuse to offer the woman.[8] There is a saving for an employment agency if it proves that it acted in reliance on a statement made to it by the employer that the employer could lawfully refuse to employ a woman, that its action would not be unlawful and that it was reasonable for it to rely on the statement.[9] There is criminal liability on a person who knowingly or recklessly makes a statement which is in a material respect false or misleading.[10]

[1] Sex Discrimination Act 1975, s. 9.

[2] *Ibid.*, s. 9 (1).

[3] This provision does not apply to benefits, facilities or services of any description if the principal is concerned with the provision of benefits, facilities or services of that description to the public, or to a section of the public to which the woman belongs unless that provision differs in a material respect from the provision of benefits, facilities or services by the principal to his contract workers; Sex Discrimination Act 1975, s. 9 (4). See note to s. 6 (7), above.

[4] Sex Discrimination Act 1975, s. 9 (2).

[5] *Ibid.*, s. 9 (3).

[6] "Employment agency" means a person who, for profit or not, provides services for the purpose of finding employment for workers or supplying employers with workers; Sex Discrimination Act 1975, s. 82 (1).

[7] *Ibid.*, s. 15 (1).

[8] *Ibid.*, s. 15 (4).

[9] *Ibid.*, s. 15 (5).

[10] *Ibid.*, s. 15 (6).

Section 38 makes it unlawful to publish or cause to be published an advertisement which indicates or might be reasonably understood as indicating any intention to discriminate unlawfully and the use of job descriptions with sexual connotations (such as "waiter", "salesgirl", "postman" or "stewardess") is taken as showing an indication to discriminate in that way unless the advertisement includes an indication to the contrary.[1] There are provisions, similar to that mentioned in connection with employment agencies, so far as the publication of an advertisement in reliance on a statement made to him by the person who caused it to be published, to the effect that the publication would not be unlawful and that it was reasonable for him to rely on the statement.[2] A person who knowingly or recklessly makes such a statement which is in a material respect false, or misleading, commits an offence.[3]

[1] The sanctions are the issue of a non-discrimination notice pursuant to

Sex Discrimination Act 1975, s. 67; see p. 41, below, or application to a county court for an injunction, *ibid.*, s. 72.
² *Ibid.*, s. 38 (4).
³ *Ibid.*, s. 38 (5).

In addition there are provisions of the Sex Discrimination Act 1975 which seek to prevent organisations of workers, organisations of employers and other organisations whose members carry on a particular profession or trade for the purposes of which the organisation exists, from discriminating unlawfully.[1] It is unlawful for an authority or body which can confer authorisation or qualifications to discriminate on the grounds of sex[2] and vocational training bodies, which include industrial training boards, the Manpower Services Commission, the Employment Service Agency, the Training Services Agency and other associations which comprise employers and have as their principal objects, or one of them, affording employees access to facilities to discriminate against women.[3] There are provisions which make it unlawful for a firm consisting of six or more partners to discriminate against a woman in relation to a position as a partner in the firm[4] and in making an appointment by a Minister of the Crown, or Government Department, to an office or post no act should be done which would be unlawful discrimination if the Crown were an employer for the purposes of the Sex Discrimination Act.[5]

[1] Sex Discrimination Act 1975, s. 12.
[2] *Ibid.*, s. 13.
[3] *Ibid.*, s. 14.
[4] *Ibid.*, s. 11. The specified number of partners may be amended by order of the Secretary of State, s. 80 (1) (*d*).
[5] *Ibid.*, s. 86.

There are savings to cover the cases of sports, games and other activities[1] of a competitive nature where the physical strength, stamina or other physique of the average woman puts her at a disadvantage to the average man and also with regard to life assurance and accident insurance policies[2] and charities.[3]

[1] Sex Discrimination Act 1975, s. 44.
[2] *Ibid.*, s. 45.
[3] *Ibid.*, s. 43.

A person is guilty of a discriminatory practice on the application by him of a requirement or condition resulting in an act of discrimination which is unlawful by virtue of any provision of Part II of the Act, or which would be likely to result in such an act of discrimination if the persons to whom it is applied were not all one sex. If and so long as the person applies the discriminatory practice, or he operates practices or other arrangements which in any circumstances would call for the application by him of a discriminatory practice he contravenes section 37. Proceedings in respect of contravention of this provision may only be brought by the Equal Opportunities Commission.[1] Similarly, it is unlawful for a person who has authority over another person, or in accordance with whose wishes that other person is accustomed to act, to instruct him to do any act which is unlawful by virtue of Part II of the Sex Discrimination Act 1975, or procure or attempt to procure the doing by him of any such act.[2] Again it is unlawful to induce, or attempt to induce, a person to do any act in contravention of Part II of the Act, by providing or offering to provide him with any benefit, or subjecting, or threatening to subject, him to any detriment.[3] This applies whether the offer is direct or indirect.[4]

[1] Sex Discrimination Act 1975, s. 37 (3).
[2] *Ibid.,* s. 39.
[3] *Ibid.,* s. 40 (1).
[4] *Ibid.,* s. 40 (2).

A person who knowingly aids another person to do an unlawful act himself is guilty of an unlawful act[1] and anything done by a person in the course of his employment is treated as done by his employer as well as by him, whether or not it was done with the employer's knowledge or approval.[2] However, in proceedings taken under the Sex Discrimination Act 1975 against any person in respect of an act alleged to have been done by an employee of his, it is a defence for the person to prove that he took such steps as were reasonably practicable to prevent the employee from doing that act, or from doing in the course of his employment acts of that description.[3]

[1] Sex Discrimination Act 1975, s. 42.
[2] *Ibid.,* s. 41
[3] *Ibid.,* s. 41 (3).

In certain cases the Act does allow discrimination to take place. For instance when a training body affords one sex only access to facilities for training, which would help to fit them for that work, or encourages women only, or men only, to take advantage of opportunities of doing that work when it appears to the training body that any time within the 12 months immediately preceding the doing of the discriminatory act, there were no persons of the sex in question doing the work in Great Britain, or the number of persons of that sex doing the work in Great Britain was comparatively small.[1] There are other provisions relating to discriminatory training both by employers and training bodies in sections 47 and 48. Section 77 contains restrictions on contracting out of the Sex Discrimination Act 1975 and the Equal Pay Act 1970.[2]

[1] Sex Discrimination Act, 1975, s. 47.

[2] It reads as follows:

"77.—(1) A term of a contract is void where—

*(a)* its inclusion renders the making of the contract unlawful by virtue of this Act, or

*(b)* it is included in furtherance of an act rendered unlawful by this Act, or

*(c)* it provides for the doing of an act which would be rendered unlawful by this Act.

(2) Subsection (1) does not apply to a term the inclusion of which constitutes, or is in furtherance of, or provides for, unlawful discrimination against a party to the contract, but the term shall be unenforceable against that party.

(3) A term in a contract which purports to exclude or limit any provision of this Act or the Equal Pay Act 1970 is unenforceable by any person in whose favour the term would operate apart from this subsection.

(4) Subsection (3) does not apply—

*(a)* to a contract settling a complaint to which section 63 (1) of this Act or section 2 of the Equal Pay Act 1970 applies where the contract is made with the assistance of a conciliation officer;

*(b)* to a contract settling a claim to which section 66 applies.

(5) On the application of any person interested in a contract to which subsection (2) applies, a county court or sheriff court may make such order as it thinks just for removing or modifying any term made unenforceable by that subsection; but such an order shall not be made unless all persons affected have been given notice of the application (except where under rules of court notice may be dispensed with) and have been afforded an opportunity to make representations to the court.

(6) An order under subsection (5) may include provision as respects any period before the making of the order."

## (4) *Relationship with the Equal Pay Act 1970*

In the broadest of terms if an employer contravenes the equality clause then the employee's ground for complaint lies under the Equal Pay Act 1970 in other cases of discrimination then the Sex Discrimination Act 1975 applies. The position is dealt with by section 8, sub-sections (2) to (5) of the Sex Discrimination Act 1975[1] which are as follows:

> "(2) Section 1 (1) of the Equal Pay Act 1970 (as set out in sub-section (1) above) does not apply in determining for the purposes of section 6 (1) (*b*) of this Act the terms on which employment is offered.
>
> (3) Where a person offers a woman employment on certain terms, and if she accepted the offer then, by virtue of an equality clause, any of those terms would fall to be modified, or any additional term would fall to be included, the offer shall be taken to contravene section 6 (1) (*b*).
>
> (4) Where a person offers a woman employment on certain terms, and sub-section (3) would apply but for the fact that, on her acceptance of the offer, section 1 (3) of the Equal Pay Act 1970 (as set out in sub-section (1) above) would prevent the equality clause from operating, the offer shall be taken not to contravene section 6 (1) (*b*).
>
> (5) An act does not contravene section 6 (2) if:
>
> (*a*) it contravenes a term modified or included by virtue of an equality clause, or
>
> (*b*) it would contravene such a term but for the fact that the equality clause is prevented from operating by section 1 (3) of the Equal Pay Act 1970."

[1] See also *Meeks* v. *National Union of Agricultural and Allied Workers*, [1976] I.R.L.R. 198.

(5) *Enforcement*

(a) *By industrial tribunals.* If an employee, or prospective employee, considers she has been discriminated against contrary to Part II of the Act she may present a complaint to an industrial tribunal.[1] This should be done before the end of the period of three months beginning when the act complained of was done,[2] unless the tribunal considers that in all the circumstances of the case it is just and equitable to consider the complaint out of time.[3] If the tribunal finds that the complaint is well founded it will make such of the following orders as it considers just and equitable:

(i) An order declaring the rights of the complainant and the respondent in relation to the act to which the complaint relates;

(ii) An order requiring the respondent to pay to the complainant compensation of an amount corresponding to any damages he may have been ordered by a county court if the complaint had been under other provisions of the Act[4]; and

(iii) A recommendation that the employer take within a specified period appearing to the tribunal to be practicable for the purposes of obviating, or reducing, the adverse effect on the complainant of any act of discrimination to which the complaint relates. If the employer without reasonable justification fails to comply with recommendations made by an industrial tribunal, then if it thinks it is just and equitable to do so, it may increase the amount of compensation required to the complainant in respect of the complaint and if an order to pay compensation had not previously been made it may make such an order.[5]

[1] Sex Discrimination Act 1975, s. 63. For the role of conciliation officers, see Chapter 9, below.

[2] *Ibid.*, s. 76 (1). Section 76 (6) is as follows:

"(6) For the purposes of this section:
  (a) where the inclusion of any term in a contract renders the making of the contract an unlawful act that act shall be treated as extending throughout the duration of the contract, and
  (b) any act extending over a period shall be treated as done at the end of that period, and
  (c) a deliberate omission shall be treated as done when the person in question decided upon it,

and in the absence of evidence establishing the contrary a person shall be taken for the purposes of this section to decide upon an omission when he does an act inconsistent with doing the omitted act or, if he has done no such inconsistent act, when the period expires within which he might reasonably have been expected to do the omitted act if it was to be done."

[3] Sex Discrimination Act 1975, s. 76 (5).

[4] With the same maximum as that prescribed under Trade Union and Labour Relations Act 1974. Sch. 1, para. 20, at present £5,200. See p. 356, below. There are provisions to avoid duplicity of compensation where the discrimination amounts to unfair dismissal as well. See p. 372, below.

[5] Sex Discrimination Act 1975, s. 65.

There are specific rules to cover the "overlap" between a complaint under the Sex Discrimination Act 1975 and under the unfair dismissal provisions of the Trade Union and Labour Relations Act 1974.[1] The limitation of £5,200 on compensation applies. The procedure for obtaining information[2] and also for obtaining a written statement of reasons for dismissal[3] may be of assistance in preparing for the hearing.

[1] See p. 372, below.

[2] See p. 42, below.
[3] See p. 152, below.

(b) *Equal Opportunities Commission*. The Equal Opportunities Commission may play two distinct types of role in connection with discrimination in the employment field. It can take a positive action by issuing non-discrimination notices[1] and itself instituting legal proceedings in respect of discrimination, and also it has powers to assist individual complainants on the ground that the case raises the question of principle, or it is unreasonable having regard to the complexity of the case, or the applicant's position in relation to the respondent or other person involved, or any other matter, to expect the applicant to deal with the case unaided.[2] The Commission also has power to conduct formal investigations either of its own volition or when required to do so by the Secretary of State.[3] A non-discrimination notice may be issued during the course of the formal investigation if the Commission decides that a breach of the Sex Discrimination Act 1975 or the Equal Pay Act 1970 has occurred.[4] The requirement as to non-discrimination notices are beyond the bounds of this book but there is a right of appeal against the notice[5] and the Commission is obliged to establish and maintain a register of such notices which have become final.[6]

[1] Sex Discrimination Act 1975, s. 67.
[2] *Ibid.*, s. 75 (1).
[3] *Ibid.*, s. 57. See the Sex Discrimination (Formal Investigations) Regulations 1975, S.I. 1975 No. 1993.
[4] Sex Discrimination Act 1975, s. 67 (2).
[5] *Ibid.*, s. 68.
[6] *Ibid.*, s. 70.

If during a period of five years beginning on the date on which either, a non-discrimination notice served on an employer became final, or a court or tribunal has determined that an employer had committed an unlawful discriminatory act, or an act in breach of a term modified or included by virtue of an equality clause under section 2 of the Equal Pay Act 1970, it appears to the Commission that unless the employer is restrained he is likely to commit one or more further such acts the Commission may apply to a county court for an injunction restraining him from doing so. If the court is satisfied that the application is well founded it may grant the injunction in the terms applied for, or in more limited terms.[1]

The Commission should not allege that a person to whom proceedings relate has done an act which is within the jurisdiction of the industrial tribunal unless a finding by the industrial tribunal that he did the act, has become final.[2]

[1] Sex Discrimination Act 1975, s. 71 (1).

[2] *Ibid.*, s. 71 (2). With a view to making an application under s. 71 (1) (and also s. 72 (4) which relates to discrimination in advertising and pressure and instructions to discriminate) the Commission may present a complaint to an industrial tribunal that the respondent has done an act within the tribunal's jurisdiction. The tribunal can make similar orders to those mentioned above, other than an act for compensation; *ibid.*, s. 73 (1). A finding by an industrial tribunal under the Equal Pay Act 1970 or the Sex Discrimination Act 1975, if final is treated as conclusive by the county court on an application under s. 71 (1) or s. 72 (4) or in proceedings on an equality clause or by an industrial tribunal on a complaint made by a person affected by the act or in relation to an equality clause; s. 73 (3).

The circumstances in which the Commission may assist an individual are set out in section 75 of the Act. In cases where the section applies the Commission may give advice with, or without, the assistance of a solicitor or counsel, arrange for representation and assist in attempts to procure a settlement.

(c) *Obtaining information.* Under the provisions of the Sex Discrimination Act 1975 the Secretary of State is empowered to prescribe forms to assist aggrieved persons to question the respondent on his reasons for doing any relevant act, or on any matter which may be relevant.[1] The Sex Discrimination (Questions and Replies) Order 1975[2] has been made in pursuance of these powers and sets out a form of questionnaire to be completed by the aggrieved person as well as a reply by the respondent. The forms are available both from the Equal Opportunities Commission and from local offices of the Employment Service Agency and the Department of Employment. Where the aggrieved person questions the respondent, whether using the prescribed form or not, the questions and the replies of the respondent are admissable as evidence in proceedings.

If it appears to the court or tribunal that the respondent deliberately and without reasonable excuse omitted to reply within a reasonable period, or that his reply is evasive or equivocal, the court or tribunal may draw any inference from that fact that it considers just and equitable to draw, including an inference that the respondent committed an unlawful act.[3] In proceedings before an industrial tribunal[4] a question and reply is only admissible as evidence when the question was served before a complaint had been presented to a tribunal, if it was so served within the period of three months beginning when the act complained of was done, and where it was served when a complaint had been presented to a tribunal either, if it was so served within the period of 21 days beginning with the day on which the complaint was presented, or if it was so served later with leave given, and within a period specified by a direction of the tribunal.

[1] Sex Discrimination Act 1975, s. 74.
[2] S.I. 1975 No. 2048.
[3] Sex Discrimination Act 1975, s. 74 (2).
[4] See the Sex Discrimination (Questions and Replies) Order 1975, S.I. 1975 No. 2048, para. 5. For the position as to proceedings before courts see *ibid.*, para. 4.

The question and reply procedure may be of great assistance in preparing cases for hearing before industrial tribunals in employment cases. For this reason it may be important from the employee's point of view that they are raised of the employer at the appropriate time and, from the employer's point of view, that they are properly replied to.

## Trade union membership and activities

It will be seen[1] that an employee has protection from dismissal in connection with trade union activities and membership and in addition the Employment Protection Act 1975[2] gives the employee the right not to have action (short of dismissal) taken against him as an individual by his employer for the purpose of

"(a) preventing or deterring him from being or seeking to become a member of an independent trade union, or penalising him for doing so; or
(b) preventing or deterring him from taking part in the activities of an independent trade union at any appropriate time, or penalising him for doing so; or
(c) compelling him to be or become a member of a trade union which is not independent."[3]

[1] See p. 294, below.
[2] Section 53. Subject to the limited exceptions contained in the Employment Protection Act 1975, s. 118 (2) any agreement to exclude or limit them is void; *ibid.*, s. 118 (1), see p. 55, below.
[3] *Ibid.*, s. 53 (1).

"Appropriate time"[1] means time which is either outside working hours (i.e. when in accordance with his contract of employment the employee is required to be at work), or is a time within them which in accordance with arrangements agreed with, or consent given by, his employer it is permissible to take part in these activities.[2] If a union membership agreement is in force and the employee is of the same class, or if not, is of the same grade or category of employees, for whom it is the practice in accordance with the union membership agreement to belong to a specified independent trade union,[3] or one of a number of specified independent trade unions, the right to take part in union activities extends to activities on the employer's premises only if that union is the specified union.[4]

[1] Employment Protection Act 1975, s. 53 (1).

[2] *Ibid.*, s. 53 (2) and see *Post Office* v. *Crouch*, [1974] 1 All E.R. 229; [1974] 1 W.L.R. 89, H.L. for a decision on a similar earlier provision.

[3] A specified union for this purpose is the union specified in the union membership agreement, or is a trade union accepted by the parties as being the equivalent of a union so specified. It also includes unions when the Advisory, Conciliation and Arbitration Service has made an operative recommendation for recognition of that union covering the employee, or the union has referred a recognition issue to the Service and the Service has not declined to proceed, the union has not withdrawn the reference, or from the reference, and the issue has not been settled or reported under the Employment Protection Act 1975, s. 12; *ibid.*, s. 53 (5).

[4] *Ibid.*, s. 53 (4).

An employee who genuinely objects on the grounds of religious belief to being a member of any trade union whatsoever, has the right not to have action short of dismissal taken against him by the employer for the purposes of compelling him to join a trade union.

An employee can present a complaint to an industrial tribunal on the ground that action has been taken against him in contravention of these rights.[1] The application must be made before the end of the period of three months beginning with the date on which there occurred the action complained of, or the last of the actions, if it is part of a series of similar actions. If the tribunal is satisfied that it was not reasonably practicable for the complaint to be presented within three months, the complaint may be presented within such further period as the tribunal considers reasonable.[2] If the tribunal finds a complaint well founded it will make a declaration to the effect and may award compensation. In the proceedings, the onus of proof is on the employer to show the purpose for which the action was taken against the complainant, and that it was not such a purpose referred to in section 53 (1) (*a*) to (*c*) or sub-section (6). In determining any question as to whether action was taken, the purpose for which it was taken, or in determining compensation, no account is taken of any pressure which by calling, organising, or procuring a strike, or other industrial action, or threatening to do so, was exercised on the employer to take the action complained of and the questions are determined as if no such pressure had been exercised.[3] If the action was taken for the purpose of safe-guarding national security the complaint will be dismissed[4] and a certificate signed by or on behalf of the Minister of the Crown is conclusive evidence of this.[5] The compensation which the tribunal may award is such as the tribunal considers just and equitable in all the circumstances, having regard to the infringement of the employee's rights and to any loss sustained by the complainant attributable to the action.[6] The loss includes all expenses reasonably incurred in consequence of the action complained of and loss of any benefit he might reasonably have expected to have had but for the action.[7] The employee is under a duty to mitigate his loss just as under a claim for damages at common law.[8] The tribunal will reduce the amount of where it finds that the action complained of was to some extent caused, or contributed to, by any action of the complainant, by such proportion as it considers just and equitable having regard to that finding.[9] These provisions do not apply to an employee who is the husband or wife of the employer, a sharefisherman and employment where under the contract of employment the employee ordinarily works outside Great Britain.[10]

[1] Employment Protection Act 1975, s. 54 (1). The assistance of a conciliation officer may also be sought; see *ibid.*, s. 108.

[2] *Ibid.*, s. 54 (2).

[3] *Ibid.*, s. 55 (2).

[4] *Ibid.*, s. 55 (3).

[5] *Ibid.*, s. 55 (4).

[6] *Ibid.*, s. 56 (1).

[7] *Ibid.*, s. 56 (2).

[8] *Ibid.*, s. 56 (3).

[9] *Ibid.*, s. 56 (5).

[10] *Ibid.*, s. 119. For details of the order extending operation of the provision to employment for the purpose of activities in the territorial waters of the United Kingdom (other than those adjacent to Northern Ireland) and activities connected with the exploration of the sea bed or subsoil or the exploitation of

their natural resources in any area designated by order under the Continental Shelf Act 1964 being activities carried out on or from an offshore installation in any such area, see p. 62. Crown servants are included in the class which benefits from those provisions, with the exception of those in the armed forces and women's services administered by the Defence Council, *ibid.*, s. 127. House of Commons staff are also included; *ibid.*, s. 122.

## Rehabilitation of Offenders Act 1974

The Rehabilitation of Offenders Act 1974 provides that a rehabilitated person[1] shall be treated in all respects as if he had no convictions. A conviction which is spent under the terms of the Act, or the failure to disclose it, shall not be a proper ground for dismissing or excluding the rehabilitated person from any office or employment, or prejudice him in any way in any office or employment.[2] The Secretary of State has power[3] to make orders excluding or modifying the application of this requirement and has done so.[4] The excluded classes of professions, occupations and employment, include medical practitioners, barristers, solicitors, chartered accountants, judicial appointments and appointments in connection with the administration of justice, school teachers and youth club employees. These employees, or prospective employees should give details of spent convictions, if at the time details are requested they are informed that by virtue of the Rehabilitation of Offenders Act 1974 (Exceptions) Order 1975 the details should be disclosed.[5] In addition section 4 does not apply to any action taken for the purpose of safeguarding national security.

[1] A rehabilitated person is defined in the Act as a person whose convictions are spent. The period after which a conviction becomes spent varies from six months to ten years, depending on the gravity of the offence and does not apply to some sentences.

[2] Rehabilitation of Offender Act 1974, s. 4 (3).

[3] *Ibid.*, s. 4 (4).

[4] Rehabilitation of Offenders Act 1974 (Exceptions) Order 1975, S.I. 1975 No. 1023.

[5] In the case of the first four named professions the questions which should be answered relate to admission to the professions, *ibid.*, art. 3(a) (i).

# Chapter 2

# REMUNERATION AND TIME OFF

## REMUNERATION

Before the intervention of legislation the parties were free to decide the terms of the contract which existed between them. They would agree as to the amount of remuneration and when it would be paid. Statute has now taken away much of that freedom and at times an employee is entitled to payment whether or not he performs work for his employer. In addition, as part of the policies of successive governments to deal with inflation and other economic phenomena, attempts have been made to regulate the quantum of wages paid to large numbers of employees. A recent example being the Remuneration, Charges and Grants Act 1975.[1] Section 1 of that Act provides that whilst the section is in force, if an employer limits the amount of remuneration paid to an employee, and that limitation is no greater than necessary to keep the remuneration within the limits set out in the White Paper *The Attack on Inflation*, he is not liable for breach of contract by reason only that the remuneration is less than that which would be payable under an agreement entered into before the Act. This particular statute is expected to be short-lived but is typical of an approach which restricts the freedom of the parties to employment contracts to decide for themselves the obligations which govern their relationship.[1]

[1] See also Counter Inflation (Temporary Provisions) Act 1972, s. 3.

At common law the word "remuneration" if unqualified in any way includes more than just the cash payment in the form of wages or salary.

In *R. v. Postmaster-General*, BLACKBURN, J., said:[1]

"... I think the word 'remuneration' means a *quid pro quo*. If a man gives his services, whatever consideration he gets for giving his services seems to me a remuneration for them."

And a later passage in his judgment reads:[2]

"I liken it to a case of a domestic servant who receives wages at a certain rate, and also has board and lodging. There seems to me no doubt that his receipt of the board and lodging is part of the remuneration, and if he was dismissed improperly or unlawfully, the measure of the damages would be not only the money paid to him, but the money and money's worth in remuneration for his services, which he would have received if the contract had been carried out;..."

In *Skailes* v. *Blue Anchor Line, Ltd.* COZENS-HARDY, M.R., said[3] with reference to the meaning of "remuneration" in section 13 of the (now repealed) Workmen's Compensation Act 1906:

"Now 'remuneration' is not the same thing as salary or cash payment by the employer. The word 'remuneration' is only found in section 13 of the Act, and in Schedule 1, paragraph 2 (a), and this latter paragraph satisfies me that remuneration involves precisely the same consideration as earnings, I do not think it is open to this Court, after our decision in *Dothie* v. *Robert Macandrew & Co.*[4] to take any other view. We there held that the value of board and lodging must be brought into account in considering whether the remuneration of the deceased man exceeded £250, and that the mere cash salary was not to be solely regarded."[5]

[1] (1876), 1 Q.B.D. 658, at p. 663; (on appeal (1878), 3 Q.B.D. 428, C.A.).
[2] *Ibid.*, at p. 664.
[3] [1911] 1 K.B. 360, at p. 362, C.A.
[4] [1908] 1 K.B. 803.
[5] See also *Costello* v. *Pigeon (Owners)*, [1913] A.C. 407, at p. 412, H.L.

In *Pauley* v. *Kenaldo, Ltd.* a decision on the Catering Wages Act 1943, BIRKETT, L.J., said:[1]

"... a person may be none the less a servant by reason of the fact that his remuneration consists solely of tips."

Thus many of the "fringe benefits" received by employees are included in the term "remuneration", as for example, use of a company car, pension and life assurance schemes, and the provision of rent free accommodation. In *S. and U. Stores, Ltd.* v. *Wilkes*,[2] the words "average weekly rate of remuneration"[3] were examined by the National Industrial Relations Court in connection with a

payment of "expenses" to an employee. The Court held that any
sum which was paid by way of reimbursement, or on account, of
expenditure incurred by the employee has to be examined in
broad terms to see whether the whole or any part of it represents
a profit, or surplus, in the hands of the employee. The profit
element is part of the employee's remuneration. *Gould* v. *Balliol
College Oxford*[4] was a case which turned on the subtle distinction
between a service occupant and a service tenant. An industrial
tribunal was required to determine the correct particulars which
ought to have been given to the employee and defined them as
follows:

> "Remuneration:
> (1) Basic wage per week of 48 hours is £11. The employee
>     is entitled to free occupancy of the College House which
>     he at present occupies.
> (2) Overtime rate per hour is 5s.
> Remuneration is paid weekly in arrears."

Statutory definitions are often drawn very widely, for instance
in the Remuneration, Charges and Grants Act 1975 remuneration
is defined[5] as including "any benefit, facility or advantage, whether
in money or otherwise, provided by the employer or some other
person under arrangements with the employer, whether for the
first-mentioned person or otherwise, by reason of the fact that the
employer employs him . . .".

[1] [1953] 1 All E.R. 226, at p. 228.
[2] (1974), 9 I.T.R. 415, N.I.R.C.
[3] Appearing in Contracts of Employment Act 1963, Sch. 2, para. 3 (now
repealed but similar phrases appear in Employment Protection Act 1975, Sch. 4,
Part II). In *Wilkes* case the Court were determining the amount of a redundancy payment.
[4] (1966), 1 I.T.R. 534.
[5] By s. 7.

Apart from statutory regulation the parties to a contract of
employment are at liberty to make such arrangements with regard
to remuneration, and the other terms of their relationship as they
wish. In practice, however, the theoretical equality of the contracting parties, if it ever existed, disappeared long ago, and the provisions of individual agreements are often dictated by external
influences. Of these the two most often encountered are statutory

regulation and collective agreements made between employers and their representatives and trade unions.

## (a) Statute

In certain trades and industries minimum remuneration and holidays are fixed in accordance with statute, for example minimum rates of wages, time off and other terms and conditions for agricultural workers are decided by the Agricultural Wages Board and for certain other industries by Wages Councils under the Wages Councils Act 1959.

Section 90[1] of the Employment Protection Act 1975 empowers the Secretary of State for Employment by way of statutory instrument to provide that a Wages Council shall become a statutory joint industrial council as defined by section 91 of that Act. Such orders may be made on the application of the nominated employers' association or trade union, or by the Secretary of State on his own volition after consulting the nominated employers and trade unions. Further, if the Secretary of State is of the opinion that in the event of the abolition of the statutory joint industrial council, adequate machinery would be established for the regulation of the remuneration and other terms and conditions of employment of workers within the council's field of operation he may abolish that council by order. The statutory joint industrial council has powers similar to those of Wages Councils. In addition there are statutory provisions governing payment of wages for those in some occupations. For example:

(i) *Agricultural Wages Act* 1948. The Agricultural Wages Act 1948 prohibits the reckoning of any benefits and additions other than those defined by an Order of the Agricultural Wages Board.[2] The employer may not deduct more than the value determined by the Order for the benefits or additions defined, and must pay the balance in cash.[3]

---

[1] Which came into force on 1st January 1976, the Employment Protection Act 1975 (Commencement No. 1) Order 1975, S.I. 1975 No. 1938.

[2] Agricultural Wages Act 1948, ss. 7 and 11 (1) (a).

[3] *Jones* v. *Harris*, [1927] 1 K.B. 425; *Hayes* v. *Curtis* (1928), 139 L.T. 312; (only permitted benefits cottage board and lodging; price of milk deducted—not permissible); *Hughes* v. *Davies* (1929), 94 J.P. 48 (washing and mending done by employer—not a permitted benefit); *Williams* v. *Smith*, [1934] 2 K.B. 158 (board and lodging); *Long Eaton Co-operative Society, Ltd.* v. *Smith*, [1949] 2 K.B. 144; [1949] 1 All E.R. 633 (letting of premises a separate and independent transaction).

(ii) *Wages Councils Act* 1959. Many industries are governed by orders regulating wages made under the Wages Councils Act 1959. In such a case the method of calculating the remuneration must be in accordance with section 14 of the Wages Councils Act, which is as follows (incorporating amendments):

"(1) Subject to the provisions of this part of this Act, any reference in this Part of this Act to remuneration shall be construed as a reference to the amount obtained or to be obtained in cash by the worker from his employer after allowing for the worker's necessary expenditure, if any, in connection with his employment, and clear of all deductions in respect of any matter whatsoever, except any deduction lawfully made—

(a) under the Income Tax Acts the enactments relating to social security or any enactment requiring or authorising deductions to be made for the purposes of a superannuation scheme;

(b) at the request in writing of the worker, either for the purposes of a superannuation scheme or a thrift scheme or for any purpose in the carrying out of which the employer has no beneficial financial interest, whether directly or indirectly; or

(c) in pursuance of, or in accordance with, such a contract in that behalf as is mentioned in section one, two or three of the Truck Act 1896, and in accordance with the provisions of that section.

(2) Notwithstanding anything in sub-section (1) of this section, orders under section 11 of this Act may contain provisions authorising specified benefits or advantages, being benefits or advantages provided, in pursuance of the terms and conditions of the employment of workers, by the employer or by some other person under arrangements with the employer and not being benefits or advantages the provision of which is illegal by virtue of the Truck Acts 1831 to 1940, or of any other enactment, to be reckoned as payment of wages by the employer in lieu of payment in cash, and defining the value at which any such benefits or advantages are to be reckoned.

(3) If any payment is made by a worker in respect of any

benefit or advantage provided as mentioned in the foregoing sub-section, then —

   (*a*)  if the benefit or advantage is authorised by virtue of that sub-section to be reckoned as therein mentioned, the amount of the payment shall be deducted from the defined value for the purposes of the reckoning;

   (*b*)  if the benefit or advantage is authorised by virtue of that sub-section to be reckoned as therein mentioned, any excess of the amount of the payment over the defined value shall be treated for the purposes of sub-section (1) of this section as if it had been a deduction not being one of the excepted deductions therein mentioned;

   (*c*)  if the benefit or advantage is specified in a wages regulation order as one which has been taken into account in fixing the statutory minimum remuneration, the whole of the payment shall be treated for the purposes of sub-section (1) of this section as if it had been a deduction not being one of the excepted deductions therein mentioned.

(4) Nothing in this section shall be construed as authorising the making of any deduction, or the giving of remuneration in any manner, which is illegal by virtue of the Truck Acts 1831 to 1940, or of any other enactment."

(iii) *The Truck Acts* 1831–1940. The Truck Acts prohibit deductions from the wages of most manual workers, other than deductions specifically permitted by the Acts. Reference must be made to the Acts themselves for the detailed provisions, but broadly speaking the main permitted deductions are:

(*a*)  Deductions from wages for the supply of certain specified things, articles, money, or services, provided the employee has signed a written agreement for such deduction (Truck Act 1831, section 23).

(*b*)  Deductions from wages towards the cost of sharpening or repairing tools, if by an agreement separate from the contract of hiring (Truck Amendment Act 1887, section 8).

(*c*)  Food, non-intoxicating drink, a cottage, or other allowances or privileges are permissible in addition to money wages as remuneration for "a servant in husbandry" (Truck Amendment Act 1887, section 4).

(*d*)  Fines, deductions for bad work, for the use of tools, machines, and various similar matters are dealt with by the Truck Act 1896.

## (b) Collective agreements

One of the major factors dealt with in agreements between employers or employers' associations and trade unions is the question of wages and wage rates. There is a presumption that such collective agreements are not legally enforceable as such,[1] but although they do not automatically form part of an individual's contract of employment, they may expressly or impliedly be incorporated in it.[2] If an agreement containing details of remuneration is so incorporated in the employee's individual contract of employment, then he is entitled to rely on it in actions for remuneration.[3] Indeed since the requirement to furnish employees with written statements of the major terms of their contracts of employment it has been common practice for the employer to refer to collective agreements which give details of remuneration and wages rates.

[1] If made before 1st December 1971 or after 31st December 1974.

[2] See *National Coal Board* v. *Galley*, [1958] 1 All E.R. 91; [1958] 1 W.L.R. 16, C.A.; *Chappell* v. *Times Newspapers, Ltd.,* [1975] 2 All E.R. 233, C.A.

[3] The employee may not be bound by variations in a collective agreement incorporated in his individual contract of employment if he leaves the union. *Cf.* a decision of an industrial tribunal in *Singh* v. *British Steel Corporation,* [1974] I.R.L.R. 131, T.

In *Camden Exhibition and Display Ltd.,* v. *Lynott,*[1] Lord DENNING, M.R., said with regard to the negotiated working rules of the National Joint Council for the exhibition industry:

"In an ordinary contract of employment a man is bound to work his proper hours during his working week. But he is not bound to do overtime. Overtime is a matter for agreement between him and his employers. Do these working rules alter the position? It seems to me that, since the Contracts of Employment Act 1963, these working rules are incorporated into the terms of employment of all men in the industry. A notice was issued under that Act saying to every man: Your rate of wages, hours of work, holidays and holiday pay are in accordance with the provisions of the constitution and working rule agreement issued by and under the authority of the National Joint Council. In view of that notice these working rules are not only a collective agreement between the union and the employers. They are incorporated into the contract of employment of each man, insofar as they are applicable to his situation."

[1] [1966] 1 Q.B. 555, at p. 562; [1965] 3 All E.R. 28, C.A. per Lord DENNING, at p. 31 and per DAVIES, L.J., at p. 33.

A statute may provide that contracts in a particular trade or industry shall be governed by the terms of a collective agreement, in which case the incorporation of the terms of the collective agreement in the agreement of the individual employee is effected not by the express or implied terms of the contract but by statute. The Dock Labour Scheme which applies to dock work (as therein defined) is an example.[1]

[1] See the Dock Workers (Regulation of Employment) Act 1946 and S. R. & O. 1947 No. 1189, as amended by S.I. 1960 No. 2029, S.I. 1961 No. 2107 and S.I. 1967 No. 1252. The Dock Work Regulation Bill should also be considered.

Further, there are powers for the Central Arbitration Committee established by the Employment Protection Act 1975 to make awards relating to the terms and conditions of employment of employees.[1] Any term and condition which by such an award an employer is required to observe in respect of the employee is treated as being part of the contract of employment of such employees.[2]

[1] Employment Protection Act 1975, s. 21 (3).
[2] *Ibid.*, s. 21 (6).

## ITEMISED PAY STATEMENTS

Sections 81 to 84 of the Employment Protection Act 1975 make provision for employees to be provided by their employers at, or before, the time of payment of wages or salary, with an itemised written pay statement containing the particulars set out in section 81. They are:

"(*a*) the gross amount of the wages or salary;
(*b*) the amounts of any variable and, subject to section 82 below, any fixed deductions from that gross amount and the purposes for which they are made;

(c) the net amount of wages or salary payable; and
(d) where different parts of the net amount are paid in different ways, the amount and method of payment of each part-payment."[1]

[1] Any agreement (other than to refrain from instituting or continuing any proceedings before an industrial tribunal after a conciliation officer has taken action pursuant to s. 108 (3) or (4)) to exclude or limit the operation of this provision or to refrain from instituting or continuing proceedings before an industrial tribunal is void; Employment Protection Act 1975, s. 118. The right extends to those in Crown employment other than those in the armed and women's services, *ibid.*, s. 121.

The provisions are not yet in force but come into operation on 6th April 1977; the Employment Protection Act 1975 (Commencement No. 5) Order 1976, S.I. 1976 No. 1379.

The statement given in accordance with the requirements need not contain separate particulars of fixed deductions, if it instead contains an aggregate amount of fixed deductions, and the employer has given to the employee at the time, or before, a pay statement is given, a written standing statement of fixed deductions which contains particulars of the amount of the deduction, the intervals at which the deduction is made and the purpose for which it is made, in respect of each deduction comprised in the aggregate amount.[1] The standing statement may be amended from time to time by notice in writing given by the employer to the employee containing particulars of the amendment and within 12 months of the date on which the first standing statement was given, and at intervals of not more than 12 months thereafter, the statement should be reissued in consolidated form incorporating any amendments.[2] The standing statement which is effective on the date on which it is given ceases to be effective for the purposes of section 81 on the expiration of the period of 12 months beginning with the date it was given, or the date on which it was last reissued. The Secretary of State for Employment has power by order to add or remove items from the specified particulars and to shorten or extend the period of 12 months.[3]

[1] Employment Protection Act 1975, s. 82 (1).
[2] *Ibid.*, s. 82 (3).
[3] *Ibid.*, s. 83.

If the employer does not provide the pay statement as required the employee may require a reference to be made to an industrial tribunal to determine what particulars ought to be included in the statement.[1] When a statement, or a standing statement of fixed deductions which purports to comply with sections 81 and 82 (1) has been given to an employee and a question arises as to the particulars which ought to have been included, either the employer, or the employee, may require the question to be referred to and determined by the industrial tribunal[2] (in this connection a question as to the particulars which ought to have been included does not include a question as to the accuracy of an amount stated in any such particulars). The application may be made while the employment continues, or within three months of the date on which the employment ceased.[3]

[1] Employment Protection Act 1975, s. 84 (1). Note the difficult wording of the sub-section. The assistance of a conciliation officer may also be sought; see *ibid.*, s. 108. See p. 386, below.
[2] *Ibid.*, s. 84 (2).
[3] *Ibid.*, s. 84 (4).

Should the tribunal find that the employer has failed to give a pay statement in accordance with section 81, or that the pay statement, or standing statement of fixed deductions, does not, in relation to a deduction, constitute the particulars required by section 82 (1), the tribunal will make a declaration to that effect and when it finds further that any unnotified deduction had been made from the pay of the employee during the period of 13 weeks immediately preceding the date of the application for the reference (whether or not the deduction was made in breach of contract) it may order the employer to pay the employee a sum not exceeding the deduction made without the employer giving the employee particulars of that deduction in any pay statement or standing statement of fixed deductions, as required.[1]

[1] Employment Protection Act 1975, s. 84 (5).

The provisions as to itemised pay statements will not apply[1] to an employee who is the spouse of the employer, to merchant seamen, to share fishermen or to employees who ordinarily work outside Great Britain.[2] Nor do they apply initially to an employee whose employment normally involves less than 16 hours[3] weekly except that if the employment relationship ceases to be governed by a contract normally involving 16 hours or more weekly and becomes governed by a contract usually involving eight hours or more though less than 16 hours per week for a period of 26 weeks the employee will be treated as if he is employed under contract for 16 hours or more weekly. In calculating the period of 26 weeks no account is taken of a week where the employee works for 16 hours or more, takes part in a strike or lock out, or a period where there is no contract of employment but the week counts for the provisions of Schedule 1 of the Contracts of Employment Act 1972.[4] If the employee whose relationship with his employer is governed by a contract of employment which usually involves eight hours or more but less than 16 weekly has been continuously employed for a period of five years or more, he will be treated as if his contract normally involves employment for 16 hours or more weekly, and so will be entitled to an itemised pay statement in respect of that employment.[5]

[1] For more detailed explanation see p. 61, below, and also Employment Protection Act 1975, s. 119.
[2] See p. 61, below, for a fuller exposition of these exclusions.
[3] See *ibid.*, s. 119 (8).
[4] See p. 226, below.
[5] Employment Protection Act 1975, s. 119 (11).

## SUSPENSION

In some cases the contract of employment contains power for the employer to temporarily suspend the employee for misconduct. Such a power can exist only by statute,[1] or by an express or implied term in the contract.[2] It is not contrary to the Truck Act 1896, section 1.[3] An established practice at a particular factory may be incorporated in a workman's contract of service whether he knows of it or not; he is presumed to have accepted employment on the same terms as those applied to other members of the factory.[4] The same may apply to an established practice in a particular trade or district. The legal effect of the power to suspend is dependent upon the precise nature of the particular power under consideration.[5]

[1] *Wallwork* v. *Fielding*, [1922] 2 K.B. 66.
[2] *Warburton* v. *Taff Vale Rail, Co.* (1902), 18 T.L.R. 420.
[3] *Marshall* v. *English Electric Co., Ltd.*, [1945] 1 All E.R. 653, at p. 655, C.A.: *Sagar* v. *Ridehalgh & Son, Ltd.,* [1931] 1 Ch. 310, C.A.
[4] See *Marshall's* case, *supra.*
[5] See p. 63, below as to the employer's duty to provide work.

In *Bird* v. *British Celanese, Ltd.*[1] the employer was entitled "temporarily to suspend the workman from his employment ... if he was guilty of misconduct or breach of duty or breach of an order". Explaining this clause SCOTT, L.J., said in the course of his judgment[2]:

> "The suspense clause may act in two ways. It may be a merciful substitute for the procedure of dismissal, and a possible re-engagement. Under the suspense clause the right to wages ceases and the wages are not earned, and no deduction can be made from wages which are not payable. In the present case, as the workman was adjudged guilty of serious mis- conduct, the operation of the clause was merely merciful. It enabled the workman, when the suspension ended, to claim as of right to continue in his old job. The clause operates in accordance with its terms; the whole contract is suspended, in the sense that the operation of the mutual obligations of both parties is suspended; the workman ceases to be under any present duty to work, and the employer ceases to be under any consequential duty to pay. That is the natural meaning of the word 'suspend' when applied to a contract of employ- ment, and I think it is also its legal meaning."

[1] [1945] 1 K.B. 336; [1945] 1 All E.R. 488, C.A.
[2] [1945] 1 K.B. 336, at p. 341.

The case of *Hanley* v. *Pease and Partners, Ltd.*[1] is illustrative of the legal rights which may arise if an employer purports to suspend an employee when he has no power to do so. A workman absented himself from work for one day without leave from his employers. The employers did not dismiss him, but suspended him from working on the following day, as a result of which he was prevented from earning a day's wages. It was held that the employee's claim in such circumstances is technically one for damages for refusing to allow him to perform his contract of service; further, that although the employers might have a right to damages against the employee, they had no right to suspend him in that by so doing they were taking upon themselves to assess their own damages at one day's wages. After declining to dismiss the employee they had elected to treat the contract as continuing.

[1] [1915] 1 K.B. 698.

A right to suspend without payment of wages analogous to that in *Bird* v. *British Celanese, Ltd.*[1] is not a termination of the contract. However, in some cases suspension may amount to dismissal.

In *Marshall* v. *English Electric Co., Ltd.*,[2] which related to a contract of service liable to be determined by an hour's notice given by either side, there was also a well-established practice at the particular works of suspending without pay for breaches of discipline, and this was held to be a condition of employment. Lord GODDARD said[3]:

> "In my opinion what is called suspension is in truth dismissal with an intimation that at the end of so many days, or it may be hours, the man will be re-employed if he chooses to apply for reinstatement."

[1] [1945] 1 K.B. 336; [1945] 1 All E.R. 488, C.A.
[2] [1945] 1 All E.R. 653, C.A.
[3] *Ibid.*, at p. 655.

An employer who purports to exercise a right of suspension when he is not entitled to do so, can be guilty of repudiating the contract of employment and, if the employee elects to accept it as such, the employer's action may amount to dismissal. In view of the new requirement to include a note of details of disciplinary procedure in the statement issued to employees pursuant to the Contracts of Employment Act 1972, employers who wish to exercise a power of suspension as a mode of discipline should ensure that it is expressly contained in that note or the document referred to in it. An employer will find it increasingly difficult to claim to have a right to suspend employees if it is not clearly stated in disciplinary rules which are contained or referred to in the note.

## SUSPENSION ON MEDICAL GROUNDS[1]

An employee who is suspended from work on medical grounds in consequence of:
(a) any statutory requirement, or the requirement of any subordinate legislation, or
(b) any recommendation in any provision of a Code of Practice issued or approved under section 16 of the Health and Safety at Work etc. Act 1974,

which is a provision for the time being set out in Schedule 2 to the Employment Protection Act 1975, is entitled to be paid by his employer remuneration while he is so suspended for a period not exceeding 26 weeks.[2] The provisions leading to suspension on medical grounds set out in that Schedule are:

| | | |
|---|---|---|
| 1. The Paints and Colours Manufacture Regulations 1907. | S.R. & O. 1907 No. 17 | Reg. 5. |
| 2. The Yarn (Dyed by Lead Compounds) Heading Regulations 1907. | S.R. & O. 1907 No. 616 | Reg. 4. |
| 3. The Vitreous Enamelling Regulations 1908. | S.R. & O. 1908 No. 1258 | Reg. 10. |
| 4. The Tinning of Metal Hollow-ware, Iron Drums and Harness Furniture Regulations 1909. | S.R. & O. 1909 No. 720 | Reg. 6. |
| 5. The Lead Smelting and Manufacture Regulations 1911. | S.R. & O. 1911 No. 752 | Reg. 13. |
| 6. The Lead Compounds Manufacture Regulations 1921. | S.R. & O. 1921 No. 1443 | Reg. 11. |
| 7. The India Rubber Regulations 1922. | S.R. & O. 1922 No. 329 | Reg. 12. |
| 8. The Chemical Works Regulations 1922. | S.R. & O. 1922 No. 731 | Reg. 30. |
| 9. The Electric Accumulator Regulations 1925. | S.R. & O. 1925 No. 28 | Reg. 13. |
| 10. The Lead Paint Regulations 1927. | S.R. & O. 1927 No. 847 | Reg. 6. |
| 11. The Pottery (Health and Welfare) Special Regulations 1950. | S.I. 1950 No. 65 | Reg. 7. |
| 12. The Factories Act 1961 | 1961 c. 34 | Section 75(2) (including that section as extended by section 128). |
| 13. The Ionising Radiations (Unsealed Radioactive Substances) Regulations 1968. | S.I. 1968 No. 780 | Regs. 12 and 33. |
| 14. The Ionising Radiations (Sealed Sources) Regulations 1969. | S.I. 1969 No. 808 | Regs. 11 and 30. |

15. The Radioactive Substances  S.I. 1970 No. 1827  Reg. 14.
    (Road Transport Workers)
    (Great Britain) Regula-
    tions 1970.[3]
16. The Radioactive Substances  S.I. 1975 No. 1522
    (Road Transport Workers)
    (Great Britain) (Amend-
    ment) Regulations 1975.[4]

[1] These provisions came into force on 1st June 1976; Employment Protection Act 1975 (Commencement No. 4) Order 1976, S.I. 1976 No. 530. Crown employees other than those in the armed and women's services are included.

[2] Employment Protection Act 1975, s. 29 (1).

[3] The Secretary of State for Employment can add or remove provisions from Schedule 2; *ibid.*, s. 29 (3). It should be noted that if an employee is dismissed by reason of any such requirement or recommendation as is referred to in s. 29 (1) the qualifying period for the unfair dismissal provisions is reduced to four weeks; s. 29 (4). The usual restrictions on contracting out apply, *ibid.*, s. 118.

[4] Added by the Employment Protection (Medical Suspension) Order 1976, S.I. 1976 No. 659.

The employee is regarded as suspended from work if he continues to be employed by the employer (i.e., the contract of employment still exists) but he is not provided with work, or does not perform the work which he normally performed before the suspension.[1] The provisions for payment on suspension for medical grounds do not apply unless the employee has been continuously employed for four weeks ending with the last complete week before the day on which the suspension begins.[2] The employee is not entitled to remuneration by virtue of these provisions if he is incapable of work by reason of disease, or bodily or mental disablement,[3] nor if he is the husband or wife of the employer,[4] is a dock worker unless he is wholly or mainly engaged in work which is not dock work as defined by the Dock Labour Scheme, is a share fisherman, or under his contract of employment the employee ordinarily works outside Great Britain.[5] The provisions do not apply to employment under a contract for a fixed term of 12 weeks or less, or to employment under a contract made in contemplation of a performance of a specific task which is not expected to last for more than 12 weeks, unless in either case, the employee has been continuously employed for a period of more than 12 weeks.[6]

[1] Employment Protection Act 1975, s. 29 (2).

[2] *Ibid.*, s. 30 (1). In this connection the position of part-time workers should be considered.

³ *Ibid.*, s. 30 (2).
⁴ *Ibid.*, s. 119.
⁵ *Ibid.*, s. 119 but note the power of the Secretary of State to extend the provisions in s. 127. The only order now in force, the Employment Protection (Offshore Employment) Order 1976, S.I. 1976 No. 766, applies the provisions to—

(a) any activities (other than activities connected with a ship which is in the course of navigation or is a survey ship or is engaged in dredging or fishing) in the territorial waters:

(b) any activities connected with the exploration of the sea bed or subsoil or the exploitation of their natural resources in any designated area (other than an area or part of an area in which the law of Northern Ireland applies) being activities carried out on or from an offshore installation in any such designated area. The provisions of the Employment Protection Act 1975 in force on 21st June 1976 are applied to these activities subject to the modifications that s. 119 has effect as if—

(i) the reference in sub-s. (5) to Great Britain included the territorial waters and the waters in any designated area (other than an area or part of an area in which the law of Northern Ireland applies);

(ii) sub-sections (6), (12), (13) and (14) were omitted.

"Designated area" means any area designated under s. 1 (7) of the Continental Shelf Act 1964.

⁶ Employment Protection Act 1975, s. 119 (7).

The employee is not entitled to remuneration on suspension for medical grounds by virtue of section 29 of the Employment Protection Act 1975 if the employer has offered to provide him with suitable alternative work, whether or not work which the employee is under his contract, or was under the contract in force before the suspension, employed to perform and the employee has unreasonably refused to perform that work, or he does not comply with reasonable requirements imposed by his employer with a view to ensuring his services are available.[1] The remuneration payable is a week's pay for each week of suspension and in proportion for any part of a week.[2] Part II of Schedule 4 of the Employment Protection Act 1975[3] applies for calculating a week's pay and the calculation date is the day before that on which the suspension begins.[4] The statutory right to remuneration does not affect any contractual right to pay, and payment under a contractual obligation goes towards discharging the statutory liability and vice versa,[5] so that the employee is entitled to receive either contractual payment or statutory payment whichever is the greater.

[1] Employment Protection Act 1975, s. 30 (3).
[2] *Ibid.*, s. 31, subject to the usual limit (at present £80 per week).
[3] See p. 247, below.
[4] Employment Protection Act 1975, s. 31 (2). In the usual way "week"

in relation to an employee whose remuneration is calculated weekly by a week ending with a day other than a Saturday means a week ending with that other day and in relation to any other employee means a week ending on Saturday.

[5] *Ibid.,* s. 31 (1).

An employee can present a complaint to an industrial tribunal that his employer has failed to pay the whole or any part of the remuneration to which he is entitled under section 29.[1] The complaint must be presented before the end of the period of three months beginning with the day in respect of which the complaint is made, or within such further period as the tribunal considers reasonable when it is satisfied that it was not reasonably practicable for the complaint to be presented within that period.[2] If it finds the complaint well founded, the tribunal must order the employer to pay to the employee the amount of remuneration due to him.[3]

[1] Employment Protection Act 1975, s. 32 (1). The assistance of a conciliation officer may also be sought; *ibid.,* s. 108. See Chapter 9, below.

[2] Employment Protection Act 1975, s. 32 (2).

[3] *Ibid.,* s. 32 (3).

When an employer engages an employee to replace an employee suspended as is referred to in section 29, and informs the new employee in writing on engaging him that his employment will be terminated at the end of the suspension, if he dismisses the new employee in order to allow the suspended employee to resume his original work, then for the purposes of the unfair dismissal provisions the reason for the dismissal is an "other substantial reason of a kind such as to justify dismissal".[1] On a complaint to an industrial tribunal by the dismissed employee claiming compensation for unfair dismissal, the employer will still have to satisfy the tribunal that in the circumstances he acted reasonably in treating the reason as a sufficient reason for dismissing the employee, if he is to successfully resist the claim.

[1] Employment Protection Act 1975, s. 33, and see Trade Union and Labour Relations Act 1974, Sch. 1, para. 6 (1) (*b*), at p. 294, below. See precedent in Appendix 6.

## LAY-OFF AND SHORT-TIME

The old common law cases indicate that the employer is not under an obligation to provide work for the employees save in special circumstances[1] such as for those employees on piecework[2] and actors.[3] In *Turner* v. *Sawdon & Co.*[4] it was said:

> "In my opinion it is not right to stretch the meaning of the words 'engage and employ' as they have been stretched in this case. The meaning of those words is that the servant is retained in the service for a period of four years at fixed wages, but there is no bargain that the servant shall be kept at work during that period."

[1] *R.* v. *Welch* (1853), 2 E. & B. 357; *Aspdin* v. *Austin* (1844), 5 Q.B. 671; *Dunn* v. *Sayles* (1844), 5 Q.B. 685.
[2] *Whittle* v. *Frankland* (1862), 2 B. & S. 49.
[3] *Fechter* v. *Montgomery* (1863), 33 Beav. 22.
[4] [1901] 2 K.B. 653; (1901), 135 L.T. 222. Smith, M. R., at p. 225.

The term "lay-off", except when used in connection with the Redundancy Payments Act 1965 where it has a technical meaning,[1] is not a clearly defined legal concept. It is often used by employers and employees but not always in the same sense and appears to be used to cover at least two distinct situations. The first is where the contract of employment is terminated. The termination can be by dismissal, agreement between the parties, or frustration, so that the employment comes to an end and there is no existing employment relationship between the employer and the employee. If the employee is subsequently re-employed by the employer the interim period may be spoken of as one of lay-off.[2] The second alternative arises when, either by agreement at the time, or as a result of a provision in the contract, the employment relationship subsists between the employer and the employee, but the obligations on the employer to provide work for the employee is temporarily suspended. The stipulation as to lay-off in these cases can be either express or implied, and an implied term has been found to arise by way of custom of the trade or of the individual business. During this type of lay-off there may be a contractual obligation on the employer to make payment of wages, or of a guaranteed minimum wage, and but for the suspension of the employer's obligation to provide work (if such there be), the relationship of employer and employee continues.

[1] See p. 223, below.
[2] *McCarthy* v. *Burroughs Machines, Ltd.* (1975), 10 I.T.R. 46, but see *Sneddon* v. *Ivorycrete (Builders), Ltd.* (1966), 1 I.T.R. 538, where it was held that dismissal could not be a "lay-off".

An example of this type of lay-off occurred in *Puttick* v. *John Wright & Sons (Blackwall), Ltd.*[1] when Lord THOMPSON delivering the judgment of the Court said:

"We think it quite possible to envisage circumstances in which A may consider it in his best interests to undertake to do such work of a particular kind as B provides for him, A holding himself available to do such work as required and being paid only for the work he actually does, while B undertakes to make available to A such work of that particular kind as from time to time comes to hand. In such an arrangement between A and B, A in effect agrees to be "temporarily suspended" or "laid off" for such periods as no work is in fact available. It may well be that in the present case the parties never put their minds to the full legal implications of such an arrangement, but it does not seem to be disputed that such an arrangement was in fact what they contemplated and intended and believed they had entered into. This is in our view borne out by the history of the relationship between the parties, particularly the basic continuity of the appellant's employment with the respondents over some 23 years, the fact that at no time when he was laid off was he given notice of dismissal and the fact that he always held himself available for work from the respondents and they always gave him work to do with only very short periods of interruption between jobs. We are unable to find anything in any of the quoted cases to suggest that such an arrangement does not amount to a contract of employment binding in its terms."

[1] (1972), 7 I.T.R. 438, at p. 442, N.I.R.C.

In this sense of the word lay-off the obligations which continue during the suspension of work vary from case to case. In some situations the relationship between the parties is still close, payment being made to the employee who reports to the place of work regularly, in others no payment is due to the employee, he collects unemployment pay and returns to work only when required.

Lay-off has been considered by the courts only rarely in recent times and the present position is far from clear.[1] If the lay-off is of a type which amounts to dismissal then it is treated as such for the purposes of the employee's claims both under the terms of his contract and arising from the employee's statutory rights. It is unlikely that the courts or tribunals will accept that lay-off does not operate as a dismissal unless a clear term of the contract, such as an express agreement to that effect, can be shown[2] and if employers wish to rely on such a right to lay-off they will be well advised to include it expressly in the rules which are referred to in the statement given to the employee pursuant to section 4 of the Contracts of Employment Act 1972. When lay-off of this type takes place the employer will be liable to pay the employee any guaranteed wage prescribed by contract or statute. The provisions of the Redundancy Payments Act 1965 may also have to be considered.

[1] Otherwise than in its technical sense in redundancy cases.
[2] See p. 193, below.

When the employer provides the employee work and payment for less than the normal number of hours per week it is said that the employee is on "short time". The position is very similar to that of lay-off. Unless the employer has the power pursuant to the contract of employment to reduce the number of hours or payment, a unilateral attempt at introducing short-time could amount to repudiation of the contract by the employer and hence dismissal. An employer who claims to have the right to put his employees on to short-time is best advised to express it in documentary form available to the employees. When an attempt to put employees on short-time amounts to dismissal then all the effects of dismissal have to be considered in the usual way. If there is a contractual right for the employees to be placed on short-time working the employer should consider his contractual and statutory obligations to provide a guaranteed minimum wage.[1] The provisions of sections 5 to 8 of the Redundancy Payments Act 1965 may also be relevant.

[1] The effect so far as guarantee payments to be paid pursuant to the Employment Protection Act 1975 is not clear. See p. 167, below.

## GUARANTEE PAYMENTS[1]

Section 22 (1) of the Employment Protection Act 1975 provides:

"22.—(1) Where an employee throughout a day[2] during

any part of which he would normally be required to work in accordance with his contract of employment is not provided with work by his employer by reason of—

(a) a diminution in the requirements of the employer's business for work of the kind which the employee is employed to do,[3] or

(b) any other occurrence affecting the normal working of the employer's business in relation to work of the kind which the employee is employed to do,

he shall, subject to the following provisions of this Act, be entitled to be paid by his employer a payment, referred to in this Act as a guarantee payment, in respect of that day and hereafter in this section and sections 23 to 26 below:

(i) such a day is referred to as a 'workless day', and

(ii) 'workless period' has a corresponding meaning."

[1] These provisions are not yet in force. It is anticipated that they will be introduced during 1977. Employment Protection Act 1975, s. 112 enables the Secretary of State for Employment to make Regulations to govern the relationship between guarantee payments and unemployment benefit.

[2] "Day" means the period of 24 hours from midnight to midnight. Where a period of employment straddles midnight, if the longer period is worked before midnight then the period of employment is treated as falling wholly on the first day. In other cases it is treated as falling wholly on the second day; Employment Protection Act 1975, s. 22 (2). Section 22 would not appear to cover short-time working.

[3] This is similar to part of the definition of redundancy. See p.      , below.

The requirement for guarantee payments does not apply if the employer is the spouse of the employee,[1] to registered dock workers unless he is in employment by virtue of which the employee is wholly or mainly engaged in work which is not dock work as defined by any scheme for the time being in force under the statutory provisions for the regulation of dock work,[1] to share fishermen,[1] or to employment under a contract where the employee ordinarily works outside Great Britain.[2] Nor do the provisions apply to employment under a contract for a fixed term of 12 weeks or less, or to employment under a contract made in contemplation of the performance of a specific task which is not expected to last for more than 12 weeks, unless in either case, the employee has been continuously employed for a period of more than 12 weeks.[1]

[1] Employment Protection Act 1975, s. 119.

To be entitled to a guarantee payment an employee has to have been continuously employed[1] for a period of four weeks ending with the last complete week before the workless day. He is not entitled to a guarantee payment if the failure to provide the employee with work occurs in consequence of a trade dispute[2] involving any employee of the employer, or of an associated employer.[3] The employee will not be entitled to a guarantee payment in respect of a workless day if his employer has offered to provide alternative work for that day which is suitable in all the circumstances, whether or not it is work the employee is contractually bound to perform and the employee has unreasonably refused the offer, or he does not comply with reasonable requirements imposed by his employer with a view to ensuring that his services are available.[4]

[1] Continuous employment is defined by reference to Contracts of Employment Act 1972, Sch. 1. It must be remembered that certain part-time employees may not qualify because their weeks of employment do not count. See p.   , below.

[2] Trade dispute" is as defined in Trade Union and Labour Relations Act 1974, s. 29.

[3] Employment Protection Act 1975, s. 23 (1). But not other employers, for instance non-associated suppliers. For definition of associated employers see Trade Union and Labour Relations Act 1974, s. 30 (5) and p. 202, below.

[4] *Ibid.*, 2. 23 (2).

Subject to the limits set out below the amount of a guarantee payment payable to an employee in respect of any day is the sum produced by multiplying the number of normal working hours on that day by the guaranteed hourly rate.[1] No guarantee payment is payable in respect of a day if there are no normal working hours on that day.[1] The guaranteed hourly rate is the amount of a week's pay[2] divided by the employee's normal working hours in a week under the contract of employment in force on the day in respect of which the guarantee payment is payable or, if the number of normal working hours in a week differs from week to week, or over a longer period, it is the amount of one week's pay[2] divided by the average number of such hours over the 12 week period ending with the last complete week before the day in respect of which the guarantee payment is payable.

If the employee has not been employed for a sufficient period it is the amount of one week's pay divided by a number which fairly represents the number of normal working hours in a week[3] having regard to the average number of normal working hours in a week which the employee could expect in accordance with the terms of his contract and the average number of such hours of other employees engaged in relevant comparable employment with the same employer, as appropriate in the circumstances. If an employee's contract has been varied or a new contract has been entered into in connection with a period of short-time working these provisions have effect as if for references to the day in respect of which guarantee payment is payable there is substituted reference to the last day on which the original contract was in force.[4]

[1] Employment Protection Act 1975, s. 24 (1).
[2] Calculated in accordance with Employment Protection Act 1975, Part II, Sch. 4. The calculation date is the day in respect of which the guarantee payment is payable, subject to s. 24 (4).
[3] *Ibid.*, s. 24 (2).
[4] *Ibid.,* s. 24 (4).

The amount of guarantee payment payable to an employee in respect of any day shall not exceed £6[1] and the employee is not entitled to guarantee payments in respect of more than the specified number of days in any three month period commencing on 1st February, 1st May, 1st August and 1st November in each year.[2] The "specified number of days" is the number of days, not exceeding five, on which the employee normally works in a week under the contract of employment in force on the day in respect of which the guarantee payment is claimed, or where the number of days varies from week to week or over a longer period, the average number of such days, not exceeding five, calculated by dividing the total number of such days during the period of 12 weeks ending with the last complete week before the day in respect of which the guarantee payment is claimed, by 12 and rounding up the resulting figure to the next whole number. If the employee has not been employed for that period of 12 weeks the specified number of days is the number which fairly represents the number of the employee's normal working days in a week, not exceeding five, having regard to the average number of normal working days in a week which the employee could expect in accordance with terms of his contract and the average number of such days of other employees engaged in relevant comparable employment with the same employer, as appropriate in the circumstances.[3] If an employee's contract has been varied, or a new contract entered into, in connection with a period of short-time working then in calculating the specified number of days references to the day in respect of which the guarantee payment is claimed are construed as if they are to the last day on which the original contract was in force.

[1] Employment Protection Act 1975, s. 25 (1). This may be varied by order of the Secretary of State for Employment, s. 25 (5).

[2] *Ibid.*, s. 25 (2). The period may be varied by order of the Secretary of State from time to time.

[3] *Ibid.*, s. 25 (3).

The provisions as to guarantee payments do not affect the validity of contractual rights to payment during absence from work and payment under the contract in respect of a workless day goes towards discharging the statutory liability to pay a guarantee payment in respect of that day, and payment of a guarantee payment goes towards discharging the contractual liability.[1] The effect is that the employee should receive whichever is the greater of the payments due under the statutory scheme and under his contract. The payment under the contract is treated as paid in respect of a workless day if it is expressed to be calculated or payable by reference to that day to the extent that it is so expressed, and in any other case to the extent that it represents guaranteed remuneration rather than remuneration for work actually done, and is referable to that day when apportioned relatively between that day and any other workless period falling within the period in respect of which the remuneration is paid.[2]

[1] Employment Protection Act 1975, s. 26 (2).

[2] *Ibid.*, s. 26 (3).

The Secretary of State for Employment may by order provide that the provisions of the Employment Protection Act 1975 relating to guarantee payments and, so far as they apply for the purpose of these provisions, Schedule 4 of the Act (relating to calculation of normal working hours and a week's pay) shall have effect subject to modifications and adaptations as may be prescribed by the order.[1]

[1] Employment Protection Act 1975, s. 26 (4).

An employee may present a complaint to the industrial tribunal that his employer has failed to pay the whole or any part of a guarantee payment to which the employee is entitled.[1] The complaint should be presented before the end of the period of three months beginning with the day in respect of which the complaint as to the guarantee payment is made, or if it is satisfied that it was not reasonably practicable for the complaint to be presented in that time within such further period as the tribunal considers reasonable.[2] When a tribunal finds a complaint well founded it will order the employer to pay to the complainant the amount of the guarantee payment it finds due to him.[3]

[1] Employment Protection Act 1975, s. 27 (1).
[2] *Ibid.*, s. 27 (2).
[3] *Ibid.*, s. 27 (3).

The Secretary of State for Employment may by order (which can be varied or revoked from time to time) exclude employees from the operation of the statutory guarantee payment scheme. There must be in force a collective agreement or wages order whereby the employees to whom the agreement or order relates have a right to guaranteed remuneration.[1] The Secretary of State will not make the order unless the agreement provides procedure to be followed (whether upon arbitration or otherwise) in cases where an employee claims his employer has failed to pay the whole or any part of any guaranteed remuneration to which the employee is entitled under the agreement and that the procedure includes the right to arbitration or adjudication by an independent referee or body, in cases where (by reason of an equality of votes or otherwise) a decision cannot otherwise be reached, or the agreement indicates that the employee can present a complaint to an industrial tribunal that his employer has failed to pay the whole or any part of any guaranteed payment to which the employee is entitled under the agreement.[2] The application to the Secretary of State has to be by all parties to the agreement or, as the case may be of the council or Board making the order and the appropriate Minister has to be satisfied that the provisions as to statutory guarantee payments should not apply to those employees.[3]

[1] Employment Protection Act 1975, s. 28.
[2] *Ibid.*, s. 28 (4). When such an order is in force industrial tribunals have jurisdiction to decide such matters.
[3] "Wages order" means an order under Wages Councils Act 1959, s. 11 and s. 3 of the Agricultural Wages Act 1948. "Appropriate Minister" is the Secretary

of State for Employment in all cases other than under the Agricultural Wages Act 1948 when it is the Minister of Agriculture, Fisheries and Food; Employment Protection Act 1975, s. 28 (2).

Any other agreement (other than to refrain from instituting or continuing any proceedings before an industrial tribunal where a conciliation officer has taken action as mentioned in Employment Protection Act 1975, s. 108 (3) or (4)) to exclude or limit the operation of the provisions as to guarantee payments, or to refrain from instituting or continuing proceedings before an industrial tribunal is void; *ibid.*, s. 118.

## SICKNESS AND INJURY

### (1) **Employees other than apprentices**

There is no universal rule of law that an employee is entitled to wages or other remuneration during sickness. The position may be clarified by sub-dividing the various principles of law as follows:

(i) The contract of employment may be terminated if the illness is so severe or of such long duration as seriously to interfere with or frustrate the business purpose of the contract. This is part of the general law of contract.[1]

[1] *Marshall* v. *Harland and Wolff*, [1972] 2 All E.R. 715; [1972] 1 W.L.R. 899, N.I.R.C.; *Poussard* v. *Spiers and Pond* (1876), 1 Q.B.D. 410 (opera-singer— unable to perform on the opening and early performances—employers justified in rescinding contract); *Storey* v. *Fulham Steel Works Co.* (1907), 24 T.L.R. 89, C.A. (*held* no frustration).

(ii) An employee may disentitle himself by the terms of his contract of employment, either express or implied, from remuneration during temporary illness. The question to be asked is: what were the terms of the contract between employer and employee, and what did those terms provide in regard to payment of wages during absence by reason of illness? The ordinary principles of the law of contract must be applied, and the right to wages depends on whether the consideration therefor has been performed. It must therefore be ascertained from the contract whether the consideration for the payment of wages is the actual performance of the work, or whether mere readiness and willingness, if of ability to do so, is the consideration.[1]

[1] *Petrie* v. *MacFisheries, Ltd.*, [1940] 1 K.B. 258, [1939] 4 All E.R. 281, C.A.; explaining *Marrison* v. *Bell*, [1939] 2 K.B. 187, [1939] 1 All E.R. 745, C.A.;

*O'Grady* v. *M. Saper, Ltd.*, [1940] 2 K.B. 469, at p. 473; [1940] 3 All E.R. 527, C.A.

(iii) When payment is for piecework the consideration for the wages will be the actual performance of the work. In the case of employment by the hour the actual performance of the work is likely to be the consideration for the wages.[1] Similarly when payment is by the day, the actual performance of each day's work is likely to be the consideration for that day's wages.[2] When payment is by the week much depends on the nature of the work. In the case of employees engaged for a longer period, usually the consideration will be found to be the mere readiness and willingness to do the work, if of ability to do so, and not the actual performance of the work.[3]

[1] *Hancock* v. *B.S.A. Tools, Ltd.*, [1939] 3 All E.R. 538 (notice displayed in works—hourly basis—custom of trade—driller).

[2] *Hanley* v. *Pease & Partners*, [1915] 1 K.B. 698.

[3] On this subject in general see A. T. Denning, "Wages During Sickness", 55 L.Q.R. 353.

(iv) If under the terms of his contract, express or implied, the employee is entitled to wages during temporary sickness, he is entitled during such absence to receive his full remuneration in accordance with the terms of his employment. This may, in certain circumstances, include a bonus.[1] Benefits payable under the social security legislation are additional benefits and, in the absence of agreement, express or implied, to the contrary, wages must be paid in full even though sickness benefit is being received.[2] The position may be different when the employer contributes to a Friendly Society Fund, and the facts must be fully investigated to ascertain the employee's rights.[3]

[1] *Orman* v. *Saville Sportswear, Ltd.*, [1960] 3 All E.R. 105; [1960] 1 W.L.R. 1055 (production manager).

[2] *Marrison* v. *Bell*, [1939] 2 K.B. 187; [1939] 1 All E.R. 745, C.A.

[3] *Niblett* v. *Midland Rail, Co.* (1907), 23 T.L.R. 240.

An implied term for payment during sickness may arise from the known practice of a particular employer, which has been acted upon in the past. It is, of course, always open to the employer to terminate the employment by giving proper notice during the absence of the employee while sick. It is only when the contract is treated as still subsisting that the above statement of the law will apply. It is in the interests of both parties that the precise right, if any, to remuneration during absence while incapacitated be defined at the time of engagement and clarified in the contract of employment and there is an obligation on the employer to give details of any provisions for sick pay in the written particulars of the contract of employment issued pursuant to the Contracts of Employment Act 1972.

### (2) Apprentices

A contract of apprenticeship differs from a mere contract of service in that the covenants are independent and not inter-dependent; thus the performance of the master's covenant does not depend on the performance by the apprentice of his obliga-tions.[1] None the less it is an implied term of a contract of apprenticeship that the apprentice's covenant to serve depends on his capacity to do so, in the sense that incapacity in the nature of permanent illness is an excuse for non-performance by the master.[2] Temporary illness of an apprentice does not however discharge a contract.[3]

[1] *Winstone* v. *Linn* (1823), 1 B. & C. 460; *Phillips* v. *Clift* (1859), 4 H. & N. 168. See also

[2] *Boast* v. *Firth* (1868), L.R. 4 C.P. 1; *cf.* R. v. *Hales-Owen* (*Inhabitants*) (1718), 1 Stra. 99.

[3] *Patten* v. *Wood* (1887), 51 J.P. 549.

## PREGNANCY—MATERNITY PAY AND THE RIGHT TO RETURN TO WORK[1]

An employee absent from work wholly or partly because of pregnancy or confinement has two important rights. If she fulfils the necessary requirements she is entitled to maternity pay[2] and has the right to return to work after the confinement.[3]

[1] Any agreement (other than where a conciliation officer has taken action and the agreement is to refrain from instituting or continuing any proceedings before an industrial tribunal) to exclude or limit the operation of these provisions or to refrain from instituting or continuing proceedings before an industrial tribunal is void; Employment Protection Act 1975, s. 118.

[2] The provisions as to maternity pay are not yet in force. They will come into force on 6th April 1977; Employment Protection Act 1975 (Commencement No. 4) Order 1976, S.I. 1976 No. 530.

[3] Those parts of the Employment Protection Act 1975 dealing with the right to return to work after confinement came into force on 1st June 1976. "Confinement" means the birth of a living child, or the birth of a child whether living or dead after 28 weeks of pregnancy; Employment Protection Act 1975, s. 52.

The employee is entitled to these rights whether or not the contract of employment subsists during her absence so long as

"(a) she continues to be employed by her employer (whether or not she is at work) until immediately before the beginning of the 11th week before the expected week of confinement;

(b) she has at the beginning of that 11th week been continuously employed for a period of not less than two years; and

(c) she informs her employer (in writing if he so requests) at least three weeks before her absence begins or, if that is not reasonably practicable, as soon as reasonably practicable:

(i) that she will be (or is) absent from work wholly or partly because of pregnancy or confinement, and

(ii) in the case of the right to return, that she intends to return to work with her employer."[1]

[1] Employment Protection Act 1975, s. 35 (2).

An employee who is dismissed because at the effective date of termination, she is because of her pregnancy incapable of doing the work which she is employed to do, or because of her pregnancy she cannot, or will not, be able to continue after that date without contravention of a statutory duty of restriction, and was not re-engaged in accordance with section 34 (2) of the Employment Protection Act 1975, is entitled to the two benefits notwithstanding that she ceased to be employed before the beginning of the eleventh week before the expected week of confinement, if, but for that dismissal, she would at the beginning of that eleventh week have been continuously employed for the qualifying two year period.[1] She is not entitled to the right to return to work unless she informs the employer in writing, if he so requests, before or as soon as reasonably practicable after the dismissal takes effect that she intends to return to work with him.[2] If the employer so requests the employee should produce for inspection a certificate from a medical practitioner or certified midwife[3] stating the expected week of the confinement[4] and if she does not do so she may lose her entitlement.

[1] This period may be varied by order of the Secretary of State; Employment Protection Act 1975, s. 35 (5). Some part-time employees may not qualify because their weeks of employment may not count.

[2] Employment Protection Act 1975, s. 35 (3).

[3] Defined in Employment Protection Act 1975, s. 52.

[4] *Ibid.*, s. 35 (4). "Expected week of confinement" means a period of seven days beginning with midnight between Saturday and Sunday in which it is expected that the confinement will take place; section 52.

Employees who are employed by their husbands are excluded, as are share fisherwomen and those who under their contract of employment ordinarily work outside Great Britain.[1]

[1] Employment Protection Act 1975, s. 119. The provisions apply to Crown Servants with appropriate amendments; *ibid.*, s. 121. The armed services and women's services administered by the Defence Council are excluded but House of Commons staff are included. Offshore employment is included in certain circumstances, see p. 62, above.

## Maternity pay

Maternity pay is paid in respect of a period, or periods not exceeding (in aggregate, if applicable) six weeks[1] during which the employee is absent from work wholly or partly because of pregnancy or confinement.[2] The employee is not entitled to maternity pay for any absence before the eleventh week before the expected week of confinement and her payment period (or periods) consists of the first six weeks of absence starting on or after the beginning of that eleventh week.[3] When the employee does not tell the employer that she is, or will be, absent from work wholly or partly because of pregnancy or confinement, or does not give a certificate stating the expected week of confinement when requested, she is not entitled to maternity pay for any part of that period until she gives the employer that information or certificate, but when she supplies these she is entitled to be paid in respect of that part of the period or periods which fall before she did so.[4]

[1] This period may be varied by order of the Secretary of State for Employment; Employment Protection Act 1975, s. 36 (3).

[2] *Ibid.*, s. 36 (1).

[3] *Ibid.*, s. 36 (2).

[4] *Ibid.*, s. 36 (4).

Maternity pay is nine-tenths of a week's pay[1] for each week during which it is payable reduced by the amount of maternity allowance payable for that week under Part 1, Schedule 4 of the Social Security Act 1975, whether or not the employee is entitled to the whole or part of that allowance.[2] Maternity pay accrues from day to day and in calculating the amount of the payment, Sundays and other days prescribed under section 22 (10) of the Social Security Act 1975 are disregarded, and the amount payable for any other day is taken as one-sixth of the amount of maternity pay for the week in which the day falls.[3] As with other benefits under the Employment Protection Act 1975, the right to maternity pay does not affect contractual rights, the sum recoverable under the statutory obligation is set against that recoverable under the contract and the effect is that the employee receives whichever is the higher.[4] An employee may present a complaint to an industrial tribunal against her employer that he has failed to pay the whole or part of maternity pay due to her.[5] The complaint has to be presented to the tribunal before the end of the period of three months beginning with the last day of the payment period, or if the industrial tribunal is satisfied that it was not reasonably practicable for the complaint to be presented within that time, such further period as the tribunal considers reasonable.[6] An industrial tribunal finding the claim well founded will order the employer to pay to the complainant the amount of maternity pay it finds due to her.[7]

[1] Defined in Employment Protection Act 1975, Sch. 4. The calculation date is the last day on which the employee worked under the contract of employment in force immediately before the beginning of her absence.

[2] Employment Protection Act 1975, s. 37 (1).

[3] *Ibid.*, s. 37 (2).

[4] *Ibid.*, s. 37 (3) and (4). I.e., the lower is set off against the higher.

[5] *Ibid.*, s. 38 (1). The assistance of a conciliation officer may also be sought; *ibid.*, s. 108 and see Chapter 9.

[6] *Ibid.*, s. 38 (2).

[7] *Ibid.*, s. 38 (3).

A "Maternity Pay Fund" is to be established under the control and management of the Secretary of State for Employment[1] and section 39 sets out rules for its management and the investment of monies of which it is comprised. Contributions to the Maternity Pay Fund are made by employers by increasing the Social Security secondary Class I contribution by 0.05% of the employee's earnings for the purposes of the Social Security Act 1975. There are provisions to enable advances to be made to the Maternity Pay Fund from the National Loans Fund.[2] Subject to any regulations made under section 42 of the Employment Protection Act 1975,[3] the Secretary of State should pay out of the Maternity Pay Fund to an employer who has paid maternity pay to an employee to whom he is liable to pay it, and who makes the appropriate claim, the whole of the maternity payment so paid, by way of rebate.[4] There is a discretion for the Secretary of State if he thinks fit and is satisfied that it would be just and equitable to do so having regard to all relevant circumstances, to pay the rebate to an employer who has paid maternity pay to an employee whose complaint to an industrial tribunal was dismissed, or would not be entertained by the tribunal, by reason of the time limit for presenting the complaint.[5] When the employer pays a sum due to the employee under the terms of the contract of employment during absence due to pregnancy or confinement it is treated as maternity pay for the purposes of rebate to the extent that it extinguishes the employer's liability to pay maternity pay, or if it would fall within the discretion of the Secretary of State mentioned above, it would extinguish the liability if the claim was not time barred.[6]

[1] Employment Protection Act 1975, s. 39 (1), which comes into operation on 6th April 1977.

[2] See *ibid.*, s. 41.

[3] There are no such regulations at present. The Secretary of State for Employment will make regulations as to making claims for rebates and may in particular require the claim to be made within a time limit and that it be supported by such evidence as may be prescribed; Employment Protection Act 1975, s. 42 (4).

[4] *Ibid.*, s. 42 (1).

[5] *Ibid.*, s. 42 (2).

[6] *Ibid.*, s. 42 (3).

An employee who claims that her employer is liable to pay her maternity pay and that she has taken all reasonable steps (other than proceedings to enforce a tribunal award) to recover payment from her employer or that her employer is insolvent[1] and the whole or any part of the maternity pay remains unpaid can apply for payment to the Secretary of State.[2] If he is satisfied that the claim is well founded, he will pay out of the Maternity Pay Fund the amount of the maternity pay which appears to him to be unpaid.[3] When an application is made the Secretary of State may require the employer to provide him with such information as he reasonably requires for determining whether the application is well founded and he may require any person having custody or control of any records or other documents to produce for examination on behalf of the Secretary of State, any such documents in that person's custody, or under his control, which are of the same description as the Secretary of State may require.[4] The Secretary of State's request should be in writing and can be varied or revoked by subsequent notice. Refusal or wilful neglect to furnish information or produce a document so requested may lead to a fine not exceeding £100 on summary conviction,[5] and if an employer claiming rebate, or an employee claiming payment from the Maternity Pay Fund, or in purporting to comply with such a notice, knowingly or recklessly makes any false statement he is liable on summary conviction to a fine not exceeding £400.[6] The payment from the Maternity Pay Fund is treated for the purposes of discharging any liability of the employer to the employee as if it had been made by the employer.[7]

[1] As defined in Employment Protection Act 1975, s. 69, see p. 380, below.
[2] *Ibid.*, s. 43 (1).
[3] *Ibid.*, s. 43 (2).
[4] *Ibid.*, s. 47 (1), but not in relation to Crown employment, *ibid.*, s. 121 (1).
[5] *Ibid.*, s. 47 (3).
[6] *Ibid.*, s. 47 (4).
[7] *Ibid.*, s. 43 (3).

When the Secretary of State makes such a payment and it appears to him that the employer's default was without reasonable excuse he may recover from the employer such amount (not exceeding the amount of the maternity pay the employer has failed to pay)[1] which the Secretary of State considers appropriate and the sum recovered is paid into the Maternity Pay Fund.[2] Should the Secretary of State make a payment out of the Redundancy Fund in accordance with the insolvency provisions of the Employment Protection Act 1975[3] and the payment in whole or in part represents arrears of pay, then in ascertaining the sum to be paid from the Maternity Pay Fund, the amount paid as arrears of wages will be treated as directly paid by the employer, if in respect of a contractual obligation of the employer to pay the employee within the maternity payment period.[4] If the Secretary of State makes a payment from the Redundancy Fund under the insolvency provisions and the payment, if it had been made by the employer to the employee, would have attracted a rebate from the Maternity Pay

Fund, then the Secretary of State shall pay from the Maternity Pay Fund into the Redundancy Fund an amount corresponding to the amount of rebate which would have been so payable.[5]

[1] Employment Protection Act 1975, s. 44 (1).
[2] *Ibid.*, s. 44 (2).
[3] See Chapter 8, below.
[4] *Ibid.*, s. 45 (1).
[5] *Ibid.*, s. 45 (2).

An employer who claims a rebate, or an employee who claims payment from the Maternity Pay Fund, may present a claim to an industrial tribunal that the Secretary of State has failed to make a payment, or has paid too little.[1] When the claim is that the Secretary of State has refused a rebate, or has paid too little, in a case where payment is in his discretion,[2] the employer may also appeal to an industrial tribunal. The complaint or appeal must be presented within the period of three months beginning with the date on which the relevant decision of the Secretary of State was communicated to the complainant or appellant or, when the tribunal is satisfied that it was not reasonably practicable for the complaint or appeal to be presented to the tribunal within that period, within such further period as the tribunal considers reasonable.[3] In cases where the tribunal finds that the Secretary of State ought to make the payment, or further payment, it will make a declaration to that effect and declare the amount of the payment which he ought to make.[4] In deciding cases when payment was made to an employee after a tribunal had dismissed, or would not entertain a claim by the employee because it was time barred, then if the tribunal is satisfied that it is just and equitable having regard to all the circumstances, that a rebate, or a further payment of rebate, should be made, the tribunal will determine accordingly and the Secretary of State should comply with the determination.[5]

[1] Employment Protection Act 1975, s. 46 (1).
[2] That is, under Employment Protection Act 1975, s. 42 (2); see p. 78, above.
[3] Employment Protection Act 1975, s. 46 (5).
[4] *Ibid.*, s. 46 (2).
[5] *Ibid.*, s. 46 (3).

## Right to return to work

The right to return to work of an employee who has been absent from work wholly or partly because of pregnancy or confinement, is a right to return to work with her original employer or where appropriate, his successor, at any time before the end of the period of 29 weeks beginning with the week in which the date of the confinement falls, in the job in which she was employed under the original contract of employment and on terms and conditions not less favourable than those which would have been applicable if she had not been so absent. When an employee is so entitled to return to work but it is not practicable by reason of redundancy for the employer to permit her to return to work, she is entitled when there is a suitable vacancy to be offered alternative employment by the employer (or his successor), or an associated employer,[1] under a new contract[2] of employment, such that the work to be done under the contract is of a kind which is both suitable in relation to the employee and appropriate for her to do in the circumstances, and the provisions of the new contract as to capacity and place in which she is employed and as to the other terms and conditions of her employment, are not substantially less favourable to her than if she had returned to work in the job which she was employed to do under the contract she worked under immediately before her absence. If because she was pregnant, or for another reason connected with her pregnancy, she was employed under a new contract of employment[3] the contract under which she was employed immediately before she entered into the later contract is the relevant one, or if there was more than one later contract, the first of the later contracts.[4]

[1] For definition see p.      , below.
[2] Employment Protection Act 1975, s. 48 (4).
[3] Under Employment Protection Act 1975, s. 34 (2) which is discussed at p.    , below.
[4] *Ibid.*, s. 48 (5). See s. 52 for definition of "original" contract of employment.

The employee exercises the right to return to work by notifying the employer, who may be her original employer, or a successor of that employer, at least one week before the day on which she proposes to return of her proposal to return on that day ("the notified day of return").[1] The employer may postpone the employee's return to work until a date not more than four weeks after the notified day of return, if he informs her before that day that for specified reasons he is postponing her return until the new date and accordingly she will be entitled to return to work with him on the new date.[2] The employee may postpone her return to work until a day not exceeding four weeks from the notified day of return, notwithstanding that the day falls after the end of the 29 week period, and when no date of return has been notified to the employer, extend the time during which she may exercise her right to return so that she returns to work not later than four weeks from the expiration of the period of 29 weeks, if before the notified date of return or, as the case may be, the expiration of the 29 week period, she gives the employer a certificate from a registered medical practitioner stating that by reason of disease, or bodily or mental disability, she will be incapable of work on the notified day of return, or the expiration of that period, as the case may be.[3] Where the employee has notified a date of return but there is an interruption of work (whether due to industrial action or for some other reason) which renders it unreasonable to expect the employee to return to work on the notified day of return, she may instead return to work when work resumes after the interruption or as soon as reasonably practicable thereafter.[4] When no day of return has been notified and there is such an interruption of work rendering it unreasonable to expect the employee to return to work before the expiration of the 29 week period, or which appears likely to have that effect, and in consequence the employee does not notify a day of return the employee may exercise the right to return to work so that she returns at any time before the end of the period of 14 days from the end of the interruption not withstanding that she returned outside the 29 week period.[5] When an employee has exercised the right to extend the period, or refrained from notifying the day of return in circumstances described in sub-section (6), the provisions as to return to work apply as if references to the expiration of the further period of four weeks, or as the case may be, the period of 14 days from the end of the interruption of work, was substituted for the references to the expiration of the 29 week period.[6]

[1] The phrase "notified day of return" may be construed differently in certain cases where the employee's return is postponed under Employment Protection Act 1975, s. 49 (2) or (3) (*a*) or the employee returns to work later because of an interruption of work under s. 49 (5), s. 50 and Sch. 3 of the Act; *ibid.*, s. 49 (8).

[2] *Ibid.*, s. 49 (2).

[3] *Ibid.*, s. 49 (3). The right of postponement or extension may be exercised only once in connection with the same return to work; *ibid.*, s. 49 (4).

[4] *Ibid.*, s. 49 (5).

[5] *Ibid.*, s. 49 (6).

[6] *Ibid.*, s. 49 (7).

An employee who is entitled to return to work and has exercised the right in accordance with the Employment Protection Act 1975,[1] but is not permitted to return is treated for the purposes of the Redundancy Payments Act 1965, the unfair dismissal provisions of the Trade Union and Labour Relations Act 1974 and the Employment Protection Act 1975, as if she had been employed until the notified day of return and if she would not otherwise be so treated,[2] as having been continuously employed until that day. She is also treated as if she had been dismissed with effect from that day for the reason that she was not permitted to return.[3] The employee may be entitled to claim for redundancy payments, compensation for unfair dismissal or both.[4]

[1] Employment Protection Act 1975, s. 49.

[2] For the rules as to continuity of employment, see p. 226, below.

[3] Employment Protection Act 1975, s. 50. For the position if the employee is dismissed during the period of absence see p. 322, below.

[4] See Chapters 6 and 7, below.

When an employer engages a replacement and on engaging the employee informs him in writing that his employment will be terminated on the return to work of another employee, who is or will be absent wholly or partly because of pregnancy or confinement, and then dismisses that employee in order to make it possible to give work to the employee (who was formerly pregnant) then the dismissal is regarded as having been for "a substantial reason of a kind such as to justify the dismissal" of an employee holding the position the employee held for the purpose of the Trade Union and Labour Relations Act 1974, Schedule 1, paragraph 6 (1) (*b*). However, if an employer is to successfully deny a claim for unfair dismissal he still has to satisfy the tribunal that he acted reasonably in treating it as a sufficient reason for the dismissal.[1]

[1] Employment Protection Act 1975, s. 51.

When an employee has a contractual right to return to work in addition to the statutory right she may not exercise the two rights separately, but may, in returning to work, take advantage of whichever right is, in any particular respect, more favourable. The provisions of sections 48 to 50 and Schedule 3 of the Employment Protection Act 1975 apply (subject to any modifications necessary to give effect to more favourable contractual terms) to the exercise

of the composite rights as they apply to the statutory right to return
to work.[1]

[1] Employment Protection Act 1975, Sch. 3, para. 5, which may be amended
or modified by statutory instrument; see Sch. 3, para. 5 (2).

## HOLIDAYS

Holidays with pay are now a common practice, but there is no
duty on an employer, apart from statute, to allow his employees
holidays, with or without pay, unless the contract contains a term,
express or implied, to that effect. A term may be implied by custom
as in *R.* v. *Stoke-upon-Trent (Inhabitants).*[1]

[1] (1843), 5 Q.B. 303.

As with other terms of contracts of employment those relating
to holidays should be expressed without ambiguity to prevent misunderstandings. In particular the position when an employee leaves
before taking a holiday should be covered, and also the question
whether a holiday accrues from day to day or requires a completed
minimum period of work before the employer is entitled to a
holiday with pay. In *Hurt* v. *Sheffield Corporation,*[1] a resolution
provided that

> "... all the workmen in the employ of the Corporation with
> not less than twelve months' service shall have one week's
> holiday in each year between the beginning of April and the
> end of October with pay..."

A workman who was dismissed and whose employment ended on
5th August was held not to be entitled to a week's wages in lieu of a
holiday which he had not had. On the wording of the resolution it
was decided that he must in fact be in the service of the Corporation
during the whole period from the beginning of April to the end of
October in order to be entitled to the holiday or payment in lieu.
The contract being lawfully terminated at an earlier date the
employer had committed no breach of contract.

[1] (1916), 85 L.J.K.B. 1684.

The first statute to govern holidays with pay was the Holidays
with Pay Act 1938, now largely repealed.[1] In many types of

employment the power to make orders for payment during holidays is vested in wages councils under the Wages Councils Act 1959. Statutory joint industrial councils have similar powers. Every wages council still in existence has made provision entitling workers to have holidays with pay. In agriculture the power to direct holidays with pay lies with the Agricultural Wages Board.

The provisions of the Factories Act 1961, section 94, govern holidays for women and young people in factories.[2]

[1] By the Statute Law (Repeats) Act 1975.

[2] See also s. 90, and the Factories Act Holiday (Different Days for Different Sets) Regulations 1947, S.R. & O. 1947 No. 184.

## TIME OFF WORK IN CERTAIN CIRCUMSTANCES

### (a) For trade union officials to carry out trade union duties[1]

An employer should permit an employee who is an official[2] of an independent trade union[3] recognised by him to take time off during working hours with pay to carry out those duties of his as such an official, which are concerned with industrial relations between his employer and any associated employer and their employees, or to undergo training in respect of industrial relations which is relevant to carrying out of those duties and approved by the Trades Union Congress, or by the independent trade union of which he is an official. The amount of time off, and the purposes for which, the occasions on which, and any conditions subject to which, time off may be taken are those that are reasonable in all circumstances having regard to the relevant provisions of the Code of Practice issued by the Advisory Conciliation and Arbitration Service. The Service will be issuing a Code of Practice providing practical guidance as to the time off to be permitted by an employer to a trade union official for carrying out official trade union duties and a trade union member, for time off for trade union activities.[4] In particular the Code will provide guidance on the circumstances in which a trade union official is to be permitted to take time off in respect of duties connected with industrial action.[5]

[1] These provisions were not in force on 1st June 1976.

[2] "Official" is defined in Trade Union and Labour Relations Act 1974, s. 30:

"'official', in relation to a trade union, means any person who is an officer of the union or of a branch or section of the union or who (not being such an officer) is a person elected or appointed in accordance with the rules of the union to be a representative of its members or of some of them, including any person so elected or appointed who is an employee of the same employer as the members, or one or more of the members, whom he is to represent."

[3] "Independent trade union" is defined in Trade Union and Labour Relations Act 1974, s. 30:

"'independent trade union' means a trade union which—
(*a*) is not under the domination or control of an employer or a group of employers or of one or more employers' associations; and
(*b*) is not liable to interference by an employer or any such group or association (arising out of the provision of financial or material support or by any other means whatsoever) tending towards such control."

A trade union is recognised if it is recognised for purposes of collective bargaining but also if the Service has made an operative recommendation for recognition.

[4] Employment Protection Act 1975, s. 6.
[5] *Ibid.*, s. 57 (3).

The amount to be paid to the employee when he has taken time off in accordance with such permission is calculated in accordance with the formula laid down in section 57. Where the employee's remuneration for work he would ordinarily have been doing during the time does not vary with the amount of the work done it is as if he had worked for the whole of that time.[1] In other cases the amount is calculated by reference to the average hourly earnings for the work he would ordinarily have carried out. The figure for the average hourly earnings is the average hourly earnings of the employee concerned, or if no fair estimate can be made of those earnings, the average hourly earnings for work of that description of persons in comparable employment with the same employer. If there are no such persons a figure of average hourly earnings which is reasonable in the circumstances is used.[2] The amount of any payment which the employer is contractually bound to pay goes towards discharging the statutory liability to pay the employee during his absence, and vice versa[3] but, subject to this, the right does not affect the right to be paid remuneration in pursuance of the contract of employment.

[1] Employment Protection Act 1975, s. 57 (4).
[2] *Ibid.*, s. 57 (5).
[3] *Ibid.*, s. 57 (7).

An employee who is an official of an independent trade union recognised by the employer may present a complaint to an industrial tribunal that his employer has failed to permit him to take time off as required by section 57 of the Employment Protection Act 1975, or pay him in accordance with it.[1]

[1] Employment Protection Act 1975, s. 57 (8).

These provisions do not apply to employment where the employee is the spouse of the employer,[1] to share fishermen,[1] employment under a contract of employment where the employee ordinarily works outside Great Britain[2] or to part-time employees.[3]

[1] Employment Protection Act 1975, s. 119.

[2] *Ibid.*, s. 119. Under s. 127 the Secretary of State for Employment can extend the provisions to cover employment for the purposes of activities in the territorial waters of the United Kingdom and off-shore installations. See p. 62 above.

[3] Employment Protection Act 1975, s. 119 (8). The usual rules as to part-time employees apply.

The Secretary of State can by order provide that the provisions do not apply to other persons and vary and revoke them and the existing exclusions.

The provisions have effect in relation to Crown employment as they do to other employment with appropriate amendments, armed forces and women's services excluded; Employment Protection Act 1975, s. 121. Members of the House of Commons staff are also included; *ibid.*, s. 122. Restrictions on contracting out of all the provisions of the Employment Protection Act 1975 (including all those relating to time off) are contained in s. 118.

## (b) For trade union activities

The employer should permit an employee who is the member of an appropriate trade union[1] to have time off during working hours for taking part in any trade union activity[1] to which section 58 applies. That is to trade activities of an appropriate trade union of which the employee is a member and any activities in relation to which the employee is acting as a representative of such union but excluding activities which themselves consist of industrial action whether or not in contemplation or furtherance of a trade dispute. The amount of time off and the purposes for which, the occasion on which and any conditions subject to which the time off may be so taken are those which are reasonable in all the circumstances having regard to the Code of Practice to be prepared by the Advisory, Conciliation and Arbitration Service in relation to time off in such circumstances.[2] The Code will provide in

87

particular, practical guidance on the question whether and the circumstances in which a trade union member is to be permitted to take time off for trade union activities connected with industrial action.[3] It is to be noted that there is no requirement in this case for the time off to be taken with pay but the employee may present a complaint to an industrial tribunal that the employer has failed to permit the time off.

[1] "Appropriate trade union" and "appropriate trade union activities" are described in s. 58 (2), as follows:

"(2) In this section "appropriate trade union", in relation to an employee of any description, means an independent trade union which is recognised by his employer in respect of that description of employee, and the trade union activities to which this section applies are—
(a) any activities of an appropriate trade union of which the employee is a member; and
(b) any activities, whether or not falling within paragraph (a) above, in relation to which the employee is acting as a representative of such a union,
excluding activities which themselves consist of industrial action whether or not in contemplation or furtherance of a trade dispute."

Employment Protection Act 1975, s. 58, was not in force on 1st August 1976.
[2] Employment Protection Act 1975, s. 58 (3).
[3] *Ibid.*, s. 58 (4).

Employees who are the spouses of their employers are excluded, as are share fishermen, employees under their contract of employment ordinarily work outside Great Britain and part-time employees.[1]

[1] See p. 87, notes [2] and [3], above.

### (c) Time off for public duties

An employer shall permit his employee to take time off in accordance with section 59 of the Employment Protection Act 1975 for carrying out public duties as a justice of the peace, member of a local authority,[1] member of any statutory tribunal, member of a Regional Health Authority or Area Health Authority,[1] member of the managing or governing body of an educational establishment maintained by a local education authority[1] and as a member of a water authority.[2] The duties of those, other than those of justices of the peace, to which the section applies are attendances at meetings of the body, or of any of its committees or subcommittees, and the doing of any other thing approved by the body or of any of a class so approved, for the purpose of the discharge of the functions of the body, or of any of its committees or sub-committees. The amount of time off which the employee is permitted, and the occasions on which, and any conditions subject to which, the time off may be so taken are those which are reasonable in all the circumstances, having regard in particular to how much time is required for the performance of the duties in question and how much time off is required for the performance of the particular duties, how much time off the employee has already been permitted for trade union duties and activities and public duties, and the circumstances of the employer's business, and the effect of the employee's absence on the running of the business.[3] There is no requirement for time off in accordance with these provisions to be with pay.

[1] Defined in Employment Protection Act 1975, s. 59 (2). These provisions were not in force on 1st August 1976.

[2] *Ibid.*, s. 59 (1). The Secretary of State may by order add to, remove or alter the description of any such office or body; *ibid.*, s. 59 (5).

[3] There is no express provision for the issue of a Code of Practice to assist by giving guidance in these cases.

An employee may present a complaint to an industrial tribunal that his employer failed to permit him to take time off as required by the section. The provisions as to time off for public duties do not apply to employment where the employee is the employer's husband or wife, a share fisherman, employment where the employee ordinarily works outside Great Britain, part-time employees and merchant seamen.[1]

[1] See p. 87, notes [2] and [3], above. So far as Crown servants are concerned if the terms of an employee's employment restrict the right to take part in certain political activities and activities which may conflict with his official functions nothing in Employment Protection Act 1975, s. 59 shall require him to be allowed time off for public duties in connection with any such activities; *ibid.*, s. 121 (8).

## (d) For employees dismissed by reason of redundancy to look for work or make arrangements for training

Section 61 of the Employment Protection Act 1975 gives some employees dismissed by reason of redundancy the right to be allowed time off to look for new employment and to make arrangements for training for future employment. This is discussed more fully in Chapter 6 (Redundancy).[1]

[1] See p. 270, below.

## (e) **Complaints to industrial tribunals**

Complaints by an employee relating to time off for trade union duties or activities and public duties should be presented within three months of the date when the failure occurred, or within such further period as the tribunal considers reasonable in a case where it is satisfied that it was not reasonably practicable for the complaint to be presented within the period of three months.[2] When it finds that a complaint of an employer's failure to permit the employee to take time off is well founded, the tribunal will make a declaration to that effect and may award compensation to be paid by the employer to the employee of such amount as the tribunal considers just and equitable in all the circumstances, having regard to the employer's default and to the loss sustained by the employee which is attributable to the matters complained of.[3] When the complaint was in respect of trade union duties and the tribunal finds that the employer has failed to pay the employee the whole or part of the amount required to be paid under section 57 of the Employment Protection Act 1975 the tribunal must order the employer to pay to the employee the sum which the tribunal finds due to him.[4]

[1] The assistance of a conciliation officer may also be sought; Employment Protection Act 1975, s. 108. See also Chapter 9, below.

[2] *Ibid.*, s. 60 (1).

[3] *Ibid.*, s. 60 (2).

[4] *Ibid.*, s. 60 (3).

# Chapter 3

# WRITTEN PARTICULARS OF TERMS OF EMPLOYMENT

## SCOPE OF THE PROVISIONS

Section 4 of the Contracts of Employment Act 1972 (as amended) requires employers to give to each employee a written statement with the particulars required by that section not later than 13 weeks after the beginning of the employee's period of employment with the employer. The employee must be notified of any changes in these terms. In order to reduce the paperwork it is possible for the employer to refer employees to documents, such as collective agreements or works rules which are reasonably accessible to them.

The Contracts of Employment Act 1972 applies to employees.

> "'employee' means an individual who has entered into or works under (or, where the employment has ceased, worked under) a contract with an employer, whether the contract be for manual labour, clerical work or otherwise, be expressed or implied, oral or in writing, and whether it be a contract of service or of apprenticeship; and cognate expressions shall be construed accordingly."[1]

[1] Contracts of Employment Act 1972, s. 11 (1).

Thus the provisions of the Act do not apply to contracts for services.[1] Special cases have to be considered as follows:

(1) A dock worker registered pursuant to a Dock Labour Scheme is excluded, except when he is engaged in work which is not dock-work as defined by the Scheme.[2] For example, a registered dock worker who obtains temporary release from the Dock Labour Scheme to take up employment of a different kind nonetheless retains his name on the register during the period of release and when he is engaged

in work which is not dock work he should be supplied with a notice pursuant to section 4.

[1] For the distinction between contracts of service and contracts for services see p. 2, above.

[2] Contracts of Employment Act 1972, s. 9 (1).

(2) **Employees in the Merchant Navy and fishing fleets who work on registered ships are excluded from the provisions of the Act. For the detailed provisions see Contracts of Employment Act 1972, section 9 (2).**[1]

[1] Section 9 (2) provides as follows:

"(2) The foregoing sections of this Act shall not apply to:
(a) a person employed as master of or a seaman on a seagoing British ship having a gross registered tonnage of 80 tons or more, including a person ordinarily employed as a seaman who is employed in or about such a ship in port by the owner or charterer of the ship to do work of a kind ordinarily done by a seaman on such a ship while it is in port, or
(b) [repealed]
(c) a person employed as a skipper of or a seaman on a fishing boat for the time being required to be registered under section 373 of the said Act."
The 'said Act' being the Merchant Shipping Act 1894.

(3) **Where the employee is the husband or wife of the employer there is no need to supply a statement pursuant to section 4.**[1] **It should be borne in mind that if the employer is a limited company (even where it is predominantly under the control of one person) it is a separate legal entity and the required particulars must be given.**[2] **This is also the case where the employer is a partnership of which the employee's spouse is a member.**[3]

[1] Contracts of Employment Act 1972, s. 9 (3).

[2] *Booth* v. *Helliwell*, [1914] 3 K.B. 252; *Lee* v. *Lee's Air Farming, Ltd.*, [1961] A.C. 12; [1960] 3 All E.R. 420.

[3] See, for instance, *Bernstein* v. *Bernstein Brothers* (1969), 1 I.T.R. 106.

(4) **Those employed for less than 13 weeks are excluded. Written particulars of terms of employment need not be given to any employee who serves less than 13 weeks with the same employer.**[1] **This is because section 4 (1) of the Contracts of Employment Act 1972 requires the employer to give the employee written particulars of employment "not later than 13 weeks after the beginning of an employee's period of employment with an employer…"**

[1] The day on which the employment began is to be excluded in calculating the 13 weeks; see *Goldsmith's Co.* v. *West Metropolitan Rail. Co.*, [1904] 1 K.B. 1, C.A.; and *Stewart* v. *Chapman*, [1951] 2 K.B. 792; [1951] 2 All E.R. 613.

(5) Employees who have a written contract containing the terms to be notified under section 4 need not be given written particulars. The written contract of employment can be in several documents and must contain details of each matter which is to be notified. In these cases, to rely on the exclusion, it is necessary for a copy of the contract, together with variations from time to time, to be given to the employee, or he should have reasonable opportunities of reading the document in the course of his employment, or the copy should be made reasonably accessible to him in some other way.[1] In addition, a note as required by section 4 (2)[2] should be given to the employee, or he must have reasonable opportunities of reading such a note in the course of his employment, or the note should be made reasonably accessible to him in some other way.

If at any time the employee ceases to come within the exclusion, the employer should give the employee a written statement in accordance with section 4 not more than one month after that date.[3]

[1] Contracts of Employment Act 1972, s. 6. But the contract must be made available to the employee. See, for example, *Grantham* v. *Harford*, [1968] C.L.Y. 1384. County Court.

[2] See p. 99, below.

[3] Contracts of Employment Act 1972, proviso to s. 6.

(6) Part-time employees—At present there is no requirement to supply a statement pursuant to section 4 when the hours of employment of the employee are normally less than 21 hours weekly. The provisions of section 4 apply to an employee who at any time comes or ceases to come within the exception as if the period of employment terminated or began at that time.[1] There are new provisions to be introduced by the Employment Protection Act 1975 to reduce the above-mentioned number of hours from 21 to 16. In addition new sub-sections (8) and (9) will include certain employments within the scope of the section where the contract of employment normally involves employment for eight hours or more.[2] See p. 94, below. An employee who at any time

comes or ceases to come within the new exceptions for part-time employees will be treated as if a period of employment terminated or began at that time.[3] The present position is governed by section 4 (7) which states:

"(7) No account shall be taken under this section of employment during any period when the hours of employment are normally less than twenty-one hours weekly, and this section shall apply to an employee who at any time comes or ceases to come within the exception in this sub-section as if a period of employment terminated or began at that time."

[1] Contracts of Employment Act 1972, s. 4 (7).
[2] These provisions are not yet in force and it is expected that they will be introduced during autumn 1976.
[3] Contracts of Employment Act 1972, s. 4 (7) in amended form.

After the implementation of the amending provisions that sub-section together with new sub-sections (8), (9) and (10) will read as follows:

"(7) [Subject to the following provisions of this section] no account shall be taken under this section of employment during any period when the hours of employment are normally less than [sixteen hours] weekly, and this section shall apply to an employee who at any time comes or ceases to come within the exception in this sub-section as if a period of employment terminated or began at that time.

[(8) If the employee's relations with his employer cease to be governed by a contract which normally involves work for sixteen hours or more weekly and become governed by a contract which normally involves employment for eight hours or more, but less than sixteen hours, weekly, the employee shall nevertheless for a period of twenty-six weeks computed in accordance with the next following sub-section be treated for the purposes of the foregoing sub-section as if his contract normally involved employment for sixteen hours or more weekly.

(9) In computing the said period of twenty-six weeks no account shall be taken of any week:
(a) during which the employee is in fact employed for sixteen hours or more;

(b) during which the employee takes part in a strike (as defined in paragraph 11 of Schedule 1 to this Act), or is absent from work because of a lock-out (as so defined) by his employer; or

(c) during which there is no contract of employment but which, by virtue of paragraph 5 (1) of Schedule 1 to this Act, counts in computing a period of continuous employment.

(10) An employee whose relations with his employer are governed by a contract of employment which normally involves employment for eight hours or more, but less than sixteen hours, weekly shall nevertheless, if he has been continuously employed for a period of five years or more (computed in accordance with Schedule 1 to this Act) be treated for the purposes of sub-section (7) of this section as if his contract normally involved employment for sixteen hours or more weekly.]"

The words introduced by the Employment Protection Act 1975 are shown in square brackets. Although these provisions are not yet in force it is likely that they will be implemented during autumn 1976.

The limits of 16 and eight hours per week may be reduced by order of the Secretary of State for Employment after approval by both Houses of Parliament.[1] If such an order is made, it can contain transitional, supplemental and incidental provisions and will affect periods before the order takes effect as well as after.[2]

[1] Contracts of Employment Act 1972, s. 10 (1) (as substituted by the Employment Protection Act 1975).
[2] *Ibid.*, s. 10 (3).

(7) Civil servants are not the subject of the provisions of the Contracts of Employment Act 1972, relating to written particulars of the major terms of the contract of employment, because the Crown is not bound by statute unless the contrary is expressly stated or reasonably implied.[1] This rule was followed in *Wood* v. *Leeds United Hospitals*,[2] when it was *held* that the Contracts of Employment Act did not apply to a Crown servant who worked in the National Health Service.

[1] See p. 14, above.
[2] (1974), 9 I.T.R. 352, N.I.R.C.

(8) Members of police forces are not employees in the strict legal sense[1] and so the provisions do not apply to them. Members of the armed forces are in the employment of the Crown and the Crown is not bound.

[1] See p. 14, above.

(9) Those who work under contracts of service with local authorities are included in the provisions relating to written statements of major terms of employment contracts. The definition of an employee as "an individual who has entered into or work under a contract with an employer, whether the contract be for manual labour, clerical work or otherwise", in section 11 of the Act is in the same words as section 8 of the Industrial Court, Act 1919, which was held to apply to local government officers in *National Association of Local Government Officers* v. *Bolton Corporation*.[1]

[1] [1943] A.C. 166; [1942] 2 All E.R. 425, H.L.

(10) In considering the position of employees of public bodies it may be necessary to consider whether the body concerned is "an emanation of the Crown" or perhaps more accurately, "a servant or agent of the Crown". If the body is within this category it may shelter under the Crown umbrella by invoking the presumption that the Crown is not bound by a statute unless it is so provided.[1]

National corporations are not emanations of the Crown, their employees are not in the position of civil servants and are consequently covered by the Act. For instance, in *Tamlin* v. *Hannaford*,[2] the British Transport Commission was held to be bound by the Rent Restriction Acts and to have none of the immunity of the Crown. Thus employees of such august bodies as the Bank of England, the British Broadcasting Corporation, the Commonwealth Development Corporation, the National Coal Board and others are all included.

[1] See p. 15, above.
[2] [1950] 1 K.B. 18; [1949] 2 All E.R. 327.

(11) The provisions as to written statements do not apply in relation to employment during any period when the employee is engaged in work wholly or mainly outside Great

Britain, unless the employee ordinarily works in Great Britain and the work outside Great Britain is for the same employer.[1] Subject to this exclusion the provisions apply whatever the law governing the contract between the employer and the employee.[2]

[1] Contracts of Employment Act 1972, s. 12 (1).
[2] *Ibid.*, s. 12 (2).

There is power in section 127 of the Employment Protection Act 1975 for the provisions as to statement of terms and particulars of employment to be extended by Order in Council to employment for the purpose of any activity in the territorial waters of the United Kingdom, or connected with the exploration of the sea bed or subsoil or the exploitation of their natural resources in any area which is designated by order under section 1 (7) of the Continental Shelf Act 1964.[1]

[1] By virtue of the Employment Protection (Offshore Employment) Order 1976, S.I. 1976 No. 766, which came into operation on 21st June 1976, the Contracts of Employment Act 1972 applies to employment for the purposes of the following activities:

(a) any activities (other than activities connected with a ship which is in the course of navigation or is a survey ship or is engaged in dredging or fishing) in the territorial waters;

(b) any activities connected with the exploration of the sea bed or subsoil or the exploitation of their natural resources in any designated area (other than an area or part of an area in which the law of Northern Ireland applies) being activities carried out on or from an offshore installation in any such designated area.

The Order does not apply to employment wholly or mainly for the purposes of any activities connected with the Frigg Field Reservoir or the Ekofisk Field. In applying the Contracts of Employment Act 1972 under the Order, s. 9 (2) (a) has effect as if the word "British" was omitted and references in s. 12 (1) and Sch. 1, para. 1 (2) to Great Britain are treated as including the territorial waters and the waters in any designated area (other than an area or part of an area in which the law of Northern Ireland applies).

(12) Additional excluded categories may be prescribed by the Secretary of State for Employment by statutory instrument laid before Parliament and approved by each House. Such orders can be revoked or varied by later orders and can contain transitional or other supplemental or incidental provisions as appear to the Secretary of State to be expedient.[1]

[1] Contracts of Employment Act 1972, ss. 9 (5), (6) and (7).

There are additional powers for the Secretary of State by statutory instrument to vary or revoke the provisions as to the exclusion of merchant seamen and the husband or wife of the employer.

When an employer at any time comes or ceases to come within the exceptions provided for by or under section 9, the provisions as to notice shall apply as if a period of employment terminated or began at that time.[1]

[1] Contracts of Employment Act 1972, s. 9 (4).

## WRITTEN PARTICULARS

Section 4 (1) to (6) of the Contracts of Employment Act 1972 (as amended) provides as follows:

"4.—(1) Not later than thirteen weeks after the beginning of an employee's period of employment with an employer, the employer shall give to the employee a written statement identifying the parties, specifying the date when the employment began, [stating whether any employment with a previous employer counts as part of the employee's period of continuous employment with him, and if so specifying the date on which the continuous period of employment began] and giving the following particulars of the terms of employment as at a specified date not more than one week before the statement is given, that is—

(a) the scale or rate of remuneration, or the method of calculating remuneration,

(b) the intervals at which remuneration is paid (that is, whether weekly or monthly or by some other period),

(c) any terms and conditions relating to hours of work (including any terms and conditions relating to normal working hours),

(d) any terms and conditions relating to:
   (i) entitlement to holidays, including public holidays, and holiday pay (the particulars given being sufficient to enable the employee's entitlement, including any entitlement to accrued holiday pay on the termination of employment, to be precisely calculated),
   (ii) incapacity for work due to sickness or injury,

98

including any provisions for sick pay,

(iii) pensions and pension schemes, and

(*e*) the length of notice which the employee is obliged to give and entitled to receive to determine his contract of employment [and

(*f*) the title of the job which the employee is employed to do:]

Provided that paragraph (*d*) (iii) of this sub-section shall not apply to the employees of any body or authority if the employees' pension rights depend on the terms of a pension scheme established under any provision contained in or having effect under an Act of Parliament and the body or authority are required by any such provision to give to new employees information concerning their pension rights, or concerning the determination of questions affecting their pension rights.

(2) [Subject to sub-section (2A) of this section] every statement given to an employee under sub-section (1) of this section shall include a note:

[(*a*) specifying any disciplinary rules applicable to the employee, or referring to a document which is reasonably accessible to the employee and which specifies such rules;

(*b*) specifying, by description or otherwise:

(i) a person to whom the employee can apply if he is dissatisfied with any disciplinary decision relating to him; and

(ii) a person to whom the employee can apply for the purpose of seeking redress of any grievance relating to his employment,

and the manner in which any such applications should be made; and

(*c*) where there are further steps consequent upon any such application, explaining those steps or referring to a document which is reasonably accessible to the employee and which explains them,] (and—

(*d*) stating whether a contracting-out certificate is in force for the employment in respect of which the statement is given),

and any reference in sub-section (5) of this section, in sub-sections (1) or (3) of section 5 of this Act or in sub-sections (1) to (6) of section 8 of this Act to that which is, or is to be, included, given or referred to in a statement under sub-section (1) of this section shall be construed as including a reference to a note under this sub-section, and any reference to that which is, or is to be, included, given or referred to in a statement under section 5 (1) of this Act shall be construed accordingly.

[(2A) The provisions of paragraphs (*b*) to (*d*) of sub-section (2) of this section shall not apply to rules, disciplinary decisions, grievances or procedures relating to health or safety at work.]

(3) If there are no particulars to be entered under any of the heads of paragraph (*d*) or under any of the other provisions of sub-section (1) of this section, that fact shall be stated.

(4) If the contract is for a fixed term, the statement given under sub-section (1) of this section shall state the date when the contract expires.

(5) A statement given under sub-section (1) of this section may, for all or any of the particulars to be given by the statement, refer the employee to some document which the employee has reasonable opportunities of reading in the course of his employment or which is made reasonably accessible to him in some other way.

(6) If not more than six months after the termination of an employee's period of employment, a further period of employment is begun with the same employer, and the terms of employment are the same, no statement need be given under sub-section (1) of this section in respect of the second period of employment, but without prejudice to the operation of sub-section (1) of the next following section if there is a change in the terms of employment."[1]

[1] The words in square brackets were inserted by the Employment Protection Act 1975 with effect from 1st June 1976. See the Employment Protection Act 1975 (Commencement No. 4) Order 1976, S.I. 1976 No. 530.

The words in round brackets are introduced by the Social Security Pensions Act 1975, s. 30. This replaces the amendment and addition to the Contracts of Employment Act 1972. s. 4 to be effected by the Social Security Act 1973. It is expected to come into force on 6th April 1978.

"*... the employer shall give to the employee ...*". It is not sufficient for the employee to be told, or shown, the terms of the contract. In *Green* v. *Moyses Stevens, Ltd.*, [1974] I.R.L.R. 274, at p. 275, the terms of the employee's contract were displayed on the Staff Notice Board. The tribunal *held* that this was not sufficient. "The purpose of the Act is that the employee shall have in his or her possession a document which can be referred to to find out what the conditions of employment are. In some cases, as for instance sickness benefit schemes or pension schemes, there can be reference to other documents, but it is not enough to provide on a notice board a statement which may or may not apply to a particular employee."

"...*identifying the parties*...". It is important that the correct employer is identified on the statement. If not the person who purports to be the employer may be stopped from denying that it is the employer, see *Smith* v. *Blandford Gee Cementation Co., Ltd.*, [1970] 3 All E.R. 154, D.C.

"...*specifying the date when the employment began*...". "...*specifying the date on which the continuous period of employment began*...". It is most important for employees to ensure that this information is given correctly. If not the employee's position relating to certain statutory rights may be prejudiced. An example occurred in *Soutar* v. *Fisher* (1975), 10 I.T.R. 38, T, when doubts arose as to whether the continuity of an employee's employment had been broken by dismissal during a strike. After the employee's return to work he was given, and in due course did not object to, a statement under the Contracts of Employment Act which gave the date of return after the strike as the commencement date. The tribunal *held* that the employee was not entitled to go beyond that date in computing his period of continuous employment.

"...*scale or rate of remuneration, or the method of calculating remuneration*...". This should be set out in detail. See p. 47, above, for discussion of remuneration, which includes matters other than mere financial benefit. The intervals at which remuneration is paid should also be given.

As with other particulars this information should be expressed in clear and unambiguous terms. In *Owens* v. *Multilux Ltd.*, [1974] I.R.L.R. 113, N.I.R.C., the terms of an agreement between the employers and employee were that the employee would be appointed managing director of the company at "a salary of £2,500 net of deductions". A statement pursuant to section 4 of the Contracts of Employment Act 1972 was not given to the employee. On the termination of his employment the employee asked a Scottish tribunal to determine the terms of the statement which should have been given to him pursuant to the Act, and in particular that the salary should be expressed as being net of income tax. It is illegal under section 189 of the Companies Act 1948 to pay a director remuneration free of income tax and the National Industrial Relations Court *held* that the employee was entitled to a salary of £2,500 per annum gross. Although the tribunal was not asked to enforce the terms of the agreement the purpose of the reference was so that the employee could in due course do so and the Court considered that the tribunal was unable to determine that the salary should be paid free of tax. See also *Rees* v. *Kraken International, Ltd.,* [1975] I.R.L.R. 342, T.

"*...any terms and conditions relating to hours of work...*". If overtime is obligatory it should be expressed to be so. It will be seen at p. 304, below, that if the employee is not bound to work overtime and is dismissed for refusing to do so it is likely to be held to be unfair. Contrast *Cole* v. *Midland Display, Ltd.,* [1973] I.R.L.R. 62, N.I.R.C., when a foreman was appointed on "staff basis" and this was *held* by the tribunal (and upheld by the Court) to include an obligation on the employee to work overtime. Such ambiguous terms should never be used.

"*...entitlement to holidays...*". The terms and conditions referred to in sub-section 4 (1) (d) (i) should be carefully prepared because difficulty is often encountered in determining the employee's entitlement on the termination of employment.

"*...incapacity for work due to sickness or injury...*". This should be dealt with as clearly as possible, as with the other terms and conditions. If there are rules as to the lodgement of medical certificates these should be mentioned, in addition to provisions regarding payment. If the employer does make payment for absence during illness he will usually expect to recover from the employee the amount of any Social Security benefit received during the period of absence and this should be specified. From the employer's point of view such benefits are best referred to as those "payable", so that the onus is on the employee to collect them. See p. 73, above.

"*...pensions and pension schemes...*". Should there be no pension scheme that fact should be expressed. The requirement does not apply to the employees of bodies where there is a statutory pension scheme which obliges the employer to give information concerning the employee's pension rights, or as to determination of questions affecting those pension rights. See proviso to section 4 (1).

"*...notice...*". The provisions of section 1 of the Contracts of Employment Act 1972 appear to have had a normative effect on the notice to be given by employers, but if the period of notice is not specified in the written particulars which are given to the employee, the court or tribunal may well hold that the employee is entitled to longer notice. In *Cuthbertson* v. *A.M.L. Distributors, Ltd.*, [1975] I.R.L.R. 228 , T, no written particulars had been given to the employee and when he applied to a tribunal to determine the period of notice which should have been specified it was *held* that if particulars had been given to the employee who was the Marketing Services Manager the parties would not have contemplated a contract which provided the statutory minimum period of notice. The tribunal found that there was no implied term or custom as to notice and decided that section 8 of the Contracts of Employment Act 1972 did not give jurisdiction to determine more than that the employee was entitled to reasonable notice. It did not specify the actual length of notice.

Where a contract of employment is for a fixed term the date of expiry should be given in the written particulars—sub-section (4).

"...*the title of the job which the employee is employed to do*...". This is a new requirement of the Employment Protection Act 1975. It is not necessary for there to be a job description although it may benefit both parties to the contract of employment if the perameters within which the employee is expected to work are set out in the statement.

Note should be made of sub-section (3) which requires that if there are no particulars to be entered in the statement under any of the heads of paragraph (*d*) or other provisions of sub-section (1) for that matter, that fact should be stated.

"...*disciplinary rules*...". This requirement was inserted in the Contracts of Employment Act 1972 by the Employment Protection Act 1975 and it is most likely that it will be fulfilled by referring to another document containing the rules. When preparing such rules it is of great importance that all disciplinary procedures and punishments, if any, are carefully set out. Employers who do not have a contractual right to do so may be held to have repudiated the contract of employment by purporting to suspend, fine or lay-off employees. See for example *Lethaby* v. *Horsman Andrews and Knill, Ltd.*, [1975] I.R.L.R. 119, T, where the employer claimed to have the right to deduct money from a coalman's wages for short delivery. There was no evidence of a specific agreement as to this. When the money was deducted and the employee collected his cards a tribunal found that he had been dismissed.

The person to whom application is to be made when the employee is dissatisfied with the disciplinary decision, or for the purpose of seeking any redress of grievance relating to the employment, is best specified by description, except in cases of very small businesses.

"*... contracting out certificate ...*". This is a certificate issued by the Occupational Pensions Board that an occupational pension scheme is contracted-out in respect of the employment to which it relates; Social Security Pensions Act 1975, s. 30 (1). An industrial tribunal is not authorised or required to determine any question whether an employment is, has been or will be contracted out employment; *ibid.*, s. 30 (5).

*Sub-section (2A).* This exclusion should be noted. It could have been more happily phrased but appears to accept that there may be separate disciplinary procedures relating solely to matters of health or safety at work.

*Sub-section (3).* The absence of contractual stipulations and procedures can be as important as the content of those that exist and this should be stated.

*Sub-section (4).* The position of fixed term contracts has been discussed at p. 127, below. The meaning of the expression "fixed term contract" is explained at p. 164 and 282, below.

*Sub-section (5).* The opportunity of referring to other documents will be of importance where collective agreements are embodied in the individual contracts of employment and to deal with holiday rules, sickness and pension schemes. These tend to be bulky and susceptible of change from time to time.

*Sub-section (6).* It will be noted that if there is a break of employment of not less than six months and the employee is engaged on the same terms, it is not necessary for a new statement to be given to the employees. However, unless the two periods of employment are to be treated as continuous it will not be advantageous to employers to utilise this rule since the original statement would give a date for commencement of continuous employment prior to the break in employment. As a matter of practice it will be best to give employees new statements in every case where there is a break in continuity of employment.

Section 7 of the Contracts of Employment Act 1972 enables the Secretary of State for Employment by order, to require further particulars as specified in the order to be included in the statement given pursuant to the Act.

## CHANGES IN TERMS OF EMPLOYMENT

Section 5 of the Contracts of Employment Act 1972 covers situations when there are changes in the terms of employment. It is as follows:

"5.—(1) If after the date to which a statement given under section 4 (1) of this Act relates there is a change in the terms of employment to be included, or referred to, in that statement, the employer shall, not more than one month after the change, inform the employee of the nature of the change by a written statement and, if he does not leave a copy of the statement with the employee, shall preserve the statement and ensure that the employee has reasonable opportunities of reading it in the course of his employment, or that it is made reasonably accessible to him in some other way.

(2) A statement given under sub-section (1) of this section may, for all or any of the particulars to be given by the statement, refer the employee to some document which the employee has reasonable opportunities of reading in the course of his employment, or which is made reasonably accessible to him in some other way.

(3) If the employer in referring in the statement given under section 4 (1) of this Act, or under sub-section (1) of this section, to any such document indicates to the employee that future changes in the terms the particulars of which are given in the document will be entered up in the document (or recorded by some other means for the information of persons referring to the document), the employer need not under sub-section (1) of this section inform the employee of any such change which is duly entered up or recorded not more than one month after the change is made.

(4) Where, after an employer has given to an employee a written statement in accordance with section 4 (1) of this Act:
(a) the name of the employer (whether an individual or a body corporate or partnership) is changed, without any change in the identity of the employer, or
(b) the identity of the employer is changed, in such circumstances that, in accordance with paragraph 9 or paragraph 10 of Schedule 1 to this Act, the continuity of the employee's period of employment is not broken,

and (in either case) the change does not involve any change in the terms (other than the names of the parties) included or referred to in the statement, then, the person who, immediately after the change, is the employer shall not be required to give to the employee a statement in accordance with section 4 (1) of this Act, but [subject to sub-section (5) of this section] the change shall be treated as a change falling within sub-section (1) of this section.

[(5) A written statement under this section which informs an employee of such a change in his terms of employment as is referred to in sub-section (4) (*b*) of this section shall specify the date on which the employee's continuous period of employment began.]"[1]

[1] The words in square brackets were introduced by the Employment Protection Act 1975 with effect from 1st June 1976.

"...*change*...". The word "change" in this section appears to be used as an equivalent of the more accepted word used habitually in the law of contract, "variation". The individual nature of the contract must not be lost sight of, and a change or variation in a contract cannot be unilateral and imposed at the will of the employer, but must be by agreement, tacit or otherwise: *Cowey* v. *Liberian Operations, Ltd.*, [1966] 2 Lloyd's Rep. 45. A variation means an alteration in the contractual obligation by mutual agreement of both parties. It is different from a forebearance or concession which is known as a waiver. A variation of the contract need not be in writing but a written statement of the change should be provided for the employee not more than a month after it has taken place.

"...*paragraph 9 or paragraph 10 of Schedule 1 to this Act*...". These are the paragraphs which deal with transfer of trade or business or undertaking and cases where employees are taken into employment by associated employers. See p. 240 and 241, below, respectively.

## EFFECT OF THE WRITTEN PARTICULARS

It was said by the tribunal in *Moore* v. *R. H. McCulloch, Ltd.*,[1] "It should perhaps be added that particulars of a contract of employment delivered under the Contracts of Employment Act [1972] by the employer to the employee, are not conclusive evidence of what the terms of the contract of employment were."[2] However, it may be extremely difficult for an employer in proceedings before a court or tribunal to claim that the statement by him wrongly sets out terms and conditions of employment when it is to the employee's advantage to contend that the statement is correct.[3] Considerable care should be exercised in preparing these statements.

[1] (1966), 1 I.T.R. 484, T.

[2] At p. 486.

[3] But see *Gascol Conversions, Ltd.* v. *Mercer* (1974), 9 I.T.R. 282, at p. 286, C.A., where it was said by Lord DENNING, M.R. when discussing a statement of terms and conditions of employment,

"It is well settled that where there is a written contract of employment, as there was here, and the parties have reduced it to writing, it is the writing which governs their relations. It is not permissible to say they intended something different."

The document given to the employee only has to provide the particulars required as above, and it is not necessary for other terms of the contract of employment to be included. On the other hand there are circumstances where it is preferable for stipulations of the contract not required to be recorded in the written particulars, to be set out. Each case must be looked at individually, but the place of employment should invariably be specified where the employer has a contractual right to require the employee to move within a geographic area, or from site to site. If the appointment is probationary or temporary this should be stated, as should any special requirements for the employee to fulfil.

It is undoubtedly good practice for the employer to obtain the signature of the employee to the copy of the statement which he retains for his records, although there is no statutory requirement as to this. An interesting case on the point is *Turner* v. *Yates Wine Lodges, Ltd.*[1] when the employee was given a statement under section 4 of the Contracts of Employment Act 1972. He sought advice from his trade union as to whether to sign a copy for the employers. The employers claimed that since the employee had not signed his copy of the statement under the Act he had resigned. Mr. Turner's application involved other matters but the tribunal had no difficulty in deciding that he was dismissed. It was not unreasonable for the employee to take advice on the statement which had been given to him.

[1] [1972] I.R.L.R. 84, T.

## REFERENCE TO AN INDUSTRIAL TRIBUNAL

Where an employer is required to give an employee a written statement under sections 4 (1) and 5 (1) of the Contracts of Employment Act 1972 within specified time limits and the employer fails to do this, the employee may require a reference to an industrial tribunal to determine the particulars which should have been included or referred to in the statement so as to comply with the requirements of the sections.[1] Similarly, when a statement, which purports to be a statement in accordance with them, has been given to the employee and a question arises as to the particulars which ought to have been included or referred to, to comply with sections 4 and 5, either the employer, or the employee can require the question to be referred to a tribunal.[2] This is also the case where a question relates to the particulars entered up in a document, or recorded by other means, as is mentioned in section 5 (3).[3]

[1] Contracts of Employment Act 1972, s. 8 (1).
[2] *Ibid.*, s. 8 (2).
[3] *Ibid.*, s. 8 (3).

When no statement has been given to the employee, the tribunal determines particulars being those which ought to have been included or referred to in a written statement, and the employer is deemed to have given the employee a statement in which the particulars are included.[1] On other references to an industrial tribunal it may either confirm the particulars, amend them, or substitute others as it determines to be appropriate, and the statement shall be deemed to have been given, entered up, or recorded, as the case may be, in accordance with the tribunal's decision.[2]

[1] Contracts of Employment Act 1972, s. 8 (4).
[2] *Ibid.*, s. 8 (5).

The reference to the industrial tribunal can be made at any time during the employment (after the time in which the employer has to give the statement), and after the employment has terminated, if made before the end of the period of three months beginning with the date on which the employment ceased.[1]

[1] Contracts of Employment Act 1972, s. 8 (8). This time limit is applied even when the ex-employee did not know that his terms of employment had

changed and so was unable to refer the matter to the tribunal within the time limit. In *Grimes* v. *London Borough of Sutton*, (1973), 8 I.T.R. 217, N.I.R.C., at p. 221, Sir Hugh Griffiths said when discussing the equitable doctrine that the running of time was postponed by fraud:

> "In a suitable case it may well be that the courts will be prepared to develop this equitable doctrine and to apply it to postpone the operation of a time limit in a statute where otherwise a plaintiff might suffer a real injustice by reason of the unconscionable behaviour of the defendant. We are, however, satisfied that this is not a case in which it would be appropriate to take such a course. It is difficult to see what real advantage the appellant would gain if he did succeed in obtaining a statement of the terms upon which he was employed in 1968, five years ago, and now, two years after his employment has ceased. It is even more difficult to see what hardship or injustice he will suffer if he does not obtain the statement; there are no proceedings he can take upon it under the Contracts of Employment Act 1972, and the fact that he does not obtain it in no way prevents him from bringing an action for breach of contract to obtain financial redress if he thinks that he has such a cause for action. Nor is there any material upon which the tribunal or this Court could properly conclude that a *prima facie* case existed of that type of unconscionable behaviour on the part of the respondents that would justify invoking the doctrine of equitable fraud."

For the position where the obligation to provide the written statement of particulars of employment, or of a change in those particulars, arose prior to 7th December 1965 see Contracts of Employment Act 1963, s. 5. *Cf.* Redundancy Payments Act 1965, s. 38 and Contracts of Employment Act 1972, s. 13 (7).

# Chapter 4

# THE EMPLOYEE'S DUTY OF GOOD FAITH

## LOYALTY AND THE DUTY TO ACCOUNT TO THE EMPLOYER

A basic element of the relationship of employer and employee at common law is the obligation of the employee to render loyal service to the employer. The employee must be faithful to his employer both in dealing with the employer's property and in exercising the trust which the employer places in him. He should not accept any payment or inducement from other persons to influence him in the activities which he carries on for his employer.[1] When performing his services he should do so entirely for the employer's benefit and should not further his own interests (save in earning remuneration), or those of any third party contrary to his employer's interests. It is a breach of this obligation if he makes secret profits for himself in carrying out his duties and he must account for any such profits to his employer. For instance, in *Boston Deep Sea Fishing and Ice Co.* v. *Ansell*[2] the employee, who was the employing company's managing director, placed contracts with shipbuilders and received a secret commission. He also made arrangements on the company's behalf, as if in his own name, which resulted in him receiving monies from a third party. Although this state of affairs did not come to light until after the employee was dismissed (before the time of his fixed term contract had expired), it was held that the acceptance of secret commission was a sufficient ground to enable the employers to dismiss the employee. The other benefits which the employee had received were bonuses which were paid to him in his personal capacity as a shareholder in the third party and could not have been received by the employer. The employee was held liable to account to the employer for these bonuses. Although the company could not have received them itself, by acting in a way to further his own interests, he had abused the trust placed in him by his employer.

[1] *Bartram & Sons* v. *Lloyd* (1903), 88 L.T. 286; *Harrington* v. *Victoria Graving Dock Co.* (1878), 3 Q.B.D. 549.

## Loyalty and the duty to account to the employer

[2] (1888), 39 Ch.D. 339, C.A.; *Sinclair* v. *Neighbour*, [1967] 2 Q.B. 279; [1966] 3 All E.R. 988.

The obligation to account to the employer extends to circumstances where the monies arise as a result of criminal actions. *Reading* v. *A. -G.*[1] was a case where a British Army Sergeant in Egypt used his position to enable a criminal practice to be carried on. As a result of the sergeant accompanying lorries in uniform, making it unlikely that they would be stopped by the civilian police, it was easier for criminals to participate in trade in illicit alcoholic spirits. The employee made an enormous profit in doing this, which was claimed by the Crown. In delivering his judgment in the House of Lords, Lord OAKSEY said:

> "I do not think there is any difficulty in imputing to a servant an implied promise that he will account to his master for any moneys he may receive in the course of his master's business, or by the use of his master's property, or by the use of his position as his master's servant. There is nothing illegal in such a promise. On the contrary, in substance it is the basis for the equitable principle that an agent is accountable for profits made in the course of his agency without the knowledge and consent of his principal and no less accountable if the profits arise out of corrupt transactions."

[1] [1951] A.C. 507; [1951] 1 All E.R. 617, at p. 621, H.L.

When information which would benefit his employer comes into an employee's possession he should disclose it to the employer and should not terminate his employment to utilise the information for his own benefit, or pass it on to some third party.[1] The employee is also under a duty to disclose to his employer the fraud of fellow employees, but not each and every discrepancy by them.[2] Employees should not take part-time employment which competes with, and harms, the business of their employers. This application of the duty of loyalty was made in *Hivac, Ltd.* v. *Park Royal Scientific Instruments, Ltd.*[3] The employees, who were skilled workers, were employed by a company making hearing aids and in their spare time worked for a direct competitor, and also persuaded other employees of the employer to work for the competitor on a part-time basis. Although no confidential information was passed on by the part-time employees, the plaintiffs were granted an interlocutory injunction to prevent the defendants (the part-time employers) employing the employees of the employer on this basis. It was said that in judging the duty of the employees in such cases, all circumstances had to be looked at, but the employees had deliberately set themselves on a course which would harm their employers and so were in breach of this duty of loyalty to them. MORTON, L.J., said:

"In all the circumstances of the case, have these five employees observed the obligations of good faith and fidelity? I do not propose to recapitulate the facts, but I must start from this point, that the work done for the defendants was done in what is usually described as the employees' spare time. No cases were cited to us in which work so done was held to be a breach of the obligation of fidelity to the employer. I do not propose to express any view of such a general nature as that all work done for a firm in the same line of business as the employers in the spare time of the employees is a breach of contract, but I do say that in my view the obligation of fidelity subsists so long as the contract of service subsists, and even in his spare time an employee does owe that obligation of fidelity."

[1] *Cranleigh Precision Engineering, Ltd.* v. *Bryant*, [1964] 3 All E.R. 289; [1965] I W.L.R. 1293.
[2] *Swain* v. *West (Butchers), Ltd.*, [1936] 3 All E.R. 261, C.A.
[3] [1946] I All E.R. 350, at p. 357.

In *Sanders* v. *Parry*[1] an employed solicitor agreed with one of his principal's clients that he would commence practice on his own account and the client would instruct the defendant to carry out his legal work for a period of seven years. The employee left his principal's employ for this purpose and at the same time his secretary also terminated her employment with the principal and shortly afterwards joined him in the new practice. It was held that during employment there is a duty on the employee to protect his employer's interests and to maintain his contacts. By accepting the offer from the client the employee was looking after his own interests and was in breach of the duty of good faith and fidelity. If the employee had known his secretary was dissatisfied it was his duty to give the opportunity to his principal of dealing with any complaint which she may have had.

[1] [1967] 2 All E.R. 803.

## CONFIDENTIALITY

The duty of the employee to look after and preserve the employer's property extends to the employer's physical property[1] and also his intangible property such as his trade secrets, lists of customers and secret processes. The obligation exists while the employee is employed and continues after the employment has terminated. The former employee is free to compete with his ex-employer, either directly by operating his own business, or as an employee of another employer, so long as he does not disclose, or make use of, confidential information belonging to the employer.[2] The extent of this duty is not entirely clear although it has been considered by the Courts on a number of occasions. Perhaps the most famous case is *Robb* v. *Green*.[3] There the defendant was a manager of the plaintiff's business. Before he left his employment he copied out lists of his employer's customers to enable him to approach those customers on behalf of the business which he intended to operate when the employment terminated. The Court had no difficulty in deciding that the employee was obligated to the employer to keep good faith between them, which the employee had clearly broken by copying out the lists for his own purposes.

[1] *Leck* v. *Maestaer* (1807), 1 Camp 138 N.P.; *Superlux* v. *Plaisted* (1958), *Times*, December 12; *Cranleigh Precision Engineering, Ltd.* v. *Bryant*, [1964] 3 All E.R. 289; [1965] 1 W.L.R. 1293.

[2] See for example *Hart* v. *Colley* (1880) reported at 6 T.L.R. 216.

[3] [1895] 2 Q.B., 315, C.A.; *Floydd* v. *Cheney*, [1970] 1 All E.R. 446, at p. 449.

What is protected is a type of "property" of the employer and it is extremely difficult to define the extent of that property. The best that can be said is that each case is looked at on its facts to ascertain if the employer has an interest which he properly seeks to protect. For instance in *Wessex Dairies, Ltd.* v. *Smith*[1] a milkman solicited business from his employer's customers when he intended to leave the employment to commence business on his own account. This was found to be an obvious infringement of the employee's obligations. When former employees of a furniture polish manufacturers set up a business in competition with their former employers to sell a similar product, under a name which would manifestly be confused with that of the employers, an injunction was granted to prevent the trade continuing.[2]

[1] [1935] 2 K.B. 80, C.A.
[2] *Liquid Veneer Co., Ltd.* v. *Scott*, [1912] R.P.C. 639.

The employee must be allowed to use his own skill and expertise acquired while working for the employer but is not entitled to make use of any information which is special or peculiar to his employer. CROSS, J., in *Printers and Finishers, Ltd.* v. *Holloway*[1] tried to differentiate between the two interests. He said:

> "The mere fact that the confidential information is not embodied in a document but is carried away by the employee in his head is not, of course, of itself a reason against the granting of an injunction to prevent its use or disclosure by him. If the information in question can fairly be regarded as a separate part of the employee's stock of knowledge which a man of ordinary honesty and intelligence would recognise to be the property of his old employer and not his own to do as he likes with, then the court, if it thinks that there is a danger of the information being used or disclosed by the ex-employee to the detriment of the old employer, will do what it can to prevent that result by granting an injunction. Thus an ex-employee will be restrained from using or disclosing a chemical formula or a list of customers which he has committed to memory."

[1] [1964] 3 All E.R. 731, at pp. 735 and 736. It had been said in the past that the distinction was that the employee was entitled to utilise the information he memorised but no more. *Cf. Worsley & Co., Ltd.* v. *Cooper*, [1939] 1 All E.R. 290.

The judge envisaged a case where the ex-employee told his new employers how the former employers had overcome minor difficulties encountered in the manufacturing process. He continued:

> "Recalling matters of this sort is, to my mind, quite unlike memorising a formula or list of customers or what was said (obviously in confidence) at a particular meeting. The employee might well not realise that the feature or expedient in question was in fact peculiar to his late employer's process and factory; but even if he did such knowledge is not readily separable from his general knowledge of the ... process and his acquired skill in manipulating a ... plant, and I do not

think that any man of average intelligence and honesty would think that there was anything improper in his putting his memory of particular features of his late employer's plant at the disposal of his new employer. The law will defeat its own object if it seeks to enforce in this field standards which would be rejected by the ordinary man. After all, this involves no hardship on the employer. Although the law will not enforce a covenant directed against competition by an ex-employee it will enforce a covenant reasonably necessary to protect trade secrets (see the recent case of *Commercial Plastics, Ltd.* v. *Vincent*),[1] in which the plaintiff only failed because the covenant was too widely drawn as regards area."

[1] [1965] 1 Q.B. 623; [1964] 3 All E.R. 546.

In addition to the duty of confidentiality which arises from the employment relationship, the rules of equity which apply generally to information communicated in confidence have to be considered.[1] For instance in *Seager* v. *Copydex, Ltd.*,[1] an inventor had in confidence provided a potential customer with details of an invention which he had not then patented. Later the customer, who had not made a bargain with the inventor, sought to patent a similar invention himself. When considering the inventor's claims, Lord DENNING, M.R., said in the Court of Appeal:

"The law on this subject does not depend on any implied contract. It depends on the broad principle of equity that he who has received information in confidence shall not take unfair advantage of it. He must not make use of it to the prejudice of him who gave it without obtaining his consent. The principle is clear enough when the whole of the information is private. The difficulty arises when the information is in part public and in part private. As for instance in this case.... When the information is mixed, being partly public and partly private, then the recipient must take special care to use only the material which is in the public domain. He should go to the public source and get it: or, at any rate, not be in a better position than if he had gone to the public source. He should not get a start over others by using the information which he received in confidence. At any rate, he should not get a start without paying for it. It may not be a case for injunction but only for damages, depending on the worth of the confidential information to him in saving him time and trouble."

[1] [1967] 2 All E.R. 415, at p. 417. See for example *Terrapin* v. *Builders Supply Co.* (*Hayes*), [1960] R.P.C. 301.

An exception to the obligation of confidentiality arises when it is in the public interest to disclose the matters which the employer has revealed to the employee. This was expressed by Lord DENNING, M.R., in *Initial Services, Ltd.* v. *Putterill*[1] in the following way:

"In support of the appeal, counsel for Initial Services, Ltd. said that in the employment of every servant there is implied an obligation that he will not, before or after his service, disclose information or documents which he has received in confidence. Now I quite agree that there is such an obligation. It is imposed by law. But it is subject to exceptions. Take a simple instance. Suppose a master tells his servant: 'I am going to falsify these sale notes and deceive the customers. You are not to say anything about it to anyone.' If the master thereafter falsifies the sale notes, the servant is entitled to say: 'I am not going to stay any longer in the service of a man who does such a thing. I will leave him and report it to the customers.' It was so held in the case of *Gartside* v. *Outram*.[2] Counsel suggested that this exception was confined to case where the master has been 'guilty of a crime or fraud'; but I do not think that it is so limited. It extends to any misconduct of such a nature that it ought in the public interest to be disclosed to others. WOOD, V.-C., put it in a vivid phrase:[2] 'There is no confidence as to the disclosure of iniquity.'"

[1] [1967] 3 All E.R. 145, at p. 148.
[2] (1856), 26 L.J.Ch. 113, at pp. 114 and 116.

Notwithstanding this, it was held in *Bent's Brewery Co., Ltd.* v. *Hogan*[1] that an employee should not disclose confidential employment to his trade union. It is not certain whether this would be the common law rule today, but the situation must be affected by the provisions of the Employment Protection Act 1975 as to the disclosure of information to representatives of independent trade unions and the Code of Practice relating to this about to be issued by the Advisory, Conciliation and Arbitration Service.

[1] [1945] 2 All E.R. 570 (where the information related to payments to employees).

## RESTRICTIVE AGREEMENTS

As a result of uncertainties surrounding the common law obligation of confidentiality on employees, employers often try to obtain express covenants or agreements from their employees to restrict their activities, insofar as they involve the disclosure of information which is peculiar to the employer. It is usual for the restraint to operate both whilst the contract subsists and after its termination. Whether or not a restraint on trade is enforceable depends on its reasonableness, both from the point of view of the public and of the parties to it. To be valid a restraint must be

"reasonable ... in reference to the interests of the parties concerned and reasonable in reference to the interests of the public, so framed and so guarded as to afford adequate protection to the party in whose favour it is imposed, while at the same time it is in no way injurious to the public."[1]

[1] Per Lord MACNAUGHTEN in *Nordenfelt* v. *Maxim Nordenfelt Guns and Ammunition Co.*, [1894] A.C. 535, at p. 565.

The Courts look with great care at restrictive covenants and agreements in view of the economic imbalance between the parties. The tests which are to be applied were explained by SELLERS, L.J., in the Court of Appeal in *Gledhow Autoparts, Ltd.* v. *Delaney*[1] as follows:

"... first, that it is for the covenantee to show that the restriction sought to be imposed on the covenantor goes no further than is reasonable for the protection of his business; secondly, that the restraint must be reasonable not only in the interests of the covenantee but in the interests of both the contracting parties; and thirdly, that an employer is not entitled by a covenant taken from his employee to protect himself after the employment has ceased against his former servant's competition, although a purchaser of goodwill is entitled to protect himself against such competition on the part of the vendor."

[1] [1965] 3 All E.R. 288, at p. 291, C.A.

In Delaney's case the restrictions sought to prohibit transactions with potential, as well as existing, customers and the covenant was held to be invalid. In applying the test of reasonableness all the circumstances are looked at to see if the agreement is reasonable. *Instone* v. *A. Schroeder Music Publishing Co., Ltd.*[1] is a recent case, not actually involving a contract of service, when the question of reasonableness was examined by the Court of Appeal. An unknown song-writer, aged 21, entered into an agreement with a music publisher giving the publisher the exclusive right to his song-writing services for five years, renewable in certain circumstances for a further period of five years. The publisher could at any time determine the agreement on a month's notice and there was no obligation on it to exploit the writer's songs. It was held that the contract was unreasonable, as it operated in restraint of trade and in view of its "one-sided" nature, RUSSELL, L.J., said:[2]

> "this contract is restrictive of the ability of the plaintiff to turn to account his compositions to an extent and in a manner that is against the public interest."

[1] [1974] 1 All E.R. 171, C.A. See also *Clifford Davis Management, Ltd.* v. *W.E.A. Records, Ltd.*, [1975] 1 All E.R. 237, C.A.
[2] *Ibid.*, at p. 178.

A covenant the effect of which would be to prevent an employee working in a similar business for a period of seven years after leaving the employer's employment was held by the House of Lords to be void.[1] The contract was contrary to public policy because it would have prevented both the employee and the world at large from having the benefit of the employee's skills.

Attempts to ensure that restrictions are reasonable usually involve limitations on their application, for instance by restricting the employee from dealing with existing customers or suppliers of the employer and no more, or by providing that the restraint is in respect of a closely defined geographic area only. In addition such agreements are frequently expressed to apply within a time limit after the expiration of the termination of employment. Each case falls to be decided on its merits. In one situation which was brought before the Courts, albeit some time ago, a world-wide restriction was considered to be reasonable,[1] as was a covenant not to engage in a solicitor's practice within seven miles of a country town.[2] A covenant not to engage in trade as a tailor within a three mile radius has been upheld[3] and so has a restriction which forbade an estate agent from acting in any capacity as such agent within three miles of a town for three years after the ending of the employment.[4]

However, in *Commercial Plastics, Ltd.* v. *Vincent*[5] an agreement "not to seek employment with any of our competitors ... for at least one year after leaving our employ" was held to be void because there was no geographic restriction and the description of the area of operations to which the restriction applied was too wide.

[1] *Herbert Morris, Ltd.* v. *Saxelby*, [1916] 1 A.C. 688.
[1] *Nordenfelt case*, above.
[2] *Fitch* v. *Dewes*, [1921] A.C. 158, H.L.
[3] *Putsman* v. *Taylor*, [1927] 1 K.B. 741.
[4] *Calvert Hunt and Barden* v. *Elton* (1974) 233 Estates Gazette 391.
[5] [1965] 1 Q.B. 623; [1964] 3 All E.R. 546.

A provision in an agreement may be a restraint on trade even though not expressed as such.[1] In *Eastham* v. *Newcastle Football Club, Ltd.*[2] the football clubs who were members of the Football Association had agreed to a rule that if a footballer's employment contract was terminated other football clubs would not employ him without the consent of the previous club. This agreement was held to be void as being in restraint of trade because it restricted the freedom of footballers to earn their living.

[1] *Stenhouse Australia, Ltd.* v. *Phillips*, [1974] A.C. 391; [1974] 1 All E.R. 117, P.C. when one of the obligations was to pay half of an insurance broker's gross commission to the former employer was dealt with as an agreement in restraint of trade; *Wyatt* v. *Kreglinger and Fernau*, [1933] 1 K.B. 793; *Bull* v. *Pitney-Bowes, Ltd.*, [1966] 3 All E.R. 384; [1967] 1 W.L.R. 273.
[2] [1964] Ch. 413; [1963] 3 All E.R. 139; *Cooke* v. *Football Association* (1972), *Times*, 24th March.

If the restriction which the employer has sought to impose is found to be void by the court it will not substitute a reasonable covenant in its place.[1] In such circumstances all the employer can do is to rely on the obligation of confidentiality at common law. The serious difficulty for employers is that they are unable to know whether agreements entered into by their employees are enforceable, until the restriction has been considered by the court, by which time it is too late for the matter to be put right. In drafting restrictions for inclusion in service agreements great care should be exercised to ensure that only such limitations as are necessary to protect the employer's proprietorial interests are included. One attempt to overcome this difficulty was to have several covenants each quite separate and severable from the other. This received a serious setback in *Attwood* v. *Lamont*[2] when the

Court of Appeal refused to apply the previous "blue pencil" approach. It considered the covenant imposed by the employer to be oppressive and would not do anything to render it enforceable. However, if the covenants are drawn in such a way as to be totally independent of each other severence may still be used to benefit the employer. In *T. Lucas & Co., Ltd. v. Mitchell*[3] one of the two restrictions which had been imposed was reasonable and the other was not. The reasonable restriction depended on the other covenant for the definition of the goods in respect of which it applied. PENNYCUICK, V.-C., said:

"I conclude then that cl 16 cannot be severed. The first restriction is unreasonable and unenforceable and the second, standing alone, would be reasonable and enforceable but as the two restrictions cannot be severed one must treat the entirety of the restrictions as being unreasonable and unenforceable. I must say I come to this conclusion with considerable regret. What is actually happening is that the defendant is canvassing the plaintiff company's customers with whom he dealt during his employment. Had cl 16 been framed as two separate restrictions there is no doubt in my mind that the plaintiff company could have prevented him from doing what he is now doing."

He was clearly of the opinion that if the two restrictions were entirely separate that it was reasonable and would have been enforceable.

[1] *Commercial Plastics, Ltd. v. Vincent*, above.
[2] [1920] 3 K.B. 571.
[3] [1972] 2 All E.R. 1035, at p. 1046.

The covenants must be limited to the circumstances which the court considers the parties had in their contemplation when the relationship was entered into.

"Another matter which requires attention is whether a restriction on trade must be treated as wholly void because it is so worded as to cover cases which may possibly arise, and to which it cannot be reasonably applied.... Agreements in restraint of trade, like other agreements, must be construed with reference to the object sought to be attained by them. In cases such as the one before us, the object is the protection of one of the parties against rivalry in trade. Such agreements cannot be properly held to apply to cases which, although covered by the words of the agreement, cannot be reasonably supposed ever to have been contemplated by the parties, and which on a rational view of the agreement are excluded from its operation by falling, in truth, outside, and not within, its real scope."[1]

[1] Per LINDLEY, M.R., in *Haynes* v. *Doman,* [1899] 2 Ch.D. 13, at pp. 24 and 25.

In *Home Counties Dairies, Ltd.* v. *Skilton*[1] it was held that a restriction not to sell dairy produce to those persons who had been customers within six months of the termination of the contract of employment was reasonable. It could be reasonably expected that such customers might return their orders to the employer even if they had left during the six month period. The only adequate solution for employers is to err on the side of caution when drawing restrictive covenants for employees to enter into.

[1] [1970] 1 All E.R. 1227; [1970] 1 W.L.R. 526.

If an employee breaks a valid restriction, or does not comply with his obligations as to confidentiality, the employer may be able to claim both damages and an injunction to prevent the breach continuing, against the employee. In many cases the remedy which will be most effective is the injunction. In addition to an injunction against the former employee, the employer may be able to obtain a similar remedy against a new employer. This can be extremely effective if obtained quickly and an interlocutory injunction[1] will often be a final solution to the employer's problem. The right to sue the former employee for damages tends to be of more academic than practical interest. In certain circumstances it may be possible to obtain an award of damages against the new employer.[2]

[1] See for instance *Standex International, Ltd.* v. *Blades,* [1976] F.S.R. 114, C.A. but contrast *Consolidated Agricultural Suppliers, Ltd.* v. *Rushmere,* (1976) *Times,* 30th June, C.A. See also *Barry Artist, Ltd.* v. *Baumal,* [1975] Law S. Gaz. 123, Ch.D.

[2] See *Printers and Finishers, Ltd.* v. *Holloway* [1964] 3 All E.R. 731; [1965] 1 W.L.R. 1.

If an employee who is still in employment at the time of the breach of the obligation as to confidentiality, or breach of a restrictive agreement which is valid, it has to be considered whether the employee has repudiated the contract of employment such as to justify dismissal, both from the point of view of the common law and the unfair dismissal provisions.[1] A breach of the duty of confidentiality would doubtless amount to a reason as to the employee's conduct for the purpose of Schedule 1, paragraph 6 (2) (*b*) of the Trade Union and Labour Relations Act 1974.[2]

[1] See pp. 144 and 290, below.

[2] But it would still be for the employer to show that in the circumstances he had acted reasonably in treating the reason as a sufficient reason for dismissing the employee. Trade Union and Labour Relations Act 1974, Sch. 1, para. 6 (8).

The Courts look on restrictions on trade during an employment or engagement, in a different light from those afterwards. It is generally regarded as less likely that a restriction during the continuance of the employment would be inimicable to the public interest.[1]

[1] See *William Robinson & Co., Ltd.* v. *Heuer*, [1898] 2 Ch.D. 451 and *Rely-A-Bell Burglar and Fire Alarm Co., Ltd.* v. *Eisler*, [1926] Ch. 609.

## INVENTIONS, COPYRIGHT AND REGISTERED DESIGNS

The question of title to inventions or improvements in processes made by employees occasionally gives rise to problems and it falls to be decided in whose ownership the invention, patent or improvement should be vested. "It is elementary that, where the employee in the course of his employment (i.e., in his employer's time and with his materials) makes an invention which it falls within his duty to make . . . he holds his interest in the invention and in any resulting patent as trustee for the employer unless he can show that he has a beneficial interest which the law recognises."[1]

[1] Per Viscount SIMONDS in *Sterling Engineering Co., Ltd.* v. *Patchett*, [1955] 1 All E.R. 369, at p. 373.

ROXBURGH, J., in *British Syphon Co., Ltd.* v. *Homewood*[1] explained the tests to be applied when deciding as to ownership of patents and improvements when there is no express agreement regarding them. In that case an employee who was a technician and advised a company which manufactured soda water syphons

on all technical matters devised a new method of dispensing sod:
water. The judge said:

> "Would it be consistent with good faith, as between master
> and servant, that he should in that position be entitled to make
> some invention in relation to a matter concerning a part of the
> plaintiff's business and either keep it from his employer, if
> and when asked about the problem, or even sell it to a rival
> and say: 'Well, yes, I know the answer to your problem, but I
> have already sold it to your rival'? In my judgment, that
> cannot be consistent with a relationship of good faith between
> a master and a technical adviser. It seems to me that he has a
> duty not to put himself in a position in which he may have
> personal reasons for not giving his employer the best advice
> which it is his duty to give if and when asked to give it. What
> I am saying only relates to matters concerning the business of
> his employer. That, of course, is quite clear; but, in matters of
> that type, it seems to me that he has a duty to be free from
> any personal reason for not giving his employer the best
> possible advice. A fortiori, it seems to me that he is not entitled
> to put himself into the position of being able to say: 'You
> retained me to advise you, and I will tell you what I advise.
> Do it this way, but you will have to buy the method from
> your rival, because I have just sold it to him, having invented
> it yesterday'. That seems to me to be reasoning which, in the
> absence of authority, makes it right and proper for me to
> decide that this invention (which, in my judgment, plainly
> relates to and concerns the business of the plaintiffs, viz., the
> distribution of soda water to the public in containers of a
> satisfactory character), if made during a time during which
> the chief technician is standing by under the terms of his
> employment, must be held to be in equity the property of the
> employer."

[1] [1956] 2 All E.R. 897, at p. 898.

Whenever there is a likelihood that an employee will make
inventions and discoveries there should be an express agreement
as to their ownership and provision made for application for, and
ownership of, the resulting patent.[1] Section 56 (2) of the Patents
Act 1949 reads as follows:

> "(2) In proceedings before the court between an employer

and a person who is or was at the material time his employee, or upon an application made to the comptroller under sub-section (1) of this section, the court or comptroller may, unless satisfied that one or other of the parties is entitled, to the exclusion of the other, to the benefit of an invention made by the employee, by order provide for the apportionment between them of the benefit of the invention, and of any patent granted or to be granted in respect thereof, in such manner as the court or comptroller considers."

[1] The agreement must not be an unreasonable restraint on trade; *Electric Transmission* v. *Dannenberg* (1949), 66 R.P.C. 183.

At first sight this would appear to present a useful opportunity for resolving difficulties between employers and employees as to the ownership of patents. However, in *Sterling Engineering Co., Ltd.* v. *Patchett*,[1] Viscount SIMONDS, having explained the common law rule, went on to consider the operation of section 56 (2).

"The word 'entitled' refers to legal right. The court must, therefore, determine the legal rights, just as it must determine them in any other case, and, if the issue is, as it is here, whether one party is entitled to the exclusion of the other, it must decide that question 'Aye' or 'No' and, having decided it in the affirmative, it is not for the court to say that it is not satisfied. So here, having examined every plea which has been adduced to support the contention that the respondent has some beneficial interest in the patents and rejected them all, the court must declare itself satisfied that the company is entitled, to the exclusion of the respondent, and decline the jurisdiction conferred by the sub-section."

[1] [1955] 1 All E.R. 369, at p. 374, H.L.

Thus making it clear that in cases where the ownership is vested in the employer there is no opportunity to apportion its benefit under the section. This means that situations where section 56 (2) will be of use are likely to be extremely rare.

Section 56 (1) of the Patents Act 1949 provides:

"(1) Where a dispute arises between an employer and a person who is or was at the material time his employee as to the rights of the parties in respect of an invention made by the employee either alone or jointly with other employees or in respect of any patent granted or to be granted in respect thereof, the comptroller may, upon application made to him in the prescribed manner by either of the parties, and after giving to each of them an opportunity to be heard, determine the matter in dispute, and may make such orders for giving effect to his decision as he considers expedient:

Provided that if it appears to the comptroller upon any application under this section that the matter in dispute involves questions which would more properly be determined by the court, he may decline to deal therewith."[1]

A decision of the Comptroller General of Patents, Designs and Trade Marks under this sub-section has the same effect as between two parties and those claiming under them as a decision of the court[2] and is subject to appeal to the Appeal Tribunal.[3]

[1] See for example *Re Selz's, Ltd.'s Application* (1953), 71 R.P.C. 158.
[2] Patents Act 1949, s. 56 (3).
[3] *Ibid.*, s. 56 (4).

The position of copyright material prepared by employees is dealt with in section 4 of the Copyright Act 1956. Sub-sections (2), (3), (4) and (5) are set out below:

"(2) Where a literary, dramatic or artistic work is made by the author in the course of his employment by the proprietor of a newspaper, magazine or similar periodical under a contract of service or apprenticeship, and is so made for the purpose of publication in a newspaper, magazine or similar periodical, the said proprietor shall be entitled to the copyright in the work in so far as the copyright relates to publication of the work in any newspaper, magazine or similar periodical, or to reproduction of the work for the purpose of its being so published; but in all other respects the author shall be entitled to any copyright subsisting in the work by virtue of this Part of this Act.

(3) Subject to the last preceding sub-section, where a person commissions the taking of a photograph, or the painting or drawing of a portrait, or the making of an engraving, and pays or agrees to pay for it in money or money's worth, and the work is made in pursuance of that commission, the person who so commissioned the work shall be entitled to any copyright subsisting therein by virtue of this Part of this Act.

(4) Where, in a case not falling within either of the two last preceding sub-sections, a work is made in the course of the author's employment by another person under a contract of service or apprenticeship, that other person shall be entitled to any copyright subsisting in the work by virtue of this Part of this Act.

(5) Each of the three last preceding sub-sections shall have effect subject, in any particular case, to any agreement excluding the operation thereof in that case."

[1] See *Byrne* v. *Statist Co.*, [1914] 1 K.B. 622 (translations in spare time belonged to employee) and *Stevenson, Jordan and Harrison, Ltd.* v. *Macdonald and Evans*, [1952] 1 T.L.R. 101, C.A. (accountants lectures vested in employee).

There are no statutory provisions relating to registered designs prepared by employees, but the employer is entitled to ownership in the design if it is produced by the employee in the course of his employment.

# Chapter 5

# TERMINATION

## TERMINATION OF EMPLOYMENT CONTRACTS

### Performance

A contract of employment may be for a fixed period or for carrying out a particular task and that task only. The general law of contract provides that in such cases when the time expires or the task is performed, and the other stipulations have been complied with, the contract is discharged. The common law regards the relationship of employer and employee as entirely one of contract and after compliance with all the provisions of the agreement the parties are released from their obligations *inter se*.

The expiry of a fixed term contract amounts to dismissal for the purposes of the Redundancy Payments Act 1965[1] and the unfair dismissal provisions,[2] and in certain unusual circumstances, notice is necessary pursuant to the Contracts of Employment Act 1972.[3] In *Whiles* v. *Harold Wesley, Ltd.*[4] an industrial tribunal considered the position when a book-keeper (whose employment under another contract had previously terminated) was employed to complete the books "until about the end of February or, perhaps, and it is not quite clear which, until the work had been completed". The employer wrote to the employee during February paying her until the end of the month "as your work is now completed". The tribunal held that the case "almost certainly" fell within section 3 (1) (b)[5] of the Redundancy Payments Act 1965, or if not, amounted to a case of dismissal by the employer. It is likely that the expiry of a contract to perform a certain task, rather than work for a fixed term (in the temporal sense), will be treated as a dismissal for statutory purposes.

[1] Redundancy Payments Act 1965, s. 3 (2) (b). See p. 190, below.
[2] Trade Union and Labour Relations Act 1974, Sch. 1, para. 5 (2) (b). See p. 286, below.
[3] See p. 138, below.
[4] (1966), 1 I.T.R. 342, T.
[5] Now replaced by Redundancy Payments Act 1965, s. 3 (2) (b), introduced by the Employment Protection Act 1975. See p. 190 below.

## Agreement

A contract of employment may be terminated by agreement between the parties in the same way as any other contract.[1] This agreement may finally discharge the relationship of employer and employee or terminate the existing contract substituting a new one in its place.[2] The new agreement may bring the contract of employment to an end without further obligation on either party, may provide for payment to be made by one to the other or contain other terms. Unless it is under seal the agreement (being itself a contract) should be supported by consideration, but this can be the release of executory promises contained in the original employment contract.

[1] *R.* v. *Bottesford (Inhabitants)* (1825), 4 B. & C. 84.
[2] *R.* v. *Buckingham (Inhabitants)* (1834), 5 B. & Ad. 953.

The advent of statutory rights which depend upon the employer having terminated the contract of employment has resulted in the courts and tribunals looking closely at circumstances which, at first sight, may appear to be instances of termination of employment by agreement, especially if they occur after notice of termination has been given by the employer. In *Lees* v. *Arthur Greaves (Lees), Ltd.*[1] the employee was given six months' notice to expire on 31st March 1972. He left the employment on 28th January, so the employers contended, by agreement (the date was of particular importance because the unfair dismissal provisions of the Industrial Relations Act 1971 came into force on 28th February 1972). The majority in the Court of Appeal expressly approved the statement by Sir JOHN DONALDSON in the National Industrial Relations Court in *McAlwane* v. *Boughton Estates, Ltd.*:[2]

"We would further suggest that it would be a very rare case, indeed, in which it could properly be found that the employer and the employee had got together and, notwithstanding that there was a current notice of termination of the employment, agreed mutually to terminate the contract, particularly when one realises the financial consequences to the employee involved in such an agreement."

[1] [1974] 2 All E.R. 393, C.A.; but see *Hempel* v. *Parrish* (1968), 3 I.T.R. 240, T.
[2] [1973] I.C.R. 470, at p. 473.

When termination takes place by agreement it will probably be in the employer's interests to record the terms in writing so that it is clear that a dismissal did not take place. A dismissal disguised as termination by agreement will remain a dismissal and care must be exercised to ensure that it is evident that no undue pressure has been applied, and that the termination is by mutual agreement.

## Frustration and supervening impossibility of performance

The doctrines of discharge by frustration and supervening impossibility of performance apply to contracts of employment. Indeed the personal nature of the relationship means that they are particularly susceptible to determination in this way. If performance of the contract becomes impossible, or it cannot be performed in the manner contemplated when it was entered into, it may be discharged. An early example occurred in *Poussard* v. *Spiers and Pond*[1] where an opera singer was unable to perform at the opening of a new opera because of illness and her contract was held to be frustrated. In another case[2] a doctor employed as School Medical Officer by Preston Corporation was interned for nine months during the Second World War and the resulting absence from his post brought the contract to an end.

[1] (1876), 1 Q.B.D. 410. See also *Condor* v. *The Barron Knights,* [1966] 1 W.L.R. 87.

[2] *Unger* v. *Preston Corporation,* [1942] 1 All E.R. 200.

Situations where the doctrines have to be considered include the following:

### (a) *Death of the employer or employee*

Unless there is a provision in the contract to the contrary the death of either party to the contract will discharge it.[1] Where the employer is a partnership the death of a partner will terminate the contract of employment if it is dependent upon the deceased's membership of the partnership.[2] There are special provisions in the Redundancy Payments Act 1965 and in the unfair dismissal provisions which may apply on the death of either party.[3]

[1] *Farrow* v. *Wilson* (1869), L.R. 4 C.P. 744.

[2] *Robson* v. *Drummond* (1813), 2 B. & Ad. 303.

[3] See pp. 253 and 366, below, respectively.

### (b) *Physical impossibility*

The contract may also be discharged if it becomes physically impossible to perform. For instance, illness of the employee going to the root of the relationship, will bring the contract to an end, as in *Poussard's* case, above.

In another reported decision[1] a contract of apprenticeship was terminated when the apprentice contracted a permanent illness. Other cases of physical impossibility are encountered where the employee is, through no fault of his own, put in a position, where he cannot render the service he has agreed to carry out for his employer.[2]

[1] *Boast* v. *Firth* (1868), L.R. 4 C.P. 1.
[2] *Unger* v. *Preston Corporation*, [1942] 1 All E.R. 200.

In a case under the Redundancy Payments Act 1965, Sir JOHN DONALDSON explained the tests to be applied in determining whether a contract of employment had been frustrated by the employee's illness.[1]

"The tribunal must ask itself: 'Was the employee's incapacity, looked at before the purported dismissal, of such a nature, or did it appear likely to continue for such a period, that further performance of his obligation in the future would either be impossible or would be a thing radically different from that undertaken by him and agreed to be accepted by the employer under the agreed terms of his employment?'

In considering the answer to this question, the tribunal should take account of—

(i) *The terms of the contract, including the provisions as to sickness pay*
The whole basis of weekly employment may be destroyed more quickly than that of monthly employment and that in turn more quickly than annual employment. When the contract provides for sick pay, it is plain that the contract cannot be frustrated so long as the employee returns to work, or appears likely to return to work, within the period during which such sick pay is payable. But the converse is not necessarily true, for the right to sick pay may expire before the incapacity has gone on, or appears likely to go on, for so long as to make a return to work impossible or radically different from the obligations undertaken under the contract of employment.

(ii) *How long the employment was likely to last in the absence of sickness*

The relationship is less likely to survive if the employment was inherently temporary in its nature or for the duration of a particular job, than if it was expected to be long term or even life long.

(iii) *The nature of the employment*

Where the employee is one of many in the same category, the relationship is more likely to survive the period of incapacity than if he occupies a key post which must be filled and filled on a permanent basis if his absence is prolonged.

(iv) *The nature of the illness or injury and how long it has already continued and the prospects of recovery*

The greater the degree of incapacity and the longer the period over which it has persisted and is likely to persist, the more likely it is that the relationship has been destroyed.

(v) *The period of past employment*

A relationship which is of long standing is not so easily destroyed as one which has but a short history. This is good sense and, we think, no less good law, even if it involves some implied and scarcely detectable change in the contract of employment year by year as the duration of the relationship lengthens. The legal basis is that over a long period of service the parties must be assumed to have contemplated a longer period or periods of sickness than over a shorter period.

These factors are inter-related and cumulative, but are not necessarily exhaustive of those which have to be taken into account. The question is and remains—

'Was the employee's incapacity, looked at before the purported dismissal, of such a nature, or did it appear likely to continue for such a period, that further performance of his obligations in the future would either be impossible or would be a thing radically different from that undertaken by him and accepted by the employer under the agreed terms of his employment?'

Any other factors which bear upon this issue must also be considered."

[1] *Marshall* v. *Harland and Wolff, Ltd.,* (No. 2) I.T.R. 150, at p. 154, N.I.R.C. (1972), 7.

Applying the test in *Marshall's* case the National Industrial Relations Court decided the contract was not frustrated even though Mr. Marshall had been absent from work for 18 months.

Each case where frustration is considered must be looked at on its own facts to determine whether the tests laid down in *Marshall's* case apply. For instance in *Hare* v. *Murphy Brothers, Ltd.*[1] the employee was sentenced to a year in prison and the Court of Appeal held that this frustrated the contract.

[1] (1975), 10 I.T.R. 1, C.A. See also *Wandby* v. *H.F.M. (Transport) Co., Ltd.*; [1976] I.R.L.R. 35, T (driver employed by employers for eight months. One month in prison *held* to frustrate contract).

(c) *Legal impossibility*

The parties may be released from their obligations if it becomes legally impossible to comply with them. This usually arises as a result of new statute law, Act of State, or change in the law of a foreign jurisdiction in some way governing the contract or the work to be carried out in accordance with it.

In *Reilly* v. *R.,*[1] Reilly was appointed a member of the Federal Appeal Board but when the position was abolished by statute his contract was frustrated.

The new situation need not go as far as making the employee's position obsolete, it is sufficient if another essential requirement of the contract is vitiated, for instance the method of calculation of remuneration.[2]

[1] [1934] A.C. 176, P.C.
[2] *Studholme* v. *South Western Gas Board,* [1954] 1 All E.R. 462.

The determination of the contract of employment in accordance with the doctrines of frustration and supervening impossibility of performance, does not amount to a breach entitling the employee to damages or payment in lieu of notice. The claim of an employee whose engagement has been so terminated is limited to the wages and other benefits accrued due to the time of dissolution. The rules as to frustration and impossibility of performance applied to contracts of employment are those generally prevailing and when relevant the Law Reform (Frustrated Contracts) Act 1943, may have to be considered.

## Notice

Employment contracts may contain express provisions enabling either party to terminate the contract upon notice being given to the other. There is no requirement that notice to be given by the employer is the same as that given by the employee or, save where expressly so provided, for the notice to terminate to be in writing.[1]

[1] For provisions requiring the employer to give reasons for dismissal in certain circumstances, see p. 152, below.

One of the requirements of the Contracts of Employment Act 1972 and of its predecessor,[1] is that details of the notice to which the employee is entitled should be given in the written particulars handed to the employee. In addition that Act lays down minimum periods of notice which apply to the majority of employment contracts.[2] When the Act applies and the employee is entitled to notice of determination of the contract, the period should be either that expressed or implied in the contract, or the statutory minimum period, whichever is the longer.[3]

[1] Contracts of Employment Act 1963.
[2] See p. 135, below.
[3] Contracts of Employment Act 1972, s. 1 (3).

Difficulties are encountered where the length of notice is not dealt with expressly. Only very rarely are the Courts prepared to accept that the parties intended employment to be for life.[1] In all other cases where the contract is not for a fixed period or task, a term will be implied as to the notice necessary for termination. Two approaches are adopted to this problem. The first is to ascertain from the contract and surrounding circumstances whether there is a period of notice which the employer and employee must have intended to be applicable thereto. Many factors may be taken into account in showing that the parties had in mind specific provisions as to notice. In the older cases reference was made to usages and customs of particular trades, and a distinction grew up between customs which had been judicially noticed and those which had not.[2] These usages and customs were established when society was evolving slowly, being common knowledge amongst those to whom they applied, but their relevance today is questionable.

[1] *Salt* v. *Power Plant Co. Ltd.*, [1936] 3 All E.R. 322; *Wallis* v. *Day* (1837), 2 M. & W. 273. But see *Ivory* v. *Palmer*, [1975] I.C.R. 340, C.A., where the Court of Appeal by majority upheld the decision of a County Court that an employment contract was for life in surprising circumstances and also *McClelland* v. *Northern Ireland General Hospital Services Board*, [1957] 2 All E.R. 129; [1957] 1 W.L.R. 594, H.L.

[2] *Paxton* v. *Courtney* (1860), 2 F. & F. 131, quoted by HORRIDGE, J., in *Produce Brokers Co., Ltd.* v. *Olympia Oil and Cake Co., Ltd.*, [1916] 2 K.B. 296, at p. 298.


In *Richardson and Another* v. *Koefod*,[1] a long recognised custom was considered by the Court of Appeal. The contract of employment for the Manageress of a Wimpy Bar did not stipulate the notice to be given until the employee had worked for 26 weeks or more, when the periods laid down by the Contracts of Employment Act 1963, were to apply. A few weeks after the employment commenced she was dismissed, notice in excess of a month being given. The employers then sought to obtain possession of the flat which the manageress occupied as part of her duties. At first instance the County Court Judge found that there was a general hiring, and the old custom that such hiring was for a year applied. On appeal his decision was reversed, it was held that the custom did not apply, and the manageress was entitled to reasonable notice which she had received. Lord DENNING, M.R., said:

> "The time has now come to state explicitly that there is no presumption of a yearly hiring. In the absence of express stipulation, the rule is that every contract of service is determinable by reasonable notice. The length of notice depends on the circumstances of the case."

[1] [1969] 3 All E.R. 1264; [1969] 1 W.L.R. 1812.


Although great care should now be exercised before reliance is placed on custom to indicate the length of notice, it may be that such well established rules as that relating to domestic service which provides that the contract may be terminated at any time by a month's notice, or at the end of the first month by a fortnight's notice,[1] will still be relevant.

[1] *Moult* v. *Halliday*, [1898] 1 Q.B. 125; *George* v. *Davies*, [1911] 2 K.B. 445.

The second approach operates where the contract is silent as to notice and it cannot be said that the parties clearly intended a specific period to apply. In such cases the Courts will imply that the relationship can be terminated on reasonable notice by either party.[1]

[1] *Payzu, Ltd.* v. *Hannaford*, [1918] 2 K.B. 348; *S. W. Strange, Ltd.* v. *Mann*, [1965] 1 All E.R. 1069; [1965] 1 W.L.R. 629 (three months held to be reasonable notice—manager of credit betting business).

Problems frequently arise (for example in calculating damages on wrongful dismissal) as to what is reasonable notice. Reasonableness is a question of fact which depends upon the circumstances of the particular case and although no definite rules can be laid down some help may be found in the reports. A ship's Chief Officer has been held to be entitled to 12 months' notice,[1] a photographer and journalist six months,[2] and three months' notice was reasonable for the manager of a bookmaker's credit department.[3]

[1] *Savage* v. *British India Steam Navigation Co., Ltd.* (1930), 46 T.L.R. 294.
[2] *Bauman* v. *Hulton Press, Ltd.*, [1952] 2 All E.R. 1121.
[3] *S. W. Strange, Ltd.* v. *Mann*, [1965] 1 All E.R. 1069; [1965] 1 W.L.R. 629.

However, previous decisions must be referred to with caution, and should be used as no more than a guide. This uncertainty makes it difficult to advise with accuracy, and decided cases show considerable variation, even in the same type of employment.

The requirements as to notice contained in the Contracts of Employment Act 1972, have undoubtedly had a restrictive effect with regard to the length of notice, and in many instances it may be difficult, if not impossible, to argue that the employee is entitled to notice longer than that required by the Act. This is so even where the balance of reasonableness is heavily on that side, for the statutory minimum period will have been expressed in the statement given pursuant to the Act, which will in many cases have been accepted as being correct by the employee.

## Statutory provisions as to notice
Section 1 of the Contracts of Employment Act 1972 lays down statutory minima for the notice to terminate many contracts of employment. It reads as follows:[1]

"1.—(1) The notice required to be given by an employer to terminate the contract of employment of a person who has been continuously employed[2] for [four weeks] or more—

(a)   shall be not less than one week's notice if his period of continuous employment is less than two years;

[(b)   shall be not less than one week's notice for each year of continuous employment if his period of continuous employment is two years or more but less than 12 years; and

(c)   shall be not less than 12 weeks' notice if his period of continuous employment is 12 years or more].

(2)[3] The notice required to be given by an employee who has been continuously employed for [four weeks] or more to terminate his contract of employment shall be not less than one week.

(3)[4] Any provision for shorter notice in any contract of employment with a person who has been continuously employed for [four weeks] or more shall have effect subject to the foregoing sub-sections, but this section shall not be taken to prevent either party from waiving his right to notice on any occasion, or from accepting a payment in lieu of notice.

(4)[5] Any contract of employment of a person who has been continuously employed for [twelve weeks] or more which is a contract for a term certain of four weeks or less shall have effect as if it were for an indefinite period and, accordingly, sub-sections (1) and (2) of this section shall apply to the contract.

(5)[6] Schedule 1 to this Act shall apply for the purposes of this and the next following section for ascertaining the length of an employee's period of employment and whether that period of employment has been continuous.

(6)[7] It is hereby declared that this section does not affect any right of either party to treat the contract as terminable without notice by reason of such conduct by the other party as would have enabled him so to treat it before the passing of this Act."

[1] Incorporating amendments made by the Employment Protection Act 1975. The words introduced by that Act are shown in square brackets. The amendments became operative on 1st June 1976; see the Employment Protection Act 1975 (Commencement No. 4) Order 1976, S.I. 1976 No. 530. The words "four weeks" were formerly "thirteen weeks" and in sub-section (4) "twelve weeks" was previously "thirteen weeks". Sub-section (1) read:

"(1) The notice required to be given by an employer to terminate the contract of employment of a person who has been continuously employed for thirteen weeks or more:

(a) shall be not less than one week's notice if his period of continuous employment is less than two years.

(b) shall be not less than two weeks' notice if his period of continuous employment is two years or more but less than five years.

(c) shall be not less than 'four weeks' notice if his period of continuous employment is five years or more but less than ten years,

(d) shall be not less than six weeks' notice if his period of continuous employment is ten years or more but less than fifteen years, and

(e) shall be not less than eight weeks' notice if his period of continuous employment is fifteen years or more."

[2] "... *continuously employed* ...". In the majority of cases calculation of a period of continuous employment should prove of little difficulty since the employer will have provided most employees to whom the section applies, with a statement in accordance with the Contracts of Employment Act 1972 setting out of date from which the period is to be calculated. See p. 98, above. In difficult cases Sch. 1 of the Contracts of Employment Act 1972 will have to be referred to and this is discussed in detail in Chapter 6, below. Continuous employment need not be pursuant to one contract but can be under a succession of them; *Re Mack Trucks (Britain), Ltd.*, [1967] 1 All E.R. 977; [1967] 1 W.L.R. 780.

[3] *Sub-section* (2). The minimum notice which an employee has to give to his employer to terminate the contract of employment is not less than one week. It is of course possible to increase this by agreement but it is to be noted that the statutory provision with regard to notice by the employee does not vary with the length of service.

[4] *Sub-section* (3). If the contract provides for shorter notice it is of no effect, but the parties at the time may waive notice, or the employee accept payment in lieu of notice. There appears to be no power to waive payment in such cases. Section 2, Contracts of Employment Act 1972 makes provision for payment during notice and unless "a contract" in sub-section 2 (4) means "an employment contract only" any agreement to exclude or limit the employer's obligations is void. Section 40 (4) of the Redundancy Payments Act 1965 deals with extension of the period of notice in relation to that Act, where the employee takes part in a strike during the currency of the notice. See p. 205 below.

[5] *Sub-section* (4). In a fixed term contract no notice is necessary, and a series of short fixed term contracts might, in the absence of this sub-section, defeat the object of the Act. This sub-section enables a person who has in fact been employed for twelve weeks or more, under a contract for a term certain of four weeks or less, to receive the statutory notice under section 1 (1) and requires him to give not less than one week's notice under section 1 (2).

[6] *Sub-section* (5). The provisions of Schedule 1 of the Contracts of Employment Act 1972 are discussed in more detail at p. 266 below.

[7] *Sub-section* (6). This sub-section was included out of an abundance of caution. It makes clear beyond doubt that the existing common law position, enabling an employer or employee to terminate the contract summarily, is preserved. The effect upon statutory rights of dismissal is less clear. The reason for the exercise of the right may well be conduct of the employee but need not

be so, and it may be necessary to consider whether the minimum period of notice laid down by the Contracts of Employment Act 1972 are excluded by section 1 (6). When a purported exercise of suspension of an employee by an employer amounts to a termination of contract and the suspension arose because of the conduct of the employee, it may fall within section 1 (6) if the conduct of the employee was such as to enable the employer "to treat the contract as terminable without notice".

The section applies to employees, as defined by section 11 (1)[1] of the Contracts of Employment Act 1972 and covers all employees other than those mentioned below, whether or not the contract was entered into before or after the commencement of the Act. It does not apply to registered dock workers engaged on dock work,[2] most merchant seamen and fishermen,[3] civil servants,[4] employees who are engaged in work wholly or mainly outside Great Britain[5] and members of the police. Those part-time workers excluded from the provisions as to written particulars of the contract of employment are not within the notice provisions either.[6] These exclusions are dealt with more fully in the Chapter on Written Particulars of Employment.[7] In addition fixed term contracts[8] are excluded, except where the employee has been continuously employed for 12 weeks or more under a contract which is a contract for a term certain of four weeks or less. The purpose of this limitation on the exclusion is to prevent the Act being avoided by a succession of short-term contracts. Normally for fixed-term contracts there is no requirement pursuant to section 1 because no notice is required to terminate such a contract and the parties know from the beginning when it will end. The requirement does not apply to a person employed under a contract made in contemplation of a specific task not expected to last for more than 12 weeks, unless the employee is continuously employed for more than 12 weeks.[9]

[1] See p. 91, above. In general terms employees are those serving under contracts of service.

[2] See p. 91, above.

[3] See p. 92, above.

[4] See p. 95, above.

[5] See p. 96, above, and also the power of the Secretary of State for Employment to include those in employment for the purposes of the activities in the territorial waters of the United Kingdom or connected with the exploration of the seabed or subsoil or the exploitation of their natural resources in any area designated by order under section 1 (7) of the Continental Shelf Act 1964; Employment Protection Act 1975, s. 127, and the order made under that section referred to at p. 97, above.

[6] See p. 93, above. At present those normally working 21 hours per week or more are included. In due course this will be reduced so that those normally

working 16 hours per week will also be covered, and in certain circumstances those normally working eight hours per week.
[7] Chapter 3.
[8] For a detailed examination of fixed term contracts, see p. 164, below.
[9] Contracts of Employment Act 1972, s. 9 (2A).

## Rights during the period of notice

Section 2 of the Contracts of Employment Act 1972 sets out the rights of the employee during the period of notice. This provides that Schedule 2 of the Act, as now substituted by the Employment Protection Act 1975,[1] has effect in all cases to which section 1 applies (whether notice is given by the employee or the employer), except where the notice to be given by the employer to terminate the contract must be at least one week more than the notice required by the Act. In which case the provision of the Contracts of Employment Act 1972 as to rights of the employee during the period of notice do not apply.[2]

[1] Employment Protection Act 1975, Sch. 5.

[2] When the statutory provisions as to the rights of the employee during the period of notice do not apply the position depends entirely on the terms of the contract existing between the parties.

Section 2 stipulates:

"2.—(1) If an employer gives notice to terminate the contract of employment of a person who has been continuously employed for [four weeks] or more, the provisions of Schedule 2 to this Act shall have effect as respects the liability of the employer for the period of notice required by section 1 (1) of this Act.

(2) If an employee who has been continuously employed for [four weeks] or more gives notice to terminate his contract of employment, the provisions of Schedule 2 to this Act shall have effect as respects the liability of the employer for the period of notice required by section 1 (2) of this Act.

(3) This section shall not apply in relation to a notice given by the employer or the employee if the notice to be given by the employer to terminate the contract must be at least one week more than the notice required by section 1 (1) of this Act.

(4) So far as a contract purports to exclude or limit the obligations imposed on an employer by this section it shall be void."[1]

[1] The words in square brackets were substituted for "thirteen weeks" by Employment Protection Act 1975, Sch. 16, Part II.

An employee whose contract of employment is governed by normal working hours and who works throughout the currency of the notice is paid under his subsisting contract and is protected by it. No additional safeguards are necessary for such an employee, except where he is absent from work, for example as a result of sickness, and his contract does not contain provisions as beneficial as those of Schedule 2.

In deciding the protection afforded by Schedule 2 it first has to be determined whether or not the employment is one for which there are normal working hours. Assistance in construing the words "normal working hours" is to be gained from Part I of Schedule 4 of the Employment Protection Act 1975 which provides:

"1. For the purposes of this Schedule the cases where there are normal working hours include cases where the employee is entitled to overtime pay when employed for more than a fixed number of hours in a week or other period, and, subject to paragraph 2 below, in those cases that fixed number of hours shall be the normal working hours.

2. If in such a case:

(a) the contract of employment fixes the number, or the minimum number, of hours of employment in the said week or other period (whether or not it also provides for the reduction of that number or minimum in certain circumstances), and

(b) that number or minimum number of hours exceeds the number of hours without overtime,

that number or minimum number of hours (and not the number of hours without overtime) shall be the normal working hours."

Thus if there is a contractually fixed number, or minimum fixed number, of overtime hours they are included as normal working hours but otherwise they are excluded from the calculation. When considering paragraph 1 of Schedule 2 to the Contracts of Employment Act 1963 which was in similar terms Lord DENNING, M.R., said in the Court of Appeal in *Tarmac Roadstone Holdings Ltd.* v. *Peacock*:[1]

"Those provisions are very complicated, but on analysis, they can be applied to these situations—

First, where there is a fixed number of compulsory working hours, and thereafter overtime is voluntary on both sides—so that the employer is not bound to employ the man for any overtime and the employee is not bound to serve it— then, although the overtime is worked regularly each week, nevertheless being voluntary, it does not count as part of the normal working hours. Such a situation is covered by [paragraph 1].

Second, when there is a fixed number of compulsory working hours and in addition a fixed period of overtime which is obligatory on both sides—so that the employer is bound to provide that overtime and the employee bound to serve it—then that fixed period of overtime is added to the fixed period of compulsory working hours so that the total number counts as the normal working hours. Such a situation is covered by [paragraph 2]. In short, 'guaranteed overtime' counts as part of normal working hours.

Third, where there is a fixed number of compulsory working hours, and overtime is obligatory on the man if asked but not on the employer—so that the employer is entitled to call on the man to work overtime but is not bound to call upon him to do so: then the overtime does not come within the normal working hours. Such a case seems to me to come within [paragraph 1]. It comes within the words 'the employee is entitled to overtime pay when employed for more than a fixed number of hours in a week. . . .' It does not come within the words of [paragraph 2], because the contract of employment does not 'fix' the number of hours of employment. The overtime is not fixed but is at the option of the employer."

[1] (1973), 8 I.T.R. 300, C.A., at p. 303. Substituted in square brackets are references to the corresponding provisions in the 1975 Act. See also *Gascol Conversions, Ltd.* v. *Mercer* (1974), 9 I.T.R. 282, C.A.

To fall within Employment Protection Act 1975, Schedule 4, paragraph 2, the obligation to work overtime must arise from a contractual duty of the employer to provide the work and the employee to carry it out. In *Peacock's* case the employee's hours of work were fixed by reference to a national agreement which gave the normal working hours as 40 per week. There was obligation to work overtime "if required to do so" and regularly the employees worked 57 hours per week. It was held that since the employers were only obliged to employ the employees for 40 hours, the number of "normal working hours" per week was 40.

Where the employee is employed under a contract of employment with normal working hours, and during any part of those normal working hours, the employee is ready and willing to work but the employer provides no work for him, or he is incapable of work because of sickness or injury, or he is absent in accordance with the terms of his employment relating to holidays, then the employer is liable to pay the employee for that part of the normal working hours in respect of which he was so absent, a sum not less than the remuneration for that part of his normal working hours calculated at the average hourly rate of remuneration produced by dividing a week's pay[1] by the number of normal working hours.

[1] "Week's pay" is defined in Employment Protection Act 1975, Sch. 4. See p. 247, below.

In situations where there are no normal working hours the employer should pay the employee for each week of the period of notice, not less than a week's pay.[1] The week's pay is computed in accordance with Schedule 4 of the Employment Protection Act 1975, which in broad terms, defines it as the average weekly rate of remuneration during the previous 12 weeks. In the case of contracts both with and without normal working hours the calculation date for Schedule 4 of the Employment Protection Act 1975 is the day preceding the first day of the period of notice.[2] It should be noted that the obligation on the employer is conditional on the employee being ready and willing to do work of a reasonable nature and amount to earn a week's pay, save when the employee is incapable of work because of sickness or injury, or is absent in accordance with the terms of the contract of employment as to holidays.

[1] Contracts of Employment Act 1972, Sch. 2, para. 3 (as amended).
[2] *Ibid.*, Sch. 2, para. 1 (2).

Whether or not there are normal working hours applicable payments made by way of sick pay, holiday pay or otherwise go towards meeting the employer's liability[1] and, if the notice has been given by the employee, the employer is not obliged to pay him in accordance with the Schedule, unless and until the employee leaves the service of the employer in pursuance of the notice.[2]

Again, in both instances, where sick pay is paid to the employee in cases of absence for sickness or injury, and in calculating the amount of such payment sickness benefit or industrial injury benefit is taken into account, the amount of those benefits is treated as being paid by the employer.[3]

[1] In respect of the relevant part of the period of notice; Contracts of Employment Act 1972, Sch. 2, paras. 2 (2) and 3 (3).
[2] *Ibid.*, Sch. 2, paras. 2 (3) and 3 (4).
[3] *Ibid.*, Sch. 2, para. 4. Under the Contracts of Employment Act 1963, as originally enacted, sickness and industrial injury benefits received from State schemes were not taken into account. See p. 73, above.

The employer is not liable to make payments in accordance with the Schedule in respect of a period of absence with leave granted by the employer at the request of the employee[1] (including any time off in accordance with the provisions of the Employment Protection Act 1975 as to time off for trade union duties and activities, public duties or to look for work or make arrangements for training).[2] No payment is due in consequence of a notice to terminate given by the employee, if after the notice is given and on or before termination of the contract, the employee takes part in a strike of the employer's employees.[3] No payments will be due in respect of any period of notice after the employer has rightfully treated a breach of the contract of employment by the employee as terminating the contract.[4]

[1] Contracts of Employment Act 1972, Sch. 2, para. 5.
[2] See Employment Protection Act 1975, ss. 57, 58, 59 and 61 and p. 85, above.
[3] Contracts of Employment Act 1972, Sch. 2, para. 6. "Strike" is defined in Contracts of Employment Act 1972, Sch. 1, see p. 238, below.
[4] Contracts of Employment Act 1972, Sch. 2, para. 7 (2).

Should the employer fail to give the notice required by the Contracts of Employment Act 1972 the rights conferred by section 2 and Schedule 2 of the Act are taken into account in arriving at the employer's liability for the breach.[1] If the employer breaks the contract during the period of notice any payments made after the breach go towards mitigating the damages payable to the employee for loss of earnings due during the period of notice.[2]

[1] Contracts of Employment Act 1972, s. 3.
[2] Contracts of Employment Act 1972, Sch. 2, para. 7 (1).

Even if the employer gives the correct notice and pays all the sums due to the employee pursuant to his contractual obligations this may not absolve the employer from liability to the employee. The law relating to redundancy and unfair dismissal has to be considered. If the employee is unfairly dismissed the tribunal may order reinstatement or re-engagement, or compensation. If the employee is redundant only, a redundancy payment may be ordered.

[1] See pp. 347 and 242, below.

## Repudiation and wrongful dismissal

If an employer or employee repudiates the contract of employment the relationship may be terminated. A party to a contract is guilty of repudiatory conduct if he acts in such a manner as to indicate that he no longer considers himself bound by, or does not intend to comply with, his obligations under it.[1] Not every breach entitles the innocent party to rescind the contract, but the misconduct must be such as goes to the foundation or "root" of the relationship itself.[2]

[1] *Freeth* v. *Burr* (1874), L.R. 9 C.P. 208.
[2] *Mersey Steel and Iron Co.* v. *Naylor, Benzon & Co.* (1884), 9 App. Cas. 434.

It is probable that it is not necessary for repudiation by an employer of the employment contract to be "accepted" by the employee to bring it to an end. In *Sanders* v. *Ernest A. Neale, Ltd.*[1] Sir JOHN DONALDSON said: "... the obvious, and indeed the only, explanation is that repudiation of a contract of employment is an exception to the general rule. It terminates the contract without the necessity for acceptance by the injured party." The opposing view that the usual rule of contract law applies, namely that the injured party has the right to elect to bring the contract to an end by clearly showing that he considers himself released from the obligations, does have some support[2] but the special nature of employment contracts is now generally accepted. There may be certain situations where a contract of employment can survive a wrongful dismissal by the employer but such cases are likely to be extremely rare.[3] In practice, however, the employee has little alternative but to treat the contract as at an end, and claim damages for wrongful dismissal since he will not be able to render the service required by the contract, and is under a duty to mitigate the loss consequent upon his employer's breach.

The repudiation may be by either the employer, or the employee, and can take place before the time the performance of the contract has arrived, when it is known as "anticipatory repudiation".[4] The most frequently encountered example of repudiation by an employer is where he wrongfully dismisses the employee when the employee's right to bring action for damages following such dismissal, is in theory an action for wrongful repudiation of the contract.[5] Repudiation by the employer is not confined to wrongful dismissal and includes other conduct failing within the definition outlined above. For example, the test was satisfied when the employer failed to comply with an important stipulation of the contract,[6] when the master of a ship treated a seaman with unreasonable harshness,[7] when the employer exposed the employee to unacceptable dangers,[8] when the employer gave notice he was to move his plant depot[9] and when an employer refused to pay an agreed guaranteed minimum wage.[10] Other examples will be found in the Chapters dealing with redundancy and unfair dismissal.[11] In such cases, the employee can accept the repudiation by summarily terminating the employment.

[1] [1974] I.C.R. 565, at p. 571, N.I.R.C.; *Kolatsis v. Rockware Glass, Ltd.,* [1974] I.C.R. 580, at p. 583, N.I.R.C. See also the judgment of Lord DENNING, M.R., in *Hill v. C. A. Parsons, Ltd.,* [1972] Ch. 305; [1971] 3 All E.R. 1345; but contrast SACHS, L.J., *Vine v. National Dock Labour Board,* [1957] A.C. 488; [1956] 2 All E.R. 939; *Cranleigh Precision Engineering, Ltd. v. Bryant,* [1964] 3 All E.R. 289; [1965] 1 W.L.R. 1293.

[2] See the Judgments of SALMON and SACHS, L.JJ., in the *Decro-Wall-International S.A. v. Practitioners in Marketing, Ltd.,* [1971] 2 All E.R. 216; [1971] 1 W.L.R. 361; and also *Denmark Productions, Ltd. v. Boscobel Productions, Ltd.,* [1969] 1 Q.B. 699; [1968] 3 All E.R. 513.

[3] See *Hill v. C. A. Parsons, Ltd.* (above) and *Sanders v. Ernest A. Neale Ltd.* (above). "The existence and extent of the *Hill v. Parsons* exception is of great general importance and it would be helpful if more light could be thrown on it by the Court of Appeal or the House of Lords" (*ibid.,* at p. 571). See also p. 158 below.

[4] *Hochster v. De La Tour* (1853), 2 E. & B. 678.

[5] *Re Rubel Bronze & Metal Co. v. Vos,* [1918] 1 K.B. 315.

[6] *The Castilia* (1822), 1 Hag. Adm. 59.

[7] *Edward v. Trevellick* (1854), 4 E. & B. 59.

[8] *Limland v. Stephens* (1801), 3 Esp. 269.

[9] *Maher v. Fram Gerard, Ltd.,* [1974] 1 All E.R. 449, N.I.R.C.

[10] *Powell Duffryn Wagon Co., Ltd. v. House,* [1974] I.T.R. 46, N.I.R.C.

[11] Chapters 6 and 7, below.

Where repudiation is by the employee, the employer

frequently decides to treat the contract at an end by summarily dismissing him. To justify summary dismissal the employee must be guilty of conduct which is inconsistent with the express or implied conditions of service.[1] On entering into a contract of employment an employee is not under a duty to disclose his prior misconduct or criminal convictions,[2] unless requested to do so by the employer, and when they subsequently come to light, the employer is not entitled to rely on them as grounds for summary dismissal except where the employee has been guilty of misrepresentation or fraud.[3] Not all misconduct by an employee is of sufficient gravity to warrant summary dismissal,[4] and when considering whether or not the employer has the right to dismiss summarily a distinction must be drawn between employee's subject to contracts of service, and apprentices subject to contracts of apprenticeship.

[1] *Clouston & Co., Ltd.* v. *Corry,* [1906] A.C. 122, P.C., at p. 129.
[2] *Healey* v. *Société Anonyme Française Rubastic,* [1917] 1 K.B. 946; *Hands* v. *Simpson Fawcett & Co., Ltd.* (1928), 44 T.L.R. 295; *Bell* v. *Lever Brothers, Ltd.,* [1932] A.C. 161, and see p. 46, above.
[3] See p. 46 for the effect of Rehabilitation of Offenders Act 1974.
[4] *Laws* v. *London Chronicle (Indicator Newspapers), Ltd.,* [1959] 2 All E.R. 285, at p. 287, C.A.; [1959] 1 W.L.R. 698, at p. 700.

(i) *Employees subject to a contract of service.* Before deciding whether or not the right to summary dismissal exists it is necessary to look at the obligations of the employee under the contract of service. There must be a grave breach of such an obligation in order to justify summary dismissal by the employer. A catalogue of breaches which have been held in the past to justify such dismissal will be found in all the standard works on the law of contract, but whether conduct of sufficient gravity exists in the given circumstances is a question of fact in each case. The conduct, according to PARKE, J.,[1] must come within the ambit of "moral misconduct, either pecuniary or otherwise, wilful disobedience, or habitual neglect".

[1] *Callo* v. *Brouncker* (1831), 4 C. & P. 518.

In a more recent case[1] Lord EVERSHED explained the law as follows:

"... since a contract of service is but an example of contracts in general, so that the general law of contract will be

146

applicable, it follows that, if summary dismissal is claimed to be justifiable, the question must be whether the conduct complained of is such as to show the servant to have disregarded the essential conditions of the contract of service. It is, no doubt, therefore, generally true that wilful disobedience of an order will justify summary dismissal, since wilful disobedience of a lawful and reasonable order shows a disregard —a complete disregard—of a condition essential to the contract of service, namely, the condition that the servant must obey the proper orders of the master and that, unless he does so, the relationship is, so to speak, struck at fundamentally."

[1] *Laws* v. *London Chronicle (Indicator Newspapers), Ltd.,* [1959] 2 All E.R. 285, C.A., at p. 287; [1959] 1 W.L.R. 698, at p. 700.

Each set of circumstances has to be looked at individually to see whether the employee's conduct amounted to a repudiation of the contract.

In *Edwards* v. *Levy*,[1] HILL, J., said: "...a single instance of insolence on the part of a gentleman employed in such a capacity [newspaper critic] would hardly justify dismissal...." In *Wilson* v. *Racher*[2] the Court of Appeal had to consider the case of a gardener who, when provoked, had used foul and offensive language on one occasion in front of his employer and his employer's wife and children. The employee, who was dismissed as a result, claimed damages for wrongful dismissal. The decision of the County Court judge, which was upheld, was that the employee was wrongfully dismissed. EDMUND DAVIES, L.J., said: "In these circumstances would it be just to say that the plaintiff's use of this extremely bad language on a solitary occasion made impossible the continuance of the master and servant relationship, and showed that the plaintiff had indeed resolved to follow a line of conduct which made the continuance of the relationship impossible?" He continued:

"In my judgment, in the light of the findings of fact the judge arrived at a just decision. That is not to say that language such as that employed by the plaintiff is to be tolerated. On the contrary, it requires very special circumstances to entitle a servant who expresses his feelings in such a grossly improper way to succeed in an action for wrongful

147

dismissal. But there were special circumstances here, and they were of the defendant's own creation. The plaintiff, probably lacking the educational advantages of the defendant, and finding himself in a frustrating situation despite his efforts to escape from it, fell into the error of explosively using this language. To say that he ought to be kicked out because on this solitary occasion he fell into such grave error would, in my judgment, be wrong."

[1] (1860), 2 F. & F. 94.
[2] [1974] I.C.R. 428, C.A.

Examples of conduct held to be sufficient to amount to repudiation are; taking money from the till even though subsequently repaid,[1] persistent insolence to the employer's wife,[2] incompetence,[3] and speculation on the Stock Exchange by a confidential clerk.[4] In seeking to justify summary dismissal an employer may rely on misconduct which came to his knowledge after the dismissal has taken place.[5]

[1] *Sinclair* v. *Neighbour*, [1967] 2 Q.B. 279; [1966] 3 All E.R. 988.
[2] *Pepper* v. *Webb*, [1969] 2 All E.R. 216; [1969] 1 W.L.R. 514.
[3] *Harmer* v. *Cornelius* (1858), 5 C.B. N.S. 236.
[4] *Pearce* v. *Foster* (1886), 17 Q.B.D. 536.
[5] *Cyril Leonard & Co., Ltd.* v. *Simo Securities, Ltd.*, [1971] 3 All E.R. 1318; [1972] 1 W.L.R. 80, C.A.

(ii) *Apprentices.* Summary dismissal, i.e., dismissal without notice, is more limited in the case of apprentices than when the relationship is merely that of employer and employee. This is probably due to the historical development and peculiar nature of the relationship. In earlier days masters of apprentices had considerable powers without the need of recourse to the Courts; further, the contract being one for the benefit of an infant, special circumstances under the law of contract had to be applied.

Although the case-law is old and to some extent apprenticeship has itself been overtaken by other methods of training, apprenticeship is still extensively used in some industries. A surprisingly modern view was expressed by SHEARMAN, J., in *Waterman* v. *Fryer*[1] in 1922 when he surveyed the law and its gradual development as social conditions changed:

"The action was brought claiming damages against the master for putting an end to the contract, and the defence was that the conduct of the plaintiff was such that the defendant was entitled to put an end to it. The authorities show that in the early days there was the greatest reluctance to break any contract of apprenticeship. It was considered of very great importance that children should be taught a trade, and the Courts, in view of the great power which masters then had over apprentices, who generally resided with them, held that the obligation of the apprentice to serve and that of the master to teach were not interdependent but independent covenants. It was at the bottom of the reasoning in the older cases that the master could make the apprentice serve, even though the latter was unwilling. That is practically impossible nowadays; but formerly, the apprentice lived in the master's house, and could be locked up, deprived of food, or chastised; and society tolerated that state of things. The master was in the position of a schoolmaster and could be made to teach. He could not defend an action, still less could he put an end to an apprenticeship deed, because he had it in his power to make the apprentice do all that the apprentice had bound himself to do. When we come to the later cases we find, as not infrequently happens in the history of cases, that the Courts, in view of social changes, found themselves able to distinguish when not absolutely bound by authority; and we find that in later cases, when an action was brought for failing to maintain and teach, it was an answer to that action to say, as in *Hughes* v. *Humphreys*,[1] that the apprentice had absented himself for good, and that that fact was an answer to the action, because there was no longer any power to enforce the duties on him; or as in *Raymond* v. *Minton*,[2] that the apprentice would not be taught, and by his own acts had prevented the master from teaching him. Then in 1891 came the case of *Learoyd* v. *Brook*.[3] There the apprentice had been habitually stealing money from his master's till, and A. L. SMITH, J., in a considered judgment extended the principle of *Hughes* v. *Humphreys*[4]—though he did not mention the case—and *Raymond* v. *Minton*,[2] and said that where there is habitual and systematic conduct, arising out of the character of the apprentice, which renders it impossible that the work of service and of teaching should continue, the master is at liberty to put an end to the contract. I think the principle laid down in that case was that if there has been a course of conduct which renders it impossible in the interests of the master, of the community, and, it may be said, of the apprentice himself, that the relationship should continue, then the master is entitled to put an end to the contract. I have no doubt that habitual intemperance would come within the same principle.

Now, did the facts in this case come within that principle? The facts found were, that the plaintiff habitually acted and was determined so to act that he might get dismissed. The county court judge said that no self-respecting master could have continued to tolerate such conduct. But then the learned judge did not go on to find as a fact that the master was justified in putting an end to the apprenticeship, and that the case came within the principle of *Learoyd* v. *Brook*[3]; he founded his decision on the ground that there was conduct by the apprentice which amounted to a repudiation of the contract, and that the master was then at liberty to accept or refuse the repudiation and had accepted it; and, therefore, that there was by conduct a new contract between them. I need not add anything to what my Lord has said on that part of the case. The county court judge could not hold that there had been an effective repudiation unless he was satisfied it was for the benefit of the infant; but he did not decide that. There is evidence upon which he may so decide if he thinks fit. I agree that the case should go back to him to decide this question."

[1] (1827), 6 B. & C. 680.
[2] (1866), L.R. 1 Exch. 244.
[3] [1891] 1 Q.B. 431.
[4] (1827), 6 B. & C. 680.

Exceptionally bad conduct is necessary to justify summary dismissal of an apprentice. Nonetheless in many contracts of apprenticeship, conduct which falls short of that giving the right to summary dismissal may, under the terms of the contract itself, give the master a remedy. For instance, the contract may permit termination by notice before the end of the full period of apprenticeship if the apprentice "be wilfully disobedient or be slothful or negligent or otherwise grossly misbehave himself."[1] However, the effects of such stipulations remain to be tested in modern circumstances and apprenticeship deeds in current use make frequent reference to arbitration to resolve differences.[2]

Whether or not an employee's employment has been rightfully or wrongfully terminated it remains to be considered whether the dismissal was by reason of redundancy or unfair.

[1] See, for instance, *Newell* v. *Gillingham Corporation*, [1941] 1 All E.R. 522.

[2] For instance, the Agreement of Service of Craft Apprentices issued by the Heating, Ventilating and Domestic Engineers' National Joint Industrial Council.

## Insolvency of the employer

Where the employer is an individual his bankruptcy may not operate as a determination of the employment contract[1] but it is usual for the Trustee in Bankruptcy to dismiss employees on his appointment. The making of a compulsory winding up order,[2] or the appointment of a Receiver by the Court,[3] of a corporate employer automatically determines employment contracts, as does the appointment of a Receiver by debenture-holders, if there is no provision making him the company's agent.[4] Most modern debentures provide that the Receiver shall be the agent of the company, in which case the appointment out of court does not terminate the contracts of employment.[5] If there is a determination of the employment relationship in accordance with the above rules it operates as a wrongful dismissal unless proper notice has been given. For the effect of insolvency on the employees' claims, see p. 379, below.

[1] *Thomas* v. *Williams* (1834), 1 Ad. & El. 685. If the employee is an apprentice both he and the employer may terminate the employment by giving notice to the Trustee in Bankruptcy; Bankruptcy Act 1914, s. 34 (1).

[2] *Re Oriental Bank Corporation (McDowall's Case)* (1886), 32 Ch.D. 366.

[3] See *Re Foster Clark Ltd.'s Indenture Trust, Loveland* v. *Horscroft*, [1966] 1 All E.R. 43; [1966] 1 W.L.R. 125; *Reid* v. *Explosives Co.* (1887), 19 Q.B.D. 264, C.A.

[4] If the contract of employment depends on the personality of the employer.

[5] *Re Mack Trucks (Britain), Ltd.*, [1967] 1 All E.R. 977; [1967] 1 W.L.R. 780.

## Statutory rights of dismissal

In some cases statutes give employers the right to dismiss their employees in specified circumstances or at will. For instance, sections 105, 106 and 107 of the now repealed Local Government Act 1933, provided that the officers concerned held office "during the pleasure of" the local authority. Effectively this meant that the Authority had the right to terminate their employment without notice and without giving a reason for its action. Such statutory rights are now very rare but should always be considered in situations involving employees of statutory and public bodies.

## Written statement of reasons for dismissal

An employee[1] who on the effective date of termination[2] had been, or will have been, continuously employed for a period of 26 weeks ending with the last complete week before that date,[3] is entitled to be provided by his employer on request within 14 days of that request, with a written statement giving particulars of the reasons for his dismissal, where he is given notice of termination of the contract of employment by his employer, his contract of employment is terminated by his employer without notice, or, where he is employed under a contract for a fixed term, that term expires without being renewed under the same contract.[4] A complaint may be presented to an industrial tribunal by the employee against the employer on the ground that the employer unreasonably refused to provide the written statement, or that the particulars of reasons given in purported compliance with this requirement are inadequate or untrue.[5] The complaint has to be made within the time limit applicable for a complaint under the unfair dismissal provisions[6] and if the tribunal finds that the complaint is well founded it may make a declaration as to what it finds the employer's reasons for dismissing the employee, and it must make an award that the employer pay the employee a sum equal to the amount of two weeks' pay.[7] The written statement provided under section 70 of the Employment Protection Act 1975 is admissible in evidence in any proceedings. Accordingly it is of great importance to the employer and employee. No doubt considerable weight will be given to the contents of the written statement by industrial tribunals and it should be carefully prepared by the employer and preserved by the employee.

[1] As defined in Trade Union and Labour Relations Act 1974, s. 30 (1).
[2] See p. 292, below.
[3] Employment Protection Act 1975, s. 70 (2) and see Trade Union and Labour Relations Act 1974, Sch. 1, para. 5 (6), discussed at p. 292, below if the employee is dismissed shortly before 26 weeks.
[4] Employment Protection Act 1975, s. 70 (1), which came into force on 1st June 1976; Employment Protection Act 1975 (Commencement No. 4) Order 1976; S.I. 1976 No. 530.
[5] Employment Protection Act 1975, s. 70 (4).
[6] *Ibid.*, 70 (5). See p. 339, below.
[7] Calculated in accordance with Employment Protection Act 1975, Part II,

Sch. 4. For the purposes of the calculation where the dismissal was with notice the calculation date is the date on which the employer's notice was given. In any other case it is the effective date of termination; Employment Protection Act 1975, s. 70(6). It should be noted that the award is mandatory and is subject to the usual limit (at present £80 per week).

The employee is entitled to be provided with the statement whatever the reason for the dismissal and even if the employee has been rightfully and fairly dismissed the employer should comply with his request for written particulars of the reason of the dismissal. If he does not do so the tribunal will make the award in favour of the employee.

The requirements as to the provision of written statements of reasons for dismissal do not apply when the employee is the spouse of the employer, nor when the employee is a registered dock worker unless he is wholly or mainly engaged in work which is not dock work as defined by the Dock Labour Scheme, is a share fisherman or when the employee under his contract of employment ordinarily works outside Great Britain.[1] Part-time employees may not qualify if their employment is not sufficient to amount to 26 weeks' continuous employment.[2]

[1] Employment Protection Act 1975, s. 119. See p. 62, above, for details of extension to cover employment in connection with territorial waters and off-shore oil installations. The exclusions may be extended, limited, varied or revoked by order of the Secretary of State for Employment, see *ibid.*, s. 119 (15). For more detailed examination of exclusions, see p. 61, above.

[2] See p. 226, below.

# EMPLOYEES' REMEDIES ON BREACH OF CONTRACT

## Damages

The employee is wrongfully dismissed when his employer terminates his contract without sufficient cause, in the case of a contract for a fixed period, prior to the expiration of the term, or where the contract is terminable on notice, without giving proper notice. It has been noted[1] that where the employee has repudiated the contract his employer is entitled to dismiss him summarily, and where that occurs the employee has been rightfully dismissed. If the employer has repudiated the contract the employee can summarily determine the relationship and sue for breach.

[1] See p. 146, above.

Where an employer has purported to dismiss the employee, even though not in accordance with the procedure laid down in the contract, it has been held that the employee cannot treat the contract as still subsisting but must proceed as if wrongfully dismissed.

If there is a term of the contract providing for liquidated damages, for instance the payment of wages for a period in lieu of notice, that is the sum which is payable. This is often the case when the period of notice is short. Where there is no such stipulation the employee can recover damages for the loss he has sustained, and the usual rules for calculation of damages on breach of contract apply.

For the employee engaged in employment terminable by notice, the starting point in the calculation is the total of the benefits he would have been entitled to receive if proper notice had been given at the time of the wrongful dismissal.[1] If the contract is for a fixed period, that figure is the sum of the benefits which would have accrued due from the time of actual termination, to the earliest time at which the contract could rightfully have been terminated. In addition to salary there may be included amounts in respect of commission,[2] pension benefits,[2] gratuities[3] and pension and life assurance contributions,[4] which the employer has contracted to provide, but only in so far as the employer was bound to provide them. Non-obligatory benefits cannot be included.[5]

[1] In appropriate cases of the Contracts of Employment Act 1972, Sch. 2 should be considered. See p. 139, above.

[2] *Bold* v. *Brough, Nicholson & Hall, Ltd.*, [1963] 3 All E.R. 849; [1964] 1 W.L.R. 201; *The Rubel Bronze and Metal Co.* v. *Vos*, [1918] 1 K.B. 315.

[3] *Manubens* v. *Leon*, [1919] 1 K.B. 208.

[4] *Achland* v. *Sentinel Insurance Co., Ltd.*, [1959] 2 Lloyd's Rep. 683.

[5] *Lavarack* v. *Woods of Colchester, Ltd.*, [1967] 1 Q.B. 278; [1966] 3 All E.R. 683. Contrast the position when assessing compensation for unfair dismissal, see p. 362, below.

From the figures so calculated should be deducted all items which should be taken into account in minimising or mitigating damages. Deductions frequently occurring, are the actual earnings of the employee during the period,[1] and/or unemployment benefit.[2] This is an application of the rule that the plaintiff is entitled to no more than be restored to his former position.

[1] *Parsons* v. *B.N.M. Laboratories Ltd.*, [1963] 2 All E.R. 658.

[2] But not social security supplementary benefits; *Basnett* v. *J. and A. Jackson, Ltd.*, [1976] I.C.R. 63, Q.B.D. but contrast *Slingsby* v. *News of the World Organisation, Ltd.*, (1970) unreported. The better view is that a statutory redundancy payment is not deductible; *Basnett's* case, above; *Millington* v. *T. M. Goodwin & Sons, Ltd.*, [1975] I.C.R. 104, Q.B.D. and *Yorkshire Engineering and Welding Co., Ltd.* v. *Burnham* [1974] I.C.R. 77, N.I.R.C. in which *Stocks* v. *Magna Merchants, Ltd.*, [1973] 2 All E.R. 329, [1973] I.W.L.R. 1505 was not followed.

The effect of this last deduction may not be as great as first appears. Paragraph 7 (1) (*d*) of the Social Security (Unemployment, Sickness and Invalidity Benefit) Regulations 1975[1] provides "a day shall not be treated as a day of unemployment if it is a day in respect of which the person receives a payment (whether or not a payment made in pursuance of a legally enforceable obligation) in lieu either of notice or of the remuneration which he would have received for that day had his employment not been terminated, so however that this sub-paragraph shall not apply to any day which does not fall within the period of one year from the date on which the employment of that person terminated". It has been held[2] that a payment made in consideration of resignation falls within this paragraph.[3]

[1] S.I. 1975 No. 564.
[2] National Insurance Tribunal Decision R(U) 9/73.
[3] But see *Parry* v. *Cleaver*, [1970] A.C.1.; [1969] 1 All E.R. 555, H.L., when in a personal accident case the House of Lords held by a majority of one that a disability pension was not deductible in calculating loss of earning capacity. In *Basnett* v. *J. and A. Jackson, Ltd.*, [1976] I.C.R. 63, Q.B.D. CRICHTON, J. held that supplementary benefits were not deductible. See also *Foxley* v. *Olton*, [1965] 2 Q.B. 306; [1964] 3 All E.R. 248, n.

The employee is under a duty to find alternative employment in respect of which earnings will be taken into account but he cannot be expected to take any job; it must be suitable to his circumstances and status. In *Yetton* v. *Eastwoods Froy, Ltd.*,[1] BLAIN, J., said:

"The basic principle of damages is *restitutio in integrum*: the plaintiff should have what he has lost through the defendant's fault; but, of course, if a plaintiff in fact, in the case of a contract of service, earns something elsewhere through being at liberty so to do, then he has lost that much less as the consequence of the default. Moreover, if he can minimise his loss by a reasonable course of conduct, he should do so, though the onus is on the defaulting defendant to show that it could be, or could have been, done and is not being, and has not been, done. Thus, the opportunity to reduce damages by finding reasonable (I repeat reasonable) alternative employment, should be taken and, indeed, sought, whether such employment is by the same defaulting employer or by someone else; in either case the test being whether it is reasonable to refuse it or not in the circumstances of each case."

[1] [1966] 3 All E.R. 353, at p. 362.

Taxation is taken into account as shown below[1] and the total sum payable may be reduced because damages are paid earlier than the salary and benefits would have been received if the contract had continued. In addition to these damages, the employee can recover the wages and benefits accrued due at the time of termination.[2]

[1] See p. 373, below.
[2] See *The Halcyon Skies,* [1976] 1 All E.R. 856; [1976] W.L.R. 514 (pension contributions were deducted from the employee's wages).

There is another pecuniary remedy available to the employee, that of an action for *quantum meruit*. Proceedings for an award of damages on this basis are rarely encountered in relation to employment contracts other than those where the employee has agreed to carry out a task certain.[1] The claim is for reasonable payment for the work carried out prior to the termination, and precludes claims for future loss and wages accrued due.[2]

[1] For example, writing a book, *Planché* v. *Colburn* (1831), C. & P. 58, N.P.
[2] *Lilley* v. *Elwin* (1848), 11 Q.B. 742.

Where the contract is repudiated by the employer before the time for actual performance by the employee has arrived,[1] the employee can immediately proceed for damages if he wishes, or he may wait until the time for performance before presenting proceedings. In such cases the question of *quantum meruit* does not arise.

[1] *Hochster* v. *De La Tour* (1853), 2 E. & B. 678.

Apprentices who are wrongfully dismissed can recover damages for the loss of future prospects and the opportunity of completing their apprenticeship,[1] and artists such as actors and authors may be able to recover additional damages for a missed chance of furthering their reputation and careers.[2] It was generally thought that for other employees it was not possible to recover damages for reduction in prestige or injured feelings. This view was based on the decision of the House of Lords in *Addis* v. *Gramophone Co., Ltd.*[3] However, the recent decision of LAWTON, J., in *Cox* v. *Philips Industries, Ltd.*[4] has raised doubts as to whether this is so in all situations. The employee became a "product leader" but in due course found himself in a position where he had vague responsibilities and little constructive work to carry out. This made him anxious and depressed. When he discussed his position with his employers he was told to accept the state of affairs as it was, or be made redundant. He decided to "accept" redundancy and received his entitlement to salary in lieu of notice but then claimed damages for his emotional distress. Mr. Cox was awarded damages of £500 by the Queen's Bench Division. The full implications of this decision are yet to be revealed.

[1] *Dunk* v. *George Waller & Son, Ltd.*, [1970] 2 Q.B. 163; [1970] 2 All E.R. 630.

[2] *Herbert Clayton and Jack Waller, Ltd.* v. *Oliver*, [1930] A.C. 209; *Withers* v. *General Theatre Corporation, Ltd.*, [1933] 2 K.B. 536.

[3] [1909] A.C. 488; *Re Golomb and William Porter & Co., Ltd.'s Arbitration* (1931), 144 L.T. 583.

[4] (1975), 119 Sol. Jo. 760.

When considering claims for damages for wrongful dismissal it is also necessary to consider the possibility of claims for redundancy payment and reinstatement or re-engagement and compensation for unfair dismissal.[1]

[1] See pp. 242 and 347, below.

## Equitable remedies

In *Hill* v. *C. A. Parsons & Co., Ltd.*[1] an injunction was granted to an employee in very unusual circumstances. As a result of pressure brought upon the employers by a trade union which was attempting to establish a closed shop, Mr. Hill was given one month's notice by his employers to terminate his employment. He held a senior position with the company which, said the majority of the Court of Appeal, entitled him to reasonable notice of at least six months. The length of notice was of crucial significance for if the employee had been given six months' notice by the time it expired the provisions of the now repealed Industrial Relations Act 1971 would have been in force. The Court, by a majority, granted Mr. Hill an injunction restraining his employers from acting on the dismissal. Such cases are however very rare. In *Chappell* v. *Times Newspapers, Ltd.*,[2] STEPHENSON, L.J., said:

> "In this developing situation there may arise cases in which it is proper for the court to exercise its discretion in favour of a workman and grant an injunction which will hold an employer against his will to the continued performance of his contract of employment. Such a case was *Hill* v. *C. A. V. Parsons & Co. Ltd.* [1972] Ch. 305; [1971] 3 All E.R. 1345; but it was 'highly exceptional', as Sachs, L.J., said at p. 317; and was in my judgment rightly described by Sir John Donaldson when presiding in the National Industrial Relations Court in *Sanders* v. *Ernest A. Neale Ltd.* [1974] 3 All E.R. 327, at p. 333, as 'unusual, if not unique'. Like Stamp, L.J., dissenting in *Hill C. A. Parsons & Co. Ltd.* [1972] Ch. 305, at p. 323: 'I would be far from holding that in a changed and changing world there can be no new exception to the general rule' that a court will not grant an injunction in aid of specific performance of a contract of personal service, so that if the servant has been wrongfully dismissed, it will consider his contract unilaterally terminated by the master and leave the servant to his remedy in damages. I would not, however, look for new categories in which to pigeonhole new exceptions to this rule as it works either for the employer or the employee, but I would make exceptions in accordance with the general principle on which discretionary remedies are granted, namely, where, and only where, an injunction is required by justice and equity in a particular case, and, at the interim stage, by the balance of convenience. Applying those general principles, I do not find this a suitable case for making an exception to this sensible but flexible rule."

[1] [1972] 1 Ch. 305; [1971] 3 All E.R. 1345, C.A.
[2] [1975] 2 All E.R. 233, at p. 241, C.A.

The Courts have recently shown a far greater inclination than in the past to grant judicial declarations and it may be that in the future the declaration will play an important role in employment law.[1]

[1] *Cf, Vine* v. *National Dock Labour Board,* [1957] A.C. 488; [1956] 3 All E.R. 939, H.L. See Zamir, *The Declaratory Judgment,* London 1962, for an account of the use of declaratory judgments.

# Chapter 6

# REDUNDANCY

## SCOPE OF THE REDUNDANCY PAYMENTS ACT 1965[1]

The Redundancy Payments Act 1965 was a totally new development in the law of employment. It came into force on the 6th December 1965[2] and its two main objects were to require employers to make redundancy payments to employees dismissed by reason of redundancy as defined by the Act, and to establish a central Redundancy Fund financed by employers' contributions, from which those making redundancy payments to employees are to recover part of the cost. The purpose of a redundancy payment appears to be to compensate an employee for the loss of his job in certain circumstances, irrespective of whether unemployment ensues.[3] An employer is liable to make a redundancy payment to his employee if he is dismissed by reason of redundancy, or laid off or kept on short-time as specified in the Act, if the employee has been continuously employed for two years or more.

[1] The Act is discussed incorporating all amendments to 1st August 1976. For the sake of convenience the position of women absent from work as a result of pregnancy or confinement is dealt with at p. 322, below.

[2] See S.I. 1965 No. 1757.

[3] The logic behind the Act is confused, but for a statement as to its policy and purpose see *Wynes* v. *Southrepps Broiler Hall Farm, Ltd.* (1968), 3 I.T.R. 407, T, and *Lloyd* v. *Brassey.* [1969] 2 Q.B. 98; [1969] 1 All E.R. 382, C.A.

Contracting out of the Act is prohibited, and any agreement purporting to exclude or limit its operation is void, except for the special provisions contained in section 11 (1) relating to exemption orders,[1] and in the circumstances of section 15 which relates to fixed term[2] contracts.[3] By virtue of section 56 (4) it is immaterial whether the law, apart from the Act, which governs a contract is that of Great Britain or elsewhere.

[1] See p. 19, above.

[2] See p. 164, below.

[3] In *Godridge* v. *Yorkshire Imperial Metals, Ltd.* (1968), 3 I.T.R. 30 T, an agreement between a union and employers that two premises be regarded as

one for the purposes of Redundancy Payments Act 1965, s. 2 (4) was *held* to be void.

Disputes which arise as to the right to a redundancy payment or the amount of the payment should be referred to and determined by industrial tribunals.[1]

[1] Redundancy Payments Act 1965, s. 9.

Although the Redundancy Payments Act 1965 does not apply in Northern Ireland similar legislation is in force there. The Redundancy Payments Northern Ireland Reciprocal Arrangements Regulations 1965[1] make reciprocal provisions so that in computing continuous employment on a dismissal by reason of redundancy in Great Britain, an employee can include service with his employer, or an associated employer,[2] in Northern Ireland. There are equivalent provisions effective in Northern Ireland.[3] Whether a dismissal was by reason of redundancy has to be considered when considering if an employee has been unfairly dismissed.[4] An employee dismissed by reason of redundancy may have a right to take time off to look for work and make arrangements for training.[5]

[1] S.I. 1965 No. 2027.
[2] For definition of associated employers see p. 211, below.
[3] Contracts of Employment and Redundancy Payments Act (Northern Ireland) 1965.
[4] See p. 294, below.
[5] See p. 270, below.

## THOSE WHO ARE NOT WITHIN THE REDUNDANCY PAYMENTS ACT 1965

The Redundancy Payments Act 1965 applies to employees, i.e., those persons working under a contract of service rather than a contract for services. See p. 2, above. Section 25 (1) of the Act states that "... 'employee' means an individual who has entered into or works under (or in the case of a contract which has been terminated, worked under) a contract with an employer, whether the contract is for manual labour, clerical work or otherwise, is express or implied, oral or in writing, and whether it is a contract of service or apprenticeship, ...". The word "employer" and any reference to employment are construed accordingly. The definition is similar to that contained in the Contracts of Employment Act 1972. There are, however, certain additional types of employment not within this definition which have been made subject to the Act by specific provisions. Section 49, for instance, makes appropriate provision for employees who are employed neither under a contract of service nor in the public appointments covered by section 41, but in respect of whom redundancy fund contributions are payable. Section 41 provides for rebates in respect of payments analogous to redundancy payments made by the Crown and certain public authorities.

It is for the applicant to prove that he is an employee, see *Hammett* v. *Livingstone Control, Ltd.* (1970), 5 I.T.R. 136, D.C., where the Divisional Court upheld the decision of the tribunal that the applicant, a demonstrator, paid a fee and allowed to carry on other business activities, was not an employee.

**Tribunal Decisions:**

*J. C. King, Ltd.* v. *Valencia* (1966), 1 I.T.R. 67, T ("selling agent"—weekly wage plus commission. *Held:* contract of service and therefore "employee").

*Robinson* v. *George Sorby, Ltd.* (1967), 2 I.T.R. 148, T (managing director who was controlling shareholder—no legal argument. *Held:* not "employee"). But see *Nottingham Egg Packers and Distributors, Ltd.* v. *McCarthy and Haslett* (1967), 2 I.T.R. 223, T, and *Adamson* v. *Arthur M. Smith (Hull), Ltd.* (1967), 2 I.T.R. 224, T (working directors and shareholders held to be "employees").

Other decisions on the position of directors of companies are: *Trussed Steel Concrete Co., Ltd.* v. *Green*, [1946] Ch. 115; and *Lee* v. *Lee's Air Farming, Ltd.*, [1961] A.C. 12; [1960] 3 All E.R. 420.

*Ferguson* v. *Telford Grier, Mackay Co., Ltd.* (1967), 2 I.T.R. 387, T (secretary and director of company).

*Howarth* v. *Howarth (Garments), Ltd.* (1968), 5 K.I.R. 25, T (managing director—onus on applicant to prove himself employee).

*Hill* v. *Barrie* (1967), 2 I.T.R. 206, T (taxicab driver *held* not to be an employee).

*Burgess* v. *O'Brien* (1966), 1 I.T.R. 164, T (salaried partner—not dismissed—dissolution of partnership).

*Park* v. *Orr* (1966), 1 I.T.R. 488, T (chaplain on staff of

industrial mission—not employee).
*Jones and Jones* v. *Minister of Labour* (1967), 2 I.T.R. 9, T.

The position of an "off the clock" taxi driver was considered by the National Industrial Relations Court in *Challinor* v. *Taylor* (1972), 7 I.T.R. 104, N.I.R.C. (The taxi owner supplied the fuel and paid the maintenance of the taxi receiving 65% of the clocked takings at the end of each week. The Court *held* that the tribunal were not wrong in deciding that the driver was not an employee.) *Yates* v. *Lancashire County Council* (1975), 10 I.T.R. 20, T (police officer employed in public office and was not employed for the purposes of the Redundancy Payments Act). For chief constables and chief and assistant chief officers of fire brigades see the Redundancy Payments Termination of Employment Regulations 1965, S.I. 1965 No. 2022. See p. 173, below.

Although the Redundancy Payments Act 1965, applies to those serving under contracts of service there are a number of exclusions and special circumstances to be considered as follows:

(1) An employee dismissed with notice, or without notice, on a ground entitling the employer to dismiss him summarily by reason of the employee's conduct cannot claim a redundancy payment as of right.[1]

[1] Redundancy Payments Act 1965, ss. 2 (2) and 10. See pp. 177 and 207, below. See also *ibid.*, s. 10.

(2) An employee who has been dismissed but has unreasonably refused an offer by the employer of a contract on the same terms, or an offer of some other suitable employment is not entitled to a redundancy payment.[1]

[1] Redundancy Payments Act 1965, s. 2 and p. 209, below.

(3) There is no obligation to make a redundancy payment to a person employed under a contract entered into before the 6th December 1965 for a fixed term of two years or more.[1] This provision does not apply however to contracts of apprenticeship,[1] or to a contract with a mariner, other than a share fisherman.[2] An explanation of "fixed term" appears in (4) below.

[1] Redundancy Payments Act 1965, s. 15 (1).
[2] *Ibid.*, s. 20 (2). For a case where the provisions of s. 15 (1) were considered see *Pope* v. *Frank Willis & Sons, Ltd.* (1968), I.T.R. 87, T (contract "for five years" from 1st March 1964. Industrial tribunal *held* section 15 (1) applied).

(4) There is power in the case of a fixed term contract[1] of two years or more, made after the 5th August 1965 to exclude the obligation to make a redundancy payment in respect of the expiry of that term, without it being renewed. The agreement to exclude the redundancy payment must be made before the expiration of the term and it is usual to include it in the service agreement when it is entered into. However the agreement to exclude the operation of the Act may be made at any time before the term expires.[2] The agreement must however be in writing. It is permissible to include an exclusion of this type in a contract of apprenticeship.[3]

If there is such an agreement and the fixed term is renewed the original exclusion agreement is not construed as applying to the term as renewed, but if it is sought to rely on this provision a new agreement in writing to exclude the right to redundancy payment must be entered into.[4]

The exclusion does not apply to contracts with mariners (including apprentices) on a British ship other than share fishermen.[5]

---

[1] A fixed term contract is one for a term with definite starting and ending dates, which is not capable of being determined, save in cases of termination by breach or operation of law. For the position in relation to employees in some offshore employments see (8) below.

In *British Broadcasting Corporation* v. *Iouannou*, [1975] Q.B. 781; [1975] 2 All E.R. 999, C.A., the employee had worked for the B.B.C. under a written contract for three years terminable on three months' notice. This was renewed for a further two years, and then a further year's employment determinable on three months' notice, to take effect at the end of that period of three years, was offered. The contract contained a provision purporting to exclude the right to a redundancy payment on expiry of the final year and the employers contended that it was effective. In the Court of Appeal two points arose. First, was the contract one for a fixed term in view of the provision enabling it to be terminated by notice. It was decided that it was not, Lord DENNING, M.R., said (at p. 90):

"In my opinion a "fixed term" is one which cannot be unfixed by notice. To be a "fixed term", the parties must be bound for the term stated in the agreement: and unable to determine it by notice on either side. If it were only determinable for misconduct, it would, I think, be a "fixed term"—because that is imported by the common law anyway. But determination by notice is destructive of any "fixed term"."

Secondly, was the term for two years or more. Again the Court held that it was not. The Master of the Rolls said in this context:

"I do not think it is necessary in these cases to inquire whether there is a 'renewal' of a previous contract of employment or a 're-engagement' under a new contract of employment. That is too fine a distinction for ordinary mortals to comprehend. Suffice it to say that you must always take the final contract which expires, and on the expiration of which he claims redundancy payment or compensation for unfair dismissal. If the final contract is for a fixed term of two years or more, it is permissible for the employee in writing to agree to exclude his rights, so long as he does it before the term expires. If the final contract is for less than two years, as for instance for a fixed term of one year, then he cannot exclude his right. It matters not whether the final contract is a renewal or re-engagement. It is the final contract alone which matters in this regard. If more than two years fixed, he can contract out of his rights. If less than two years he cannot."

See also *Fuller-Shapcott* v. *Chilton Electric, Ltd.* (1970), 5 I.T.R. 186, T (contract for ten years and to continue until determined by at least six months' notice. *Held* that contract was not for fixed term and redundancy payment awarded), *Warren* v. *D. Ferranti Ltd.* (1968), 3 I.T.R. 284, T (contract could be terminated at any time after the 30th June 1967 on three months' notice. *Held* not fixed term).

[2] Redundancy Payments Act 1965, s. 15 (2).

[3] For the position where the employee is engaged in employment in United Kingdom territorial waters or offshore installations see (8) below.

[4] Redundancy Payments Act 1965, s. 15 (4).

[5] Redundancy Payments Act 1965, s. 20.

(5) A registered dock worker[1] is not entitled to a redundancy payment unless he was wholly or mainly engaged on work which was not dock work.[2] There is of course a separate regime applicable to such persons which is outside the scope of this work.

[1] Includes limited dock workers who are excluded from the provisions of the Act. See *Castle and Castle* v. *Cawood Wharton & Co., Ltd.* (1966), 1 I.T.R. 560, T and *Humphrys* v. *Beck and Pollilzer Warehousing, Ltd.* (1966), 1 I.T.R. 467, T.

[2] In *McNee* v. *R. O. Edwards & Co., Ltd.* (1972), 7 I.T.R. 11, T, a registered dock worker had worked in a timber yard in a clerical capacity before the termination of his employment. The tribunal *held* that the employee was not entitled to redundancy payment. The definition of dock work in the Dock Labour Scheme is very wide and the local agreement was such that under its terms a dock worker could have been put on such work.

(6) A member of a crew of a fishing vessel who is not remunerated in respect of the employment, otherwise than by a share in profits, or gross earnings, of the vessel (commonly called "share fishermen") is excluded.[1]

[1] Redundancy Payments Act 1965, s. 16 (2). The Secretary of State may determine, with the approval of the Treasury, to make payments to employers in respect of share fishermen out of the Redundancy Fund, provided that the

Chapter 6 Redundancy

amounts to be paid do not exceed the amount paid into the Redundancy
Fund from the appropriate employment protection allocation from all secondary
Class I contributions pursuant to the Social Security Act 1975, paid by the
employer in respect of the employees; *ibid.*, s. 31. The section is applied
by Redundancy Payments Share Fishermen Regulations 1966, S.I. 1966 No.
145, para. 4.

(7) The Act does not apply where the employer is the
husband or wife of the employee.[1]

[1] Redundancy Payments Act 1965, s. 16 (3). In *Bernstein v. Bernstein
Brothers* (1969), 4 I.T.R. 106, T, the tribunal held that a wife of a partner was
not excluded by s. 16 (3).

(8) Employment wholly or partially abroad.[1] When under
the contract of employment the employee ordinarily works outside Great Britain and on the relevant date of termination he is
outside Great Britain then no redundancy payment is payable.[2]
If the contract of employment provides for the employee
ordinarily to work in Great Britain, he is entitled to a redundancy
payment even if he is outside Great Britain when the contract
terminates.[3] When an employee ordinarily works outside Great
Britain he is only entitled to a redundancy payment if at the
relevant date he is in Great Britain in accordance with instructions
given to him by his employer.[4]

[1] Subject to what is said in note [2] below the position is governed by
Redundancy Payments Act 1965, s. 17. Section 17 does not apply to a mariner
who is a person employed as a master, seaman or apprentice in a British ship
who is ordinarily resident in Great Britain; *ibid.*, ss. 17 (7) and 20. Subject
only to the exclusions below such persons are subject to the redundancy payments scheme. For "relevant date of termination", see p. 208, below.

[2] Employment Protection Act 1975, s. 127 enables Orders in Council to
be made to extend the operation of the Redundancy Payments Act 1965, the
Contracts of Employment Act 1972, the Trade Union and Labour Relations
Act 1974 and the 1975 Act itself to cover employment for the purposes of any
activities in United Kingdom territorial waters, or connected with the exploration of the seabed or subsoil, or the exploitation of their natural resources
in any area designated under the Continental Shelf Act 1964, s. 1 (7). The
Employment Protection (Offshore Employment) Order 1976, S.I. 1976 No. 766,
has been made under this power. The Order which came into operation on 21st
June 1976 applies to employment for the purposes of the following activities:

(a) any activities (other than activities connected with a ship which is in the
course of navigation or is a survey ship or is engaged in dredging or fishing)
in the territorial waters;
(b) any activities connected with the exploration of the sea bed or subsoil or the
exploitation of their natural resources in any designated area (other than an

166

area or part of an area in which the law of Northern Ireland applies) being activities carried out on or from an offshore installation in any such designated area.

The Order does not apply to any employment wholly or mainly for the purpose of any activities connected with the Frigg Field Reservoir or the Ekofisk Field.

The Redundancy Payments Act 1965 is applied for such purposes as are relevant to or in relation to persons in employment to which the Order relates as follows:

(1) Sections 20 and 57 are not applied.
(2) There are the following modifications:—
    (a) section 15 has effect as if—
        (i) for the words in sub-section (1) "before the appointed day whether before or after the passing of this Act" there were substituted the words "before 21st June 1976";
        (ii) sub-section (5) were omitted;
    (b) the references in section 17 (1) and (2) to Great Britain are treated as including the territorial waters and the waters in any designated area (other than an area or part of an area in which the law of Northern Ireland applies).
(3) The application by the Order of the provisions of the 1965 Act does not affect the exclusion of any merchant seaman from the Act by the Redundancy Payments (Merchant Seamen Exclusion) Order 1973 or the disregarding pursuant to Article 4 of that Order of any period of employment.

³ Redundancy Payments Act 1965, s. 17 (1).

⁴ *Ibid.*, s. 17 (2). When considering a case of an employee who works partly in Great Britain and partly abroad refer to *Roux International Ltd.* v. *Licudi* (1975), 10 I.T.R. 162, D.C. An employee who worked from an office in his home in London but had travelled a great deal on the Continent was dismissed. He applied to a tribunal seeking a redundancy payment. The employer contended that there was no jurisdiction. DONALDSON, J. held that since the employee was in Great Britain at the time of his dismissal on the employer's instructions he was entitled to a redundancy payment. He went on to say, (at p. 166):

"A contract of employment can require the employee to work ordinarily in Great Britain with visits abroad, or to work ordinarily partly in Great Britain and partly abroad. It is only the latter category, of which Mr. Licudi's contract is an example, which gives rise to any difficulty. Although I have not found the construction of section 17 easy, I have come to the conclusion that such contracts are unaffected by sub-sections (1) and (2) and are governed by sub-section (3). This sub-section, whilst preserving continuity of employment, reduces reckonable service to the extent that the employment is in fact abroad. As a matter of construction the expression in sub-sections (1) and (2), 'works outside Great Britain,' is clear and means that, *de minimis* apart, all the work is done outside Great Britain. The inclusion of the word 'ordinarily' slightly widens the *de minimis* concept leaving an employee without a right to claim a redundancy payment if his work in Great Britain, albeit done under and in accordance with the contract of employment, is extra-ordinary or exceptional."

This view has been doubted in *Portec (U.K.), Ltd.* v. *Mogensen*, [1976] I.R.L.R. 209, E.A.T. a decision relating to the unfair dismissal provisions. BRISTOW, J., concluded, *obiter*, that only sub-sections (1) and (2) deal with whether the employee is entitled to a redundancy payment or not.
See also *Maulik* v. *Air India* (1974), 9 I.T.R. 348, N.I.R.C., for an example of similar provisions in Trade Union and Labour Relations Act 1974, Sch. 1, para. 9 (2).

In deciding whether the employee has been employed for the requisite period, and the quantum of the redundancy payment, weeks of employment count, before 5th July 1948, if Class I National Insurance contributions would have been payable by the employer if the National Insurance legislation was in force, from that date to 6th April 1975, weeks only count if Class I National Insurance contributions were payable in respect of them, and from that date until 31st May 1976 a week will not count if the employee was not during that week an employed earner for the purposes of the Social Security Act 1975. From the last date, the week will not count if the employee was outside Great Britain during the whole or part of the week and he was not during that week an employed earner for the purposes of the Social Security Act 1975, in respect of whom a secondary Class I contribution was payable. There are provisions in the new section 17 (6) of the Redundancy Payments Act 1965 for determining matters of doubt in these cases.[1] However, where as a result of the above rules, a week does not count in computing the period of continuous employment it does not break the continuity of employment.[2]

[1] Redundancy Payments Act 1965, s. 17 (6), as substituted by the Employment Protection Act 1975, provides:

"(6) Any question arising under this section—
(a) whether an employer's contribution was paid, or was or would have been payable, as mentioned in sub-section (3) or (4) of this section; or
(b) whether a person was an employed earner for the purposes of the Social Security Act 1975 and if so whether a secondary Class I contribution was payable in respect of him under that Act,
shall be determined by the Secretary of State; and any legislation (including regulations) as to the determination of questions which under that Act the Secretary of State is empowered to determine (including provisions as to the reference of questions for decision, or as to appeals, to the High Court or the Court of Session) shall apply to the determination of any question by the Secretary of State under this section.".

[2] Redundancy Payments Act 1965, s. 17 (5), as substituted by the Employment Protection Act 1975.

(9) Domestic employees *prima facie* benefit from the redundany payments scheme. A household is treated as a business, and its maintenance, the carrying on of that business.[1] The employee is not entitled to a redundancy payment if the employer is the father, mother, grandfather, grandmother, step-father, step-mother, son, daughter, grandson, grand-daughter, step-son, step-daughter, brother, sister, half brother or half sister of the employer.[2] There are special provisions should the employer die[3] but otherwise the usual rules apply.

[1] Redundancy Payments Act 1965, s. 19 (1).
[2] *Ibid.*, s. 19 (2).
[3] See p. 253, below.

(10) **Crown Servants** are not entitled to redundancy payments since the Act is not expressed to bind the Crown.[1]

The Act does not apply to public offices for the purpose of the Superannuation Act 1972, or to employment which is treated for the purposes of pensions and superannuation benefits as service in the civil service of the State.[2] These exclusions apply to employees of certain public bodies such as the **Forestry Commission** and the **Nature Conservancy** who are not technically Crown Servants but whose conditions of employment are similar.

Employment by the bodies specified in Schedule 3 of the Redundancy Payments Act 1965 is excluded as well.[3] In general terms these are National Health Service employees. The Schedule is construed technically[4] and reference must be made to it in each case.

[1] Redundancy Payments Act 1965, s. 16 (4) (*a*).
[2] Redundancy Payments Act 1965, s. 16 (4) (*b*). In *Robinson* v. *County of London Territorial and Auxiliary Forces* (1967), 2 I.T.R. 652, T, the industrial tribunal held that Part I of the Redundancy Payments Act 1965 (that part dealing with redundancy payments) does not apply to employment by Territorial Army Associations but in *Kenward* v. *Borridaile* (1968), 3 I.T.R. 257, T, a tribunal determined that a Combined Cadet Force School Staff Instructor did not fall within the exclusion of section 16 (4).
See Employment Protection Act 1975, s. 121 (3) for the application of other provisions of employment law.
[3] Redundancy Payments Act 1965, s. 16 (4) (*c*). Schedule 3, as amended by the National Health Service Reorganisation Act 1973 and the National Health Service (Scotland) Act 1972 is as follows:

"Section 16          SCHEDULE 3

NATIONAL HEALTH SERVICE EMPLOYERS

[1. A Regional Health Authority, Area Health Authority, special health authority, Health Board or the Common Services Agency for the Scottish Health Service.]

. . .                                    . . .

4. The Dental Estimates Board.

. . .

7. Any joint committee constituted under . . . [section 13 (8) of the National Health Service (Scotland) Act 1972].

8. The Public Health Laboratory Service Board."

The provisions of Sch. 3 may be varied or revoked by order of the Secretary of State complying with the provisions of section 16, *ibid*. See section 16 (6) (*b*), *ibid*.

⁴ For instance in *Mason* v. *Plymouth and District Hospital Management Committee* (1973), 8 I.T.R. 334, T, a tribunal held that an employee of a Hospital Management Committee was entitled to redundancy payment because that Committee was not included in the schedule although similar bodies were.

Where payments are made to employees of public bodies which are analagous to redundancy payments pursuant to the Act rebates may be had from the Redundancy Fund.

A Government undertaking has been given with regard to those employees who are excluded under these provisions, see Hansard, Standing Committee D, Official Report for 3rd June, p. 437 and 15th June, p. 471, 1965.

(11) Redundancy payments are not payable to any person in respect of employment in any capacity under the Government of an overseas territory.[1]

¹ Redundancy Payments Act 1965, s. 16 (5). See for example *Antoni and Louka* v. *United Kingdom Area Exchange* (1968), 3 I.T.R. 136, T (no power to award a redundancy payment to a hairdresser employed by the U.S.A. Government in Great Britain) but contrast *Bagga* v. *Heavy Electricals (India), Ltd.* (1972), 7 I.T.R. 70, N.I.R.C., (although not raised in notice of appeal "somewhat unlikely" that a company whose capital was wholly owned by the Indian Government could avail itself of the exemption). For the possibility of payments from the Redundancy Fund see *ibid.*, s. 31.

(12) Employees who have reached retirement age (65 for a man, 60 for a woman), by the Saturday of the week in which the dismissal takes place are not entitled to a redundancy payment.[1] When the employee is over 64, (if a man) or 59, (if a woman) the payment is reduced by one twelfth of the total which would otherwise be payable, for every whole month which has elapsed since the 64th or 59th birthday, as the case may be by the relevant date.

[1] Redundancy Payments Act 1965, Sch. 1, para. 4 (2). For an example of the application of this rule see *Swithenbank* v. *Platt Brothers & Co., Ltd.* (1968), 3 I.T.R. 134, T. See p. 243, below.

(13) Redundancy payments do not become payable until there has been a minimum of two years continuous service[1] with an employer after the age of 18 years.[2]

[1] See p. 226, below.
[2] Redundancy Payments Act 1965, Sch. 1, para. 1 (1).

(14) At the present time employees normally working for less than 21 hours per week do not qualify for a redundancy payment.[1] There are provisions in the Employment Protection Act 1975[2] which will alter the requirement so that employees whose hours of employment are normally 16 or more per week will qualify.[3] In addition it is provided that if the employee's relations with the employers cease to be governed by a contract normally involving work for 16 hours or more weekly and become governed by a contract which normally involves employment of eight hours or more, but less than 16 hours weekly, the employee shall for a period of 26 weeks for the purposes of calculating continuity be treated as if his contract normally involved employment for 16 hours or more weekly. In computing this period of 26 weeks no account is taken of any week:

    (a) During which the employee is in fact employed for 16 hours or more;

    (b) During which the employee takes part in a strike[4] as defined in Schedule 1 of the Contracts of Employment Act 1972 or is absent from work because of a lock-out (as similarly defined) by his employer; or

    (c) During which there is no contract of employment but which by virtue of paragraph 5 (1) of Schedule 1 to the Contracts of Employment Act 1972, counts in computing a period of continuous employment.

In addition under these new rules an employee whose relations with his employer are governed by a contract of employment which normally involves employment for eight hours or more, but less than 16 hours, weekly shall nevertheless if he has been continuously employed for a period of five years or more (computed in accordance with Schedule 1 of the Contracts of

Employment Act 1972) be treated as if his contract normally involved employment for 16 hours or more weekly.[5]

[1] See Redundancy Payments Act 1965, Sch. 1 and Contracts of Employment Act 1972, Sch. 1. For a more detailed discussion see p. 226, below.
[2] Not yet in force. It is anticipated that these provisions will be introduced during autumn 1976.
[3] See p. 230, below.
[4] See p. 231, below.
[5] Contracts of Employment Act 1972, Sch. 1, para. 4. See p. 231, below. See also *ibid.*, Sch. 1, para. 4c.

(15) The majority of merchant seamen are excluded by virtue of The Redundancy Payments (Merchant Seamen Exclusion) Order 1973.[1] They are covered by a special scheme applicable to their industry known as the National Maritime Board Redundancy Payments Agreement.

[1] S.I. 1973 No. 1281, para. 3. The definition of "merchant seamen" does not include persons employed in the fishing industry, or employed on board a ship otherwise than by the owner, manager or charterer, except a person employed as a radio officer; *ibid.*, para. 2 (2).

(16) Employers or employers' associations and the relevant trade union or unions representing employees may agree on a redundancy scheme which in their view is more suitable than the statutory scheme and in such a case they can apply to the Secretary of State for Employment for an exemption order under section 11 of the Redundancy Payments Act 1965. If the Secretary of State is satisfied as to the provisions of the agreement then he may make the order.[1] The Secretary of State will not make such an order in respect of an agreement unless it indicates the willingness of the parties to it to submit to an industrial tribunal questions arising under the agreement as to the right of an employee to a payment on the termination of his employment, or as to the amount of such a payment, as if the payment were a redundancy payment and the question arose under the Redundancy Payments Act. Orders made under this section are extremely rare.[2] Where an order is in force a person who immediately before the relevant date is an employee to whom the agreement relates is not entitled to a redundancy payment pursuant to the Act and an industrial tribunal has jurisdiction in relation to any question arising under the agreement as to the right of an employee to a payment on the termination of his employment or as to the amount of such payment.[3]

[1] Redundancy Payments Act 1965, s. 11 (1).
[2] The only orders at the moment are: S.I. 1969 No. 207, (affecting employees of Centrax Limited and associated companies) and S.I. 1970 No. 354 (relating to North of Scotland Hydro Electricity Board and South of Scotland Electricity Board).
[3] Redundancy Payments Act 1965, s. 11 (3).

(17) Section 49 of the Redundancy Payments Act 1965 enables the Secretary of State for Employment to make regulations relating to employment in certain offices in respect of which the office holders are technically not employees under a contract of service. The effect of such regulations is that the office holders concerned are treated as employees for the purposes of the Redundancy Payments Act 1965. The Redundancy Payments Office Holders Regulations 1965[1] have been made pursuant to this power and bring such persons as justices' clerks and registrars of births and deaths within the scope of the Act.

[1] S.I. 1965 No. 2007. Also includes a rent officer or depty rent officer appointed under the Rent Act 1965 and medical inspectors appointed under the Aliens Order 1953 and the Commonwealth Immigrants Act 1962.

(18) The Redundancy Payments Termination of Employment Regulations 1965[1] bring redundant Chief Constables and Chief Fire Officers and Assistant Chief Fire Officers within the scope of the Redundancy Payments Act 1965 and they are treated as employees for the purposes of its provisions.

[1] S.I. 1965 No. 2022 made pursuant to Redundancy Payments Act 1965, s. 50.

(19) The Secretary of State may by order provide that the statutory redundancy payments scheme does not apply to persons or employments as prescribed by the order, or shall apply to persons or employments so prescribed. He may also in the same way vary, or revoke, exclusions which now exist and vary and revoke orders made under these provisions.[1] There is power for the Secretary of State to make regulations providing that the Redundancy Payments Act has effect in relation to any person who by virtue of any statutory provisions is transferred to, or becomes a member of, a body specified in those provisions, but at a time so specified ceases to be a member of that body, subject to certain conditions.[2]

[1] Redundancy Payments Act 1965, s. 16 (6). The Redundancy Payments (Merchant Seamen Exclusion) Order 1973, S.I. 1973 No. 1251, is made under this section. See (15), above.

[2] Redundancy Payments Act 1965, s. 50. See for instance the Redundancy Payments Termination of Employment Regulations 1965, S.I. 1965 No. 2022, discussed at (18) above.

(20) There are special rules applicable under the unfair dismissal provisions when an employee is dismissed by reason of redundancy.[1]

[1] See p. 294, below.

## REDUNDANCY

Broadly speaking an employer is required to make a redundancy payment to an employee who has been continuously employed for the requisite period of two years, if the employee is:

(a) dismissed by his employer by reason of redundancy, or
(b) laid-off or kept on short-time as defined in the Act; Redundancy Payments Act 1965, section 1 (1). For consideration of the provisions as to lay-off and short-time see p. 233, below.

Section 1 (2) of the Redundancy Payment Act states:
"(2) For the purposes of this Act an employee who is dismissed shall be taken to be dismissed by reason of redundancy if the dismissal is attributable wholly or mainly to—
(*a*) the fact that his employer has ceased, or intends to cease, to carry on the business for the purposes of which the employee was employed by him, or has ceased, or intends to cease, to carry on that business in the place where the employee was so employed, or
(*b*) the fact that the requirements of that business for employees to carry out work of a particular kind, or for employees to carry out work of a particular kind in the place where he was so employed, have ceased or diminished or are expected to cease or diminish."

Where an employee is dismissed by his employer and neither of the conditions specified in paragraphs (*a*) and (*b*) of section 1 (2) is fulfilled, but one or other of those conditions would be fulfilled if the business of the employer together with the business, or businesses, of his associated employers were treated as one business, that condition is taken to be fulfilled in relation to the dismissal of the employee; Redundancy Payments Act 1965, section 48 (3) as substituted by the Employment Protection Act 1975. For "associated employers" see p. 211, below. The situation when an employee given notice because of redundancy is dismissed for misconduct, other than taking part in a strike, takes part in a strike, or anticipates the expiry of the notice is dealt with at pp. 207, 205 and 202, below, respectively.

This sub-section has been construed on many occasions and must therefore be considered in detail.

"... *dismissed* ...". Dismissal is discussed at p. 187, below.

*Onus of proof.* Unless the contrary is proved an employee who has been dismissed by his employer shall be presumed to have been so dismissed by reason of redundancy, Redundancy Payments Act 1965, section 9 (2). Thus the burden of proof rests on the employer and he has to prove to the tribunal on the balance of probabilities that the employee is not redundant. Since this would involve proof of a negative, the onus is usually discharged by proving a reason for dismissal other than redundancy. In *Parkes v. B. and M. (Bodyworks), Ltd.* (1972), 7 I.T.R. 48; N.I.R.C., the employers gave as reasons for the dismissal of a paint sprayer, a specific complaint of faulty workmanship in connection with repainting a lorry and also, an unsatisfactory attitude towards the foreman. The tribunal stated that although they were uncertain as to the reasons given by the employer, they found that on the balance of probabilities there was not sufficient evidence to find redundancy. This decision was upheld on appeal to the National Industrial Relations Court because it was considered that the tribunal was saying "... there was sufficient evidence, on the balance of probabilities to negative redundancy ..." See the judgment of SACCHS, L.J., in *Hindle v. Percival Boats, Ltd.*, [1969] 1 All E.R. 836; [1969] 1 W.L.R. 174; C. A. and *Wagstaff v. Trade and Industrial Press, Ltd.* (1967), 3 K.I.R. 339, D.C.

"... *attributable* ...". Difficulty has been experienced in deciding whether a subjective or objective text is to be applied in determining whether a dismissal is "attributable" to redundancy. WIDGERY, L.J. (as he then was), in *Hindle v. Percival Boats, Ltd.*

(1969), 4 I.T.R. 86, C.A., said (at p. 97):

> "I agree that the tribunal must look at the facts objectively to discover the true causes to which the dismissal is attributable but I do not find the distinction between objective and subjective tests to be either helpful or conclusive.
>
> The dismissal is attributable to the facts which caused it to occur. The tribunal must consider the evidence to see what those facts were and must bear in mind that the claimant succeeds on this issue unless the employer demonstrates that a diminution in the requirements of the business was *not* the main cause. The employer's evidence may be highly material because he knows what prompted him to dismiss the claimant and if his evidence is believed it may go a long way to establishing the true causes of his action. It must also be remembered that the employer is often entitled to dismiss his employee on due notice without assigning any reason at all. He may think that the employee is a bad influence in the works, or suspect him of pilfering or wish to replace him by a younger man. If dismissal then follows, the employer does not assume the obligation of proving that his suspicions were well founded or of persuading the tribunal that any reasonable employer would have acted as he did. All he must do is prove that redundancy was *not* the main cause and he does this by proving that the requirements of the business for workers of the relevant kind had not diminished. It is not the policy of this Act to reward long service and good conduct, as such, but only to compensate an employee who is dismissed for redundancy as defined in section 1."

"... *wholly or mainly* ...". There may be cases where there are several reasons for dismissal, for instance it could be due to a combination of circumstances such as redundancy, and unsuitability or lack of ability. It will have to be considered whether the employee has been unfairly dismissed, but he will be entitled to a redundancy payment only if the dismissal is attributable "wholly or mainly" to redundancy. Dismissal may, in some cases, be due neither to redundancy, nor misconduct, as in *Arnold* v. *Thomas Harrington, Ltd.*, [1969] 1 Q.B. 312; [1967] 2 All E.R. 866, D.C., where the reason for dismissal was to regain possession of a flat. In this connection reference may also be made to the judgment of WIDGERY, L.J. in *Hindle* v. *Percival Boats, Ltd.* (above) and also

*North Riding Garages, Ltd.* v. *Butterwick*, [1967] 2 Q.B. 56; [1967] 1 All E.R. 644, D.C.

In *Mac Fisheries, Ltd.* v. *Willgloss* (1972), 7 I.T.R. 57, N.I.R.C., the Court dealt with a case where both redundancy and inefficiency operated towards the dismissal. Lord THOMPSON in delivering the decision of the Court said, (at p. 58) "It seems to us that, broadly speaking the employer can discharge this onus in two ways.... In the first place, if the employer negatives the proposition that "the requirements of the employer's business for employees to carry out work of a particular kind has diminished or was expected to diminish", then the employee's case must fail. If on the other hand a "redundancy situation" is established by the evidence to the satisfaction of the tribunal, then the employers must go on to establish to the tribunal's satisfaction that the dismissal was not attributable wholly or mainly to the redundancy situation". Lord THOMPSON went on to say that where two causes contributed to the dismissal it is for the industrial tribunal to decide whether the employers have discharged the onus of proving that redundancy was not the sole, or main, cause of dismissal. The tribunal had taken the view that the employers had not proved that the cause other than redundancy went more towards the dismissal than the redundancy, so the employers must fail in their appeal.

Section 2 (2) of the Redundancy Payments Act 1965, (which can only apply where redundancy may be a reason for dismissal) provides that an employee is not entitled to a redundancy payment if the employer is entitled to terminate his employment without notice and does so summarily, or by giving shorter notice than that appropriate if the employer had not been entitled to terminate summarily, or if he gives the normal notice or longer and the notice includes, or is accompanied by, a statement in writing that the employer would be entitled to terminate without notice by reason of the employee's conduct. It should be remembered in this respect that the Contracts of Employment Act 1972 specifically preserves the common law rights of dismissal without notice. An example of a case where an employer, by concession, allowed an employee some notice although less than that to which he would have been entitled apart from the misconduct is to be found in *Hambling* v. *Marsden Builders, Ltd.* (1966), 1 I.T.R. 494, T. It is section 2 (2) (*c*) which covers the case where an employer allows the employee to work out his full notice notwithstanding his misconduct. In order to avoid being required to make a redundancy payment in these circumstances the employer must give the requisite statement in writing under sub-section (2) (*c*). See Appendix 9, Form 1. For interpretations of the sub-section see *Statham* v. *Hadlow's Garages, Ltd.* (1967), 2 I.T.R. 656, T, and *Essen* v. *Vanden Plas (England) 1923, Ltd.* (1966), 1 I.T.R. 186, T. A case involving misconduct discovered after the dismissal is *X* v. *Y, Ltd.* (1969), 4 I.T.R. 204, T. For a case where section 2 (2) was considered in a strike situation see *Simmonds* v. *Hoover, Ltd.*, [1976] *Times*, 20th July, E.A.T. where it was held that the employers were entitled to dismiss the employee as a result of his conduct while he was on strike and notwithstanding that the dismissal was by reason of redundancy. Since the dismissal was without notice section 2 (2) applied to defeat his claim. The employee was not able to find any assistance from section 10.

What is the effect if the employer does not give a notice in writing to the employee? In *Fleming* v. *Ritches, Ltd.* (1966), 1 I.T.R. 304, T, the tribunal held that an employer who is entitled to dismiss an employee summarily but instead gives notice without an accompanying statement specified in section 2 (2) (*c*), is not thereby precluded from proving that the employee was not redundant in order to discharge the onus under section 9 (2) (*b*). Reference may again be made to *Essen* v. *Vanden Plas (England) 1923, Ltd.* (above); and also *Abraham* v. *Beech* (1967), 2 I.T.R. 186, T.

"... *business* ..."; "... *employer* ...". Redundancy Payments Act 1965, section 25 (1) states that "business" includes a trade or profession and includes any activity carried on by a body of persons, whether corporate or unincorporate. The definition of business was discussed in *Lloyd* v. *Brassey*, [1969] 2 Q.B. 98; [1969] 1 All E.R. 382; C.A. and *Kenmir* v. *Frizzell*, [1968] 1 All E.R. 414; [1968] 1 W.L.R. 329, D.C., "activity" in this context means "the combination of operations undertaken by the corporate body whether or not amounting to a business trade or profession in the ordinary sense" per DIPLOCK, L.J., in *Dallow Industrial Properties, Ltd.* v. *Else*, [1967] 2 Q.B. 449 at p. 448, D.C. "Employer" is construed in accordance with the definition of employee in section 25 (1) (see p. 161). In some circumstances a company which was not the applicant's employer can be held to be estopped from denying that it was the employer; see *Smith* v. *Blandford*

*Gee Construction, Ltd.*, [1970] All E.R. 154, D.C., where the Divisional Court held that a respondent company was estopped from denying that it was the applicant's employer after it had served on the employee a statement under the Contracts of Employment Act 1972 which contained a provision that the employment was with the respondent company, although it was not so.

"... *ceased* ...". means ceased either permanently or temporarily and from whatever cause and "*diminish*" has a corresponding meaning; Redundancy Payments Act 1965, section 25 (3).

"... *work of a particular kind* ...". Section 1 (2) (*a*) covers a complete closedown of a business or a transfer of its location, section 1 (2) (*b*) on the other hand makes as a test of redundancy the question whether there has been any reduction in the requirements for workers to carry out work of the particular kind rather than of work *simpliciter*. An example of redundancy within this sub-section is the case of an employer deciding that the same amount of work can be done by fewer employees, as a result of which some employees are dismissed. Another instance may arise when employee B becomes surplus and is transferred to the work of employee A who thereby becomes surplus and is dismissed, e.g., on the basis of "last in first out"; employee A is then regarded as redundant for the purpose of the Act. See *W. Gimber & Sons, Ltd.* v. *Spurrett* (1967), 2 I.T.R. 308, D.C. "Work of a particular kind" does not mean "work of a particular kind on the existing terms and conditions of employment"; *Chapman* v. *Goonvean and Rostowrack China Clay Co., Ltd.*, [1973] 2 All E.R. 1063; [1973] 1 W.L.R. 678, C.A. in which employees whose employment was treated as terminated claimed redundancy payments when their employers withdrew a free bus service because of its increased *per capita* cost. The Court of Appeal decided that the absence of the bus service could not be said to result in the employer's requirement for work of a particular kind to have ceased or diminished. BUCKLEY, L.J., explained the position (at p. 1070) as follows:

"The section does not pose the question, what might be expected to happen if the employees were not dismissed but continued under their prior contracts of employment. It poses the question whether the employers' requirement for employees to carry out work of the particular kind in question is expected to cease or diminish. That is a question which needs to be answered objectively in the light of all the circumstances affecting the employers' business, but not, in my opinion, with any special relation to the particular contracts of employment under which the dismissed employees were previously employed."

In *Vaux and Associated Breweries, Ltd.* v. *Ward* (No. 2) (1970), 5 I.T.R. 62, D.C., the applicant, aged 57, had been dismissed because the respondents wished to give a public house, where she was a barmaid, a modern image and replace her with a younger girl. The Divisional Court said the question was whether the requirement of the business for employees to carry out work of a particular kind had ceased or diminished, not whether there had been a diminution in the requirement for a barmaid of her type. In that case the type of work was the same and it was held that the applicant's application for a redundancy payment failed.

In *Bromby and Hoare, Ltd.* v. *Evans* (1972), 7 I.T.R. 76, N.I.R.C. it was decided that "requirements" in the sub-section means "needs". The employer had an increasing amount of work on hand but decided that it could be more efficiently carried out by self employed persons rather than employees. The tribunal decision awarding a redundancy payment was upheld because the appellants needs for employees had dimished since they had decided that the work could be carried out better by self employed men. In considering an appeal to the Court of Appeal in *Johnson* v. *Nottinghamshire Combined Police Authority* (1974), 9 I.T.R. 164, C.A. DENNING, M.R., said at p. 167:

"It is settled by those cases that an employer is entitled to reorganise his business so as to improve its efficiency and, in so doing, to propose to his staff a change in the terms and conditions of their employment: and to dispense with their services if they do not agree. Such a change does not automatically give the staff a right to redundancy payments. It only does so if the change in the terms and conditions is due to a redundancy situation. The question in every case is: Was the change due to a redundancy situation, or not? If the change is due to a redundancy situation, he is entitled to a redundancy payment. If it is not due to it, he is not.

Typical of redundancy situations are these: There may be a recession in trade so that not so many men are needed.

There may be a change in the kind of work done, as from wood to fibre-glass, so that woodworkers are no longer needed (see *Hindle* v. *Percival Boats, Ltd.* [above]). The business may be no longer profitable so that the employer has to cut down somewhere. Or, he may be overstaffed. The employer may meet such a situation by dispensing with the services of some of the men: or alternatively he may lower the wages: or put them on part time. If he does it by making a change in the terms and conditions of employment, it is due to a redundancy situation. Those who lose or leave their work in consequence are entitled to redundancy payments."

Compare *Kykot* v. *Smith Hartley, Ltd.*, [1975] I.R.L.R. 372, D.C. (nightworkers required to change to rotating day shifts when at the same time there was a reduction in the number of employees was held to be redundancy).

When deciding whether the requirements of a business for employees to carry out work of a particular kind have ceased or diminished or are expected to cease or diminish the overall requirements of the business are looked at. In *North Riding Garages, Ltd.* v. *Butterwick* (1967), 2 I.T.R. 229, D.C., WIDGERY, J. (as he then was) said at p. 232:

"It is, we think, important to observe that a claim under section 1, sub-section (2) (*b*) is conditional upon a change in the requirements of the business. If the requirement for the business for employees to carry out work of a particular kind increases or remains constant no redundancy payment can be claimed by an employee, in work of that kind, whose dismissal is attributable to personal deficiencies which prevent him from satisfying his employer. The very fact of dismissal shows that the employee's services are no longer required by his employer and that he may, in a popular sense, be said to have become redundant, but if the dismissal was attributable to age, physical disability or inability to meet his employer's standards he was not dismissed on account of redundancy within the meaning of the Act. For the purpose of this Act an employee who remains in the same kind of work is expected to adapt himself to new methods and techniques and cannot complain if his employer insists on higher standards of efficiency than those previously required; but if new methods alter the nature of the work required to be done it may follow that no requirement remains for employees to do work of the particular kind which has been superseded and that they are truly redundant. Thus if a motor manufacturer decides to use plastics instead of wood in the bodywork of his cars and dismisses his woodworkers, they may well be entitled to redundancy payments on the footing that their dismissal is attributable to a cessation of the requirement of the business for employees to carry out work of a particular kind, namely woodworking."

See also *European Chefs (Catering), Ltd.* v. *Currell* (1971), 6 I.T.R. 37, D.C.

It is, of course, essential to decide the particular kind of work carried out by the employee. This should be made easier by the requirement of the Contracts of Employment Act 1972, inserted by the Employment Protection Act 1975, that the statement issued pursuant to the earlier act should include the title of the job which the employee is employed to do. However, considerable difficulties in this regard have been experienced in the past. In *Amos* v. *Max Arc, Ltd.* (1973), 8 I.T.R. 65, N.I.R.C., the Court considered a case where metal workers who had previously worked with stainless steel were asked to change to black metal. Sir JOHN DONALDSON said "the phrase 'work of a particular kind', in Section 1 (2) (b) of the Act, means, in our judgment, work which is distinguished from other work of the same general kind by requiring special aptitudes, skills or knowledge". In *Amos's* case this had not been sufficiently considered by the tribunal and the case was remitted for this purpose. Another instance occurred in *Lane Fox and Co., Ltd.* v. *Binns* (1972), 7 I.T.R. 125, N.I.R.C., where the tribunal had decided that a man who had formerly been a brick-layer but had for some time performed as personal assistant and chaffeur to the company chairman, was a brick-layer and the National Industrial Relations Court upheld this decision. In *O'Donnell* v. *George Wimpey & Co., Ltd.* (1972), 7 I.T.R. 343, N.I.R.C. a labourer who had been put on lighter work because of failing eyesight was *held* to be a labourer and so not redundant when dismissed, when there was no suitable light work for him. But see *Weed* v. *A. E. Smith & Son (Kettering), Ltd.* (1972), 7 I.T.R. 352, N.I.R.C. when a paint sprayer was given a job as a clerk-receptionist after suffering a heart attack. He

Redundancy

performed the new tasks for 18 months and it was *held* that his employment had changed to that of clerk/receptionist. The question for the tribunal to decide is what are the employee's terms of employment. Does his contract restrict him to one kind of work. In *O'Neill* v. *Merseyside Plumbing Co., Ltd.* (1973), 8 I.T.R. 122, N.I.R.C., the case was remitted to the tribunal to determine this when an employee who had been carrying out gas-fitting was dismissed for refusing to do general plumbing, there being no gas-fitting work available for him.

At one time it was suggested that if an employee had been partly responsible for the redundancy situation arising he may not be entitled to a redundancy payment. However, in *Sanders* v. *Ernest A. Neale, Ltd.*, [1974] I.C.R. 565, at p. 573, N.I.R.C., this idea was finally dispelled. Sir JOHN DONALDSON said:

"The court would like to take this opportunity of exorcising the ghost of self-induced redundancy. It can certainly occur, but as such it has no legal significance. Interruption of service due to industrial action can cause customers to look to competitors or to turn to substitute materials or services. This can lead to a diminution in the requirements of the business for employees to carry out work of a particular kind and to workers being dismissed. But the mere fact that the employees' action created the redundancy situation does not disentitle them to a redundancy payment. The entitlement depends upon the words of the statute and there is no room for any general consideration of whether it is equitable that the employee should receive a payment."

"*... place where he was so employed ...*". The contract of employment may provide that the geographical place where the employee works may be changed by the employer. If the employer is entitled to transfer the employee and he is dismissed because he refuses to be transferred, the dismissal is not by reason of redundancy. Therefore it is essential to establish the exact terms of the contract. In some instances there are express terms permitting transfer by the employer, cf. *Briggs* v. *Imperial Chemical Industries, Ltd.* (1968), 3 I.T.R. 276, D.C. (transfer within a factory), *Parry* v. *Holst & Co., Ltd.* (1968), 3 I.T.R. 317, D.C. (transfer from South Wales to Somerset), and *Joel* v. *Cammell Laird (Ship-*

*Repairers), Ltd.* (1968), 3 I.T.R. 206, T (incorporation of collective agreement made subsequent to employment).

In other cases a term allowing "transferability" may be implied. In *O'Brien Pritchard and Browning* v. *Associated Fire Alarms, Ltd.*, [1969] 1 All E.R. 93; [1968] 1 W.L.R. 1916, C.A., the Court of Appeal decided that whether such a term could be implied was a point of law and not of fact, and thus was subject of appeal. Each case must be judged on its merits, and in that instance, it was held that a term could not be implied enabling the employer to require electricians to work beyond daily travelling distance of Liverpool. The employees who were dismissed for refusing to work outside the area were entitled to redundancy payments. On the other hand in *Stevenson* v. *Tees-side Bridge and Engineering, Ltd.*, [1971] 1 All E.R. 296, D.C., the Divisional Court dismissed an appeal from a tribunal which had held there to be an implied term that a steel erector could be sent to any of his employers' sites. If the employers seek to rely on a clause allowing transfer they must invoke it when they seek to do so; *R. H. McCulloch, Ltd.* v. *Moore*, [1968] 1 Q.B. 360; [1967] 2 All E.R. 290, D.C.

In *Lister* v. *Fram Gerard, Ltd.* (1973), 8 I.T.R. 610, N.I.R.C. A turner was employed at a plant depot in Swindon. A term of the National Working Rule Agreement was that the employee could be required to transfer from site to site. The employers wished to transfer Mr. Litster to their depot at Aldington. It was *held* that the agreement did not entitle the employers to transfer the employee; "site" meant civil engineering sites and did not include permanent depots.

*Sutcliffe* v. *Hawker Siddley Aviation, Ltd.* (1974), 9 I.T.R. 58, N.I.R.C. (contract to work anywhere in the United Kingdom. Employee required to work long distance from his home. *Held* no redundancy).

*United Kingdom Atomic Energy Authority* v. *Claydon* (1974), 9 I.T.R. 185, N.I.R.C. (requirement to work at any of employees establishments in Great Britain or in posts overseas).

*Rowbotham* v. *Arthur Lee & Sons Ltd.* (1975), 10 I.T.R. 145, D.C. (discussion of "implied" terms in contract to enable transfer).

It is clear from the above decisions that any employer who wishes to have the right to transfer the geographic location of employment must include a provision to that effect in the contract of employment. The position is similar for the application of the unfair dismissal provisions.

**In the following cases the employee was held not to be redundant:**

*Hindle* v. *Percival Boats, Ltd.*, [1969] 1 All E.R. 836, [1969] 1 W.L.R. 174 C.A. (Hindle skilled wood craftsman employed by boat builders and repairers. Earlier employees dismissed because of movement to glass fibre boats but Hindle was retained for repair work. He was an excellent skilled craftsman but was dismissed because he took such a long time in doing a thorough job).

*J. Styles & Son, Ltd.* v. *Saunders* (1968), 3 I.T.R. 126, D.C. (one-eyed carpenter, although contract permitted transfer he refused to go to site where exposed to danger to existing eye).

*Malton* v. *Crystal of Scarborough, Ltd.* (1971), 6 I.T.R. 106, D.C. (redundancy situation but dismissed because of unsatisfactory work).

*Stride* v. *Moore (Metal Spinners), Ltd.* (1968), 3 I.T.R. 117, D.C. (redundancy situation but dismissed because of unsatisfactory work).

*Jones* v. *Star Associated Holdings, Ltd.* (1970), 5 I.T.R. 178, D.C. (manager of Casino and Theatre, employer reduced applicant's status to Theatre Manager only and appointed new Casino Manager).

*Vaux and Associated Breweries, Ltd.* v. *Ward, (No. 2)* (1970), 5 I.T.R. 62, D.C. (elderly barmaid replaced by younger girl).

*Wagstaff* v. *The Trade and Industrial Press, Ltd.* (1968), 3 I.T.R. 1, D.C. (employers dissatisfied with employee).

*North Riding Garages, Ltd.* v. *Butterwick*, [1967] 2 Q.B. 56; [1967] 1 All E.R. 644, D.C.

*Arnold* v. *Thomas Harrington, Ltd.*, [1969] 1 Q.B. 312; [1967] 2 All E.R. 866, D.C. (reason for dismissal to obtain possession of flat).

*Auld* v. *Trocoll Industries (Scotland), Ltd.* (1971), 6 I.T.R. 64, D.C., C.S. (dispute with his employers resulted in dismissal).

*Jones* v. *Wagon Repairs, Ltd.* (1968), 361, D.C. (employee away sick for 6 months returned to work for a month and then away for further 18 months. Divisional Court *held* contract frustrated not entitled to redundancy payment even though other employees were dismissed for redundancy by the employer).

*Bradley* v. *Plastocraft Products (Darwen), Ltd.* (1971), 6 I.T.R. 217, D.C. (clash of personalities with chairman).

*Kleboe* v. *Ayr City Council* (1972) I.T.R. 201, N.I.R.C. (art teacher dismissed when unable to comply with statutory requirement for registration—the business was that of teaching children not teaching by unregistered lecturer).

*Blakely* v. *Chemetron Ltd.* (1972), 7 I.T.R. 224, N.I.R.C. (change to night shift not a change in requirement for work of a particular kind).

*Johnson* v. *Nottinghamshire Combined Police Authority,* [1974] 1 All E.R. 1082; [1974] 1 W.L.R. 358, C.A. (change for clerical workers to shift working—no diminution of work).

**Industrial Tribunal decisions**

*Brownlie* v. *Purvis* (1968), 3 I.T.R. 375 (employee having purchased employer's farm).

*Wren* v. *Wiltshire County Council* (1969), 4 I.T.R. 251 (unqualified teacher dismissed for replacement by qualified teacher).

*Miller* v. *British Railway Workshops* (1968), 3 I.T.R. 89 (employee refused to carry out night shift working agreed between Unions and Employers).

*Garnett* v. *Dawson Brothers (Lymington), Ltd.* (1966), 1 I.T.R. 375 (employer's reasons "rude, disagreeable and unco-operative").

*Boswell and Hardy* v. *W. W. Howard Brothers & Co., Ltd.* (1966), 1 I.T.R. 387 (dismissal because co-employees threatened to strike).

*Vincent* v. *William Campbell & Sons (Biscuits), Ltd.* (1966), 1 I.T.R. 319 (refusal to obey order).

*Hodgkinson* v. *Braintree and Bocking Urban District Council* (1966), 1 I.T.R. 258 (need for dustmen).

*Crowe* v. *Lewden Metal Products, Ltd.* (1967), 2 I.T.R. 68 ("gross breach of terms of employment" justifying dismissal).

*Mackenzie* v. *William Paton, Ltd.* (1966), 1 I.T.R. 507. (*Held:* unqualified cost accountant replaced by qualified cost accountant because employers considered him unable to install and run system —not dismissed by reason of redundancy).

**In the following cases the employee was held to be redundant and redundancy payments were awarded:**

*Hall* v. *Farrington Data Processing, Ltd.* (1969), 4 I.T.R. 230, D.C. (branch manager of Cardiff Office offered employment as salesman with same salary on closing of office).

*Monckton* v. *Atkins* (1969), 4 I.T.R. 254, D.C. (gamekeeper whose work was reduced because of foot and mouth disease. His employer did not appear before tribunal).

*Etherington* v. *Henry Greenham (1929), Ltd.* (1969), 4 I.T.R.

226, D.C. (employee told he was to be replaced by younger man, but not replaced. Presumption of redundancy not rebutted). *Walley* v. *Morgan* (1969), 4 I.T.R. 122, D.C. (farm worker persuaded employer to dismiss him shortly after foot and mouth outbreak). *Watts Watts & Co., Ltd.* v. *Steeley* (1968), 3 I.T.R. 363, D.C. (ship's Master off sick for month during which Chief Officer takes over as Captain. Employers no longer required his services but preferred the Chief Officer who was a foreign going captain). *Royle* v. *Pointer Group Holdings, Ltd.* (1971), 6 I.T.R. 124, D.C. (oil tanker driver dismissed for refusing to do general haulage work). *City Tote Ltd.* v. *Johnson* (1972), 7 I.T.R. 44, N.I.R.C. (security man doing some photographic work transferred to photography department after reorganisation). *Marshall* v. *Harland and Wolff, Ltd.* (No. 2) (1972), 7 I.T.R. 150, N.I.R.C. (an employee incapable of work at the time can be held to be entitled to a redundancy payment).

**Industrial Tribunal decisions**
*Sartin* v. *Co-operative Retail Services, Ltd.* (1969), 4 I.T.R. 392, T (manager of counter shop dismissed after change to supermarket).
*Irvine* v. *National Fishcuring Co., Ltd.* (1966), 1 I.T.R. 151, T (applicant's job taken over by lower-paid employee).

DISMISSAL

**(i) Generally**
A redundancy payment may be payable in the following circumstances:
(1) If the employer terminates the contract of employment by notice—Redundancy Payments Act 1965, section 3 (2) (*a*).
(2) If the employer terminates the contract of employment without notice—Redundancy Payments Act 1965, section 3 (2) (*a*).
(3) When a fixed term contract expires without being renewed under the same contract—Redundancy Payments Act 1965, section 3 (2) (*b*).[1]

---

[1] Subject to Redundancy Payments Act 1965, s. 15; see p. 163, above.

(4) If the employee terminates the contract of employment, whether with or without notice, in circumstances entitling him to do so by reason of the employer's conduct, apart from a lock-out—Redundancy Payments Act 1965, section 3 (2) (*c*) and section 10 (4).[1]

[1] See p. 190, below.

(5) If the employee anticipates the expiry of the employer's notice by himself giving notice, the relevant date being the date when the employee's notice expires; but a redundancy payment is not obligatory if before the expiry of the notice the employer gives a notice in accordance with section 4 (3), with which the employee does not comply. The matter is then referred to a tribunal to determine whether or not there should be a redundancy payment.

Apart from the rigorous provisions relating to lay-off and short time,[1] there can be no redundancy payment unless the employee is first dismissed within the meaning of the Act. Section 3 defines dismissal, and there have been many decisions dealing with the fine distinctions which this section has produced. It will be seen that, broadly speaking, an employee is dismissed (1) when the contract is terminated by the employer, or (2) on expiry of a fixed-term contract, or (3) if the employee with justification "walks out". In relation to (1) and (2) there is no "dismissal" if the employee is re-engaged on the termination of the employment, or, within four weeks of termination subject to the provisions as to trial periods.[2]

[1] See p. 233, below.
[2] See p. 197, below.

Even though a situation of redundancy exists there can be no redundancy payment where the employee himself terminates the employment, except within the provisions of section 3 (2) (*c*) when the employee justifiably "walks out", or when the employee anticipates the expiry of the employer's notice of dismissal within the provisions of section 4. Warning by an employer that employment will be terminated at some future unspecified date is not a dismissal, and if as a result the employee finds fresh employment he is not entitled to a redundancy payment.[1] If employer and employee agree to part company there is no dismissal and no redundancy payment can ensure.

[1] *Morton Sundour Fabrics, Ltd.* v. *Shaw* (1967), 2 I.T.R. 84, D.C.

Voluntary redundancies can occur when the agreement between the employer and the employee is that the employer will determine the employee's employment.[1] The varied reasons why the employment has come to an end have presented the industrial tribunals and courts with numerous problems turning on the question whether or not what has occured amounts to a dismissal within the meaning of the Redundancy Payments Act 1965. The most important matters to consider are the terms and conditions of the contract, and in this respect the statement given under the Contracts of Employment Act 1972 can be of immense importance. It may be relevant, for instance, to ascertain whether a mobile operator can be expected to move from place to place to different sites. The distance involved in a move may be of significance. A business moving from "John o'Groats to Lands End" is different from "down the street or across the road".[2] An employee's leaving may amount to dismissal within section 3 (2) (*c*) if the employee leaves, whether with or without notice,[3] by reason of the employer's conduct. The Act does recognise the right of both employer and employee to determine the contract of employment where the other party has been guilty of repudiatory conduct.

[1] See *Burton, Allton and Johnson, Ltd.* v. *Peck*, [1975] I.R.L.R. 87, D.C.
[2] See *Margiotta Porter and Fookes* v. *Mount Charlotte Investments, Ltd.* (1966), 1 I.T.R. 465, T.
[3] Before 1st June 1976 when the appropriate provisions of the Employment Protection Act 1975 were introduced the employee had to leave without notice.

Section 3 (1) and (2) of the Redundancy Payments Act 1965 as substituted by the Employment Protection Act 1975 provides as follows:[1]

"3.—(1) In this Part of this Act, "dismiss" and "dismissal" shall be construed in accordance with the provisions of this section and the next following section.

(2) Subject to the following provisions of this section and to the next following section, an employee shall be treated as dismissed by his employer, if, but only if—

(*a*) the contract under which he is employed by the employer is terminated by the employer, whether it is so terminated by notice or without notice,[2] or

(b) where under that contract he is employed for a fixed term,[3] that term expires without being renewed under the same contract, or

(c) the employee terminates that contract, with or without notice, in circumstances (not falling within section 10 (4) of this Act) such that he is entitled to terminate it without notice by reason of the employer's conduct."

[1] The substitution came into effect on 1st June 1976. Section 3 (1) formerly read:

"3—(1) For the purposes of this Part of this Act an employee shall, subject to the following provisions of this Part of this Act, be taken to be dismissed by his employer if, but only if:

(a) the contract under which he is employed by the employer is terminated by the employer, whether it is so terminated by notice or without notice, or

(b) where under that contract he is employed for a fixed term, that term expires without being renewed under the same contract, or

(c) the employee terminates that contract without notice in circumstances (not falling within section 10 (4) of this Act) such that he is entitled so to terminate it by reason of the employer's conduct."

[2] "... *without notice* ...". Where the dismissal without notice is justified by the employee's conduct meriting summary dismissal the provisions of the Redundancy Payments Act 1965, s. 2 (2) have to be considered. Section 2 (2) is discussed at p. 177, above, summary dismissal, at p. 144, above.

[3] "... fixed term ...". The position at common law has been discussed at p. 127, above. For the special provisions relating to some fixed term contracts, see p. 163, above.

See section 22 for implied and constructive termination of contracts, p. 203, below.

*Onus of proof.* The burden is on the applicant to show that he was dismissed. For an early example see *Connop* v. *Unit Metal Construction, Ltd.* (1966), 1 I.T.R. 486, T.

*Decisions relevant to section 3 (2) (a):* made under the original section 3 (1) (a) which was in similar terms assist in resolving difficulties.

Particular problems arise in deciding whether a contract has been terminated or consensually varied by the parties. Such a case came to be considered by the Court of Appeal in *Marriott* v. *Oxford and District Co-operative Society, Ltd. (No. 2)*, [1970] 1 Q.B.

# Dismissal

186; [1969] 3 All E.R. 1126, C.A. The employers wrote to the employee stating that as a result of reorganisation they did not require him as an electrical foreman. However, they wished to retain his services and were prepared to do so reducing his wages by £3 per week. Mr. Marriott objected and after discussions another letter was written by the employers stating that the arrangement to reduce his wages by £3 had been rescinded but they would be reduced by £1 per week subject to review after three months. He left after 3 or 4 weeks having been paid less the £1 reduction for two or three weeks. The Court of Appeal *held* that the second letter was a dismissal falling within section 3 (1) (a) the predecessor of section 3 (2) (a) in that the employer clearly stated that they would not fulfil their contract with Mr. Marriott. He had not been party ot a consensual variation by receiving reduced wages for two or three weeks since he had never accepted the position. Lord DENNING, M.R., said (at p. 1128 "If the parties agree consensually to vary the terms of the contract of employment, or to rescind it and substitute a new contract of employment, the plain fact is that the contract is not terminated by the employers but by consent". WINN, L.J., said (at p. 1129):

> "The workman might agree with the employer that he prefers, rather than to have his contract terminated, to accept different, perhaps less advantageous, working conditions than he has hitherto enjoyed—either permanently, or, more probably, for a short time—to see if co-operating together they can pull the ship out of shallow water. That is the effect of an agreement which itself is made while the contract of employment still exists in order to achieve, inter alia, the object of avoiding a termination of that contract of employment".

The cases have to be looked at with great care, especially in the light of the "trial period" provisions introduced by the Employment Protection Act 1975, (see p. 197, below), but help may be available from *Lowe* v. *East Lancashire Paper Mill Co., Ltd.* (1970), 5 I.T.R. 132, D.C., where a stock clerk returned to work after being away ill for four months and his employer said that if he returned he did so as a load conveyer with a reduction of £3 a week in his wages. He considered the matter carefully, contacted his union and others to discuss the matter, eventually agreeing to work under the renewed terms without protest. He left after four weeks. The Court upheld the decision of the industrial tribunal that there had been a consensual variation of the terms of his contract. See *McDonnell* v. *Taylor & Son (Successors), Ltd.* (1970), 5 I.T.R. 256, D.C. (*held* consensual variation pieceworker put on hourly wage), *Hempel* v. *Parrish* (1968), 3 I.T.R. 240, D.C. (employer and employee agreed that the employee should work for another amployer on a temporary basis) and *Spelman* v. *George Garnham* (1968), 3 I.T.R. 370, D.C. (consensual variation accepting employment for $17\frac{1}{2}$ hours per week).

In some instances it is clear that there has been no consensual variation and the employer has repudiated the contract. For instance, *Gresham Furniture, Ltd.* v. *Wall* (1970), 5 I.T.R. 171, D.C. (Mr. Wall employed by two companies controlled by the same person, one ceased to trade and he was told that his wages would be reduced. The Divisional Court said the tribunal was correct in deciding that the employers had repudiated the contract.)

The variation must be truly consensual to enable the employer to avoid payment on this ground and may not be so even if the employee works under the new terms for a short time; see *Shields Furniture, Ltd.* v. *Goff*, [1973] 2 All E.R. 653, N.I.R.C. and *Sheet Metal Components, Ltd.* v. *Plumridge* (1974), 9 I.T.R. 238, N.I.R.C.

The contract of employment may enable the employer to transfer the employee from one type of work to another.

*Atherton* v. *John Crankshaw Co., Ltd.* (1970), 5 I.T.R. 201, D.C. (hand moulder who made gulley piping on piecework rates was required to do other hand moulding jobs at hourly rates. The Divisional Court *held* that there was no dismissal since his contract enabled his employer to do this). *Simms Motor Units, Ltd.* v. *Hindes* (1971), 6 I.T.R. 113, D.C. (employee moved from injector assembly work to pump assembly work), *Imperial Chemical Industries, Ltd.* v. *McCullum* (1969), 4 I.T.R. 24, C.S. (transfer to another occupation within the employee's trade but with lower rate of payment). See the decision of the Court of Appeal in *Charles* v. *Spiralynx (1933), Ltd.* (1970), 5 I.T.R. 82, C.A., where the employees were not entitled by the contract to transfer their employees to their new premises. Contrast *Bective Electrical Co., Ltd.* v. *Warren* (1968), 3 I.T.R. 119, D.C., and see cases on transfer of ownership of business and section 3 (2) (c), below.

Other helpful decisions relevant to the sub-section are:
*Horsell* v. *Heath* (1966), 1 I.T.R. 332, T, (no presumption that employee has been dismissed—tribunal unable to decide which version correct—applicant failed to establish that he was dismissed). *Brownlie* v. *Purvis* (1968), 3 I.T.R. 375, T (applicant purchased farm from employer—not dismissal but voluntary termination); contrast *Harris* v. *Hugo* (1968), 3 I.T.R. 138, T (employee given notice and during notice negotiated to purchase business which he did—redundancy payment awarded) and *Scott* v. *Executors of A. E. Marchant, dcd.* (1969), 4 I.T.R. 319, T (employee given the business).

*Burgess* v. *O'Brien* (1966), 4 I.T.R. 164, T (partner remunerated by salary and commission and not by share of profits—no dismissal but dissolution of partnership by mutual consent).

*Sweeney* v. *Englehard Industries, Ltd.* (1966), 1 I.T.R. 317, T (the employee himself terminated the employment and was not dismissed).

*Miller* v. *Nettle Accessories, Ltd.* (1966), 1 I.T.R. 328, T (notice of dismissal rescinded but *held* to operate as dismissal if alternative employment rejected).

*Burchell* v. *Clark's Bakeries (Finchley), Ltd.* (1966), 1 I.T.R. 396, T (employee terminated contract himself because he refused to work at contract rate—previously paid more than contract rate).

*Sneddon* v. *Ivorycrete (Builders), Ltd.* (1966), 1 I.T.R. 538, T (dismissal not lay-off—no provision in working agreement for suspension).

*Jones* v. *Harry Sherman, Ltd.* (1969), 4 I.T.R. 63, T (lay-off not permitted by contract amounted to dismissal).

*Glenboig Union Fireclay Co., Ltd.* v. *Stewart* (1971), 6 I.T.R. 14, C.S. (employee off sick and works closed and he was told that when he was fit again he would be offered work by associated company. *Held*: that the employee was dismissed when the works closed down and that his services were no longer required).

*Thomas (Deceased)* v. *John Drake & Co., Ltd.* (1971), 6 I.T.R. 146, T (employee off sick for nine months, employers wrote "in view of your protracted illness ... any contract of employment must now be considered terminated as from today". *Held*: that letter amounted to dismissal). See *Jones* v. *Wagon Repairs, Ltd.* (1968), 2 I.T.R. 361, D.C., and "frustration" at p. 204, below.

*Gallagher* v. *Union Transit Co., Ltd.* (1969), 4 I.T.R. 214, T (notice to terminate employment cannot be unilaterally extended or withdrawn).

*Bryan* v. *George Wimpey & Co., Ltd.* (1968), 3 I.T.R. 28, T (notice cannot be withdrawn).

*Brown* v. *Brekkes, Ltd.* (1970), 5 I.T.R. 300, T (employee stayed on at employer's request after he had given notice to terminate employment and the contract terminated when the depot closed down. *Held:* dismissed).

*R. J. Hewitt (Wholesale Fruiters), Ltd.* v. *Russell* (1969), 4 I.T.R. 260, D.C. (employee rude to employer and employer purported to accept the repudiation. *Held:* that employee had not meant to treat contract as at an end and was dismissed by employer).

*Dinnen* v. *Barrow in Furness Corporation* (1969), 4 I.T.R. 107, T (employee who worked full time for one department and then part time for another department at the Corporation was dismissed from full time job. Industrial tribunal *held* dismissed).

*Steadman* v. *Halsales, Ltd.* (1967), 2 I.T.R. 77, T (dismissal is unilateral in character, and if an employer and employee agree that it is in their best interests to part company that is not dismissal.

*Jones* v. *W. C. Youngman, Ltd.* (1966), 1 I.T.R. 463, T (contract not confined to night work—refusal to work on day shift—no dismissal).

*Dubiel* v. *William Park & Co. Forgemasters, Ltd.* (1967), 2 I.T.R. 268, T (dismissal without notice under forerunner of section 3 (2) (a)).

*Goode and Cooper, Ltd.* v. *Thompson,* [1974] I.R.L.R. 111, N.I.R.C. (general manager to be demoted to foreman. *Held* to amount to repudiation of contract and hence dismissal).

*G.K.N. (Cwmbran), Ltd.* v. *Lloyd* (1972), 7 I.T.R. 160, N.I.R.C. (core straightener on day-work told to work as labourer on shift work—£7 a week drop in wages—*held* dismissed).

*Weed* v. *A. E. Smith & Son (Kettering), Ltd.* (1972), 7 I.T.R. 352, N.I.R.C. (paint sprayer employed as a clerk/receptionist for over 12 months required to return to job as sprayer—dismissed since he was employed as a clerk/receptionist at time of dismissal).

*E. and J. Davis Transport, Ltd.* v. *Chattaway* (1972), 7 I.T.R. 361, N.I.R.C. (the employers discontinued road licences after industrial dispute with drivers—*held* dismissal).

*Maher* v. *Fram Gerrard, Ltd.,* [1974] 1 All E.R. 449, N.I.R.C. (employee told employers were closing depot and proposed to move him to another some distance away. He gave notice before he was told of the date of move. *Held* the employers were not entitled to require him to move and therefore they had repudiated their contract amounting to dismissal).

    *Powell Duffryn Wagon Co., Ltd.* v. *House* (1974), I.T.R. 46, N.I.R.C. (refused to pay guaranteed minimum wage amounted to repudiation of the contract and dismissal).

    *Sanders* v. *Ernest Neale, Ltd.,* [1974] 3 All E.R. 327, N.I.R.C. (employees working to rule were told that unless they undertook to work normally by 11th May 1972 they would be regarded as being in breach of contract and dismissed. Employers sent the employees their cards and closed the factory. This amounted to dismissal even though repudiation was not "accepted" by the employees).

    *McCarthy* v. *Burroughs Machine, Ltd.* (1975), 10 I.T.R. 46, T (employee laid off without pay. No power to do so in contract —lay off amounted to dismissal).

    *Rowbotham* v. *Arthur Lee & Sons, Ltd.* (1975), 10 I.T.R. 145, D.C. (no power to require employee to move—dismissal).

    An employee who is expressly invited to resign when his job is at an end is dismissed for these purposes. See *East Sussex County Council* v. *Walker* (1972), 7 I.T.R. 280, N.I.R.C. The fact that the employee agreed to his selection for redundancy does not prevent the termination from amounting to a dismissal. See *Burton, Allton and Johnson, Ltd.* v. *Peck,* [1975], I.C.R. 193, D.C., where the employee had been absent for over a year. Whilst he was away the employers had indicated that it would be in Mr. Peck's interest to accept a redundancy payment if it could have been paid to him. When he returned his employers had no job for him. The Divisional Court upheld the tribunal's decision that the employee had been dismissed notwithstanding his consent to redundancy.

    The notice must be more than a general indication of an intention to dismiss.

    *Morton Sundour Fabrics, Ltd.* v. *Shaw* (1967), 2 I.T.R. 84, D.C. (Warning that employment would be terminated at some future unspecified date—not termination—employee himself terminated employment by finding new job—no redundancy payment.) The following is an extract from the judgment of WIDGERY, J.: "In exactly the same way as a notice to quit in the context of the law of landlord and tenant must specify the date on which it was intended to take effect, so a notice to terminate a contract of employment must specify the date on which it was intended that the employment come to an end, or at least the notice must contain facts from which an inference of a definite date of termination could be drawn. The contract could not be terminated by the employer announcing that at some future date he intended that the employment should cease." See also *Phillips* v. *Morganite Carbon, Ltd.* (1967), 2 I.T.R. 53, T, but contrast the decision of an industrial tribunal in *Hudson* v. *Fuller-Shapcott* (1970), 5 I.T.R. 266, T (in October told her employment would end in February but left earlier with employer's implied consent).

See also *Tunnel Holdings, Ltd.* v. *Woolf* (1976), 11 I.T.R. 75, D.C.

*Decisions relevant to section 3 (2) (c)*: having been taken under a similar sub-section, as originally enacted.

An employee's leaving may amount to dismissal within section 3 (2) (c) if the employee leaves by reason of the employer's conduct.

In *O'Reilly* v. *Hotpoint, Ltd.* (1970), 5 I.T.R. 68, D.C., an employee was off sick and eventually the employers ceased to pay him transfering him to the "holding department". When he was fit enough to return to work the employers had no work for him. Divisional Court *held* that by not providing the employee with work the employers had repudiated the contract of employment and he was entitled to treat himself as dismissed. An employee can be made redundant although off sick.

An unusual situation was considered by the Court of Appeal in *Duckworth* v. *P. F. Farnish & Co., Ltd.* (1970), 5 I.T.R. 17 where an employee was with consent loaned to other employers for a few days. After about 10 days the employee was paid by the second employers and told his first employers would not take him back. The employee later wrote to the first employers to terminate the contract with them. It was *held* that there was a termination within the meaning of section 3 (1) (c), the forerunner of section 3 (2) (c). The court pointed out that whether the conduct falls within the sub-section is a matter of law based on the facts of the case.

Examples of decisions on the earlier sub-section are:

*Broadhurst* v. *H. Buchan & Son* (1969), 4 I.T.R. 247, T (failure to pay wages fell within section 3 (1) (c)).

*Callison* v. *Ford Motor Co., Ltd.* (1969), 4 I.T.R. 74, T

(employee regraded as result of agreement between employers and union. The industrial tribunal *held* that the employers conduct did not fall within sub-section 3 (1) (c)).

*Stannard, Gent, Halsy and Field* v. *Dexion, Ltd.* (1966), 1 I.T.R. 274, T (requirement to do work in a different department of a different nature but within employees' grade as general production workers—not conduct within s. 3 (1) (c)).

*Skillen* v. *Eastwoods Froy, Ltd.* (1967), 2 I.T.R. 112, T (reduction in status—subordinate position—conduct entitling employee to terminate his contract summarily—therefore dismissed).

*Ramage* v. *Harper-Mackay, Ltd.* (1966), 1 I.T.R. 503, T (representative told he would work in warehouse—section 3 (1) (c) applied).

*Saunders* v. *Paladin Coachworks, Ltd.* (1968), 3 I.T.R. 51, D.C. (employee entitled to treat contract of employment as repudiated by employers but did not do so and terminated employment himself. No dismissal—no redundancy payment).

When an employee terminates his contract of employment without notice being entitled to do so by reason of a lock-out by his employer then section 3 (2) (c) does not apply. See Redundancy Payments Act 1965, section 10 (4).

## (ii) Renewal and re-engagement

In certain circumstances where an employee's contract is renewed, or he is re-engaged under a new contract of employment, then he is not regarded as being dismissed. The provisions governing this are set out in section 3, sub-sections (3)–(8) which are included in the Redundany Payments Act 1965 by the Employment Protection Act 1975. They are as follows:

"(3) If an employee's contract of employment is renewed, or he is re-engaged under a new contract of employment in pursuance of an offer (whether in writing or not) made by his employer before the ending of his employment under the previous contract, and the renewal or re-engagement takes effect either immediately on the ending of that employment or after an interval of not more than four weeks thereafter, then, subject to sub-sections (5) to (8) of this section, the employee shall not be regarded as having been dismissed by his employer by reason of the ending of his employment under the previous contract.

(4) For the purposes of the application of the last preceding sub-section to a contract under which the employment ends on a Friday, Saturday or Sunday—

(a) the renewal or re-engagement shall be treated as taking effect immediately on the ending of the employment if it takes effect on or before the Monday after that Friday, Saturday or Sunday, and

(b) the interval of four weeks referred to in that sub-section shall be calculated as if the employment had ended on that Monday.

(5) If in a case to which sub-section (3) of this section applies, the provisions of the contract as renewed, or the new contract, as to the capacity and place in which the employee is employed, and as to the other terms and conditions of his employment, differ (wholly or in part) from the corresponding provisions of the previous contract, there shall be a trial period in relation to the contract as renewed, or the new contract (whether or not there has been a previous trial period under this section).

(6) The trial period shall begin with the ending of the employee's employment under the previous contract and end with the expiration of the period of four weeks beginning with the date on which the employee starts work under the contract as renewed, or the new contract, or such longer period as may be agreed in accordance with the next following sub-section for the purpose of retraining the employee for employment under that contract.

(7) Any such agreement shall—

(a) be made between the employer and the employee or his representative before the employee starts work under the contract as renewed or, as the case may be, the new contract;

(b) be in writing;

(c) specify the date of the end of the trial period; and

(d) specify the terms and conditions of employment which will apply in the employee's case after the end of that period.

(8) If during the trial period—

(a) the employee, for whatever reason, terminates the contract, or gives notice to terminate it and the contract is thereafter, in consequence, terminated; or (*b*) the employer, for a reason connected with or arising out of the change to the renewed, or new, employment, terminates the contract, or gives notice to terminate it and the contract is thereafter, in.consequence, terminated.

then, unless the employee's contract of employment is again renewed, or he is again re-engaged under a new contract of employment, in circumstances such that sub-section (3) above again applies, he shall be treated as having been dismissed on the date on which his employment under the previous contract or, if there has been more than one trial period, the original contract ended for the reason for which he was then dismissed or would have been dismissed had the offer (or original offer) of renewed, or new, employment not been made, or, as the case may be, for the reason which resulted in that offer being made."

The sub-sections should be read in conjunction with section 2 (5) of the Redundancy Payments Act 1965 (as amended) which relates to cases where the offer of the new contract or re-engagement has been refused. See p. 209, below.

The principal changes brought about in this connection by the Employment Protection Act 1975, (which changes came into effect on 1st June 1976) are that it is no longer necessary for the offer of renewal, or re-engagement, to be in writing. If the provisions of the new contract as to the capacity and place in which the employee is employed, and as to the other terms and conditions, do not differ from the corresponding provisions of the previous contract and it takes effect immediately, or after an interval of not more than four weeks after the ending of the contract of employment, then the employer is not regarded as having dismissed the employee and there is no trial period. If, on the other hand, the terms differ from the previous contract, (in whole or in part), there is a trial period in relation, to the contract as renewed, or to the new contract. This is so whether or not there has been a previous trial period under these provisions (section 3 (5)). For an employer to take advantage of the trial period rules it is necessary for the renewed, or new, contract to take effect immediately on the ending of the employment or after an interval of not more than four weeks. When calculating this time, if the employment ends on Friday, Saturday or Sunday, the renewal or re-engagement is treated as taking effect immediately if it takes effect on the following Monday, and the interval of four weeks is computed as if the employment had ended on that Monday (section 3 (4)).

The trial period beings with the ending of the employment under the previous contract, and ends with the expiration of the period of four weeks beginning with the date on which the employee starts work under the renewed, or new, contract, unless it was agreed that the period be longer pursuant to the provisions of section 3, sub-section (7). An example of circumstances when it is likely that advantage of the power to lengthen the trial period, is a situation where re-training is necessary for the employee to undertake new tasks. If the employee terminates the contract, for whatever reason, during the trial period, or the employer does so for a reason connected with, or arising out of, the renewed or new employment then, unless the employee's contract is again renewed or he is re-engaged, he is treated as being dismissed.

Although these provisions are new, some assistance may be gained from examining decisions under the original section 3 (2). It was clear that the onus of proof lay on the employer to show that the sub-section applied; *Kitching* v. *Wall, Watson and Taylor* (1967), 2 I.T.R. 464, T, *Ubsdell* v. *Paterson*, [1973] 1 All E.R. 685, N.I.R.C. and *Cartin* v. *Bottley Garage, Ltd.* (1973), 8 I.T.R. 150, N.I.R.C. It is suggested that under the new sub-section the burden of proof will remain with the employer. If the terms differed from those of the previous contract under the sub-section which has now been repealed, it was essential that the offer should be in writing and the important terms had to be made clear to the employee. Notwithstanding the abolition of the requirement that the offer should be in writing all the important terms of the offer should be fully available to the employee, at least by the end of the trial period.

The offer must be a serious and proper one with a realistic estimate of future earnings; *Clarke* v. *Wolsey*, [1975] I.R.L.R. 154, T. Although far less likely to arise in view of the new provisions as to trial period a novel point was dealt with in *Eaton* v. *R.K.B.* (*Furmston*), *Ltd.* (1972), 7 I.T.R. 348, N.I.R.C. The employers moved their operation and offered to provide transport to collect the employee each day from a pick-up point not far from his home. After the move when the employee had accepted the offer the employers told him that they would collect him from a point further from his house. This proposed change was not explained to the employee prior to acceptance of the offer and he terminated his contract. It was *held* that the terms intended were not offered to the employee so that he was unable to apply his mind to it. The decision in the case may have been different if a proper offer had been made on the terms which were intended.

It is likely that the effect of the introduction of a trial period will be that the notion of "conditional acceptance" which had been advanced in *Bond* v. *Harbour and General Works, Ltd.* (1967), 2 I.T.R. 340, T, and *Fouracre* v. *National Coal Board* (1971), 2 I.T.R. 53, D.C., will no longer be utilised. See also *Ubsdell* v. *Paterson* and *Cartin* v. *Bottley Garage, Ltd.* (above). For the renewal or re-engagement to result in the termination of the previous employment not being regarded as dismissal, the offer of renewal or re-engagement must be made before the ending of the contract and it is still safer from the employer's point of view for the offer to be in writing. See for example *Ubsdell* v. *Paterson*, [1973] 1 All E.R. 685, N.I.R.C. when the employers had not discharged the onus of proof that the sub-section's predecessor had been complied with.

If the ex-employee is treated as dismissed after an offer of renewal or re-engagement, the employer may seek to claim that the employee is not entitled to a redundancy payment because of the employee's unreasonable refusal of the offer. See p. 209, below.

"... *renewal* ..." includes extension. Redundancy Payments Act, 1965, section 5 6 (1).

"...*re-engagement*..." is construed as reference to re-engagement by the employer, or an associated employer, see below, (save on the change of ownership of a business). Two employers are treated as associated if one is a company of which the other (directly or indirectly) has control, or if both are companies of which a third person (directly or indirectly) has control.

The provisions of section 3, sub-sections (3)–(8) may apply on the change of ownership of a business when they may assume considerable importance. See p. 216, below.

*Associated employers.* References to re-engagement are construed as references to re-engagement by an employer, or by any associated employer, and to an offer made by an employer as to an offer made by an associated employer; Redundancy

Payments Act 1965, section 48 (1), as substituted by Employment Protection Act 1975, Schedule 16, Part I, paragraph 18. This does not affect the operation of Redundancy Payments Act 1965, section 13, on the change of ownership of a business; Redundancy Payments Act 1965, section 48 (2), as substituted. Two employers are treated as associated if one is a company of which the other (directly or indirectly) has control, or if both are companies of which a third person (directly or indirectly) has control; Redundancy Payments Act 1965, section 48 (4).

*Death of Employer.* See p. 253, below.

## (iii) **Employee anticipating expiry of employer's notice**[1]

If an employer gives notice to the employee and during the period equal to the minimum period of notice (prescribed by statute or the contract) which expires at the time the employers notice actually expires,[2] the employee gives notice in writing to terminate the contract earlier than the date on which the employer's notice is due to expire, the employee is taken as being dismissed, save that the "relevant date" is the date on which the employee's notice expires.[3] The employer can serve a counter-notice in writing, requiring the employee to withdraw his notice and continue employment until the date on which the employer's notice expires, stating that unless he does so the employer will contest any liability to pay the employee a redundancy payment in respect of the termination of the contract of employment.[4] In such circumstances, if on a reference to an industrial tribunal it appears to the tribunal, having regard both to the reasons for which the employee seeks to terminate he employment and those for which the employer requires him to continue in it, to be just and equitable that the employee shall receive the whole or part of any redundancy payment to which he would have been entitled but for the provisions of section 4, then the tribunal may award to the employee the whole or such part of the redundancy payment as the tribunal thinks fit.

---

[1] See Redundancy Payments Act 1965, s. 4.
[2] Called "the obligatory period" and defined in Redundancy Payments Act 1965, s. 4 (5).
[3] Redundancy Payments Act 1965, s. 4 (2) and see precedents, p. 481, below.
[4] *Ibid.*, s. 4 (3).

Decisions relevant to section 4 are: *Armitt* v. *McLauchlan* (1966), 1 I.T.R. 280, T (where the employee was *held* to have left voluntarily. Notice by the employer and subsequent oral notice by the employee before commencement of the obligatory period) and *Meger* v. *Greens Foodfare, Ltd.* (1966), 1 I.T.R. 244, T (majority decision. Oral notice given by the employee and accepted by the employer—application for redundancy payment dismissed). However, situations where section 4 applies must be distinguished from those where the employer acquiesces in an employees request to leave earlier than required by the notice. In *McAlwane* v. *Boughton Estates, Ltd.*, [1973] 2 All E.R. 299, N.I.R.C., an appeal against a decision of a tribunal that an employee had not been dismissed, when after receipt of his employers notice, it had been agreed orally that the employee could leave a week before the notice expired, was successful and the case remitted to the tribunal to determine whether the employee had been unfairly dismissed or dismissed by reason of redundancy.

### (iv) Implied or constructive termination of contract

If any act of an employer, or an event affecting an employer, (including in the case of an individual, his death) operates in accordance with any enactment or rule of law so as to terminate an employment contract then for the purposes of the Redundancy Payments Act 1965, that act or event is treated as a termination of the contract by the employer; Redundancy Payments Act 1965, section 22. The most common examples of this occur on the death of an individual employer, or the compulsory or voluntary winding-up of a company. The special rules applicable on the death of an employer are dealt with at p. 253, below.

If in cases of implied or constructive termination of contract, other than as a result of the employer's death,[1] the employee's contract is not renewed and he is not re-engaged,[2] so as to be treated under the renewal and re-engagement provisions (including those as to trial period) set out above, as not having been dismissed, he is taken as having been dismissed by reason of redundancy, if the circumstances in which his contract was not so renewed, or he was not re-engaged, are wholly or mainly attributable to the grounds specified in the statutory definition of redundancy. It is to be noted that the employee is not automatically entitled to a redundancy payment. He is only so entitled if his contract is not renewed, or he is not re-engaged, in the circumstances amounting to redundancy.[3]

[1] See p. 253, below.

[2] For these purposes, section 1 (2) (a) of the Redundancy Payments Act 1965, insofar as it relates to the employer ceasing or intending to cease to carry on the business, shall be construed as if reference to the employer included a reference to any person to whom in consequence of the act or event in question power to dispose of the business has passed; *ibid.*, section 22 (3). The most frequently encountered examples of this are liquidators and receivers appointed by the Court. See *McEwan* v. *Upper Clyde Shipbuilders, Ltd. (in liquidation)* (1972), 7 I.T.R. 296, T, when the liquidator of a shipbuilding company was *held* to have renewed the employee's contract in circumstances falling within section 3. Contrast *Golding and Howard* v. *Fire, Auto and Marine Insurance Co. Ltd., (in liquidation)* (1968), I.T.R. 372, T. See also *British Airports Authority* v. *Fenerty* (1976), 11 I.T.R. 84, Q.B.D., where the court found that when an airport policeman was transferred with his consent to the Metropolitan Police Force pursuant to a statutory instrument the termination of his contract with the Authority did not fall within the Redundancy Payments Act 1965, s. 22 (1). The termination flowed from the statutory instrument and the employee's consent.

[3] For instance in *Narang* v. *Trustees of J. Hodge (deceased)* (1969), 4 I.T.R. 81, T, where the employee refused to continue to work for the deceased employer's widow after the death of the employer and was *held* not entitled to a redundancy payment.

## (v) Frustration

If the contract of employment is frustrated there can be no dismissal unless Redundancy Payments Act 1965, s. 22 applies, see p. 203, above. Reference should be made to p. 129, above, and to *Marshall* v. *Harland and Wolff, Ltd. (No. 2)* (1972), 7 I.T.R. 150, N.I.R.C. In that case an employee had been off work for 18 months sick when the employers decided to close down their works. The employee thought he might be able to work in the near future. On the facts it was *held* that the employee was entitled to a redundancy payment. Contrast *Scarr* v. *F. W. Goodyear & Son, Ltd.,* [1975] I.R.L.R. 166, T, where considerable absences through illness were *held* to frustrate the contract.

The burden of proof in frustration lies on the employers. See *Farmer* v. *Willow Dye Works, Ltd.* (1972), 7 I.T.R. 226, N.I.R.C. (employee absent for four months, had been similar absences previously and further serious operation in prospect. The employers retained the employee's cards. *Held* not frustrated), and *Puttick* v. *John Wright & Sons (Blackwell), Ltd.* (1972), 7 I.T.R. 438, N.I.R.C. (no frustration) but see *Harrison* v. *George Wimpey & Co., Ltd.* (1972), 7 I.T.R. 188, N.I.R.C., when the judgment of the National Industrial Relations Court included the statement, "where an employee conducts himself as to lead a reasonable employer to believe that the employee has terminated the contract, the contract is then terminated". It continued:

> "Before we part with this matter we would like to say a word about the industrial relations aspects of the case. We wish to affirm that it is an employee's duty, when he is away sick, to keep his employer fully informed as to the progress he is making towards recovery, in order that the employer may know that his employee intends to return for further work. Equally we regard it as very important that an employer, who is minded to treat the employment as having come to an end for any reason, should communicate so far as he can with the employee, stating his intentions. In that way a great deal of misunderstanding can be avoided, as indeed it might conceivably have been avoided in this case. But that it not a matter which goes directly to the merits of this appeal; it is a matter of general industrial relations."

An example of a case where close contact was maintained between the parties during the employee's absence is *Hebden v. Forsey & Son* (1973), 8 I.T.R. 656. N.I.R.C., when an absence of 18 months was *held* not to amount to frustration. See also *Scarr v. F. W. Goodyear & Sons, Ltd.*, [1975] I.R.L.R. 166, T, where an absence of about three years after a previous absence was found to have frustrated the employment contract.

The appointment of a receiver out of court who is an agent of the company does not of itself determine current service contracts; *Re Mack Trucks (Britain), Ltd.*, [1967] 1 All E.R. 977; [1967] 1 W.L.R. 780, Ch.D., applying *Re Foster Clark Ltd.'s Indenture Trusts, Loveland v. Horscroft*, [1966] 1 All E.R. 43, Ch.D. See also *Deaway Trading, Ltd. v. Calverley*, [1973] 3 All E.R. 776, N.I.R.C., where a receiver and manager of a company who was appointed by the debenture holders was an agent of the company, and later a liquidator was appointed in a creditors voluntary winding up. The business was then sold and the court *held* that there was continuity.

### (vi) Strikes during period of employer's notice[1]

Section 40 of the Redundancy Payments Act 1965, provides a safeguard for an employer if the employee takes part in a strike during the period of his notice given on dismissal by reason of redundancy. If during the period of notice the employee strikes, the employer may serve on him a written notice ("a notice of extension")[2] requesting him to agree to extend the employment contract beyond the time of expiry of the dismissal notice by an additional period comprising as many available days as the number of working days lost by striking.[3] The notice of extension should be served prior to the expiry of the dismissal notice. The additional period is called "the proposed period of extension". It is immaterial whether there has been one or more strikes during the period of notice; a single notice of extension is sufficient.[4] The notice of extension should indicate the employer's reasons for the request and should state that unless, either the employee complies with the request, or the employer is satisfied that in consequence of sickness, injury or otherwise the employee is unable to comply with it, or that notwithstanding that he is able to comply with it in the circumstances it is reasonable for him not to do so, then the employer will contest any liability to a redundancy payment in respect of the dismissal.[2] To comply the employee must attend at his proper or usual place of work on each of the days during the proposed period of extension and be ready and willing to work.[5] Signifying his agreement to the request in any other way is not good enough within the technical provisions of the section, although it would be taken into account by a tribunal in the proceedings mentioned below.

[1] For the situation when the employee is guilty of misconduct see p. 207.
[2] Redundancy Payments Act 1965, s. 40 (1).
[3] See specimen notice at p. 484, below.
[4] Redundancy Payments Act 1965, s. 40 (8).
[5] Contracts of Employment Act 1972, s. 2 and Sch. 2 of that Act apply accordingly as if the period of notice required under s. 1 of that Act were extended to a corresponding extent, *ibid.*, s. 40 (4).

If the employee does not comply with the request, he is not entitled to a redundancy payment in respect of that dismissal in circumstances where his employer does not agree to pay it and should he wish to persist with his claim he must apply to the tribunal.[1] When a notice of extension has been served and it appears to the tribunal that the employee has not complied with the request, and the employer has not agreed to pay a redundancy payment in respect of the dismissal in question but that the employee was unable to comply with the request, or it was

## Dismissal

reasonable for him not to comply with it,[2] the tribunal may determine that the employer is liable to pay to the employee the whole of the redundancy payment which would otherwise be due, or such part of it as the tribunal thinks fit.[3]

[1] Redundancy Payments Act 1965, s. 40 (5).

[2] In circumstances were in consequence of sickness, injury or otherwise he is unable to comply with it, (or that notwithstanding that he is able to comply with it) in the circumstances it is reasonable for him not to do so; see Redundancy Payments Act 1965, s. 40 (2) (b).

[3] Ibid., s. 40 (6). For a case which shows that taking part in a strike can be misconduct notwithstanding ibid., s. 10 (1), see Simmonds v. Hoover, Ltd., (1976) Times, 20th July, E.A.T.

### (vii) Misconduct during notice

Where after he has been given notice by his employer to terminate his contract, at any time within the obligatory period[1] of the employer's notice, or where the employee has given notice to the employer under the provisions as to lay-off or short-time, an employee's contract is terminated by his employer who is entitled to terminate it without notice by reason of the employee's conduct, otherwise than taking part in a strike,[2] either without notice, or by giving shorter notice than that which in the absence of such conduct the employer would be required to give to terminate the contract, or by giving notice which includes, or is accompanied by, a statement in writing that the employer would by reason of the employee's conduct be entitled to terminate the contract without notice, section 10 of the Redundancy Payments Act 1965 has to be considered.[3] Under sub-section (3) of that section, if on a reference to a tribunal it appears to the tribunal, in the circumstances of the case to be just and equitable that the employee should receive the whole, or part, of any redundancy payment to which he would have been entitled apart from the provisions of section 2 (2), the tribunal should determine that the employer is liable to pay to the employee, the whole of the redundancy payment, or such part of it, as the tribunal thinks fit.[3]

[1] As defined in Redundancy Payments Act 1965, s. 4 (5). If the actual notice is the minimum required by statute or contract, (whichever is the longer), the actual period of notice, in any other case that period which being equal to that minimum period expires at the time when the employer's notice expires.

[2] But see Simmonds v. Hoover, Ltd., (1976). Times, 20th July, E.A.T., where

it was held that the employers were entitled at common law to terminate the contract of a man on strike without notice and in accordance with Redundancy Payments Act 1965, s. 2 (2), no redundancy payment was payable.

³ Redundancy Payments Act 1965, s. 10 (3). In *Cairns* v. *Burnside Shoe Repairs* (1967), 2 I.T.R. 75, T, two-thirds of the redundancy payment was paid; in *Jarmain* v. *Pollard, Son & Co., Ltd.* (1967), 2 I.T.R. 406, T, £90 out of £180 was awarded—larceny after seven years service with the company. In *Clark* v. *E. N. Heath & Co., Ltd.* (1967), 2 I.T.R. 42, T, the whole of the redundancy payment was paid. See also *ibid.*, s. 10 (1).

## (viii) Relevant date

Section 3, sub-sections (9) and (10)¹ define "relevant date"² in relation to dismissal. They are as follows:

"(9) Subject to the next following sub-section and to the next following section, in this Part of this Act, 'the relevant date', in relation to the dismissal of an employee—

(a) where his contract of employment is terminated by notice, whether given by his employer or by the employee, means the date on which that notice expires;

(b) where his contract of employment is terminated without notice, means the date on which the termination takes effect;

(c) where he is employed under a contract for a fixed term and that term expires as mentioned in sub-section (2) (b) of this section, means the date on which that term expires; and

(d) where he is treated, by virtue of sub-section (8) of this section, as having been dismissed on the termination of his employment under a previous contract, means—

(i) for the purposes of section 21 of this Act, the date which is the relevant date as defined by paragraph (a), (b) or (c) of this sub-section in relation to the renewed, or new, contract, or, where there has been more than one trial period, the last such contract; and

(ii) for any other purpose, the date which is the relevant date as defined by paragraph (a), (b) or (c) of this sub-section in relation to the previous contract, or, where there has been more than one trial period, the original contract.

(10) Where the notice required to be given by an employer to terminate a contract of employment by section 1 (1) of the Contracts of Employment Act 1972 (minimum period of

notice) would, if duly given when notice of termination was given by the employer, or (where no notice was given) when the contract of employment was terminated by the employer, expire on a date later than the relevant date as defined by the last preceding sub-section, then for the purposes of section 8 (1) of, and paragraphs 1 (1) and 5 (7) of Schedule 1 to, this Act, that later date shall be treated as the relevant date in relation to the dismissal."

[1] Inserted by Employment Protection Act 1975, Sch. 16, Part I, para 3.
[2] Relevant date is used in calculating periods of continuous employment. See p. 226, below. When calculating redundancy payments the relevant date is construed as the Saturday of the week in which it falls; Redundancy Payments Act 1965, Sch. 1, paras. 8 and 9.

The provisions of sub-section (10), which was inserted by the Employment Protection Act 1975, are very important. When less than the period of notice required to be given by section 1 (1) of the Contracts of Employment Act 1972, or no notice, has been given on termination by the employer, the date on which the minimum notice, if it had been given would have expired is the relevant date for the purpose of ascertaining if the employee has been employed for the requisite period and the multiplier in calculating a redundancy payment.

## REFUSAL OF OFFER OF RENEWAL OR RE-ENGAGEMENT

An employee who has been dismissed within the meaning of the Redundancy Payments Act 1965 but who unreasonably refuses an offer made by the employer of a contract on the same terms or an offer of some other suitable employment subject to the provisions for a trial period, is not entitled to a redundancy payment.

Section 2, sub-sections (3) to (6) of the Redundancy Payments Act 1965 (as substituted by the Employment Protection Act 1975) provides as follows:

"(3) If an employer makes an employee an offer (whether in writing or not) before the ending of his employment under the previous contract to renew his contract of employment, or to re-engage him under a new contract of employment, so that the renewal or re-engagement would take effect either immediately on the ending of his employment under the previous contract or after an interval of not more than four weeks thereafter the provisions of sub-sections (5) and (6) of this section shall have effect

(4) For the purposes of the application of the last preceding sub-section to a contract under which the employment ends on a Friday, Saturday or Sunday—

(a) the renewal or re-engagement shall be treated as taking effect immediately on the ending of the employment under the previous contract if it takes effect on or before the next Monday after that Friday, Saturday or Sunday; and

(b) the interval of four weeks shall be calculated as if the employment had ended on that Monday.

(5) If an employer makes an employee such an offer as is referred to in sub-section (3) of this section and either—

(a) the provisions of the contract as renewed, or of the new contract, as to the capacity and place in which he would be employed, and as to the other terms and conditions of his employment, would not differ from the corresponding provisions of the previous contract; or

(b) the first mentioned provisions would differ (wholly or in part) from those corresponding provisions, but the offer constitutes an offer of suitable employment in relation to the employee;

and in either case the employee unreasonably refuses that offer, he shall not be entitled to a redundancy payment by reason of his dismissal.

(6) If an employee's contract of employment is renewed, or he is re-engaged under a new contract of employment, in pursuance of such an offer as is referred to in sub-section (3) of this section, and the provisions of the contract as renewed, or of the new contract, as to the capacity and place in which he is employed, and as to the other terms and conditions of his employment, differ (wholly or in part) from the corresponding provisions of the previous contract but the employment is suitable in relation to the employee, and during the trial period referred to in section 3 of this Act the employee unreasonably terminates the contract, or unreason-

ably gives notice to terminate it and the contract is thereafter, in consequence, terminated, he shall not be entitled to a redundancy payment by reason of his dismissal from employment under the previous contract."

[1] The new sub-sections were substituted for section 2, sub-sections (3) and (4) with effect from 1st June 1976. Previously the section 2, sub-sections (3) and (4) had read:

"(3) An employee shall not be entitled to a redundancy payment by reason of dismissal if before the relevant date the employer has offered to renew his contract of employment, or to re-engage him under a new contract, so that—

(a) the provisions of the contract as renewed, or of the new contract, as the case may be, as to the capacity and place in which he would be employed, and as to the other terms and conditions of his employment, would not differ from the corresponding provisions of the contract as in force immediately before his dismissal, and

(b) the renewal or re-engagement would take effect on or before the relevant date,

and the employee has unreasonably refused that offer.

(4) An employee shall not be entitled to a redundancy payment by reason of dismissal if before the relevant date the employer has made to him an offer in writing to renew his contract of employment, or to re-engage him under a new contract, so that in accordance with the particulars specified in the offer the provisions of the contract as renewed or of the new contract, as the case may be, as to the capacity and place in which he would be employed, and as to the other terms and conditions of his employment, would differ (wholly or in part) from he corresponding provisions of the contract as in force immediately before his dismissal, but—

(a) the offer constitutes an offer of suitable employment in relation to the employee, and

(b) the renewal or re-engagement would take effect on or before the relevant date or not later than four weeks after that date,

and the employee has unreasonably refused that offer."

Except in cases where there is a change in ownership of a business, references in Part I of the Redundancy Payments Act 1965 (that Part dealing with entitlement to redundancy payments) to re-engagement by the employer are construed as references to re-engagement by the employer or any associated employer. Similarly, references to offers made by the employer are construed as including references to offers made by associated employers.[1] Any two employers are treated as associated if one is a company of which the other (directly or indirectly) has control, or if both are companies of which a third person (directly or indirectly) has control.[2]

[1] Redundancy Payment Act 1965, s. 48 (1) and (2), as substituted by Employment Protection Act 1975, Sch. 16, Part 1, para. 18. See p. 197, above
[2] Redundancy payments Act 1965, s. 48 (4).

There is provision for the businesses of associated employers to be considered as one business in some situations. When an employee is dismissed but neither of the conditions specified in sub-sections (*a*) and (*b*) of section 1 (2)[1] of the Redundancy Payments Act 1965 is fulfilled but one or other of those conditions would be satisfied if the business of the employer together with the business of his associated employer were treated as one business, then the condition in the definition of redundancy is taken as being satisfied.

[1] Definition of redundancy, see p. 174, above.

"... *before the ending of his employment* ...". It is essential that the offer to renew or re-engage is made before the ending of the previous contract of employment. The amended section no longer requires the offer to be in writing and difficult questions of proof are likely to arise where a written offer is not made. *Nuttall* v. *Redfern* (1972), 7 I.T.R. 409, T (the employer was selling her business and dismissed the employee who expected the employment to end on 26th January. Completion of the sale did not take place on that day and it was mutually agreed to extend the time and the offer upon which it was ought to rely was made during the extended period. *Held* the provisions of the former sub-section were complied with). *Smith* v. *Brown Bayley Steels, Ltd.* (1973), 8 I.T.R. 606, T. (written offers of employment were posted to the employees before the determination of their contracts of employment but did not arrive until after the dismissal had taken effect. *Held* the offer was not effective until it was communicated to the offeree). See also *Craney* v. *Wm. Agnew, Ltd.* (1966), 1 I.T.R. 518, T, and *Baker* v. *Gill* (1971), 6 I.T.R. 61, D.C. (a case on the former section 3 (2) (*b*).

"...*renew* ...". Renewal as defined in Redundancy Payments Act 1965, section 56 (1) includes extension.

*Change of ownership of business.* Section 2, sub-sections (3) to

(5) regularly have to be considered on the change of ownership of a business. See p.    , below. On the change of ownership of a business when the new owner offers to renew the employee's contract of employment or to re-engage him, the offer is not treated as one whereby the provisions of his renewed contract, or of the new contract, differ from the corresponding provisions of the old contract in force immediately before the dismissal, by reason only that the new owner would be substituted for the previous owner as the employer and no account is taken of that substitution in determining whether the refusal of the offer was unreasonable. Section 13 (4), *ibid.*, (as amended).

*Onus of proof:* The burden of proof is on the employer to establish that he offered suitable employment in relation to the employee and that the employee unreasonably refused that offer. It is also for the employer to show that the offer would take effect within the time limits laid down and that the other technical requirements would be complied with. This was clearly established in *Jones* v. *Aston Cabinet Co., Ltd.* (1973) I.T.R. 356, N.I.R.C.

*Offer of employment with another employer.* An employer who procures this is not making an offer of alternative employment within the terms of the sub-section; see *Farquharson* v. *Ross* (1966), 1 I.T.R. 335, T, and *Scott* v. *Salisbury and Chandler* (1970), 5 I.T.R. 22, T, where a tribunal held that on a dissolution of partnership an offer by one partner on his own account was not an offer falling within the provisions of the forerunner of the present sub-section. What if no offer of renewal or re-engagement is made because the employee has indicated that he is not willing to accept any such offer? In *Simpson* v. *Dickinson* (1973), 8 I.T.R. 40, N.I.R.C., it was conceded that the exclusion provided by section 2 could not be relied upon by the employer. Even in circumstances where the employer knows that the employee will refuse it is necessary for the employer to make the offer. In *Simpson's* case the principle of estoppel did not assist the employer notwithstanding that the employee had stated in the clearest of terms that she did not wish to be re-engaged.

*Sub-section (5) (a).* When the provisions of the contract as renewed or the new contract do not differ from the corresponding provisions of the previous contract the question of suitability does not arise, the only issue for the industrial tribunal to determine is whether the employee unreasonably refused the offer.

*Sub-section* (5) (b). In *Carron* v. *Robinson* (1967), 2 I.T.R. 484, C.S. The Court of Session in considering the previous sub-section held that the tribunal must first decide whether the employment is suitable before considering if the employee was unreasonable to refuse the offer. This suggestion was canvassed in *Morganite Crucible Ltd.* v. *Street*, [1972] 2 All E.R. 411; [1972] I W.L.R. 918, N.I.R.C., but the National Industrial Relations Court did not wish to express any opinion on the point.

"... *offer of suitable employment* ...". This is a question of fact and degree for the industral tribunal to decide, see *Collier* v. *Smith's Dock Co., Ltd.* (1969), 4 I.T.R. 338, D.C., and *Hitchcock* v. *St. Anne's Hosiery Co., Ltd.* (1971), 6 I.T.R. 98, D.C., being looked at in relation to the employee in question. In *Taylor* v. *Kent County Council*, [1969] 2 All E.R. 1080; [1969] 3 W.L.R. 156, D.C. Lord PARKER, C.J. dealing with section 2 as originally enacted said:

> "... it does seem to me that by the words 'suitable employment', suitability means employment which is substantially equivalent to the employment which has ceased. Section 2 (3) which I read at the beginning is dealing with the case where the fundamental terms are the same, and then no offer in writing is needed, but when they differ, then it has to be put in writing and must be suitable. I, for my part, think that what is meant by 'suitable' in relation to the employee means conditions of employment which are reasonably equivalent to those under the previous employment, not the same, because then sub-section (3) would apply, but it does not seem to me that, by 'suitable employment', is meant employment of an entirely different nature but in respect of which the salary is going to be the same."

See also *Goode and Cooper, Ltd.* v. *Thompson*, [1974] I.R.L.R. 111, N.I.R.C., where employment as a foreman was not suitable for a former general manager even though no reduction in salary. Suitability is to be considered in the light of facts known at the time when the offer was made; *Smith* v. *Spicers Ltd.* (1966), I I.T.R. 470, T. Other cases which may be referred to for general guidance include *Johnston* v. *St. Cuthbert's Co-operatives Association Ltd.* (1969), 4 I.T.R. 137, C.S. and *Eltringham* v. *Sunderland Co-operative Society, Ltd.* (1971), 6 I.T.R. 121, D.C.

## Refusal of offer of renewal or re-engagement

"... *unreasonably refused that offer*...". In *Pilkington* v. *Pickstone* (1966), 1 I.T.R. 363, T, a tribunal dismissing an employee's application gave the following reasons which are a useful statement of the principles even today "the applicant may have acted and decided 'reasonably' in what he believed to be his own personal interests, and may have obtained certain advantages from employment (which he had obtained)..., but we hold that the reasonableness or otherwise of his refusal must for the purposes of section 2 of the Act be considered as between the employer (or his successor) and the employee, or in relation to special circumstances affecting the employee personally. We do not consider that a personal preference for a complete change of employment is a circumstance which (however 'reasonable' from the employee's own standpoint) is intended by the Act to be a ground for such a claim for compensation under the statute".

In *Freer* v. *Kayser Bondor, Ltd.* (1967), 2 I.T.R. 4, T, the reason for redundancy was considered to be relevant to the question of reasonableness.

## Decisions under section 2 (3) and (4) as originally enacted

(1) *Unreasonable rejection of employer's offer*

*Johnston* v. *St. Cuthbert's Co-operative Association, Ltd.* (1969), 4 I.T.R. 137, C.S. (office worker offered post on same terms save that office at Fountainbridge, Edinburgh and not Portobello).

*Hitchcock* v. *St. Ann's Hosiery Co., Ltd.* (1971), 6 I.T.R. 98, D.C. (offered work at Newark instead of Nottingham, other terms comparable, employers would pay travelling expenses for nine months and alter shifts to suit travelling arrangements).

*Collier* v. *Smith's Dock Co., Ltd.* (1969), 4 I.T.R. 338, D.C. (chargehand shipwright transferred to other dockyard as shipwright).

*Eltringham* v. *Sunderland Co-operative Society, Ltd.* (1971), 6 I.T.R. 121, D.C. (branch manager of shop offered job as assistant manager with prospects—status "is not the only consideration").

*Morganite Crucible Ltd.* v. *Street*, [1972] 2 All E.R. 411; [1972] 1 W.L.R. 918, N.I.R.C. (one reason given by clerk/typist for refusal to accept an offer of alternative employment was that she thought that the new employment would only last between 12 to 18 months. Sir JOHN DONALDSON (at p. 413) said, "In our judgment save in exceptional cases, if the offer is of regular employment, the time which it is anticipated that the employment will last is irrelevant either under the heading of 'suitability' or 'reasonableness'. There may be exceptional cases which would qualify the general rule, but we are satisfied that that should be the general rule." If the offer is of "regular" (as opposed to "temporary") employment the length of time which it is likely to last is not to be taken into account in assessing either suitability or reasonableness.

*(2) Employment not suitable and/or reasonably rejected by employee*

*Taylor* v. *Kent County Council* (1969), I.T.R. 294, D.C. (on amalgamation of schools a headmaster with 10 years experience offered post in pool of mobile staff. *Held* unsuitable).

*Lee* v. *British Wagon Co., Ltd.* (1970) I.T.R. 192, D.C. (branch manager of finance company offered post as new business representative).

*Allied Ironfounders, Ltd.* v. *Macken* (1971), I.T.R. 109, D.C. (refused double shift work because he had to attend invalid wife).

*Universal Fisher Engineering, Ltd.* v. *Stratton* (1972), 7 I.T.R. 66, N.I.R.C. (shift worker working four nights per week offered job on different work five nights per week. *Held* suitable employment but reasonably refused).

*E. & J. Davis Transport, Ltd.* v. *Chataway* (1972), 7 I.T.R. 361, N.I.R.C. (offer made to all employees in context of an industrial dispute. *Held* not suitable offer for all employees).

*Harris* v. *Turner & Sons (Joinery), Ltd.* (1973), 8 I.T.R. 29, N.I.R.C. (joiner who had been promoted to "apprentice instructor" paid at higher rate than other joiners and "on the staff", offered job as joiner. *Held* not suitable. Regard should be had to the employee's status and history) but contrast *Kane* v. *Raine & Co., Ltd.*, [1974] 1 C.R. 300, N.I.R.C., where a slight change of status did not render the new employment unsuitable.

*Thomas Wragg & Son, Ltd.* v. *Wood*, [1976] I.C.R. 313, E.A.T. (after notice was given by his employers an employee obtained other employment to begin immediately the notice expired. Offer of alternative employment not made until the day before the notice was due to expire).

## CHANGE OF OWNERSHIP OF BUSINESS

The Redundancy Payments Act 1965, (as amended) contains

special rules which have effect when a change occurs in the ownership of a business. Section 13 (1) provides:

"13 (1) The provisions of this section shall have effect where—

(a) a change occurs (whether by virtue of a sale or other disposition or by operation of law) in the ownership of a business for the purposes of which a person is employed, or of a part of such a business, and

(b) in connection with that change the person by whom the employee is employed immediately before the change occurs (in this section referred to as "the previous owner") terminates the employee's contract of employment, whether by notice or without notice."

**Meaning of "change of ownership"[1]**

It will be seen that the provisions as to change of ownership of a business overlap with the rules governing continuity of employment.[1] The Contracts of Employment Act 1972, Schedule 1, paragraph 9 (2) contains provisions which apply if "... a trade or business ... is transferred from one person to another ..." rather than on the change of ownership of a business. This paragraph first appeared as paragraph 10 (2) of Schedule 1 of the Contracts of Employment Act 1963, and doubts were expressed at one time as to whether the two expressions differed. However, these were allayed in *Lloyd* v. *Brassey*, [1969] 2 Q.B. 98; [1969] 1 All E.R. 382, C.A. when it was made clear that they had the same meaning, (see also the earlier decision of the Divisional Court in *Dallow Industrial Properties, Ltd.* v. *Else*, [1967] 2 Q.B. 449; [1967] 2 All E.R. 30, D.C. Difficulty has frequently been experienced in deciding whether or not a business has been transferred when there has been no assignment of good-will.

[1] See p. 240, below.

In *Lloyd* v. *Brassey*, above, the employee was a farm worker. The purchaser of farm land also bought some of the live and dead stock at the farm auction but he did not pay for, or take an assignment of, the good-will of the farming business. The purchaser engaged Mr. Lloyd who had been employed by the vendor on slightly better terms than those that he had previously enjoyed. It was *held* that there was a change in ownership of the farming business and that there was a continuity of employment.

Lord DENNING, M.R. said (at p. 384):

"If the new owner takes over the business as a going concern
—so that the business remains the same business but in different
hands—and the employee keeps the same job with the new
owner then he is not entitled to redundancy payment. His
period is deemed to continue without a break in the same
job: so that, if he is afterwards dismissed by the new owner for
redundancy, his payment is calculated on the whole period in
that job."

He continued (at p. 385):

"In my opinion the business of farming consists of cultivating
the land, ploughing, sowing, grazing, keeping cows, making
hay, and so forth. The land itself is the essence of the business;
and when the land, together with the buildings, is sold, the
business is necessarily sold with it. It remains the same
business but it changes hands. When the land is occupied by
a tenant farmer who goes out, and a new tenant farmer
comes in, there is again a change in ownership of the business,
namely, the business of farming that particular land. As a rule
the outgoing farmer sells his animals and equipment separately
by auction. The incoming farmer does not take them all
over, lock, stock and barrel. He buys those he wants and
not the others. But that makes no difference. The live stock
and dead stock are only ancillary to the business of the farm.
They are not the essence of it. The essence is the land,
together with the buildings."

However, it is clear that the mere transfer of physical assets
is not enough. In *Woodhouse and Staton* v. *Peter Brotherhood, Ltd*
(1972), 7 I.T.R. 110, C.A., two long-serving employees worked
for a company which manufactured diesel engines and decided to
move elsewhere. It sold the factory to Peter Brotherhood
Limited ("Brotherhoods"). Brotherhoods used the factory for
manufacture of their own (differing) products but employed all
the employees previously employed by the former employers. In
due course Brotherhoods dismissed the employees by reason of
redundancy and the question for the court to decide was whether
the employees could include service with their former employers
in computing the redundancy payment. In delivering his judgment
in the Court of Appeal, DENNING, M.R. referred to the passage

at p. 384 in his judgment in *Lloyd* v. *Brassey*, (set out above) and continued:

"To that passage I would now add this: if the new owner does *not* take over the business as a going concern, but only takes over the physical assets—using them in a *different* business —then the workman is entitled to redundancy payment from the outgoing owner. He may be taken on by the new owner straight away and thus loses no wages, but nevertheless he is entitled to redundancy payment from the outgoing owner. It is, in a real sense, compensation for long service with that owner. In due course, if he serves more than two years with the new owner, and is afterwards dismissed by the new owner for redundancy, he will be entitled to redundancy payment from the new owner, calculated on his length of service with him."

The circumstances were very different from the Lloyd's case, there the business both before and after the change was one of farming, whilst the business carried on at the factory in Brotherhoods' case had changed. It was formerly the manufacture of diesel engines but became the manufacture of spinning machines etc. *Crompton* v. *Truly Fair (International), Ltd.* (1975), 10 I.T.R. 114, D.C., was a somewhat similar case where a factory used for the production of children's clothes was later used for the manufacture of trousers. The Queen's Bench Division *held* that there was no change in the ownership of the business.

There may be a transfer of a separate and self-contained part of a larger business.

In *McLeod* v. *John Rostron & Sons, Ltd.* (1972), 7 I.T.R. 144, N.I.R.C., a paper manufacturer ran a fleet of eighty vehicles. The transport division was in due course sold to a separate contractor. The contractor engaged the applicant who was formerly a driver with the paper manufacturer. Delivering the decision of the court, Sir JOHN DONALDSON said (at p. 147):

"In our judgment, whether or not a particular transaction is properly described as a change in ownership of a separate, self-contained part of a business is a question of fact and of scale. We say "of scale" because as was pointed out during the course of argument, practical problems arise on the application of s. 13 (1) (*a*) to, for example, the firm with a small cleaning department which decides to go over to contract cleaning and the small shop with one or two delivery vans which sells its vans to road carriers, the employees in each case being taken on by the new providers of the services. In our judgment, where there is a single employee or only two or three employees who are so taken over, it is the fact that there are so few of them which usually makes it impossible to say that what is transferred is a separate and self-contained part of a business. But here, of course, we are dealing with a very much larger unit, of some 80 vehicles and a commensurate number of employees."

It was held that the continuity was not broken. This case should be contrasted with *Newlin Oil Co., Ltd.* v. *Trafford* (1974), 9 I.T.R. 324, N.I.R.C., when on an alteration of marketing arrangements for oil distribution 40% of the customers of one employer were transferred to another. The employee was then employed by the company to which the transfer was made. *Held* not a change of ownership of a business and *Port Talbot Engineering Co., Ltd.* v. *Passmore*, [1975] I.C.R. 234, D.C., where it was *held* that there was no continuity of employment when employees were employed by successive employers who succeeded in competitive tenders for the same work.

Examples where a change of ownership of a business was found to have taken place are:

*G. D. Ault (Isle of Wight), Ltd.* v. *Gregory* (1967), 2 I.T.R. 301, D.C. (transfer of part of transferor's business which itself formed a separate and self-contained unit of operation).

*Robinson* v. *Bournemouth Corporation* (1970), 5 I.T.R. 100, T (transfer of surveying department of Bournemouth College of Technology to Portsmouth College of Technology).

*Baker* v. *Gill* (1971), 6 I.T.R. 61, D.C. (adjoining landowner purchased farm. *Held:* transfer of business but section 3 (2) not complied with).

*Rose* v. *Henry Trickett & Son, Ltd.* (1971), 6 I.T.R. 116, D.C. (transfer of building and works contractors business by respondents who also owned haulage contractors business).

*Watts, Watts & Co., Ltd.* v. *Steeley* (1968), 3 I.T.R. 363, D.C. (transfer of all shipowning company's vessels).

*Winter* v. *Deepsaun Garages, Ltd.* (1969), 4 I.T.R. 162, T (applicant employed at same petrol station by several employers.

*Held*: that there was continuity of employment).

## Effect of change of ownership of business

Having established that there has been a change in ownership of a business and that in connection with the change the employer terminates the contract of employment of the employee, Redundancy Payments Act 1975, section 13, sub-sections (2)–(6)[1] have to be considered. They are as follows:

"(2) If, by agreement with the employee, the person who immediately after the change occurs is the owner of the business or of the part of the business in question, as the case may be (in this section referred to as "the new owner") renews the employee's contract of employment (with the substitution of the new owner for the previous owner) or re-engages him under a new contract of employment, [sub-sections (3) to (10) of section 3] of this Act shall have effect as if the renewal or re-engagement had been a renewal or re-engagement by the previous owner (without any substitution of the new owner for the previous owner).

(3) If the new owner offers to renew the employee's contract of employment (with the substitution of the new owner for the previous owner) or to re-engage him under a new contract of employment, [sub-sections (3) to (6) of section 2 of this Act shall have effect, subject to the next following sub-section, in relation to that offer as they would have had effect in relation to the like offer made by the previous owner].

(4) For the purposes of the operation, in accordance with the last preceding sub-section, of [sub-sections (3) to (6)] of section 2 of this Act in relation to an offer made by the new owner,—

(*a*) the offer shall not be treated as one whereby the provisions of the contract as renewed, or of the new contract, as the case may be would differ from the corresponding provisions of the contract as in force immediately before the dismissal by reason only that the new owner would be substituted for the previous owner as the employer, and

(*b*) no account shall be taken of that substitution in determining whether the refusal of the offer was unreasonable, [or, as the case may be, whether the employee acted reasonably in terminating the renewed, or new, employment during the trial period referred to in section 3 of this Act].

(5) The preceding provisions of this section shall have effect (subject to the necessary modifications) in relation to a case where—

(a) the person by whom a business, or part of a business, is owned immediately before a change is one of the persons by whom (whether as partners, trustees or otherwise) it is owned immediately after the change, or

(b) the persons by whom a business, or part of a business, is owned immediately before a change (whether as partners, trustees or otherwise) include the person by whom, or include one or more of the persons by whom, it is owned immediately after the change,

as those provisions have effect where the previous owner and the new owner are wholly different persons.

(6) Nothing in this section shall be construed as requiring any variation of a contract of employment by agreement between the parties to be treated as constituting a termination of the contract."

[1] The sub-sections are shown as amended. The words in square brackets were inserted by the Employment Protection Act 1975. Since no authorities are quoted with regard to the sub-sections they are not shown as originally enacted.

Thus if there has been a transfer of the business the provisions dealing with re-engagement and renewal of the employee's contract may apply and the offer is treated as if being one of renewal or re-engagement within those sections.[1] When there is any doubt whether a business has changed hands and the employee is employed by the purchaser of assets, the employee should always claim a redundancy payment from his former employer as soon as possible to protect his interests.

[1] See discussion of Redundancy Payments Act 1965, s. 2 at p. 209, and s. 3 at p. 197, above.

There are special provisions which are applicable on the death of the employer.[1]

[1] See p. 253, below.

Section 13 A of the Redundancy Payments Act 1965 (which

is added to that Act by Employment Protection Act 1975, section 120 (2), applies the provisions of section 13 to a transfer of functions from a person not acting on behalf of the Crown to a Minister of the Crown, government department or any other officer or body exercising functions on behalf of the Crown as it applies to a transfer of a business. Sections 2 (4) to (6) and 3 (3) to (10) apply as if the reference in them to employment under a contract of employment was to employment otherwise than under a contract of employment.

## LAY-OFF AND SHORT-TIME

Under section 6 of the Redundancy Payments Act 1965, an employee is entitled to a redundancy payment if, after lay-off or short-time lasting four or more consecutive weeks, or a total of six or more weeks (of which not more than three were consecutive) in any thirteen weeks, he leaves after giving the proper notice. This "notice of intention to claim" which must be in writing, has to be given four weeks or less after the end of the period of lay-off or short-time or of the 13 week period.[1] When an employee has given notice of his intention to claim he is not entitled to a redundancy payment in pursuance of the notice unless he terminates his employment by a week's notice[2] which is given before the end of the period allowed for this purpose.[3] If he is obliged by his contract to give more than a week's notice to terminate the employment then the reference to a week's notice is construed as being to the minimum period of notice he is required to give to bring his employment to an end. The employee is not entitled to a redundancy payment by virtue of his notice of intention to claim, if the employer dismisses him, (but this is without prejudice to the usual rules as to redundancy payments which may apply to the dismissal). Within seven days after service of the notice of intention to claim the employer can serve on the employee a notice in writing "the counter-notice" contesting liability to pay a redundancy payment in pursuance of the notice of intention to claim, stating that on the date of the notice of intention to claim it was reasonably expected that the employee, (if he continued to be employed by the same employer) would, not later than four weeks after that date, enter upon a period of employment[4] of not less than thirteen weeks during which he would not be laid-off or on short-time for any week.[5]

[1] Redundancy Payments Act 1965, s. 6 (1). For definition of week see *ibid.*, s. 5 (3), p. 229, below.
[2] This notice must be a full seven days notice; *Homson* v. *F.M.S.* (*Farm Products*), *Ltd.* (1967), 2 I.T.R. 326, T, and see *Vennard* v. *Deal* (1969), 4 I.T.R. 315, T.
[3] Redundancy Payments Act 1965, s. 6 (3). For a definition of the period allowed refer to *ibid.*, s. 7 (5), which defines it as follows:

"(a) if the employer does not give a counter-notice within seven days after the service of the notice of intention to claim, that period is three weeks after the end of those seven days;
(b) if the employer gives a counter-notice within those seven days, but withdraws it by a subsequent notice in writing, that period is three weeks after the sercice of the notice of withdrawal; or
(c) if the employer gives a counter-notice within those seven days and does so withdraw it, and a question as to the right of the employee to a redundancy payment in pursuance of the notice of intention to claim is referred to a tribunal, that period is three weeks after the tribunal has notified to the employee its decision on that reference."
For (c) no account is taken of any appeal from a tribunal's decision.
[4] The period of employment refers to employment under the contract of employment in relation to which the employee was laid off. *Neepsend Steel and Tool Corporation, Ltd.* v. *Vaughan*, [1972] 3 All E.R. 725, N.I.R.C., where the employment offered differed from that previously carried out and s. 6 (4) was held not to have been complied with.
[5] Redundancy Payments Act 1965, s. 6 (4).

It is conclusively presumed that the condition for a valid counter-notice has not been complied with if the employee continues or has continued for four weeks after the notice of intention to claim was served, to be employed by the same employer and he is, or has been, laid off or kept on short time for each of those weeks.[1]

[1] Redundancy Payments Act 1965, s. 7 (1).

If a counter-notice is served and not subsequently withdrawn by notice in writing the employee is not entitled to a redundancy payment in pursuance of his notice of intention to claim except in accordance with a decision of an industrial tribunal.[1]

[1] Redundancy Payments Act 1965, s. 7 (4).

Lay-off and short-time are defined in section 5 of the Redundancy Payments Act 1965.[1] Section 5 (1) provides:

"(1) Where an employee is employed under a contract on such terms and conditions that his remuneration thereunder depends on his being provided by the employer with work of the kind which he is employed to do, he shall for the purposes of this Part of this Act be taken to be laid off for any week in respect of which, by reason that the employer does not provide such work for him, he is not entitled to any remuneration under the contract."[2]

[1] It is important to distinguish between lay-off and short-time and dismissal; the decision of an industrial tribunal in *Sneddon* v. *Ivorycrete (Builders), Ltd.* (1966), 1 I.T.R. 538, T, is illustrative. The employers wished to lay off an employee for about three weeks, but his trade union advised that there was no provision in the working agreement for suspension and the employee should be dismissed. He was dismissed and after about three weeks was recalled to work. He refused and claimed redundancy payment. The employers contended that he was laid off and not dismissed, but the tribunal decided (by majority) that he had been dismissed and pointed out that in law the contract of employment was still in being in a case of lay off, (though in a modified form), whereas it was terminated where an employee is dismissed. Reference may also be made to *Jones* v. *Harry Sherman, Ltd.* (1969), 4 I.T.R. 63, T, and *Powell Duffryn Wagon Co., Ltd.* v. *House*, [1974] I.C.R. 123, N.I.R.C. As is illustrated by *Sneddon's* case not all contracts contain the power for the employer to lay-off their employees and great care must be exercised before purporting to lay-off an employee.

[2] For a discussion of the meaining of "lay-off" at common law see p. 63, above. The definition in s. 5 (1) is probably not restricted to piecework employment alone; *Hulse* v. *Harry Perry (t/a Arthur Perry & Son)*, [1975] I.R.L.R. 181, T, explaining *obiter dicta* in *Powell Duffryn Wagon Co., Ltd.* v. *House* (above). Contrast the judgment of Lord PARKER, C.J. in *Hanson* v. *Wood (Abingdon Process Engravers)*, (1968), 3 I.T.R. 46, D.C.

Section 5 (2), (2A) and (3) defines short-time:

"(2) Where by reason of a diminution in the work provided for an employee (being work of a kind which under his contract the employee is employed to do) the employee's remuneration for any week is less than half a week's pay, he shall for the purposes of this Part of this Act be taken to be kept on short-time for that week.

[(2A) For the purposes of Part II of Schedule 4 to the Employment Protection Act 1975 as it applies for the calculation of a week's pay for the purposes of the last preceding sub-section, the calculation date is the day immediately preceding the first of the four or, as the case may be, the

six weeks referred to in section 6 (1) of this Act.]
(3) In this section and in sections 6 and 7 of this Act 'week', in relation to the employee whose remuneration is calculated weekly by a week ending on a day other than Saturday, means a week ending with that other day, and, in relation to any other employee, means a week ending with Saturday."[1]

[1] The words in square brackets were added by the Employment Protection Act 1975. Before this amendment after the words "half a week's pay" in section 5, sub-section (2), the words "(calculated in accordance with Schedule 2 to this Act)" appeared. A week's pay is now as defined in Schedule 4 to the Employment Protection Act 1975. See p. 247, below.

For the purpose of the provisions as to lay-off and short-time it is immaterial whether a series of weeks consists wholly of weeks during which the employee is laid off or kept on short-time, or partly one and partly of the other.[1] However, no account is taken of any week in which the employee is laid-off or kept on short-time where the lay-off or short-time is wholly or mainly attributable to a strike or lock out, whether or not the strike or lock-out is in the trade industry in which the employee is employed, and whether or not it is in Great Britain or elsewhere.[2]

[1] Redundancy Payments Act 1965, s. 7 (2).
[2] *Ibid.*, s. 7 (3). For decisions as to lay-off see for example *Taylor* v. *Dunbar (Builders), Ltd.* (1966), 1, I.T.R. 249, T (*held* that the conditions required by section 6 (1) (*a*) had been satisfied but the employers had served a counter-notice in the terms of section 6 (5), and it was reasonably to be expected that the employee would have entered upon a period of normal employment as specified in section 6 (4), therefore no redundancy payment). See also *Vennard* v. *Deal* (1969), 4 I.T.R. 315, T, (applicant served notice of intention to claim and employer did not serve counter-notice. However, no entitlement to redundancy payment since contract was not terminated) and *Hulse* v. *Harry Perry (t/a Arthur Perry & Son)*, [1975] I.R.L.R. 181, T (counter-notice served but not sufficient evidence as at the date of the claim that it was reasonably to be expected that the applicant would within four weeks enter upon a period of employment as required by the statute).

## THE REQUISITE PERIOD AND CONTINUITY OF EMPLOYMENT

It has already been seen that for the employee to be entitled to a redundancy payment, it is a condition that the employee dismissed by reason of redundancy has been continuously employed for the requisite period. This requisite period is the period of two years ending with the relevant date,[1] excluding any week which began before the employee attained the age of 18 years.[2] Continuity of employment is determined in accordance with Schedule 1 of the Contracts of Employment Act 1972.

[1] See p. 208, above.
[2] Redundancy Payments Act 1965, s. 8 (1).

This Schedule, which is based on that to the Contracts of Employment Act 1963, is referred to for calculating the period of continuity of employment for many statutory purposes including the Redundancy Payments Act 1965, the Trade Union and Labour Relations Act 1974, and the Employment Protection Act 1975, as well as in the Contracts of Employment Act 1972, itself.

When dealing with continuity of employment for the purposes of the Redundancy Payments Act 1965, it is essential to note that section 9 (2) lays down that for the purpose of any reference to an industrial tribunal a person's employment during any period shall, unless the contrary is proved be presumed to have been continuous.[1] Thus the onus of proof is on the employer, if he alleges that employment has not been continuous, to prove that there was no continuity. This would involve proving a negative and is usually done by producing evidence of the break in the continuity. See for example an early case in *Binks and Kersley* v. *Weymann's, Ltd.*,[2] where the onus of proof was not discharged. In the interesting case of *Cole* v. *Fred Stacey, Ltd.*[3] the tribunal decided that an agreement between employers and an employee whereby he was paid expenses which were not true expenses, so as to reduce his income tax liability was an illegal contract and employment under it could not be used by the employee to show that he had been continuously employed for the requisite period.

[1] There is a similar presumption for other purposes; Trade Union and Labour Relations Act 1974, Sch. 1, para. 30 (2) and Employment Protection Act 1975, s. 126 (5).
[2] (1966), 1 I.T.R. 265, T.
[3] (1974), 9 I.T.R. 11, T.

In some situations an employer may be estopped from denying that an employee has been continuously employed for a period when he was not so employed. *Evenden* v. *Guildford City Association Football Club, Ltd.*[1] is a case where this occurred.

A groundsman at a football ground was employed by a supporters' club and after 13 years employment with them he became employed by the football club itself doing similar work to that which he had previously carried out. At the time of the change it was agreed by the football club that the employee's service would remain unbroken. It was held that the employer was estopped from denying that the employment with the supporters' club was continuous with that of the football club.

[1] [1975] Q.B. 917; [1975] 3 All E.R. 269, C.A.

If an employee is treated as not having been dismissed by virtue of a renewal or re-engagement pursuant to Redundancy Payments Act 1965, section 3 (3)[1] and when an employee is re-instated or re-engaged by his employer, or engaged by a successor, or associated employer, following the presentation of a claim to an industrial tribunal for unfair dismissal, or after the intervention of a conciliation officer, then any week which falls within the interval beginning with the date of dismissal and ending with the date of renewal, reinstatement, re-engagement, or engagement as the case may be counts in the computation of the employee's period of continuous employment and its continuity is preserved. If the terms of the re-engagement or engagement include provision for the employee to repay the amount of the redundancy payment paid in respect of the dismissal, section 24 of the Redundancy Payments Act 1965, which requires the period of continuity to be broken when a redundancy payment is paid does not apply if those provisions are complied with.[2]

That section states that if a redundancy payment is paid to an employee who is dismissed, or laid-off, or put on short-time, within the meaning of the Act but the contract of employment is renewed, or he is re-engaged, the continuity of the period of employment is treated as being broken at the date which was the relevant date in respect of the payment of the redundancy payment. Accordingly no account is taken in any subsequent calculation of the period of employment of any time before that date. Payment includes actual payment by the employer and also payment made by the Secretary of State for Employment. Similar provisions to section 24 apply when, instead of a redundancy payment, a payment has been made under section 1 of the Superannuation Act 1972 or similar payments to other public employees[3] so that the continuity is broken by such payment.[4]

# The requisite period and continuity of employment

[1] Redundancy Payments Act 1965, s. 8 (3) (as amended).
[2] The Industrial Relations (Continuity of Employment) Regulations 1976, S.I. 1976 No. 660. The position is similar if the reinstatement, re-engagement or engagement takes place after a claim has been made in accordance with a dismissals procedure agreement designated by an order under Trade Union and Labour Relations Act 1974, Sch. 1, para. 13.
[3] Redundancy Payments Act 1965, s. 41 (3).
[4] Ibid., s. 24A. Added by Employment Protection Act 1975, s. 120 (3). There is also a similar exclusion to that relating to s. 24 on reinstatement or re-engagement; Labour Relations (Continuity of Employment) Regulations 1976, reg. 5.

A period of employment for the purpose of the Contracts of Employment Act is computed in weeks,[1] but for redundancy and other purposes reference is made to a year or years. A year means 52 weeks (whether continuous or discontinuous) which count in computing a period of employment.[1] Save where there is specific provision to the contrary a week which doesn't count under the provisions of Schedule 1 breaks the continuity of the period of employment.[2]

[1] Contracts of Employment Act 1972, Sch. 1, para. 1. "Week" means a week ending with a Saturday. A week may count as a week if the minimum number of hours, or more, is worked even though a full week has not been worked. See for instance *Coulson* v. *City of London Polytechnic*, [1976] I.R.L.R. 212, E.A.T. and p. 231, below.
[2] Ibid., Sch. 1, para. 2.

It frequently happens in a period of long service with one employer that the employer and employee enter into a succession of new contracts, for example on promotion or other reasons and paragraph 1 does not require that "continuous" employment should be pursuant to a single contract of service; per PENNYCUIK, J. in *Mack Tracks (Britain), Ltd.*[1] The provisions of the First Schedule to the Contracts of Employment Act 1972 have effect for the purpose of computing an employee's period of employment but for no other purpose in relation to Crown employment and to persons in Crown employment as they have effect in relation to other employment and to other employees with appropriate amendments so far as construction is concerned.[2] This does not apply to service as a member of the naval, military or air forces of the Crown or of any women's service administered by the Defence Council but does apply to employment by any association for the purposes of Auxiliary Forces Act 1963.[3]

[1] [1967] 1 All E.R. 977; [1967] 1 W.L.R. 780, Ch.D.; *Loggie* v. *Alexander Hall & Son (Builders), Ltd.* (1969), 4 I.T.R. 390, T.
[2] Contracts of Employment Act 1972, Sch. 1, para. 10A. Added by Employment Protection Act 1975, s. 120 (1). The provisions of the Schedule also apply to members of House of Commons Staff, *ibid.*, s. 122 (1).
[3] Contracts of Employment Act 1972. Sch. 1, para. 10A (3).

## (1) Part-time employment

At the moment any week during the whole or part of which the employee's relations with the employer are governed by a contract of employment which normally involves employment for 21 hours or more weekly counts in computing a period of employment,[1] as does any week in which the employee is employed for 21 hours or more.[2]

[1] Contracts of Employment Act 1972, Sch. 1, para. 4. See *Kincey* v. *Pardey and Johnson, Ltd.* (1966), 1 I.T.R. 182, T (no continuity when 22½ hours worked the one week and 19 the next) and *Middle* v. *Edward Saunders & Son, Ltd.* (1966), 1 I.T.R. 361, T (continuity broken by a period of 11 months when only 19½ hours worked each week, by agreement). The hours of employment of an employee who is required by the terms of his employment to live on the premises where he works shall be the hours during which he is on duty or during which his services may be required; *ibid.*, Sch. 1, para. 11 (2).

[2] *Ibid.*, para. 3. There is power for the Secretary of State for Employment to reduce the number of hours by statutory instrument but it is unlikely that this power will be used before the amendments mentioned below are brought into effect.

Under the provisions of Part II, Schedule 16 to the Employment Protection Act 1975[1] amendments are made to the first Schedule to the Contracts of Employment Act 1972 to reduce the minimum number of weekly hours when computing a period of employment. These provisions have not been brought into force at the time of going to press,[2] but under them any week in which the employee is employed for 16 hours, or more, counts in computing the period of employment as does any week during the whole or part of which the employee's relations with the employer are governed by a contract of employment which normally involves employment for 16 hours or more weekly. The reduction in number of hours per week introduced by the Employment Protection Act 1975 will, when effective, apply both in respect of periods before and after the commencement of the relevant provisions of that Act. By virtue of new paragraphs 4A, 4B and 4C[3] certain employees who do not normally work the minimum number of hours can in some situations include weeks in the computation.

[1] Paragraph 13 of that Part of that Schedule.
[2] They are expected to come into force during autumn 1976.
[3] Added by Employment Protection Act 1975, Sch. 16, Part II, para. 14. This paragraph is not yet in force and so paras. 4A, 4B and 4C do not appear in Contracts of Employment Act 1972, Sch. 1 at present.

Under these new rules if an employee's relations with his employer cease to be governed by a contract which normally involves work for 16 or more hours per week and become governed by a contract which normally involves employment for eight hours or more per week but less than 16 hours weekly and, but for that change, the later weeks would count in computing a period of employment or would not break the continuity of a period of employment, then those later weeks count in computing a period of employment, or as the case may be, do not break the continuity, notwithstanding the change. Not more than 26 weeks at the reduced hourly rate will count between any two periods when the contract of employment normally involves employment for 16 hours or more weekly, but in computing the 26 weeks no account is taken of any week which otherwise counts in computing a period of employment, or does not break the continuity of a period of employment.[1]

[1] Contracts of Employment Act 1972, Sch. 1, para. 4A, when inserted by provisions of the Employment Protection Act 1975 which are not yet operative.

If an employee, on the date by reference to which the length of any period of employment falls to be ascertained, has been continuously employed for a period of five years or more and his relations with the employer are governed, or have from time to time been governed, by a contract of employment which normally involves employment for eight hours or more but less than sixteen hours weekly, then for the purpose of computing weeks which count and continuity of employment he is treated as if engaged under a contract normally involving sixteen hours or more weekly and as if the contract had normally involved employment for sixteen hours or more weekly during that period.[1]

[1] Contracts of Employment Act 1972, Sch. 1, para. 4A when inserted by the provisions of Employment Protection Act 1975 which are not yet operative. In computing for these purposes an employee's period of employment

the provisions of Sch. 1 apply but as if for the words "sixteen hours" in paras. 3 and 4 the words "eight hours" were substituted: *ibid.*, Sch. 1, para. 4B (3).

When an employee has at any time during the relevant period of employment been continuously employed for a period which qualifies him for any right requiring a qualifying period of continuous employment computed in accordance with Schedule 1 of the Contracts of Employment Act 1972 (including the "requisite period" for the purpose of the Redundancy Payments Act 1965), he is regarded as continuing to satisfy the requirement until in a week subsequent to the time at which the employee qualified for that right his relations with the employer are governed by a contract of employment which normally involves employment for less than eight hours weekly and he is employed in that week for less than 16 hours. The relevant period of employment for these purposes is the period of employment ending on the date by reference to which the length of any period of employment falls to be ascertained, which would be continuous if, at all relevant times, the employee's relations with the employer had been governed by a contract of employment which normally involved the employee for 16 hours or more weekly.[1]

[1] Contracts of Employment Act 1972, Sch. 1, para. 4C, not yet in force. If in a case in which an employee is entitled to any right by virtue of these provisions it is necessary for the purpose of ascertaining the amount of his entitlement to determine for what period he has been continuously employed (as in the case of redundancy) he is to be regarded for that purpose as having been continuously employed throughout the relevant period; *ibid.*, Sch. 1, para. 4C (4).

There is power for the Secretary of State for Employment by order of both Houses of Parliament to substitute a reference to lower numbers of hours per week than 16 or 8 as the case may be.[1]

[1] New sections, to, Contracts of Employment Act 1972. Not yet substituted. This power does not extend to the requirement of eight hours in paragraph 4A.

### (2) Temporary absences

When the contract of employment subsists during a temporary absence the above rules may determine whether or not a week counts and continuity is preserved. In addition Schedule 1 of the Contracts of Employment Act 1972 provides that if in any week for the whole or part of the week the employee is:

(a) incapable of working in consequence of sickness or injury,[1] or

(b) absent from work on account of a temporary cessation of work other than a temporary cessation of work on account of a strike in which the employee takes part,[2] or

(c) absent from work in circumstances such that by arrangement or custom he is regarded as continuing in the employment of his employer,[3] or

(d) she [sic] is absent from work wholly or partly because of pregnancy or confinement,[4]

that week counts as a period of employment notwithstanding that it does not fall under paragraph 3, 4 or 4A of the Schedule.

[1] Contracts of Employment Act 1972, Sch. 1, para. 5 (1) (a). Not more than 26 weeks count under this paragraph between any of the periods falling under paragraphs 3, 4 and 4A of the Schedule. See for instance *Tarbuck* v. *L. E. Wilson & Co., Ltd.* (1967), 2 I.T.R. 157, T (absence in excess of 26 weeks but contract continued. *Held* continuity not broken) and *Thompson* v. *Monteiths, Ltd.* (1967), 2 I.T.R. 205, T.

[2] *Ibid.*, Sch. 1, para. 5 (1) (b). "... *temporary cessation of work* ...": This phrase does not apply to a temporary cessation of work on account of a strike in which the employee takes part. If, however, there is a strike in another plant or section of an industry, employees who do not themselves strike but are involved in a temporary cessation of work do not have such period of enforced idleness subtracted from their continuous period of employment.

Further, under Schedule 1, paragraph 6 (1), which applies to industrial disputes after the Act comes into force, a week does not count under paragraphs 4, 4A, 5 and 5A if in that week, or any part of it, the employee takes part in a strike.

The words in paragraph 5 (1) (b) have been interpreted by the House of Lords in *Fitzgerald* v. *Hall Russell & Co., Ltd.* (1970), 5 I.T.R. 1, H.L., when during the course of his judgment Lord UPJOHN said (at p. 16), "In my opinion, the words 'absent from work on account of temporary cessation of work' mean that he was laid off or dismissed because his employer had no longer work available for him personally any longer..." "...So the question —was the cessation temporary?—in most cases cannot be answered at the time of dismissal..." "...you must look at the original dismissal with hindsight, that is to say, with knowledge of all that has happened since the original dismissal until the second dismissal, and then decide whether in all the circumstances of the case the original dismissal can properly be described as due to a *temporary* cessation of work..."

In that case a welder was first employed by the respondents in 1958, and in November 1962 he was discharged because of a shortage of work. Nearly eight weeks later matters had improved and he was re-engaged. During the interim period the applicant had not obtained employment elsewhere in the hope that the respondents would re-employ him. The House of Lords remitted the case to the industrial tribunal to enable it to reconsider whether the cessation of work was temporary in the light of the guidance given by the House.

In deciding whether a period of cessation of work was temporary or not, a subjective approach is adopted. In *Hunter* v. *Smith's Dock Co., Ltd.*, [1968] 2 All E.R. 81; [1968] 1 W.L.R. 1865, WINN, L.J. said "for my own part I do not think that this test under 5 (1) (*b*) is only satisfied where it can be shown there has been a cessation of all work, or all work of any one department, formerly carried out at a place where the employee was employed" and this dictum was approved by the House of Lords in *Fitzgerald's* case. The earlier decision concerned an applicant, a ship's riveter, who began working for the respondents in the 1920s, but was periodically stood off for short periods not exceeding 40 days. On these occasions there was no provision for re-engagement but when riveting work was available Mr. Hunter was re-employed. It was held by the Divisional Court that the absences, particularly one of 31 days in 1964/5 did not break the continuity of employment.

The Court of Appeal in *Thompson* v, *Bristol Channel Ship Repairers and Engineers, Ltd.* (1970), 5 I.T.R. 85, C.A., considered a case of a painter and fitter who was laid off from January to April 1962 as a result of a lack of work. Although he was unemployed for part of this period he did obtain employment with one of the respondent's competitors for 10 weeks, but on the understanding that he could return to his former employers when they had sufficient work available. The employee was finally dismissed in 1967 in circumstances of redundancy. The Court held that the period of four months was a "temporary cessation of work" and the applicant could include his earlier period of employment in calculating the redundancy payment due to him. But see *Newsham* v. *Dunlop Textiles, Ltd.* (*No.* 2) (1969), 4 I.T.R. 268, D.C. (absence of six weeks after fire at mill, treated as termination. Divisional Court *held* broke continuity). In *Bentley Engineering Co., Ltd.* v. *Crown*, [1976] I.C.R., 225, D.C., PHILLIPS, J. examined the earlier decisions and stated (at p. 228): "... paragraph 5 (1) (*b*) poses three questions: was there a cessation of the employee's work or job; was the employee absent on account of that cessation; and ... was the cessation a temporary one? That those are the right questions was not challenged in this appeal; they were followed by the tribunal, and they are helpful. But I do think that some caution is needed because, although they are a helpful guide and anybody confronted with this problem should follow them, at the end of the day one has to go back to the words of the statute, which I have read. And it is probably helpful if, after considering the particular questions I have mentioned, a tribunal does go back and look at the question in the round to see whether it is satisfied that the claimant was absent from work on account of a temporary cessation of work." Applying those tests and looking at the circumstances "as the historian of a completed chapter of events" the Court upheld the decisions of an industrial tribunal that absences of 21 months and two years (during the shorter one of which that employee took other employment) were absences which fell within para. 5 (1) (*b*) notwithstanding that after the absence the employees worked in different jobs for an associated company of their former employer.

³ Contracts of Employment Act 1972, Sch. 1, para. 5 (1) (*c*). "... *absent from*

*work in circumstances such that, by arrangement or custom, he is regarded as continuing in the employment of his employer for all or any purposes ...".* These words cover, for example, the case of an employee absent with or without consent and unpaid who has not received back his insurance card, or his P45 income tax form, or been told that he is no longer required. See also *Murray* v. *Kelvin Electronics Co.* (1967), 2 I.T.R. 622 (break ignored for purposes of pension and holidays—continuity not broken); and *Cann* v. *Co-operative Retail Services, Ltd.* (1967), 2 I.T.R. 649.

[4] Contracts of Employment Act 1972, Sch. 1, para. 5 (1) (*d*). Inserted by Employment Protection Act 1975, Sch. 16, Part II, para. 15, with effect from 1st June 1976; the Employment Protection Act 1975 (Commencement No. 4) Order 1976. Not more than 26 weeks count under this paragraph between any periods falling under paragraphs 3, 4 and 4A of the Schedule. If an employee returns to work in accordance with Employment Protection Act 1975, s. 49 after a period of absence from work wholly or partly occasioned by pregnancy or confinement, every week during that period counts notwithstanding that it would not otherwise do so; *ibid.*, Sch. 1, para. 5A.

When an employee is entitled to claim re-instatement under the National Service Act 1948, and is re-employed by his former employer within six months at the end of his whole time service the period of service did not break the continuity of employment. The reference to the National Service Act includes reference to Part II of that Act as applied or extended by other statutes, for instance the Re-instatement Civil Employment Act 1950 and the Army Reserve Act 1962.[1]

[1] Contracts of Employment Act 1972, Sch. 1, para. 8.

The Contracts of Employment Act 1972, Schedule 1, paragraph 1 (2), provides that for the purpose of computing an employee's period of employment (but for no other purpose) the provisions of the Schedule apply to periods during which the employee is engaged in work wholly or mainly outside Great Britain and periods during which the employee is excluded by or under the Contracts of Employment Act 1972, section 9, as they apply to other periods. For the purposes of the Redundancy Payments Act 1965 special provisions apply so far as persons employed outside Great Britain for the whole or any part of a week are concerned[1] and where an employee is employed in employment which is excluded from the benefit of the Redundancy Payments Act 1965 because the employee is a merchant seaman[2] it is disregarded in ascertaining whether the employee has been employed for the requisite period or in calculating a redundancy payment.[3]

However, such employment does not break the continuity of that person's period of employment.[3]

[1] See p. 166, above. These rules apply on calculation of entitlement to, and amount of, redundancy payments.

[2] Redundancy Payments (Merchant Seaman Exclusion) Order 1973, S.I. 1973 No. 1281. See p. 172, above

[3] Redundancy Payments (Merchant Seaman Exclusion) Order 1973, para. 4, above.

An interesting point arose in *Clarke Chapman-John Thompson v. Walters*, [1972] 1 All E.R. 614; [1972] 1 W.L.R. 378, N.I.R.C. The applicant and others went on strike and when he returned to work was informed that he was discharged and would be allowed to apply for employment again which he did. Some of the employees started back to work immediately but the applicant was not required to return for 16 days. It was necessary to decide whether the 16 days absence broke the continuity of employment for the requisite period ending with the relevant date. The court held that Mr. Walters had been continuously employed. He had not resumed work after the strike because there was a temporary cessation of work the exclusion as to the temporary cessation of work on account of a strike means a strike in which the employee is currently taking part and not "a temporary cessation of work as a consequence of a strike in which the employee is taking part or has theretofor taken part". A somewhat similar problem was considered in *Kolatsis v. Rockware Glass, Ltd.*, [1974] 3 All E.R. 555, N.I.R.C. The employee was dismissed whilst in Cyprus after a holiday having been unable to return home because of ill health. In due course he returned and was told that he could either start on another shift immediately, or on his old shift in 10 days time. He preferred his old shift, and made the appropriate arrangements. It was held that continuity of employment was not broken, the interval of absence between the incapacity because of sickness and return was absence on account of a temporary cessation of work.

*Other decisions include:*

*Moore v. James Clarkson & Co., Ltd.* (1970), 5 I.T.R. 298, T (3 months' absence to look after son—employers retaining cards—no breach in continuity).

*Brogan v. Highams, Ltd.* (1969), 4 I.T.R. 387, T (employee

arranged termination to obtain accrued holiday pay. Tribunal *held* break in continuity).

*Loggie* v. *Alexander Hall & Son (Builders), Ltd.* (1969), 4 I.T.R. 390, T (to obtain transfer employee gave notice to determine employment at one site on Friday. On following Monday he commended working for the same employers at different site. *Held:* continuity not broken).

*Lappin* v. *Fairfield-Rowan, Ltd.* (1967), 2 I.T.R. 8, T (4 weeks' absence during which he took other job. *Held:* broke continuity).

The employee in *Wishart* v. *National Coal Board* (1974), 7 I.T.R. 320, N.I.R.C., worked for the Coal Board but requiring lighter work was employed by a contractor working for the Coal Board for 18 months. During that time he remained in the Mineworkers Pension Scheme. It was held that the period did not break the continuity (for the purposes of calculating redundancy payment) because the employers regarded the employee as not having left the industry permanently and by custom they regarded him as continuing in their employ and continuity was not broken and see *Taylor* v. *Triumph Motors British Leyland U.K., Ltd. and Secretary of State for Employment*, [1975] I.R.L.R. 369, T.

In *Lane* v. *Wolverhampton Die Casting Co., Ltd.* (1967), 2 I.T.R. 120, T, the following explanation of paragraph 5 (1) (*c*) was given "... reinstatement, even on all the same terms and conditions as before, cannot amount to an arrangement by which the employee is 'regarded as continuing in the employment of his employer for all or any purposes'. An agreement to 'take back' into employment necessarily involves that meanwhile the employment is broken: unless there is ... some specific term of the agreement by which *during absence* he is for some purpose still treated as an employee." See also *Smith* v. *G. K. Purdy Trawlers, Ltd.* (1966), 1 I.T.R. 508, T (Chief engineer of trawler working on shore between voyages); *Jones* v. *National Coal Board* (1966), 1 I.T.R. 474, T (absence of nearly four years because of industrial disease—not within 5 (1) (*c*)); *Walker* v. *Staines Kitchen Equipment Co., Ltd.* (1967), 2 I.T.R. 21, T; *Binks and Kersley* v. *Weymann's, Ltd.* (1966), 1 I.T.R. 265, T; *Bennett* v. *G. W. Thompson, Ltd.* (1966), 1 I.T.R. 173, T; *Barry* v. *D. Murphy & Son, Ltd.* (1967), 2 I.T.R. 134, T (casual worker—laid off from time to time—*Held* (by majority) employment continuous within 5 (1) (*c*)); *Gray* v. *Burntisland Shipbuilding Co.* (1967, 2 I.T.R. 255, T (shipbuilders

—three weeks' absence—regarded as continuing employment.)
*Southern Electricity Board* v. *Collins*, [1969] 1 Q.B. 83, [1969]
2 All E.R. 1168, D.C. (claimant transferred to Central Electricity
Generating Board for 6½ months. Divisional Court *held* employment not continuous).

*Alexander* v. *McMillan* (1969), 4 I.T.R. 171, T (loan of employee for 18 months to new employer who paid wages. Tribunal *held* no break in continuity).

*Logan* v. *G.U.S. Transport, Ltd.* (1969), 4 I.T.R. 287, T (employee left one company on Saturday and commenced working for associated company on following Monday. Tribunal *held* continuity broken).

*Rhodes* v. *Pontins, Ltd.* (1971), 6 I.T.R. 88, T (cricketer employed by respondents during winter, played cricket full time in summer. Tribunal *held* no continuity, employment broken every year).

*McAree* v. *G.K.N. Sankey, Ltd.*, [1976] I.R.L.R. 58, D.C. (employee dismissed in aftermath of an industrial dispute reengaged two months later. Tribunal decision that dismissal amount to a break in service upheld).

## (3) Strikes and lock-outs

Continuity of employment is not broken if during a week or weeks the employee takes part in a strike. Weeks in which the employee takes part in a strike if they began after 6th July 1964 do not count in the computation of a period of employment but those beforehand do.[1] A " 'strike' means the cessation of work by a body of persons employed acting in combination, or a concerted refusal or a refusal under a common understanding of any number of persons employed to continue to work for an employer in consequence of a dispute, done as a means of compelling their employer or any person or body of persons employed, or to aid other employees in compelling their employer or body of persons employed, to accept or not to accept terms or conditions of or affecting employment"; unless the context otherwise requires.[2]

[1] Contracts of Employment Act 1972, Sch. 1, para. 6 (1) (2).
[2] *Ibid.*, Sch. 1, para. 11 (1).

A strike includes an unofficial as well as an official strike[1] and for this purpose can continue after the employee has been dismissed.[2]

## The requisite period and continuity of employment

[1] *Underwood* v. *N. G. Bailey & Co., Ltd.* (1967), I.T.R. 420.
[2] See *Bloomfield* v. *Springfield Hosiery Finishing Co.* (1972), I.T.R. 89, N.I.R.C., the applicant was dismissed while on strike but later agreement was reached between the parties and he returned to work. After less than two years he was dismissed because of redundancy. Sir JOHN DONALDSON, in delivering the judgment of the National Industrial Relations Court, said (at p. 94):

> "The fact that the employer terminates their contracts of employment does not take them outside this category, unless and until he engages other persons on a permanent basis to do the work which the strikers had been doing or he permanently discontinues the activity in which they were employed. Similarly the fact that the striker takes other temporary employment pending the settlement of the dispute, does not prevent him claiming that he is taking part in a strike."

See *Clarke Chapman-John Thompson, Ltd.* v. *Walters*, [1972] 1 All E.R. 614; [1972] 1 W.L.R. 378, N.I.R.C., for a case where there was a temporary cessation of work after the strike had finished to allow an orderly return to work.

In *McGorry* v. *Earls Court Stand Fitting Co., Ltd.* (1973), 8 I.T.R. 109, N.I.R.C., the employee was dismissed *as being redundant* whilst on strike but the Court *held* that continuity was preserved because there was a temporary cessation of work between the dismissal and return to work. It was not decided whether the "strike" rules would have had similar effect. The argument being that *Bloomfield's* case did not apply, since the reason for the dismissal was that the employee was not a person who would have been employed but for the strike because he was at the time redundant. In *Soutar* v. *Fisher* (1975), I.T.R. 38, T, during a strike the employer dismissed the employees. In due course he took them back but refused to withdraw the notices of dismissal. The employees did not reject new statements pursuant to the Contracts of Employment Act 1972 giving the date of resumption of work as date of commencement of employment. A tribunal decided that by not taking positive steps to amend the statement under the Contracts of Employment Act 1972 the employees accepted that their period of employment began at the time of the resumption after the strike.

A lock-out does not break continuity of employment.[1] A "'lock-out' means the closing of a place of employment, or the suspension of work, or the refusal by an employer to continue to employ any number of persons employed by him in consequence of a dispute, done with a view to compelling those persons, or to aid another employer in compelling persons employed by him, to accept terms or conditions of or affecting employment;" unless the context otherwise requires.[2]

[1] Contracts of Employment Act 1972, Sch. 1, para. 7.
[2] *Ibid.*, Sch. 1, para. 11 (1).

## (4) Change of employer

The usual rule is that employment is only continuous if it is
employment by one employer.[1] There are however certain
exceptions:

a. As has already been mentioned there are rules to preserve
the continuity of employment if a trade, or business or undertaking (whether or not it is an undertaking established by or
under Act of Parliament) is transferred from one person to
another. The period of employment with the trade, or business or
undertaking at the time of transfer counts as a period of employment with the transferee and the transfer does not break
continuity of the period of employment.[2]

[1] Contracts of Employment Act 1972, Sch. 1, para. 9 (1).
[2] *Ibid.*, Sch. 1, para. 9 (2).

In *Lloyd* v. *Brassey*,[1] [1969] 2 Q.B. 98; [1969] 1 All E.R.
382, Lord DENNING, M.R. said "... the words 'a trade or business
or undertaking is transferred from one person to another' clearly
have the same meaning as a 'change in the ownership of a
business' in section 13, Redundancy Payments Act, 1965 ...".
Accordingly reference should be made to the decisions which
have been mentioned in connection with that section.[2] *Lord
Advocate* v. *De Rosa*, [1974] 2 All E.R. 849; [1974] 1 W.L.R. 946,
H.L., is a case where the weakness of legislation by reference is
highlighted when dealing with a question of continuity of employment. Mr. de Rosa was employed by one company and there was a
transfer of business to another company which took immediate
effect. The employee's employment was not interrupted but after
the transfer he worked for the new employer on differing terms.
At the time there was a requirement that if the employer wished
to claim that there was no dismissal pursuant to the rules as to
offer and re-engagement, then if the terms differed, the offer
should have been made in writing prior to the transfer, which
it was not. In due course Mr. de Rosa was made redundant and
claimed a redundancy payment based on employment with both
employers. The House of Lords having examined the several
references to Schedule 1 of the Contracts of Employment Act
1972 contained in the Redundancy Payments Act 1965, and also
the provisions of sections 3 and 13 of that Act unanimously
held that the paragraph which is now paragraph 9 (2) applied
and for the purpose of calculating redundancy payments continuity

was preserved. The period of employment with the former employer counted notwithstanding that at the time of the transfer of the business Mr. de Rosa could have claimed a redundancy payment against him.[3]

[1] [1969] 1 All E.R. 382, at p. 384.
[2] See p. 216, above.
[3] The possibility of double payment is avoided by Redundancy Payments Act 1965, s. 24.

This certainly applies when the Contracts of Employment Act 1972, Schedule 1 is referred to for the purpose of computing *quantum* of a redundancy payment and it is probable that the same reasoning would be used with regard to computation of the requisite period, i.e., governing *entitlement* to a redundancy payment.

b. There is express provision in Contracts of Employment Act 1972, Schedule 1, paragraph 9 (3) to preserve the continuity of employment when under an Act of Parliament a contract of employment is modified and another body corporate is substituted as the employer. Continuity is preserved and the period of employment with the former employer counts with the new employer.

c. If an employee is taken into the employment of another employer which at the time he is taken into employment is an associated employer of the first named employer then similar rules apply, continuity is preserved as is the period of employment which ranks as with the second employer.[1] Associated employer is defined as for other purposes of the Redundancy Payments Act 1965 this time by the Contracts of Employment Act 1972, Schedule 1, paragraph 10 (2), as amended. Any two employers are to be treated as associated if one is a company of which the other (directly or indirectly) has control, or if both are companies of which a third person (directly or indirectly) has control.[2]

[1] Contracts of Employment Act 1972, Sch. 1, para. 10 (1), as substituted by the Employment Protection Act 1975, Sch. 16, Part II, para. 19.
[2] In *Southern Electricity Board* v. *Collins* [1969] 2 All E.R. 1168, D.C., it was held that two public corporations were not associated "companies" for the purpose of the paragraph which was amended by the Employment Protection Act 1975. This is still likely to be the case. See also *Spencer* v. *Miller Brothers and Battley Ltd.* (1968), 3 I.T.R. 371, T, where there was a voluntary period of unemployment before the employee was engaged by an associated company. *Held* no continuity. However, in *Binns* v. *Versil, Ltd.*, [1975] I.R.L.R. 273, T,

where the employee left a job with his employer for employment with an associated company without the acquiescence of the employers continuity was *held* to be preserved.

d. If on the death of an employer the employee is taken into the employment of the personal representatives or trustees of the deceased, the employee's period of employment at the time of death counts as a period with the employer's personal representatives or trustees and the death shall not break the contunuity.[1]

[1] Contracts of Employment Act 1972, Sch. 1, para. 9 (4).

e. Similarly if there is a change of partners, personal representatives, or trustees, who employ an employee, the employee's period of employment at the time of the change counts as a period of employment with the partners, personal representatives, or trustees after the change and does not break the continuity of employment.[1]

[1] Contracts of Employment Act 1972, Sch. 1, para. 9 (5). In *Harold Fielding Ltd.* v. *Mansi*, [1974] 1 All E.R. 1035 N.I.R.C., the employee had been employed by a partnership when presenting a theatrical show and immediately afterwards he was employed on a different show by one of the partners individually. The National Industrial Relations Court *held* that there was no continuity of employment to enable the applicant to claim that he has been employed for the requisite period. First, paragraph 9 (5) did not appear to cover a case where there was only a sole proprietor after the change and secondly the two theatrical productions were separate ventures and so not covered by the Schedule.

## REDUNDANCY PAYMENTS

### (i) Calculation of redundancy payments[1]

Redundancy payments are calculated by reference to periods of continuous employment ending with the relevant date and reckoning backwards the number of years of continuous employment falling within the period and allowing:

(a) $1\frac{1}{2}$ weeks' pay for each such year of employment which consists wholly of weeks in which the employee was not below the age of 41 years;

(b) 1 week's pay for each such year of employment (not falling with (a)) which consists entirely of weeks in which the employee was not below the age of 22 years;

(c) $\frac{1}{2}$ a week's pay for each such year (not falling with (a) or (b)) and in respect of which the employee was over the age of 18 years.

When reckoning the number of years no account of any year is taken beyond 20 years. When the relevant date is after the employee's 64th birthday if a man (59th birthday if a woman) the amount of a redundancy payment is reduced by one-twelfth for each complete month of employment prior to the relevant date after that birthday.[2]

Continuous employment is defined by reference to Schedule 1 of the Contracts of Employment Act 1972 but as if any week that began before the employee attained the age of 18 years were excluded and the continuity of employment is not broken if there is a renewal or re-engagement within the meaning of section 3 (3) of the Redundancy Payments Act 1965[3] and the period of any interval before such renewal or re-engagement counts as a period of employment for this purpose.[4]

Where the relevant date is as defined by section 3 (10) (i.e., as if the minimum statutory notice had been given) the period of the interval between the actual date of dismissal and the relevant date counts notwithstanding that it would not do so under the terms of Schedule 1 of the Contracts of Employment Act 1972.[5] The provisions of the Schedule have already been discussed but it is important to see that the limitations imposed by the Redundancy Payments Act 1965, Schedule 1, paragraph 1 (1) (as amended) are not overlooked.[6]

[1] When using Schedule 1 of the Redundancy Payments Act 1965 to calculate redundancy payments if the relevant date does not occur at the end of a week references to the relevant date are construed as references to the end of the week in which the relevant date falls. Save in the expression "week's pay" week means a week ending with a Saturday.

[2] See *Swithenbank* v. *Platt Brothers & Co., Ltd.* (1968), 3 I.T.R. 134, T.

[3] See p. 197, above. For the position where the employee works abroad consider also p. 166, above.

[4] Section 8 (3) and Redundancy Payments Act 1965, Sch. 1, para. 1. See p. 228, above.

[5] Redundancy Payments Act 1965, Sch. 1, para. 1 (1) (c) as added by the Employment Protection Act 1975.

[6] See *Lord Advocate* v. *De Rosa*, [1974] 2 All E.R. 849; [1974] 1 W.L.R. 946, H.L. where the possibility of differing effects of Sch. 1 to the Contracts of Employment Act 1972 in the light of the difference in the references to it was discussed.

By virtue of section 85 of the Employment Protection Act

1975, Schedule 4 of that Act has effect for calculating a week's pay in computations under the Redundancy Payments Act 1965.[1]

[1] Before 1st June 1976 "week's pay" was defined by reference to Contracts of Employment Act 1972, Sch. 2; Redundancy Payments Act 1965, Sch. 1, para. 5 (1) (as originally enacted). By virtue of the Employment Protection (Commencement No. 4) Order 1976, S.I. 1976 No. 530 the new paragraph 5 of the Redundancy Payments Act 1965 which is found in Employment Protection Act 1975, Sch. 16, para. 21 is brought into effect on 1st June 1976.

For the purpose of calculating redundancy payments the calculation date for use in making computations in accordance with Schedule 4 of the Employment Protection Act 1975 is the date on which notice would have been given by the employer had the contract been terminable by notice, and had it been terminated by giving such notice as was the minimum notice necessary in accordance with section 1 of the Contracts of Employment Act 1972, to terminate the contract of employment and that notice had expired on the relevant date.[1] When ascertaining the calculation date for the purpose of Schedule 4 of the Employment Protection Act 1975 in cases where employment has been terminated during the trial period, the relevant date is the date as determined in accordance with section 3 (9) of the Redundancy Payments Act 1965, even if section 3 (10) applies for other purposes.[2] Where the occasion for payment of a redundancy payment is a result of the statutory provisions as to short-time and lay-off the calculation date for the purposes of Schedule 4 of the Employment Protection Act 1975 is the day immediately preceding the first of the four or, as the case may be, the six weeks referred to in Section 6 (1) of the Redundancy Payments Act 1965.[3]

[1] Redundancy Payments Act 1965, Sch. 1, para. 5 (as amended). For "relevant date", see p. 208, above.
[2] *Ibid.*, Sch. 1, para. 5 (3).
[3] *Ibid.*, s. 5 (2A).

When calculating a redundancy payment there is a statutory limit to a week's pay which has to be taken into account and this is £80.[1] The Secretary of State has power to vary this limit by order when carrying out the annual review of limit required by section 86 of the Employment Protection Act 1975. There may be transitional and incidental provisions in any order made pursuant to that section.[2]

The amount of redundancy payment may be reduced in accordance with regulations made under section 14 of the Redundancy Payments Act 1965 where the redundant employee has a right or claim (whether legally enforceable or not) to a periodical payment, or lump sum, by way of pension annuity or superannuation allowance in respect of his employment by the employer. The present rules are contained in the Redundancy Payments Pensions Regulations 1965.[1] These must be looked at in detail when they are applicable. Broadly they apply when there is a statutory scheme, or a scheme or arrangement established by an irrevocable trust, or secured by a contract of assurance, or an annuity contract with an insurance company, registered friendly society, or industrial and provident society, for provision of periodical payments, or a lump sum,[2] by way of pension, gratuity or superannuation allowance, having for its' object or one of its' objects, the provision of retirement benefits for persons serving in particular employments.[3] Payments made to an employee which consist solely of a return of his own contributions, with or without interest, payments to an employee which are attributable solely to additional voluntary contributions by that employee made in accordance with the scheme or arrangement, and periodical payments, or lump sums, which represent statutory compensation[4] are all ignored.[5]

¹ S.I. 1965 No. 1932.
² There is no requirement that the lump sum should be secured as mentioned when it has been paid.
³ Redundancy Payments Pensions Regulations 1965, para. 3 (1). Certain other arrangements are also included, for instance some schemes equivalent to those of the Civil Service and certain Commonwealth pension arrangements.
⁴ As is mentioned in Redundancy Payments Act 1965, s. 47 (1).
⁵ Redundancy Payments Pensions Regulations 1965, para. 3 (3).

The right to the payment may be excluded or reduced where an employee who is entitled, or but for the Regulations would be entitled, to a redundancy payment from an employer, has a right or claim to a benefit as mentioned above for himself which is to be paid by reference to the employee's period of continuous employment with that employer, and if it is a lump sum is to be paid, or if it is a periodical payment is to begin to accrue, at the time when the employee leaves the employment with that employer, or within 90 weeks thereafter. In addition if the pension consists of periodical payments the conditions specified in paragraph 4 (2) of the Regulations must be satisfied. For the right to be exercised the employer must by notice in writing to the employee claim to exclude the right of the employee to a redundancy payment, or reduce its amount to the extent permitted, and the employee in those circumstances is not entitled to a redundancy payment or, as the case may be, entitled only to the reduced amount.[1] The right of the employer to exclude, or reduce, the amount of the redundancy payment is discretionary, and if he pays the full amount of the redundancy payment without exercising his right to reduce or eliminate it he will still receive from the Redundancy Fund a rebate calculated by reference to the redundancy payment which would otherwise be payable.[2]

[1] Redundancy Payments Pensions Regulations 1965, para. 5. If by virtue of a statutory provision an employee's remuneration is payable to him by a person other than his employer any reference to employer is construed as a reference to the person paying the remuneration, *ibid.*, para. 6.
[2] I.e., on the full amount.

The Secretary of State is empowered[1] to make provision by regulation for securing that where a person is entitled to compensation under a statutory provision for loss of employment, or loss, or diminution, of emoluments or pension rights, in consequence of the operation of another statutory provision, the amount of any redundancy payment to which the employee is also entitled should be set off against the compensation which is otherwise payable. The Redundancy Payments Statutory Compensation Regulations 1965[2] have been made under this power and the amount of compensation payable pursuant to the listed statutory compensation provisions should be reduce. by the amount of the redundancy payment paid to the employee under the Redundancy Payments Act 1965.[3] For the effect on a redundancy payment when the employee is guilty of misconduct, takes part in a strike during notice, or is guilty of other misconduct during notice, see pp 177, 205 and 207, above respectively.

[1] By Redundancy Payments Act 1965, s. 47.
[2] S.I. 1965 No. 1988.
[3] Redundancy Payments Statutory Compensation Regulations 1965, para. 4.

## (ii) A week's pay

Part II of Schedule 4 of the Employment Protection Act 1975 sets out the method of calculating a week's pay.[1]

[1] Prior to its full introduction by the Employment Protection Act 1975 (Commencement No. 4) Order 1976, the Contracts of Employment Act 1972, Sch. 2 applied as originally enacted.

Where there are normal working hours for an employee when employed under the contract of employment in force on the calculation date,[1] if the employee's remuneration[2] for employment in the normal working hours whether by the hour, week, or other period, does not vary with the amount done, the amount of a week's pay is the amount[3] which is payable by the employer under the contract of employment in force on the calculation date if the employee works throughout his normal working hours in a week.[4] Paragraph 4 provides for cases where there are normal working hours for an employee when employed under the contract of employment in force at the calculation date, and he is required under the contract to work during those hours on days of the week, or at times of the day which differ from week to week, or over a longer period, so that the remuneration payable for, or apportionable to, any week varies according to the incidence of the days or times. The amount of a week's pay is the amount of remuneration for the average weekly number of normal working hours at the average hourly rate.[5] The average is taken over a 12 week period.[6]

[1] For an explanation of when there are and are not, normal working hours see p. 140, above.

[2] For remuneration, see p. 47, above. In general terms it means all financial benefits to which the employee is contractually entitled. If a similar approach is applied to the word "remuneration" in Sch. 4 as was used in relation to Contracts of Employment Act 1972, Sch. 2, benefits in kind will be disregarded, as will payments from third parties, but the profit element in "expenses" will be included; *S. and U. Stores, Ltd.* v. *Wilkes*, [1974] 3 All E.R. 401, N.I.R.C.

[3] I.e., the contractual gross pay; see *Murphy Telecommunications (Systems), Ltd.* v. *Henderson and Craig*, [1974] I.R.L.R. 51, N.I.R.C.

[4] Employment Protection Act 1975, Sch. 4, para. 3 (2). References to remuneration varying with the amount of work done include references to remuneration which may include commission or similar payment which varies in amount; *ibid.*, Sch. 4, para. 3 (4).

[5] *Ibid.*, Sch. 4, para. 4 (2).

[6] *Ibid.*, Sch. 4, para. 4 (3) and (4). Where the calculation date is the last day of a week the 12-week period ends with that week, in other cases it is the 12-week period ending with the last complete week before the calculation date. "Week" means for an employee whose remuneration is calculated weekly by a week

ending with a day other than Saturday, a week ending with that other day, and for other employees, means a week ending with Saturday; *ibid.*, Sch. 4, para. 8 (*b*).

In other cases of employments for which there are normal working hours, the amount of a week's pay is the amount of remuneration for the number of normal working hours in a week calculated at the average hourly rate of remuneration payable by the employer to the employee in respect of the period of 12 weeks (a) where the calculation date is the last day of the week, ending with that week; or (b) in any other case ending with the last complete week before the calculation date.[1]

[1] Employment Protection Act 1975, Sch. 4, para. 3 (3). For "week", see note on p. 247, above.

In arriving at the average hourly rate of remuneration only the hours when the employee was working, and only the remuneration payable for, or apportionable to, those hours of work will be brought in; and if for any of the 12 weeks mentioned no remuneration was payable by the employer to the employee, account shall be taken of remuneration in earlier weeks so as to bring the number of weeks of which account is taken up to 12.[1] Where in arriving at the hourly rate of remuneration account has to be taken of remuneration payable for, or apportionable to, work done in hours other than normal working hours, and the amount of that remuneration is greater than it would have been if the work had been done in normal working hours, account is taken of that remuneration as if the work had been done in normal working hours and the amount of that remuneration had been reduced accordingly.[2] In such a case where the minimum number of hours of employment exceeds the number of hours without overtime[3] the remuneration for the hours other than normal working hours is taken as if the work had been done in "non-overtime hours" and the amount of the remuneration had been reduced accordingly.[4]

[1] Employment Protection Act 1975, Sch. 4, para. 5 (1).
[2] *Ibid.*, Sch. 4, para. 5 (2).
[3] I.e., falling within Employment Protection Act 1975, Sch. 4, para. 2.
[4] *Ibid.*, Sch. 4, para. 5 (3).

Differing rules apply to employments when under the contract of employment in force on the calculation date there are no normal working hours for the employee.[1] The amount of a week's pay in this situation, is the amount of the employee's average weekly remuneration in the period of 12 weeks ending on the calculation date, if it is the last day of the week, or in any other case ending with the last complete week before the calculation date.[2] No account is taken of a week in which no remuneration was payable by the employer to the employee and remuneration in earlier weeks is brought in so as to bring the number of weeks of which account is taken to 12.[3]

[1] Employment Protection Act 1975, Sch. 4, para. 6.
[2] *Ibid.*, Sch. 4, para. 6 (2).
[3] *Ibid.*, Sch. 4, para. 6 (3).

Both where there are, and are not, normal working hours applicable to the employment if the employee has not been employed for a sufficient period to enable a calculation to be made as above the amount of a week's pay is the amount which fairly represents the week's pay. The tribunal in determining that amount applies the above provisions as it considers appropriate, and may have regard to such of the following considerations as it thinks fit:

(a) Any remuneration received by the employee in respect of the employment in question;

(b) The amount offered to the employee as remuneration in respect of the employment in question;

(c) The remuneration receivable by other persons engaged in the relevant comparable employment with the same employer;

(d) The remuneration received by other persons engaged in relevant comparable employment with other employers.[1]

Account is taken of work with former employers where continuity has been preserved for the purposes of Schedule 1 to the Contracts of Employment Act 1972.[2]

If bonuses or other payments are receivable but do not coincide with the periods for which the remuneration or other payments are calculated then they are apportioned in such manner as the tribunal considers to be just.[3] The Secretary of State may by regulation provide that in prescribed cases the amount of a week's pay shall be calculated in such manner as the regulations may prescribe.[4]

[1] Employment Protection Act 1975, Sch. 4, para. 7.
[2] *Ibid.*, Sch. 4, para. 8 (*a*).
[3] *Ibid.*, Sch. 4, para. 9.
[4] *Ibid.*, Sch. 4, para. 10.

## (iii) **Written statement of amount of redundancy payment**

On making a redundancy payment, otherwise than in pursuance of a decision of an industrial tribunal, which specifies the amount of the payment to be made, the employer should give to the employee a written statement indicating how the payment has been calculated.[1] Forms for this purpose are available from local offices of the Department of Employment although there is no statutory requirement to use them. An employer who fails to comply, without reasonable excuse, is guilty of an offence and is liable on summary conviction to a fine not exceeding £20.[2] In addition the employee can require the employer to provide such a statement by a notice in writing[3] within such period, (not being less than one week beginning with the day on which the notice is given) as may be specified in the notice. If the employer without reasonable excuse fails to comply with that notice he is guilty of an offence and is liable,[4] if it is his first conviction to a fine not exceeding £20, or in any other case to a fine not exceeding £100. The form supplied by the Department of Employment, a duplicate of which is used as a receipt for the redundancy payment and is normally sent to the Department on the application for a redundancy rebate, is a very convenient vehicle for setting out this information.[5]

---

[1] Redundancy Payments Act 1965, 2. 18 (1).

[2] *Ibid.*, s. 18 (2). See also, *ibid.*, s. 52 (1), discussed at p. 273, below.

[3] See Appendix 7, Form 4, below.

[4] Redundancy Payments Act 1965, s. 18 (3).

[5] If a payment is made to an employee which is in excess of his legal entitlement for payment in lieu of notice, holiday pay and the like, the excess cannot be regarded as attributable to a redundancy payment due, unless section 18 of the Redundancy Payments Act 1965 is complied with by providing the required written statement. An example is *Collin* v. *Flexiform, Ltd.* (1966), 1 I.T.R. 253, T, when payment in lieu of notice was more than that legally due. This was held not to include redundancy payment. *Pratt* v. *Gordon* (1966), 1 I.T.R. 537, T, and *Power* v. *E.M.I. Astral, Ltd.* (1966), 1 I.T.R. 482, T, are also relevant. Contrast *Bagga* v. *Heavy Electricals (India) Ltd.* (1972), 7 I.T.R. 70, N.I.R.C. The applicant who was dismissed by reason of redundancy wrote to his former employers claiming a redundancy payment. After some delay the employers replied "that as adequate compensation as per section 14 Redundancy Payments Act on the termination of your services, the management have agreed to pay you gratuity". A payment was made of exactly the sum due under the Redundancy Payments Act 1965, but section 14 of that Act was not relevant, and the employers thought that their liability to make redundancy payments arose under the Superannuation Act 1965. They did however realise that the payment was such as was due in a redundancy situation. The decision of the

*Time limit in which to claim for a redundancy payment*

industrial tribunal holding that the payment was a redundancy payment was upheld.

## TIME LIMIT IN WHICH TO CLAIM FOR A REDUNDANCY PAYMENT

Section 21 of the Redundancy Payments Act 1965, as amended,[1] provides:

"21.—[(1)] Notwithstanding anything in the preceding provisions of this Part of this Act, an employee shall not be entitled to a redundancy payment unless, before the end of the period of six months beginning with the relevant date,—

(a) the payment has been agreed and paid, or

(b) the employee has made a claim for the payment by notice in writing given to the employer, or

(c) a question as to the right of the employee to the payment, or as to the amount of the payment, has been referred to a tribunal in accordance with regulations made under Part III of this Act, [or

(d) a complaint relating to his dismissal has been presented by the employee under paragraph 17 of Schedule 1 to the Trade Union and Labour Relations Act 1974.

(2) An employee shall not by virtue of the preceding subsection lose his right to a redundancy payment if, during the period of six months immediately following the period mentioned in that subsection, the employee—

(a) makes such a claim as is referred to in paragraph (b) of that subsection,

(b) refers to a tribunal such a question as is referred to in paragraph (c) of that subsection, or

(c) makes such a complaint as is referred to in paragraph (d) of that subsection,

and it appears to the tribunal to be just and equitable that the employee should receive a redundancy payment having regard to the reason shown by the employee for his failure to take any such step as is referred to in paragraph (a), (b) or (c) of this subsection within the period mentioned in the preceding subsection, and to all the other relevant circumstances]."

[1] By virtue of the Employment Protection Act 1975 (Commencement No. 4) Order 1976, S.I. 1976 No. 530, the amendments to the Redundancy Payments Act 1965, s. 21 made by Employment Protection Act 1975, Sch. 16, Part I, para. 9 were introduced. The words added are shown in square brackets. Previously the subsection now numbered (1) constituted the entire section. Under s. 21 prior to its amendment failure to claim in time was a bar to the right to a redundancy payment, not merely the remedy, *Secretary of State for Employment* v. *Atkins Auto Laundries, Ltd.*, [1972] 1 All E.R. 987; [1972] 1 W.L.R. 507. The time limit applies to the right to a redundancy payment but does not apply to claims as to its amount; *Bentley Engineering Co., Ltd.* v. *Crown*, [1976] I.C.R. 225, D.C.

Sub-section (2) was added by the Employment Protection Act 1975, to cover, in particular, the case where a claim for a redundancy payment was made orally within the six-month period and did not fall within section 21, sub-section (1) (b) because it was not made in writing. The new sub-section is not limited to such instances but can cover a wide variety of situations where it appears to the tribunal to be just and equitable that the employee should receive a redundancy payment. There are special provisions which apply on the death of the employee.

"*. . . 6 months . . .*", Prior to the amendment carried out by the Employment Protection Act 1975, there was a tendency to look liberally at section 21. In *McCutcheon* v. *Sykes Macfarlane Ltd.* (1967), 2 I.T.R. 621, T, an application posted within the six months but received after the expiry of the time was held valid. The applicant in *Hetherington* v. *Dependable Products Ltd.* (1971), 6 I.T.R. 1 C.A., did not apply to the industrial tribunal within the six-month period but a union official wrote to the employers "re the position of Mrs. Hetherington, who was made redundant whilst off sick". In the Court of Appeal Lord DENNING, M.R., said that the requirements as to notice should be construed liberally in favour of the employee but that the letter from the union official could not be held to be such notice. Contrast *Gerrard* v. *James Linton & Co., Ltd.* (1969), 4 I.T.R. 135, D.C., where the letter referred to taking the case to the tribunal. This was found by the Divisional Court to be sufficient notice in writing. It is possible that cases like these will now be dealt with by the exercise of the tribunal's new discretion.

"*. . . the relevant date . . .*": This is defined in the Redundancy Payments Act 1965, section 3 (9) (added by Employment Protection Act 1975, see p. 208, above) as being: (1) when the contract of employment is terminated by notice, whether given by the employer or the employee, the date on which the notice expires; or (2) where the contract is terminated without notice the date on which the termination takes effect; or (3) where the employee is employed under a conttact for a fixed term which expires and is not renewed, the date of expiry; or (4) where there is a trial period pursuant to section 3 of the Redundancy Payments Act 1965 (see p. 197, above) and within the trial period the employee terminates the contract (for whatever reason), or the employer terminates the contract, or gives notice to terminate it and it is later terminated for a reason connected with or arising out of the change to the renewed or new contract, the date (for the purposes of Redundancy Payments Act 1965, s. 21 only; Redundancy Payments Act 1965, s. 3 (9) (*d*) (i)) is that specified in (a), (b) or (c) above in relation to the renewed contract, or if there has been more than one trial period, the last such contract; or (5) where the employee anticipates the expiry of the employer's notice by giving notice himself, the date on which the employee's notice expires (Redundancy Payments Act 1965, s. 4 (2)).

*section 21 (1) (b)* "...*to the employer...*". In *Stoughton* v. *Bancroft Folding Machines, Ltd.* (1967), 2 I.T.R. 32, T, notice given to a director in his personal capacity was held not to constitute notice to the company. It was further held that a letter to the employer from the applicant's solicitors "reserving the rights of our client" under the Redundancy Payment Act 1965 was not a claim under section 21 (1) (*b*).

If the employee dies before the end of the six-month period beginning with the relevant date the initial period of six months is extended to a year; Redundancy Payments Act 1965, Schedule 4, paragraph 20 (1). If the former employee dies after the period of six months from the relevant date and before the end of the following period of six months the "discretionary" period of six months is extended to one year; Redundancy Payments Act 1965, Schedule 4, paragraph 20 (2).

## DEATH OF EMPLOYER OR OF EMPLOYEE

### (i) Death of employer

The death of an individual employer terminates the employment of the employee and as such operates as a dismissal.[1] If the contract is not renewed or the employee is not re-engaged under a new contract under the provisions of Redundancy Payments Act 1965, section 3 (3) he is taken as being dismissed by reason of redundancy if the fact that he is not so re-engaged is wholly or mainly attributable to redundancy as defined in Redundancy Payments Act, 1965, section 1 (2).[2]

[1] Redundancy Payments Act 1965, s. 22 (1).

[2] *Ibid.*, s. 22 (2). Section 3 (3) applies as substituted for the purpose by *ibid.*, Sch. 4, para. 3. See *Narang* v. *Trustees of J. Hodge (deceased)* (1969), 4 I.T.R. 81, T, where an application for a redundancy payment made by an employee who refused to work for his dead employer's widow was dismissed.

By virtue of section 23 of the Redundancy Payments Act 1965 the provisions of Part I of Schedule 4 (as amended by the Employment Protection Act 1975) apply.[1] This provides that when an employee's contract is terminated by the death of his employer, he is not entitled to a redundancy payment if he is re-engaged by the personal representative to take effect not later than eight weeks after the death, provided that if the provisions of the contract as renewed, or the new contract, as to the capacity and place in which the employee is employed or as to the other terms and conditions of his employment, differ (wholly or in part) from the corresponding provisions of the previous contract the rules as to trial period on offer of renewal or re-engagement apply, save that reference to the employer shall be construed as reference to the personal representatives of the deceased employer.[2]

[1] Redundancy Payments Act 1965, Sch. 4 is amended by Employment Protection Act 1975, Sch. 16, Part I, paras. 23–34 and is discussed in its amended form.

[2] Redundancy Payments Act 1965, Sch. 4, paras. 3 and 4 (as amended). For the rules as to trial period, see p. 197, above.

Redundancy Payments Act 1965, Schedule 4, paragraph 4 (as amended) provides that an employee is not entitled to a redundancy payment if he unreasonably refuses such an offer of re-engagement by the personal representatives, if the employment offered is either on the same terms as before, or if on different terms, suitable in relation to the employee.[1] In deciding whether the employment offered is suitable or whether the employee acted unreasonably in refusing it, the mere fact that the personal representative is now the employer is irrelevant.[2]

# Death of employer or of employee

[1] See p. 209, above.
[2] Redundancy Payments Act 1965, Sch. 4, para. 5 (a).

If the employee has been laid-off or put on short-time immediately before the employer's death and has not served notice of intention to claim, Redundancy Payments Act 1965, Schedule 4, paragraph 7 (as amended) contains provisions for aggregating a period before death with that afterwards as if the week in which the former employer died and the first week of employment by the personal representative were consecutive weeks. The periods of four and 13 weeks are construed accordingly. Paragraphs 8–10 of Schedule 4 deal with cases where the employee has served notice of intended claim within the four weeks preceding the death.[1]

[1] If the employee had not, by the date of death, terminated the contract in accordance with the provisions as to lay-off and short-time discussed at p. 223, above, if he is not re-engaged or his contract is not renewed within four weeks after the service of notice of intention to claim the usual provisions apply as if the employer had not died and the employee had terminated the employment by notice expiring at the end of the four weeks; Redundancy Payments Act 1965, Sch. 4, para. 9. If the contract is renewed, or the employee re-engaged, and the employee was laid-off or put on short-time for one or more weeks before the employer's death and he is laid off or kept on short-time by the personal representative for the week or more weeks following the renewal or re-engagement the weeks are treated as consecutive and the periods for lay-off and short-time are extended by any week or weeks any part of which was after the death of the deceased employer and before the date on which the renewal or re-engagement took effect; Redundancy Payments Act 1965, Sch. 4, para. 10.

Where the employee is a domestic servant employed in a private household[1] references to personal representative are construed as including references to any person (e.g., a relative) to whom management of the household has passed in consequence of the death, otherwise than on a sale or other disposal for valuable consideration.[2]

[1] Redundancy Payments Act 1965, s. 19 (1). See p. 169, above.
[2] Ibid., Sch. 4, para. 13.

There are special provisions relating to the death of an insolvent employer contained in section 32 (5) (b).

On a renewal or re-engagement by a personal representative within the provisions mentioned above the employee is not regarded as having been dismissed and continuity is preserved.[1] The obligations of personal representatives so far as payment of a redundancy payment which is payable as a result of the termination occasioned by the death is a liability which is treated as accruing immediately before the former employer's death.[2]

[1] Redundancy Payments Act 1965, Sch. 4, para. 3, as substituted by Employment Protection Act 1975, Sch. 16, Part I, para. 23.
[2] Redundancy Payments Act 1965, Sch. 4, para. 15.

## (ii) Death of the employee

There are provisions in Part II of Schedule 4 of the Redundancy Payments Act 1965 to cover cases where the employee dies after notice has been given, where notice has been given and an offer to renew the employment contract or re-engage the employee has been made and also if the employee dies during the trial period.[1] If there is no personal representative of the deceased employee, tribunal proceedings may be instituted, or contained, on behalf of the estate of the deceased employee by such other persons as the tribunal may appoint, being either a person authorised by the employee to act in connection with the proceedings before his death, or the widower, widow, child, father, mother, brother or sister of the deceased employee.[2] References to a personal representative are construed as including such person.[3] In such a case any award made by the tribunal shall be in such terms and shall be enforceable in such manner as may be provided by regulations made by the Secretary of State.[4] For the effect of death on the time limits in which to claim redundancy payments, see p. 253, above.

[1] Redundancy Payments Act 1965, Sch. 4, paras. 16–22. If an employee has been given notice and dies before it expires the notice is treated as expiring on the date of the employee's death; *ibid.*, Sch. 4, para. 16 (1). Other notices are treated as expiring on that date; *ibid.*, Sch. 4, para. 17A and offers to renew, or re-engage, both before and during the trial period defeat a claim "if it would have been unreasonable" for the employee to refuse them; *ibid.*, Sch. 4, paras. 17 and 17A.
[2] Redundancy Payments Act 1965, Sch. 4, para. 21A. Inserted by Employment Protection Act 1975, Sch. 16, Part I, para. 34.
[3] Redundancy Payments Act 1965, Sch. 4, para. 21A (2).
[4] *Ibid.*, Sch. 4, para. 21A (2). The regulations are made in accordance with Employment Protection Act 1975, s. 123; Redundancy Payments Act 1965, Sch. 4, para. 21A (3). See the Industrial Tribunals Awards (Enforcement in Case of Death) Regulations 1976, S.I. 1976 No. 663, discussed at p. 411, below.

## REBATES AND THE REDUNDANCY FUND

The Redundancy Fund was established by section 26 of the Redundancy Payments Act 1965 and is under the control and management of the Secretary of State for Employment. It is financed by employers from an allocation from the secondary Class I contribution paid in respect of the employed earners under the Social Security Act 1975 and may receive advances from the National Loans Fund.

### (1) Payments out of the Redundancy Fund to employers

An employer who is liable to, and makes a redundancy payment, or is liable to make a payment under an agreement the subject of an order under section 11 of the Redundancy Payments Act 1965, on the termination of employment and has made that payment, is entitled to a rebate from the Redundancy Fund.[1] No rebate is payable if the payment made pursuant to an agreement in respect of which an order has been made under the Redundancy Payments Act 1965, section 11 is made by virtue of a period of employment, computed in accordance with the agreement, which is less than 104 weeks.[2] Prior to the passing of the Employment Protection Act 1975, if an employer made the payment voluntarily after the employee's claim was time-barred then no rebate was payable.[3] The new sub-section 30 (2A) of the Redundancy Payments Act 1965 gives the Secretary of State for Employment a discretion to make payment of the rebate if he is satisfied that it would be just and equitable to do so having regard to the relevant circumstances. If the Secretary of State refuses to pay a rebate in such a case then the employer can appeal to an industrial tribunal and if it is satisfied that having regard to all the relevant circumstances it is just and equitable for the rebate to be paid, it determines accordingly and the Secretary of State should comply with the determination.[4]

[1] Redundancy Payments Act 1965, s. 30 (1). A rebate is also payable to an employer who by virtue of an award by the Central Arbitration Committee in respect of an agreement in respect of which an exemption order has been made under section 11, (see p. 173, above) is liable to make, and has made, a payment to an employee on the termination of his contract of employment; section 30 (1) (c). See also Redundancy Payments Act 1965, Sch. 5, paras. 8 and 9.

[2] Redundancy Payments Act 1965, s. 30 (2).

# Chapter 6 Redundancy

[3] *Secretary of State for Employment* v. *Atkins Auto Laundries, Ltd.*, [1972] 1 All E.R. 987; [1972] 1 W.L.R. 507, N.I.R.C.

[4] Redundancy Payments Act 1965, s. 34 (3A), added by Employment Protection Act 1975, Sch. 16, Part I, para. 16.

Since the Redundancy Rebates Act 1969 the amount of the rebate has been one half of the redundancy payment payable in accordance with Schedule 1 of the Redundancy Payments Act 1965.[1] In the case of an agreement which is exempted under section 11 the rebate payable is that which would have been payable in respect of a payment calculated under the rules of the exempted agreement for the purpose of computing the period of employment, but under the rules of the Redundancy Payments Act 1965, (as amended) for all other purposes. If the amount of the payment is less than the redundancy payment which would have been payable then the amount of the rebate is one-half of the payment actually paid.

[1] Redundancy Payments Act 1965, Sch. 5, as amended. If the redundancy payment is reduced in accordance with provisions of the Act, or statutory instrument, the rebate is reduced in proportion. On 22nd July 1976 the Chancellor of the Exchequer announced the Government's intention to reduce the amount of rebate to 40% of the redundancy payment payable. If this is implemented references in the text to "one half" should be changed to "40%".

The employer should notify the local office of the Department of Employment prior to the effective date of dismissal.[1] If there are 10 or more employees in the same establishment whose contracts are to terminate or are expected to terminate on the same day or within a period of not more than six days, not less than 21 days notice should be given before the terminations (or first of them) are to, or are expected to, take effect.[2] In other cases prior notice should be given not less than 14 days before the date on which the termination of the contract of employment is to take effect or is expected to take effect.[2] The Regulations prescribe the information which is to be given and the local offices of the Employment Services Agency have forms readily available which are convenient to use. If the employer fails to give the required advance notice then the employer's rebate can be reduced by the Secretary of State by up to 1/10th if it appears to him that the employer failed to give the notice without reasonable excuse. The reduction can be of such proportion as appears to be appropriate in the circumstances.[3] An employer who is aggrieved about the decision of the Secretary of State to reduce the rebate may appeal to an industrial tribunal which can determine that the employer should have the full amount of the rebate, or can increase, or reduce, the amount of the reduction within the 10 per cent limit.[4]

[1] Redundancy Payments Rebates Regulations 1965, S.I. 1965 No. 1893, (as amended).
[2] Redundancy Payments Rebates Regulations 1965, above, para. 3. This obligation is quite separate from that to notify the Secretary of State under Employment Protection Act 1975, s. 100, see p. 267, below.
[3] Redundancy Payments Act 1965, s. 30 (6), subject to the 10% maximum. There is also a separate right to reduce the rebate under the provisions in the Employment Protection Act, 1975, see p. 268, below.
[4] *Ibid.*, 2. 34 (4).

The claim for rebate should be made within six months of the day on which the employer made the payment in respect of which rebate is claimed, or within such further period of the Secretary of State in his discretion allows.[1] If the original application is incomplete, or defective in some way, and the form requires amendment, the claim can be made within four weeks of it being referred back to the employer by the Secretary of State, or within four weeks of the expiry of the six month period.[2]

[1] Redundancy Payments Rebates Regulations 1965, reg. 5.
[2] *Ibid.*, reg. 7. The form must specify the employee or employees to which it relates if this is to apply.

The claim should be made in writing specifying the day on which the employment terminated and indicate how the payment was calculated.[1] Unless the requirement is waived the claim form should be accompanied by a receipt for the redundancy payment signed by the employee.[2] The Employment Service Agency has available forms for making claims together with others which are particularly useful being (if used in duplicate), both receipts and statements as to calculation of the redundancy payment, to accompany claim forms. The Secretary of State has power to require further evidence and information to be determine the right of a person to, or the amount of, a rebate.[3] In proceedings for rebate it is possible for the industrial tribunal to look again at the amount of redundancy payments. In *Crest Hotels, Ltd.* v. *Secretary of State for Employment*[4] an industrial tribunal awarded an employee £111 redundancy payment but on hearing an application by the employer for rebate it became apparent that only £19 was properly payable. The tribunal held that it could look again at the computation of redundancy payments and a rebate calculated by reference to the £19 was ordered. *North Western Electricity Board* v. *Secretary of State for Employment*[5] was a case where a redundancy payment had been paid but subsequently a wage award was "back-dated" to before the dismissals took effect. Further redundancy payments were paid and the employer sought to obtain rebates in respect of the extra payments. The tribunal held that the employers were entitled to the rebate in cases where the employees had made application to the employers within the time limit. The discretion of the Secretary of State would apply as far as payments to the other employees are concerned.[6]

[1] Redundancy Payments Rebates Regulations 1965, reg. 5.

[2] *Ibid.*, reg. 6(2).

[3] *Ibid.*, reg. 6 (1).

[4] (1971) 6 I.T.R. 142, T, but the original award cannot be re-opened on such application; *Oliver* v. *R. F. Tilney & Son, Ltd.* (1967), 2 I.T.R. 183, T.

[5] (1973), 8 I.T.R. 209. As to the effect of the time limit on the *quantum* of a redundancy payment see *Bentley Engineering Co., Ltd.* v. *Crown*, [1976] I.C.R. 225, D.C.

[6] If the Secretary of State makes payment of rebate as a result of a mistake of fact he can recover the rebate wrongly paid; *Secretary of State for Employment* v. *Wellworthy, Ltd.* (*No. 2*), [1976] I.C.R. 13, D.C. It is the High Court and not an industrial tribunal which has jurisdiction to deal with such a claim; *Secretary of State for Employment* v. *Wellworthy, Ltd.*, [1973] 3 All E.R. 488.


If an employer in providing information required by the Secretary of State under the Regulations makes a statement which he knows to be false in a material particular, or recklessly makes such a statement, or produces a document which to his knowledge is wilfully falsified he is guilty of an offence.[1] A person guilty of such an offence is liable on summary conviction to a fine not exceeding £100, or to imprisonment for a term of three months, or both, or on conviction on endictment to a fine, or to imprisonment for a term not exceeding two years, or both.[2]

[1] Redundancy Payments Act 1965, s. 30(7).

[2] *Ibid.*, s. 30(8). See also s. 52, discussed at p. 273, below.


Section 41 of the Redundancy Payments Act 1965 makes

provision for the payment of appropriate sums from the Redundancy Fund in respect of payments akin to redundancy payments made to persons by certain public bodies[1] and section 43 makes somewhat similar provisions to cover employment under the Government of an overseas territory in respect of whom Social Security contributions as employed persons are made. Broadly speaking the payment from the Redundancy Fund is the sum which appears to the Secretary of State to be equal to that which would have been payable by way of rebate if a redundancy payment had been payable and had been paid.[2] In certain cases payments may be made from the Redundancy Fund in respect of employees who are excluded from the statutory redundancy payments scheme.[3]

[1] It includes payment to those in public offices for the purposes of the Superannuation Acts 1965 to 1972, civil servants, employees of bodies listed in Redundancy Payments Act 1965, Sch. 3 and those remunerated out of the revenues of the Duchy of Lancaster, the Duchy of Cornwall, the Queen's Civil List and Her Majesty's Privy Purse; Redundancy Payments Act 1965, s. 41 (1).

[2] See *ibid.*, s. 41 (4) and s. 43 (3).

[3] *Ibid.*, s. 31.

## (2) Payments out of the Redundancy Fund to employees

When an employee has taken all reasonable steps (other than legal proceedings) to recover a redundancy payment from his employer and the employer has refused or failed to pay it, or has paid part, and refused, or failed, to pay the balance, or the employer is insolvent and the whole or part of the redundancy payment remains unpaid the employee may apply to the Secretary of State for Employment for payment from the Redundancy Fund.[1] When the Secretary of State is satisfied of the employee's entitlement, that the employee has taken all reasonable steps to obtain payment from the employer, or the employer is insolvent and the redundancy payment or part of it remains unpaid, he must make a redundancy payment computed in accordance with Schedule 1 of the Redundancy Payments Act 1965.[2] So long as the employee is not affected by an agreement exempted under section 11 the sum paid is the whole of the redundancy payment less any amount already paid.[2] If the Secretary of State is satisfied that a sum is due under an exempted agreement and that the employee's right arises by virtue of a period of employment (computed in accordance with the provisions of the agreement) which is not less than 104 weeks, he must similarly make a payment; the payment is either the payment due to the employee under the agreement or the payment in respect of which rebate is payable to the employer whichever is the less, reduced by any part payment made by the employer.[2] In cases where the employer admits his liability to make a payment but fails to pay, application to a tribunal is not a necessary "step to recover payment" within section 32 (1); see *Jeffrey* v. *Grey*.[3] An employee can claim against the employer before a tribunal even though the employer is insolvent; *Barcza* v. *Poomac Restaurants, Ltd.*[4]

[1] Redundancy Payments Act 1965, s. 32. The phrase "legal proceedings" does not include any proceedings before a tribunal but includes any proceedings to enforce a decision or award of a tribunal; *ibid.*, s. 32 (7).

[2] *Ibid.*, s. 32 (2) and Sch. 6.

[3] (1967), 2 I.T.R. 335, T.

[4] (1968), 3 I.T.R. 234, T.

If the Secretary of State makes a payment all rights and remedies of the employee with respect to the employer's payment (or if appropriate that part paid from the Redundancy Fund) are transferred to and vest in the Secretary of State. Any decision of a tribunal requiring the employer's payment to be paid to the employee has effect as if it required that payment, or as the case may be, that part of it paid from the Fund to be paid to the Secretary of State for payment into the Redundancy Fund.[1] Insolvency is defined for these purposes by section 32 (5) of the Redundancy Payments Act 1965 (as amended) as being, in the case of an individual, if he has become bankrupt, or made a composition, or arrangement, with his creditors, or a receiving order is made against him,[2] or he has died and an order has been made under section 130 of the Bankruptcy Act 1914 for the administration of his estate according to the law of bankruptcy, or by virtue of an order of a court his estate is being administered in accordance with the rules set out in Part I of Schedule 1 to the Administration of Estates Act 1925, or where the employer is a company, a winding up order has been with respect to it, or a resolution for voluntary winding up has been passed, or a receiver or manager of its undertaking has been duly appointed, or possession has been taken by, or on behalf of, the holders of any debentures secured by a floating charge, of any property of the company comprised in or subject to the charge.[3] In cases of insolvency where the Secretary of State makes payment to the employee he is able to prove in the insolvency for half the amount of the redundancy payment. When the employer has failed, or refused, to pay (or pay the whole of) a redundancy payment in circumstances where it appears to the Secretary of State to have been without reasonable excuse he may withhold the rebate, or part of it, as he considered appropriate.[4] An employer who claims a rebate which is withheld or reduced by the Secretary of State may refer the matter to an industrial tribunal.[5] An employee who has made a claim to the Secretary of State for payment under section 32 may refer the matter to the tribunal to determine liability, or the amount of any payment to be made.[5] A tribunal does not have jurisdiction to decide whether or not employees have rightly received redundancy payments paid to them on a reference by the Secretary of State.[6]

[1] Redundancy Payments Act 1965, s. 32 (3).

[2] The reference to a receiving order was added by Employment Protection Act 1975, Sch. 16, Part I, para. 14; see *Pollard* v. *Teako (Swiss) Ltd.* (1967), 2 I.T.R. 357, T.

[3] A company may not be able to pay its debts and yet not be insolvent within the meaning of Redundancy Payments Act 1965, s. 32 (5).

[4] Redundancy Payments Act 1965, s. 32 (4).

[5] *Ibid.*, s. 34 (1).

[6] *Secretary of State for Employment* v. *Wellworthy, Ltd.*, [1973] 3 All E.R. 488, N.I.R.C.; *Secretary of State for Employment* v. *Nortons (Cardiff), Ltd.* (1972), 7 I.T.R. 136, T (as to this point). This is within the jurisdiction of the High Court; *Secretary of State for Employment* v. *Wellworthy, Ltd. (No. 2),* [1976] I.C.R. 13, Q.B.D.

## PROCEDURE FOR HANDLING REDUNDANCIES

Part IV of the Employment Protection Act 1975[1] introduces a new statutory procedure for handling redundancies. This has two elements, consultation and notification. For the purposes of proceedings involving these procedures, dismissals and proposed dismissals shall be presumed to be by reason of redundancy unless the contrary is proved.[2]

[1] Which came into force on 8th March 1976.

[2] Employment Protection Act 1975, s. 106 (2), and see p. 175, above as to the general presumption of redundancy.

### (a) Consultation

Consultation should begin at the earliest opportunity and if the employer is proposing to dismiss as redundant 100 or more employees at one establishment within a period of 90 days or less, it must begin at least 90 days before the first of those dismissals takes effect; when the employer proposes to dismiss as redundant 10 or more employees at one establishment within a period of 30 days or less, it must begin at least 60 days before the first of those dismissals takes effect.[1] No account is taken in computing the figures of employees who are to be dismissed because they are redundant, of those employees in respect of whom redundancy consultation has already begun.[2] The consultation should be with representatives of the independent trade union recognised[3] by the employer in respect of employees of the description of the employee to be made redundant. The employer should disclose in writing to the trade union representatives:

"(*a*) the reasons for his proposals;
 (*b*) the numbers and descriptions of employees whom it is proposed to dismiss as redundant;
 (*c*) the total number of employees of any such description employed by the employer at the establishment in question;
 (*d*) the proposed method of selecting the employees who may be dismissed; and
 (*e*) the proposed method of carrying out the dismissals, with due regard to any agreed procedure, including the period over which the dismissals are to take effect."

The employer is obliged in the course of consultation to consider representations made by the trade union representatives and to reply to them and, if he rejects any of them, to state his reasons.[4] If there are special circumstances rendering it not reasonably practicable to carry out such consultation the employer shall take all such steps towards compliance as are reasonably practicable.[5] It is in order for the employer to give notice to the employees during the period of consultation.

[1] Employment Protection Act 1975, s. 99 (3). There is no requirement for a minimum period of continuous service for any employees for the provisions to apply.
 [2] Employment Protection Act 1975, s. 99 (4).
 [3] For definition see Employment Protection Act 1975, s. 106. A union is treated as recognised not only if it is recognised for the purposes of collective bargaining but also if the Advisory Conciliation and Arbitration Service has made a recommendation for recognition which is operative within the meaning of *ibid.*, s. 15.

⁴ Employment Protection Act 1975, s. 99 (7). There is no requirement that the reasons should be reasonable.
⁵ *Ibid.*, s. 99 (8).

## (b) Failure to consult

An appropriate trade union may present a case to an industrial tribunal on the ground that an employer has dismissed as redundant, or is proposing to dismiss as redundant, one or more employees and has not complied with the consultation obligations.[1] An individual employee is not able to present a complaint. The onus of proof in this respect is on the trade union[2] save that if the employer seeks to show that he did not comply with the obligation because of special circumstances rendering it not reasonably practicable to do so, it is for the employer to show that there were such circumstances and that he took all steps towards compliance with the requirements as were reasonably practicable in the circumstances.

[1] Employment Protection Act 1975, s. 101. The tribunal will refer the matter to the Advisory Conciliation and Arbitration Service so that conciliation may be attempted. See p. 386, below.
[2] Subject to the presumption which will operate so far as reasons for the dismissal are concerned.

If the tribunal finds that the complaint is well founded it must make a declaration to that effect and may also make a protective award.[1] A protective award is an award that in respect of such descriptions of employee as may be specified, being employees who have been dismissed, or whom it is proposed to dismiss, as redundant, and in respect of whose dismissal or proposed dismissal the employer has failed to comply with the consultation requirements, the employer shall pay remuneration for a "protected period".[2] The protected period is a period, beginning with the date on which the first of the dismissals to which the complaint relates takes effect, or the date of the award, whichever is the earlier, of such length as the tribunal determines as being just and equitable in all circumstances having regard to the seriousness of the employer's default in complying with the consultation requirement. The period must not exceed 90 days when the 90-day consultation period was applicable or 60 days when the 60-day period applied. In any other case the protected period should not exceed 28 days.[3] The complaint to the industrial tribunal must be made before the proposed dismissal takes effect, or before the end of a period of three months beginning with the date on which the dismissal takes effect, or such further period as the tribunal considers reasonable in a case where it is satisfied that it was not reasonably practicable for the complaint to be presented within the period of three months.[4]

[1] Employment Protection Act 1975, s. 101 (3).
[2] *Ibid.*, s. 101 (4).
[3] *Ibid.*, s. 101 (5).
[4] *Ibid.*, s. 101 (6).

If a protective award is made every employee of the description to which the award relates is entitled to be paid remuneration for the protected period.[1] This is calculated at the weekly rate of a week's pay as defined in the Employment Protection Act 1975.[2] Payment made to an employee under, or by way of damages for breach of, a contract of employment during the protected period goes towards discharging the employer's liability to pay remuneration under the protective award and vice versa.[3] An employee is not entitled to remuneration during the protected period unless he would have been so entitled under his contract of employment or by virtue of Schedule 2 of the Contracts of Employment Act 1972 (as amended)[4] nor is he entitled to remuneration, where he is fairly dismissed during the period for a reason other than redundancy, or when he unreasonably terminates the contract of employment, in respect of any period during which but for the dismissal or termination he would have been so employed.[5]

[1] Employment Protection Act 1975, s. 102 (1).
[2] *Ibid.*, Sch. 4, Part II. The calculation date is, either is the usual date for redundancy purposes if the dismissal has taken effect and in other cases it is the date on which the protective award was made; *ibid.*, s. 106 (3).
[3] *Ibid.*, s. 102 (3).
[4] *Ibid.*, s. 102 (4). See p. 139, above. This applies in respect of a period during which the employee is employed by the employer.
[5] *Ibid.*, s. 102 (5).

There are special provisions to cover situations where the employer makes an offer, (whether in writing or not), to renew the contract of employment or re-engage the employee under a new contract, when the renewal or re-engagement would take effect before or during the protected period.[1] If the provision of the renewed contract, or the new contract, (as the case may be)

would not differ as to the capacity or place in which he would
be employed and as to the other terms and conditions of his
employment, or they differ, but the offer constitutes an offer of
suitable employment in relation to the employee, if he unreasonably refuses the offer he is not entitled to any remuneration
under the protective award in respect of any period during which,
but for the refusal, he would have been employed.[2] There are
similar provisions as to a trial period of four weeks, or longer if
agreed in accordance with the statutory procedure, as applicable
on other offers of employment or re-engagement.[3]

[1] Employment Protection Act 1975, s. 102 (6) to (11).
[2] *Ibid.*, s. 102 (7).
[3] *Ibid.*, s. 102 (8) to (11). See p. 197, above.

An employee[1] can present a complaint to an industrial
tribunal on the ground that a protective award relates to him and
his employer has failed wholly, or in part, to pay his remuneration
under the award. The complaint should be presented before the
end of the period of three months beginning with the day, or if
applicable, last of the days in respect of which the complaint is
made of failure to pay remuneration, or within such further
period as the tribunal considers reasonable in a case where it is
satisfied it was not reasonably practicable for the complaint to be
presented within the period of three months.[2] If the industrial
tribunal finds the complaint is well founded it must order the
employer to pay the amount of remuneration due to him.[3]

[1] It should be noted that the individual employee and not the trade union
makes the complaint under this head.
[2] Employment Protection Act 1975, s. 103 (2).
[3] *Ibid.*, s. 103 (3).

### (c) Notice to the Secretary of State

An employer who proposes to dismiss as redundant 100 or
more employees at one establishment within a period of 90 days
or less, must notify the Secretary of State for Employment, in
writing, of his proposal at least 90 days before the first of the
dismissals takes effect, or if he proposes to dismiss 10 or more
employees at one establishment within a period of 30 days or
less, he should notify the Secretary of State in writing at least
60 days before the first of the dismissals takes place.[1] When the
notice relates to employees of a description in respect of which an

independent trade union is recognised by the employer he should give a copy of the notice to the representatives of that trade union.[1] The form and particulars to be given to the Secretary of State have been prescribed by him and copies of the form are obtainable from local offices of the Department of Employment. If it is a case where consultation is required the notice should identify the trade union concerned and state the date when consultation began.[2] On receiving the notice the Secretary of State may in writing require the employer to give him such further information as he specifies. There is a similar proviso to that relating to consultation, in that if there are special circumstances rendering it not reasonably practicable for the employer to comply with the requirements as to notice, he is obliged to take all steps towards compliance with that requirement as are reasonably practicable in those circumstances.[3]

[1] Employment Protection Act 1975, s. 100 (1).
[2] *Ibid.*, s. 100 (3).
[3] *Ibid.*, s. 100 (6).

### (d) Failure to notify the Secretary of State

If an employer fails to give notice to the Secretary of State as required by section 100 of the Employment Protection Act 1975 there are two possible remedies, which are only available in the alternative.[1]

If the employer is entitled to a rebate from the redundancy fund in respect of a dismissed employee, the Secretary of State may reduce the rebate by such proportion (not exceeding one-tenth), as appears to the Secretary of State to be appropriate in the circumstances.[2] If the employer is dissatisfied as to the reduction he may appeal to an industrial tribunal. If the tribunal is satisfied that a rebate was reduced to any extent and should not have been reduced or should have been reduced by a greater or lesser proportion, the tribunal shall determine accordingly and the Secretary of State shall comply with the determination.[3] The appeal to the tribunal should be made within three months beginning with the date on which the decision of the Secretary of State was communicated to the employer, or in such other period as the tribunal considers reasonable in a case where it is satisfied that it was not reasonably practicable for the appeal to be presented within the three month period.[4]

The other action which can be taken is for proceedings to be instituted by, or with the consent of, the Secretary of State.[5] Proceedings cannot be instituted for the failure to comply with the provisions as to notification, if the Secretary of State has reduced a rebate under those provisions. The employer is liable on summary conviction to a fine not exceeding four hundred pounds in such proceedings.[6] A document signed by or on behalf of the Secretary of State certifying that no reduction in rebate has been made, is conclusive evidence of that fact.[7] Officers of the Department of Employment may be authorised to conduct the proceedings themselves before magistrates courts.[8]

[1] Employment Protection Act 1975, s. 104 (2).
[2] *Ibid.*, s. 104 (1).
[3] *Ibid.*, s. 104 (4).
[4] *Ibid.*, s. 104 (3).
[5] *Ibid.*, s. 105 (2).
[6] *Ibid.*, s. 105 (1).
[7] *Ibid.*, s. 105 (5).
[8] *Ibid.*, s. 105 (3).

## (e) General

There is provision for the Secretary of State for Employment, by order, to vary the periods given above (with certain limitations) subject to approval by both Houses of Parliament.[1] The Secretary of State may make an order adapting, modifying or excluding any of the consultation and notification provisions in certain circumstances. For such an order to be made there must be a collective agreement in force relating to the employees concerned, which establishes arrangements for providing alternative employment for employees to which it relates if dismissed as redundant, or arrangements for handling redundancies. All parties to the agreement must apply to the Secretary of State and he must be satisfied that the arrangements on the whole are at least as favourable as those created by the Employment Protection Act.[2] The agreement must contain independent arbitration or adjudication arrangements, or indicate that an aggrieved employee can complain to an industrial tribunal on the ground that the employer or another person has not complied with the provisions of the agreement.[3] An order so made may confer on an industrial tribunal such powers and duties as the Secretary of State considers appropriate.[4]

The provisions as to handling redundancies do not apply to Crown employment.[5]

[1] Employment Protection Act 1975, s. 106 (4).
[2] *Ibid.*, s. 107 (1).
[3] *Ibid.*, s. 107 (2).
[4] *Ibid.*, s. 107 (3). There have been no such orders at the moment.
[5] Employment Protection Act 1975, s. 121 (1). The provisions do not apply to dock workers unless they are wholly or mainly engaged in work which is not dock work, as defined by a Dock Labour Scheme, sharefishermen, merchant seamen and those who under their contract of employment ordinarily work outside Great Britain, (subject the order pursuant to the Employment Protection Act 1975, s. 127). In addition they do not apply to the fixed term contracts referred to in Employment Protection Act 1975, s. 119 (7) where the employee has not been continuously employed for more than 12 weeks.

## TIME OFF TO LOOK FOR WORK AND MAKE ARRANGEMENTS FOR TRAINING[1]

An employee who is given notice of dismissal by reason of redundancy, and who, at the later of the date on which his notice is due to expire, and the date on which it would expire if it was the minimum statutory required notice,[2] will have been, or would have been, as the case may be, continuously employed for two years[3] or more, is entitled before the expiration of his notice to be allowed reasonable time off during his working hours in order to look for new employment, or make arrangements for training for future employment.[4]

[1] These provisions came into force on 1st June 1976. They apply to Crown servants other than members of the armed forces and women's services administered by the Defence Council; Employment Protection Act 1975, s. 121. They also apply to members of the staff of the Houses of Commons, *ibid.*, s. 122.
[2] Required by the Contracts of Employment Act 1972.
[3] Employment Protection Act 1975, s. 61 (2).
[4] *Ibid.*, s. 61 (1).

An employee who is accordingly allowed time off during his working hours shall be entitled to be paid remuneration by his employer for the period of absence at the appropriate hourly rate. This is the amount of a week's pay[1] divided by the number of normal working hours in a week for that employee when employed under the contract of employment in force on the day when the notice was given, or when the number of such normal working hours differs from week to week, or over a longer period, the average number of such hours calculated by dividing the number of the employee's normal working hours during the period of 12 weeks ending with the last complete week before the date on which notice was given, by 12. The amount of the employer's liability does not exceed in respect of the notice period of any employee, two-fifths of a week's pay for that employee.[2] If an employer unreasonably refuses to allow an employee time off under section 61 of the Employment Protection Act 1975 the employee is entitled to be paid at an amount equal to the remuneration which would have been paid if he had been allowed time off, subject to the above limitation, and he may present a complaint to an industrial tribunal that his employer has unreasonably refused to allow him time off under the provisions, or has failed to pay the whole or any part of any amount to which the employee is entitled in respect thereof.[3] If the tribunal finds the grounds of the complaint well founded it should make a declaration to that effect and order the employer to pay to the employee the amount due to him.[4] The aggregate amount of the employer's liability to pay remuneration and the amount awarded by the tribunal is subject to the limitation of two-fifths of a week's pay[5] and the statutory provisions do not affect the right of an employee to remuneration under his contract of employment,[6] but the amount of any contractual remuneration in respect of the period when he takes the time off goes towards discharging liability under section 61 and vice versa.[7]

[1] Calculated in accordance with Employment Protection Act 1975, Sch. 4, Part II. The calculation date for these purposes is day on which the employers notice was given; *ibid.*, s. 61 (5). "Week" in relation to an employee whose remuneration is calculated weekly by a week ending with a day other than Saturday means a week ending with that other day, otherwise it means a week ending with a Saturday; *ibid.*, s. 61 (6).

[2] Employment Protection Act 1975, s. 61 (11). There is no such restriction on the length of time off, (presumably without pay if not provided for in the contract of employment).

[3] Employment Protection Act 1975, s. 61 (8). For the role of conciliation officers, see p. 386, below.

[4] *Ibid.*, s. 61 (10).

[5] *Ibid.*, s. 61 (11).

[6] *Ibid.*, s. 61 (12).

[7] *Ibid.*, s. 61 (13).

The industrial tribunal has jurisdiction to entertain complaints under section 61 only if the complaint is presented to the tribunal within the period of three months beginning with the day on which it is alleged that the time off should have been allowed, or within such further period as the tribunal considers reasonable, in a case where it is satisfied that it was not reasonably practicable for the complaint to be presented within the period of three months.[1]

[1] Employment Protection Act 1975, s. 61 (9).

The provisions as to time off in these circumstances do not apply to employment where the employee is the husband or wife of the employer, he is a registered dock worker, unless in employment by virtue of which the employee is wholly or mainly engaged in work which is not dock work, he is a share fisherman, a merchant seaman, or is engaged in employment where under his contract he ordinarily works outside Great Britain.[1] They do not cover part-time employees who do not qualify because of the requirement for two years continuous employment.[2]

[1] Now including certain offshore installations; see p. 62, above.
[2] For a discussion of part-time employees and impending changes see p. 226, above.

## MISCELLANEOUS PROVISIONS OF THE REDUNDANCY PAYMENTS ACT 1965

The Employment Protection Act 1975 substitutes a new section 12 in the Redundancy Payments Act 1965 which deals with claims as to extension of terms and conditions. Briefly this states that a claim as to recognised terms and conditions and the general level of terms and conditions may be reported to the Advisory Conciliation and Arbitration Services and by them to the Central Arbitration Committee notwithstanding that it relates to redundancy. The Committee may make an award which becomes an implied term in the contract.

When by virtue of a statutory provision an employee's remuneration is payable to him by a person other than his employer, section 51 and Schedule 8 of the Redundancy Payments Act 1965 provide that reference to the "employer" should be construed as reference to the person responsible for paying remuneration.

Section 53 of the Redundancy Payments Act 1965 sets out the rules applicable for serving notices pursuant to the Act. A notice to be given by an employer to an employee may be delivered to the employee, or left at his usual or last known place of residence or sent to him by post there. Notices to the employer may be given either by the employee himself, or by a person authorised by him to act on his behalf, and can be delivered to the employer, sent by post addressed to him at the place where the employee is, or was, employed by him or, if arrangements in this behalf have been made by the employer can be given by being delivered to a person designated by the employee is pursuance of the arrangements or left for such a person at a place so designated, or sent by post to that person at the designated address. Notices left for a person at the appropriate place mentioned above are presumed, unless the contrary is proved, to have been received by him on the day on which it was left there.

When a criminal offence under the Redundancy Payments Act 1965 committed by a body corporate is proved to have been committed with the consent or connivance of, or to be attributable to any neglect on the part of any director, manager, secretary, or other similar officer of the body corporate, or any person purporting to act in any such capacity, he is guilty of the offence as well as the body corporate and is liable to be proceeded against and be punished accordingly.[1]

[1] Redundancy Payments Act 1965, s. 52 (1). "Director" is defined in *ibid.*, s. 52 (2).

# Chapter 7

# UNFAIR DISMISSAL

## SCOPE OF THE PROVISIONS

The right not to be unfairly dismissed was first contained in the ill-fated Industrial Relations Act 1971, but on the repeal of that Act reappeared in Schedule 1 to the Trade Union and Labour Relations Act 1974. The main object of the unfair dismissal provisions is to protect the employee from the weak position which arises from the contractual basis of the employment relationship at common law. Until the recent spate of legislation in the employment field, the employee could be dismissed without cause, or reason and, in the vast majority of cases, was entitled to recover very little from the employer.[1]

[1] See p. 153, above.

An employee who is covered by the Act has a right not to be unfairly dismissed by his employer[1] and if he claims that he is so dismissed, he can make a complaint to an industrial tribunal. These tribunals have exclusive jurisdiction to hear such complaints.[2] The unfair dismissal provisions apply to all cases of employment under a contract of service unless excluded by the provisions of the Schedule.[3]

[1] Trade Union and Labour Relations Act 1974, Sch. 1, para. 4.
[2] *Ibid.*, Sch. 1, para. 4 (1).
[3] *Ibid.*, Sch. 1, para. 4 (2). It is immaterial whether the law which governs a person's employment (apart from the Act) is the law of the United Kingdom, or a part of the United Kingdom, or not; *ibid.*, s. 30 (6).

Contracting out of the unfair dismissal provisions is not allowed, except for dismissal procedures agreements designated under paragraph 13, and fixed term contracts referred to in paragraph 12. Subject to these exceptions, and agreements concluded where action has been taken by a conciliation officer, and union membership agreements, any agreement to exclude or limit the provisions relating to unfair dismissal is void, as is any agreement to preclude a person from making a complaint to or bringing any proceedings before an industrial tribunal.[1] For this reason great care must be exercised in settling claims for compensation for unfair dismissal.

[1] Trade Union and Labour Relations Act 1974, Sch. 1, para. 32. See *Council of Engineering Institutions* v. *Maddison,* (1976) *Times,* 3rd August, E.A.T.

The provisions discussed are those in force at the date of going to press except for those amendments and additions wrought by the Employment Protection Act 1975 which have not yet been implemented but are also referred to.

## THOSE WHO ARE, AND ARE NOT, PROTECTED BY THE UNFAIR DISMISSAL PROVISIONS

The right not to be unfairly dismissed applies to employees only. An employee is an individual who has entered into, or works under (or where the employment has ceased), worked under, a contract of service or apprenticeship (whether express, implied, oral or in writing) otherwise than in the police service.[1] Thus the benefit of the unfair dismissal provisions does not enure for the benefit of those working under contracts for services. Reference should be made to the decisions on the distinction between contracts of service and contracts for services which were given when discussing the position at common law and under the Redundancy Payments Act 1965.[2] There are a number of exclusions and special circumstances to be considered as follows:

(1) Where the employer is the husband, or wife, of the employee, the unfair dismissal provisions do not apply; Schedule 1, Trade Union and Labour Relations Act 1974, Schedule 1, paragraph 9 (1) (b). Prior to the implementation of the Employment Protection Act 1975 this exclusion applied to certain other close relatives. It is unlikely that the exclusion is applicable where the employee had been employed by a partnership in which the spouse was a partner.[3]

[1] Trade Union and Labour Relations Act 1974, Sch. 1, para. 4, and s. 30 (1). See also p. 2, above.
[2] See p. 2 and 161, above, respectively.
[3] *Bernstein* v. *Bernstein Brothers* (1969), 4 I.T.R. 106, T (a case under the

Redundancy Payments Act 1965). This paragraph may be varied, added to, or excluded by order of the Secretary of State; Trade Union and Labour Relations Act 1974, Sch. 1, para. 11 (2).

(2) The unfair dismissal provisions do not apply to a registered dock worker as defined by the Dock Labour Scheme unless by virtue of the employment, the employee is wholly, or mainly, engaged in work which is not dock work as defined by the scheme.[1]

[1] Trade Union and Labour Relations Act 1974, Sch. 1, para. 9 (1) (c). See p. 165, above, for discussion of the similar exclusion from the provisions of the Redundancy Payments Act 1965. The paragraph may be varied, added to, or excluded, by order of the Secretary of State; Trade Union and Labour Relations Act 1974, Sch. 1, para. 11 (2).

(3) Employment as a master, or as a member of the crew of a fishing vessel, where the employee is not remunerated otherwise than by a share in the profits, or gross earnings, of the vessel (a "share fisherman") is excluded. Paragraph 9 (1) (d), Schedule 1, Trade Union and Labour Relations Act 1974.[1]

[1] See p. 165, above, for a discussion of the similar exclusion from the provisions of the Redundancy Payments Act 1965. This exclusion may be varied, added to, or excluded by order of the Secretary of State; Trade Union and Labour Relations Act 1974, Sch. 1, para. 11 (2).

(4) The unfair dismissal provisions do not apply to any employment, where under his contract of employment, the employee ordinarily works outside Great Britain; Trade Union and Labour Relations Act 1974, Schedule 1, paragraph 9 (2). Persons employed to work on board a ship registered in the United Kingdom (not being a ship registered at a port outside Great Britain) are regarded as persons who under their contracts ordinarily work in Great Britain, unless the employment is wholly outside Great Britain, or the employee is not ordinarily resident in Great Britain.[1] There is power contained in section 127 of the Employment Protection Act 1975 for the unfair dismissal provisions to be applied to employment for the purposes of any activities in the territorial waters of the United Kingdom, or connected with the exploration of the seabed, or subsoil, or the exploitation of their natural resources in any area designated by order under section 1 (7) of the Continental Shelf Act 1964.[2]

*Those who are, and are not, protected*

¹ Trade Union and Labour Relations Act 1974, Sch. 1. para. 9 (3). In *Maulik* v. *Air India*, [1974] I.C.R. 528, N.I.R.C. the employee had worked for Air India and its predecessors for 27½ years, 12½ years inside India and 15 in London. At the time of his dismissal he was their operations manager in England and since his appointment had spent marginally over half of his time outside Great Britain. Sir JOHN DONALDSON giving the judgment of the court said that the question was whether *under* his contract of employment the employee ordinarily works outside Great Britain. Mr. Maulik's contract did not require him to work at any place. He was obliged to leave when posted and work away from London. Thus the employee's contract was outside the unfair dismissal provisions. In *Portec (U.K.), Ltd.* v. *Mogensen,* [1976] I.R.L.R. 209, E.A.T. an employee divided his time between Wales and Paris and received a living allowance while in Wales. The industrial tribunal found that since he ordinarily worked in Great Britain it could not be said he ordinarily worked outside Great Britain. On appeal this was reversed and it was said that when the employee was required to work in Wales he was ordinarily working in Great Britain and when required to work in Paris he was ordinarily working outside Great Britain. An employee who ordinarily worked outside Great Britain could not bring proceedings under the unfair dismissal provisions. It appears from this case that para. 9 (3) may be construed differently from Redundancy Payments Act 1965, s. 17. See p. 164, above. The exclusion may be varied, added to, or excluded by order of the Secretary of State; *ibid.,* Sch. 1. para. 11 (2).

² This power has been exercised and the Employment Protection (Offshore Employment) Order 1976, S.I. 1976 No. 766 came into force on 21st June 1976. Subject as below the Trade Union and Labour Relations Act 1974 is applied to employment for the purposes of the following activities:

(a) any activities (other than activities connected with a ship which is in the course of navigation or is a survey ship or is engaged in dredging or fishing) in the territorial waters;

(b) any activities connected with the exploration of the sea bed or subsoil or the exploitation of their natural resources in any designated area (other than an area or part of an area in which the law of Northern Ireland applies) being activities carried out on or from an offshore installation in any such designated area.

The order does not apply to any employment wholly or mainly for the purposes of any activities connected with the Frigg Field Reservoir or the Ekofisk field. Sections 1 (1) and (3), 19, 21, 22, 23, 24, 25 (2) and 31 (5) do not apply. Schedule 1 applies with modifications so that para. 27 is not applied and the Schedule has effect as if para. 9 (3) were omitted. The reference in para. 9 (2) to Great Britain has effect as if the territorial waters, and waters in any designated area (other than an area or part of an area in which the law of Northern Ireland applies) were included and in para. 12 (a) the words "before the 21st June 1976" are treated as substituted for "before 28th February 1972".

(5) An employee who on, or before, the effective date of termination¹ attained the age, which in the undertaking in which he was employed, was the normal retiring age for an employee holding the position which he held, or if a man attained the age of

65, or, if a woman, attained the age of 60 is excluded; Trade Union and Labour Relations Act 1974, Schedule 1, paragraph 10 (*b*).[2] Even if an employee would be excluded from the unfair dismissal provisions under this sub-paragraph the exclusion does not apply if it is shown that the reason (or if more than one, the principal reason) for the dismissal was an inadmissible reason.[3]

[1] See p. 292, below.
[2] This exclusion was examined in *Ord* v. *Maidstone and District Hospital Management Committee* (1974), 9 I.T.R. 243, N.I.R.C. Mr. Ord was a mental health officer who was dismissed 15 months after attaining the age of 60. In the National Health Service 60 is the "pensionable age" but employees may remain in employment thereafter if permitted to do so by the employer. Mental health officers do not normally retire at 60. In giving the judgment of the National Industrial Relations Court Sir JOHN DONALDSON stated (at p. 246):

"the words 'normal retiring age' should be given their ordinary meaning. The ordinary meaning is 'the age at which the employees concerned usually retire.' It has nothing to do with whether the employees are or are not then entitled to a pension. Still less has it anything to do with a notional chronological landmark indicating the beginning of a period during which it is the policy of the employer to consider whether and when to compulsorily retire the employee".

Mr. Ord was not excluded from the benefit of the provisions. The provisions of Sch. 1, para. 10 may be varied, added to, or excluded by order of the Secretary of State; Trade Union and Labour Relations Act 1974, Sch. 1, para. 11 (2).
[3] Trade Union and Labour Relations Act 1974, Sch. 1, para. 11 (1). See p. 316, below.

(6) Except as set out below an employee does not have the benefit of the unfair dismissal provisions, unless he has been continuously employed for a period of not less than 26 weeks, ending with the effective date of termination.[1] When calculating the qualifying period account must be taken of the provisions of paragraph 5 (6) of Schedule 1[2] of the Trade Union and Labour Relations Act 1974, which provide that the effective date of termination is to be the date when a notice of the minimum period necessary under section 1 (1) of the Contracts of Employment Act 1972 would have expired, if given when notice of termination was given, or if there was no notice, when the contract was terminated by the employer, if later than the effective date of termination as otherwise defined.[3] Continuous employment is calculated in accordance with Schedule 1 of the Contracts of Employment Act 1972.[4]

[1] Trade Union and Labour Relations Act 1974, Sch. 1, para. 10 (*a*). For "effective date of termination" see below. The paragraph may be varied, added to, or excluded by order of the Secretary of State; *ibid.*, Sch. 1, para. 11 (2).

[2] Added by the Employment Protection Act 1975, Sch. 16, Part III, para. 10.

[3] The period during the interval between the actual date of termination and the effective date of termination counts as a period of employment; Trade Union and Labour Relations Act 1974, Sch. 1, para. 30 (1A). Previously if the contract of employment was wrongfully terminated immediately before completion of the qualifying period the employee was not protected; *Dixon* v. *Stenor, Ltd.* (1973), 8 I.T.R. 141, N.I.R.C.

[4] Trade Union and Labour Relations Act 1974, Sch. 1, para. 30 (1). For the purpose of proceedings for unfair dismissal a person's employment shall, unless the contrary is shown, be presumed to have been continuous; *ibid.*, Sch. 1, para. 30 (2). The Secretary of State may make provision for preserving the continuity of a person's employment for the purpose of the Contracts of Employment Act 1972, Sch. 1, or for the purposes of that Schedule as applied by, or under, any enactment specified in the Regulations in certain circumstances; Trade Union and Labour Relations Act 1974, Sch. 1, para. 30 (3). For a discussion of continuous employment see p. 226, above. There are requirements as to the minimum number of hours worked, or contracted to be worked, in each week for the week to count. In accordance with Contracts of Employment Act 1972, Sch. 1, weeks may count during part of which only the employee was employed. Thus in *Coulson* v. *City of London Polytechnic*, [1976] I.R.L.R. 212, E.A.T. an employee was able to count the whole of the week in which his employment started and the whole of the week in which it terminated in computing the 26 weeks.

The exclusion of employees who have not been continuously employed for the minimum period does not apply to the dismissal of employees if it is shown that the reason (or if more than one, the principal reason) for the dismissal was an inadmissible reason.[1] If an employee is dismissed on medical grounds by reason of any requirement imposed by, or under any provision of any enactment or of any instrument made under any enactment or any recommendation in any provision of a code of practice issued or approved under the Health and Safety at Work Act 1974, s. 16, which is a provision for the time being specified in the Employment Protection Act 1975, Sch. 2, then the qualifying period is reduced from 26 weeks to four weeks.[2]

[1] See p.    , below.

[2] Employment Protection Act 1975, s. 29 (4). This provision came into force on 1st June 1976. The reason may well amount to a reason within the Trade Union and Labour Relations Act 1974, Sch. 1, para. 6 (2) (*d*) (see p.    , below), but it will remain for the employer to satisfy the tribunal that he has acted reasonably as required by the Trade Union and Labour Relations Act 1974, Sch. 1, para. 6 (8).

(7) Those employed in police service are not included in the unfair dismissal provisions because they are excluded from the definition of employees.[1] Police service means service:

"(a) In England and Wales as a member of a police force or as a special constable;
(b) As a constable within the meaning of the Police (Scotland) Act 1967;
(c) As a member of any constabulary maintained by virtue of any enactment; or
(d) In any other capacity by virtue of which a person has the powers or privileges of a constable."[2]

[1] Trade Union and Labour Relations Act 1974, s. 30 (1). See p. 275, above.
[2] *Ibid.*, s. 30 (1).

(8) Members of the Naval, Military or Air Forces of the Crown or of any women's service administered by the Defence Council are excluded.[1] Other persons in Crown employment are included, references to "employee" in the unfair dismissal provisions being construed as references to Crown employee and reference to dismissal as if to the termination of Crown employment.[2] Crown employment means "employment under or for the purposes of a government department, or any officer or body exercising on behalf of the Crown functions conferred by any enactment,"[3] other than the military personnel mentioned above. A Crown employee is a person who is for the time being in Crown employment, or (where it has ceased) was in Crown employment. Any reference to redundancy so far as Crown employees are concerned is construed as a reference to the existence of circumstances treated as equivalent to redundancy in accordance with section 41 (3) of the Redundancy Payments Act 1965.[4] Associations established for the purposes of the Auxiliary Forces Act 1953 are treated as if they are government departments and employment by them is treated as Crown Employment.[5]

[1] Trade Union and Labour Relations Act 1974, Sch. 1, para. 33.
[2] *Ibid.*, Sch. 1, para. 33 (3).
[3] *Ibid.*, Sch. 1, para. 33 (2).
[4] *Ibid.*, Sch. 1, para. 33 (3) (*c*), and see p. 261, above.
[5] *Ibid.*, Sch. 1, para. 33 (4). None of the bodies specified in Sch. 3 to the Redundancy Payments Act 1965 (see p. 169, above) are regarded as performing functions on behalf of the Crown, their employees are not regarded as being employed under or for the purposes of a government department and employ-

ment by them is not Crown employment for the purposes of para. 33; Trade Union and Labour Relations Act 1974, Sch. 1, para. 33 (4) (*a*). See (10), p. 281, below.

(9) Cases involving national security. If on a complaint before an industrial tribunal under the unfair dismissal provisions it is shown that the action to which the complaint relates was taken for the purpose of safe-guarding national security the industrial tribunal should dismiss the complaint.[1] A certificate purporting to be signed by or on behalf of, a Minister of the Crown certifying that the action specified in the certificate was taken for the purpose of safe-guarding national security, or that a particular request for information could not be complied with except by disclosing information the disclosure of which would be against the interests of national security, is treated as conclusive evidence of the facts so certified.[2]

[1] Trade Union and Labour Relations Act 1974, Sch. 1, para. 18 (1).
[2] *Ibid.*, Sch. 1, para. 18 (2).

(10) **Employment by the National Health Service bodies** set out in the Third Schedule to the Redundancy Payments Act 1965 (as amended) is included in the unfair dismissal provisions in the usual way.[1] If there are statutory schemes equivalent to redundancy applicable in such cases references to redundancy under the Redundancy Payments Act 1965 under the unfair dismissal provisions are treated as references to circumstances equivalent to redundancy in accordance with those arrangements.[2]

[1] Trade Union and Labour Relations Act 1974, Sch. 1, para. 33 (4).
[2] *Ibid.*, Sch. 1, para. 33 (4A). Added by Employment Protection Act 1975, Sch. 16, Part III, para. 34.

(11) **Until 1st October 1976** any employment in an undertaking in which immediately before the effective date of termination[1] there was in aggregate (including the dismissal employee) less than four employees who had been continuously employed for a period of not less than 13 weeks, whether they were, or had been, all employed at the same place, or different places, was excluded from the unfair dismissal provisions.[2]

Paragraph 14 (1) (*a*) of Schedule 16 of the Employment Protection Act 1975 provides for the abolition of this exclusion from the unfair dismissal provisions and comes into effect on

1st October, 1976. The exclusion did not operate if the reason (or if more than one the principal reason) for the dismissal was an inadmissible reason.[3]

[1] See p. 292, below.

[2] Trade Union and Labour Relations Act 1974, Sch. 1, para. 9 (1) (*a*). This provision and its predecessor (which was in similar terms) have been considered by the National Industrial Relations Court on several occasions. In *Margetts* v. *Underwood (Zelah), Ltd.* (1973), 8 I.T.R. 478, N.I.R.C., it was decided that directors who were only discharging their functions as directors were not employees for the purposes and in *Haque* v. *A. Stitchen & Co. (1937), Ltd.* (1973), 8 I.T.R. 553, N.I.R.C., it was held that part-time employees whose periods of employment did not count within Schedule 1 of the Contracts of Employment Act 1972 could not be included to raise the number over four. The employer in *Kapur* v. *Shields* (1975), 10 I.T.R. 173, D.C., carried on the business of letting houses divided into flats, on his own account and through companies in which he and his family were the only shareholders. The employee was the only employee at one property. In the Divisional Court, PHILLIPS, J., said (at p. 180): "In short, for the purpose of counting the number of employees one is concerned only with whether they are employed in the undertaking and not with who employs them." In *Boston* v. *Chilton*, 5th February 1974, N.I.R.C. (unreported), Sir HUGH GRIFFITHS said that the burden of proof to show that employment fell within the exclusion was on the employer. Reference may also be made to *Mayhew* v. *Richard Alexander & Son*, [1973] 3 All E.R. 39, N.I.R.C., where it was held that the four employees must each have a minimum of 13 weeks' service.

[3] For inadmissible reason, see p. 316, below.

(12) Fixed term contracts require special consideration. The unfair dismissal provisions do not apply:

"(*a*) to dismissal from employment under a contract for a fixed term of two years or more, where the contract was made before 28th February 1972 and is not a contract of apprenticeship, and the dismissal consists only of the expiry of that term without its being renewed, or

(*b*) to dismissal from employment under a contract for a fixed term of two years or more, where the dismissal consists only of the expiry of that term without its being renewed, if before the term so expires the employee has agreed in writing to exclude any claim in respect of rights under that paragraph in relation to that contract."[1]

[1] Trade Union and Labour Relations Act 1974, Sch. 1, para. 12. In deciding whether a contract is for a fixed term the cases cited at p. 164, above should be looked at. In particular, *British Broadcasting Corporation* v. *Ioannou*, [1975] Q.B. 781; [1975] 2 All E.R. 999. C.A., where Lord DENNING, M.R., stated that a fixed term contract is one which is not determinable by

notice on either side. The employee in *Weston* v. *University College, Swansea* (1975), 10 I.T.R. 60, T, was appointed as a lecturer for a three-year probationary period and at the end of that period the employment was terminated. An industrial tribunal in Cardiff held that the contract was not for a fixed term and that it had jurisdiction to entertain a claim alleging that the employee had been unfairly dismissed.

The power to agree to exclude the unfair dismissal provisions is similar to that to exclude the provisions of the Redundancy Payments Act 1965, see p. 164, above. When the contract is such that it is covered by paragraph 12 (*b*), the written agreement to exclude the unfair dismissal rights may be in a service agreement but need not necessarily be so. The agreement must be made before the term expires. It can be in an apprenticeship agreement. Where there is no valid exclusion whether or not an employee has been dismissed fairly on the expiration of a fixed term depends on the facts of the case; *Terry* v. *East Sussex County Council*, (1976), *Times*, 3rd August, E.A.T.

In Trade Union and Labour Relations Act 1974, Sch. 1, para. 12, as it applies to employees treated as unfairly dismissed by virtue of Employment Protection Act 1975, s. 34 (1) and (2), 1st June 1976 is substituted for 28th February 1972 in sub-paragraph (*a*); Employment Protection Act 1975, s. 34 (6).

(13) By virtue of Trade Union and Labour Relations Act 1974, Schedule 1, paragraph 13, there is power to exclude the operation of the unfair dismissal provisions in respect of dismissal procedures agreements. It reads as follows:

"13.—(1) An application may be made jointly to the Secretary of state by all the parties to a dismissal procedures agreement to make an order designating that agreement for the purposes of this paragraph.
(2) On any such application the Secretary of State may make such an order of he is satisfied—
    (*a*)  that every trade union which is a party to the dismissal procedures agreement is an independent trade union;
    (*b*)  that the agreement provides for procedures to be followed in cases where an employee claims that he has been, or is in the course of being, unfairly dismissed;
    (*c*)  that those procedures are available without discrimination to all employees falling within any description to which the agreement applies;

(*d*) that the remedies provided by the agreement in respect of unfair dismissal are on the whole as beneficial as (but not necessarily identical with) those provided in respect of unfair dismissal by this Schedule;

(*e*) that the procedures provided by the agreement include a right to arbitration or adjudication by an independent referee, or by a tribunal or other independent body, in cases where (by reason of an equality of votes or for any other reason) a decision cannot otherwise be reached; and

(*f*) that the provisions of the agreement are such that it can be determined with reasonable certainty whether a particular employee is one to whom the agreement applies or not.

(3) Where a dismissal procedures agreement is designated by an order under this paragraph which is for the time being in force, the provisions of that agreement relating to dismissal shall have effect in substitution for any rights under paragraph 4 above; and accordingly that paragraph shall not apply to the dismissal of an employee from any employment if it is employment to which, and he is an employee to whom, those provisions of the agreement apply."[1]

Paragraph 14 lays down the procedures for the order designating the dismissals procedure agreement to be revoked. The revocation order may contain transitional provisions.[2]

Unless an agreement has been designated by order of the Secretary of State for Employment for the purpose of paragraph 13 or it falls within the other provisions mentioned above it cannot exclude the right to complain to the industrial tribunal alleging that the employee has been unfairly dismissed. If a collective agreement contains an appeals procedure which is applicable on dismissal, in view of the time limit for presenting complaints, it is important for the complaint to the industrial tribunal to be made as soon as possible. The tribunal will usually be prepared to postpone the hearing of the complaint until the procedure contained in the agreement has been gone through.[3]

---

[1] Paragraph 13 (3) does not apply to the right not to be unfairly dismissed for any reason mentioned in Employment Protection Act 1975, s. 34 (1) and (2) (the section dealing with dismissal on grounds of pregnancy); Employment Protection Act 1975, s. 34 (7).

[2] Trade Union and Labour Relations Act 1974, Sch. 1, para. 14 (3).

[3] See *MacDonald* v. *South Cambridgeshire Rural District Council* (1973), 8

I.T.R. 557, N.I.R.C., where an ex-employee pursued his domestic remedies but when they were exhausted found that he could not present a complaint for unfair dismissal because it was time-barred.

(14) There are special provisions relating to teachers in aided schools.[1] When such a teacher is dismissed by the governors or managers of the school in pursuance of a request of the local education authority under paragraph (*a*) of the proviso to section 24 (2) of the Education Act 1944 the unfair provisions have effect as if the local education authority had at all material times been the teacher's employer[2] and the local education authority had dismissed him and the reason, or principal reason, for which they did so had been the reason, or principal reason, for which they required the dismissal.[3]

[1] Contained in Trade Union and Labour Relations Act 1974, Sch. 1, para. 27. As a result of the amendment to para. 27 (1) made by the Employment Protection Act 1975, this also applies to dismissals in connection with pregnancy and confinement.

[2] Trade Union and Labour Relations Act 1974, Sch. 1, para. 27 (1) (*a*).

[3] *Ibid.*, Sch. 1, para. 27 (1) (*b*). There are similar modifications applicable so far as remedies are concerned; *ibid.*, Sch. 1, para. 27 (2) as amended by the Employment Protection Act 1975, Sch. 16, Part III, para. 27.

(15) If there is a union membership agreement (as defined by the Trade Union and Labour Relations Act 1974) in force then paragraph 6 (5) may have to be considered.[1]

[1] See p. 316, below.

(16) House of Commons staff: section 122 of the Employment Protection Act 1975 states that the unfair dismissal provisions apply to relevant members of House of Commons staff as they apply to persons in Crown employment. This provision does not apply to members of the staff of the House of Lords.

(17) Part-time employees: Trade Union and Labour Relations Act 1974. Schedule 1, paragraph 9 (1) (*f*) excluded any employment under a contract which normally involved employment for less that 21 hours weekly, from the unfair dismissal provisions.[1] This was repealed by the Employment Protection Act 1975[2] and the repeal came into effect on 1st June 1976. Since the paragraph was repealed the only requirement as to the number of hours worked is that in respect of the requirement as to the qualifying period of continuous employment.[3]

[1] The requirement was in addition to that for continuous employment. See dismissal for inadmissible reasons at p. 316, below.
[2] Employment Protection Act 1975, Sch. 16, Part III, para. 14 (1) (c).
[3] See p. 278, above.

(18) An employer who is entitled to diplomatic privilege is not bound by the Trade Union and Labour Relations Act 1974 even though the exemption is not expressed in it. In *Omerri* v. *Uganda High Commission*,[1] Sir JOHN DONALDSON said: "The basis of diplomatic immunity is that of international law, international comity and respect of one sovereign state for another. It is mutual. In foreign countries, British missions enjoy the same immunity as this country and its courts extend to foreign and Commonwealth missions in London. It has always been a matter of general law. It is not to be thought from the fact that Parliament did not mention diplomatic missions, that Parliament intended, in breach of international law and the accepted standards of international behaviour, to make foreign and Commonwealth missions subject to the Act."

[1] (1973), 8 I.T.R. 14 at p. 15, N.I.R.C.

## DISMISSAL

For the purposes of the unfair dismissal provisions dismissal is defined in the Trade Union and Labour Relations Act 1974, Schedule 1, para. 5. Sub-paragraphs (1) to (3) (as amended), are as follows:

"5.—(1) In this Schedule 'dismissal' and 'dismiss' shall be construed in accordance with the following provisions of this paragraph.
(2) Subject to sub-paragraph (3) below, an employee shall be treated for the purposes of this Act as dismissed by his employer, if, but only if,—
  (a) the contract under which he is employed by the employer is terminated by the employer, whether it is so terminated by notice or without notice, ; or
  (b) where under that contract he is employed for a fixed term, that term expires without being renewed under the same contract; or

(*c*) the employee terminates that contract, with or without notice, in circumstances such that he is entitled to terminate it without notice by reason of the employer's conduct.

(3) Where an employer gives notice to an employee to terminate his contract of employment and, at a time within the ... period of that notice, the employee gives notice ... to the employer to terminate the contract of employment on a date earlier than the date on which the employer's notice is due to expire, the employee shall for the purposes of this Schedule be taken to be dismissed by his employer, and the reasons for the dismissal shall be taken to be the reasons for which the employer's notice is given.[1]

[1] The words omitted from paragraph 5 (3) are "obligatory" and "in writing", respectively. See Employment Protection Act 1975, Sch. 16, Part III, para. 8.

Paragraph 5 (3) does not apply in a case where an employer gives notice to an employee to terminate her contract of employment for the reason that, at the effective date of termination she is or will have become because of her pregnancy, incapable of adequately doing the work for which she is employed, or because of her pregnancy, she cannot or will not be able to continue after that date to do that work without contravention (either by her or her employer) of a duty or restriction imposed by or under any enactment.[1]

[1] Employment Protection Act 1975, s. 34 (5).

The definition of dismissal contained in paragraph 5 (2) is very similar to that in section 3 (2) of the Redundancy Payments Act 1965 (as amended), and guidance can be obtained from the decisions made under that sub-section, see p. 187, above.

The onus of proof to show that dismissal has taken place is on the employee. See for example *Dudar* v. *Leys Malleable Casting Co., Ltd.*, [1973] I.R.L.R. 51, T, and also *G.E.C. Telecommunications Ltd.* v. *McAllister*, [1975] I.R.L.R. 346, D.C. If the dismissal is denied by the employers it is usual for the employee to call his evidence first to support the allegation of dismissal.

Action taken by employers which does not constitute an express written, or oral, notice of dismissal but which may amount to a repudiation of the contract often gives rise to difficulties, and reference should be made to the cases discussed in the Chapter on Redundancy. The employer may ask the employee to perform a task which he is not willing to carry out, and he may be told that if he does not comply the employee will be treated as having terminated his contract, or having resigned. In other situations the employee is informed that unless he resigns he will be dismissed. Both of these situations amount to dismissal.

In *Jones* v. *Liverpool Corporation* (1974), 9 I.T.R. 34, N.I.R.C., after a dispute which lead to the employee's suspension, the employer wrote to the employee informing him that he was instructed to return to work on 1st March 1973 and in the event of his failing to do so the employee's employment "will be deemed to be terminated" from that date. The employee did not return and payment was made to him in lieu of notice. The employee complained to the industrial tribunal seeking compensation for unfair dismissal and the tribunal found that the employee had not been dismissed. On appeal to the National Industrial Relations Court it was *held* that the employee had been dismissed. The employer had in effect said that if the employee disobeyed the instructions the employer would treat the contract as terminated and this was clearly shown by payment of money in lieu of notice. The case was remitted to another tribunal to determine whether or not the dismissal was fair.

*Sutcliffe* v. *Hawker Siddley Aviation Ltd.* (1974), 9 I.T.R. 58, N.I.R.C., is an example of a fairly common type of situation. The employer (who had power to do so under the terms of the contract of employment) requested Mr. Sutcliffe to accept a posting some distance from the R.A.F. station where he worked. He indicated that he did not wish to be moved and the employers wrote to him "Would you please let [us] have immediate confirmation that you accept the posting or that you intend to resign your employment with this company"; the employee resigned. The tribunal found the employee to have been dismissed but not unfairly. He appealed. Sir JOHN DONALDSON, delivering the judgment of the National Industrial Relations Court, said: "The members of this court fully accept that an employer can place his employee in such a position in which the employee really has no option but to tender his notice. In such a situation the reality is, and the finding of any court or tribunal ought to be, that the employee is dismissed. So far as the facts of this case are concerned we are by no means sure that we would agree with the decision of the tribunal. But there is no appeal against it...". See also *McMillan* v. *Securicor Ltd.* (1972), 7 I.T.R. 428, T (clerk "asked to resign" *held* to be dismissed); *East Sussex County Council* v. *Walker* (1972), 7 I.T.R. 280, N.I.R.C. (similar facts—a redundancy case); and *Pascoe* v. *Hallen and Medway Ltd.*, [1975] I.R.L.R. 116, T (employee told she would be dismissed if she did not resign *held* dismissed).

When the action of the employer is such as to amount to repudiation of the contract this can be dismissal for the purpose of the unfair dismissal provisions.

*Middlemass* v. *Greenwood and Batley Ltd.*, [1972] I.R.L.R. 3, T (employee demoted from sales manager to representative. *Held* dismissal).

*Jewell* v. *Neptune Concrete, Ltd.*, [1975] I.R.L.R. 147, T (employer purported to lay-off employee when there was no power to do so in the contract. *Held* dismissed).

See also *McCarthy* v. *Burroughs Machines, Ltd.* (1975), 10 I.T.R. 42, T (a redundancy case).

*Stewart* v. *Swan Hunter Shipbuilders, Ltd.*, [1975] I.R.L.R. 143, T (crane driver offered other job which was not acceptable to him. Although there was an agreement with the union he could be transferred—the employee was not aware of this. *Held* dismissed).

*Singh* v. *British Steel Corporation*, [1974] I.R.L.R. 131, T (employers tried unilaterally to vary contract after agreement with trade union to which employee no longer paid dues. *Held* dismissal but fair because the employee failed to act reasonably).

*Wares* v. *Caithness Leather Products Ltd.*, [1974] I.R.L.R. 162, T (employee left early prior to holiday thinking that it had been agreed. After holiday most unpleasant interview when foul language was used. Employee gave a week's notice. *Held* dismissed).

*Breach* v. *Epsylon Industries, Ltd.*, [1976] I.R.L.R. 180, E.A.T. (failure to provide work for the employee may amount to repudiation of the contract).

There must of course be a termination of the contract as a result of the employer's conduct. See *Crapper* v. *Butler Machine Co.*, [1973] I.R.L.R. 194, T (the employee was demoted having previously been a foreman. He was offered other employment which he accepted and worked under. *Held* no dismissal since the employer's repudiation was not accepted by the employee). But for this to apply the employer's conduct has to amount to a repudiation. For instance, in *Elliott* v. *Waldair Construction Ltd.*, [1975] I.R.L.R. 104, T, it did not do so. The employee refused to transfer to a different vehicle because he anticipated that he would earn less overtime payment so he resigned. It was *held* he was not dismissed because the employers could transfer him to this vehicle.

It often has to be considered whether an employee has repudiated the employment contract when he purports to transfer an employee from one geographic location to another. Such situations are discussed in detail at p. 192, above.

When the employee is guilty of wilful disobedience this may be treated by the employer as bringing the contract to an end and there is no dismissal. See for example *London* v. *James Laidlaw & Sons*, [1974] I.R.L.R. 136, T, where an employee refused to work in the rain even though contractually bound to do so and having received express orders. He was asked to collect his cards. *Held* not dismissed.

*Aguirre* v. *James Smart (Restorations) Ltd.*, [1974] I.R.L.R. 198, T (employee not allowed to return after walking out during argument with manager. Had been warned about walking out. *Held* not dismissed).

If the employee is under notice to terminate his employment given by the employer the courts and tribunals are slow to find that the employment was terminated by agreement prior to the expiry of the notice. See *Lees* v. *Arthur Greaves (Lees) Ltd.*, [1974] 2 All E.R. 393, C.A., and *Glacier Metal Co., Ltd.* v. *Dyer*, [1974] 3 All E.R. 21, N.I.R.C.

An employer does not dismiss an employee by refusing to allow him to withdraw a notice served by the employee and accepted by the employer. *Brennan* v. *Lindley & Co., Ltd.*, [1974] I.R.L.R. 153, N.I.R.C., but when the employer has repudiated the contract then if the employee accepts that repudiation by himself giving notice he is dismissed, *Maher* v. *Fram Gerrard, Ltd.*, [1974] 1 All E.R. 449, N.I.R.C., a redundancy case. In *Bishop* v. *John Brignell & Co. (Builders), Ltd.* (1974), 9 I.T.R. 307, C.A., the employee said to the managing director, "If you are not satisfied with me, I am going and I am giving you a week's notice." To which the director replied: "I do not want you working for me under those conditions. If you want to leave you can leave tonight." Later the employee was given his cards. The Court of Appeal upheld a decision that he was dismissed.

If the contract is frustrated there can be no dismissal. The employee in *Hare* v. *Murphy Brothers, Ltd.* (1975), 10 I.T.R. 1, C.A., had worked for the employer for over 25 years but was sentenced to 12 months' imprisonment for an offence which was in no way connected with his employment. On his release after eight months (with remission), he asked for his job back but was told that if was filled and that the employers did not have a suitable job for him. The Court of Appeal decided that the imprisonment was a frustrating event and so there was no dismissal. LAWTON, L.J., said (at p. 4): "There may be exceptional cases, for example when a man gets a very short sentence; but that is not this case and, in my judgment, for the reasons already given, a sentence as long as 12 months made it impossible for this man's contract of personal service to subsist."

Other examples when frustration was discussed include *Marshall* v. *Harland and Wolff Ltd.* (No. 2) (1972), 7 I.T.R. 150, N.I.R.C.—a redundancy case and *Hebden* v. *Forsey and Son* (1973), 8 I.T.R. 656, N.I.R.C., also a redundancy case. See p. 129, above, for a more detailed discussion of the doctrine of frustration and employment contracts.

Prior to the commencement of the relevant provisions of the Employment Protection Act 1975 the requirements of sub-paragraph (3) were more stringent and if the employee wished to terminate the contract prior to the expiry of his employer's notice he had to give notice in writing during the obligatory period of notice. Now he is empowered to give his notice at any time after the employer has given notice and there are no formal require-ments for the notice. In circumstances where sub-paragraph (3) applies the employee is taken to be dismissed by his employer notwithstanding any earlier leaving. In this connection regard should be had to the decisions discussed when dealing with Redundancy Payments Act 1965, s. 4 (see p. 202, above). In *McAlwane* v. *Boughton Estates, Ltd.*, [1973] 2 All E.R. 299, N.I.R.C., an employee was *held* to have been dismissed when after notice it was agreed that he should leave before the notice expired. *Springbank Sand and Gravel Co., Ltd.* v. *Craig*, [1973] I.R.L.R. 278, N.I.R.C., was a case where on giving notice the employer indicated that it was not necessary for the employee to work during the notice period. It was *held* that the employee had been dismissed even though he did not return. In neither *McAlwane's* nor *Craig's* cases were the requirements of sub-paragraph (3) complied with. It is to be hoped that the sub-paragraph in its amended form will avoid the necessity for a too legalistic approach to be adopted when considering the parties actions after notice to terminate the contract of employment has been given by the employer, although the employee is still required to give "notice to the employer to terminate the contract of employment".

Note should be made of the exclusion of paragraph 5 (3) in certain cases of dismissal of pregnant employees.

## EFFECTIVE DATE OF TERMINATION

The Trade Union and Labour Relations Act 1974, Schedule 1, paragraph 5, sub-paragraphs (5) and (6) determine "the effective date of termination".

"(5) In this Schedule 'the effective date of termination'—

(*a*) in relation to an employee whose contract of employment is terminated by notice, whether given by his employer or by the employee, means the date on which that notice expires;

(*b*) in relation to an employee whose contract of employment is terminated without notice, means the date on which the termination takes effect; and

(*c*) in relation to an employee who is employed under a contract for a fixed term, where that term expires without being renewed under the same contract, means the date on which that term expires.

[(6) Where the notice required to be given by an employer by section 1 (1) of the Contracts of Employment Act 1972 (minimum period of notice) would, if duly given when notice of termination was given by the employer, or (where no notice was given) when the contract of employment was terminated by the employer, expire on a date later than the effective date of termination as defined by sub-paragraph (5) above, that later date shall be treated as the effective date of termination in relation to the dismissal for the purposes of paragraph 10 (*a*) below and of sections 70 (2), 74 (3) and 75 (6) of the Employment Protection Act 1975 (written statement of reasons for dismissal and calculation of basic award of compensation for unfair dismissal).]"

The new provisions of sub-paragraph (6) shown in square brackets introduced by the Employment Protection Act 1975, Schedule 16, Part III, paragraph 11, mean that in the specified circumstances the effective date of termination will be later than the actual date of termination of the employment if no notice, or less than the minimum required by section 1 (1) of the Contracts of Employment Act 1972, has been given to the employee. Trade Union and Labour Relations Act 1974, Schedule 1, paragraph 10 (a), requires a qualifying period of not less than 26 weeks continuous employment ending with the effective date of termination, for the right not to be unfairly dismissed to arise. It is to be noted that the alteration is for the purposes listed only and not for all purposes.

Once notice has been given by the employer the effective date of termination is the date when it expires, even if the employee is allowed, or ordered, to attend work no longer; *Brindle* v. *H. W. Smith (Cabinets), Ltd.* (1973), 8 I.T.R. 69, C.A. (a case where the notice straddled the coming into force of the unfair dismissal provisions of the Industrial Relations Act 1971). However, if the employer terminates the employment with immediate effect then, subject to the new sub-paragraph (6) of paragraph 5, the effective date of termination is when the termination takes place. See *Dedman* v. *British Building and Engineering Appliances, Ltd.*, [1974] 1 All E.R. 520; [1974] 1 W.L.R. 171, C.A., where on 5th May 1972 the employee was handed a letter stating that the employers had "no alternative but to terminate" the employment "immediately". The Court of Appeal found that the effective date of termination of Mr. Dedman's employment was 5th May 1972, notwithstanding that the employee was given a cheque for a full month's salary plus a month's pay in lieu of notice.

Note should be made of the different rule applicable to the construction of "effective date of termination" in certain cases where the employee claims to be entitled to return to work under the rules governing those absent through pregnancy and confinement. See Employment Protection Act 1975, Schedule 3, paragraph 2 (3), and p. 320, below.

## THE MEANING OF UNFAIR

The Trade Union and Labour Relations Act 1974, Schedule 1,

paragraph 6, provides:

"6.—(1) In determining for the purposes of this Schedule whether the dismissal of an employee was fair or unfair, it shall be for the employer to show—

(a) what was the reason (or, if there was more than one, the principal reason) for the dismissal; and

(b) that it was a reason falling within sub-paragraph (2) below, or some other substantial reason of a kind such as to justify the dismissal of an employee holding the position which that employee held.

(2) In sub-paragraph (1) (b) above the reference to a reason falling within this sub-paragraph is a reference to a reason which—

(a) related to the capability or qualifications of the employee for performing work of the kind which he was employed by the employer to do; or

(b) related to the conduct of the employee; or

(c) was that the employee was redundant; or

(d) was that the employee could not continue to work in the position which he held without contravention (either on his part or on that of his employer) of a duty or restriction imposed by or under an enactment.

(3) Where the employer has fulfilled the requirements of sub-paragraph (1) above, then, subject to paragraphs 7 and 8 below, the question whether the dismissal was fair or unfair shall be determined in accordance with the following provisions of this paragraph.

(4) For the purposes of this Schedule the dismissal of an employee by an employer shall be regarded as having been unfair if the reason for it (or, if more than one, the principal reason) was that the employee—

(a) was, or proposed to become, a member of an independent trade union;

(b) had taken, or proposed to take, part at any appropriate time in the activities of an independent trade union; or

(c) had refused, or proposed to refuse, to become or remain a member of a trade union which was not an independent trade union.

[(4A) In sub-paragraph (4) above, 'appropriate time' in relation to an employee taking part in the activities of a trade union, means time which either—

(*a*) is outside his working hours; or

(*b*) is a time within his working hours at which, in accordance with arrangements agreed with or consent given by his employer, it is permissible for him to take part in those activities;

and in this sub-paragraph 'working hours', in relation to an employee, means any time when, in accordance with his contract of employment, he is required to be at work.]

(5) Dismissal of an employee by an employer shall be regarded as fair for the purposes of this Schedule if—

(*a*) it is the practice, in accordance with a union membership agreement, for [employees for the time being] of the same class as the dismissed employee to belong to a specified independent trade union, or to one of a number of specified independent trade unions; and

(*b*) the reason for the dismissal was that the employee was not a member of the specified union or one of the specified unions, or had refused or proposed to refuse to become or remain a member of that union or one of those unions;

unless the employee genuinely objects on grounds of religious belief to being a member of any trade union whatsoever ... in which case the dismissal shall be regarded as unfair.

[(5A) For the purposes of sub-paragraph (5) above a union shall be treated as specified for the purposes of or in relation to a union membership agreement (in a case where it would not otherwise be so treated) if—

(*a*) the Service has made a recommendation for recognition covering the employee in question which is operative within the meaning of section 15 of the Employment Protection Act 1975; or

(*b*) the union has referred a recognition issue (within the meaning of that Act) covering that employee to the Advisory, Conciliation and Arbitration Service under section 11 of that Act and the Service has not declined to proceed on the reference under section 12 of that Act, the union has not withdrawn the reference, or from the reference, and the issue has not been settled or reported on under that section.]

(6) Any reason by virtue of which a dismissal is to be regarded as unfair in consequence of sub-paragraph (4) or (5)

above is hereafter in this Schedule referred to as an inadmissible reason.

(7) Where the reason or principal reason for the dismissal of an employee was that he was redundant, but is shown that the circumstances constituting the redundancy applied equally to one or more other employees in the same undertaking who held positions similar to that held by him and who have not yet been dismissed by the employer, and either—

(a) that the reason (or, if more than one, the principal reason) for which he was selected for dismissal was an inadmissible reason; or

(b) that he was selected for dismissal in contravention of a customary arrangement or agreed procedure relating to redundancy and there were no special reasons justifying a departure from that arrangement or procedure in his case;

then, for the purposes of this Schedule the dismissal shall be regarded as unfair.

(8) Subject to sub-paragraphs (4) to (7) above, the determination of the question whether the dismissal was fair or unfair, having regard to the reason shown by the employer, shall depend on whether the employer can satisfy the tribunal that in the circumstances (having regard to equity and the substantial merits of the case) he acted reasonably in treating it as a sufficient reason for dismissing the employee.

(9) In this paragraph [unless the context otherwise requires, references to a trade union include references to a branch or section of a trade union, and], in relation to an employee:

(a) 'capability' means capability assessed by reference to skill, aptitude, health or any other physical or mental quality;

(b) 'qualifications' means any degree, diploma or other academic, technical or professional qualification relevant to the position which the employee held; and

(c) any reference to redundancy or to being redundant shall be construed as a reference to the existence of one or other of the facts specified in paragraphs (a) and (b) of section 1 (2) of the Redundancy Payments Act 1965.''

Sub-paragraphs (4A) and (5A) were added by paragraphs 11 and 12, respectively, Employment Protection Act 1975, Schedule 16, Part III. The alteration to sub-paragraph (5) was carried out by the Trade Union and Labour Relations (Amendment) Act 1976, sections 1 (e) and 3 (5). The words in square brackets replaced

the words "all the employees of that employer or all employees".
Before the repeal the words "or as any reasonable grounds to being
a member of a particular trade union" appeared in sub-paragraph
(5) after "being a member of any trade union whatsoever". The
words added to sub-paragraph (9) were included by the Trade
Union and Labour Relations (Amendment) Act 1976, section 3 (6).

It is necessary for the paragraph to be examined in great detail.
"... *it shall be for the employer to show* ...". The burden of proof
lies on the employer to show the reason for the dismissal and that it
falls within the provisions of sub-paragraph (2) (*a*), (*b*), (*c*) and (*d*),
or was some other substantial reason of a kind such as to justify
dismissal of the employee: *Earl* v. *Slater and Wheeler (Airlyne) Ltd.*,
[1973] 1 All E.R. 145; [1973] 1 W.L.R. 51, N.I.R.C. Subject to
the special provisions relating to redundancies and trade union
membership and activities, for the dismissal to be fair the employer
then has to satisfy the tribunal that in the circumstances (having
regard to equity and the substantial merits of the case) he acted
reasonably in treating it as a sufficient reason for dismissing the
employee. Reference to previous decisions must be made with
great caution. Every case where unfair dismissal is alleged depends
on its own facts and the cases which are cited must be treated as
examples only. They can be no more than that.
"... *reason falling within sub-paragraph (2) below,* ...". In *Earl* v.
*Slater and Wheeler (Airlyne), Ltd.* above, Sir JOHN DONALDSON
explained (at p. 3) that the test to ascertain whether a dismissal
is fair operates in two stages:

> "In the first stage it is for the employer to show what was the
> principal or only reason for the dismissal and that it was a
> potentially valid reason, that is to say a reason falling within
> [sub-paragraph 1 (b)] 'or some other substantial reason of a
> kind such as to justify the dismissal of an employee holding
> the position which that employee held'. If the employer fails
> to discharge this burden, the tribunal must find that the
> dismissal was unfair."

The second stage, which is dealt with below, is determining
whether the dismissal was fair, or unfair, in accordance with the
following provisions of the paragraph.
*Rigby* v. *British Steel Corporation* (1973), 8 I.T.R. 191,
N.I.R.C., was a case where the employer did not appear before the

tribunal. It could not therefore discharge the onus of proof which rested on it and so the National Industrial Relations Court *held* that the employer had not shown that the dismissal took place for an acceptable reason and the employee was unfairly dismissed.

When determining the reasons or reason for the dismissal all the circumstances surrounding it are looked at to find the reason for the dismissal not just the final incident which leads to it. Giving judgment on an appeal by the employee in *Turner* v. *Wadham Stringer Commercials (Portsmouth) Ltd.*, [1974] I.R.L.R. 83, N.I.R.C., Sir HUGH GRIFFITHS said, when considering the employee's conduct which had led to the dismissal, "[counsel's] point, as we understand it is that 'the reason' referred to in [now paragraph 6 (1) (*a*)] is 'the reason' which immediately precipitates the dismissal. It may be quite a trivial matter and, although it is trivial and merely the trigger, that is the sole reason referred to. Accordingly he says, one looks in isolation at what happens on the day of the dismissal and one must then elect and find to which of the matters set out in [paragraph 6 (2)] it related. We do not adopt this construction of the section. [Paragraph 6 (1)] charges the tribunal with the duty of deciding as a matter of common-sense why the employee was dismissed." Mr. Turner was an employee who had worked his way through the employer's organisation to become assistant general manager. He was alleged not to have conducted himself satisfactorily and to be of insufficient calibre for senior management. The employers wrote to him complaining about certain activities of his wife, and demoting him to be sales manager. The tribunal found that he was not unfairly dismissed and his appeal failed.

It will be difficult for employers to go beyond the reasons which they specify in the written statement of reasons for dismissal which may be required under section 101 of the Employment Protection Act 1975. Because of this great care should be taken when preparing this statement.

*Tribunal decisions:*

*Betts* v. *Berrisford*, [1974] I.R.L.R. 271, T (employer heard rumour that the employee was to set up in competition. *Held* not sufficient reason).

*Yates* v. *British Leyland U.K. Ltd.*, [1974] I.R.L.R. 367, T (allegation that employee had urinated on the floor, not established in evidence. *Held* employer had not proved the reason for the dismissal).

*O'Brien* v. *International Harvester Co. of Great Britain*, [1974] I.R.L.R. 374, T (employee away from work sick. When representatives of the employers called it appeared that the employee had been engaged in hard physical labour and the employers thought that he was malingering. The letter of dismissal stated that the employee was dismissed because he was medically unfit. The tribunal *held* that the employers had not proved the reason for the dismissal and his claim succeeded).

*Whitaker* v. *Milk Marketing Board*, [1973] I.R.L.R. 100, T (the employee was an artificial insemination operator. He was dismissed after a series of complaints. No evidence was called from farmers to substantiate the complaints. Tribunal *held* that the employers had not proved a reason for the dismissal falling within the specified categories).

*Ellerker* v. *Waudbys of Weatherby, Ltd.*, [1973] I.R.L.R. 195, T (argument between the company secretary and the employee's wife was *held* not to be a acceptable reason for dismissal).

*Jury* v. *Jones Stroud Co., Ltd.*, [1975] I.R.L.R. 56, T (the employee who was a foreman told his employers that he was hoping to emigrate and would give two months' notice of leaving. The employers made arrangements to promote another employee to the position of foreman in three months' time. The employee was given notice and he asked what would happen if he hadn't sold his house in time. He was told he could have another job with lower status and rate of pay. It was *held* that the knowledge that the employee would be leaving was not a reason falling within paragraph 6 (1) (*b*), or (2), but as the employee had obtained other employment he received no compensation).

## Reason related to the employee's capability or qualifications

*Capability.* The tests of capability can be both physical and mental. The definition of "capability" is contained in paragraph (9), sub-paragraph (*a*) and of "qualifications" in paragraph (9), sub-paragraph (*b*).

(a) *Physical.* In *Kyte* v. *Greater London Council*, [1974] I.R.L.R. 8, N.I.R.C., the employee was a painter and decorator and as a result of an accident to his leg could only do light work. A new system of payment was introduced which was based on the output of a group of employees. An offer of inside work was made and refused by the employee. The employers notified him that he would be retired because of incapacity. The National Industrial Relations Court upheld a decision of the tribunal that Mr. Kyte was fairly dismissed.

*Lucking* v. *May and Barker, Ltd.*, [1974] I.R.L.R. 151, N.I.R.C., is a somewhat similar case. An employee who had to be on her feet most of the day injured her foot and was away for six months. It was not known whether she would return. The National Industrial Relations Court upheld the tribunal's decision that the employers had ground to dismiss the employee by reason of her incapacity.

The employee in *Tan* v. *Berry Brothers and Rudd, Ltd.*, [1974] I.R.L.R. 244, N.I.R.C., was regularly absent because of health problems. His job as a cellar-man involved lifting heavy weights. The Court said that the rules as to frustration expressed in *Marshall* v. *Harland and Wolff, Ltd.* (No. 2) (1972), 7 I.T.R. 150, N.I.R.C., were not relevant when dealing with a case such as that of Mr. Tan. Termination by frustration was totally different from termination by dismissal. The employee in Tan's case had been dismissed and employers had proved that it was for a reason relating to his capability.

Other cases on the point include *Casey* v. *Joseph Dawson, Ltd.*, [1973] I.R.L.R. 15, T (employee suffered from very serious ulcers. The employers transferred him to a department where there was lighter work. The employee did not like this and requested to be transferred to his old department where he was less easily "covered". He was dismissed after absence due to ill health. *Held* dismissal because of lack of capability).

*Fitzpatrick* v. *Hobourn Eaton (Manufacturing) Co., Ltd.*, [1973] I.R.L.R. 17, T (the employee suffered from dermatitis. Could not work machines because exposure to oils aggravated the illness. *Held* the reason relating to the employee's capability).

(b) *Mental.* In *Abernethy* v. *Mott Hay and Anderson* (1974), 9 I.T.R. 251, C.A., the employers claimed to have dismissed the employee, a senior civil engineer, because he was redundant. There was no scheme available on which he could work from head office, although he was offered and refused site work. Having examined the provisions of sub-paragraph 6 (2) (*a*) and 6 (9) (*a*), Lord DENNING, M.R., said (at p. 254): "In this particular case the reason was the inflexibility of Mr. Abernethy and his lack of adaptability. That seems to me to come within his aptitude and mental qualities. He had not the capability for performing the work he was em-

ployed to do. That was a reason to justify his dismissal." See also
*A. J. Dunning & Sons (Shop Fitters), Ltd.* v. *Jacomb* (1973), 8 I.T.R.
453 N.I.R.C., which is a case where the employee was a shop-
fitter's contracts manager. He did not get on well with his employers' customers, being uncooperative and unbending. The
National Industrial Relations Court *held* that the reason for the
dismissal related to his capability to perform the work he was
employed to do. In *Hopper* v. *Feedex, Ltd.*, [1974] I.R.L.R. 99,
N.I.R.C., the employee was a successful pig-man who was
promoted to pig farm manager. He was dismissed because he did
not have the ability for this job. The National Industrial Relations
Court said that here was a reason affecting the capability of the
employee to carry out the work he was employed to do.

See other tribunal decisions:

*O'Hagan* v. *Firestone Tyre and Rubber Co., Ltd.*, [1974]
I.R.L.R. 226, T (industrial relations manager without previous
experience. There were complaints about his conduct. He was
unable to create good personal relationships with the departments
of his employers and the trade unions. *Held* a reason going to the
employee's capability).

*Okerke* v. *The Post Office*, [1974] I.R.L.R. 170, T (several
complaints as to conduct of a clerical officer and his ability to
perform his job speedily and accurately. *Held* were reasons affecting
his capability).

*Allan* v. *F. W. Farnsworth, Ltd.*, [1974] I.R.L.R. 370, T (after
serious road accident an employee returned to work and was
transferred from job in bakery to butchery department. One day
he fainted at work and was dismissed because of risk of danger if
there was a recurrence. *Held* this was a reason as to the capability
of the employee though dismissal was unfair).

*Qualifications.* The lack of qualifications for the job represents
a less common reason than dismissal for lack of capability. An
example is *Blackman* v. *The Post Office* (1974), 9 I.T.R. 122,
N.I.R.C. Mr. Blackman was employed by the Post Office on the
basis that he would pass an aptitude test. He took the test on three
occasions but failed each time. The trade union would not agree to
waive the requirement of the aptitude test. The National Industrial
Relations Court found this was a reason falling within the
provisions relating to qualifications and, furthermore, fell in the
category of "some other substantial reason" for the employers

action. Trustworthiness is not a qualification within the meaning of the sub-paragraph; *Singh* v. *London County Bus Service, Ltd.*, [1976] I.R.L.R. 176, E.A.T.

## Reason related to conduct of the employee

Reasons relating to the employee's conduct are the most frequently encountered reasons given by employers for dismissal. The majority of cases where the dismissal takes place as a result of conduct by the employee are readily dealt with. Difficulties arise when dealing with the condition that the employer must have acted reasonably.

The "circumstances" which the industrial tribunal should consider in deciding whether the employer's action was reasonable are the circumstances as they existed at the time of the dismissal. Matters of which the employer was not aware prior to the dismissal cannot be relied upon by him to show that dismissal was fair. An example is *W. Devis & Sons, Ltd.* v. *Atkins,* [1976] 2 All E.R. 822, D.C. The employee was the manager of an abattoir and the employers became dissatisfied as to his disobedience of their directions for purchasing cattle. After dismissal evidence came to light of gross misconduct by the employee, namely that of taking a secret commission from the vendors of the cattle. It has been seen at p. 148 when discussing *Cyril Leonard* v. *Simo Securities Trust, Ltd.*, [1971] 3 All E.R. 1318, C.A., that evidence discovered after the dismissal could be used to justify a dismissal in an action for wrongful dismissal. However, in *Atkins'* case, PHILLIPS, J., said that matters coming to light after the dismissal could be used to prove prior events on which the dismissal was based, but they were not admissible as to the reason for the dismissal. There are two types of case:

(1) Where an employee was dismissed for a reason, say drunkenness, which on the facts known at the time of dismissal was difficult to establish; later events proving the drunkenness may be admissible; see for instance *Da Costa* v. *Optolis,* [1976] I.R.L.R. 178, E.A.T., or

(2) where the employee was dismissed for a particular reason, as in *Atkins'* case for general disobedience and incompetence, and then later it was discovered that he had been guilty of some serious misconduct which was quite different. The gross misconducts could of course have an effect on the amount of compensation.

Examples of conduct which have been considered by tribunals to be reasons for dismissal include:

(a) Inefficiency and failure to comply with employer's orders:

*Green* v. *Moyses Stevens, Ltd.*, [1974] I.R.L.R. 274, T (despatch manager refused to carry out filing of despatch returns despite repeated requests. The tribunal found that the employer's reason for dismissal was this refusal).

*Boobier* v. *Johnsons Cleaners (Southern), Ltd.*, [1974] I.R.L.R. 329, T (inefficient manager. *Held* reason was his conduct, but not reasonable in the circumstances).

*Bussey* v. *C.S.W. Engineering, Ltd.*, [1973] I.R.L.R. 9, T (driver/labourer slow and dilatory. *Held* dismissal because of the employee's conduct but that the employers did not act reasonably).

*Hilti (Great Britain), Ltd.* v. *Windridge* (1974), 9 I.R.T. 197, N.I.R.C. (salesman falsified return to obtain commission. *Held* reason for dismissal related to his conduct, but was not fair).

*Dalton* v. *Burtons Gold Medal Biscuits, Ltd.*, [1974] I.R.L.R. 45, N.I.R.C. (employee "clocked in" a fellow worker despite clear rules that this practice would result in instant dismissal. He was summarily dismissed. The National Industrial Relations Court upheld the decision of the tribunal that the dismissal was by reason of the employee's conduct).

*Turner* v. *Pleasurama Casinos, Ltd.*, [1976] I.R.L.R. 151, D.C. (Inspector dismissed for failing to spot a single instance of fraud. Tribunal's decision that because of gravity of mistakes in gambling the dismissal was fair was upheld on appeal).

(b) Absenteeism:

*Mooney* v. *Rowntree Mackintosh, Ltd.*, [1974] I.R.L.R. 277, T (long history of absenteeism after warnings. *Held* that the reason related to his conduct and was fair).

*Moore* v. *Central Electricity Generating Board (Midlands Region)*, [1974] I.R.L.R. 296, T (employee had periods of absence through illness and lateness and was held in custody for a month by police following an offence for which he subsequently received a suspended sentence. In giving its reasons the tribunal said at p. 297: "We do not think that there is a hard and fast period whereby if the employee exceeds it, he can be fairly dismissed. Each case must be treated differently. It depends on a variety of factors. Examples are the nature of the applicant's work, the reasons for the absences, his record with his employer and the warning he has been given").

*Ross* v. *Aquascutum, Ltd.*, [1973] I.R.L.R. 107, T (night watchman spent up to two hours each night away from the building. *Held* employee's conduct was reason for the dismissal which was fair).

*Willcox* v. *Hants and Sussex Aviation, Ltd.*, [1975] I.R.L.R. 133, T (employee did not return after Christmas holiday because of death of her dog. Dismissed because she did not produce doctor's note for the absence on the first day even though she was not contractually bound to produce note until three days' absence. *Held* to be unfair dismissal).

*Ali* v. *Tillotsons Containers, Ltd.*, [1975] I.R.L.R. 272, T (employee who was part of a team was warned about absences which were because of ill health. The absences continued and a written warning was given. Then after six months a check revealed that the employee still had a poor attendance record, although there was some improvement, and he was dismissed. The tribunal by a majority *held* that he was fairly dismissed).

*Gillanders* v. *Riding Hall Carpets, Ltd.*, [1974] I.R.L.R. 327, T (supervisor's contract said hours were 40 per week on shifts to be agreed with the manager. The employers tried to introduce a new rota system with the employee doing more weekend work. The complainant objected and, when he was fit after illness, refused to work the shifts. He was summarily dismissed. The tribunal *held* that it was necessary for there to be an agreement to alter the hours. The employee should have been given a warning and summary dismissal was unfair. The compensation was reduced by 75% because of the employee's uncooperative attitude).

*Muggeridge* v. *East Anglia Plastics, Ltd.*, [1973] I.R.L.R. 163, T (female employees asked to adapt hours of work but did not wish to do so because of domestic commitments. They were given notice. *Held* the requirements were not unusual or onerous. Although not contractually bound to do the work inability to accept the advised hours was a reason relating to the employees conduct), but contrast *Burns* v. *Ideal Timber Products, Ltd.*, (1975), 10 I.T.R. 14, T (employee worked as hand sander and with others was not satisfied as to working conditions. Employers requested non-obligatory overtime which employees refused to do. This led to dismissal. *Held* unfairly dismissed but applicant had contributed to the dismissal). See also *Graham* v. *Anthony Todd (Haulage), Ltd.*,

[1975] I.R.L.R. 45, T (where an apprentice was dismissed for refusing to work voluntary overtime. *Held* to be unfairly dismissed).
*Wallace* v. *E. J. Guy, Ltd.*, (1973), 8 I.T.R. 154, N.I.R.C.
(employee dismissed after he had refused to carry out pipe bending
work because the employers would not pay extra 2p per hour.
There was a practice of negotiating bonuses individually at the
factory. *Held* unfairly dismissed).

*Henderson* v. *Masson Scott Thrissell Engineering, Ltd.*, [1974]
I.R.L.R. 98, N.I.R.C. (employee thought person in office was
holding up letter re merit bonus. In fact it was still the subject
of negotiation with the trade union. He was abusive to drawing
office manager and filing clerk. *Held* dismissal fair).

*Lamsdale* v. *Her Majesty's Stationery Office*, [1975] I.R.L.R.
239, T (director of industrial relations refused to attend meeting to
discuss an industrial dispute despite oral and written requests to
attend. Later he circulated documents criticising management. The
matter was investigated by a higher level of management and
he was dismissed. The job was advertised before his last appeal
was heard. *Held* fair).

(c) Insubordination, non-cooperative attitude and breach of rules:

*Farnborough* v. *The Governors of Edinburgh College of Art*,
[1974] I.R.L.R. 245, N.I.R.C. (an art lecturer did not agree with
the allocation of work. Was ordered to comply but refused to
lecture. Fairly dismissed).

*Kemp* v. *Robin Knitwear, Ltd.*, [1974] I.R.L.R. 69, T (an employee had previously worked for an associated company but for
two or three years had worked exclusively for respondants. She
refused to assist in an associated company's warehouse when there
was not enough work with her employers. Tribunal *held* that employee was under no contractual obligation to work for the other
company and so was not guilty of misconduct).

*Shortland* v. *Chantrill*, [1975] I.R.L.R. 208, N.I.R.C.
(managing director criticised apprentice's work and he said to the
managing director, "You couldn't have done any f...... better".
He was instantly dismissed. Tribunal *held* that he was unfairly
dismissed. It was an isolated instance and particular care should
be used in dealing with apprentices. A warning or period of
suspension would have been the proper punishment. Although the
National Industrial Relations Court remitted the case to the
tribunal to recalculate the compensation they approved the finding

that the dismissal was unfair). See also *King* v. *Motorway Tyres and Accessories, Ltd.*, [1975] I.R.L.R. 51, T (an otherwise able employee told branch manager to "f... off" during an argument. He was instantly dismissed. *Held* unfairly dismissed).

*Blake* v. *Berkel Auto Scale Co., Ltd.*, [1974] I.R.L.R. 272, T (contrary to rules of which he was aware the employee bought a second-hand scale and sold it at a profit. He used the company van and other employees in the dealings. He was summarily dismissed. *Held*, as the employee knew of the rule, he was fairly dismissed).

*Blanchard* v. *D.R.E. Holdings (1971), Ltd.*, [1974] I.R.L.R. 266, T (travelling sales manager found to be drunk during working hours. He was not dismissed until two days later even though director stayed in the same hotel with him. *Held*, although the conduct warranted severe censure, if it merited summary dismissal should have taken place immediately).

*Hutchins* v. *British Railways Board*, [1974] I.R.L.R. 303, T (fight with other employee. Disciplinary hearing with procedural defects. *Held* unfairly dismissed).

*Whitlow* v. *Alkanet Construction, Ltd.*, [1975] I.R.L.R. 321, T (a carpenter was asked to carry out work at the chief executive's house. He indulged in love-play and sexual intercourse with the chief executive's wife and was dismissed. *Held* dismissal fair).

*Spiller* v. *F. J. Wallis, Ltd.*, [1975] I.R.L.R. 362, T (female employee had "an association" with a married employee and was dismissed pursuant to a well known company rule which said that this type of conduct would result in dismissal. *Held* dismissal fair).

(d) Dishonest and criminal action of employee:

*Fowler* v. *Cammell Laird (Shipbuilders), Ltd.*, [1973] I.R.L.R. 72, T (an employee convicted of theft of other employee's car mirror from car left in company car park. Tribunal *held* dismissal fair). Contrast *Donson and Frudd* v. *Conoco, Ltd.*, [1973] I.R.L.R. 258, T (tanker drivers convicted of theft of scaffolding pipes unconnected with employment. Not dismissed until their appeals against conviction failed. The dismissal *held* unfair, though 50% contribution).

*O'Brien* v. *Boots Pure Drug Co.*, [1973] I.R.L.R. 261, T (shop assistant had items in her possession which had not dealt with in accordance with company staff sales practice. *Held* unfair dismissal.

The person exercising power of dismissal should look at the
individuals' circumstances).

*How* v. *Tesco Stores, Ltd.*, [1974] I.R.L.R. 194, T (contrary to
company rule 50 pence removed from till for private purposes.
Summary dismissal and procedure not gone through correctly.
*Held* unfair).

*Gardiner* v. *Newport County Borough Council*, [1974] I.R.L.R.
262, T (lecturer teaching 16- and 17-year-olds convicted of an
offence of gross indecency in public lavatories. Claim for compensation for unfair dismissal failed).

*Creffield* v. *British Broadcasting Corporation*, [1975] I.R.L.R. 23,
T (film cameraman was convicted of sexual offences involving girl
under 16 he had met in the course of his employment. He also
introduced her to a friend of his who was a prostitute. The
applicant was often sent on location for filming. *Held* by majority
that dismissal was fair).

*Budgen & Co.* v. *Thomas,* [1976] I.C.R. 344, E.A.T. (the
employee a cashier admitted to security officer that although she
had placed money in the till she had not "rung up" the sale. She
signed a statement to that effect. The officer reported to head office
which dismissed the employee. She was not given the opportunity
of explaining herself to the level of management which took the
decisions to dismiss. *Held* unfair).

*Carr* v. *Alexander Russell, Ltd.*, [1976] I.R.L.R. 220, C.S.
(employee who was away from work ill was caught "red handed"
by police stealing cable from the employers. The employers
operated a disciplinary procedure but not in cases of gross misconduct. *Held* fairly dismissed).

**Redundancy**

As we have reasons relating to the capability, qualifications
and conduct of the employee it is not sufficient for an employer
who wishes to show that the dismissal of his employee was fair
for him to prove that the reason or principal reason for the
dismissal was that the employee was redundant. Where the reason
for the dismissal is redundancy sub-paragraphs (7) and (8) have to
be considered. Sub-paragraph (7) does not exhaustively define the
circumstances where an employee dismissed by reason of redundancy can be unfairly dismissed; *Rigby* v. *British Steel Corporation*
(1973), 8 I.T.R. 191, N.I.R.C. Thus dismissal by reason of
redundancy is also unfair if either of the conditions in sub-para-

graphs (7) (*a*) or (*b*) is satisfied, or the employer fails to show that he acted reasonably in accordance with sub-paragraph (8).

For the purposes of proceedings, where an employee claims to have been unfairly dismissed the onus of proof is on the employer to show the reason for dismissal, and this applies in cases of redundancy just as it does in others. It will be recollected that for the purposes of a claim under the Redundancy Payments Act 1965, the onus of proof is on the employer to disprove redundancy. Thus it is possible in the case of an application for both compensation for unfair dismissal and for redundancy payments, for the employer to fail to discharge the onus of proof so far as the unfair dismissal application is concerned, and yet for the tribunal to resolve that for the purposes of the Redundancy Payments Act 1965 the employee was dismissed by reason of redundancy. An example is:

*Midland Foot Comfort Centre* v. *Richmond* (1973), 8 I.T.R. 223, N.I.R.C. The employers claimed to have dismissed the employee because of misconduct and inefficiency. The tribunal rejected these contentions and awarded the employee a redundancy payment and compensation for unfair dismissal. In delivering the judgment of the National Industrial Relations Court, Sir JOHN DONALDSON said, at p. 227:

> "We accept that where there are claims under both the 1965 and the [1974] Acts, the tribunal in considering the claim to a redundancy payment must take full account of the employer's evidence as to the reason for the dismissal even if, as will usually be the case, this evidence is primarily addressed to rebutting the claim that the dismissal was unfair. If the tribunal is satisfied that the reason was redundancy, no problem arises. If it is left in doubt as to the true reason, the dismissal is unfair and the presumption provided by the 1965 Act, entitles the applicant to a redundancy payment. But if the tribunal is satisfied on the evidence that the principal reason for the dismissal was other than redundancy and was not a [paragraph 6 (1)] reason, e.g. an unreasonable personal dislike of the employee, the dismissal will be unfair but the claim to a redundancy payment will fail because the presumption of dismissal for redundancy will have been rebutted. Of course, in such an event, the amount of the award of compensation will reflect the loss of accrued rights to a redundancy payment in the event of dismissal for that reason and the likeli-

hood that, if not dismissed for other reasons, the employee would have been dismissed for redundancy and received that payment." See Trade Union and Labour Relations Act 1974, Sch. 1, para. 23.

Prior to the implementation of the Employment Protection Act 1975 there were difficulties and anomalies in computing compensation when the employee was both redundant and unfairly dismissed. Now sections 75 (8) and 76 (7) of the Employment Protection Act 1975 effectively cover such cases. From the employee's point of view there is now far less reason to show that he was dismissed by reason of redundancy as well as unfairly dismissed.

A tribunal is not bound to find that an employee had been dismissed by reason of redundancy even if the dismissal has been expressed as such. See *Abernethy* v. *Mott Hay and Anderson* (1974), 9 I.T.R. 251, N.I.R.C., where, notwithstanding that the employers thought that the employee was redundant the tribunal found that dismissal occurred because of his lack of capability. This decision was upheld on appeal. If the possibility that selection for redundancy was made for an inadmissible reason has been raised it must be considered by the tribunal. When the National Industrial Relations Court found that a tribunal had not looked at the somewhat similar provisions in the now repealed Industrial Relations Act 1971, in determining why an employee was chosen for redundancy, the case was remitted to the tribunal for rehearing: *Axe* v. *British Domestic Appliances, Ltd.* (1973), 8 I.T.R. 126, N.I.R.C.

For a discussion of inadmissible reasons, see p. 316, below.

(a) *Unfair selection for redundancy*

In *Bessenden Properties* v. *Corness* (1974), 9 I.T.R. 128; affd. [1974] I.R.L.R. 338, C.A., the employers purported to lay-off the employee when they had no power to do so. This was *held* to be a dismissal due to redundancy. The tribunal found that the dismissal was unfair because a junior member of staff was retained by the employers. They said that the usual custom of the industry "last in, first out" was not applied. In the National Industrial Relations Court Sir JOHN DONALDSON said (at p. 130), that he did not consider that a usual custom in the industry amounted to a customary arrangement. "In our judgment what is contemplated by this section—though we do not seek to define it in this case—is something which is so well known, so certain and so clear as to amount in effect to an implied 'procedure' as contrasted with the express 'agreed procedure' which is the alternative contemplated by the paragraph." The decision of the tribunal that "last in, first out" was the customary arrangement was wrong but the finding that the employers did not act reasonably was correct and the determination of unfair dismissal was upheld. The duty of the industrial tribunal is to decide whether the employers acted reasonably and not whether had they been the employers the same decision would have been taken; *Grundy (Teddington), Ltd.* v. *Willis*, [1976] I.R.L.R. 118, D.C.

Whether or not an employee has been dismissed in breach of an agreed procedure is a question of fact for the tribunal to decide. In *Gibb* v. *Lanarkshire Bolt*, [1973] I.T.R. 53, N.I.R.C., a tribunal had determined that an employee had been dismissed in accordance with an agreed procedure and the National Industrial Relations Court refused to interfere with the decision. Before it can come to this decision, however, the industrial tribunal must find that there is a customary arrangement, or agreed procedure. If one or other does not exist then sub-paragraph (7) is not relevant to the question to be determined by them. The decision of the tribunal in *British Olivetti, Ltd.* v. *Kay*, [1975] I.R.L.R. 29, D.C., did not make it clear whether the tribunal had concluded that the applicant was unfairly dismissed in breach of a customary arrangement, or agreed procedure, or whether it considered the dismissal on the grounds of redundancy to be unreasonable. The Divisional Court remitted the case to a newly constituted tribunal to look again at the facts to determine the issues. See also *Hollies* v. *Principal Pattern and Engineering Co.*, [1973] I.R.L.R. 165, T (the longest serving employee dismissed because redundant. Other employees were retained. There was no agreed procedure or consultation. The tribunal said that regard should have been had to the length of service and the dismissal was therefore unfair. One-third of the compensation was deducted because the employee was "unenthusiastic").

*Dorrell* v. *Engineering Developments (Farnborough), Ltd.*, [1975] I.R.L.R. 234, T (employee had longer continuous service with employers but shorter cumulative service than another employee not dismissed. It was *held* that the usual application of "last in, first out" is in respect of continuous service and therefore the dismissal was unfair.

The agreed procedure need not always be "last in, first out". In *Boothby* v. *Kingston Craftsmen, Ltd.*, [1975] I.R.L.R. 138, T, the employee was a painter and was selected for redundancy after consultation with the union following an agreed procedure. An employee with shorter service was retained. The tribunal *held* that the dismissal was in accordance with the procedure and was fair. However, the customary arrangement must be brought to the attention of the employee who is dismissed. In *Keepin* v. *Hurn Brothers, Ltd.*, [1975] I.R.L.R. 141, T, the employee was chosen for dismissal on a basis used previously, and one thing that had been taken into account was that he was not a union member. The employee who had been asked to join the union had not been told that if he did not do so he was more likely to be made redundant. The tribunal *held* the dismissal to be unfair. The effect of not being a member of the union should have been explained to the employee.

*Gargrave* v. *Hotel and Catering Industry Training Board*, [1974] I.R.L.R. 85, N.I.R.C. (an employee was dismissed as redundant. The procedure agreement said that within grades "last in, first out" should be applied. The employee claimed that other employees should have been dismissed in departments not affected by the redundancy since they had less service. The employers and the union contended that the employee was selected in accordance with the scheme. The National Industrial Relations Court was satisfied that an agreed procedure should be looked at in the context of, and applied to, those employees in the field of activity affected by the redundancy situation and who were engaged in the same type and category of work).

*Sudders* v. *The Prestige Group, Ltd.*, [1975] I.R.L.R. 367, T (employee dismissed had more continuous service but less cumulative service than an employee who was retained. The principle of "last in, first out" applied but the complainant was dismissed. The employers had issued a policy statement clearly saying that breaks of service not exceeding a year in certain circumstances did not break the continuity of employment and the retained employee's break in service fell within this category. *Held*, the dismissal was fair).

*Shaw* v. *Garden King Frozen Foods, Ltd.*, [1975] I.R.L.R. 98, T (an employee employed for over a year and became an attendant at the effluent plant. After alteration to the system it became obvious that only one attendant was required and not two. The employee was made redundant in preference to another who had only a month's service but was far more efficient. He had not been warned about inefficiency. The dismissal was *held* to be unfair, good management could have improved the employee's standard of performance).

#### (b) *Reasonableness in connection with redundancy*

When considering whether an employer has acted reasonably in dismissing an employee by reason of redundancy, as with other cases where the reason for dismissal has been proved, reference should be made to the Code of Practice. Paragraphs 44, 45, 46, 52, 53 and 65 have particular relevance in redundancy cases.

As has been seen the reason of redundancy is subject to the provisions of the Trade Union and Labour Relations Act 1974, Schedule 1, paragraph 6 (8), in the same way as the other reasons for dismissal, see *Clarkson International Tools, Ltd.* v. *Short*, [1973] I.R.L.R. 90, N.I.R.C. It is for the employer to prove that he acted reasonably and if he does not appear at the hearing the tribunal should find the employee was unfairly dismissed as well as redundant; *Rigby* v. *British Steel Corporation* (1973), 8 I.T.R. 191, N.I.R.C.

In *Vokes, Ltd.* v. *Bear* (1974), 9 I.T.R. 85, N.I.R.C., the employee was a work manager who became redundant after a takeover. He was given no notice, no attempt was made to place him elsewhere in the group, and he was not assisted in finding alternative employment. A tribunal awarded him compensation for unfair dismissal. In considering the application of paragraph 6 (8) Sir HUGH GRIFFITHS said (at p. 88):

> " 'The circumstances' embrace all relevant matters that should weigh with a good employer when deciding at a given moment in time whether or not he should dismiss his employee. The sub-section is focusing the tribunal's attention upon 'the dismissal', that is, the dismissal on the 2nd March. The question they have to ask themselves is whether on the 2nd March the employer was acting reasonably in treating redundancy as a sufficient reason for dismissing Mr. Bear on that date. The tribunal are entitled to take into account all the circumstances affecting both the employer and the employee at the time of the dismissal.
>
> "The position is somewhat analogous to the case of a warning. An employer may have good grounds for thinking

that a man is not capable of doing his job properly, but in the general run of cases it will not be reasonable for him to regard that lack of capability as a sufficient reason for dismissing him until he is given a warning so that the man has the chance to show if he can do better. So in this case there was a redundancy situation but there was no compelling reason why the axe should fall until the employer had done his best to help the employee."

See also *Marcus* v. *Geo. Wimpey & Co., Ltd.*, [1974] I.R.L.R. 356, T (the employee was a dumper driver who had previously been a labourer and was employed for seven years. He was transferred to a site as a matter of urgency since the employee he was replacing had been taken ill. During the first week he was told that the site was closing down and he was to be made redundant. Other employees with less service were retained to avoid disturbing "gangs". The tribunal *held* that there was no agreement or procedure for redundancies. Since other employees with less service had been retained the employers did not act reasonably).

*Farthing* v. *Midland Household Stores, Ltd.*, [1974] I.R.L.R. 354, T (on reduction of internal auditors the claimant was chosen for redundancy even though junior employees were retained. There were minor criticisms of his ability. In giving its decision the tribunal said: "As to what weight ought to be given to seniority, it is very difficult and might be a mistake to lay down a hard and fast rule, but the principle must apply regardless of the nature of the employment, namely, that the longer an employee goes on working for the same employer the more dependent he becomes on him, and the employer owes a corresponding moral duty to avoid dismissing the employee if reasonably possible. In cases of sufficient gravity, a senior employee may have to be dismissed, but it should be avoided if possible").

*O'Reilly* v. *Welwyn and Hatfield District Council*, [1975] I.R.L.R. 334, T ("temporary cashier" dismissed because of redundancy situation of punch card operators. She was not told her job was in danger or warned that she should apply for a permanent position. *Held* dismissed unfair).

*Hammond-Scott* v. *Elizabeth Arden, Ltd.* (1976), 11 I.T.R. 33, T (long-serving female employee aged 53 took post in 1972 because it was understood that she would retain it until she was 60. Dismissed by reason of redundancy in 1975. *Held*, unfair).

**Sub-paragraph (2) (*d*) ... "that the employee could not continue to work ... without contravention ... of a duty or restriction ... under an enactment ..."**

This is a ground which arises only rarely and many of the cases have involved employees disqualified from driving. *Appleyard v. F. M. Smith (Hull), Ltd.*, [1972] I.R.L.R. 19, T (an employee employed as driver lost licence. *Held* fairly dismissed). *Fearn v. Tayford Motor Co., Ltd.*, [1975] I.R.L.R. 336, T (a used-vehicle supervisor where driving was an important part of the job. Lost his licence for 12 months. Dismissal *held* fair).

In *Pearman v. J. I. Case Co., Ltd.*, [1974] I.R.L.R. 309, T, an interesting problem arose. The applicant was the United Kingdom "director" of marketing although he was not actually a director of the company. He was an undischarged bankrupt. The tribunal *held* that since he had no formal office with the company his occupation of the position was not in breach of section 187 of the Companies Act 1948 and so his dismissal because of the bankruptcy was unfair. The employers had not discharged the onus of proof which rested on them.

When the reason for the dismissal under this head is on medical grounds regard should be had to Employment Protection Act 1975, section 29 (4). See p. 59, above.

**Sub-paragraph 6 (1) (*b*) "... some other substantial reason of a kind such as to justify dismissal of an employee holding the position which the employee held ..."**

As with other grounds which the employers may seek to show to persuade the tribunal that the dismissal was fair this depends very largely on questions of fact. It is to be stressed that the reason does not have to justify dismissal at this stage in the tribunal's determination it only has to be a reason which could justify dismissal; *Mercia Rubber Mouldings, Ltd. v. Lingwood*, [1974] I.R.L.R. 82, N.I.R.C. The words "some other substantial reason" do not have to be construed *ejusdem generis* with the reasons in sub-paragraph (2). See *R.S. Components, Ltd. v. Irwin*, [1974] 1 All E.R. 41, N.I.R.C.

If a person engaged as a replacement for an employee suspended on medical grounds pursuant to Employment Protection Act 1975, section 33, is dismissed, provided that the requirements laid down in that section have been complied with, the dismissal is regarded as having been for a substantial reason of a kind such as to justify dismissal of an employee holding the position which the employee held, for the purposes of paragraph 6 (1) (*b*). See p. 63, above. Similarly, if a person engaged as a replacement for an employee absent, wholly or partly, because of pregnancy, or confinement, is dismissed in accordance with Employment Protection Act 1975, section 51, provided the requirements of that section have been complied with, then for the purposes of paragraph 6 (1) (*b*), the dismissal is regarded as having been for a substantial reason of a kind such as to justify dismissal of an employee holding the position which the employee held. See p. 294, above. In both cases for the employer to successfully claim the employee was fairly dismissed he has to prove that paragraph 6 (8) has been complied with.

*Cases where "other substantial reason" has been shown*
   *Treganowan* v. *Robert Knee & Co., Ltd.* (1975), 10 I.T.R. 121, D.C. (friction arose in employer's offices as a result of colleagues dislike of promiscuous activities of dismissed employee which she continually discussed at work. Dismissal *held* fair).
   *Robinson* v. *Flitwick Frames, Ltd.*, [1975] I.R.L.R. 261, T (employee was not contractually obliged to work overtime but a meeting of all in his section agreed to do so to get work out on time. Although nothing was said at the meeting the employee refused to work overtime and was dismissed. *Held* dismissal fair).
   *Flude* v. *Post Office*, [1975] I.R.L.R. 330, T (employee was on a year's trial period. Had already received warning as to conduct. Had an altercation with another employee and was dismissed during trial period as not satisfactory. *Held* dismissal fell within paragraph 6 (1) (*b*)).
   *Knighton* v. *Henry Rhodes, Ltd.*, [1974] I.R.L.R. 71, T (the employers were rearranging maintenance department. The employee was a maintenance fitter and as a result would have to do one week in six on night shift. He said he did not want nights and was offered the job as chargehand fitter during the day. He refused and was dismissed. *Held* refusal to accept variation of contract was another substantial reason).
   *R.S. Components, Ltd.* v. *Irwin* (1973), 8 I.T.R. 569, N.I.R.C. (employer sought to impose a restrictive covenant on the employee to prevent soliciting customers in the area covered by him within 12 months of his leaving the company's employ. Dismissed because he refused to sign. *Held* to fall within the meaning of the

forerunner of sub-paragraph 6 (1) (*b*)).
*Gorfin* v. *Distressed Gentlefolks Aid Association*, [1973] I.R.L.R.
290, T (employee was cause of dissention amongst staff. *Held* "other
substantial reason for dismissal").
*Muggeridge and Slade* v. *East Anglia Plastics, Ltd.*, [1973]
I.R.L.R. 163, T (employee refused to adapt hours to suit employer's request which was not unreasonable. *Held* "other substantial reason").
*Farr* v. *Hoveringham Gravels, Ltd.*, [1972] I.R.L.R. 104, T (an
employee who when accepting promotion agreed to move house
subsequently refused to do so and was dismissed. *Held* "other
substantial reason").
*Blackman* v. *Post Office* (1974), 9 I.T.R. 122, N.I.R.C. (employee had failed test required by agreement between employers
and trade union. *Held* to fall within the sub-paragraph).
*Foot* v. *Eastern Counties Timber Co., Ltd.*, [1972] I.R.L.R. 83, T
(employee's husband set up rival business near subsidiary of the
employer. Reason for dismissal *held* to fall within the terms of the
sub-paragraph's predecessor).

*Cases where "other substantial reason" not shown*
*Betts* v. *Berrisford*, [1974] I.R.L.R. 271, T (employee told the
employer that he would be leaving and it was rumoured that he
was to work for competitors. He was dismissed. Tribunal *held*
that this was not a substantial reason justifying the action).
*Bumpus* v. *Standard Life Assurance Co., Ltd.*, [1974] I.R.L.R.
232, T (employers were reorganising their activities. The employee
refused to fit in. *Held* not substantial reason justifying dismissal).

### Dismissal for inadmissible reasons

A reason by virtue of which a dismissal is regarded as unfair
in consequence of sub-paragraph 6 (4) or (5) is referred to as an
inadmissible reason. The reasons set out in sub-paragraph 6 (4)
if the reason (or, if more than one, the principal reason) for the
dismissal automatically make the dismissal unfair. There is no
requirement for reasonableness. Sub-paragraph 6 (5) outlines
circumstances in "closed shop" situations where a dismissal is automatically regarded as fair, except in the one instance when it is
unfair.

The definition of "independent trade union" appears in Trade
Union and Labour Relations Act, section 30 (1), see p. 86, above.

That section (as amended by the Trade Union and Labour Relations (Amendment) Act 1976) also defines "union membership agreement" as follows:

"... 'union membership agreement' means an agreement or arrangement which—
(a) is made by or on behalf of, or otherwise exists between, one or more independent trade unions and one or more employers or employers' associations; and
(b) relates to employees of an identifiable class; and
(c) has the effect [in practice of requiring the employees for the time being of the class to which it relates (whether or not there is a condition to that effect in their contract of employment) to] be or become a member of the union or one of the unions which is or are parties to the agreement or arrangement or of another [specified] independent trade union."

The words in square brackets are added by the Trade Union and Labour Relations (Amendment) Act 1976, section 3 (3). That Act also adds a new sub-section (5A) to section 30 of the Trade Union and Labour Relations Act 1974. It is:

"(5A) For the purposes of this Act employees are to be treated, in relation to a union membership agreement, as belonging to the same class if they have been identified as such by the parties to the agreement, and employees may be so identified by reference to any characteristics or circumstances whatsoever."

The provisions of Schedule 1 of paragraph 6 (4), (4A), (5) and (5A) of the Trade Union and Labour Relations Act 1974 differ from those enacted in the Industrial Relations Act 1971. As has been seen, the exclusions from the unfair dismissal provisions on the ground that the employee does not have the minimum qualifying period of employment, that he was employed in a small business and because he was over retiring age, do not apply when the dismissal is for an inadmissible reason.

An example of a case falling within the terms of sub-paragraph 6 (4) (b) is *Miller* v. *Rafique*, [1975] I.R.L.R. 70, T. A solicitor's secretary agreed with her employer on her appointment that she could leave early one hour per month to attend meetings of her independent trade union. The employee indicated that she was applying for another job and after this was told that she must stick strictly to the working hours. She took the hour off and was dismissed the next day. An industrial tribunal *held* that dismissal was unfair because of breach of paragraph 6 (4). It was an appropriate time to attend a trade union meeting because in view of the agreement she was contractually entitled to the time off and so her attendance at the meeting was outside working hours. However, the activities must be related to a trade union and not be solely of a type undertaken by a trade union. See *Gardner* v. *Peeks Retail, Ltd.*, [1975] I.R.L.R. 244, T. An employee who did not have the qualifying period of continuous service made various complaints to the management about the unsatisfactory state of the staff room and failure to display a statutory poster. The tribunal *held* that the employee's activities were not in connection with a trade union and the unfair dismissal provisions did not apply. An unofficial strike has been held by a tribunal not to amount to "trade union activities"; *McQuade* v. *Scotbeef, Ltd.*, [1975] I.R.L.R. 332, T. See also *Sarvent* v. *Central Electricity Generating Board*, [1976] I.R.L.R. 66, T, and *Lyon and Scherk* v. *St. James Press, Ltd.*, [1976] I.R.L.R. 215, E.A.T.

Paragraph 6 (5) enables an employer to dismiss an employee who is not a member of the specified union pursuant to a union membership agreement where it is the practice of employees of the same class as the dismissed employee to belong to a specified union, unless the employee genuinely objects on grounds of religious belief to being a member of any trade union whatsoever. From an employer's point of view the difficulty is that he has to decide whether there is a genuine religious belief applicable in the circumstances. The burden of proof to show that conditions (a) and (b) had been complied with lies on the employer. It is then for the employee to justify his refusal to join the trade union by proving that he genuinely objects on grounds of religious belief to being a member of any trade union whatsoever. Before the amendments made by the Trade Union and Labour Relations (Amendment) Act 1976 there was an additional escape for the employee if he had reasonable grounds for not joining a particular trade union, but this is no longer applicable.

### Dismissal in connection with industrial action

Employment Protection Act 1975, Schedule 16, Part III, paragraph 13, substitutes a new paragraph 7 for paragraphs 7 and 8 of

Schedule 1 of the Trade Union and Labour Relations Act 1974 as originally enacted. It is as follows:

"7.—(1) The provisions of this paragraph shall have effect in relation to an employee who claims that he has been unfairly dismissed by his employer where at the date of dismissal—
(a) the employer was conducting or instituting a lock-out; or
(b) the employee was taking part in a strike or other industrial action.

(2) In such a case an industrial tribunal shall not determine whether the dismissal was fair or unfair unless it is shown—
(a) that one or more relevant employees of the same employer have not been dismissed; or
(b) that one or more such employees have been offered re-engagement, and that the employee concerned has not been offered re-engagement.

(3) Where it is shown that the condition referred to in paragraph (b) of sub-paragraph (2) above is fulfilled, the provisions of paragraph 6 above and of section 34 of the Employment Protection Act 1975 shall have effect as if in that paragraph and that section for any reference to the reason or principal reason for which the employee was dismissed there were substituted a reference to the reason or principal reason for which he has not been offered re-engagement.

(4) Paragraph 21 (4) below shall apply in relation to a complaint to which sub-paragraph (3) above applies as if for references to the effective date of termination there were substituted a reference to the first date on which any relevant employee was offered re-engagement.

(5) In this paragraph—
(a) 'date of dismissal' means—
  (i) where the employee's contract of employment was terminated by notice, the date on which the employer's notice was given; and
  (ii) in any other case, the effective date of termination.
(b) 'relevant employees' means—
  (i) in relation to a lock-out, employees who were directly interested in the trade dispute in contemplation of furtherance of which the lock-out occurred; and
  (ii) in relation to a strike or other industrial action, employees who took part in it; and

(*c*) any reference to an offer of re-engagement is a reference to an offer (made either by the original employer or by a successor of that employer or an associated employer) to re-engage an employee, either in the job which he held immediately before the date of dismissal or in a different job which would be reasonably suitable in his case."

Employment Protection Act 1975, section 34, relates to dismissal on the grounds of pregnancy, see p. 320, below. Trade Union and Labour Relations Act 1974, Schedule 1, paragraph 21 (4), relates to the time limit on presenting complaints before industrial tribunals, see p. 339, below.

Although paragraph 7 differs from paragraphs 7 and 8 as originally enacted some assistance may be gained by referring to decisions under them, for instance *Thompson* v. *Eaton, Ltd.*, [1976] Law Soc. Gaz. 485, E.A.T. and *Stock* v. *Frank Jones (Tipton), Ltd.*, [1976] Law Soc. Gaz. 349, E.A.T.

**Unfair dismissal and pregnancy**

An employee is treated for the purposes of Trade Union and Labour Relations Act 1974, Schedule 1, as unfairly dismissed if the reason, or principal reason, for her dismissal is that she is pregnant, or is any other reason connected with her pregnancy, unless at the effective date of termination she is, or will have become, because of her pregnancy, incapable of adequately doing the work which she is employed to do, or that because of her pregnancy she cannot, or will not be able to continue after that date to do that work without contravention (either by her or by her employer) of a duty or restriction imposed by or under any enactment; Employment Protection Act 1975, section 34 (1). In addition an employee is treated as unfairly dismissed if her employer dismisses her for one of the last mentioned reasons, but neither he, nor any successor of his, where there is a suitable available vacancy, makes her an offer before, or on the effective date of termination, to engage her under a new contract; *ibid.*, section 34 (2). The new employment contract must take effect immediately on the ending of employment under the previous contract, or, where that employment ends on a Friday, Saturday or Sunday, on or before the next Monday after that day. It must be such that the work to be done under it is of a kind which is both suitable in relation to the employee, and appropriate for her to do in the circumstances, and its provisions as to the capacity and place in which she is employed and as the other terms and conditions of her employment, must not be substantially less favourable to her than the corresponding provisions of the previous contract. When an employee makes a complaint of unfair dismissal on the ground of failure to offer to so engage an employee, it is for the employer to show that he or a successor made an offer to engage her in compliance with the requirements or, as the case may be that there was no suitable vacancy for her; *ibid.*, section 34 (4).

If an employee exercising her right to return to work in accordance with section 49 of the Employment Protection Act 1975 (see p. 80, above), is not permitted to return to work then she is treated for the purposes of the unfair dismissal provisions and the Redundancy Payments Act 1965 as if she had been employed until the notified day of return and, if she would not otherwise be so treated, as having been continuously employed until that day, and as if she had been dismissed with effect from that day for the reason for which she was not permitted to return; Employment Protection Act 1975, section 50 (1).

By virtue of the Employment Protection Act 1975, Schedule 3, paragraph (1), the Trade Union and Labour Relations Act 1974, Schedule 1, paragraph 6, has effect as if a new sub-paragraph (8) were substituted. The effect of this is that subject to paragraphs (4), (6) and (7) of paragraph 6, the determination of the question whether the dismissal was fair, or unfair, having regard to the reason shown by the employer will depend on whether the employer can satisfy the tribunal, that, in the circumstances (having regard to equity and the substantial merits of the case), he would have been acting reasonably in treating it as a sufficient reason for dismissing the employee if she had not been absent from work. In circumstances where section 48 (4) of the Employment Protection Act 1975 applies (i.e. where the employee is entitled to return to work but it is not practicable by reason of redundancy for the employer to permit her so to return to work, she is entitled, where there is a suitable vacancy, to be offered alternative employment with her employer (or his successor) or an associated employer, under a new contract of employment complying with section 48 (5), see p. 81, above). If no offer is made of the alternative employment then the dismissal is automatically treated as unfair dismissal; Employment Protection Act 1975, Schedule 3, paragraph 2 (2). References in the unfair dismissal provisions to "effective date of termination" and "date of termination of employment" are construed as references to the notified day of return, and the provisions of Trade Union and Labour Relations Act 1974, Schedule 1, paragraphs 5, 6 (5), 9 to 14 and 30 (1A), and Employment Protection Act 1975, sections 72 (7), 74 (4), (6) and (7) and 75 (1) to (3) and (6) do not apply. For the purposes of the Employment Protection Act 1975, Schedule 4, Part II, the calculation date is the last day on which the employee worked under the original contract of employment.

When an employee is entitled to return to work under the provisions of the Employment Protection Act 1975 relating to pregnancy, and her contract of employment continues to subsist during the period of her absence, but she is dismissed by her employer during that period, after the beginning of the 11th week before the expected week of confinement, the provisions of Employment Protection Act 1975, Schedule 3, paragraph 4, must be considered. In the application of the Trade Union and Labour Relations Act 1974, Schedule 1, to such a dismissal, paragraphs 6 (5), 9, 10, 11, 13 and 14 do not apply, and the dismissal does not affect the employee's right to return to work, but compensation in any unfair dismissal proceedings arising out of that dismissal is assessed without regard to the employee's right to return, and that right shall be exercisable only on her repaying any redundancy payment, or compensation for unfair dismissal paid in respect of that dismissal, if the employer requests such repayment.

So far as the construction of the rules relating to redundancy is concerned the Redundancy Payments Act 1965 applies as if the relevant date, except where the context otherwise requires, is the notified day of return and references to a renewal, or re-engagement, taking effect immediately on the ending of employment, or after no more than four weeks thereafter, are construed as references to a renewal, or re-engagement, taking effect on the notified day of the return, or not more than four weeks after that day; Employment Protection Act 1975, Schedule 3, paragraph 3. Other provisions of the Redundancy Payments Act 1965 are appropriately amended by that Schedule. If, in proceedings arising out of a failure to permit an employee to return to work, the employer shows that the reason for the failure is that the employee is redundant and that the employee was dismissed or, had she continued to be employed by him, would have been dismissed, by reason of redundancy during her absence, on a day earlier than the notified day of return and falling after the 11th week before the expected week of confinement, then for the purposes of the Redundancy Payments Act 1965 the employee is not treated as having been dismissed with effect from the notified day of return, but is treated, if she would not otherwise be so treated, as having been continuously employed until that earlier day and as having been dismissed by reason of redundancy with effect from that day; Employment Protection Act 1975, Schedule 3, paragraph 6.

The Secretary of State has power, by order to amend the provisions of Employment Protection Act 1975, Schedule 3, and to modify its application to any description of case. See p. 76, above for details of those not covered by these rights since they differ from the usual exclusions from the right to redundancy payments and remedies for unfair dismissal.

When the procedure laid down by Employment Protection Act 1975, section 51 (see p. 83, above), has been complied with on the engagement of a replacement for a person absent wholly or partly because of pregnancy or confinement, and the replacement is dismissed in order to make it possible to give work to the other employee, then the dismissal is regarded as having been for a substantial reason of a kind such as to justify dismissal of an employee holding the position which the employee held.

### Sub-paragraph 6 (8)—Did the employer act reasonably in the circumstances?

The determination of a question whether the dismissal was fair, or unfair, when the employer has shown that the reason for the dismissal fell within sub-paragraphs 6 (1) (a) or (b) depends upon whether he can satisfy the tribunal that in the circumstances (having regard to the equity and substantial merits of the case) he acted reasonably in treating the reason as a sufficient reason for dismissing the employee. This factor is examined by the industrial tribunal after the reason for dismissal has been shown to it and, as with many other matters concerning unfair dismissal, depends to a large extent on the facts which the tribunal determines.

Each case is looked at in the light of these, and although previous decisions are of interest they must be treated with great caution. All that can be done is to highlight some of those factors which have particular relevance in determining the question of reasonableness. The majority of the cases given below were decided under section 24 (6) of the Industrial Relations Act 1971 which although it is replaced by Trade Union and Labour Relations Act 1974, Schedule 1, paragraph 6 (8), was not in exactly the same terms. In particular under section 24 (6) of the Industrial Relations Act 1971 the onus of proof was not so clearly placed on the employer.

The tribunals will pay attention to such matters as whether, or not, Codes of Practice have been complied with, whether the employee has received warnings of the consequences of continuance, or repetition, of the conduct upon which the employers seek to rely, whether a warning, or warnings, were properly given, the length of time the employee has been employed by the employer, his status, and whether the employer acted fairly in the employment situation. If the appointment was a probationary one this will probably be taken into account, see for instance *Hamblin* v. *London Borough of Ealing*, [1975] I.R.L.R. 354, T. Disciplinary procedures may be looked at to see whether they are fair, and if in the circumstances they were properly applied. The interests of both the employer and the employee should be considered. For instance in *James* v. *Waltham Holy Cross Urban District Council* (1973), 8 I.T.R. 467, N.I.R.C., the tribunal had to consider whether a local authority acted reasonably. The employee was a building maintenance officer who was aggrieved because the work on which he was engaged was being transferred from one department to another. When a grievance procedure was introduced he made a formal complaint. However, when asked to particularise his objections he refused to answer, and the matter was referred to the appropriate council sub-committee; at the meeting of which the employee was rude to the councillors. They reported to the Finance and General Purposes Committee which resolved to dismiss Mr. James with a month's notice. He appealed against the decision to the appeals committee under the appropriate procedure and in due course the council confirmed the dismissal. The employee did not have an opportunity of seeing the appeals committee report which indicated that the employee should not be dismissed and criticised both sides. The tribunal *held* that the employee had been fairly dismissed. In the National Industrial Relations Court Sir JOHN DONALDSON said the reason for the dismissal was the employee's lack of cooperation. If the dismissal had been because of the application of the grievance procedure it would almost certainly have been unfair "... for we cannot conceive of circumstances in which it would be reasonable to dismiss an employee solely because he had a grievance or exercised his right to use a grievance procedure". The court continued: "An employer's duty is to be fair both to the employee and to the business in all the circumstances. . . . This duty of fairness both to the employee and to the business is only the general rule. All else is but a particular application of that general rule."

The court found that the tribunal should have enquired as to the recommendations of the appeals committee about whose recommendations it was not told until after the tribunal's decision and reasons had been given. The court concluded that the recommendations of the appeals committee were relevant and should have been considered when determining the reasonableness, or otherwise, of the decision. The case was remitted to the tribunal for reconsideration in the light of the determination by the appeals committee.

The court also drew attention to the fact that the notice of dismissal expired after the appeals committee had met and heard the appeal, but before the council decided to confirm the dismissal. It hoped that consideration would be given in future to the possibility of giving notice of such length that the decision to dismiss can be affirmed, or withdrawn, before it takes effect.

On the question of balancing the interests of the parties concerned, see also *Lucking* v. *May and Baker, Ltd.*, [1974] I.R.L.R. 151, N.I.R.C.

The reasons, or facts, giving rise to the reason for the dismissal should be made generally known to the employee at the time of the dismissal. See the judgment of Lord DENNING, M.R., in *Abernethy* v. *Mott, Hay and Anderson*, [1974] I.R.L.R. 213, C.A., and *St. Anne's Board Mill Co., Ltd.* v. *Brien* (1973), 8 I.T.R. 463, N.I.R.C. In the latter case the dismissed employees who were cable pullers refused to work with another employee ("Mr. White") because they thought he was responsible for an accident which had taken place approximately 12 months earlier. The employers investigated the matter carefully and came to the conclusion that Mr. White was not responsible for the accident, but another employee, who admitted the fact, was at fault. The employees still said that they would not work with Mr. White and they were told that unless they did work with him they would be dismissed. The employees refused and were given notice. The National Industrial Relations Court said that the tribunal were wrong in endeavouring to ascertain who was responsible for the accident, they should have looked at the situation at the time of dismissal to ascertain whether the employer's action was fair in the context in which it was taken. Since the employers had investigated the matter properly the dismissal was fair. In *Merseyside and North Wales Electricity Board* v. *Taylor* (1975), 10 I.T.R. 52, D.C., the employee had been employed for 38 years. He had been promoted to a job which involved considerable physical effort. Later he began to suffer from heart trouble, there were several medical examinations, after which it appeared that the employee may be fit enough for sedentary or semi-sedentary work only. No suitable work was available and the employee was "prematurely retired". Further evidence to health was obtained after the dismissal by the Board and the employee's union. O'CONNER, J., in the Divisional Court found that circumstances in section 24 (6) of the Industrial Relations Act 1971 referred to matters applying at the date of, or prior to, the dismissal. Subsequent events cannot be relevant. See also *W. Devis & Sons, Ltd.* v. *Atkins,* [1976] 2 All E.R. 822, D.C. The duty of the tribunal is to decide whether the employers acted reasonably, not whether the employee committed the acts alleged against him; *Ferodo, Ltd.* v. *Barnes,* [1976] Law Soc. Gaz. 595, E.A.T.

Although each case must be decided on its merits an employer cannot be called on to create a special job for an employee. If the employer does have light work available the circumstances may be such that it is proper to offer the employee an opportunity of doing that work. Contrast with *Todd* v. *North Eastern Electricity Board,* [1975] I.R.L.R. 130, T, where it was *held* that the employers should have offered the employee an available post as a clerical assistant when a skin complaint affecting his feet made it difficult for the employee to perform his job as an arrears collector.

What is the position if, before dismissing the employee, the employer seeks a replacement? Sir HUGH GRIFFITHS said in *Judge International, Ltd.* v. *Moss,* [1973] I.R.L.R. 208, N.I.R.C., when considering Industrial Relations Act 1971, section 24 (6), that although the question of reasonableness is looked at at the time of the dismissal, the fact that the employers were already looking for a replacement in no way affected the employee's capability, or the question whether he might prove capable if given more time, and so did not make the dismissal unreasonable.

In the usual case the employee should have an opportunity of giving an explanation of his conduct. In a case before the Court of

Session, *Jamieson* v. *Aberdeen County Council*, [1975] I.R.L.R. 349, C.S., Lord McDONALD said: "The essence of the unfair dismissal was that the appellant was not given an opportunity of being heard, not what might have happened if he had been heard. No matter what an employee has done it is always unfair to dismiss him without giving him a chance to offer an explanation. This does not mean, however, that an employer is bound to ignore a long history of unsatisfactory service on the part of the employee, nor in my opinion does it mean that an Industrial Tribunal must ignore it for the purposes of [compensation]." See also *Shipside (Ruthin), Ltd.* v. *Transport and General Workers Union*, [1973] I.R.L.R. 244, N.I.R.C.

The longer an employee has worked for the employers the greater the amount of consideration he can expect to be given by them. *Tiptools, Ltd.* v. *Curtis*, [1973] I.R.L.R. 276, N.I.R.C., is a case where the employee had been with the employer for 19 years, in fact since he was 15 years of age. On several occasions he had been warned about his poor work, but other people had been warned as well. The National Industrial Relations Court said that Mr. Curtis should have been given a serious warning telling him that unless his standards improved he would have to leave. "One surely should have expected that some special consideration would have been given to a man who had been employed with the company since the age of 15." See also *Hilti (Great Britain), Ltd.* v. *Windridge*, [1974] I.R.L.R. 53, N.I.R.C. (commission obtained under false pretences. *Held* although employee's conduct was dishonest judged against a background of 11 years' employment the offence did not warrant dismissal); but contrast *Dalton* v. *Burtons Gold Medal Biscuits, Ltd.*, [1974] I.R.L.R. 45, N.I.R.C. There, an employee with 20 years' service was dismissed after he had "clocked-in" a fellow employee contrary to the works rules. The rules were clear and well-known, and warning notices were displayed by the clock. Counsel for the employee contended that paragraph 133 of the Code of Practice meant that no employee should be dismissed for a first breach of discipline, except in the case of gross misconduct and this was not gross misconduct. The Court *held* that it is not possible to provide a legal definition of gross misconduct which will fit the circumstances of every case. "It would in each case be a matter of fact to consider whether it was gross misconduct or not. Furthermore the Code of Practice is only a guide. It does not bind the employers it does not bind the

Court.... Although it was undoubtedly a severe punishment, one has to take into account the ample warning of the consequences of the type of conduct had been given and the pernicious effect which laxity in enforcing these warnings may have upon practices which could develop all too quickly under factory conditions."

The fact that the dismissal is in breach of the employment contract is not a circumstance to be taken into account in deciding if the employer has acted reasonably. See *Treganowen* v. *Robert Knee & Co., Ltd.* (1975), 10 I.T.R. 121, D.C. The employee was dismissed because of the personality clash which had arisen where she worked. She boasted about her relationship with a boy little more than half her age and this irritated her fellow employees. The employee was dismissed summarily. It was pointed out that having decided that there was a dismissal and a reason for it, it falls for the tribunal to decide what are the relevant circumstances and did the employer act reasonably in treating the reason as being sufficient to dismiss the employee. PHILLIPS, J., stated that the rules of unfair dismissal were totally different from wrongful dismissal. The tribunal was not concerned as to whether the dismissal was summary, or whether notice was given by the employer, in determining whether the dismissal was reasonable for the purposes of paragraph 6 (8). It could be relevant in determining other matters of fact, for instance, the real reason for the dismissal, what is to be believed, etc., but no more.

### (a) *Code of Practice*

Great importance is attached to the "Code of Practice" and the implementation of its guidance and failure to do so have been determining factors in many cases. The Secretary of State has a duty to maintain a code of practice containing such practical guidance as would be helpful for the purpose of promoting good industrial relations. The Code of Practice which was brought into effect under the Industrial Relations Act 1971 remains in effect for the purposes of the unfair dismissal provisions; Employment Protection Act 1975, Schedule 17, paragraph 4. Although not legally binding on the parties a failure on the part of any person to observe any provision of a Code of Practice which is for the time being in force under the Trade Union and Labour Relations Act 1974, Schedule 1, whilst not rendering the party liable in proceedings, is admissible in evidence before industrial tribunals, and any provision of the code which appears to the tribunal to be relevant to any question which arises is taken into account by the tribunal in determining that question; Trade Union and Labour Relations Act 1974, Schedule 1, paragraph 3, Employment Protection Act 1975, Schedule 17, paragraph 4.

Under the Employment Protection Act 1975, section 6, the Advisory, Conciliation and Arbitration Service has power to issue Codes of Practice containing such practical guidance as the Service thinks fit for the purpose of promoting the improvement of industrial relations. Subject to the approval of the Secretary of State for Employment, and of both Houses of Parliament, these Codes come into effect on such day as the Secretary of State may appoint. The Advisory, Conciliation and Arbitration Service has issued a draft Code of Practice relating to Disciplinary Practice and Procedures and further Codes will follow in due course. A failure on the part of any person to observe any provisions of a Code of Practice made pursuant to section 6 of the Employment Protection Act 1975 does not itself render any person liable to proceedings but in proceedings before an industrial tribunal (and the Central Arbitration Committee) any Code of Practice issued under the section is admissible in evidence and if any provision of such a Code appears to the tribunal (or Committee) to be relevant to any question arising in the proceedings, it should be taken into account in determining the question.

As will be seen from many of the cases mentioned below the Code of Practice, originally issued under the Industrial Relations Act 1971, has often been considered by industrial tribunals in deciding whether dismissal is fair.

The paragraphs of the Code of Practice issued under the 1971 Act which are most frequently cited before industrial tribunal are numbers 130–133 which are as follows:

"Disciplinary Procedures.

**130** Management should ensure that fair and effective arrangements exist for dealing with disciplinary matters. These should be agreed with employee representatives or trade unions concerned and should provide for full and speedy consideration by management of all the relevant facts. There should be a formal procedure, except in very small establishments where there is close personal contact between the employer and his employees.

**131** Management should make known to each employee:

  (i)  its disciplinary rules and the agreed procedure;

  (ii)  the type of circumstances which can lead to suspension or dismissal.

**132**  The procedure should be in writing and should:

  (i)  specify who has the authority to take various forms of disciplinary action, and ensure that supervisors do not have the power to dismiss without reference to more senior management;

  (ii)  give the employee the opportunity to state his case and the right to be accompanied by his employee representative;

  (iii)  provide for a right of appeal, wherever practicable, to a level of management not previously involved;

  (iv)  provide for independent arbitration if the parties to the procedure wish it.

**133**  Where there has been misconduct, the disciplinary action to be taken will depend on the circumstances, including the nature of the misconduct. But normally the procedure should operate as follows:

  (i)  the first step should be an oral warning or, in the case of more serious misconduct, a written warning setting out the circumstances;

  (ii)  no employee should be dismissed for a first breach of discipline except in the case of gross misconduct;

  (iii)  action on any further misconduct, for example, final warning, suspension without pay or dismissal, should be recorded in writing;

  (iv)  details of any disciplinary action should be given in writing to the employee and, if he so wishes, to his employee representative;

  (v)  no disciplinary action should be taken against a shop steward until the circumstances of the case have been discussed with a full-time official of the union concerned."

The obligation is for the tribunal to take into account the provisions of the Code of Practice; this does not mean that because the Code has not been complied with to the letter that the dismissal is unfair. The Code is not binding although it is very important. See for example *Dacres* v. *Walls Meat Co., Ltd.*, [1976] I.R.L.R. 20, D.C. (where the absence of an employee's representative when employee asked to explain a fight in a slaughterhouse did not render the dismissal unfair).

(b) *Disciplinary and grievance procedures*

In many cases the tribunal will look at the grievance or disciplinary procedures adopted by the employers to see if the necessary facilities have been made available to the dismissed employee, and whether, or not, they have been properly applied. The absence of a grievance procedure as recommended by the Code of Practice does not automatically make the dismissal unfair. It is one of the factors which the tribunal has to take into account in deciding whether the dismissal was fair or unfair. See *Henderson* v. *Masson Scott Thrissel Engineering, Ltd.*, [1974] I.R.L.R. 98, N.I.R.C. In *Earl* v. *Slater and Wheeler (Airlyne), Ltd.*, [1973] 1 All E.R. 145; [1973] 1 W.L.R. 51, N.I.R.C., it was said by the National Industrial Relations Court: "Whilst we do not say that in all circumstances the employee must be given an opportunity of stating his case, the only exception can be the case where there can be no explanation which would cause the employers to refrain from dismissing the employee. This must be a very rare situation." The provisions of the Code of Practice relating to appeals procedure must be viewed in the light of the circumstances of the individual case. For instance, paragraph 132 of the Code of Practice provides that there should be a right of appeal whenever practicable to a level of management not personally involved. The recommendation is relevant to large companies when the responsibility for dismissal lies below the level of top management, and in such cases it is generally advisable for there to be an appeal to a higher level of management. This cannot however apply to some small family companies where the person taking the decision to discharge is the highest level of management in the company and it is not practicable to have an appeal beyond him: *Tiptools, Ltd.* v. *Curtis*, [1973] I.R.L.R. 276, N.I.R.C.

If there is a procedure it should be followed properly. In *Wells* v. *E. and A. West, Ltd.*, [1975] I.R.L.R. 269, T, the agreed procedure provided for a warning to be followed by a period of suspension. The employee was given three warnings but no suspension. The tribunal found that the dismissal was unfair. It is not necessary for the employee to be given opportunity to make representations orally; see for example *Ayanlowo* v. *Inland Revenue Commissioners*, [1975] I.R.L.R. 253, C.A. The employee was a probationary tax officer. He was given a final warning in January and was dismissed in September 1973 when he was told he had a right to make written representations. He wrote to the Board referring to an earlier letter which they had not received. The Board asked for and were supplied with a copy and the dismissal became operative. In the Court of Appeal, BUCKLEY, L.J., said that it was not necessary for the employee to have a right to an oral hearing.

## (c) *Warnings*

Paragraph 133 of the Code of Practice lays great stress on warnings and they clearly are important if an employer is to succeed in contending that a dismissal is fair. However, it is not an absolute requirement, in that every case depends upon its own facts and it is for the tribunal to determine whether the employer acted reasonably in the circumstances. As Lord THOMPSON said in *Farnborough* v. *Governors of Edinburgh College of Art*, [1974] I.R.L.R. 245, N.I.R.C.: "There is no such rule of law that is as unfair to dismiss an employee without first warning him of the risk of dismissal if he does not mend his ways. In each case must depend on its own circumstances". In that case a lecturer refused, despite an order, to take certain classes. The employee was not warned that if he did not comply he would be dismissed. The dismissal was held to be reasonable. In *McKinney* v. *Bieganek*, [1973] I.R.L.R. 311, N.I.R.C., Sir JOHN DONALDSON said: "It is correct that in terms of the Code of Practice and decisions of this Court, it is sound industrial practice to give warnings. Indeed, common fairness requires that warnings should be given. But it is not right to say, as a matter of law, in every case and in every circumstance warnings must be given. There are cases in which the conduct of the employee is such that there is no reason or rule for a warning and immediate dismissal follows reasonably". The employee's conduct complained of, in the case under consideration, was an aggressive attitude over a long period towards colleagues and the Court *held* that this should have been the subject of warnings before the dismissal took place.

Whether an employee has been given a warning is a matter of substance and not a matter of procedure only. See *A. J. Dunning & Sons (Shop Fitters), Ltd.* v. *Jacomb* (1973), 8 I.T.R. 453, N.I.R.C. But to determine if the warning is sufficient is essentially a matter for the industrial tribunal; *Atkin* v. *Enfield Group Hospital Management Committee*, [1975] I.R.L.R. 217, C.A., and *Hopper* v. *Feedex, Ltd.*, [1974] I.R.L.R. 99, N.I.R.C.

In *Winterhalter Gastronom, Ltd.* v. *Webb* (1973), 8 I.T.R. 313,

N.I.R.C., it was suggested that because of the terms of the Code of Practice warnings were restricted to cases where there has been misconduct, but not where it was the employee's capability which was the reason for the dismissal. Sir HUGH GRIFFITHS said:

"We do not agree. There are many situations in which a man's apparent capabilities may be stretched when he knows what is demanded of him; many do not know they are capable of jumping the five-barred gate until the bull is close behind them. No doubt there may be cases in which giving warning to a director would be neither necessary nor achieve any useful purpose. But, each case must depend upon its own particular facts and it is, in the view of this Court, quite impossible to say as a matter of law that there can never be circumstances in which it is necessary to give warning to a director before dismissing him."

It was also submitted in that case that the position of Mr. Webb as the director of the company made a warning unnecessary. As a matter of law it was made clear that it is impossible to say that status as a director made it unnecessary for the employer to give the employee a warning. A warning is not an absolute essential before a dismissal for lack of capability, or a series of misdeeds, can be fair, but if the employee has not been given a chance to improve and the dismissal was "like a bolt from the blue", "it would go a long way towards establishing unfair dismissal". "We do not go so far as to say that it would be conclusive in all cases but it would certainly be very congent evidence to weigh on the side of the employee in considering whether a dismissal was fair or unfair," per Sir HUGH GRIFFITHS in *O'Hara* v. *Fram Gerrard. Ltd.*, [1973] I.R.L.R. 94, N.I.R.C. 95.

Other cases on warnings include *Judge International, Ltd.* v. *Moss*, [1973] I.R.L.R. 208, N.I.R.C. (in a reply to an inquiry as to the employer's omission to give a salary increase the employee was told that it was because he was not carrying out his job with sufficient forcefulness to justify an increase. Found to be a sufficient warning).

In a case where it was customary for the employees to bargain with the employer over particular wage rates, they refused to do so on one occasion when the employee thought that the work which they required was outside the scope of his employment. The National Industrial Relations Court over-ruled an industrial tribunal's decision and stated that the employers should have warned the employee that the consequences of the refusal to carry out the work would result in dismissal; *Wallace v. E. J. Guy, Ltd.* (1973), 8 I.T.R. 154, N.I.R.C.

*Lamsdale v. H.M. Stationery Office*, [1975] I.R.L.R. 239, T (the Director of Industrial Relations had openly defied orders given by his superiors. The tribunal said that the dismissal was not unfair even though warnings had not been given. If the employee is not in doubt as to the seriousness of the nature of his activities a warning would serve no purpose). See also the extract from *James v. Waltham Holy Cross Urban District Council* (1973), 8 I.T.R. 472, N.I.R.C., cited at p. 324, above.

*Moore v. Aluminium Platers (Leeds), Ltd.*, [1976] I.R.L.R. 23, D.C. (it was not clear whether further work had been carried out after final warning. The decision that the employee was not unfairly dismissed was upheld. The overall position has to be looked to see if the final decision would have been different if the employer had waited longer).

(d) *Decisions where the dismissal was held to be fair*

*Carr v. Alexander Russell, Ltd.*, [1976] I.R.L.R. 220, C.S. (employee accused by police of theft from employers during absence through industrial injury. The employee was apparently caught in the act and when the employers learnt of this he was summarily dismissed. The Court of Session *held* that the decision was fair even though the employee did not have the chance to explain himself and the employers did not investigate the circumstances of the theft. Suspension was impractical in view of the time likely to elapse for the employee to be brought to court. It would have been improper for the employers to hold an internal inquiry while the criminal proceedings were pending.

*Coulson v. Felixtowe Dock and Rail Co.*, [1975] I.R.L.R. 11, T (an employee was absent as a result of ill health for considerable periods of time. On his return he was given light work and later asked to return to his old job. If he could not do so he was to be regraded. He was, and was given, opportunity to discuss this with the managing director who gave him a further six months to prove his fitness. During that period the employee said he was fit to resume his former position, but after a week doing it was away sick. After six weeks' absence he was dismissed. *Held* fair even though no warnings and though dismissed during the six month period).

*Spiller* v. *F. J. Wallis, Ltd.*, [1975] I.R.L.R. 362, T (female employee was "having an association" with a senior employee. There was a company rule making it clear that such conduct would lead to dismissal. *Held* fair).

*Pascoe* v. *Hallen and Medway*, [1975] I.R.L.R. 116, T (employee suffered from asthma and held a green card as a disabled person. She had suffered from periodic attacks at work and eventually had three months off work. She was dismissed on her return to work. *Held* fair because of the disruption caused at work when she had asthmatic attacks).

*Tovey* v. *F. and F. Robinson (Stockton-on-Tees), Ltd.*, [1975] I.R.L.R. 139, T (a new wage structure had been introduced which provided for a basic wage including 14 hours overtime. The employee refused to work overtime unless he would receive extra pay and was dismissed. *Held* fair because the employee was refusing to comply with his contract. The absence of warning did not affect the decision).

*Potter* v. *W. J. Rich & Sons*, [1975] I.R.L.R. 338, T (an employee was a driver who had previously been discharged by the employers because of bad driving. He drove a vehicle too fast leading to brake failure and an accident after which the vehicle was written off. He was dismissed and the tribunal *held* the dismissal was fair even though there was no warning. The employer's duty to the public had to be taken into account).

*Taylor* v. *Associated Country Women of the World*, [1973] I.R.L.R. 324, T (employee had a violent argument with a colleague and despite attempts at reconciliation difficulties persisted. After a further outburst Mrs. Taylor was dismissed. *Held* fair).

*Williams* v. *Mortimer Fashions, Ltd.*, [1974] I.R.L.R. 300, T (employee was the financial director of the employers. Did not provide proper information to fellow directors so that they could realise the company was running at a loss. The dismissal was *held* to be fair although no warning in view of his senior position. There was no need to give an employee a chance to do better in the future).

*Durant and Cheshire* v. *Clariston Clothing Co., Ltd.*, [1974] I.R.L.R. 360, T (employees had free transport in taxi to work, but because the numbers had reduced and fare increased the employers decided to discontinue this. The costs would have been £24 per week per employee. Several suggestions were made including paying employees for use of own car and employees to work at their own homes. The dismissal was *held* to be fair).

(e) *Decisions where the dismissal was held to be unfair*

*Morrish* v. *Henlys (Folkstone), Ltd.* [1973] 2 All E.R. 137, N.I.R.C. (driver whose duty was to record the amount of fuel drawn by him refused to allow the records to be altered to show a false figure of fuel taken and he was dismissed because of this. There was some evidence to show that there was a practice of falsification of the records. The court *held* the dismissal was unfair).

*Forgings and Presswork, Ltd.* v. *McDougall,* [1974] I.R.L.R. 243, N.I.R.C. (supervisor fought with another employee after returning from a celebration of a fellow employee's retirement and was dismissed. *Held* dismissal was unfair).

*Shortland* v. *Chantrill,* [1975] I.R.L.R. 208, D.C. (apprentice with 10 months of apprenticeship left unexpired who had not been guilty of misconduct earlier had a row with the managing director and said "you couldn't do any f...... better". Summarily dismissed. *Held* unfair).

*Wilson* v. *I.D.R. Construction, Ltd.,* [1975] I.R.L.R. 260, T (bricklayer obliged to move from site to site refused one day because his wife was ill, his car was being repaired and he did not want to do cement rendering work. He was dismissed. *Held* unfair, the employee had genuine reasons for not going and was not given the opportunity of giving an explanation).

*Thomas* v. *Budgen & Co.,* [1975] I.R.L.R. 201, T (shop cashier who did not ring up the amount of a sale on the till was interviewed by a security officer and dismissed. Tribunal *held* unfair, because she did not have a chance to explain her action to the person at the level where the decision to dismiss was taken).

*Davison* v. *Kent Meters, Ltd.,* [1975] I.R.L.R. 145, T (an employee assembled 471 out of 500 components incorrectly, but had not been shown properly how to perform the task. She only received general exaltations to do better, no actual warnings of dismissal and was refused the right to speak to higher management when sacked. *Held* the dismissal was unfair. She should have been told how to do her job properly and warned that failures could lead to dismissal).

*O'Reilly* v. *Hatfield District Council,* [1975] I.R.L.R. 334, T ("temporary cashier" not told job was in jeopardy, or warned of redundancy, although employers knew of it for four months before dismissal. *Held* dismissal unfair).

*Sherrad* v. *Tangye-Epco, Ltd.*, [1975] I.R.L.R. 106, T (an employee engaged as industrial relations adviser promoted to be deputy managing director of a company to improve industrial relations. In fact a decision taken by the board, on his advice, only made the matters worse and a strike ensued. He was dismissed. *Held* although the conduct of the employee would normally have been sufficient to justify dismissal, as the actual decision had been a joint one the dismissal was unfair).

*Lethaby* v. *Horsman Andrew and Knill, Ltd.*, [1975] I.R.L.R. 119, T (coalman employed for seven years. Part of his job was to check coal delivered and on one delivery was 2 cwt. short. He was given the option of being dismissed, or paying for the coal. *Held* the dismissal was unfair, there was no contractual right to fine the employee, and his seven years of service should have been taken into account).

*Barber* v. *Makro Self-Service Wholesalers, Ltd.*, [1975] I.R.L.R. 361, T (employee suspended without pay for taking chocolate from container and not paying for it. After 11 weeks' suspension was dismissed. *Held* although immediate dismissal would have been fair, employers acted unreasonably in suspending the employee for 11 weeks before deciding to dismiss him).

## Pressure on an employer to dismiss unfairly

Trade Union and Labour Relations Act 1974, Schedule 1, paragraph 15, provides:

"15. In determining for the purposes of this Part of this Schedule any question as to the reason, or principal reason, for which an employee was dismissed or any question whether the reason or principal reason for which an employee was dismissed was a reason fulfilling the requirements of paragraph 6 (1) (*b*) above or whether the employer acted reasonably in treating it as a sufficient reason for dismissing him, —
(*a*) no account shall be taken of any pressure which, by calling, organising, procuring or financing a strike or other industrial action, or threatening to do so, was exercised on the employer to dismiss the employee; and
(*b*) any such question shall be determined as if no such pressure had been exercised."

On making a decision on the application of an employee claiming that he has been unfairly dismissed the industrial tribunal ignores any pressure of the type to which paragraph 15 relates. An example is *Wooding* v. *Stoves, Ltd.*, [1975] I.R.L.R. 198, T. All hourly paid workers in the employer's factory were formerly members of the National Union of Domestic Appliance and Metal Workers but because they did not approve of an agreement entered into by the union all those in the Foundry Shop left the union. Afterwards a redundancy situation arose and the employers and union agreed that save for the Foundry Shop the principle of "last in, first out" would be applied in the factory rather than on the departmental basis. The union had said that if no non-union members were sent elsewhere in the factory difficulties would arise. The applicant employees were dismissed as redundant and applied for compensation for unfair dismissal. The tribunal *held* that the dismissal was unfair and that they had to ignore the pressure brought to bear by the trade union. See also *Morris* v. *Gestetner, Ltd.*, [1973] I.C.R. 587, N.I.R.C.

## THE COMPLAINT TO AN INDUSTRIAL TRIBUNAL[1]

A person alleging that he was unfairly dismissed may present a complaint against an employer to an industrial tribunal.[2] When the dismissal is with notice, the complaint may be presented before the effective date of termination and the provisions of the Trade Union and Labour Relations Act 1974 and the Employment Protection Act 1975 are construed as if references to dismissal, re-instatement, effective date of termination and the employee ceasing to be employed are altered appropriately.[3] This amendment introduced by the Employment Protection Act 1975 effectively reverses the decision in *Penrose* v. *Fairey Surveys, Ltd.*[4]

---

[1] For a discussion of the role of conciliation officers, see p. 386, below. For the relationship between complaints under the unfair dismissal provisions and the Sex Discrimination Act, see p. 355, below. Where the complaint may involve an act of racial discrimination, see p. 506, below.

[2] Trade Union and Labour Relations Act 1974, Sch. 1, para. 17.

[3] *Ibid.*, Sch. 1, para. 21 (4A). Added by Employment Protection Act 1975, Sch. 16, Part III, para. 21. Paragraph 21 (4A) reads as follows:
"(4A) An industrial tribunal shall consider a complaint under paragraph 17 of Schedule 1 above if, where the dismissal is with notice, the complaint is presented after the notice is given notwithstanding that it is presented before the effective date of termination and in relation to such a complaint the provisions of this Act and of the Employment Protection Act 1975, so far as they relate to unfair dismissal, shall have effect—

(a) as if references to a complaint by a person that he was unfairly dismissed by his employer included references to a complaint by a person that his employer has given him notice in such circumstances that he will be unfairly dismissed when the notice expires;

(b) as if references to reinstatement included references to the withdrawal of the notice by the employer;

(c) as if references to the effective date of termination included references to the date which would be the effective date of termination on the expiry of the notice; and

(d) as if references to an employee ceasing to be employed included references to an employee having been given notice of dismissal."

[4] (1974), 9 I.T.R. 41, N.I.R.C.

Paragraph 21 (4)[1] of Schedule 1 to the Trade Union and Labour Relations Act 1974 is of great importance and states:

"(4) [Subject to sub-paragraph (4A) below] an industrial tribunal shall not consider a complaint under paragraph 17 above unless it is presented to the tribunal before the end of the period of three months beginning with the effective date of termination or within such further period as the tribunal considers reasonable in a case where it is satisfied that it was not reasonably practicable for the complaint to be presented [before the end of] the period of three months."

[1] Shown as amended by Employment Protection Act 1975, Sch. 16, Part II, para. 20. The additions are in square brackets. The words "before the end of" replace "within". For the date used in place of the effective date of termination when the dismissal is in connection with an industrial dispute, see Trade Union and Labour Relations Act 1974, Sch. 1, para. 7 (4), at p. 319, above.

In view of the short time limit it is very important that complaints claiming remedies for unfair dismissal are presented to industrial tribunals as soon as possible. The requirement is jurisdictional and so cannot be waived by the parties; *Rogers* v. *Bodfari (Transport), Ltd.,* [1973] I.C.R. 325, N.I.R.C. The words "it was not reasonably practicable" have given rise to difficulties. The Court of Appeal had to consider similar wording in the Industrial Relations Act 1971, in *Dedman* v. *British Builders and Engineering Appliances, Ltd.,* [1974] 1 All E.R. 520; [1974] 1 W.L.R. 171, C.A. There, the employee after his dismissal, knew he had rights under the unfair dismissal provisions but did not know of the time limit in which to present the complaint (then four weeks). Approximately 14 days after the effective date of termination the employee consulted his legal advisers who did not advise him to make the complaint within the necessary period. The complaint was not made until seven weeks after the effective date of termination. Lord DENNING, M.R., explained the tests to be applied (at p. 526), as follows:

> "Summing up, I would suggest that in every case the tribunal should enquire into the circumstances and ask themselves whether the man or his advisers were at fault in allowing the four weeks to pass by without presenting the complaint. If he was not at fault, nor his advisers—so that he had just cause or excuse for not presenting his complaint within the four weeks—then it was 'not practicable' for him to present it within that time. The court has then a discretion to allow it to be presented out of time, if it thinks it right to do so. But, if he was at fault, or if his advisers were at fault, in allowing the four weeks to slip by, he must take the consequences. By exercising reasonable diligence, the complaint could and should have been presented in time."

SCARMAN, L.J., concurred in the approach but STAMP, L.J., dissented on this point. Mr. Dedman had consulted his lawyers during the period and so it was practicable for the complaint to be presented and the tribunal did not have jurisdiction.

It is important to note that the test is applied in two stages. First, the tribunal has to decide whether it was reasonably practicable for the complaint to be presented in time, and secondly, the tribunal determines if it is reasonable to extend the period. Although the wording of paragraph 21 (4) of Schedule 1 of the Trade Union and Labour Relations Act 1974 differs slightly from that in the corresponding provision under Industrial Relations Act 1971 it is likely that a similar approach will be adopted although with the longer period in which to present the complaint the industrial tribunals and courts are likely to be more restrictive in deciding whether it was reasonably practicable for the complaint to be presented within the limit. In *Westward Circuits, Ltd.* v. *Read* (1973), 8 I.T.R. 320, N.I.R.C., a case which was earlier than, but referred to in, Dedman's case, the employee did not know that he might have rights under the unfair dismissal provisions of the Industrial Relations Act 1971 until after the time-limit had expired.

When he found out about them he presented a complaint to a tribunal fairly promptly. The tribunal found that it was not practicable for the complaint to be presented earlier, and awarded him compensation for unfair dismissal. The employers appealed to the National Industrial Relations Court. Sir JOHN DONALDSON said (at p. 323):

"Unless and until he is put on inquiry, it is clearly impracticable for a dismissed employee to present a claim. However, once he is put on inquiry the situation is changed and the tribunal has to ask itself whether, starting from that point of time, it was practicable for that particular complainant's complaint to be presented before the expiry of the [three month] period which began with the effective date of termination of the contract of employment. Clearly, the sooner the complainant is put on inquiry and the greater the degree of information which he then acquires, the sooner it will be practicable to present the complaint. Thus, if the employment exchange tells him of his right and gives him the appropriate form, it will be practicable to present the complaint sooner than if he merely reads in the newspapers that some other person in different circumstances has been awarded compensation for unfair dismissal.

Let no one regard this judgment as a licence to complainants to sleep on their rights. Time is of the essence in all matters concerning industrial relations. There can be few, if any, workers who have not heard of the Industrial Relations Act 1971, but there have been times when the members of the Court have wondered how many people had any idea of what it provided. However, that situation is changing and the time will come when it will be difficult, if not impossible, for a complainant to persuade any tribunal that he or she was unaware in a general way of the rights conferred by the Act in relation to unfair dismissal. In the meantime, if any employers are worried at the prospects of being faced by late claims, the remedy is in their own hands. They need only tell dismissed employees that if they consider that they have been unfairly dismissed within the meaning of the Act, they are entitled to apply to an industrial tribunal for compensation and must do so within the specified period."

In *Hammond* v. *Haigh Castle & Co., Ltd.*, [1973] 2 All E.R.

289, N.I.R.C., it was held that "practicable" meant "capable of being carried out in action" or "feasible". The Court followed *Trow* v. *Ind Coope* (*West Midlands*), *Ltd.*, [1967] 2 Q.B. 899; [1967] 2 All E.R. 900, C.A., and held that the period in which the claim is to be presented includes the effective date of termination as part of the period. If the application is posted at a time when in the ordinary course of post it would have arrived within time he may have a strong case for contending that the delay in postal services made it not practicable for the complaint to be presented in time; *Sturges* v. *A. E. Farr, Ltd.*, [1975] I.C.R. 356, D.C.

The rules laid out in *Dedman's* and *Read's* cases have been applied on numerous occasions and each decision must be looked at on its own particular facts. An example is *Ruff* v. *Smith Trading as Friar Tuck Restaurant*, [1975] I.R.L.R. 275, D.C. An employee who was dismissed filled in an application form and left it with the employment exchange in good time but did not post off another form until after the (then) 28 day limit had gone by. The tribunal *held* that the application was time-barred, but on appeal to the Queen's Bench Division the case was remitted to the tribunal. When deciding whether a late application can be entertained the tribunal should clearly differentiate the two parts of the enquiry set out above. In coming to a decision whether it was reasonably practicable to present the application with the period events which take place afterwards are irrelevant. When the tribunal finds that it was not reasonably practicable to present the complaint in time, the second part of the enquiry involves the tribunal exercising its discretion whether, or not, to entertain the complaint out of time. In *Ruff's* case the application form which was in use at the time did not make reference to the time limit as the tribunal had thought, and so the case was remitted to them for further consideration. See also *Norgett* v. *Luton Industrial Co-operative Society, Ltd.*, (1976) *Times*, 23rd June, E.A.T., the first such case before the Employment Appeal Tribunal.

In view of the provisions of the Employment Protection Act 1975, section 71 (8), see p. 348, below it should be stated in the originating application whether or not the applicant wishes to be reinstated or re-engaged if the tribunal finds the grounds of the complaint well founded.

## INTERIM RELIEF

Sections 78, 79 and 80 of the Employment Protection Act 1975 provide for interim relief when an employee has been unfairly dismissed by the employer and the reason, or if more than one, the principal reason, for the dismissal was that the employee was, or proposed to become a member of a particular independent trade union,[1] or had taken, or proposed to take, part at an appropriate time[2] in the activities of a particular independent trade union of which he was, or proposed to become, a member.[3] The application has to be presented to the industrial tribunal before the end of the period of seven days immediately following the effective date of termination (whether before, on or after that date), and before the end of that period a certificate signed by an authorised official[4] of the independent trade union must be presented to the tribunal stating that the employee was on the date of the dismissal a member, or had proposed to become a member, of the union and that there appears to be reasonable grounds for supposing that the reason for the dismissal, or if more than one, the principal reason, was one alleged in the complaint.[5]

[1] Defined in Trade Union and Labour Relations Act 1974, s. 30(1). See p. 86, above.

[2] As defined in Employment Protection Act 1975, s. 53; Employment Protection Act 1975, s. 78 (10). See p. 44, above.

[3] *Ibid.*, s. 78 (1).

[4] An authorised official is an official of the union authorised by it for the purposes of Employment Protection Act 1975, s. 78; *ibid.*, s. 78 (10). A document purporting to be an authorisation and to be signed on behalf of the union is to be taken to be such authorisation unless the contrary is proved. A document purporting to be a certificate signed by such an official is to be taken as signed by him unless the contrary is proved; *ibid.*, s. 78 (11).

[5] *Ibid.*, s. 78 (2).

Tribunals have special accelerated procedure for dealing with these applications[1] and the employer receives a copy of the application and certificate and notice of the hearing at least seven days before the date of the hearing.[2] Hearings are not postponed in these cases unless the tribunal is satisfied that there are special circumstances justifying the postponement.[3]

[1] See p. 389, below. A tribunal having an application under the Employment Protection Act 1975, ss. 78 and 80, may consist of a President of

Industrial Tribunals, the chairman of the tribunal, or a member of a panel of chairmen of tribunals nominated by the President to hear such applications; *ibid.*, s. 80 (4).

[2] *Ibid.*, s. 78 (3). See p. 389, below.

[3] *Ibid.*, s. 78 (4).

If when it hears the application it appears to the tribunal that it is likely that the tribunal will find that the complainant was unfairly dismissed and the reason, or principal reason, was a reason mentioned in section 78 (1) the tribunal must announce its findings and explain to both parties if present, the powers of the tribunal under the section, and the circumstances in which it may exercise these, and shall ask the employer (if he is present) whether he is willing, pending the determination or settlement of the complaint to reinstate the employee (i.e. treat the employee in all respects as if he had not been dismissed), or if not, to re-engage him in another job on terms and conditions no less favourable than would have been applicable for him if he had not been dismissed.[1] When the employer indicates that he will reinstate the employee the tribunal will make an order to that effect.[2] In cases where the employer indicates that he is willing to re-engage the employee and specifies the terms and conditions on which he is willing to do so, the tribunal should ask the employee whether he is willing to accept the job on the terms and conditions, and if he is so willing, the tribunal will make an order to that effect, but if the employee is unwilling and the tribunal is of the opinion that the refusal is reasonable, the tribunal will make an order for the continuation of his contract of employment, but otherwise the tribunal will make no order under section 78.[3]

[1] Employment Protection Act 1975, s. 78 (5). Such terms mean, as regards seniority, pension rights and similar rights, that the period prior to the dismissal shall be regarded as continuous with his employment following the dismissal; *ibid.*, s. 78 (6).

[2] *Ibid.*, s. 78 (7).

[3] *Ibid.*, s. 78 (8).

If on the hearing of an application under section 78 the employer fails to attend before the tribunal or states that he is not willing to reinstate, or re-engage, the employee on the above terms, the tribunal will make an order to continue the contract of employment.[1] Section 79 of the Employment Protection Act 1975, lays down the provisions as to orders for the continuation of the contract of employment. It is as follows:

"79.—(1) An order for the continuation of a contract of employment under section 78 above shall be an order that the contract of employment, if it has been terminated, shall continue in force as if it had not been terminated and if not shall on its termination continue in force, in either case until the determination or settlement of the complaint and only for the purposes of pay or any other benefit derived from the employment, seniority, pension rights and other similar matters and for the purpose of determining for any purpose the period for which the employee has been continuously employed.

(2) Where the tribunal makes any such order it shall specify in the order the amount which is to be paid by the employer to the employee by way of pay in respect of each normal pay period or part of any such period falling between the date of the dismissal and the determination or settlement of the complaint and, subject to sub-section (5) below, the amount so specified shall be that which the employee could reasonably have been expected to earn during that period or part, and shall be paid, in the case of a payment for any such period falling wholly or partly after the order, on the normal pay day for that period and, in the case of a payment for any past period, within a time so specified.

(3) If an amount is payable by way of pay in pursuance of any such order in respect only of part of a normal pay period the amount shall be calculated by reference to the whole period and be reduced proportionately.

(4) Any payment made to an employee by an employer under his contract of employment, or by way of damages for breach of that contract, in respect of any normal pay period or part of any such period shall go towards discharging the employer's liability in respect of that period under sub-section (2) above, and conversely any payment under sub-section (2) above in respect of any period shall go towards discharging any liability of the employer under, or in respect of breach of, the contract of employment in respect of that period.

(5) If an employee, on or after being dismissed by his employer, receives a lump sum which, or part of which, is in lieu of wages but is not referable to any normal pay period,

the tribunal shall take the payment into account in determining the amount of pay to be payable in pursuance of any such order.

(6) For the purposes of this section the amount which an employee could reasonably have been expected to earn, his normal pay period and the normal pay day for each such period shall be determined as if he had not been dismissed."

[1] Employment Protection Act 1975, s. 78 (9).

The Act does make provision for an employer, or an employee, to apply to the tribunal at any time between the making of the order under section 78 and the determination or settlement of the complaint to which it relates for the revocation, or variation, of the order on the ground of a relevant change in the circumstances since the making of the order.[1] If on the application of an employee the tribunal is satisfied that the employer has not complied with the terms of an order to reinstate, or re-engage, the employee under these provisions, the tribunal will make an order for the continuation of the employee's contract of employment, and will order the employer to pay the employee such compensation as the tribunal considers just and equitable in the circumstances, having regard to the infringement of the employee's right to be reinstated, or re-engaged, and to any loss suffered by the employee in consequence of the non-compliance.[2] When an employee applies to the tribunal and the tribunal is satisfied that the employer has not complied with the terms of an order for the continuation of a contract of employment, then if the non-compliance consists of a failure to pay an amount by way of pay specified in the order, the tribunal will determine the amount owed at the date of the determination, and, if on that date the tribunal also determines the employee's complaint that he has been unfairly dismissed by his employer the tribunal will specify the amount separately from any other sum awarded to the employee.[3] In any other case the tribunal will order the employer to pay to the employee, such compensation as the tribunal considers just and equitable in all the circumstances having regard to the loss suffered by the employee in consequence of the non-compliance.[4]

[1] Employment Protection Act 1975, s. 80 (1). Section 78 applies to the application as it applies to an application for an order under s. 78, save that no certificate from an authorised union official is required, and if the application is by the employer for the reference in s. 78 (3), to the employer is sub-

stituted a reference to the employee; *ibid.*, s. 80 (1) (*a*) and (*b*).
² *Ibid.*, s. 80 (2).
³ *Ibid.*, s. 80 (3) (*a*).
⁴ *Ibid.*, s. 80 (3) (*b*).

## REMEDIES FOR UNFAIR DISMISSAL

### 1 Orders for reinstatement and re-engagement

When an industrial tribunal finds a complaint for unfair dismissal well-founded it has to explain to the employee what orders for reinstatement and re-engagement can be made under section 71 of the Employment Protection Act 1975 and the circumstances in which they can be made. It should ask the employee if he wishes the tribunal to make such an order and if he does so wish the tribunal may make the order.[1] The orders are for reinstatement[2] or for re-engagement[3] on terms decided by the tribunal.[4]

[1] Employment Protection Act 1975, s. 71 (1).
[2] *Ibid.*, s. 71 (3) and (4) provide as follows:
"(3) An order for reinstatement is an order that the employer shall treat the complainant in all respects as if he had not been dismissed, and on making such an order the tribunal shall specify—
(*a*) any amount payable by the employer in respect of any benefit which the complainant might reasonably be expected to have had but for the dismissal, including arrears of pay, for the period between the date of termination of employment and the date of reinstatement;
(*b*) any rights and privileges, including seniority and pension rights, which must be restored to the employee; and
(*c*) the date by which the order must be complied with.
(4) Without prejudice to the generality of sub-section (3) above, if the complainant would have benefited from an improvement in his terms and conditions of employment had he not been dismissed, an order for reinstatement shall require him to be treated as if he had benefited from that improvement from the date on which he would have done so but for being dismissed."
[3] *Ibid.*, s. 71 (5) provides as follows:
"(5) An order for re-engagement is an order that the complainant be engaged by the employer, or by a successor of the employer or by an associated employer, in employment comparable to that from which he was dismissed or other suitable employment, and on making such an order the tribunal shall specify the terms on which re-engagement is to take place including—
(*a*) the identity of the employer;
(*b*) the nature of the employment;
(*c*) the remuneration for the employment;

(d) any amount payable by the employer in respect of any benefit which the complainant might reasonably be expected to have had but for the dismissal, including arrears of pay, for the period between the date of termination of employment and the date of re-engagement;

(e) any rights and privileges, including seniority and pension rights, which must be restored to the employee; and

(f) the date by which the order must be complied with."

[4] *Ibid.*, s. 71 (2).

In exercising its discretion the tribunal should first consider whether to make an order for reinstatement, and in so doing take into account whether the employee wishes to be reinstated, whether it is practicable for the employer to comply with an order for reinstatement, and where the complainant caused, or contributed to some extent to, his dismissal, whether it would be just and equitable to order reinstatement.[1] If the tribunal decides not to make an order for reinstatement it should consider whether to make an order for re-engagement and if so on what terms.[2] In so doing the tribunal should take into account, any wish expressed by the complainant as to the nature of the order to be made, whether it is practicable for the employer, or as the case may be, a successor or associated employer to comply with an order for re-engagement, and where the employee caused, or contributed to some extent to, his dismissal whether it would be just to order re-engagement and if so on what terms.[2] Except in such a case where the tribunal takes into account contributory fault if a tribunal orders re-engagement it should do so, so far as is reasonably practicable, on terms which are as favourable as an order for reinstatement.[2]

[1] Employment Protection Act 1975, s. 71 (6).

[2] *Ibid.*, s. 71 (7). There are important distinctions between the above provisions as to reinstatement and re-engagement and those contained in the Trade Union and Labour Relations Act 1974 as originally enacted. For this reason it is unlikely that decisions based on Sch. 1, para 17 (2), will be referred to. However *Coleman and Stephenson* v. *Magnet Joinery, Ltd.*, [1974] I.R.L.R. 343, C.A., and *Bateman* v. *British Leyland U.K., Ltd.*, [1974] I.R.L.R. 101, N.I.R.C., may still be of interest.

The tribunal should not take into account in determining whether it is practicable to comply with an order for reinstatement or re-engagement, the fact that the employer has engaged a permanent replacement for the dismissed employee, unless the employer shows that it was not practicable for him to arrange for the dismissed employee's work to be done without engaging a permanent replacement, or that he engaged the replacement after the lapse of a reasonable period, without having heard from the dismissed employee that he wished to be reinstated or re-engaged, and that when the employer engaged the replacement it was no longer reasonable for him to arrange for the dismissed employee's work to done except by a permanent replacement.[1] When calculating sums payable by the employer to the employee on reinstatement or re-engagement the tribunal will take into account, so as to reduce the employer's liability, any sums received by the complainant in respect of the period between the date of termination of employment, and date of reinstatement, or re-engagement, by way of wages in lieu of notice, or ex gratia payment paid by the employer, remuneration paid in respect of employment with another employer and such other benefits as the industrial tribunal thinks appropriate in the circumstances.[2]

[1] Employment Protection Act 1975, s. 71 (8).
[2] *Ibid*., s. 71 (9).

If a tribunal makes an order that the employee be reinstated, or re-engaged and the complainant is reinstated, or as the case may be, re-engaged, but the terms of the order are not fully complied with, the industrial tribunal should make an award of compensation to be paid by the employer to be employee, of such amount as the tribunal thinks fit having regard to the loss sustained by the complainant in consequence of the failure to comply fully with the terms of the order.[1] There is a limit on the amount of such compensation of £5,200 at present.[2]

[1] Employment Protection Act 1975, s. 72 (1).
[2] Trade Union and Labour Relations Act 1974, Sch. 1, para. 20 as substituted by Employment Protection Act 1975, Sch. 16, Part III, para. 17. The limit of £5200 may be increased by order of the Secretary of State; Trade Union and Labour Relations Act 1974, Sch. 1, para. 20 (2) (as substituted as aforesaid).

If an order for reinstatement or re-engagement is made, but the complainant is not reinstated, or as the case may be re-engaged, in accordance with the order the tribunal is obliged to make an award of compensation consisting of the basic award and a compensatory award calculated in accordance with sections 73 to 76 of the Employment Protection Act 1975.[1] In addition, unless the employer satisfies the tribunal that it was not practicable to comply with the order, the tribunal will make an additional award of compensation to be paid by the employer to the employee of an amount of either, not less than 26, or more than 52, weeks' pay, or not less than 13, or more than 26, weeks' pay.[2] The higher of these two awards is made when the reason for the dismissal being unfair is as a result of an inadmissible reason (i.e. by virtue of Trade Union and Labour Relations Act 1974, Schedule 1, paragraph 6 (4) or (5)) or dismissal which is an unlawful act of discrimination (within the meaning of the Race Relations Act 1968)which is unlawful by virtue of that Act or a dismissal which is as a result of discrimination (within the meaning of the Sex Discrimination Act 1975) which is unlawful by virtue of that Act.[3]

When the employer has engaged a permanent replacement for the dismissed employee the tribunal should not take that fact into account in determining whether it was practicable to comply with an order for reinstatement or re-engagement, unless the employer shows that it was not practicable to arrange for the dismissed employee's work to be done without engaging a permanent replacement.[4]

[1] Employment Protection Act 1975, s. 72 (2) (*a*).

[2] *Ibid.*, s. 72 (2) (*b*). Weeks pay is defined in Employment Protection Act 1975, Sch. 4, Part II; see p. 247, above. If the dismissal was with notice, the calculation date is the date on which the notice was given and in any other case it is the effective date of termination; *ibid.*, s. 72 (7). The usual limit, at present £80, applies; *ibid.*, s. 72 (8).

[3] *Ibid.*, s. 72 (3).

[4] Employment Protection Act 1975, s. 72 (4).

## 2 Compensation

If on a complaint the industrial tribunal finds that the complainant was unfairly dismissed and no order is made under section 71 of the Employment Protection Act 1975 or such an order has been made but the complainant is not reinstated, or as the case may be re-engaged, in accordance with the order the tribunal will make an award of compensation for unfair dismissal.[1] The award of compensation consists of the basic award and a compensatory award.[2] If the complainant has unreasonably prevented an order for reinstatement, or re-engagement, from being complied with, then the industrial tribunal shall take this conduct into account as a failure on the part of the complainant to mitigate his loss.[3]

[1] Employment Protection Act 1975, ss. 72 (5) and 72 (2) (a).
[2] *Ibid.*, s. 73.
[3] *Ibid.*, s. 72 (6). See *Curtis* v. *James Paterson (Darlington), Ltd.* (1973), 8 I.T.R. 519; N.I.R.C.

## (a) Basic award

The rules as to calculation of the basic award are set out in the Employment Protection Act 1975, sections 74 and 75 as follows:

"74.—(1) The amount of the basic award shall be the amount calculated in accordance with sub-sections (3) to (7) and sections (1) to (6) below, subject to the following provisions of this Act, namely—

(a) sub-section (2) below (which provides for an award of two weeks' pay in certain cases);

(b) section 75 (7) below (which provides for the amount of the award to be reduced where the employee contributed to the dismissal);

(c) section 75 (8) below (which provides for the amount of the award to be reduced where the employee received a payment in respect of redundancy); and

(d) section 77 below (which prohibits double compensation where compensation in respect of the same matter is also awarded under the Sex Discrimination Act 1975).

(2) In the following cases the amount of the basic award shall be two weeks' pay—

(a) where the tribunal finds that the reason or principal reason for the dismissal of the employee was that he was redundant and the employee—

(i) by virtue of section 2 (5) or (6) of the Redundancy Payments Act 1965 (unreasonable refusal or relinquishment of suitable alternative employment) is not, or if he were otherwise entitled would not be, entitled to a redundancy payment; or

(ii) by virtue of the operation of section 3 (3) of that Act (renewal of employment or re-engagement) is not treated as dismissed for the purposes of Part I of that Act;

(b) where the amount calculated in accordance with sub-sections (3) to (7) and section 75 (1) to (7) below is less than the amount of two weeks' pay.

351

(3) The amount of the basic award shall be calculated by reference to the period, ending with the effective date of termination, during which the employee has been continuously employed, by starting at the end of that period and reckoning backwards the numbers of years of employment falling within that period, and allowing:

(*a*) one and a half weeks' pay for each such year of employment which consists wholly of weeks in which the employee was not below the age of 41;

(*b*) one week's pay for each such year of employment which consists wholly of weeks in which the employee was below the age of 41 and was not below the age of 22; and

(*c*) half a week's pay for each such year of employment which consists wholly of weeks in which the employee was below the age of 22 and was not below the age of 18.

(4) In ascertaining for the purpose of sub-section (3) above the period for which an employee has been continuously employed, where the effective date of termination falls to be determined in accordance with paragraph 5 (6) of Schedule 1 to the 1974 Act, a period falling within such an interval as is referred to in paragraph 30 (1A) of that Schedule (period of continuous employment) shall count as a period of employment notwithstanding that it does not count under Schedule 1 to the Contracts of Employment Act 1972 (computation of period of employment).

(5) Where in reckoning the number of years of employment in accordance with sub-section (3) above 20 years of employment have been reckoned no account shall be taken of any year of employment earlier than those 20 years.

(6) Where in the case of an employee the effective date of termination is after the specified anniversary the amount of the basic award calculated in accordance with sub-sections (3) to (5) above shall be reduced by the appropriate fraction.

(7) In subsection (6) above "the specified anniversary" in relation to a man means the 64th anniversary of the day of his birth, and in relation to a woman means the 59th anniversary of the day of her birth, and "the appropriate fraction" means the fraction of which—

(*a*) the numerator is the number of whole months reckoned from the specified anniversary in the period beginning with that anniversary and ending with the effective date of termination; and

(b) the denominator is 12.

75.—(1) For the purposes of Part II of Schedule 4 to this Act as it applies for the calculation of a week's pay for the purposes of section 74 above, the calculation date is, subject to sub-section (3) below, the date on which notice would have been given by the employer had the conditions referred to in sub-section (2) below been fulfilled (whether those conditions were in fact fulfilled or not).

(2) Those conditions are that the contract was terminable by notice and was terminated by the employer giving such notice as is required to terminate that contract by section 1 (1) of the Contracts of Employment Act 1972 (minimum period of notice), and that the notice expired on the effective date of termination.

(3) Where by virtue of paragraph 5 (6) of Schedule 1 to the 1974 Act a date is to be treated as the effective date of termination for the purposes of section 74 (3) above which is later than the effective date of termination as defined by paragraph 5 (5) of that Schedule, then, for the purposes of Part II of Schedule 4 to this Act as it applies for the calculation of a week's pay for the purpose of section 74 above, the calculation date is the effective date of termination by the said paragraph 5 (5).

(4) Notwithstanding anything in the said Part II, the amount of a week's pay for the purpose of calculating a basic award shall not exceed £80.

(5) The Secretary of State may, after a review under section 86 below, vary the limit referred to in subsection (4) above by order made in accordance with that section.

(6) Without prejudice to the generality of the power to make transitional provision in an order under sub-section (5) above, such an order may provide that it shall apply in the case of a dismissal in relation to which the effective date of termination for the purposes of this sub-section (as defined by paragraph 5 (6) of Schedule 1 to the 1974 Act) falls after the order comes into operation, notwithstanding that the effective date of termination for the purposes of other provisions of this Act or the 1974 Act (as defined by paragraph 5 (5) of Schedule 1 to the 1974 Act) falls before the order comes into operation.

(7) Where the tribunal finds that the dismissal was to any extent caused or contributed to by any action of the complainant it shall, except in a case where the dismissal was by reason of redundancy, reduce the amount of the basic award by such proportion as it considers just and equitable having regard to that finding.

(8) The amount of the basic award shall be reduced or, as the case may be, be further reduced, by the amount of any redundancy payment awarded by the tribunal under the Redundancy Payments Act 1965 in respect of the same dismissal or of any payment made by the employer to the employee on the ground that the dismissal was by reason of redundancy, whether in pursuance of the said Act of 1965 or otherwise."

Subject to the occasions where the basic award is two weeks pay, and to the provisions contained in section 75 (7), the amount of the basic award is similar to that of a statutory redundancy payment, although it is of course payable to those qualified for compensation for unfair dismissal. The Trade Union and Labour Relations Act 1974 did not contain this provision although when assessing compensation for unfair dismissal under that Act, loss of protection in respect of dismissal by reason of redundancy was a head of claim in the compensation; see *Norton Tool Co. Ltd.* v. *Tewson*, [1973] 1 All E.R. 183; [1973] 1 W.L.R. 45, N.I.R.C., p. 356 below.

(b) *The compensatory award*

The rules governing this are set out in sections 76 and 77 of the Employment Protection Act 1975 as follows:

"76.—(1) Subject to paragraph 20 of Schedule 1 to the 1974 Act (limit on compensation) and to section 77 below, the amount of the compensatory award shall be such amount as the tribunal considers just and equitable in all the circumstances having regard to the loss sustained by the complainant in consequence of the dismissal in so far as that loss is attributable to action taken by the employer.

(2) The said loss shall be taken to include—

(a) any expenses reasonably incurred by the complainant in consequence of the dismissal, and

(b) subject to sub-section (3) below, loss of any benefit which he might reasonably be expected to have had but for the dismissal.

(3) The said loss, in respect of any loss of any entitlement or potential entitlement to, or expectation of, a payment on account of dismissal by reason of redundancy, whether in pursuance of the Redundancy Payments Act 1965 or otherwise, shall include only the loss referable to the amount, if any, by which the amount of that payment would have exceeded the amount of a basic award (apart from any reduction under section 75 (7) or (8) above) in respect of the same dismissal.

(4) In ascertaining the said loss the tribunal shall apply the same rule concerning the duty of a person to mitigate his loss as applies to damages recoverable under the common law of England and Wales or of Scotland, as the case may be.

(5) In determining for the purposes of sub-section (1) above how far any loss sustained by the complainant was attributable to action taken by the employer no account shall be taken of any pressure which, by calling, organising, procuring or financing a strike or other industrial action, or threatening to do so, was exercised on the employer to dismiss the employee, and that question shall be determined as if no such pressure had been exercised.

(6) Where the tribunal finds that the dismissal was to any extent caused or contributed to by any action of the complainant it shall reduce the amount of the compensatory award by such proportion as it considers just and equitable having regard to that finding.

(7) If the amount of any payment made by the employer to the employee on the ground that the dismissal was by reason of redundancy, whether in pursuance of the Redundancy Payments Act 1965 or otherwise, exceeds the amount of the basic award which would be payable but for section 75 (8) above that excess shall go to reduce the amount of the compensatory award."

Section 77 of the Employment Protection Act 1975 provides that where compensation falls to be awarded in respect of any act, both under the Sex Discrimination Act 1975 and under the unfair dismissal compensation provisions, an industrial tribunal should not award compensation under the Sex Discrimination Act or under those provisions in respect of any loss or other matter which is, or has been, taken into account under the other statute by the tribunal, or another industrial tribunal, in awarding compensation on the same or another complaint in respect of that act. The aggregate of the compensation awarded under the Sex Discrimination Act and the rules as to compensation under the unfair dismissal provisions should not exceed the limit for the time being imposed by paragraph 20 of the First Schedule to the Trade Union and Labour Relations Act 1974.

Subject to the provisions relating to the loss of entitlement, or prospective entitlement to, or expectation of, redundancy payments, whether under the Redundancy Payments Act 1965 or otherwise, the provisions of the Employment Protection Act 1975, section 76 are somewhat similar to the Trade Union and Labour Relations Act 1974, Schedule 1, paragraph 19. The new paragraph 20 of that Schedule provides that the amount of compensation ordered to a person under section 72 (1) of the Employment Protection Act 1975 on a compensatory award, in accordance with section 76 shall not exceed £5,200 (the former restriction of 104 weeks pay having disappeared). This figure may be increased by order of the Secretary of State for Employment in accordance with sub-paragraph (2) of paragraph 20.

Originally there was doubt as to the effect of the limits of compensation where monies were already paid to complainants. Paragraph 20 (3) is an attempt to dispel these problems. The limit imposed by paragraph 20 applies to the amount which the industrial tribunal would, apart from the paragraph, otherwise award in respect of the subject matter of the complaint, after taking into account every payment made by the respondent to the complainant in respect of that matter and any reduction in the amount of the award required by any enactment, or rule of law.

When considering the compensatory award some of the decisions given prior to the Employment Protection Act 1975 continue to be referred to.

In *Norton Tool Co., Ltd.* v. *Tewson*, [1973] 1 All E.R. 183; [1973] 1 W.L.R. 45, N.I.R.C., the National Industrial Relations Court assessed the compensation under four heads.

(a) Immediate loss of wages. *Prima facie* the employee was held to be entitled to compensation equal to his net pay for the proper period of notice and no deduction was made in respect of earnings from another employer during that period; *Vaughan* v. *Weighpack, Ltd.* (1974), 9 I.T.R. 226, N.I.R.C. and *Blackwell* v. *G.E.C. Elliott Process Automation, Ltd.*, [1976] I.R.L.R. 144, E.A.T. If the employee is paid a sum of less than that for the proper period, then the amount actually paid is taken into account and, if he receives a sum from his former employer which exceeds his net pay for the period of notice, no compensation for loss of wages due during the period of notice is awardéd and he should bring into account under the other heads the additional sum paid to him by his former employer; *Everwear Candlewick, Ltd.* v. *Isaac* [1974] 3 All E.R. 24, N.I.R.C.; *Cawthorn and Sinclair, Ltd.* v. *Hedger* (1974), I.T.R. 171, N.I.R.C. Query the position of an ex-employee who was employed under a contract for a fixed term which had not come to an end.

(b) Manner of dismissal. The manner and circumstances of the dismissal may give rise to a risk of further loss at a later stage, for example by making him less acceptable to potential employers or exceptionally liable for selection for dismissal. Awards under this head were rare and it is only when there is cogent evidence that the manner of the dismissal caused a financial loss that it became relevant in assessing compensation; *Vaughan* v. *Weighpack, Ltd.* (above).

(c) Future loss of wages. The compensation awarded under this head depended on whether the employer had obtained other employment and estimates were made as to whether there would be losses in the future from short-time working, lay-off or unemployment. The amount awarded was the net loss after deducting future earnings, or possible future earnings, or if appropriate, unemployment pay; *Vaughan* v. *Weighpack, Ltd.* (above), and can be nil; *Donnelly* v. *Feniger and Blackburn, Ltd.* (1973), 8 I.T.R., 134, N.I.R.C. Although compensation for injured feelings has not yet been awarded as part of compensation for unfair dismissal, if emotional upset resulting from the dismissal has an effect on the length of time likely to be taken to obtain alternative employment it has properly been taken into account; *John Millar & Sons* v. *Quinn* (1974), 9 I.T.R. 277, N.I.R.C. In *Bishop* v. *John Brignell & Co. (Builders), Ltd.* (1974), 9 I.T.R. 307, C.A., there was an argument during which the employee purported to give a week's notice but the employer summarily dismissed the employee. The Court of Appeal would not interfere since the matter had not been raised before a tribunal but Lord DENNING, M.R. said, *obiter*, that he would not have limited the compensation to a week's wages because the probability was that if he was not dismissed the employment would have continued indefinitely. Future loss is looked at subjectively and so personal factors such as the applicant's age or state of health at the time of the dismissal should be taken into account; *Fougere* v. *Phoenix Motor Co. (Surrey), Ltd.,* (1976) *Times,* 7th July, E.A.T. The amount awarded may include sums in respect of loss of wages beyond the state retirement age; *Barrel Plating & Phosphating Co., Ltd.* v. *Danks,* [1976] Law Soc. Gaz. 593, E.A.T.

Under this head of claim an employee has included loss of the opportunity of completing an apprenticeship. In *Shortland* v. *Chantrill,* [1975] I.R.L.R. 208, D.C., the employee was dismissed ten months before completing his apprenticeship. The tribunal made an award including a head of compensation on this basis. GRIFFITHS, J. said that this was proper but reduced the tribunal's award because it was wrongly calculated. The judge took the difference between a fitter's wage and an advanced fitter's pay, the net loss being approximately £120 a year and by using a figure of approximately ten years purchase arrived at a figure of a little over a thousand pounds. Expected improvements in future earnings could be recovered. For instance, in *York Trailer Co., Ltd.* v. *Sparkes* (1973), 8 I.T.R. 491, N.I.R.C., the employee received compensation calculated on the basis of a highly probable future salary increase. In assessing the loss the tribunal members may take into account their own knowledge of re-employment prospects; *Donnelly* v. *Feniger & Blackburn, Ltd.,* [1973] I.C.R. 68, N.I.R.C.

(d) Loss of protection in respect of unfair dismissal. This is now of much less importance since the qualifying period for unfair dismissal is only 6 months continuous employment. Loss of protection in respect of dismissal by reason of redundancy is now covered by the basic award and 76 (3) of the Employment Protection Act 1975.

Other heads of claim indicated by decisions are:

(e) Losses in respect of pension schemes.

In *Copson* v. *Eversure Accessories, Ltd.* (1974), I.T.R. 406, N.I.R.C., Sir JOHN DONALDSON (at p. 410) summarised the rules applicable as follows:

"(a) *Burden of proof.* The burden of proving the loss and its extent lies fairly and squarely on the claimant, notwithstanding that most of the evidence will be in the possession or power of the employer. However machinery exists for enabling him to obtain this evidence. We return to this point below.

(b) There is no one right way of proving or assessing the loss, but a broad commonsense approach should be adopted. Evidence from actuaries or pension brokers would certainly be relevant and admissible, but would not usually be necessary in the type of case with which industrial tribunals are concerned.

(c) *Types of loss.* There are two distinct types of loss to which dismissal from pensionable employment can give rise. The first is the loss of the pension position which has been earned, e.g. 15 years' service towards a pension of £x in 20 years' time at the age of 65. The second is the loss of future pension opportunity, i.e. opportunity of improving this position until the time at which the pension becomes payable. They differ in important respects and have to be evaluated separately.

(d) *Loss of pension position.* Properly funded pensions are built up by the payment of periodical contributions by employers and usually also by employees. These contributions are invested under favourable taxation provisions and build up to a capital sum which at retirement age will buy an annuity equal to the amount of the pension. Thus a crude assessment of the accrued value of a worker's pension position at any point of time can be achieved by taking the sum of the contribution already paid increased by compound interest from the date of payment. The calculation of compound interest is not easy without tables, but an increase in the rate of simple interest applied to the capital sum will achieve rough and ready justice.

(e) If a claimant is dismissed shortly before he reaches pensionable age, an alternative approach is to take the capital value of the pension to which he would have become entitled and to discount it for accelerated payment.

(f) In some cases the loss under this head will have been reduced by the employer or pension fund repaying the employee's own contributions with or without interest. Credit must, of course, be given for this repayment.

(g) It must be remembered that some employees lose the

benefit of pensionable service without any fault on the part of the employer. For example they may be dismissed fairly or they may resign voluntarily in circumstances which disentitle them to any pension. If the complainant would later have found himself in this category if he had not already been unfairly dismissed, he has lost nothing. Some discount can properly be made for these factors, if it is clear that there was a real chance of the claimant failing, otherwise than because of the unfair dismissal, to qualify for a pension from his employer.

(h) The transferable pension is not very common, in the private sector, but tribunals should bear the possibility in mind. If the employee is able to transfer his pension to his new employment, he will probably have suffered no loss under this head. The same may be true if the employee on leaving becomes entitled to a paid-up pension, payable on retirement, albeit of a smaller amount than if he had remained in the service of the employer until retirement.

(i) *Loss of future pension opportunity.* If the employee had continued in his previous employment he could have gone on improving his pension position—travelled further down the road to his pension. If he can do the same in his new employment at no greater cost to himself, there is no loss under this head. But often this will not be the case.

(j) If there is no pension scheme in operation, the employee will lose the benefit of being able to pay his own contribution free of tax. This aspect of the loss will be equal to the tax on his own contributions until pensionable age, discounted for accelerated payment and the usual imponderables of the future to which we referred in (g) above.

He will also lose the benefit of the employer's contributions. These are in reality, and should be treated as, a tax free addition to wages or salary being assessed under the head of future loss of earnings. Thus the employee who is unfairly dismissed from pensionable employment at £40 per week, is really losing a wage of £42 per week if the employer's pension contribution was £2. If then he goes to new non-pensionable employment at £35 per week, his loss of future earnings is £7 and not £5 per week. Account must, of course, be taken of any contribution to the state graduated pensions scheme which was made by either the former or the new employer if these do not cancel out and the difference in benefit to the employee is significant.

We have set the position out in some detail in the hope of assisting industrial tribunals in what is, as we have said, a very difficult task. We must, however, stress that it is impossible to cover every eventuality and permutation and that there is no single right way of assessing the loss in respect of pension."

See also *Scottish Co-operative Society* v. *Lloyd* (1973), 8 I.T.R. 178, N.I.R.C.; *Cawthorn and Sinclair, Ltd.* v. *Hedger* (1974), 9 I.T.R. 171, N.I.R.C.; *Gill* v. *Harold Andrews Sheepbridge, Ltd.* (1974), 9 I.T.R. 219, N.I.R.C., and *Hilti (Great Britain), Ltd.* v. *Windridge* (1974), 9 I.T.R. 197, N.I.R.C.

The prospect that the employee will benefit from pension contributions paid by future employers should be taken into account. *John Millar & Sons* v. *Quinn* (1974), 9 I.T.R. 277, N.I.R.C.

(f) Loss of right to longer notice. The employee when he starts his new employment will probably be on shorter notice than his was with his former employers if he had been employed by them for a long time. See *Hilti (Great Britain), Ltd.* v. *Windridge* (1974), 9 I.T.R. 197, N.I.R.C. In that case it was said that this head is likely to consist of only "a very small award" in the average case. However it could be higher in some cases as a result of the change to the minimum periods of notice required by the Contracts of Employment Act 1972, as amended by the Employment Protection Act 1975.

(g) Other losses sustained by the employee. The tribunal may award compensation for other losses which are sustained by the complainant in consequence of the dismissal. The principle is that the compensation should, so far as money can do so, put the employee in the same position as if he had not been dismissed: *Vaughan* v. *Weighpack, Ltd.* (1974), 9 I.T.R. 226, N.I.R.C. The tribunal in *Narraine* v. *Fidelity Radio* (1975), 10 I.T.R. 186, T, *held* that compensation was not recoverable in respect of temporary deprivation of unemployment benefit and another tribunal in *Reed* v. *F. and J. Carroll, Ltd.* (1975), 10 I.T.R. 81, T., did not award compensation for a loss sustained by the employee as a result of a lay-off by his new employers.

Losses which are recoverable included benefits the employee might reasonably expect to have received but for the dismissal including those to which he was not contractually entitled. Removal and disturbance expenses have been awarded when the former employee has had to move to obtain other employment; *Nohar* v. *Granite Stone (Galloway), Ltd.* (1974), 9 I.T.R. 155, N.I.R.C. The loss of benefits such as the private use of a company car (including losses on the sale of a car which the former employee purchased), see for example *Nohar's* case. Even discomfort resulting from inferior accommodation may be included; *Imperial London Hotels* v. *Cooper* (1974), 9 I.T.R. 312, N.I.R.C.

In *Nohar's* case it was decided that it was not possible for an employee to recover the cost of representation before the tribunal under this head.

The tribunal in giving its decision and reasons should set out its calculation to show how the figure for compensation was reached. If the employee received a payment from his ex-employers this should be taken into account in assessing the compensatory award. See for example *Wellman Alloys, Ltd.* v. *Russell* (1973), 8 I.T.R. 632, N.I.R.C., where there had been a payment to the employee of £1,000 "for loss of office" which exceeded the amount of compensation which the tribunal would award. The award was reduced to nil. If it can be shown that the employee suffered no loss under these heads because he could have been fairly dismissed in the circumstances then he will not recover a compensatory award: *Earl* v. *Slater and Wheeler (Airlyne), Ltd.*, [1973] 1 All E.R. 145; [1973] 1 W.L.R. 51, N.I.R.C. The award can include matters to which the employee was not contractually entitled. An example is *York Trailer Co., Ltd.* v. *Sparkes* (1973), 8 I.T.R. 491, N.I.R.C. where a prospective salary increase was taken into account.

As has been seen Employment Protection Act 1975, section 76 (6) provides that where the dismissal was to any extent caused, or contributed to, by any action of the complainant, the tribunal shall reduce the award by such proportion as it considers to be just and equitable having regard to that finding. There is somewhat similar provision in section 75 (7). The extent to which decisions under Trade Union and Labour Relations Act 1974, Schedule 1, paragraph 19 (now repealed) will be followed is not certain, but in *Millington* v. *T. H. Goodwin & Sons, Ltd.* (1975),

10 I.T.R. 33, D.C., it was *held* that the correct approach under that paragraph was to assess the compensation in total, itemising it fully, and only after this sum had been worked out can the deduction be assessed.

The amount of any reduction in the amount of compensation depends on the facts of each particular case. Doubts were expressed on interpretation of the provisions of the Industrial Relations Act 1971 and the Trade Union and Labour Relations Act 1974 as to the approach to be adopted by tribunals when considering the possibility of reductions, but in *Maris* v. *Rotherham County Borough Council*, [1974] 2 All E.R. 776, N.I.R.C., the National Industrial Relations Court having reviewed the authorities used a very broad "common sense" approach taking into account all the circumstances surrounding the dismissal. This was expressly approved by PHILLIPS, J. in *Cooper* v. *British Steel Corporation* (1975), 10 I.T.R. 133, D.C., when the Court *held* that save in exceptional circumstances tribunals should not conclude that the employee has contributed towards his dismissal by anything like 100%. The amount of the reduction made by the tribunal in that case was 95%, which was altered to 70% by the appellate court. But compare *Smyth* v. *Autocar and Transporters, Ltd.*, [1975] I.C.R. 180, D.C. When tribunals do make reductions under these provisions they should state the reason for doing so. There should be no reduction if the employee is not in any way to "blame" for the dismissal. See *Morrish* v. *Henlys (Folkstone), Ltd.*, [1973] 2 All E.R. 137, N.I.R.C., and *Winterhalter Gastronom, Ltd.* v. *Webb* (1973), 8 I.T.R. 313, N.I.R.C., where no reduction was made where the dismissal took place because of lack of capability. For cases where reductions were made see *Munif* v. *Cole and Kirby, Ltd.*, [1973] I.C.R. 486, N.I.R.C. and *Springbank Sand and Gravel Co., Ltd.* v. *Craig*, [1973] I.R.L.R. 278, N.I.R.C.

The employee is under a duty to mitigate his loss and the usual rules of contract law apply.

In *Bessenden Properties* v. *Corness* (1974), I.T.R. 128; affd. [1974] I.R.L.R. 338, C.A., it was suggested by counsel for the employers that the employee should not refuse to take alternative employment solely because it was not suitable. Sir JOHN DONALDSON said:

> "We agree that this is not the test. A complainant is certainly not entitled to sit idly by and refuse all jobs unless they measure up precisely to the same criteria as the job which

he or she has lost. The proper test is to consider whether the person who is said to have failed to mitigate his damage acted reasonably in all the circumstances. In deciding whether he acted reasonably, a useful test is for the court or tribunal to ask itself, 'If the complainant had had no hope of recovering compensation from anybody else and if he had consulted merely his own interests and had acted reasonably in all the circumstances, would he have accepted the job in mitigation of the loss which he had suffered?' If the answer is 'Yes' then he should have taken the job and the fact that he is able to look towards the respondent for compensation provides him with no excuse for not doing so." (At p. 132.) See also *Archbold Freightage, Ltd.* v. *Wilson* (1974), 9 I.T.R. 133, N.I.R.C.

If matters come to light after an award of compensation which shows that the employer could have been dismissed for misconduct the tribunal may reduce the award of compensation or award no compensation under this head. See the decision of the tribunal in *McGregor* v. *Gibbings* (1975), 10 I.T.R. 64, T, and of the Divisional Court in *W. Devis & Sons, Ltd.* v. *Atkins*, [1976] 1 W.L.R. 393, D.C. If after a compensation award it comes to light as a result of events following the tribunal's decision, that it was in some way misconceived it should be considered whether or not to seek a review. The test to be applied by the tribunal in such cases is explained by Sir John Donaldson in *Yorkshire Engineering and Welding Co., Ltd.* v. *Burnham* (1973), 8 I.T.R. 621, N.I.R.C., as follows (at p. 625):

"In such circumstances the test to be applied in deciding whether or not to review a decision is as follows. The tribunal must ask itself whether the forecasts which were the basis of its decision have been falsified to a sufficiently substantial extent to invalidate the assessment and whether this occurred so soon after the decision, that a review was necessary in the interests of justice. There must be some finality in these matters. But at the same time, if very shortly after a tribunal has reached a decision it comes to its notice, upon an application for review, that the facts are so different from those which it had assumed, that the whole substratum of its award has gone, then, subject to such considerations as whether the party applying could have obtained that evidence before the hearing, there is manifestly a case for review."

The purpose of section 77 is to avoid the possibility of up to two separate awards of compensation in respect of the same losses arising when a dismissal is both an unfair dismissal and an act of discrimination under the Sex Discrimination Act 1975. The limit imposed by paragraph 20 of the Schedule 1 of the Trade Union and Labour Relations Act 1974 applies to the aggregate of the three awards.

By virtue of the Employment Protection Act 1975, section 112, the Secretary of State for Employment may by regulations make provision with regard to payment of wages, or compensation for loss of wages, or to any payment under the Employment Protection Act by an employer to an employee, or a payment by an employer to an employee of a nature similar to, or for a purpose corresponding to the purpose of, any payment under the Act, and which are the subject of proceedings before an industrial tribunal:

> (a) enabling the Secretary of State to recover from an employer, by way of total or partial recoupment of unemployment benefit or supplementary benefit, a sum not exceeding the amount of the prescribed element of the monetary award;
>
> (b) requiring or authorising the tribunal to order the payment of such a sum, by way of total or partial recoupment of either benefit, to the Secretary of State instead of to the employee;
>
> (c) requiring the tribunal to order the payment to the employee of only the excess of the prescribed element of the monetary award over the amount of any unemployment benefit or supplementary benefit shown to the tribunal to have been paid to the employee, and enabling the Secretary of State to recover from the employer, by way of total or partial recoupment of the benefit, a sum not exceeding that amount.

The "prescribed element" means so much of the award as may be prescribed by the regulations. No regulations have been made at the date of the Preface but it is expected that regulations will be made in due course and that their object will be to oblige the employer to pay to the Department of Health and Social Security a sum equal to the unemployment and supplementary benefits received by the employee resulting from the unfair dismissal. In cases where the regulations apply the employer should delay payment of compensation to the employee as therein provided until the appropriate claim has been dealt with.

## DEATH OF EMPLOYER OR OF EMPLOYEE[1]

Employment Protection Act 1975, Schedule 12, Part II provides the rules applicable when the death of either party takes place after a dismissal which is claimed to be unfair has taken place. If the employer has given notice to the employee to terminate his contract of employment and before the termination the employer, or employee, dies the unfair dismissal provisions apply as if the contract had been duly terminated by the employer by notice expiring on the date of death.[2] When the contract of employment has been terminated and Trade Union and Labour Relations Act 1974, Schedule 1, paragraph 5 (6) (the provisions which apply when notice is of less than the obligatory statutory period has been given) provides for an effective date of termination later than would otherwise have been the case and before that later date the employee or the employer dies, then sub-paragraph 5 (6) has effect as if the notice to which it refers would have expired on the date of death.[3]

[1] For institution and continuance of tribunal proceedings and rights and liabilities accruing after death, see p. 411 below.

[2] Employment Protection Act 1975, Sch. 12, para. 9.

[3] *Ibid.*, Sch. 12, para. 10.

If the employee dies before an order of reinstatement, or re-engagement, has been made the unfair dismissal provisions relating to reinstatement and re-engagement do not apply and if the industrial tribunal finds that his case was well-founded, then for the purposes of compensation the case is treated as one falling within section 72 (5) as a case in which no order under section 71 has been made.[1] When in such circumstances an order for reinstatement or re-engagement has been made, and the employee dies before it is complied with, if the employer has before the death refused to reinstate, or re-engage, the employee in accordance with the order the usual provisions as to section 72 (2) and (3) apply and compensation may be awarded for that reason unless the employer satisfies the tribunal that it was not practicable at the time of the refusal to comply with the order.[2] When there has not been a refusal the tribunal may still make an award in respect of ancillary terms of the order which were capable of fulfilment after the employee's death if the employee fails to comply with the order in just the same way as if there was a failure to comply with the order where the employee had been reinstated, or re-engaged.[3]

[1] Employment Protection Act 1975, Sch. 12, para. 11.
[2] *Ibid.*, Sch. 12, para. 12 (*a*).
[3] *Ibid.*, Sch. 12, para. 12 (*b*).

# Chapter 8

# CALCULATION OF TOTAL ENTITLEMENT ON TERMINATION

## COMPOSITE CLAIMS

As a result of the same dismissal the employee may be entitled to awards of damages, and/or compensation, against the employer under several different heads, and whilst proceedings for wrongful dismissal have to be heard by the ordinary courts, in more than one forum. An employee who commences proceedings for damages for wrongful dismissal at common law, or presents a complaint to an industrial tribunal under a particular statute, is not precluded from seeking remedies under other statutes, or the common law. The total amount recovered by the employee can consist of one, or more, of the following:

(a) Payment in lieu of notice, or damages for wrongful dismissal.[1] These claims only arise if the contract is not rightfully terminated at common law. In general, damages for wrongful dismissal do not put the dismissed employee in a position better then he would have been in if the contract had been terminated at the earliest time at which it could lawfully have been brought to an end. Although not beyond doubt, the better view is that a redundancy payment is not deducted in computing damages for wrongful dismissal. In *Stocks* v. *Magna Merchants, Ltd.*,[2] ARNOLD, J, held on assize, that a redundancy payment should be deducted in computing damages for wrongful dismissal. However this was strongly disapproved by Sir JOHN DONALDSON in *Yorkshire Engineering and Welding Co., Ltd.* v. *Burnham*,[3] when he said in the National Industrial Relations Court:

"The essence of the cause of action for wrongful dismissal is that the employee is dismissed prematurely. If it is a fixed term contract, he is dismissed before the end of the term. If it is a running contract, his contract is terminated without notice or with less notice than that to which he is entitled under the contract. The damages to which he is entitled consist of the

net loss flowing from the *premature* nature of the dismissal.
*Prima facie* the measure of damage is what the employee
would have earned between the time of dismissal and the
earliest moment at which he could properly have had his
contract terminated, less any benefits which he has received
and which he would not have received if he had been properly
dismissed, i.e. had been allowed to work until the end of the
notice or the end of the fixed term contract. We are unable
to agree with and follow *Stocks'* case because it appears to
overlook the fact that Mr. Stocks' would have received his
redundancy payment even if his contract had been allowed to
run to the end of its term, that being the earliest date upon
which it could properly have been determined. If, contrary
to our view, the decision in *Stocks'* case is correct and of
general application it would produce some very startling
results. To take simple figures, suppose that a man aged 40
or over is dismissed on account of redundancy. He is then
entitled, under the Redundancy Payments Act, 1965, to a
lump sum calculated at the rate of one-and-a-half weeks'
wages for every year of his service, provided only that he has
a minimum of 104 weeks' continuous service. If one assumes
a man with only four years' service, his redundancy payment
will amount to a sum equal to six week's pay and his entitlement to notice will be only two weeks (Contracts of Employment Act, 1972). Accordingly, if the decision in *Stocks* v.
*Magna Merchants, Ltd.*[4] is right, any employer can dismiss such
an employee summarily without wages in lieu of notice,
because the redundancy payment will be set off against and
exceed the amount of money due in lieu of notice."[5]

[1] See p. 153, above. For the position under the 1976 Race Relations Bill
see p. 505, below.
[2] [1973] 2 All E.R. 329; [1973] 1 W.L.R. 1505.
[3] [1973] I.T.R. 621, at p. 623, N.I.R.C.
[4] [1973] 2 All E.R. 329; [1973] 1 W.L.R. 1505.
[5] *Burnham's* case was approved and *Stocks* expressly disapproved in
*Millington* v. *T. H. Goodwin & Sons, Ltd.*, [1975] I.C.R. 104, Q.B.D., and
*Basnett* v. *J. and A. Jackson, Ltd.*, [1976] I.C.R. 63, Q.B.D.

When an award of compensation for unfair dismissal has
already been made, insofar as it relates to matters which would be
taken into account in calculating damages for wrongful dismissal,
it is likely that the amount of the compensation for items so taken

into account, would be deducted by the court, (or, in due course, the tribunal), in assessing damages for wrongful dismissal. For instance, if an industrial tribunal makes an award which includes an element for loss of wages during the period in respect of which the employee would have been employed, had his employment been rightfully terminated, although there is no direct authority on the point, it may be assumed that the amount of compensation awarded for loss of wages during that period, will be deducted when the damages are computed.[1] The basic award, on the other hand, is not related to the loss arising from the unlawful nature of the termination, and although it far from clear, it is considered that no part of the basic award will be taken into account when assessing damages for wrongful dismissal.[2]

[1] On the principle that the same loss cannot be recovered twice.
[2] The reasoning being similar to that in *Burnham's* case. See *Basnett* v. *J. and A. Jackson, Ltd.*, [1976] I.C.R. 63, Q.B.D.

It has been seen[1] that a compensation award consequent upon discrimination contrary to the Sex Discrimination Act 1975, although awarded by an industrial tribunal, is of an amount corresponding to any damages which the employee could have been awarded by a county court judge under the provisions of section 66 of that Act.[2] This means that the calculation is as if the claim was in tort, and the compensation can include an element in respect of injury to feelings.[3] It is probable that insofar as an award of such compensation takes into account factors which form the basis of an award for damages for wrongful dismissal, the damages would be reduced by the amount of compensation awarded in respect thereof if the damages are assessed after the compensation has been awarded.

[1] See p. 39, above.
[2] Sex Discrimination Act 1975, s. 65 (1) (*b*).
[3] *Ibid.*, s. 66 (4).

If an employee is reinstated, or re-engaged, following an order of an industrial tribunal, the loss resulting from a breach of contract could be reduced to nil and the damages would be similarly affected. A payment whether described as *ex gratia*, or not, referring expressly to a payment consequent upon wrongful dismissal, may be held to reduce the damages for such dismissal.

(b) Redundancy payments. A redundancy payment is calculated in accordance with the statutory formula and so is not affected by the amount of any damages for wrongful dismissal, payment in lieu of notice, or compensation for unfair dismissal, or discrimination. It may fall to be repaid, if after its payment, the employee is reinstated, or re-engagement, ensues.[1] In certain circumstances, a payment not expressly referrable to the Redundancy Payments Act 1965, may be held to be a redundancy payment,[2] otherwise an ex gratia payment may not go towards discharging the employer's liability for redundancy payments. A payment made in respect, or on account, of damages for wrongful dismissal will not reduce the amount of redundancy payment, nor will compensation for unfair dismissal, or compensation awarded as a result of discrimination on the ground of sex, or married status.

[1] For instance as a result of an agreement such as is mentioned in Industrial Relations (Continuity of Employment) Regulations 1972, S.I. 1972 No. 55, para. 4. See p. 228, above.

[2] See p. 250, above.

(c) Compensation for unfair dismissal. The amount of the compensatory award for unfair dismissal may be affected by the amount of damages for wrongful dismissal. If the employee has already received payment in respect of such a claim then the loss which he has suffered will be reduced to the extent that the loss has already been compensated.[1] As has been seen a court considering a case on a claim for wrongful dismissal, when compensation for unfair dismissal has been awarded, may consider that insofar as an element of the compensation was in respect of the period during which the contract would have existed, if it were rightfully terminated, then damages for wrongful dismissal should be reduced accordingly. Before the coming of the basic award, the loss of any entitlement, or potential entitlement, to a redundancy payment was taken into account in calculating compensation for unfair dismissal.[2] Employment Protection Act 1975, section 76 (3) now governs the position, and provides that such element of compensation should include only the loss referable to the amount, if any, by which the amount of that payment would have exceeded the amount of the basic award (apart from any reduction under the Employment Protection Act 1975, section 75 (7) or (8)) in respect of the same dismissal. The aggregate of compensation awarded under Sex Discrimination Act 1975, section 65 and any compensation awarded under Employment Protection Act 1975, section 72 (1) or as the case may be, which is calculated in accordance with the rules for working out the compensatory award must not exceed the limit prescribed by the Trade Union and Labour Relations Act 1974, Schedule 1, paragraph 20 (at present £5,200).[3] It is likely that there will be overlap between the heads of claim under both Acts, and when the same factors are taken into account for the purpose of calculating the sum to be paid to the employee, each factor will be taken into account only once, on the basis that the ex-employee should not recover his loss twice.[4] Gratuitous payments to the employee after the dismissal will be taken into account in computing the compensatory award for unfair dismissal.[5]

[1] See *Wellman Alloys Ltd.* v. *Russell* (1973), 8 I.T.R. 632, N.I.R.C.
[2] See *Norton Tool Co., Ltd.* v. *Tewson*, [1973] 1 All E.R. 183; [1973] 1 W.L.R. 45, N.I.R.C. and p. 358, above.
[3] Employment Protection Act 1975, s. 77 (2). *Ibid.*, s. 77 (1) provides that when compensation falls to be awarded both under the Sex Discrimination Act 1975 and the unfair dismissal provisions, an industrial tribunal shall not award compensation in respect of any loss or matter which is, or has been, taken into account in a previous award of compensation in respect of the same act.
[4] Employment Protection Act 1975, s. 77 (1).
[5] *Wellman Alloys, Ltd.* v. *Russell* (1973), 8 I.T.R. 632, N.I.R.C.

(d) Compensation for discrimination on the grounds of sex, or marital status. The principles of assessment of compensation under the Sex Discrimination Act 1975 provide that damages will be computed "in like manner as any other action in tort".[1] It is most likely that the tribunal will be careful not to duplicate an award of compensation arising from the same cause.[2] The same limit on compensation applies to the aggregate of compensation under the Sex Discrimination Act 1975 and under the Employment Protection Act 1975, section 72 (1) or, as the case may be, calculated in accordance with section 76 of that Act, as is imposed by Trade Union and Labour Relations Act 1974, Schedule 1, paragraph 20.[3] Payment of a redundancy payment will probably not affect compensation awarded under the Sex Discrimination Act 1975 and the relationship with damages for wrongful dismissal has been dealt with above. It is likely that all claims relating to the same dismissal falling within the jurisdiction of individual tribunals will be heard together if possible and compensation calculated at the same time.[4]

[1] Sex Discrimination Act 1975, s. 66 (1).

## TAXATION

There are three distinct contexts in which the effects of taxation have to be considered when making payment to an employee, or former employee, on the termination of his employment. First, taxation may have to be taken into account in calculating the sum to be paid to the former employee, secondly, it has to be decided whether the payment is deductible in computing the taxable profits of the employer, and thirdly, the taxation consequences for the recipient have to be examined.

### (a) Calculation of sum paid

Originally damages for breach of employment contracts and payments made on termination of contracts of employment were not brought into charge for tax. However provisions were introduced in the Finance Act 1960 which taxed "golden handshakes", i.e. payments made on a person's retirement, or removal, from employment (including damages awarded as a result of wrongful dismissal) leaving only the first £5,000 excluded from the charge. These provisions are effectively re-enacted by Income and Corporation Taxes Act 1970, sections 187 and 188 so that the first £5,000[1] of the sum paid after removal from office or employment, (whether or not as the result of an award of the court), is free of tax, but any excess over this sum is subject to taxation on a "top-slicing" basis.

[1] This includes the amount of any redundancy payment; Income and Corporation Taxes Act 1970, s. 412 (8). Otherwise redundancy payments are exempt from income tax under Schedule E; *ibid.*, s. 412 (1).

Unless there is a provision in the contract providing for liquidated damages by reference to gross remuneration,[1] as there is in some contracts providing for pay in lieu of notice, the employee can recover his net loss only, on a claim for breach of contract. Where the claim is for loss of earnings which, if the contract had been performed, would have been subject to tax, the damages may be reduced by the amount of the tax saving, if the sum recovered or payment is itself not taxable, or is taxable at a lower rate, in the former employee's hands. This is, of course, an application of the principle that damages paid on breach of contract will not, save in most unusual cases, put the employee in a position better than that in which he would have been had the contract continued, see p. 154, above. The rule in *British Transport Commission* v. *Gourley*[2] is still applied in calculating damages to the £5,000 ceiling, and a deduction is made from the damages equivalent to the amount of tax which would fall to be paid if the sum was received by way of emoluments, in the normal way,[3] i.e. where the notional figure for damages is less than £5,000, the adjusted notional sum is apportioned over the unexpired term of employment, or period of notice, and reduced by the tax which would be payable by the employee thereon if the same was received by way of remuneration. Where the payment is over £5,000 taxation has no effect on the amount of the excess this being chargeable under section 187. In such a case £5,000 is treated as if it were the total award for loss of income during the period in respect of which the damages are claimed, (i.e. the length of notice, or the unexpired period of a fixed term contract), the taxation likely to be charged on such income is computed and that figure is then deducted from the notional gross amount of damages.[4] It will be seen that in certain cases, for instance those involving foreign service, payments may not be caught by the Income and Corporation Taxes Act 1970, section 187.[5] In such circumstances liability to foreign taxation will be taken into account in computing the employee's or former employee's, net loss.

[1] In cases where payments to be made when the contract is determined are agreed when it is entered into the Revenue are likely to contend that they are emoluments taxable under Schedule E.

[2] [1956] A.C. 185, H.L.: See also *Beach* v. *Read Corrugated Cases, Ltd.*, [1956] 2 All E.R. 652; [1956] 1 W.L.R. 807, Q.B.D.

[3] *Parsons* v. *B.N.M. Laboratories, Ltd.*, [1964] 1 Q.B. 95; [1964] 1 All E.R. 658, C.A.; *Stewart* v. *Glentaggart*, 1963 S.L.T. 119.

[4] *Bold* v. *Brough Nicholson and Hall, Ltd.*, [1963] 3 All E.R. 849; [1964] 1 W.L.R. 201, Q.B.D. This approach is not however, beyond doubt. The amount of tax payable as a result of the charge effected by s. 187 may differ by a considerable amount from that which would be payable if the contract continued. Logically the difference between the amounts of taxation should be taken into account, since the net result after the damages have been paid should be that the ex-

employee is in no better, or worse, position than if the contracted relationship had not been wrongfully determined. See the Scottish case of *Stewart* v. *Glentaggart*, (above). But *Bold's* case has been followed by CRICHTON, J., in *Basnett* v. *J. and A. Jackson, Ltd.*, [1976] I.C.R. 63, Q.B.D. See also *Lyndale Fashion Manufacturers* v. *Rich*, [1973] 1 All E.R. 33; [1973] 1 W.L.R. 73, C.A. and *Slingsby* v. *News of the World Organisation*, (1970) 1st May (unreported).
[5] Income and Corporation Taxes Act 1970, s. 188 (2).

## (b) Consequences of payment for the employer

For an employer liable to income tax, if an individual, or partnership, or to corporation tax if a corporate body, payments made "wholly and exclusively" for the purpose of the trade profession or vocation are deductible in computing profits brought into account for such taxes.[1] Where the employer is continuing in trade payments made to an ex-employee on dismissal, or retirement, of the employee, if made at arms length, are allowable.[2] This is on the ground that such payments to former employees may affect the employer's relations with present employees and so benefit his business.

[1] Income and Corporation Taxes Act 1970, s. 130.
[2] *Smith* v. *Incorporated Council of Law Reporting*, [1914] 3 K.B. 674, K.B.D.

A payment made to compromise an action, or threat of proceedings for damages, or compensation, which is properly calculated would be so deductible. *Ex gratia* payments pose a more difficult problem. They are allowed as deductions when calculating the employer's profit only if the employer, be it an individual, or company, has considered the matter properly and thoroughly in its' own interests and those of its' trade.[1] At first sight the applications of these principles appears to be simple, but difficulties arise if the payment is made at, or close to, the time when the employer's business is sold or closes down, or when in the case of a company there are changes in the ownership of shares in the employer. On the sale of the business redundancy payments made to employees, are an allowable deduction.[2] Other payments are allowable if made from revenue sources and if they fall within the requirements set out above but not if they are set aside as part of the sale price.[3] On the cessation of a business, redundancy payments are allowed[2] but not other payments for the discontinuance of the trade. This is because they could not have been made for the benefit of the employer's trade since it was not continuing.[4] However, when the cessation is on a liquidation, which is part of a reconstruction involving a transfer of trade, so long as the payment is made before the liquidator is appointed, then it is allowable. Payment for services already rendered is also deductible even if paid after cessation.[5]

[1] *Snook & Co., Ltd.* v. *Blasdale,* [1952] T.R. 233, C.A.
[2] Income and Corporation Taxes Act 1970, s. 412 (2).
[3] *George Peters & Co.* v. *Smith*; *Williams* v. *J.J. Young & Son,* [1963] T.R. 329
[4] *Godden* v. *A. Wilsons Stores (Holdings), Ltd.,* [1962] T.R. 19, C.A.; *Strang* v. *Woodifield,* [1906] A.C. 448, H.L.
[5] *Inland Revenue Commissioners* v. *Patrick Thompson Ltd. (in liquidation),* [1956] T.R. 471, C.S. Such payments would be subject to taxation under Schedule E, in the ex-employee's hands.

When the former employee was also a shareholder in the employing company and there is a transfer of his shares at, or about, the same time as the termination of his employment, the principle in *Snook's* case is applied but the practice of the Revenue is to look more carefully at the payment to ensure that decisions as to payment and quantum have been taken solely in the company's interests. In that case DONOVAN, J., (as he then was) said:[1]

> "The mere circumstances that compensation to retiring directors is paid on a change of shareholding control does not of itself involve the consequence that such compensation can never be a deductible trading expense. So much is common ground. But it is essential in such cases that the company should prove to the Commissioners' satisfaction that it considered the question of payment wholly untrammelled by the terms of the bargain its shareholders had struck with those who were to buy their shares and came to a decision to pay solely in the interests of its trade. This may be very difficult at times, because the persons who have to take the decision are often the persons who are to get the compensation; but any difficulty in securing an independent decision by or on behalf of the Company does not do away with the necessity of securing it if a title to deduct the compensation as a trade expense is to be sought."

[1] At p. 251. See also *George J. Smith & Co., Ltd.* v. *Furlong,* [1969] 2 All E.R. 760, Ch.D.

A further difficulty can be encountered when the former employee, or director, was, or is, a member of the paying company, since the payment could be treated as being a distribution by the former employer.[1] The Revenue have stated that they give sympathetic consideration to such cases where the terminal payment was made by a continuing company at arms length, and was reasonable having regard to the circumstances and admissibility as a deduction for corporation tax purposes.[2]

[1] Income and Corporation Taxes Act 1970, s. 233.
[2] 1974 British Tax Review, p. 412.

A payment which is allowable as a deduction against the profits of the paying company cannot give rise to the possibility of capital transfer tax,[1] but if there is an element of bounty in the payment, and the payer is a close company, capital transfer tax may have to be considered.[2] If chargeable, the amount of the transfer value is apportioned to the participators, according to their rights and interests in the company. The company is liable for the tax but, if it remains unpaid after the due date, the persons to whom the amounts have been apportioned, and any individual whose estate has been increased, are liable. A person to whom not more than 5% of the value transferred has been apportioned, is not liable for any tax, and if the value of the estate of the person to whom the value has been apportioned, has increased as a result of the transfer, (i.e. he has received the payment) the amount of the increase may be deducted from the apportioned sum.

[1] Finance Act 1975, Sch. 6, para. 9.
[2] *Ibid.*, ss. 39 and 20 (1).

### (c) Consequences of payment for the employee

When a payment is made while the employment relationship subsists, (i.e. before the termination), then *prima facie* it is liable to taxation under Schedule E and the employee should receive it subject to the deduction of P.A.Y.E. Where the sum is paid after the employment relationship has been determined, then the £5,000 exemption, mentioned above, applies and a payment under £5,000 may be made gross, providing that it is properly payable as being "wholly and exclusively" for the purposes of trade and it is not taxable under Schedule E. This is also the case when the payment is made on the termination, and it is reasonable compensation, (the term includes damages for wrongful dismissal, compensation for unfair dismissal, or payment in lieu) for loss of office, or employment, there being no further obligation of service thereafter.[1] To put the matter beyond a doubt, it is preferable from the employee's point of view for the payment to be made after termination. Even if the payment is made after termination, but it in in effect payment for services rendered under the contract of employment, it is taxable under Schedule E.[2] The Revenue are also likely to challenge any payment made gross, if the ex-employee continues to carry out work for the employer after the termination.[3]

[1] *C. G. Clayton v. Lavender*, [1965] T.R. 461, Ch.D.

[2] *Hockstrasser v. Mayes*, [1960] A.C. 376; [1959] 3 All E.R. 827, H.L.; *Henry v. Foster* (1932), 145 L.T. 225, C.A. See also *Heywood v. Comptroller General of Inland Revenue*, [1975] A.C. 229; [1974] 3 All E.R. 872, P.C.

[3] Payments which are to be made gross should never be paid until the position has been cleared with the local Tax Office. See "Employers Guide to PAYE", April 1975, para. 51. If tax is not deducted when it is deductible the employer may be liable to pay to the Revenue the tax which should have been deducted and may be unable to recover it from the ex-employee. See Income Tax (Employments) Regulations 1973, S.I. 1973 No. 334, reg. 26. If the payment is accepted by the Revenue as being compensation for loss of office but exceeds £5,000 the excess should be added to the employees pay for PAYE purposes and the appropriate deduction made; *ibid.*, reg. 16. The Inspector of Taxes should be given details as soon as convenient and whenever possible he should authorise a reduced tax deduction related to the employee's potential liability; "Employers Guide to PAYE", April 1975, para. 51.

The provisions of sections 187 and 188 relate only to payments on loss of office and employment (often called compensation for loss of office) and so payments such as damages for industrial injury, or on death are not taxable under them. Payments from occupational pension schemes are also excluded, but may themselves be taxable under provisions which are beyond the scope of this book. A payment made to an employee should he enter a restrictive covenant on the termination of his employment, or when he releases the employer from such a covenant, would be taxable under different provisions.[1] To the extent that the compensation for loss of employment exceeds the sum of £5,000, increased if applicable as above, then the sum received by the employee is taxable and the method of calculation is laid down in the Income and Corporation Taxes Act 1970, Schedule 8.[2] From this Schedule it will be seen that it may be necessary for the payment to be apportioned between the sum which is damages for wrongful dismissal, redundancy payment and/or compensation for unfair dismissal, and any element which is in the nature of a gratuitous payment. The reliefs and periods over which the sums are to be apportioned may differ when there is a gratutious element in the payment. Thus the principles upon which payment is calculated may be of importance in deciding the incidence of taxation and they should be properly recorded. This is especially true in cases where there is an element of bounty in the payment since besides the differing top-slicing period, "the standard capital superannuation benefit" may be used in certain circumstances to reduce the figures bought into charge for tax. Save in cases of death it is not possible to finalise the top-slicing calculation until the end of the tax year.

[1] Income and Corporation Taxes Act 1970, s. 188 (1) (*b*).

[2] This Schedule lays down relief for "the standard capital superannuation benefit" and in certain cases of foreign service, as well as top-slicing relief and should be studied in detail.

## THE EFFECT OF INSOLVENCY ON AN EMPLOYEE'S CLAIMS[1]

As has been seen above[2] there are provisions enabling the Secretary of State to pay redundancy payments from the Redundancy Fund where the employer is unable to make payment as a result of insolvency. With the exception of the provision in the Redundancy Payments Act 1965 there were no special provisions in the recent employment legislation relating to employees claims where the employer was insolvent save for those contained in the Bankruptcy Act 1914, section 33 and the Companies Act 1948, section 319. In general terms these provide that not more than four months arrears of wages, or salary of employees together with holiday pay, not exceeding £200, ranks as a preferential debt. Under the provisions of the Employment Protection Act 1975 guarantee payments,[3] remuneration payable on suspension on medical grounds under the Employment Protection Act 1975, section 29[4] payment for time off, in accordance with section 57 (4) or 61 (3) of that Act[5] and remuneration to be paid under a protection award made by an industrial tribunal pursuant to the Employment Protection Act 1975, section 101[6] rank as preferential debts in the same way as wages accrued due under the Bankruptcy Act 1914, section 33 and the Companies Act 1948, section 319.[7] When an employee makes written application to the

Secretary of State and he is satisfied that the employer has become insolvent, and on the date the employer became insolvent,[8] or date of termination of the employee's employment, whichever is the later, the employee was entitled to the debt or any part of any debt, mentioned below the Secretary of State for Employment should pay to the employee, out of the Redundancy Fund, the amount which in the opinion of the Secretary of State he is entitled in respect of the debts.[9]

[1] The provisions discussed are contained in the Employment Protection Act 1975 and, save in respect of guarantee payments, were in force on 1st June 1976.

[2] See p. 261, above. For similar provisions relating to payment of maternity pay from the Maternity Pay Fund see p. 78, above.

[3] See p. 66, above.

[4] See p. 59, above.

[5] See p. 85 and p. 270, above.

[6] See p. 265, above.

[7] Employment Protection Act 1975, s. 63 (2).

[8] *Ibid.*, s. 69 (1) provides:

"69.—(1) For the purposes of sections 64 to 68 above an employer shall be taken to be insolvent if, but only if, in England and Wales,—

(a) he becomes bankrupt or makes a composition or arrangement with his creditors or a receiving order is made against him;

(b) he has died and an order is made under section 130 of the Bankruptcy Act 1914 for the administration of his estate according to the law of bankruptcy, or by virtue of an order of the court his estate is being administered in accordance with rules set out in Part I of Schedule 1 to the Administration of Estates Act 1925; or

(c) where the employer is a company, a winding up order is made or a resolution for voluntary winding up is passed with respect to it, or a receiver or manager of its undertaking is duly appointed, or possession is taken, by or on behalf of the holders of any debentures secured by a floating charge, of any property of the company comprised in or subject to the charge."

[9] *Ibid.*, s. 64 (1).

The debts to which the provisions apply are:

(a) Any arrears of pay in respect of a period or periods not exceeding in the aggregate eight weeks[1] (arrears of pay include, guarantee payments, remuneration on suspension on medical grounds, payment for time off in accordance with the Employment Protection Act 1975, sections 57 (4) and 61 (3) and remuneration under a protection award under that Act[2]).

(b) Any amount the employer is liable to the employee in

respect of the statutory minimum period of notice or failure to give such notice.[3]

(c) Any holiday pay in respect of a period, or periods, of holiday, not exceeding six weeks in all, to which the employee became entitled during the 12 months immediately preceding the relevant date.[4]

(d) Any basic award of compensation for unfair dismissal.[5]

(e) Any reasonable sum by way of reimbursement of the whole, or part, of any premium paid by an apprentice, or articled clerk.[6]

[1] Employment Protection Act 1975, s. 64 (3) (*a*).

[2] *Ibid.*, s. 64 (4).

[3] *Ibid.*, s. 64 (3) (*b*). The statutory minimum period of notice is that required by the Contracts of Employment Act 1972, ss. 1 (1) or (2).

[4] *Ibid.*, s. 64 (3) (*c*). "Holiday pay" means pay in respect of a holiday actually taken, or any accrued holiday pay which, under the employee's contract of employment would in the ordinary course have become payable to him in respect of the period of a holiday if his employment with the employer had continued until he became entitled to a holiday; *ibid.*, s. 69 (3).

[5] *Ibid.*, s. 64 (3) (*d*).

[6] *Ibid.*, s. 64 (3) (*e*).

The amount in respect of payments referable to time, is limited to £80 per week, reduced in proportion for lesser periods.[1] The Secretary of State may increase the limit by statutory instrument after the annual review.[2] The reasonable sum by way of reimbursement of fee, or premium, on apprenticeship, or articles of clerkship, is the sum admitted to be reasonable by the trustee in bankruptcy, or the liquidator, under Bankruptcy Act 1914, section 34 or that section as applied by Companies Act 1948, section 317 (whichever is applicable).[3] The Secretary of State will not make payment until he has received a statement from the trustee in bankruptcy, the liquidator, the receiver, or manager, or the trustee under a trust deed for the benefit of the employer's creditors, including the Official Receiver in his capacity as provisional liquidator, or interim receiver, as the case may be, ("the relevant officer"), of the amount of the debt which appears to be owed to employee on the relevant date and to remain unpaid.[4] There is a duty on the relevant officer, on the request of the Secretary of State, to provide the statement as soon as reasonably practicable,[4] but, when 6 months after application for payment was received by the Secretary of State, no payment has been made, the Secretary of State is satisfied that a payment should be made, and it appears to him that there is likely to be further delay before he receives a statement about the debt in question, the Secretary of State may on request from the applicant, or of his own volition make payment even though the statement has not been received.[5]

[1] Employment Protection Act 1975, s. 64 (5).
[2] *Ibid.*, s. 64 (6). The review carried out under s. 86.
[3] *Ibid.*, s. 64 (7).
[4] *Ibid.*, s. 64 (10).
[5] *Ibid.*, s. 64 (11).

In addition, if on application in writing by persons competent to act in respect of an occupational pension scheme,[1] the Secretary of State is satisfied that an employer has become insolvent[2] and that at the time he did so there were unpaid contributions to be paid by the employer, either on his own account, or on behalf of the employee which had been deducted from the employee's pay by way of contribution from him,[3] then the Secretary of State will pay into the resources of the scheme, out of the Redundancy Fund, the sum which in his opinion is payable in respect of such unpaid contributions.[4] The contributions payable in respect of unpaid contributions of an employer on his account shall be the least of, the balance of the contributions remaining unpaid on the date the employer became insolvent and payable by the employer on his own account to the scheme in respect of the 12 months immediately preceding that date, the amount certified by an actuary to be necessary for the purpose of meeting the liability of the scheme on dissolution to pay the benefits provided by the scheme to, or in respect of, the employees of the employer, or an amount equal to 10% of the total amount of remuneration paid, or payable, to those employees in respect of the 12 months immediately preceding the date on which the employer became insolvent.[5] The sums paid in respect of the employee's contributions will not exceed those deducted from the employees in respect of contributions to the pension scheme during the 12 months immediately preceding the date on which the employer became insolvent.[6] There are similar provisions as to statements from the relevant officer and payment after six months has elapsed since application for payment as those previously discussed.[7]

[1] "Occupational pension scheme" means any scheme or arrangement which provides, or is capable of providing, in relation to employees in any description of employment, benefits (in the form of pensions or otherwise) payable to, or in

respect of, any such employees on the termination of their employment, or on their death or retirement; Employment Protection Act 1975, s. 69 (3).
[2] As defined for the purposes of the Employment Protection Act 1975, s. 64. The definition is contained in *ibid.*, s. 69 (1). See p. 380, above.
[3] *Ibid.*, s. 65 (2).
[4] *Ibid.*, s. 65 (1).
[5] *Ibid.*, s. 65 (3). For these purposes "remuneration" includes holiday pay, maternity pay and other payments which are referred to in s. 63 (2). These are the payments mentioned above which also rank as preferential debts in the same way as wages. This definition of remuneration is contained in section 65 (4).
[6] *Ibid.*, s. 65 (5).
[7] *Ibid.*, s. 65 (7), (8) and (9).

An employee who has made application to the Secretary of State for payment of any sums from the Redundancy Fund may present a complaint to an industrial tribunal, when he claims the Secretary of State has failed to make payment, or the payment is less than should have been paid.[1] In a similar way the persons competent to act in respect of an occupational pension scheme may present a complaint to an industrial tribunal that the Secretary of State has failed to make payment to the resources of the pension scheme, or that the amount paid is less than should have been paid.[2] When the tribunal finds the Secretary of State ought to have made such payment, it should make a declaration to that effect and also declare the amount of any such payment the Secretary of State ought to make.[3] The complaint to the industrial tribunal should be made within three months of the date on which the decision of the Secretary of State was communicated to the employee, or the persons acting for the pension scheme, whichever is applicable, or if that was not reasonably practicable within such further period as is reasonable.[4]

[1] Employment Protection Act 1975, s. 66 (1).
[2] *Ibid.*, s. 66 (2).
[3] *Ibid.*, s. 66 (3).
[4] *Ibid.*, s. 66 (1), and (2), respectively.

If the Secretary of State makes payment to the employee, or into the resources of the pension scheme, in accordance with the provisions of sections 64 and 65 of the Employment Protection Act 1975, any rights or remedies in respect of the payments, or the part payment made by the Secretary of State, become rights and remedies of the Secretary of State, and any decision of an industrial tribunal requiring the employer to pay the debt is treated as if it were an order for it to be paid to the Secretary of State.[1] The rights which are vested in the Secretary of State include any right to be paid in priority to other creditors in accordance with Bankruptcy Act 1914, section 33 and Companies Act 1948, section 319 as the case may be, and the Secretary of State is entitled to be so paid in priority to other unsatisfied claims of the employee.[2] If the Secretary of State receives payment under these provisions the monies are paid into the Redundancy Fund.[3]

[1] Employment Protection Act 1975, s. 67 (1) and (3).
[2] *Ibid.*, s. 67 (2).
[3] *Ibid.*, s. 67 (4).

The Secretary of State has power to require the employer to provide him with such information as he requires to decide if the claims under Employment Protection Act 1975, sections 64 and 65 are well founded[1] and to require any person having the custody, or control, of any relevant records or documents to produce them for examination on behalf of the Secretary of State, if of a description he requires to be so produced.[2]

The requirements of the Secretary of State should be given in writing and can be varied or revoked.[3] A person who refuses, or wilfully neglects to furnish any information, or to produce any document, he has been required to furnish or produce by such a notice shall be liable on summary conviction to a fine not exceeding £100.[4] A person purporting to comply with the requirement of such a notice who knowingly, or recklessly, makes a false statement is liable on summary conviction to a fine not exceeding £400.[5]

[1] Employment Protection Act 1975, s. 68 (1) (*a*).
[2] *Ibid.*, s. 68 (1) (*b*).
[3] *Ibid.*, s. 68 (2).
[4] *Ibid.*, s. 68 (3).
[5] *Ibid.*, s. 68 (4).

All employees serving under contracts of service are entitled to take advantage of these provisions with the exception of an employee who is the spouse of the employer, a registered dock worker not being a person who is wholly or mainly engaged in work which is not dock work, a share fisherman, an employee who ordinarily works outside Great Britain and merchant seamen.[1]

It is to be noted that this protection applies to employees who are over usual retirement age.

¹ For exclusions see the Employment Protection Act 1975, s. 119. The exclusions may be varied or revoked by order of the Secretary of State, who may in the same way provide that the provisions do, or do not, apply to persons or employments of such classes as may be prescribed, subject to such exceptions and modifications as may be so prescribed; *ibid.*, s. 119 (15). For the application of the provisions to employment for the purposes of activities in the territorial waters of the United Kingdom, or connected with the exploration of the sea bed, or subsoil, or the exploitation of their natural resources in any area designated by an order under the Continental Shelf Act 1964, 2. 1 (7), see p. 62, above.

# Chapter 9

# CONCILIATION AND INDUSTRIAL TRIBUNALS

## CONCILIATION

The Employment Protection Act 1975[1] gives statutory recognition to the establishment of the Advisory, Conciliation and Arbitration Service ("A.C.A.S.") which is charged with the general duty of promoting the improvement of industrial relations and in particular of encouraging the extension of collective bargaining and the development and, where necessary, reform of collective bargaining machinery. Besides its conciliation powers in connection with trades disputes A.C.A.S. designates officers to perform the functions of conciliation officers under enactments in respect of matters which are, or could be the subject of proceedings before an industrial tribunal.[2] References to a conciliation officer in such enactments are treated as being references to officers so designated by A.C.A.S. When a complaint or claim is presented to an industrial tribunal pursuant to the Equal Pay Act 1970, the unfair dismissal provisions of the Trade Union and Labour Relations Act 1974, the Sex Discrimination Act 1975 and to the provisions granting individual employees rights under the Employment Protection Act 1975 a copy is sent by the Secretary of Tribunals to the conciliation officer.[3] It is the duty of a conciliation officer, if he is requested to do so both by the complainant and the person against whom the complaint is presented, or if in the absence of any such request, the conciliation officer considers that he could act under the appropriate sub-section with a reasonable prospect of success to endeavour to promote a settlement of the complaint without it being determined by an industrial tribunal.[4] In proceeding in accordance with these powers the conciliation officer has regard, where appropriate, to the desirability of encouraging the use of other procedures available for the settlement of grievances. In all those cases a request may be made to a conciliation officer before a complaint or claim has been presented to an industrial tribunal by the complainant, or by the person against whom the complaint could be made, for the conciliation officer to make his services available to him, and the conciliation officer then acts as if a complaint had been presented to an industrial tribunal.[5]

[1] Section 1.
[2] Employment Protection Act 1975. s. 2 (4).
[3] Industrial Tribunals (Labour Relations) Regulations 1974, S.I. 1974 No. 1386, Schedule, rule 2 (4).
[4] Trade Union and Labour Relations Act 1974, Sch. 1, para. 26 (2) (unfair dismissal—in paragraph 26 (3) it is stated that the conciliation officer shall in particular seek to promote the reinstatement or re-engagement of the complainant); Sex Discrimination Act 1975, s. 64 (1) (Equal Pay Act 1970 and the Sex Discrimination Act itself) and Employment Protection Act 1975, s. 108 (3) (the rights mentioned in s. 108 (2) of that Act as added to pursuant to s. 108 (8)).
[5] Trade Union and Labour Relations Act 1974, Sch. 1, para. 26 (4); Sex Discrimination Act 1975, s. 64 (2) and Employment Protection Act 1975, s. 108 (4).

The assistance of a conciliation officer is of particular significance when settling complaints to an industrial tribunal pursuant to the Equal Pay Act 1970, the unfair dismissal provisions of the Trade Union and Labour Relations Act 1974, the Sex Discrimination Act 1975 and the Employment Protection Act 1975. There are specific exclusions from the restrictions on contracting out of the statutes in circumstances where the contract is made with the assistance of a conciliation officer in the case of the Equal Pay Act 1970 and the Sex Discrimination Act 1975,[1] or is to refrain from presenting or proceeding with a complaint for unfair dismissal if a conciliation officer has taken action in accordance with the Trade Union and Labour Relations Act 1974, Schedule 1, paragraph 26 (2)[2] or in the case of a complaint or claim pursuant to the Employment Protection Act 1975 the agreement is to refrain from instituting or continuing any proceedings before an industrial tribunal where a conciliation officer has taken action in accordance with section 108 (3) or (4) of that Act.[3]

[1] See p. 25, above and p. 38, above.
[2] See p. 274, above.
[3] See p. 72, above.

Matters communicated to a conciliation officer in connection with the performance of his functions under the enactments mentioned above are not admissible in evidence in any proceedings before an industrial tribunal except with the consent of the person who communicated it to that officer.[1]

[1] See p. 406, below.

## CONSTITUTION OF INDUSTRIAL TRIBUNALS

The industrial tribunals were created by the Industrial Training Act 1964, section 12 for the purposes of hearing appeals against levies imposed by Industrial Training Boards. Their scope has been extended on many occasions so that they now have jurisdiction conferred by several enactments including, amongst others, the Redundancy Payments Act 1965, the Equal Pay Act 1970, the Contracts of Employment Act 1972, the Trade Union and Labour Relations Act 1974, the Sex Discrimination Act 1975 and the Employment Protection Act 1975. The Employment Protection Act 1975, section 109 makes provision for jurisdiction in respect of claims for damages for breach of contracts of employment or other contracts connected with employment, claims for sums due under such contracts and claims for the recovery of sums in pursuance of any enactment relating to the terms or performance of such contracts, to be conferred on industrial tribunals, but it is understood that this will not be done for some time.

The President of Industrial Tribunals (at present Mr. E. A. Seeley) is appointed by the Lord Chancellor subject to provisions as to resignation, retirement and revocation.[1] The chairman of each tribunal is a barrister or solicitor of not less than seven years standing appointed by the Lord Chancellor and he sits with two other members selected by the President from a panel of persons appearing to the Secretary of State for Employment, after consultation with organisations, or associations of organisations, representing employers or employed persons, to have knowledge or experience of employment in industry or commerce.[2] The tribunals sit at suitable centres throughout the United Kingdom.

[1] Industrial Tribunals (England and Wales) Regulations 1965, S.I. 1965 No. 1101, reg. 3 as amended by Industrial Tribunals (England and Wales) (Amendment) Regulations 1970, S.I. 1970 No. 941.

[2] Industrial Tribunals (England and Wales) Regulations 1965, reg. 5.

A person is appointed Secretary of Tribunals and there are Assistant Secretaries of Tribunals. The Assistant Secretaries of Tribunals can perform all functions of the Secretary of Tribunals other than the powers given by rule 1 (2).[1]

[1] Rule 11 (6). For rule 1 (2), see p. 395, below.

The procedure of industrial tribunals for the purposes discussed in this book is laid down by the Industrial Tribunals

388

(Labour Relations) Regulations 1974.[1] In cases where the Employment Protection Act 1975, section 78 is applicable (when an employee claims that he has been unfairly dismissed by his employer and that the reason for the dismissal (or, if more than one, the principal reason) was that the employee was, or proposed to become, a member of a particular independent trade union, or he had taken, or proposed to take, part at an appropriate time in the activities of a particular independent trade union of which he was or proposed to become a member)[2] and interim relief is sought then the Rules apply as modified by that section. An application presented to an industrial tribunal in accordance with section 78 should be determined by the industrial tribunal as soon as practicable after receiving the application and the tribunal should, at least seven days before the date of the hearing, give the employer a copy of the application and certificate in support together with notice of the date, time and place of hearing.[3] An industrial tribunal will not exercise its powers of postponing the hearing in the case of an application under these provisions except where the tribunal is satisfied that special circumstances exist which justify it in doing so.[4] Otherwise the usual rules apply to such applications.

[1] S.I. 1974 No. 1386 as amended by S.I. 1976 No. 661 and S.I. 1976 No. 663. The Rules of Procedure contained in the Schedule to the Regulations are the "Rules" referred to in this Chapter.

[2] See p. 343, above.

[3] Employment Protection Act 1975, s. 78 (3).

[4] *Ibid.*, s. 78 (4).

In any proceedings before an industrial tribunal under the Trade Union and Labour Relations Act 1974 the Code of Practice in effect under the Trade Union and Labour Relations Act 1974, Schedule 1, Part I, is admissible in evidence and relevant provisions should be taken into account by the tribunal in determining the question before it until that Code is superseded in whole or in part by a Code or Codes of Practice issued pursuant to the Employment Protection Act 1975.[1] Similarly in any proceedings before an industrial tribunal a Code of Practice issued under the Employment Protection Act 1975, section 6 is admissible in evidence and if any provision of such a code appears to the tribunal to be relevant to any question arising in the proceedings it shall be taken into account in determining that question. A failure on the part of any person to observe any provision of the codes of practice does not of itself render him liable to any proceedings.[2]

[1] Employment Protection Act 1975, Sch. 17, para. 4. The Code of Practice issued pursuant to the Industrial Relations Act 1971 is maintained in force for the puposes of the 1974 Act. The Government has announced its intention to provide for the issue of Codes of Practice effective in a similar way under the Sex Discrimination Act 1975 and the Race Relations Bill.
[2] Employment Protection Act 1975, s. 6 (11).

Any sum payable in pursuance of a decision of an industrial tribunal in England and Wales which has been registered in accordance with the Regulations shall, if a county court so orders, be recoverable by execution issued from the county court or otherwise as if it were payable under an order of that court.[1]

[1] Trade Union and Labour Relations Act 1974, Sch. 1, para. 25 (1).

Although the subject of a recommendation by the Lord Chancellor's Advisory Committee on Legal Aid, legal aid is not available for representation at hearings of industrial tribunals although legal advice may be given under the "Green Form Scheme"[1] in respect of employment matters. The assistance can include the drafting of documents in relation to proceedings before an industrial tribunal and even the production of proofs and documents to assist presentation of the case before the tribunal.

[1] Under the Legal Aid Act 1974. This form of legal aid is also (wrongly) called the "£25 Scheme".

## THE APPLICATION

The originating application to the industrial tribunal is made by the person seeking the tribunal's decision. It should be in writing setting out the name and address of the applicant, the name and address of the person or persons against whom relief is claimed and the grounds upon which the relief is sought. Forms for completion of originating applications are readily available from local offices of the Department of Employment and the Central and Regional Offices of Industrial Tribunals but are not essential. In *Smith* v. *Automobile Proprietary, Ltd.*[1] it fell to be decided whether a letter addressed to the Central Office of Industrial Tribunals by a prospective applicant's solicitors amounted to an originating application. Sir HUGH GRIFFITHS delivering the judgment of the now defunct National Industrial Relations Court stated (at p. 1107), "be it observed that there is no requirement that any particular form shall be used. In fact for the convenience of litigants a form has been prepared and is available throughout the country . . . but we repeat that it is not mandatory, and an application will not fail merely because the form is not used, provided such application contains the necessary information required by Rule 1." It is important to note that the requirement of rule 1 (1) (*d*) is for the "grounds on which the relief is sought" to be shown and not the relief which is sought. In *Coates* v. *C. J. Crispin, Ltd.*[2] the applicant had deleted the reference to the Industrial Relations Act 1971 (the statute which gave employees the right not to be unfairly dismissed at that time) when filling in the form of originating application then available from local offices of the Department of Employment. Thus the form read "I HEREBY APPLY for a decision of a tribunal under REDUNDANCY PAYMENTS ACT, 1965". When completing the section of the form entitled "the grounds of the application are as follows:" Mr. Coates wrote "Sir, I have been employed by Mr. Crispin for five years. About seven weeks ago approximately the first week in October, I had a disagreement about one particular job. On 25th October, he gave me one months' notice and told me I would not receive redundancy payments. Yours Mr. H. Coates."

[1] [1973] 2 All E.R. N.I.R.C. 1105. See also (1973), 8 I.T.R. 376, N.I.R.C.
[2] (1973), 8 I.T.R. 446, N.I.R.C.

During Mr. Coates' evidence it had been clear that he was in reality seeking redress for unfair dismissal. When asked by the chairman of the tribunal whether, in view of the error, the respondents were prepared to allow the case to proceed on the basis of a claim for unfair dismissal they indicated that they would not make any concessions in the matter. The National Industrial Relations Court held that the grounds which he set out suggested that what Mr. Coates was seeking was a remedy for unfair dismissal and pointed out[1] that the note to the form of application used at the time stated that the applicant was fully entitled "to amplify (and, as we would add, clarify) the grounds of his complaint at the hearing" but if the ground of complaint is dismissal "the tribunal should always be prepared on the facts to consider whether either a redundancy payment or compensation for unfair dismissal or both, is due unless, (a) on the facts the tribunal has been deprived of jurisdiction in relation to compensation for unfair dismissal by

. . . (the time bar), (b) the validity of one or other claim has been determined in previous proceedings between same parties or (c) there has been an unequivocal abandonment of one or other claim in such circumstances that even if there was an adjournment of the hearing, consideration of the abandoned claim would be unjust to the respondent employer".[2]

[1] (1973), 8 I.T.R. 446 at p. 451.
[2] At p. 452.

A tribunal has allowed a claim by an employee that he was unfairly dismissed where the applicant named a company as the employer which was not the employing company but which had a common managing director and majority shareholder. Since the respondents knew of the application and were not caused any prejudice an amendment substituting the name of the employing company as respondents was allowed.[1] Nevertheless problems often arise where the employer is a member of a group of companies and the employee though employed by one of their number, performs tasks for one or more others. Such a case was considered by the National Industrial Relations Court in *Cocking v. Sandhurst (Stationers), Ltd.*[2] when although employed by the holding company, the applicant was a director of a subsidiary which was named as the respondent in the originating application. The applicant wished to amend the application to substitute the name of his employer as the respondent. Sir JOHN DONALDSON gave the judgment of the Court and said[3]

> "In every case in which a tribunal is asked to amend a complaint by changing the basis of the claim or by adding or substituting respondents it should proceed as follows —
> (1) It should ask itself whether the unamended originating application compiled with rule 1 of the rules of procedure (see in relation to home made forms of complaint *Smith* v. *Automobile Proprietary, Ltd*).[4]
> (2) If it did not, there is no power to amend and a new originating application must be presented.
> (3) If it did, the tribunal should ask itself whether the unamended originating application was presented to the Secretary of Tribunals within the time limit appropriate to the type of claim being put forward in the amended application.

(4) If it was not, the tribunal has no power to allow the proposed amendment.

(5) If it was, the tribunal has a discretion whether to allow the amendment.

(6) In deciding whether or not to exercise its discretion to allow an amendment which will add or substitute a new party, the tribunal should only do so if it is satisfied that the mistake sought to be corrected was a genuine mistake and was not misleading or such as to cause reasonable doubt as to the identity of the person intending to claim or, as the case may be, to be claimed against.

(7) In deciding whether or not to exercise its discretion to allow an amendment, the tribunal should in every case have regard to all the circumstances of the case. In particular it should consider any injustice or hardship which may be caused to any of the parties, including those proposed to be added, if the proposed amendment were allowed or, as the case may be, refused. Rule [10] of the rules of procedure provides that a tribunal shall not normally award costs. If, however, the tribunal considered that the defect in the originating application had caused any party to incur unnecessary expense it could properly conclude that leave to amend should only be given if the party seeking to amend agreed to make some payment in respect of that expense and could order accordingly."

1 *Fellows* v. *Rock Rippers, Ltd.*, (1973), 8 I.T.R. 348.
2 (1975), 10 I.T.R. 6, N.I.R.C.
3 At p. 12.
4 See p. 390, above.

In *Smith's* case, above, the letter addressed to the Central Office of Industrial Tribunals did not set out the address of the respondents but since the respondents were the proprietary company of the R.A.C. the National Industrial Relations Court were of the opinion that the application was not rendered bad by this omission. It is suggested that the same would be true of any respondent being a company incorporated in the United Kingdom. The Registrar of Companies does not allow more than one company on the register with a particular name and since a major purpose of the address is to identify the respondent there should be no question of mistaken identity in such a case.

In *Chapman* v. *Goonvean and Rostowrack China Clay Co., Ltd.,*[1] Sir JOHN DONALDSON made another major statement of policy as to the treatment of applications and to the exercise by tribunals of their right to amend applications:

> "Accordingly, if there is the slightest doubt whether an applicant's claim is or should be for a redundancy payment or compensation for unfair dismissal, or for both ... the applicant should be encouraged to put forward or maintain both such claims until all the facts are known. The adoption of this course will not usually increase the time or expense involved as all or most of the evidence will be common to both claims. Even when the full facts are known and a decision has been made as to the true basis of claim, if there is any chance of this Court taking a different view on appeal, the claim which is considered inappropriate should be dismissed rather than withdrawn, thus allowing this Court to restore it if necessary. In all circumstances industrial tribunals should make the widest use of their powers to allow amendment of claims and to extend time limits in order to ensure that justice is done not only to the applicant, but to the respondent, who must always be granted any adjournment necessary to enable him to answer a new basis of claim which emerges at a late stage."

[1] (1973), 8 I.T.R. 77 N.I.R.C. at p. 86. Upheld on appeal (1974), 9 I.T.R. 379, C.A.

The tribunals will not entertain further applications amounting to a challenge to a previous decision. The parties cannot test a previous decision otherwise than by way of appeal.[1] Industrial tribunals will not hear applications where it has been determined that they fall outside their jurisdiction.[2]

[1] *Curtis* v. *James Paterson (Darlington) Ltd.,* (1974), 9 I.T.R. 231, N.I.R.C. A tribunal can review its decision; see p. 414, below.

[2] See for example: *Haydon* v. *South Eastern District of the Workers Education Association,* (1972), 7 I.T.R. 318, T (premature); *Tostevin* v. *News of the World, Ltd. and National Society of Operative Printers, Graphical and Media Personnel,* (1972), 7 I.T.R. 444, T (no jurisdiction as to breach of contract); *Simmons* v. *Tom Garner Motors, Ltd.,* (1972), 7 I.T.R. 246, T (clause for pay).

Applications should be sent to the Secretary of Tribunals at the Central Office of Industrial Tribunals, 93, Ebury Bridge Road, London, SW1W 8RE in England, or the Secretary, Central Office of Industrial Tribunals (Scotland), St. Andrew House, 141, West Nile Street, Glasgow G1 2RU, if the matter to which the complaint relates arose in Scotland.[1]

[1] So far as proceedings discussed in this book are concerned there is jurisdiction under the Industrial Relations (Labour Relations) Regulations 1974 where:

"(a) the respondent or one of the respondents resides or carries on business in England or Wales; or

(b) had the remedy been by way of action in the county court, the cause of action would have arisen wholly or in part in England or Wales; or

(c) the proceedings are to determine a question which has been referred to the tribunal by a court in England or Wales;" reg 3.

If the Secretary of Tribunals is of the opinion that the originating application does not seek, or the facts cannot entitle the applicant to, relief which can be granted by the industrial tribunals he can give notice of this to the applicant giving his reasons for his decision, informing the applicant that the application will not be registered unless he states in writing that he wishes to proceed with it.[1] If no such notice is forthcoming then the application will not be proceeded with by the industrial tribunal but this will not prejudice any other application made by the applicant.[2]

The better view is that a tribunal will not entertain an academic or hypothetical application where there is no dispute between the parties.[3]

An originating application is presented when it is received by the Central Office of Industrial Tribunals.[4] If the Central Office is closed when the time for presenting an originating application expires the term is extended to the next day on which the Office is open.[5]

[1] Rule 1 (2).

[2] Rule 1 (3) and (4).

[3] *Secretary of State for Employment* v. *Nortons (Cardiff), Ltd.,* (1970), 5 I.T.R. 136, T. and N.I.R.C.

[4] In *Bengey* v. *North Devon District Council,* [1976] Law Soc. Gaz. 615, E.A.T. it was held that an application was presented when it was received and accepted by an Assistant Secretary of Tribunals in a regional office.

[5] *Anglo-Continental School of English (Bournemouth), Ltd.* v. *Gardiner,* (1973), 8 I.T.R. 251, N.I.R.C.

The Secretary of Tribunals will deal with the originating application in accordance with rule 2. He enters particulars in the Register and gives the originating application a number, sends a copy (usually a photographic copy) to the respondent and informs the parties of the case number and address to which further correspondence to the Secretary of Tribunals may be sent. The notice to the respondent is accompanied by information as to the means and time for entry of appearances.[1] At the same time, in redundancy cases, a copy of the application is sent to the Secretary of State for Employment[2] and in all cases under the provisions of any enactment providing for conciliation to the Advisory Conciliation and Arbitration Service.[3] Copies of all documents and notices arising later in the proceedings are also sent to the Secretary of State for Employment or the appropriate conciliation officer as the case may be.[4]

[1] Rule 2 (1). The Secretary of Tribunals also notifies the parties that in all cases under the provisions of any enactment providing for conciliation the services of a conciliation officer are available to them.

[2] Rule 2 (2).

[3] Rule 2 (4).

[4] Rules 2 (2) and 2 (4), respectively.

## APPEARANCE BY THE RESPONDENT [1]

The respondent should within 14 days of receiving the copy of the originating application enter an appearance to the proceedings by sending to the Secretary of Tribunals written notice of appearance setting out his full name and address, stating whether or not he intends to resist the application and, if so, upon what grounds. On receipt of the appearance the Secretary of Tribunals forthwith sends a copy to any other party to the proceedings. Unless an extension of time in which to enter the appearance is granted, the respondent who does not enter an appearance in the time cannot take any part in the proceedings otherwise than to apply for such extension and to be called as a witness by another person. He can of course apply for review of a decision by the Tribunal on the grounds that he did not receive notice of the proceedings leading to the decision.[2]

[1] Rule 3.

[2] Rules 3 (2) (iv) and 9 (1) (*b*). Copies of the documents are also sent to the Secretary of State or conciliation officer if appropriate.

Power is given to the tribunal to extend the time in which an appearance may be entered[1] and if a notice of appearance is sent to the Secretary of Tribunals out of time it is deemed to include an application for such an extension. If the industrial tribunal grants the extension it should send a copy of the appearance to the other parties to the proceedings and it should not refuse an extension of time unless it has given the person seeking to enter the appearance an opportunity to show reason why the extension of time should be granted.[2] An application for extension of time can be made both before and after the time limit in which to enter the appearance has gone by. In a case where the notice of appearance did not raise the issue of the applicants capability although the respondents attempted to prove to the tribunal that the applicant's employment was terminated because of his lack of capability the National Industrial Relations Court found that the applicant had not been prejudiced and so did not remit the case to the tribunal.[3] The Chairman should, in an appropriate case, give the applicant the opportunity to call further witnesses or evidence.[4] In such instances it may be that an adjournment will be necessary for the applicant to consider the new arguments being advanced by the respondents and make appropriate arrangements for further evidence. Although the industrial tribunals frequently, in the interests of justice, are prepared to allow appearances to be entered out of time their patience is not unending. A Birmingham tribunal had to consider whether to extend the time to allow an appearance entered over 60 days after the receipt by the respondent of the originating application. In view of the explanations or excuses offered in the case the tribunal considered it not to be reasonable to extend the limit in the circumstances.[5]

[1] Rule 12 (1).
[2] Rule 3 (3).
[3] *Dean* v. *Polytechnic of North London,* (1973), 8 I.T.R. 526, N.I.R.C.
[4] *Ibid.*, at p. 529.
[5] *Cook* v. *Pardor Engineering Co., Ltd.,* (1975), 10 I.T.R. 28, T. See also *Ryan Plant Ltd.* v. *Price and Secretary of State for Employment.* [1976] I.R.L.R. 25, D.C. where in a situation where there were many applications to the tribunal extension of time to enter an appearance was granted in some cases only.

## INTERLOCUTORY MATTERS

Industrial tribunals have power, on the application of a party, or the Secretary of State (whether or not a party) to require another party to furnish further particulars of the grounds on which he relies[1] and of any facts or contentions relevant thereto, to grant discovery and inspection of documents as may be granted by a County Court and to require the attendance of any person (including a party to the proceedings) as a witness or require the production of any document relating to the matters to be determined, wherever such witness may be within Great Britain.[2] An industrial tribunal, if it thinks fit, may require the party applying for an order to give notice of the application to the other party or parties. The notice shall give particulars of the time by which and an address at which objections may be lodged if so specified by the tribunal.

---

[1] In *White* v. *University of Manchester,* [1976] I.R.L.R. 218, E.A.T. it was held that an employee who had applied should have been granted an order for further and better particulars to enable her to know the details of the case she had to meet with sufficient particularity to enable her to prepare an answer.

[2] Rule 4 (1).

If after an order for further particulars has been made it is not complied with a tribunal may either before or at the hearing dismiss the application or, as the case may be, strike out the whole or part of the notice of appearance, and where appropriate, direct that the respondents be debarred from defending altogether. The practice of the tribunals is where it appears appropriate to invite the party from whom the particulars have been requested to provide them voluntarily before making an order and this approach is also often used when an application is made for a witness order and orders for discovery or the production of documents. In *Copson* v. *Eversure Accessories, Ltd.,*[1] the National Industrial Relations Court said that industrial tribunals should be vigilant to ensure the parties are aware of these powers in appropriate cases and in such circumstances tribunals should take the initiative by telling parties that they are entitled to apply for orders. In *Dada* v. *Metal Box Co., Ltd.*[2] the National Industrial Relations Court considered the circumstances in which industrial tribunals should issue witness orders. Tribunals no longer have jurisdiction to hear claims such as that forming the substance of Mr. Dada's application, but Sir JOHN DONALDSON delivering the judgment of the Court gave the following statement of matters to be considered by industrial tribunals when considering an application for a witness order.

"We are quite clear that tribunals have a discretion in deciding whether or not to issue witness orders. There is no automatic right to witness orders. But that discretion must be exercised judicially and it must be exercised with due regard to the fact that a tribunal is dealing with litigants in person who may not have the benefit of any advice.

It seems to us that there are only two matters of which tribunals should be satisfied before they issue a witness order. The first is that the witness *prima facie* can give evidence which is relevant to issues in dispute. For that purpose they will no doubt wish to ask the applicant what evidence can be given by the person who is the proposed subject of the witness order. We do not suggest that the tribunal should ask the applicant to give a full proof of that evidence, but applicants should indicate the subject matter of the evidence and show the extent to which it is relevant. The second matter of which the tribunal should be satisfied is that it is necessary to issue a witness order. In the present case the tribunal seems to have taken the view that it would be wrong ... to issue a witness order, unless they could be satisfied that the person concerned was unwilling to attend voluntarily. We think that this policy is erroneous to the point of amounting to an error of law.

The necessity for issuing a witness order can arise in a number of ways. We agree that witnesses should always be invited to attend by the applicant before he applies for witness orders. If they agree to attend and the applicant is quite satisfied that they will attend, then it is unnecessary to issue witness orders. If in such circumstances he asks for an order, it should be refused. But there are a number of other cases which can arise. A witness may not reply to the request for an undertaking that he will attend. In those circumstances it may be necessary to issue such an order. He may refuse, in which case no problem arises for a witness order is clearly needed. Again, he may equivocate or give an answer which at any rate leaves the applicant in reasonable doubt whether the witness will attend in the absence of such an order. In such circumstances it will, of course, be a matter for the judgment of the tribunal, but we should not be in the least surprised if the tribunal thought it proper to issue a witness order. Finally, although not exclusively (because these problems arise in many shapes, forms and sizes), there is the case of the witness who says, "Certainly I will come and give evidence, but it would be very much easier for me to come if I had a witness order requiring me to come." That situation can arise if an employer is unwilling to release a witness. Again that would be a reason for granting a witness order. We do not seek in any way to fetter the discretion of tribunals. What we are saying is that tribunals should be satisfied that the witness can give relevant evidence and that it is necessary to issue a witness order. But if they are satisfied on both those matters they ought to issue such an order."

¹[1974] I.C.R. 636, N.I.R.C.
²(1974), 9 I.T.R. 390, N.I.R.C.

In *H.G.S., Ltd.* v. *Wilcox*¹ a case was remitted to a new tribunal so that a new chairman could decide whether to make a witness order directed to a third party enabling documentary evidence required by an applicant to be made available at a tribunal hearing when the chairman who had made the decision not to make the order had seen a letter prejudicial to the applicant's case.

¹[1976] I.R.L.R. 222, C.A.

When an order granting discovery, or inspection of documents, or requiring the attendance of a witness, or production of documents, has been made on an *ex parte* application the party or person to whom the order has been directed may apply to the tribunal requesting that it be varied or set aside. Notice of such application should be given to the person on whose application the order was made. The application will not be entertained in a case where a time limit has been appointed in respect of the requirement unless it is made before that time, or as the case may be, the expiration of the time so appointed.¹

¹ Rule 4 (3).

The order for discovery, inspection of documents, ordering the attendance of a witness, or production of documents, should contain a reference to the fact that under the Trade Union and Labour Relations Act 1974, Schedule 1, Part III, paragraph 21 (6) any person who without reasonable excuse fails to comply with any such request shall be liable on summary conviction to a fine not exceeding £100.¹

¹ Rule 4 (4).

The President of Industrial Tribunals or the nominated chairman fixes the date, time and place of the hearing and not less than 14 days before the hearing date the Secretary of Tribunals should send to each party entitled to receive the same notice of the hearing which contains an explanatory memorandum as to attendance at the hearing bringing witnesses and other matters.[1] It is possible for the parties to consent to a hearing being held at short notice.

[1] Rule 5 (1). The President has expressed the need for speed in bringing matters to hearing before industrial tribunals. He states that parties and their advisers "should be ready to attend a hearing at any time after the expiry of five weeks after the application was presented or three weeks after the Notice of Appearance was entered"; Practice Note, July, 1976.

Industrial tribunals can, on application, grant extensions to time limits imposed by the Rules, subject as above, both before and after the time has passed.[1] If an extension of time is granted notice is given to the parties. A party to proceedings, or in redundancy cases, the Secretary of State for Employment, can apply at any time to the tribunal for directions on any matter arising in connection with proceedings.[2] The application may be made by sending to the Secretary of Tribunals a notice stating the title of the proceedings and setting out the grounds of the application.

[1] Rule 12 (1).
[2] Rule 12 (2).

An industrial tribunal may upon application of any person, or of its own motion direct that any person appearing to the tribunal to be directly interested in the subject of the originating application be added as a respondent and give such consequential direction as it considers necessary.[1] There is a similar power, exercised in the same way, to dismiss for the proceeding a person who appears to the tribunal not to have been, or to have ceased to be, directly interested in the subject of the originating application.[2] Where there are numerous persons having the same interest in an originating application one or more of them may be cited as the person or persons against whom relief is sought and may be authorised by the tribunal whether before, or at, the hearing to defend on behalf of all the persons so interested.[3]

[1] Rule 13 (1).
[2] Rule 13 (2).
[3] Rule 13 (3).

Notices which are in writing are directed to parties at the

addresses given by them for service on the originating application, or notice of appearance, or if no address is so specified the last known address, place of business in the United Kingdom, or if a corporate body the corporation's registered or principal office.[1] A party may by notice in writing to the Secretary of Tribunal and to the other party change his address for service.[2] Where a document is not delivered, the recorded delivery postal service is used if a second set of documents or notices is sent to a party who has not entered an appearance.[3] If for any sufficient reason service of any document or notice cannot be so effected the President of Industrial Tribunals or a nominated chairman may make an order for substituted service in such manner as he may deem fit and such service shall have the same effect as service previously prescribed.[4]

[1] Rule 14 (1) (*e*).
[2] Rule 14 (2).
[3] Rule 14 (3).
[4] Rule 14 (4).

It has been seen that industrial tribunals have power to extend time limits (subject to the limitations set out above as to the extension of time for giving further particulars, granting discovery or inspection of documents) and may postpone or adjourn hearings.[1] There are most useful rules empowering the industrial tribunals to dismiss proceedings if the applicant shall at any time give notice of withdrawal[2] and permitting them to make a formal decision in accordance with a written agreement between the parties (and the Secretary of State for Employment if appropriate) as to the terms for decision.[3] At any stage of the proceedings a tribunal can order to be struck out, or amended any originating application or notice of appearance, or anything in such application or notice of appearance, on the ground that it is scandalous, frivolous or vexatious.[4] Many of the actions of industrial tribunals referred to above may be carried out by the President of Industrial Tribunals or the tribunal chairman or a nominated chairman.[5]

[1] This power is very wide (see *Jacobs* v. *Norsalta, Ltd.*, [1976] E.A.T. No. 296/76, E.A.T.) Under rule 11 (2) (*b*) (as amended) particular stress is laid on the exercise of the power to adjourn to give an opportunity for the complaint to be settled by way of conciliation and withdrawn.
[2] Rule 11 (2) (*c*)
[3] Rule 11 (2) (*d*).
[4] Rule 11 (2) (*e*).
[5] Rule 11 (4).

## THE HEARING

Hearings before industrial tribunals take place in public, unless in the opinion of the tribunal a private hearing would be appropriate for the purpose of hearing evidence which relates to matters of such a nature that it would be against the interests of national security to allow the evidence to be given in public, or for hearing evidence from any person which in the opinion of the tribunal is likely to consist of:

    (a) information which he could not disclose without contravening a prohibition imposed by or under any enactment; or

    (b) any information which has been communicated to him in confidence, or which he has otherwise obtained in consequence of the confidence reposed in him by another person; or

    (c) information the disclosure of which would cause substantial injury to the interests of any undertaking of his or any undertaking in which he works for reasons other than its effect on negotiations with respect to any of the matters mentioned in the Trade Union and Labour Relations Act 1974, section 29 (1).[1]

[1] Rule 6 (1) as amended by the Industrial Tribunals (Labour Relations) (Amendment) Regulations 1976, S.I. 1976 No. 661. The Trade Union and Labour Relations Act 1974, s. 29 (1) gives the meaning of the words "trade dispute".

In a case where Rule 6 (1) applies a member of the Council of Tribunals is entitled to attend in his official capacity.

Hearings usually take the form of oral hearings but a party who desires to submit representations in writing for consideration at the hearing may do so, provided that he sends such representations to the Secretary of Tribunals not less than seven days before the hearing at the same time sending a copy or copies to the other parties and where appropriate, to the Secretary of State for Employment.[1] If a party has failed to attend or be represented at the hearing (whether or not he has sent any written representations) the contents of his originating application or, as the case may be, or his entry of appearance may be treated by the tribunal as representations in writing. The representations contemplated by Rule 6 (3) are those given in place of evidence on oath. The Rule does not include a case where a witness who was sworn reads from his proof of evidence.[2] In *Hemus* v. *Robert Wilkes, Ltd.*,[3] a tribunal sitting in Birmingham had to consider whether affidavit evidence of persons not present at the hearing served on the applicant and the tribunal only two days prior to the hearing should be admitted in evidence where counsel for the respondents who had produced the affidavits, stated that in no circumstances would his clients call the witnesses to give evidence. After referring to the court rules applicable in such circumstances the tribunal decided that the affidavits should not be admitted since the applicant's counsel *bona fide* wanted to cross examine the witnesses but would have no opportunity to do so. The tribunal would not treat the affidavits as written representations because they were not submitted in time, but it did not make a ruling whether they had been submitted in time they would have been admissible even though not representations of parties to the proceedings.

[1] Rule 6 (3).
[2] *Hardisty* v. *Lowton Contruction Group, Ltd.*, (1973), 8 I.T.R. 603, N.I.R.C.
[3] (1974), 9 I.T.R. 248, T.

At the hearing those entitled to be present may appear in person, be represented by counsel, solicitor, representative of trade union or employers association, or any other person whom he desires to represent him.[1] The Secretary of State for Employment, if he so elects, is entitled to appear as if he were a party and be heard at any hearing on, or in connection with, an originating application in proceedings which may involve payments out of the Redundancy Fund under the provisions of any enactment.[2] Those entitled to appear may make an opening statement, give evidence, call and cross examine witnesses, and address the tribunal.[3] The tribunal may require witnesses to give evidence on oath or affirmation and administer such oath or affirmation.[4] If a party fails to appear or to be represented at the time the day is fixed for the hearing the tribunal may dispose of the application in the absence of that party or may adjourn the hearing to a later date. If the absent party has made written representations then these will be considered by the tribunal.[5]

[1] Rule 6 (6).
[2] Rule 6 (5) as substituted by the Industrial Tribunal (Labour Relations) (Amendment) Regulations 1976, S.I. 1976 No. 661, reg. 4.
[3] Rule 7 (1).
[4] Rule 7 (3).
[5] Rule 7 (2).

The hearing is accusatory and not inquisitorial. The tribunal has no duty to ensure that all the relevant evidence is before it but it is for the parties to present their cases to the tribunal.[1] The tribunal will however assist the parties in presenting their cases particularly where they are not represented or are manifestly unconversed in the legal procedure before a tribunal.[2]

[1] *Bagga* v. *Heavy Electricals (India), Ltd.,* (1972), 7 I.T.R. 70, N.I.R.C.
[2] *Craig* v. *British Railways (Scottish Region),* (1973), 8 I.T.R. 636, N.I.R.C.

Where at the hearing a party is taken by surprise, for instance because he has been mislead by a conciliation officer into believing that the case will not proceed,[1] or because the other party seeks to rely on grounds which were not referred to in the originating application or notice of appearance, the tribunal may decide that it is appropriate to grant an adjournment to reconsider the case in the light of the new circumstances and to allow the party taken by surprise to prepare his case accordingly. In *Dean* v. *Polytechnic of North London,*[2] Sir JOHN DONALDSON said "It is of the greatest importance that parties to proceedings before courts or tribunals should have the fullest opportunity of presenting their cases. If, due to the necessary informality of the proceedings, they are in any way taken by surprise they should be offered the opportunity of calling or themselves giving further evidence and if there is any need for an adjournment it should be granted without hesitation."

[1] *Berkeley Garage (Southampton), Ltd.* v. *Edmunds,* (1975), 10 I.T.R. 70. D.C.
[2] (1973), 8 I.T.R. 526, N.I.R.C.

The usual procedure is for the tribunal to call upon the person on whom the burden of proof lies to present his case first. Thus in a case of an application alleging unfair dismissal where dismissal is accepted as having taken place by the respondent employers, it is for them to present their case first and to put forward the grounds on which they allege justify the dismissal.[1] Although, as we have seen the tribunal has power to admit written representations the best evidence is given on oath. Tribunals try to adopt a flexible and informal approach and so do not apply the usual rules of evidence in every case. Parties entitled to take part in the hearing have the right to cross-examine witnesses called by the other parties or party.[2]

[1] *Gill* v. *Harold Andrews Sheepbridge, Ltd.,* (1974), 9 I.T.R. 219, N.I.R.C.

² *McBride* v. *British Railways Board*, (1972), 7 I.T.R. 84, N.I.R.C.; see also *Vickers* v. *Hudson Bros. (Middlesbrough) Ltd.*, (1970), 5 I.T.R. 259, D.C.

Occasionally tribunals are aware that there is more than one application against the same respondents and there is an inclination to hear both cases together on the grounds of economy. Such an approach should however be used with the greatest caution. *Strowger* v. *David Rosenfield, Ltd.*¹ was such a case where the tribunal ordered that the evidence of the second applicant be given after the conclusion of the evidence of the first and before evidence given on behalf of the respondent. The National Industrial Relations Court held that the tribunal had no power to make such an order. Sir JOHN BRIGHTMAN giving judgment said that there would have been no objection to hearing the two cases consecutively and the tribunal giving its decision in both cases after both cases had been closed, nor would it have been objectionable if after the close of the first applicant's case the second applicant's case was commenced and following the conclusion of the second applicant's evidence his representative had been invited to cross-examine the respondent's witnesses on the basis that both sides would agree that the evidence-in-chief given on the first application by the employer should be read into the second application so as to avoid repetition.²

¹ (1972), 7 I.T.R. 375, N.I.R.C.
² But see *Green* v. *Southampton Corporation*, [1973] I.C.R. 153, N.I.R.C. (husband and wife superintendent and matron of boys' home—tribunal *held* to be right to hear both cases together but should consider each separately). When several applications are dealt with together it is essential that in coming to a decision in an individual's case that the position of each employee is considered separately taking into account any peculiarities of his case; *John Fowler (Don Foundry), Ltd.* v. *Parkin*, [1975] I.R.L.R. 89, D.C.

Anything communicated to a conciliation officer designated by the Advisory Conciliation and Arbitration Service in connection with the performance of his function in endeavouring to promote a settlement of an issue which is being considered by an industrial tribunal is not admissible in any proceedings before the industrial tribunal except with the consent of the person who communicated it to that officer.¹ A similar provision was included in the Industrial Relations Act 1971 and it was considered by the National Industrial Relations Court in *M. and W. Grazebrook, Ltd.* v. *Wallens*.² Sir JOHN DONALDSON who delivered the judgment of the Court, pointed out that the provision was not intended to render inadmissible evidence which could have been given if there had been no communication to the conciliation officer. Documents passing between parties and those representing them and conciliation officers relating to proceedings before industrial tribunals pose a special problem and their admissibility depends upon rules of privilege established in the interests of the administration of justice. The privilege is however limited. "It exists only in relation to communications with an actual view to the litigation in hand and the mode of conduct of it. It does not exist in relation to the situation at the time when the matters complained of were arising."[3] The privilege extends to any document which was prepared solely for the purpose of communication to a conciliation officer whether in connection with his function as such or more generally with a view to achieving a settlement of the subject matter of proceedings before the tribunal. "The basis of this privilege (which extends to 'without prejudice' communications between parties or in the field of family law, to communications through marriage guidance counsellors, probation officers and others) is the public interest in achieving an agreed settlement of disputes".

[1] Trade Union and Labour Relations Act 1974, Sch. 1, para. 26 (5) (unfair dismissal); Sex Discrimination Act 1975, s. 64 (4) (Equal Pay Act 1970 and Sex Discrimination Act 1975); Employment Protection Act 1975, s. 108 (7) (rights given by the provisions set out in s. 108 (2) of that Act and any further provisions directed to be added by order of the Secretary of State under s. 108 (8)).

[2] (1973), 8 I.T.R. 258, N.I.R.C.
[3] At p. 261.

Within reasonable limits the parties before the tribunal and those representing them may present their cases as they wish but a strange situation arose before the tribunal in *Barnes* v. *B.P.C. (Business Forms), Ltd.*[1] For reasons of business efficacy counsel for the respondents asked the chairman of the tribunal hearing a case if certain witnesses who were employees of the respondents and were attending the hearing in response to witness orders could be called prior to the cross-examination of the applicant. The applicant's solicitor objected to this course of action but the chairman directed that it should take place and it did. On appeal PHILLIPS, J., in the Queens Bench Division although describing the action as unfortunate, thought that in the case before him it had worked no injustice and so found against the appellants. In view of the complex nature of the remedies available before industrial tribunals and their factual bases tribunals often determine the issue of liability separately from compensation as a preliminary matter and then examine the remedies to be granted if necessary.[2] When dealing with involved cases the hearing may take several days and in such instances the tribunal should if possible arrange for consecutive hearings take place to avoid difficulties in recalling evidence occasioned by long adjournments.[3] In practice this may not be easy to arrange since the lay members of tribunals are always part-time.

[1] (1976) 1 All E.R. 237; (1975) 1 W.L.R. 1565, D.C.
[2] See *Copson* v. *Eversure Accessories, Ltd.*, (1974), 9 I.T.R. 406, N.I.R.C.
[3] See *Barnes'* case, above.

The chairman of the tribunal should take a note of the substance of the evidence which is placed before it. He is not obliged to write down every word of evidence but justice does require that in appropriate cases an appellant should be able to refer to the evidence which was given to the tribunal. In suitable cases where an applicant or respondent can demonstrate that he has need for the notes for the purposes of considering an appeal the chairman should co-operate and provide a copy of them.[1] The practice of supplying notes of evidence was described by PHILLIPS, J., in *Thomas* v. *Aluminium Platers (Leeds) Ltd.*,[2] as being of "the greatest possible assistance" to appellate bodies. Where there is a conflict between the chairman's notes of evidence and the findings of fact in the formal reasons given by the tribunal, the appellate court is guided by the findings of facts in the reasons, unless there are compelling circumstances which lead it to the conclusion that the reasons may inaccurately state the substance of the evidence.[3]

[1] *Archbold Freightage, Ltd.* v. *Wilson*, (1974), 9 I.T.R. 133, N.I.R.C.
[2] [1976] I.R.L.R. 23, D.C.
[3] *Ogidi-Olu* v. *Guys Hospital Board of Governors*, (1974), 9 I.T.R. 70, N.I.R.C.

It has already been mentioned[1] that on certain applications if it is shown that the action to which the complaint relates was taken for the purposes of safeguarding national security the tribunal shall dismiss the complaint. A certificate purporting to be signed by or on behalf of a Minister of the Crown certifying that the action specified was taken for the purpose of safeguarding national security or that a particular request for information could not be complied with except by disclosing information the disclosure of which would have been against the interests of national security is treated as conclusive evidence of the fact so certified.[2]

[1] See p. 281, above.
[2] Trade Union and Labour Regulations Act 1974, Sch. 1, para. 18 (unfair dismissal); Employment Protection Act 1975, s. 121 (4) (rights granted by that Act).

## COSTS

Subject to two exceptions an industrial tribunal does not normally award costs but may do so where in its opinion a party to any proceedings (and if he is the respondent, whether or not he has entered an appearance) has acted frivolously or vexatiously. In such cases the tribunal may order that the party pay to another party (or to the Secretary of State where appropriate) either a specified sum in respect of the costs incurred by him or, in default of agreement the taxed amount of those costs.[1] If costs are required by an order to be taxed, they are taxed in the county court according to such of the scales prescribed by the county court rules for proceedings in the county court as the tribunal directs.[2]

[1] Rule 10 (1).
[2] Rule 10 (4).

In *Marjoram* v. *James Kilpatrick & Son, Ltd.*,[1] costs were refused by the tribunal and the following statement was made:

"Although it would appear that the application was misconceived, we are unanimously of opinion that we cannot say that the applicant acted frivolously (or, indeed, vexatiously). We are of opinion that his application was probably made seriously and *bona fide*, but in ignorance of the operation and scope of the Redundancy Payments Act 1965. We note that the Press is present, and we hope that publicity may be given to the remarks made by the respondents' representative as to the desirability of intending applicants seeking the advice of their Union officials, where they are in a position to do so, or of officials at the [Department of Employment] in appropriate circumstances."

[1] (1966), 1 I.T.R. 564.

In *Prajapati* v. *Richard Thomas and Baldwins, Ltd.*,[1] an application for costs was refused, the decision of the industrial tribunal contains the following statement of principle:

> "We take it that an application in order to be 'frivolous' must be made with knowledge that it is doomed to failure, as a 'try on'; and that 'vexatiousness' involves the same knowledge with an added intention of putting the respondents to unjustified trouble and expense. Probably all vexatious applications would also be frivolous, but perhaps the converse would not be universally true".[2]

[1] [1966] I.T.R. 339.
[2] Other tribunal decisions on the point include:
*Smith* v. *Hoffmans of London, Ltd.*, (1966), 1 I.T.R. 413, T (application ill-advised but not "frivolous" or "vexatious").
*Rolfe* v. *Ray King Transport, Ltd.*, (1966), 1 I.T.R. 454, T (costs awarded—"vexatious" behaviour—"putting in a defence which they knew was bad and putting it in for an ulterior purpose").
*Strachan* v. *Robert Bain & Sons*, (1967), 2 I.T.R. 25, T (no relevant objections notice of appearance entered without good cause—no appearance at hearing—held to have acted "frivolously").
*Craighead* v. *Dumfries and Maxwelltown Co-operative Society, Ltd.*, (1967), 2 I.T.R. 125, T (costs ordered against applicant in respect of hearing adjourned owing to failure to attend).
*Beaton* v. *Anglo-Continental School of English, Ltd.*, [1972] I.R.L.R. 42, T (costs awarded against employer). Compare *Durrant* v. *Baker Oils (U.K.) Ltd.*, [1974] I.R.L.R. 290, T (employer's conduct not vexatious).

The first exception is where on the application of a party to the proceedings the tribunal has postponed the day or time fixed for the hearing or has adjourned the hearing, when the tribunal may order costs or allowances against, or in favour of, that party.[1] Such an award may be made if irrespective of any question whether the party acted "frivolously or vexatiously" as is also the case when the second exception applies. This is where a postponement or adjournment of a hearing has been caused by the respondent when (in accordance with the Trade Union and Labour Relations Act 1974, Schedule 1, paragraph 21 (3A) on a complaint of unfair dismissal) the employee has expressed a wish to be reinstated or re-engaged which was communicated to the employer at least seven days before the hearing of the complaint, or the proceedings arise out of the employer's failure to permit the employee to return to work after an absence due to pregnancy or confinement, and the tribunal will in the absence of some special reason for failure to produce reasonable evidence as to the availability of the job from which the employee was dismissed, or as the case may be, which she held before her absence, or a comparable or suitable employment, make orders against the employer as respect any costs which occurred or any allowances paid as a result of the postponement or adjournment.[2]

[1] Rule 10 (2) (*a*) as substituted by the Industrial Tribunals (Labour Relations) (Amendment) Regulations 1976, reg. 6.
[2] Rule 10 (2) (*b*), as so substituted. See the Trade Union and Labour Relations Act 1974, Sch. 1, para. 21 (3A) inserted by Employment Protection Act 1975, Sch. 16, Part III, para. 19.

Subsistence allowances may be paid to a party, witnesses and the person representing a party, unless he is a full-time officer of a workers or employers association, or a solicitor or barrister. In addition allowances for loss of earnings occasioned by attendance at the tribunal may be granted. The allowances vary from time to time and details can be obtained from the local tribunal office. The tribunal may refuse the payment of an allowance if it considers the attendance did not reasonably justify or the applicant acted frivolously or vexatiously.[1]

[1] An appeal tribunal is unlikely to overrule a decision of an industrial tribunal as to costs and allowances since the matter being discretionary the appeal will only succeed if it can be shown that the industrial tribunal misdirected itself as to the law, *E. T. Marler* v. *Robertson*, [1974] I.C.R. 72, N.I.R.C.

## DEATH OF A PARTY

Where an employee has died tribunal proceedings may be instituted or continued by his personal representative under the provisions of the Redundancy Payments Act 1965, on a complaint of unfair dismissal and under the provisions of the Employment Protection Act 1975 conferring rights on employees. If there is no personal representative then the proceedings may be instituted or continued on behalf of the estate of the deceased employee by such person as the industrial tribunal may appoint being either a person authorised by the employee to act in connection with the proceedings before the employee's death or the widower, widow, child, father, mother, brother or sister of the deceased employee.[1] The award in these cases is made by the industrial tribunal in favour of the estate, or as the case may be, in favour of the employee who has since died, and the person appointed by the tribunal may enforce such award on behalf of the estate without his obtaining letters of administration or probate of any will and the receipt of that person shall be a sufficient discharge to the employer for any sum payable to the estate under the award.[2] Where there is no person so appointed the award made in favour of the estate, or in favour of an employee who has since died, is enforceable on behalf of the estate by the person to whom a grant of letters of administration or probate has been made in respect of that estate. The personal representative or appointed person is put in a similar position to the applicant in proceedings where death is not involved.[3]

[1] Redundancy Payments Act 1965, Sch. 4, para 21A (as inserted by the Employment Protection Act 1975, Sch. 16, Part I, para, 34)—redundancy payments; Employment Protection Act 1975, Sch. 12—unfair dismissal and the provisions of the Employment Protection Act 1975 conferring rights on employees).

[2] Industrial Tribunals Awards (Enforcement in case of Death) Regulations 1976, S.I. 1976 No. 663, made pursuant to the Employment Protection Act 1975, Sch. 12, para. 3 (2) and Redundancy Payments Act 1965, Sch. 4. para. 21A (2).

[3] Employment Protection Act 1975, Sch. 12, para. 4 (1).

The personal representative of a deceased employer may defend proceedings in a similar way but there is no corresponding provision for appointment by the tribunal of a person to act on behalf of the deceased's estate. Where under the provisions a deceased employer is liable to pay an amount and that liability has not accrued before the death of the employer in question it should be treated for all purposes as if it was a liability of the deceased employer which accrued immediately before the death.[1]

If a protective award is made pursuant to the Employment Protection Act 1975, section 101 and an employee of a description to which the award relates dies during the protected period the award shall be limited in his case as if it specified a protected period of such length as to end on the date of his death.[2]

There are specific provisions relating to death in situations of redundancy and unfair dismissal and they are discussed above.[3]

[1] Redundancy Payments Act 1965, Sch. 4, para. 15—redundancy payments; the Employment Protection Act 1975, Sch. 12, para. 6—unfair dismissal and the provisions of the Employment Protection Act 1975 conferring rights on employees.

[2] Employment Protection Act 1975, Sch. 12, para. 7. See p. 266, above.

[3] For redundancy, see p. 255, above and unfair dismissal, p. 366, above.

## THE DECISION

The decision may be by a majority or if there are only two members of the industrial tribunal the chairman has a casting vote.[1] The decision may be given orally at the hearing or can be reserved, but in either case it is recorded in a document which is signed by the chairman and contains reasons for the decision. The clerk of the tribunal sends the signed decision and reasons to the Secretary of Tribunals who enters it in the Register and sends copies to the parties and to any other person who being entitled to appear, did appear.[2] The reasons are omitted from the Register in any case where the evidence was heard in private and the tribunal so directs and in that event a specification of the reasons should be sent to the parties and to any superior court in any proceedings relating to such decision together with the copy of the entry. Tribunals should give full reasons for each part of their decision so that the parties can know why the tribunal has decided as it has and since an appeal lies on a point of law only it is desirable that an appellate body in reviewing a tribunal's decision should be able to determine upon what grounds the decision was arrived at.[3]

[1] Rule 8.
[2] Copies are also sent to the Equal Opportunities Commission in all cases under the Equal Pay Act 1970 and the Sex Discrimination Act 1975; rule 14 (6).
[3] See for example *Cooper* v. *British Steel Corporation*, (1975), 10 I.T.R. 133, D.C.; *Beardmore* v. *Westinghouse Brake and Signal Co., Ltd.*, [1975] I.R.L.R. 310, D.C.

The absence of evidence to support a finding of fact is an error of law as is a conclusion which no tribunal properly directing itself could reach on the basis of the evidence which had been given to and accepted by them. Thus a tribunal should in its reasons state what evidence it does or does not accept for the statement of reasons must provide both parties with the material which would enable them to know whether or not the tribunal has made an error of law in making its decision.[1]

[1] *Alexander Machinery (Dudley) Ltd.* v. *Crabtree*, (1974), 9 I.T.R. 182, N.I.R.C. See also *Norton Tool Co., Ltd.* v. *Tewson*, [1973] 1 All E.R. 183; [1973] 1 W.L.R. 45, N.I.R.C. and the many cases following it, for instance, *Blackwell* v. *G.E.C. Elliot Process Automation, Ltd.*, [1976] I.R.L.R. 144, E.A.T., *British Olivetti, Ltd.*, v. *Kay*, [1975] I.R.L.R. 29, D.C.

## REVIEW

The Industrial Tribunals (Industrial Relations etc.) Regulations 1972 were the first regulations which expressly gave industrial tribunals the right to review their decisions and the rule governing this right is now contained in the Industrial Tribunals (Labour Relations) Regulations 1974.[1] A tribunal has power to review, revoke or vary, by certificate under the chairman's hand, any of its decisions in a case in which a county court has power to order a new trial on grounds that:

"(a) the decision was wrongly made as a result of an error on the part of tribunal staff; or

(b) a party did not receive notice of the proceedings leading to the decision; or

(c) the decision was made in the absence of a party or a person entitled to be heard; or

(d) new evidence has become available since the making of the decision provided that its existence could not have been reasonably known of or foreseen; or

(e) the interests of justice require such a review."

[1] Rule 9 (1). Before the express power of review was given similar operations were carried out by tribunals on rare occasions, see for instance *Taylor* v. *France,* (1967), 2 I.T.R. 661, T (notice not sent); *Summers* v. *British Railways Board,* (1969), 4 I.T.R. 395, T (power to vary decision before entered in the Register).

An application for review may be refused by the President of Industrial Tribunals or the chairman of the tribunal which decided the case or a nominated chairman if in his opinion it has no reasonable prospect of success.[1] If not so refused the application is heard by the tribunal and if it is granted, the tribunal may vary or revoke the decision, or order a rehearing.[2]

[1] Rule 9 (3).
[2] Rule 9 (4).

The chairman's certificate as to revocation or variation of the tribunal's decision should be sent by the clerk of the tribunal to Secretary of Tribunals who should make such variation in the Register as is necessary, sending copies to the parties and the persons who were entitled to appear and did appear and the Equal Opportunities Commission if appropriate. The application for review may be made at the hearing but if it is not made then it should be made to the Secretary of Tribunals at any time from the date of hearing until 14 days after the date of the entry of a decision in the Register and must be in writing stating the grounds in full.[1] The industrial tribunal is empowered to extend this time limit[2] but since to do so is a discretion of the tribunal an appellate court does not have such power.[3]

[1] Rule 9 (2) as substituted by Industrial Tribunals (Labour Relations) (Amendment) Regulations 1976, S.I. 1976 No. 661, reg. 5.
[2] Rule 12.
[3] *Archbold Freightage, Ltd.* v. *Wilson,* (1974), 9 I.T.R. 133, N.I.R.C., and see also *Ryan Plant International, Ltd.* v. *Price and Secretary of State for Employment,* [1976] I.R.L.R. 25, D.C.

When making an application for review on the basis of new evidence the ordinary practice should be to submit to the tribunal the substance of the evidence which it is intended to put before the tribunal. The matter should have been investigated to the point of taking proofs and such proofs should be submitted in support of the application.[1] In *Yorkshire Engineering and Welding Development Co., Ltd.* v. *Burnham*[2] a tribunal had to consider an application for review on grounds that at the hearing the applicant had given evidence that he would only be able to earn £86.50 gross per week, whereas at the time he had already made enquiries about a post which he had subsequently taken the pay for which was greatly in excess of that sum. Sir JOHN DONALDSON delivering the decision of the National Industrial Relations Court said:[3]

"In such circumstances the test to be applied in deciding whether or not to review a decision is as follows. The tribunal must ask itself whether the forecasts which were the basis of its decision have been falsified to a sufficiently substantial extent to invalidate the assessment and whether this occurred so soon after the decision, that a review was necessary in the interests of justice. There must be some finality in these matters. But at the same time, if very shortly after a tribunal has reached a decision it comes to its notice, upon an application for review, that the facts are so different from those which it had assumed, that the whole substratum of its award has gone, then, subject to such considerations as whether the party applying could have obtained that evidence before the hearing, there is manifestly a case for review.

As the interval of time between the original decision and

the application lengthens, it becomes more and more difficult to justify a review, for two reasons: first, because of the need for certainty and finality in litigation, and second, because any tribunal which is looking into the future should recognise that the further into the future it looks, the more impossible it is to be accurate. Longer term inaccuracies do not therefore strike at the foundations of the tribunal's award because they will have been contemplated."

¹ *Simmons* v. *Medway Welding, Ltd.*, (1973), 8 I.T.R. 373, N.I.R.C.
² (1973), 8 I.T.R. 621, N.I.R.C.
³ At p. 625.

*Bateman* v. *British Leyland (U.K.) Ltd.*¹ concerned an applicant who at the first hearing by the industrial tribunal was awarded compensation based on an assumption that he had obtained a reasonably secure job with new employers. Unfortunately the new employers went out of business almost immediately and he lost the employment. A review was applied for on the grounds that there was new evidence not available to the tribunal. Although the event in respect of which the evidence was to be given had occurred since the hearing, the National Industrial Relations Court said that the tribunal was entitled to carry out a review. The fact that an estimate had been made as to the security of the job did not preclude such a decision. Where the facts which it is intended to put before the tribunal on review are known to the party seeking to put them forward at the time on the original hearing no review will be granted save in exceptional circumstances.² In one case an employee who was represented at the tribunal hearing by a union representative did not give a medical reason for refusing to accept alternative employment which had been offered to him.³ He did not tell his representative of his incapacity until after the hearing and a review was applied for. In giving his decision PHILLIPS, J., discussed the relationship between paragraphs 9 (1) (*d*) and (*e*)⁴ and reached the conclusion that paragraph (*d*) cannot be regarded as exhaustive of cases where the ground of the application is the desire to call fresh evidence. He said paragraph (*e*) was intended to be a residual category of case designed to confer a wide discretion on industrial tribunals but must be applied in practice with some regard to the kind of case which is intended to come within paragraph (*d*). Paragraph (*e*) exists for the case which although it may be put forward under paragraph (*d*) has in it some special additional circumstance which leads to the conclusion that justice does require a review, for instance a case where although all the evidence could be foreseen or indeed reasonably foreseen or actually known, it was for some reason or another not available. Having weighed the arguments for both sides the judge concluded that the majority of the tribunal was right in not granting a review. In giving his decision PHILLIPS, J., considered an earlier case of *Stevensons (Dyers), Ltd.* v. *Brennan*[5] which has been the subject of some adverse criticism. In that case the National Industrial Relations Court had, in a reserved decision, determined first, that the power of the review under the predecessor of rule 9 is a once and for all power and that when it has been used once it cannot be used again for a similar reason, and secondly, that in construing the rule no account is to be taken of the words "in which a county court has power to order a retrial". In the later case PHILLIPS, J., having carefully considered the matter decided reluctantly[6] to follow *Brennan's* case, although it is open to the Court of Appeal to decide that the familiar rules of practice which have been laid down over the years in the courts should be taken into account when deciding whether a decision should be reviewed.

[1] (1974), 9 I.T.R. 266, N.I.R.C.
[2] *Richler* v. *North Thames Gas Board*, (1973), 8 I.T.R. 177, N.I.R.C.
[3] *Flint* v. *Eastern Electricity Board* (1975), 10 I.T.R. 152, D.C.
[4] The judgment actually relates Industrial Tribunals (Industrial Relations, etc.) Regulations 1972, S.I. 1972 No. 38, Schedule rules 12 (*d*) and (*e*) which were in exactly the same terms.
[5] (1974), 9 I.T.R. 202, N.I.R.C.
[6] See [1975] I.C.R., at p. 401.

A review was not granted by a tribunal on the grounds that it was in the interests of justice when the solicitors acting for the respondents had by telephone requested an adjournment of the hearing without explanation only two and a half hours before it was due to take place and notwithstanding the request the hearing proceeded, when applying for review no explanation for their conduct was given.[1] Applications for review are looked at very much in the circumstances of each individual case.[2]

[1] *Pigott* v. *Sidney Jacobs (Bettan) Co., Ltd.*, (1973), 8 I.T.R. 367, T.
[2] See for example *Richler's* case, above.

An interesting situation arose on review in *Estorffe* v. *Smith*[1] an employee applied to an industrial tribunal for compensation for unfair dismissal and redundancy payment and at the first hearing was awarded compensation for unfair dismissal. A factor not brought to the tribunal's attention was that the employer employed three employees only[2] and the employer applied for a review. At the review hearing he produced his wages book to show that he had only three employees. The tribunal revoked that part of their decision awarding compensation for unfair dismissal, but having seen the rundown of staff from the wages book, also reversed its earlier decision not to award a redundancy payment and the appropriate sum was awarded to the employee. The National Industrial Relations Court said that having been asked to review the finding of unfair dismissal (but not redundancy) the tribunal did have power to review the previous decision as to redundancy as well. There was one decision, so it was said, although it dealt with two issues. The employer who appealed against the decision as reviewed did succeed however and the case was remitted for rehearing by another tribunal because the tribunal's attitude on the question of redundancy was a matter the employer had not come prepared to meet and if the tribunal intended to base an inference on the wages book he should have been given an opportunity of considering whether to call further evidence as to the reason why other employees had left.

[1] (1973), 8 I.T.R. 627, N.I.R.C.
[2] At present an employee of such an employer is excluded from the unfair dismissal provisions, see p. 281, above.

Once a tribunal has determined an application for review on one ground then it does not have power to entertain another application for review on that ground. The argument being that having granted or refused an application the tribunal is *functus officio*.[1] In exceptional circumstances however a second application for review may be favourably heard.[2]

Application for review is not as such an alternative or pre-liminary to an appeal to an appellate body[3] but if the result of the review could be to remove or alter the ground of appeal, or alter the findings of fact, the application should be dealt with before the hearing of the appeal. A tribunal may be able to review its decision even though notice of appeal has been filed.[4] An industrial tribunal would in such circumstances attempt to dispose of the application to review as speedily as possible. It should not be necessary to seek an extension of time for the appeal since it can be made at the same time as the application for review but if the tribunal does not dispose of the review quickly it could be that it would be appropriate to apply for an extension of the time in which to appeal.[5]

The better view is that the decision of a tribunal may be reviewed even though it is not possible to convene the same tribunal because, for instance, a member has reached retiring age, died or becomes ill.[6]

[1] *Stevensons (Dyers), Ltd.* v. *Brennan,* (1974), 9 I.T.R. 202, N.I.R.C.

[2] *Raybright T.V. Service, Ltd.* v. *Smith,* (1974), 9 I.T.R. 28, N.I.R.C.

[3] *Dean* v. *Polytechnic of North London,* (1973), 8 I.T.R. 526, N.I.R.C.

[4] *Dean's* case, above, but see *Simmons* v. *Medway Welding, Ltd.,* (1973), 8 I.T.R. 373, N.I.R.C.

[5] In such a case the appeal should always be made in time if at all possible.

[6] *Coates* v. *C. J. Crispin, Ltd.,* (1973), 8 I.T.R. 448, N.I.R.C. at p. 452. In this respect the decision of the tribunal in *Piggott* v. *Sidney Jacobs (Bettan) Co., Ltd.,* (1973), 8 I.T.R. 367, T, is considered to be wrongly decided.

# Chapter 10

# APPEALS FROM INDUSTRIAL TRIBUNALS

## GROUNDS OF APPEAL

Appeals lie to the Employment Appeal Tribunal on questions of law arising from any decision of, or arising in any proceedings before, an industrial tribunal under, or by virtue of:
(a) the Redundancy Payments Act 1965,
(b) the Equal Pay Act 1970,
(c) the Contracts of Employment Act 1972,
(d) the Trade Union and Labour Relations Act 1974,
(e) the Sex Discrimination Act 1975, and
(f) the Employment Protection Act 1975.

[1] Employment Protection Act 1975, s. 88 (1). For the position under the 1976 Race Relations Bill see p. 506, below.

No appeal lies except to the Employment Appeal Tribunal from any decision of an industrial tribunal under these statutes.[1] The restriction of the grounds of appeal to those raising matters of law is of immense importance. The determination of facts by the tribunal cannot be challenged on appeal and it is essential that the facts are properly presented to the tribunal at the hearing.

[1] Employment Protection Act 1975, s. 88 (5).

Whether, or not, there are points of law meriting an appeal depends upon the circumstances of each case. Deductions as to the legal effects of factual situations are matters of law.[1] If the facts found by the tribunal do not support the decision, an appeal may be satisfactorily prosecuted. A party may also appeal if he can show that the evidence was such that no reasonable tribunal could reach the tribunal's conclusion.[2] Questions as to the construction of statutes are clearly matters of law,[3] as are points touching on the construction of contracts,[4] and whether, or not, a term may be implied in the contract.[5] An error in reasoning by a tribunal has also been the subject of a successful appeal.[6]

[1] For instance, whether a period in prison frustrated an employment contract, *Hare v. Murphy Brothers, Ltd.*, [1974] 3 All E.R. 940, C.A.

[2] *O'Hara v. Fram Gerard, Ltd.*, [1973] I.R.L.R. 94, N.I.R.C.; *Hilti (Great Britain), Ltd. v. Windridge* (1974), 9 I.T.R. 197, N.I.R.C. Or if the tribunal assessed compensation at a figure unwarranted by the evidence, or failed to take into account some element of compensation which they were legally bound to take into account, *Nohar v. Granite Stone (Galloway), Ltd.* (1974), 9 I.T.R. 155, N.I.R.C.

[3] See for instance *Lord Advocate v. De Rosa*, [1974] 2 All E.R. 849; [1974] 1 W.L.R. 946, H.L.

[4] An example being *Cole v. Midland Display, Ltd.*, [1973] I.R.L.R. 62, N.I.R.C.

[5] *O'Brien v. Associated Fire Alarms, Ltd.*, [1969] 1 All E.R. 93; [1968] 1 W.L.R. 1916, C.A.

[6] *Mercia Rubber Holdings, Ltd. v. Lingwood*, [1974] I.C.R. 256, N.I.R.C.

Appeals from industrial tribunals have also taken place where there have been irregularities in the conduct of the hearing.[1] In *Mercia Rubber Mouldings, Ltd. v. Lingwood*,[2] the former employee was not given an opportunity to give evidence as to an important matter—relating to his possible contribution to the dismissal—the National Industrial Relations Court granted his appeal. In a somewhat similar case,[3] where an applicant was given no opportunity to cross-examine the respondent's witnesses the appeal court remitted the case to a tribunal for re-hearing. There was the same outcome when, on appeal, it appeared that the Chairman of the industrial tribunal had tried to combine the taking of evidence in two distinct cases when the tribunal did not have the jurisdiction to do so.[4] If there are irregularities, for instance when the Chairman wrongly instructs a party's solicitor as to the order in which to present evidence, it is likely that the Employment Appeal Tribunal will look to see if there is a real possibility of prejudice to the injured party. If not, the decision will not be over-ruled.[5] When a respondent was prevented by transport difficulties from attending the hearing, which proceeded in his absence, the Court of Session ordered that the case be re-heard.[6]

[1] It is usually alleged in such appeals that the rules of natural justice have not been complied with.

[2] [1974] I.C.R. 256, N.I.R.C.

[3] *McBride v. British Railways Board* (1972), 7 I.T.R. 84, N.I.R.C. See also *Estorffe v. Smith* (1973), 8 I.T.R. 627 N.I.R.C. and *H.G.S. v. Wilcox.* [1976] I.R.L.R. 232, C.A.

[4] *Strowger v. David Rosenfield, Ltd* (1972), 7 I.T.R. 375, N.I.R.C.

[5] *Barnes v. B.P.C. (Business Forms), Ltd*, [1976] 1 All E.R. 237, D.C.

[6] *Murrays (Turf Accountants)* v. *Laurie* (1972), 7 I.T.R. 22, C.S.; *Priddle* v. *Fisher & Sons*, [1968] 3 All E.R. 506; [1956] 1 W.L.R. 1478, D.C. See also *Taylor* v. *France* (1967), 2 I.T.R. 661, T (where an industrial tribunal set aside its own decision when the notice of hearing had not been sent to the respondents); *Berkeley Garage (Southampton), Ltd.* v. *Edmunds* (1975), 10 I.T.R. 70, D.C. (employer did not attend the hearing with witness because he was misled by an official of the Department of Employment).

New evidence will be admitted on appeal only in rare and exceptional cases.[1] For instance the National Industrial Relations Court refused to consider a letter which was not produced before the tribunal since no reasonable explanation of its non-production was given.[2] Sir JOHN DONALDSON said,[3] in that case:

"I have read that letter because we admitted it *de bene esse*, but we have come to the conclusion that it ought to form no part of the basis for our decision. On any view of the matter it was a letter of some importance to the appellant's case, and he had it at the time of the tribunal, and he did not choose to place it before the tribunal. Parties must not think that they can prosecute a case in front of the tribunal, appeal and come to this court, producing additional evidence which they could have placed in front of the tribunal, and then expect this court to allow them to re-open the case and add to the evidence. The rules applied by the courts are clear. Such evidence will only be admitted if some reasonable explanation can be produced for its not having been put before the tribunal of first instance and if the new evidence is credible, and if it would or might have had a decisive effect upon the decision.

In our judgment, this is a clear case where the appellant fails to satisfy the first head of those three requirements, in that he has offered no reasonable excuse for not having placed it before the tribunal originally. Therefore, we are not prepared to allow him to add that letter to the correspondence."

The Appeal Tribunal will not allow points which were not raised at the industrial tribunal hearing to be canvassed.[4]

[1] *Roux International, Ltd.* v. *Licudi* (1975), 10 I.T.R. 162, D.C. It is only in most unusual circumstances that new evidence will be admitted in view of the right of industrial tribunals to review their decisions, see above. See also *Hopper* v. *Feedex, Ltd.*, [1974] I.R.L.R. 99, N.I.R.C.; and *Sinclair* v. *Scottish Co-operative Wholesale Society, Ltd.* (1972), 7 I.T.R. 185, N.I.R.C. (where the case was remitted to the tribunal).

[2] *Bagga* v. *Heavy Electricals (India), Ltd.* (1972), 7 I.T.R. 70, N.I.R.C.
[3] At p. 72.
[4] *Stewart* v. *Alexander* (1969), 3 I.T.R. 234, C.S.; *Bishop* v. *John Brignell and Company (Builders), Ltd.* (1974), 9 I.T.R. 307, C.A.

In many cases which were formerly the subject of appeal, the right of review given to the industrial tribunals should be made use of. However, a review is not an alternative, or preliminary, to an appeal.[1]

[1] *Dean* v. *Polytechnic of North London* (1973), 8 I.T.R. 526, N.I.R.C.

It is possible for the supervisory jurisdiction of the High Court to be exercised with regard to industrial tribunals by use of the prerogative orders of certiorari, mandamus and prohibition.[1] Their use in relation to industrial tribunals is very rare, and in view of the comparative ease and cheapness of the system of review and appeals to the Employment Appeal Tribunal it is unlikely that there will be any increase in the frequency. It may also be possible to obtain a judical declaration with regard to proceedings before an industrial tribunal.[2]

[1] See the application for certiorari in *R.* v. *Industrial Tribunal, Ex parte George Green and Thompson, Ltd.* (1967), 2 I.T.R. 360. This is the only case of certiorari of which the editor is aware.
[2] See Whitesides and Hawker, "Industrial Tribunals", London, 1975, at p. 73.

## THE EMPLOYMENT APPEAL TRIBUNAL

The Employment Appeal Tribunal was created by the Employment Protection Act 1975.[1] It consists of a number of judges, nominated from time to time by the Lord Chancellor from judges of the High Court and Court of Appeal, it has at least one judge from the Court of Session, nominated by the Lord President of that Court, and such number of other members as may be appointed from time to time by Her Majesty the Queen, on the joint recommendation of the Lord Chancellor and the Secretary of State for Employment.[2] These members are persons who appear to the Lord Chancellor and the Secretary of State to have special knowledge, or experience, of industrial relations, either as representatives of employers, or of workers.[3] One of the judges is appointed President of the Employment Appeal Tribunal by the Lord Chancellor.[4] The first President is PHILLIPS, J., and the central office of the Tribunal is at 4 St. James' Square, London S.W.1, in England and St. Andrew's House, 141 West Nile Street, Glasgow G1 2RN, in Scotland.

[1] Section 87 (1). The Tribunal has some similarities to the defunct National Industrial Relations Court.

[2] Employment Protection Act 1975, s. 87 (2).

[3] *Ibid.*, s. 87 (3).

[4] *Ibid.*, s. 87 (4). Prior to the appointment, the Lord Chancellor consults with the Lord President of the Court of Session.

The members of the Employment Appeal Tribunal who are persons appointed on the joint recommendation of the Lord Chancellor and the Secretary of State for Employment, hold and vacate office subject to the terms of their appointment and to the provisions of the Employment Protection Act 1975, Schedule 6.[1]

They may resign at any time,[2] and if the Lord Chancellor, after consultation with the Secretary of State, is satisfied that the member has been absent from sittings of the Tribunal for a period longer than six consecutive months without the permission of the President of the Tribunal, or has become bankrupt, or made an arrangement with his creditors, or is incapacitated by physical, or mental, illness, or is otherwise unable, or unfit, to discharge the functions of a member, the Lord Chancellor may declare his office as a member of the Employment Appeal Tribunal to be vacant and shall notify the declaration in such manner as he thinks fit, and thereupon the office becomes vacant.[3]

[1] Employment Protection Act 1975, Sch. 6, para. 1.

[2] *Ibid.,* Sch. 6, para. 2.

[3] *Ibid.,* Sch. 6, para. 3 (1).

The Lord Chancellor can nominate another judge to act as President of the Tribunal in the temporary absence of the President,[1] and judges may be appointed to act in the place of judges nominated to the Employment Appeal Tribunal who are themselves temporarily absent.[2] Temporary lay members may be appointed jointly by Lord Chancellor and Secretary of State.[3]

[1] Employment Protection Act 1975, Sch. 6, para. 4.

[2] *Ibid.,* Sch. 6, para. 5. The appointment made when the judge who is absent was nominated by the Lord President of the Court of Session is made by him pursuant to Sch. 6, para. 6.

[3] *Ibid.,* Sch. 6, para. 7.

The Employment Appeal Tribunal, which came into being on 30th March 1976,[1] is a superior court of record and has an official seal which is judicially noticed.[2] Although the office of the Tribunal is at present at the above address, the Tribunal may sit at any time, and in any place, in Great Britain.[3] The President of the Employment Appeal Tribunal may direct that it sits in one, or more, divisions concurrently.[4] If the parties to proceedings consent, a case may be heard by a judge and one appointed member, but in default on such consent, proceedings before the Tribunal should be heard by a judge and either two, or four appointed members, so that in either case there are equal numbers of persons whose experience is as representatives of employers and of workers.[5]

[1] Employment Protection Act 1975 (Commencement No. 3) Order 1976, S.I. 1976 No. 321.
[2] Employment Protection Act 1975, Sch. 6, para. 10.
[3] *Ibid.*, Sch. 6, para. 12.
[4] *Ibid.*, Sch. 6, para. 13.
[5] *Ibid.*, Sch. 6, para. 14.

The Secretary of State appoints officers and staff of the Tribunal, subject to the approval of the Minister for the Civil Service as to numbers and terms and conditions of service.[1] There are provisions enabling the payment of remuneration and travelling and other allowances of the lay members[2] and for payment of pensions, allowances and gratuities due to or in respect of, them, and, in certain circumstances, for the payment of compensation when a person ceases to be a member.[3]

[1] Employment Protection Act 1975, Sch. 6, para. 22.
[2] *Ibid.*, Sch. 6, para. 23.
[3] *Ibid.*, Sch. 6, paras. 24 and 25.

The Lord Chancellor is empowered to make rules with respect to proceedings for the Employment Appeal Tribunal.[1] The Employment Appeal Tribunal Rules 1976[2] have been made by him pursuant to these powers. Subject to the rules for the time being in force the Tribunal has power to regulate its own procedure.[3]

[1] Employment Protection Act 1975, Sch. 6, para. 15. The rules are made after consultation with the Lord President of the Court of Session.
[2] S.I. 1976 No. 322.
[3] Employment Protection Act 1975, Sch. 6, para. 15 (2).

On disposing of an appeal the Employment Appeal Tribunal may exercise any power of the industrial tribunal from which the appeal was brought, or remit the case to the industrial tribunal,[1] and any decision, or award, of the Tribunal on an appeal shall have the same effect and may be enforced in the same manner as a decision, or award, of the industrial tribunal.[2] It has, in relation to the attendance and examination of witnesses, the production and inspection of documents, and all other matters incidental to its jurisdiction, the like powers, rights, privileges and authority, in England and Wales, as the High Court, and in Scotland, as the Court of Session.[3] However, no person may be punished for contempt of the Tribunal except by, or with consent of, a judge.[4] There are express provisions relating to fines for contempt.[5]

[1] Employment Protection Act 1975, Sch. 6, para. 19 (1).
[2] *Ibid.*, Sch. 6, para. 19 (2).
[3] *Ibid.*, Sch. 6, para. 20 (1).
[4] *Ibid.*, Sch. 6, para. 20 (2).
[5] *Ibid.*, Sch. 6, para. 21.

Legal aid is available for proceedings in the Employment Appeal Tribunal[1] subject to the Legal Aid (General) Regulations 1971 (as amended).[2]

[1] Legal Aid (Extension of Proceedings) Regulations 1976, S.I. 1976 No. 499.
[2] S.I. 1971 No. 62; amended by S.I. 1971 No. 1877, and the Legal Aid (General) (Amendment) Regulations 1976, S.I. 1976 No. 338.

## PROCEDURE

Appeals to the Employment Appeal Tribunal are instituted by serving on the Tribunal, within 42 days of the date on which the document recording the decision, or order, appealed from was sent to the appellant, a notice of appeal in, or substantially in, accordance with Form 1[1] set out in the Schedule to the Employment Appeal Tribunal Rules 1976.[2] When it appears to the Registrar that the grounds of appeal stated in the notice do not give the Tribunal jurisdiction, he will notify the appellant accordingly and inform him of the reasons for this opinion.[3] When notification has been given under this rule, the appellant may serve a fresh notice of appeal within the time remaining, or within 28 days from the date on which the Registrar's notification was sent to him, whichever is the longer period.[4] Subject to this, no further action will be taken on an appeal where the Registrar has notified the appellant that he is of the opinion that the grounds of appeal do not give the Tribunal jurisdiction, unless the President, or a judge, otherwise directs.[3]

[1] See p. 498, below.
[2] Employment Appeal Tribunal Rules 1976, S.I. 1976 No. 322, rule 3 (1). The Rules came into operation on 30th March 1976; *ibid.*, rule 1.
[3] *Ibid.*, rule 3 (2).
[4] *Ibid.*, rule 3 (3). Although there is power in rule 24 for time limits to be extended the National Industrial Relations Court was reluctant to do so in such circumstances and it is likely that the Employment Appeal Tribunal will adopt a similar approach. See *Marshall* v. *Harland and Wolff, Ltd.* (*No. 2*) (1972), 7 I.T.R. 150, N.I.R.C. See also *Middleton* v. *Vaux and Associated Breweries, Ltd.* (1972), 7 I.T.R. 129, N.I.R.C. (delay of three years—no extension) and *De Mars* v. *Gurr Johns and Angier Bird, Ltd.*, [1973] I.C.R. 35, N.I.R.C.

On receipt of the notice of appeal, the Registrar seals the original notice, and serves sealed copies on the appellant and the other parties to the proceedings before the industrial tribunal, on the Secretary of Industrial Tribunals, and on the Secretary of State for Employment in the case of an appeal under the Redundancy Payments Act 1965.[1]

[1] Employment Appeal Tribunal Rules 1976, S.I. 1976 No. 322, rule 4 and also rule 5.

The Registrar, as soon as practicable, notifies every respondent of the date which the Tribunal has appointed by which any answer must be delivered.[1] A respondent who wishes to resist an appeal, should within this time-limit deliver to the Tribunal an answer in writing, in, or substantially in, accordance with Form 3 in the Schedule to the Rules.[2] This should set out the grounds on which the respondent relies, but if he wishes to rely on any ground which is the same as the ground relied on by the industrial tribunal for making the decision, or order appealed from, it is sufficient to state this in the answer.[2] A respondent may cross-appeal by including in the answer a statement of the grounds of his cross-appeal, and in that event an appellant who wishes to resist the cross-appeal, should, within the time appointed by the Tribunal, deliver to it a reply in writing setting out the grounds on which he relies.[3] The Registrar serves a copy of every answer and reply to a cross-appeal on every party, other than the party by whom it was delivered.[4] Should the respondent not wish to resist an appeal the parties may deliver to the Tribunal an agreed draft of an order

allowing the appeal and it may, if it thinks it right to do so, make
an order allowing the appeal in the terms agreed.[5]

[1] Employment Appeal Tribunal Rules 1976, S.I. 1976 No. 322, rule 6 (1).
[2] *Ibid.*, rule 6 (2).
[3] *Ibid.*, rule 6 (3).
[4] *Ibid.*, rule 6 (4).
[5] *Ibid.*, rule 6 (5).


The Registrar, as soon as practicable, gives notice of the
arrangements made by the Employment Appeal Tribunal for
hearing the appeal to every party to the proceedings, the Secretary
of Industrial Tribunals and the Secretary of State for Employment,
in the case of an appeal under the Redundancy Payments Act 1965,
if he is not a respondent.[1] The notice should state the date
appointed by the Tribunal by which any interlocutory application
must be made.[2] On the application of any person, or on its own
motion, the Tribunal may direct that any person not already a party
to the proceedings, be added as a party, or that any party in the
proceedings shall cease to be a party, and in either case may give
such consequential directions as it considers necessary.[3]

[1] Employment Appeal Tribunal Rules 1976, S.I. 1976 No. 322, rule 7 (1).
[2] *Ibid.*, rule 7 (2).
[3] *Ibid.*, rule 8.


Interlocutory application may be made to the Tribunal by
giving notice in writing specifying the direction and order sought.[1]
The Registrar should serve a copy on every other party to the
proceedings who appears to be concerned in the matter to which
the notice relates, and should notify the applicant and every such
party of the arrangements made by the Tribunal for disposing of
the application.[2] Except in cases where the President, or a judge,
whether generally, or in a particular case, otherwise directs, an
interlocutory application is considered by a judge, who may
dispose of it himself, refer it in whole, or in part, to the Tribunal,
or to the Registrar.[3] When an application is disposed of by the
Registrar, a party who is aggrieved by his decision may appeal to a
judge, and in that case the judge may determine the appeal himself,
or refer the matter in whole, or in part, to the Tribunal.[4] Such
notice of appeal may be given to the Tribunal, either orally, or in
writing, within three days of the decision appealed from, and the
Registrar notifies every other party who appears to him to be con-

cerned with the appeal, and informs those parties and the appellant of arrangements made by the Tribunal for the disposing of it.[5] When hearing interlocutory applications the Tribunal may sit either in private, or in public.[6]

[1] Employment Appeal Tribunal Rules 1976, S.I. 1976 No. 322, rule 9 (1).
[2] *Ibid.*, rule 9 (2).
[3] *Ibid.*, rule 10.
[4] *Ibid.*, rule 11 (1).
[5] *Ibid.*, rule 11 (2).
[6] *Ibid.*, rule 12.

The Tribunal may, either on its own motion, or application, at any stage in the proceedings appoint a date for giving of directions as to the future conduct of proceedings, where it appears to it that their future conduct would thereby be facilitated.[1] The Registrar gives to each party notice of the date appointed and any party applying for directions shall, if practicable, before that date give to the Tribunal particulars of the directions which he seeks.[2] The Registrar will then take steps as may be practicable to inform the other parties of any directions which are sought.[3] On the date appointed, the Tribunal considers every application for directions, and any written representations relating to the applications submitted to the Tribunal, and gives such directions as it thinks fit for the purposes of securing the just, expeditious and economical disposal of the proceedings, including, where appropriate, directions as to conciliation to ensure that the parties are enabled to avail themselves of opportunities for conciliation.[4] Amongst other directions, the Tribunal has the right to direct as it thinks fit, as to the amendment of any notice, answer or any other document, the admission of any facts or documents, the admission in evidence of any documents, the mode in which evidence is to be given at the hearing and the consolidation of proceedings with any other proceedings pending before the Employment Appeal Tribunal.[5] In addition the Tribunal can, of course, issue directions as to the place and date of hearing,[5] and has power to deal with applications for further, or variation of directions.[6] The Tribunal may of its own motion, at any stage, give parties directions as to any steps to be taken in relation to the proceedings.[7]

[1] Employment Appeal Tribunal Rules 1976, S.I. 1976 No. 322, rule 13 (1).
[2] *Ibid.*, rule 13 (2).
[3] *Ibid.*, rule 13 (3).
[4] *Ibid.*, rule 13 (4). For conciliation, see p. 386, above.

[5] *Ibid.*, rule 13 (5).
[6] *Ibid.*, rule 13 (6).
[7] *Ibid.*, rule 14.

If a respondent fails to give an answer within the time appointed, or if a party fails to comply with an order, or direction, of the Tribunal, it may order that he be debarred from taking any further part in the proceedings or make such other order as it thinks just.[1]

[1] Employment Appeal Tribunal Rules 1976, S.I. 1976 No. 322, rule 15.

The Tribunal does have power on the application of any party, to order any person to attend before it as a witness, or to produce any document.[1] A person to whom such an order is directed shall not be treated as having failed to obey the order, unless at the time at which it was served on him, there was tendered a sufficient sum of money to cover his costs of attending before the Tribunal.[2] The Tribunal may, either on its own motion, or on application, require any evidence to be given on oath.[3]

[1] Employment Appeal Tribunal Rules 1976, S.I. 1976 No. 322, rule 16 (1).
[2] *Ibid.*, rule 16 (2).
[3] *Ibid.*, rule 17.

Time limits prescribed by the Rules, or order of the Tribunal, may be extended (whether they have already expired or not), or abridged, and the date appointed for any purposes may be altered by the Tribunal.[1] When the last day for doing any act falls on a day when the appropriate office of the Tribunal is closed, and by reason thereof the act cannot be done on that day, it may be done on the next day on which the office is open.[2]

[1] Employment Appeal Tribunal Rules 1976, S.I. 1976 No. 322, rule 24 (1). Probably the Employment Appeal Tribunal has no power to extend time limits applicable before the industrial tribunal, for instance that relating to review. Such matters are within the tribunal's discretion only. See *Archbold Freightage, Ltd.* v. *Wilson* (1974), 9 I.T.R. 133, at p. 135, N.I.R.C.
[2] *Ibid.*, rule 24 (2).

Failure to comply with requirements of the Rules does not invalidate proceedings unless the Tribunal directs otherwise.[1] The Employment Appeal Tribunal may even dispense with the taking of any step required, or authorised, by the Rules, or may direct that any such step be taken in some manner other than prescribed by the

Rules, if it considers that to do so would lead to the more expeditious, or economical, disposal of any proceedings, or would otherwise be desirable in the interests of justice.[2] The Rules lay down specific provisions as to the service of notices and documents.[3] They may be sent to any person by post to his address for service, or where no address for service has been given, to his registered office, principal place of business, head, or main office, or last known address, as the case may be. Notices, or other documents, required, or authorised, to be served on, or delivered to, the Employment Appeal Tribunal may be sent by post, or delivered to, the Registrar, in the case of a notice instituting proceedings at the central office, or any other office of the Tribunal, or in other cases at the office of the Tribunal in which the proceedings are being dealt with.[4] Notices, or documents, to be served on, or delivered to, an unincorporated body may be sent to its secretary, manager or similar officer and documents served by post shall be assumed in the absence of evidence to the contrary, to have been delivered in the normal course of post.[5] The Tribunal can inform itself in such manner as it thinks fit of the posting of any document by its officers,[7] and it has power to direct that service of any document be dispensed with, or effected otherwise than in a manner prescribed by the Rules.[8]

[1] Employment Appeal Tribunal Rules 1976, S.I. 1976 No. 322, rule 26 (1).
[2] *Ibid.*, rule 26 (2).
[3] *Ibid.*, rule 22.
[4] *Ibid.*, rule 22 (1).
[5] *Ibid.*, rule 22 (2).
[6] *Ibid.*, rule 22 (3).
[7] *Ibid.*, rule 22 (4).
[8] *Ibid.*, rule 22 (5).

## THE HEARING

The oral hearings at which any proceedings before the Tribunal are finally disposed of, take place before such members of the Tribunal as the President may nominate subject to the rule mentioned above. The hearing will normally take place in public,[1] but the Tribunal may sit in private to hear evidence which in its opinion:

(a) relates to matters of such a nature that it would be against the interests of national security to allow the evidence to be given in public; or

(b) is likely to consist (wholly or in part) of information which either:

    (i) the person giving the evidence could not disclose without contravening a prohibition imposed by, or under, any enactment; or

    (ii) has been communicated to that person in confidence, or which he otherwise obtained in consequence of the confidence reposed in him by another person; or

    (iii) is information the disclosure of which would cause substantial injury to an undertaking of the person giving the evidence, or any undertaking in which he works, for reasons other than its effect on any negotiations with respect to matters mentioned in the definition of "trade dispute" in the Trade Union and Labour Relations Act 1974.[2]

Parties may appear before the Tribunal in person, or be represented by counsel, or by a solicitor, or a representative of a trade union, or employer's association, or by any other person whom they desire to represent them.[3]

[1] Employment Appeal Tribunal Rules 1976, S.I. 1976 No. 322, rule 18 (1).
[2] *Ibid.*, rule 18 (2).
[3] Employment Protection Act 1975, Sch. 6, para. 18.

Orders of the Tribunal are drawn up by the Registrar and a copy bearing the Tribunal's seal is served by the Registrar on every party to the proceedings to which it relates, and so far as appeals from industrial tribunals are concerned, on the Secretary of Industrial Tribunals.[1] On the application of any party made within 14 days after the making of an order finally disposing of proceedings, the Tribunal should give its reasons in writing for the order, unless it was made after the delivery of a reasoned judgment.[2]

[1] Employment Appeal Tribunal Rules 1976, S.I. 1976 No. 322, rule 19 (1).
[2] *Ibid.*, rule 19 (2).

The Employment Appeal Tribunal may, either on its own motion, or on any application, review any order made by it and may on such review, revoke, or vary, the order on the grounds that it was wrongly made as a result of an error on the part of the Tribunal or its staff, a party did not receive proper notice of the proceedings leading to the order, or the interests of justice require such review.[1] The application for review should be made within 14 days of the date of the order.[2] There is power for a clerical mistake in any order arising from an accidental slip, or omission, to be corrected at any time by or on the authority of, a judge, or member.[3]

[1] Employment Appeal Tribunal Rules 1976, S.I. 1976 No. 322, rule 20 (1).
[2] *Ibid.*, rule 20 (2).
[3] *Ibid.*, rule 20 (3).

Where it appears to the Tribunal that any proceedings were unnecessary, improper or vexatious, or that there has been reasonable delay, or other unreasonable conduct in bringing, or conducting, the proceedings, the Tribunal may order that the party at fault pay to any other party the whole, or such part as it thinks fit, of the costs, or expenses incurred by that other party in connection with the proceedings.[1] When making such an order the Tribunal may assess the sum to be paid, or direct that it be assessed by a taxing officer from whose decision an appeal shall lie to a judge.[2] The judge may determine the appeal himself, or refer it to the Tribunal, which may sit either in private, or in public to deal with the appeal.[3]

[1] Employment Appeal Tribunal Rules 1976, S.I. 1976 No. 322, rule 21 (1). There are similarities between this rule and the Industrial Court Rules 1971, S.I. 1971 No. 1777, (the rules regulating procedure before the National Industrial Relations Court) rule 69(1). Some assistance in predicting the views of the Employment Appeal Tribunal as to costs may be obtained from decisions taken under that rule. For instance in *Maroof* v. *J. B. Battye & Co., Ltd.* (1973), 8 I.T.R. 489, N.I.R.C., the appellant had been told almost two months prior to the hearing that no point of law arose and there was accordingly no right of appeal and yet the appeal was not abandoned until at the hearing. An award of costs was made. See also *J. and H. Smith, Ltd.* v. *Smith* (1974), 9 I.T.R. 175, N.I.R.C., and *Penrose* v. *Fairey Surveys, Ltd.* (1974), 9 I.T.R. 41, N.I.R.C., where the circumstances of awards of costs were discussed. Also relevant are *Imperial London Hotels, Ltd.* v. *Cooper* (1974), 9 I.T.R. 312, N.I.R.C.; *Wedge* v. *F. P. A. Finnegans, Ltd.* (1973), 8 I.T.R. 476, N.I.R.C.; and *Neefjes* v. *Crystal Products Co., Ltd.* (1973), 8 I.T.R. 616, C.A. See the observations of PHILLIPS, J. in *White* v. *Manchester University*, [1976] I.R.L.R. 218, E.A.T.
[2] Employment Appeal Tribunal Rules 1976, S.I. 1976 No. 322, rule 21 (2).
[3] *Ibid.*, rule 21 (3), applying rules 11 and 12.

The Tribunal does have power at any stage in the proceedings when it appears to it there is reasonable prospect of agreement being reached between the parties, to take such steps as it thinks fit to enable them to avail themselves of any opportunities for conciliation whether by adjournment of proceedings, or otherwise.[1]

[1] Employment Appeal Tribunal Rules 1976, S.I. 1976 No. 322, rule 23. For conciliation, see p. 386, above.

Subject to the above provisions, and without prejudice to the rules laid down in the Administration of Justice Act 1960, section 13, in cases of contempt of court, an appeal lies on any question of law from a decision, or order, of the Employment Appeal Tribunal with leave of the Tribunal, or of the Court of Appeal, or as the case may be, the Court of Session, in the case of proceedings in England and Wales to the Court of Appeal, or in the case of proceedings in Scotland, to the Court of Session.[1] Subject to any order made by the Court of Appeal, or Court of Session, and to any directions given by the Tribunal, an appeal from the Tribunal shall not suspend the enforcement of any order by it.[2] Legal aid would be available on such an appeal according to the usual rules. The normal requirements apply to appeals from the Court of Appeal or Court of Session.

[1] Employment Protection Act 1975, s. 88 (4).
[2] Employment Appeal Tribunal Rules 1976, S.I. 1976 No. 322, rule 19 (3).

# Appendix 1

# CHECK-LISTS

## Check-list 1

### Check-list on Engagement

1. Is the applicant eligible for the employment?[1]
2. No discrimination on grounds of:
   (a) Sex or marital status,[2]
   (b) Race or colour.[3]
3. Is a work permit necessary?[4]
4. Consider provisions affecting disabled persons.[5]
5. Convictions for criminal offences by applicant.[6]
6. A probationary period?[7] If so ensure that it is explained and expressed as such in letter of appointment.
7. Explain the provisions of the contract which affect the applicant. A useful way of dealing with this could be to refer to the statement to be issued under the Contracts of Employment Act 1972.[8]
8. As a matter of practice, in the letter of appointment refer to the statement to be issued pursuant to the Contracts of Employment Act 1972.[9]
9. If the statement issued pursuant to the Contracts of Employment Act 1972 will refer to other documents, explain to the prospective employee where these will be available and in particular explain any rights of suspension and disciplinary rules.[10]
10. If the applicant is to be a replacement for an employee suspended on medical grounds, or for an employee absent wholly, or partly, because of pregnancy or confinement, and it is intended in due course to dismiss the replacement to allow the other employee to resume work, the statutory procedure must be gone through.[11]

[1] Specific requirements of statutes (for instance the Factories Act 1961), union membership agreements, etc. to be considered. Does the applicant have the qualifications necessary for the employment?

2 See p. 28, above.
3 See p. 500, below.
4 See p. 18, above.
5 See p. 18, above.
6 See p. 46, above.
7 This may be advantageous in resisting a claim for unfair dismissal, see p. 324, above. However, any benefit from such an arrangement will only arise if the employee is aware that the appointment is probationary when it is accepted by him.
8 If the statement is used in this way the terms of employment will be clear to the employee on engagement.
9 See p. 98, above for provisions as to the statement. There is no requirement for the statement to be supplied at this stage but to do so avoids misunderstandings.
10 It is essential that any document referred to is available to the employee when the statement under the Contracts of Employment Act 1972 has to be given to the employee, and an explanation on engagement may prevent future difficulties.
11 See Employment Protection Act 1975, s. 33 and s. 51 respectively discussed at p. 63 and 83, above. See also Appendix 5, Form 6 and Appendix 6 below.

CHECK-LIST 2

## Check-list on Preparation of Service Agreement[1]

1. Position regarding previous agreements.[2]
2. Period of employment—determination by notice?[3]
3. (a) Job description.
   (b) The possibility of appointing others to act jointly with the appointee?
   (c) Can the employee be directed to perform other functions or to transfer to other locations?[4]
4. Relationship with any associated employer of the employer.[5]
5. Applicant to devote whole of time to the employer's business?
6. Remuneration.[6]
   (a) Fixed salary?
   (b) Commission or bonuses?
   (c) Definition of profits, or turnover, for use in calculating commission or bonuses?
   (d) Accrual at daily rate?
7. Provision for increase in remuneration.[6]
   (a) "Built-in" increases in salary?
   (b) Increase by agreement?
   (c) Increase by reference to indices?

8. Pensions.
9. Payment of expenses.
10. Provision of motor vehicle.
11. Restrictive agreements.[7]
12. Employee to maintain strict secrecy:[8]
    (a) During employment,
    (b) After employment,
    (c) Restrictions on dealing with customers, or suppliers after employment?
13. Inventions and new processes—application for patents and registered designs.[9]
14. Holidays.[10]
    (a) The amount of holiday to be taken by the employee and when it should be taken.
    (b) Payment for holiday entitlement on termination.
15. Sickness:[11]
    (a) Provisions for evidence of illness, and payment during absence.
    (b) Provision for long periods of absence to enable termination of the agreement.
16. Circumstances in which the Agreement be determined prior to expiration of fixed term, or notice.[12]
17. Saving of Agreement on amalgamation, or liquidation, on re-construction of the Company.
18. Transferability of the Agreement.
19. Exclusion of provisions of redundancy, and unfair dismissal provisions on a fixed term contract for two years or more.[13]
20. Arbitration clause.
21. Proper Law.[14]
22. Note required by the Contracts of Employment Act 1972.[15]

---

[1] See specimen agreement at p. 443, below.

[2] Are there any provisions which should be "brought forward" into the new agreement?

[3] If it is intended to exclude the right to a redundancy payment and remedies for unfair dismissal on expiry consider the meaning of "fixed term" contract, see Redundancy Payments Act 1965, s. 15, discussed at p. 164, above, and Trade Union and Labour Relations Act 1974, Sch. 1, para. 12, discussed at p. 282, above.

[4] If there is not power to do this an employer may in certain circumstances be found to have repudiated the contract if he purports to change the nature of work carried out by the employee, or the location of the work. See p. 192, above.

[5] It may be intended that the employee will perform work for other persons, or may come into contact with their trade secrets.

[6] See Forms 2a–2e, below.

[7] See p. 117, above.

[8] See p. 113, above.

[9] See p. 122, above.

[10] See p. 84, above.

[11] See p. 72, above.

[12] If it is intended to exclude statutory remedies on dismissal see *British Broadcasting Corporation* v. *Iouannou,* [1975] Q.B. 781; [1975] 2 All E.R. 999, C.A., and p. 164, above.

[13] See p. 164 and 282, above and Forms at pp. 451 and 489.

[14] If there is any possibility of doubt the system of law which is to be applicable to the employment should be specified.

[15] See p. 99, above and Form 2, p. 454, below.

## CHECK-LIST 3

### Employer's Check-list on Dismissal

1. Review the position of all employees after an intial period of employment. It may be that the employer will wish to dismiss an employee by giving him no less than the minimum statutory period of notice to expire before the expiry of 26 weeks employment to avoid the unfair dismissal provisions.[1]

2. If due to redundancy, consider provisions as to consultation and notification to the Secretary of State.[2]

3. Reasons for Dismissal. Possibility of unfair dismissal[3] and/or redundancy[4] and/or discrimination on the grounds of sex or marital status[5] and/or racial discrimination.[6]

4. Is there a right to dismiss in pursuance of notices served under the rules relating to suspension on medical grounds,[7] and absence due to pregnancy and confinement?[8]

5. Procedures. Have all procedures and the codes of practice been properly complied with?[9]

6. Is the dismissal such as to affect the employers compliance with the Disabled Persons (Employment Act) 1944.[10]

7. Statement of reasons for dismissal.[11] It is best for this to be given without request but the employee has a right to require this.

8. Entitlement as to notice. Does the employees conduct warrant summary dismissal?[12] Statutory and contractual requirements as to notice.[13]

9. Payment on termination, payment during notice, accrued rights to holiday pay,[14] redundancy payments.[15]

10. Is any payment made taxable?[16]
11. Pension scheme—exercise of options.
12. If appropriate claim rebate from the Redundancy Fund.[17]

[1] See p. 278, above. The 26 weeks time limit does not apply to dismissal for inadmissible reasons, see p. 316, above; and the time limit is reduced to four weeks in certain cases of dismissal on medical grounds, see p. 278, above.

[2] See p. 263, above and Appendix 7, Forms 10, 11 and 12 below.

[3] See p. 274, above.

[4] See p. 161, above.

[5] See p. 28, above.

[6] Used in the sense of all discrimination made unlawful by the Race Relations Act 1968, see p. 500, below.

[7] See p. 63, above and Appendix 6, below.

[8] See p. 83, above and Appendix 5, Form 6, below. The employer must still act reasonably.

[9] See p. 314, above.

[10] See p. 18, above.

[11] See p. 152, above.

[12] See p. 144, above and the statement issued pursuant to the Contracts of Employment Act 1972.

[13] This, like the question of notice, should be evident from the statement of terms and conditions of employment and the holiday rules.

[14] See p. 84, above.

[15] See p. 242, above.

[16] See p. 377, above.

[17] See p. 257, above.

## CHECK-LIST 4

### Employee's Check-list on Dismissal[1]

1. Domestic remedies, appeals procedures?[2]
2. If dismissal for an inadmissible reason[3] is interim relief[4] required? If so action should be taken immediately.
3. Obtain statement of reasons for dismissal.[5]
4. If employee wishes to be reinstated, or re-engaged, inform employer.[6]
5. Application to industrial tribunal for following remedies?
   (a) redundancy payment?[7]
   (b) compensation for discrimination on grounds of sex, marital status,[8] or race?[9]
   (c) compensation for unfair dismissal?[10]
   (d) determination of statement under Contracts of Employment Act 1972, which may assist with other proceedings.[11]
6. Note carefully the time limits for the above applications.[12]

7. Conciliation.[13]
8. Wrongful dismissal.[14] Action for breach of contract in County Court or High Court, at present.[15] Consider whether to institute such proceedings prior to determination of other applications by industrial tribunals.[16]
9. Recovery of monies accrued due to employee, wages in hand, fidelity bond, holiday pay, etc.
10. Pension schemes. Are there options to exercise?
11. Employee to take steps to mitigate his loss.[17]
12. Register for unemployment benefit.

[1] The matters mentioned below should be considered as soon as notice has been given.

[2] Attempts should be made to settle the matter internally and appeal and other procedures made use of. However, if the dismissal takes effect before such procedures are exhausted, application to an industrial tribunal should not be delayed pending the outcome of the domestic proceedings. Otherwise it is possible that the other proceedings may become time-barred. See *MacDonald* v. *South Cambridgeshire Rural District Council* (1973), 8 I.T.R. 557, N.I.R.C.

[3] See p. 316, above.

[4] See p. 152, above. For procedure see p. 348, above.

[5] See p.    , above.

[6] See Employment Protection Act 1975, s. 71 (8) (*b*), discussed at p. 348, above.

[7] See p. 161, above.

[8] See p. 28, above. Consider also position under Equal Pay Act 1970 (as amended) relating to equal terms and conditions. Is there a possibility of obtaining arrears? See p. 26, above.

[9] See p. 500, below.

[10] See p. 274, above.

[11] See p. 108, above.

[12] Reference should be made to the time limits mentioned when discussing the individual remedies.

[13] See p. 386, above.

[14] See pp. 144 and 153, above.

[15] There is power for jurisdiction in respect of certain claims for damages for breach of contracts of employment, or any other contract connected with employment and other claims in connection with employment contracts to be conferred on industrial tribunals; Employment Protection Act 1975, s. 109, see p. 388, above. This power has not yet been exercised.

[16] It is possible that an industrial tribunal may, on the application of a party, adjourn proceedings before it to allow proceedings before the High Court or County Court relating to the same matter to be determined. See *Jacobs* v. *Norsalta, Ltd.,* [1976] E.A.T. no. 296/76.

[17] This applies to claims for wrongful and unfair dismissal, see p. 155 and 355, above respectively. Adequate evidence should be obtained. Letters of applications for new employment, etc. and notes of interviews should be carefully preserved.

# Appendix 2

# CONTRACTS OF EMPLOYMENT

## Form 1

### Specimen Simple Contract of Employment[1]

AN AGREEMENT made the . . . day of . . . BETWEEN . . . of . . . (hereinafter called the employer) of the one part and . . . of . . . (hereinafter called the employee) of the other part.

WHEREBY IT IS AGREED AS FOLLOWS:

    1. The employer agrees to employ the employee and the employee to serve the employer in the capacity of gardener from the . . . day of . . . 197 . . until the employment shall be determined as hereinafter provided. No employment with a previous employer counts as part of the employee's period of continuous employment with the employer.

    2. The employee shall be remunerated by a weekly wage of £ . . payable on the Friday of each week.

    3. The employee shall give to the employer one week's notice to terminate his said employment.

    4. The employer shall give to the employee the following notice to terminate his said employment, except when he is entitled to terminate the employment by summary dismissal:

(a) not less than one week, if his period of continuous employment is less than two years;

(b) not less than one week's notice for each year of continuous employment if his period of continuous employment is two years or more but less than 12 weeks; and

(c) not less than 12 weeks' notice if his period of continuous employment is 12 years or more.

    5. The normal working hours shall be from 8 a.m. to 5 p.m. from Monday to Friday inclusive and from 8 a.m. to 12 noon on Saturday when so required by the employer.

    6. The employee shall be entitled to one week's holiday with pay after completing six calendar months' work and a further two weeks after completing 12 calendar months' work which said

441

holiday shall be taken at a time convenient to the employer to be agreed at least one calendar month before the commencement of the said holiday. In each following year the employee will be entitled to three weeks' holiday with pay to be taken at a time convenient to the employer to be agreed with him. No payment will be made for holidays not taken on the termination of employment.

7. Further the employee shall be entitled to the statutory and Bank holidays with pay.

8. In the case of incapacity for work due to sickness or injury the certificate of a registered medical practitioner must be sent to the employer within 72 hours. During the continuity of the contract of employment the employer shall be entitled to deduct from the employee's wages the amount of the benefits in respect of such absence [received by the employee] from the Department of Health and Social Security [to which the employee is entitled] and the employee shall keep the employer informed of any such amounts.[2]

9. There is no pension scheme in existence and no agreement as to pension has been entered into.

10. Note:

(a) If the employee is dissatisfied with any disciplinary decision relating to him or he seeks redress of any grievance he should apply to the head gardener. If the matter is not resolved by the head gardener it should be referred to the employer and he will personally investigate the problem.[3]

[(b) No contracting-out certificate is in force in respect of the employment the subject of this agreement][4]

As WITNESS the hands of . . . and . . . the day and year first above written.[5]

Signed by the said
. . . in the presence
of:

Signed by the said
. . . in the presence
of:

[1] This is a simple form designed to avoid the necessity of giving a separate statement pursuant to the Contracts of Employment Act 1972. It contains

essential features but will no doubt require considerable adaption in practice to meet particular circumstances.

[2] See p. 73, above.

[3] There should be formal grievance and disciplinary procedures except in very small establishments where there is close personal contact between the employer and the employees. Reference should be made to the appropriate Code of Practice.

[4] This is a requirement introduced by the Social Security Pensions Act 1975. It is expected to come into force in April 1978.

[5] When the employer is a limited company the contract must be signed by a person acting under its authority. See also the Companies Act 1948, ss. 32 (1) and 36.

## FORM 2

## Specimen Service Agreement for Senior Employee/Director[1]
(with variations as to remuneration)

THIS AGREEMENT is made the            day of nineteen hundred and seventy-       BETWEEN LIMITED whose Registered Office is situate at in the County of (hereinafter called "the Company") of the one part and of            (hereinafter called "the Employee") of the other part. WHEREBY IT IS AGREED as follows:

1. This Agreement will govern the relationship between the Company and the Employee from the            day of 19   and any former agreements subsisting between the parties will cease to be of effect on that day.

2. The Company will, subject to the provisions set out below, employ the Employee and he will serve the Company as [ Director] or in such other capacity as the Board of Directors of the Company shall in its absolute discretion decide until the            day of            19   [2] [and thereafter until terminated by either party giving to the other not less than six months' notice in writing so as to expire on or at any time after the said day of            19   ]. [Provided that if the Employee ceases to be a director of the Company his employment under this Agreement will continue and he will perform executive duties on the Company's behalf.][3]

443

3. The Employee will carry out such duties and comply with such instructions as the Board of Directors of the Company shall determine from time to time [at such place or places within Great Britain as the Board of the Directors shall determine][4] and during his employment hereunder the Employee will devote the whole of his time and attention to the Company's affairs and use his best endeavours to promote its interests.

4. The Company may at any time appoint any person or persons to act jointly with the Employee in discharging his duties hereunder.[5]

5. The Employee will be entitled by way of remuneration to a salary at the rate of £ per annum. The salary will accrue from day to day and be payable in arrear on the last day of each month by equal monthly instalments.[6]

6. The Company will pay into the Pension Scheme the employer's contribution payable in respect of the Employee under that Scheme during the Employee's employment hereunder. The Employee will pay to that Scheme any employee's contributions required thereby during such period.[7]

7. The Company will repay to the Employee all expenses incurred by him with its authority in connection with his employment.

8. The Company will during his employment so long as the Employee is legally entitled to drive supply to him a motor car for his use and will bear the cost and running expenses. The Employee will pay to the Company the sum of £ per annum for his private use of the motor car and will supply the fuel for such use at his own expense.

9. The Employee will be entitled to working days' holiday in each holiday year in addition to the statutory Bank Holidays. Holidays other than Bank Holidays will be taken within the period of 12 months starting on the first day of April in each year (the "holiday year") at such times as are agreed with the Board of Directors of the Company. Holidays may not be carried forward and no payment will be made in respect of holidays which have not been taken.[8]

10. During his employment by the Company the Employee will not be engaged or interested in any business or undertaking whatsoever other than in connection with his employment hereunder and the holding of shares or securities quoted on a public stock exchange.[9]

11. The Employee will not during his employment by the Company or for one year afterwards endeavour to solicit orders or custom from any person, firm or company who within the period of one year before the termination of his employment had been a customer of the Company or any associated employer or endeavour to influence in any way the relationship between any supplier or employee and the Company or any associated employer.[9]

12. The Employee will not during his employment by the Company or afterwards communicate or divulge to any person except to those officials of the Company whose province is to know the same any confidential information relating to the business affairs processes or trade secrets of the Company or of any associated employer.[9]

13. Any invention discovery design or improvement whether or not capable of protection by letters patent registered design or otherwise made or discovered by the Employee which relates to or is connected with the business of the Company or any associated employer will belong absolutely to the Company or the associated employer as the case may be. The Employee will provide the Company or associated employer with full details and information with regard thereto and will at the expense of the Company apply or join with the Company in applying for letters patent registration of the design or other protection in the United Kingdom and in any other part of the world therefor. The Employee will at the Company's expense execute and do all instruments and things which the Company or associated employer may reasonably require to vest the absolute ownership in the said letters patent registered design or other protection in the Company or associated employer and in the meantime will hold all interests therein in trust for the Company.[10]

14. (1) If the Employee is absent from his duties as a result of sickness or injury for a period of three days or more he will produce to the Company a medical certificate in respect of such absence.

(2) If the Employee is absent from his duties as a result of sickness or injury he will be entitled to payment of his salary at the full rate less any Social Security or other benefits receivable by him for a period (whether consecutive or in aggregate) of no more than           weeks in any period of 12 months and shall thereafter be entitled to no further payment from the Company during his absence.[11]

15. The Company will be entitled to determine the Employee's employment hereunder if:

(1) the Employee breaks any term of this Agreement;
(2) the Employee neglects omits or refuses to discharge his duties hereunder or to comply with any instruction given to him by the Board of Directors of the Company;
(3) the Employee is guilty of gross misconduct or is convicted of any criminal offence involving dishonesty;
(4) the Employee is declared bankrupt or a Receiving Order is made against him or he makes or attempts to make any composition with his creditors;
(5) the Employee as a result of mental or physical illness becomes incapable of performing his duties;
(6) for a period of          weeks (whether consecutive or in aggregate) in any period of two years the Employee has been absent from his duties as a result of sickness or injury.

16. The Employee will have no claim against the Company in respect of the determination of his employment under this Agreement by reason of the liquidation of the Company for the purposes of amalgamation or reconstruction if he is offered employment on not less favourable terms than contained in this Agreement with any person firm or company which acquires the whole or substantially whole of the undertaking of the Company as a result of such amalgamation or reconstruction.[12]

17. The term "associated employer" in this Agreement means any company of which the Company has control (directly or indirectly) or which has control (directly or indirectly) over the Company or any company of which a third person having control over the Company has control whether directly or indirectly.

18. Any dispute concerning this Agreement or its construction or application will be referred to a single arbitrator in accordance with the provisions of the Arbitration Act 1950 or any statutory modification or re-enactment thereof. The arbitrator will be appointed by agreement between the parties or in default of agreement by the President for the time being of The Law Society on the application of either party.[13]

19. Notices given under this Agreement should be in writing and if to be given to the Company delivered or despatched by registered or recorded delivery post to its registered office and if to be given to the Employee handed to him or sent to his last known

residential address in Great Britain by registered or recorded delivery post. A notice despatched by post is deemed to be given three days after despatch

IN WITNESS, etc.[14]

[1] The form is a specimen only and will no doubt require adaption to meet particular circumstances. If it is desired to include a clause excluding the right to a redundancy payment and/or compensation for unfair dismissal, see p.    , above and Form 3, below. That form may be adapted for inclusion in the Service Agreement.

[2] It is intended to exclude the statutory rights on the expiration of the employment and discussion of "fixed term" contracts at p. 164, above, should be considered.

[3] The purpose of the proviso being to prevent it being contended by the employee that removal from the Board of Directors amounts to a repudiation of the contract. The clause may be adapted by the inclusion of a further provision that the employee will not resign his directorship or refuse to seek re-election as a director of the company.

[4] For decisions on the right to transfer, see p. 192, above.

[5] The clause which is self-explanatory will enable the employer to appoint an employee to act jointly with the Employee without repudiating the contract.

[6] For other clauses as remuneration, see Forms 2a–2e, below.

[7] As a result of this provision the employer's contributions to the pension scheme are part of the employee's contractual remuneration.

[8] For holidays, see p. 84, above. The requirements of the Contracts of Employment Act 1972, s. 4, as to details of holidays to be given in the written statement supplied pursuant to that section are discussed at p. 102, above.

[9] For the duty of good faith and restrictive agreements, see p. 110, above. If the employer has particular areas of knowledge which he wishes to protect these should be totally separate covenants with regard to each providing the minimum protection required, see p. 117, above.

[10] See p. 122, above. If preferred the references to registered designs may be omitted in view of their infrequent use.

[11] For consideration of the position during sickness and injury, see p. 72, above.

[12] This clause is an attempt to prevent the employee having a claim for breach of contract in situations of amalgamation and reconstruction.

[13] At the present time arbitration is thought to be a more satisfactory method of resolving some difficulties than use of the courts. It may be that in certain cases a more efficient remedy will be an application to an industrial tribunal if the power to confer jurisdiction on tribunals given by Employment Protection Act 1975, s. 109, is exercised. However, since the jurisdiction will be limited, an arbitration clause will continue to be useful for some purposes.

[14] The agreement may be under seal and is still exempt from stamp duty, see p. 8, above.

FORM 2a

## Clause providing for Specified Increases in Salary[1]

5. The Employee will be entitled to a salary at the rate of £ per annum until 31st December 1978, to a salary at the rate of £ per annum from that date until 31st December 1980 and to a salary of £ per annum for the remainder of the term of the Employee's employment hereunder. The salary to which the Employee is entitled hereunder will accrue from day to day and be payable in arrear on the last day of each month by equal monthly instalments.

[1] Clauses of this type are probably not satisfactory in times of rapid inflation. It may be that legislation will allow employers to breach salary increase clauses with impunity if they are complying with Government anti-inflation policy; see the Remuneration Charges and Grants Act 1975, s. 1 and p. 42, above.

FORM 2b

## Clause providing for Bonus by Reference to Profits[1]

5. (1) The Employee will be entitled to a salary of £ per annum payable in arrear on the last day of each month. The salary will accrue from day to day.

(2) In addition to the salary herebeforementioned the Employee will be entitled to a bonus calculated at the rate of per centum of the Company's net profits declared by the Board of Directors to be available for the purposes of bonus calculation. Such profits will be computed after making such charges and setting aside such reserves as the Board in its absolute discretion considers appropriate but before charging bonus payments payable to any other employee. A certificate of the Company's profit for such purposes given by the Secretary of the Company will be final and binding on the parties hereto. The bonus will be paid within six months of the ending of the Company's financial year. It will be deemed to accrue from day to day and if the Employee ceases to be employed by the Company for whatever reason during a financial year will be apportioned on a daily basis in respect of

the period during which the Employee was employed by the Company.

[1] The definition of profits used in this clause leaves the right to determine the profits with the Board of Directors of the Company. If a more exact definition is used difficulties may be encountered in its application. This clause may be unsatisfactory in theory but if several employees have similar provisions in their contracts it works suprisingly well in practice.

## Form 2c

### Clause providing for Commission by Reference to Turnover[1]

5. (1) The Employee will be entitled to a salary of £ per annum payable in arrear on the last day of each month. The salary will accrue from day to day.

(2) In addition to the salary hereinbefore mentioned the Employee will be entitled to a commission of     per centum of the turnover of the Company. A certificate of the Company's turnover will be given by the Company's auditors which will be final and binding on the parties hereto. The commission will be paid within six months of the Company's financial year. It will be deemed to accrue from day to day and if the Employee ceases to be employed by the Company for whatever reason during a financial year will be apportioned on a daily basis in respect of the period during which the Employee was employed by the Company.

[1] This type of clause is frequently encountered. It may be varied by including turnover over a threshold only or by using varying rates of commission for "bands" of turnover.

## Form 2d

### Variation of Salary by reference to Particulars of Changes set out in a Schedule[1]

5. The Employee will be entitled by remuneration to a salary at the rate of £     per annum from the date hereof. The

449

rate of salary may be increased as agreed between the Company and the Employee and if so agreed the particulars will be set out in the Schedule endorsed hereon and initialled by the Employee and by a[nother] director on the Company's behalf. The most recent of these particulars will be treated as if they are incorporated in this Agreement. The salary payable hereunder will accrue from day to day and be payable in arrear on the last day of each month by equal monthly instalments.

---

Schedule of increased salary in accordance with Clause 5

| Date from which new salary is to commence | Rate per annum of new salary | Initialled by Employee | Initialled on behalf of the Company |
|---|---|---|---|

[1] Theoretical difficulties can be raised regarding this clause as well as to Form 2b. However, in similar fashion it works well in actual use.

## Variation of Salary by reference to the Index of Retail Prices[1]

5. (1) Subject as mentioned below the Employee will be entitled by way of remuneration to a salary at the rate of £ per annum. The Employee's salary hereunder will accrue from day to day and will be payable in arrear on the last day of each month by equal monthly instalments.

(2) The salary payable hereunder will be reviewed on 2nd January in each year ("the review date"). The salary of the Employee during the year commencing with the review date will be the sum which is produced by multiplying the amount of salary hereinbefore provided for by the fraction in which     2 is the denominator and the numerator is the figure for the Index of Retail Prices last published by the Department of Employment (or its successor) before the review date and calculated using the same basis for its compilation as is used at the date hereof. If that basis changes and no figure for the Retail Prices

Index on that basis is published during the period of three months immediately preceding the review date the numerator is the figure which the Index would have been on the review date if the basis had not been changed. If it is impossible to calculate this figure the numerator will be such figure as is agreed between the parties or failing agreement determined by an Arbitrator in accordance with Clause 18 hereof as being a reasonable estimate of that figure.

[1] Salary increases by reference to published indices have gained in popularity during the present inflationary situation.

[2] The figure of the Retail Prices Index published immediately before the entry into the service agreement is entered here.

## Form 3

## Agreement to exclude the Right to Redundancy Payment and Remedies for Unfair Dismissal where the Employee is employed for a Fixed Term of two years or more[1]

TO: [Employer]

I                              being employed by you under a contract of employment for a fixed term of     years commencing on the                    hereby agree to exclude any right to a redundancy payment pursuant to the Redundancy Payments Act 1965 and to exclude any claim in respect of rights under paragraph 4, Schedule 1, Trade Union and Labour Relations Act 1974, and in each case in pursuance of any statutory modification or re-enactment thereof, on the expiry of that term without its being renewed.

Date..............                              Signature................................
                                                  [of Employee]

[1] See the Redundancy Payments Act 1965, s. 15, and the Trade Union and Labour Relations Act 1974, Sch. 1, para. 12, discussed at p. 164 and 282, above, respectively. There is an express provision in the Redundancy Payments Act 1965 that an agreement to exclude the right to a redundancy payment in respect of a term which is renewed is not construed as applying to the term as renewed but without prejudice to making a further such agreement; Redundancy Payments Act 1965, s. 15 (4). Probably the same would be true of the unfair dismissal provisions, see p. 164, above.

# Appendix 3

# FORMS UNDER THE CONTRACTS OF EMPLOYMENT ACT 1972

## General Form of Statement of Terms of Employment[1]

Employer:
Employee:
Address:
Particulars of the terms of your employment as at
197 .[2]
The following particulars constitute the written statement
required to be given to you under the Contracts of Employment
Act 1972, (as amended by the Employment Protection Act 1975)
in respect of your employment with the above named employer
which began on            [and which forms part of a
continuous period of employment which began on
with            .] [No employment with a previous employer
counts as part of your period of continuous employment.]

    1. *Title of Employment.*

    2. *Place of Employment.*[3]

    3. *Remuneration.* Your rate of pay will be            per
paid on the            day of each

    4. *Hours.* You are required to work            days per week from
Monday to Friday inclusive between the hours of            a.m. and
    p.m. with a break of            hour for lunch, [and in addition
you should work such over-time as may be required by your
employers].[4]

    5. *Holidays.* Holiday regulations are deposited in the
Office and are available for inspection there.[5]

    6. *Sickness or Injury.* Regulations as to payment during
absence due to sickness or injury are available for inspection in the
        Office.[5]

    7. *Pensions.* Your Employer [does not] operate[s] a pension

scheme applicable to your employment [details of which are available for inspection in the            Office]. [A contracting-out certificate is [not] in force in respect of your employment].[6]

8. *Notice.*

(1) You are obliged to give a minimum period of one week notice to terminate your employment.

(2) Except when you are in breach of your contract you are entitled to receive a minimum period of notice of:

    (a) one week for continuous service with the Company for any period of up to two years;

    (b) one week for each complete year of such service between two and twelve years;

    (c) not less than twelve weeks for such service of twelve years or more.[7]

9. *Disciplinary Rules.* A copy of the disciplinary rules applicable to your employment is available for inspection in the Office. You can apply to [the foreman of your Department] if you are dissatisfied with any disciplinary decision relating to you.[8]

10. *Redress of Grievances.* Details of procedure available in cases where you have grievance in connection with your employment are available for inspection in the            Office. Any grievance should initially be raised with [the foreman of your Department].[8]

NOTE:

The documents which are referred to as being available in the            Office are open to inspection at any time during normal working hours and future changes will be recorded in them from time to time.[5]

Dated ......      Signed ......

(Company Secretary)[9]

*Acknowledgment by employee.* I agree that the preceding provisions including those contained in the documents referred to (as varied from time to time) form the basis of my contract of employment and acknowledge receipt of a statement of which the foregoing is a true copy.

Dated this     day of     197 .

.............................[10]

    [Employee]

---

[1] This form should be readily adapted to fit most situations encountered in practice. If there are no particulars to be included under any head this should be stated.

[2] This date must be a day not more than one week before the statement is given.

[3] Although not a requirement of the Contracts of Employment Act 1972 this information is often the source of dispute and is best specified. From the employers point of view there should always be a right to transfer the employee if there is any likelihood of wishing to alter the place of employment. See the cases cited at p. 192, above.

[4] The words in brackets should be included if the employee is obliged to work overtime, but see *Pearson and Workman* v. *William Jones, Ltd.*, (1967) 2 I.T.R. 471, D.C.

[5] The employee should have reasonable opportunities of reading documents referred to in the course of his employment or they should be made reasonably accessible to him in some other way; Contracts of Employment Act 1972, s. 4 (5), see p. 100, above.

[6] This requirement of the Social Security Pensions Act 1975 is expected to come into force on 6th April 1978.

[7] The minimum periods of notice required by the Contracts of Employment Act 1972, s. 1 (1) are shown. The employees entitlement may be agreed as being longer but not shorter if the provisions of the Act as to notice apply, see p. 135, above.

[8] The practice is adopted of not drawing any distinction between particulars to be given in the written statement and the note to be included in the statement. Compare Contracts of Employment Act 1972, s. 4 (1) and (2), see p. 99, above.

[9] A signature is not required by the Contracts of Employment Act 1972 but does help avoid disputes if the contents of the statement are relevant to any dispute.

[10] There is no requirement for the employee to sign a copy of the statement, contained in the Contracts of Employment Act 1972. However, it is good practice to obtain such signature as evidence that a statement was given and received and that the employee accepts the statement as correctly setting out the terms of the employment.

## FORM 2

## Statement under Contracts of Employment Act 1972 when a Service Agreement has been entered into between the Employer and the Employee[1]

Employer:
Employee:
Address:
Particulars of the terms of your employment as at
197 .
The following particulars constitute the written statement required to be given to you under the Contracts of Employment

Act 1972, (as amended by the Employment Protection Act 1975) in respect of your employment with the above named employer which began on          [and which forms part of a continuous period of employment which began on
          with                    ]. [No employment with a previous employer counts as part of your period of continuous employment.]

Details as to the title of your job, remuneration, hours, entitlement to holidays and holiday payment, terms and conditions relating to incapacity for work due to sickness or injury, including provision for sick pay, and pensions and pension schemes are contained in a Service Agreement made between the Employer and the Employee dated the          day of 197 , a copy of which is in your possession.[2]

Your employment is for a fixed term expiring on the day of          19 [and thereafter until terminated by either party giving to the other no more than [six] months notice].

NOTE:

Rules concerning disciplinary procedures applicable to your employment are available for inspection in the Accounts Department as are rules relating to the redress of grievances. If you wish to raise a grievance or are dissatisfied with a disciplinary decision relating to you, you should contact the          Director.

The documents which are referred to as being in the Accounts Department are open to inspection at any time during normal working hours and future changes will be recorded in them from time to time.[3]

Dated ...   ....... 197          Signed ...   ..............
                              (Company Secretary)[4]

*Acknowledgment by employee.* I agree that the preceding provisions including those contained in the documents referred to (as varied from time to time) form the basis of my contract of employment and acknowledge receipt of a statement of which the foregoing is a true copy.

Dated this          day of          1976.

                    ......................[5]
                    [Employee]

[1] This form suitably adapted may present a convenient vehicle for providing an employee with whom there is a service agreement with the additional

information required by the Contracts of Employment Act 1972. The notes to Form 1 above should also be referred to.

2 Since the original service agreement should be in the possession of the employee it has been made "reasonably accessible to him in some other way". Contracts of Employment Act 1972, s. 4 (5).

3 See note 5, p. 454, above.

4 See note 9, p. 454, above.

5 See note 10, p. 454, above.

## FORM 3

## Statement of Written Particulars of Terms of Employment suitable for a Shorthand-typist[1]

To: Miss Jane Roe,
    300 Lancaster Way,
    London, W.2.

    The following particulars are given to you pursuant to the Contracts of Employment Act 1972, (as amended):

    1. The parties are as follows:

Name and Address of Employer:     John Doe, Ltd.,
        500 York Place,
        London, W.2.

Name and Address of Employee:     Jane Roe,
        300 Lancaster Way,
        London, W.2.

    2. The date when your employment began was May 1st 197 . [Your employment with Messrs. Bloggs & Co. from whom John Doe, Ltd. purchased the business and which began on June 1st 197 counts as part of your period of continuous employment with John Doe, Ltd.] [No employment with a previous employer counts as part of your period of continuous employment.]

    3. The following are the particulars of the terms of your employment as at June 15th, 197 .[2]

(a) You are employed at York Place, London as a shorthand-typist.[3]

(b) The rate of your remuneration is £—— per week.

(c) Your remuneration is paid at weekly intervals.

(d) Your normal working hours are from 9.30 a.m. to 5 p.m. Mondays to Fridays inclusive.

456

(e)  (i)  You are entitled to two weeks' holiday with pay after one completed year of service and to three weeks' holiday with pay every year after two completed years of service. Such holidays are to be taken at a time convenient to the employer between May 1st and October 30th in each year, provided that an employee whose employment is lawfully terminated before she has taken all the holiday which has accrued due is entitled to payment in lieu thereof on leaving her said employment. You are also entitled to the customary holidays with pay, i.e. New Years Day, Good Friday, Easter Monday, May Day, Spring Bank Holiday, Late Summer Bank Holiday, Christmas Day and Boxing Day.

  (ii)  In the case of incapacity for work due to sickness or injury the certificate of a registered medical practioner must be sent to the employer within 72 hours. During the continuity of the contract of employment the employer shall be entitled to deduct from the employee's wages the amount of the Social Security benefits in respect of such absence [received by the employee] [receivable by the employee] and the employee shall keep the employer informed of any such amounts.

 (iii)  Pensions and Pension Schemes: none in existence.

[There is no contracting-out certificate in force for your employment.]

(f)  The length of notice which you are obliged to give to determine your contract of employment is one week and the length of notice which you are entitled to receive unless your conduct is such that you may be summarily dismissed is as follows:

  (i)  One week if your period of continuous employment is less than two years.

  (ii)  One weeks' notice for each year of continuous employment if your period of continuous employment is two years or more but less than twelve years and

 (iii)  twelve weeks if your period of continuous employment is twelve years or more.

(g)  NOTE

If you are dissatisfied with any disciplinary decision relating to you or seek redress of any grievance relating to your employment you can apply to the person in charge of the typing pool. Details of the procedures to be followed are

posted in the staff room and the office manager's room.
Dated 20th day of June 197 .

Signed[4] J. Quill

(Company Secretary)

[1] The statement must be given to the employee not later than 13 weeks after the beginning of the employee's period of employment.

[2] This date must be a day not more than one week before the statement is given.

[3] The locality of the employment is not required to be specified by the Contracts of Employment Act 1972. If the employer may wish to later the location of the employment he should mention any right to do so.

[4] A signature is not essential under the Act, but it is included in this form to avoid any dispute which might arise in the event of the contents of the form being subsequently queried. The signature must be that of a person acting under the authority of the company. The employee should be asked to sign the employer's copy as follows:

"I have received and read a copy of the above particulars, which are correct in all respects.

Signed .....................
Date .....................,"

FORM 4

## Statement of Written Particulars pursuant to the Contracts of Employment Act 1972 for Employees subject to Orders under Wages Councils Act 1959, section 11[1]

From: [*name and address of employer*]
To: [*name and address of employee*]
You are employed as a ....... [*give job title*]
Your employment began on ...... [*insert date*]. No other employment with a previous employer counts as part of your period of continuous employment with your employer.
The following are the particulars[2] of the terms of your employment as at ...... [*insert date*][3]
1. *Remuneration*[4]
(a) Remuneration for normal working hours is at the rate of ....
a day [*week*] payable in arrear on the .... day of the week *or* [£ .... a month payable in arrear on the last day of each month].

458

(b) Overtime is calculated in accordance with the Wages Regulation (...... [*insert as appropriate*]) Order, 19  , as amended, particulars of which are contained in the notices posted up at your place of employment (as required by the Wages Councils Act, 1959) which you may read during normal working hours *or*[5] Overtime is payable on the following basis .......

(c) Commission is payable to you on the following basis .......

(d) For particulars of holiday remuneration see Clause 3 of this form.

2. *Hours of work*
   Your normal working hours are as follows:

| | | | | |
|---|---|---|---|---|
| Monday | ..a.m. to ..p.m. | Thursday | ..a.m. to ..p.m. |
| Tuesday | ..a.m. to ..p.m. | Friday | ..a.m. to ..p.m. |
| Wednesday | ..a.m. to ..p.m. | Saturday | ..a.m. to ..p.m. |

You are entitled to the following breaks .....

3. *Holidays and holiday pay*
   The terms and conditions relating to annual holidays, customary holidays and holiday pay are those contained in the Wages Regulation (...... [*insert as appropriate*]) Order, 19  , as amended, particulars of which are contained in the notices posted up at your place of employment (as required by the Wages Councils Act 1959) which you may read during normal working hours.

4. *Absence due to sickness or injury*
   (a) Subject to the production of a medical certificate if required by the employer, and subject also to the exceptions stated in paragraph (b), an employee who is absent owing to sickness, accident or disablement not arising from or attributable to his or her misconduct shall be entitled upon the completion of six months' continuous service to payment for such absence up to .... days in any year, and upon the completion of five years' continuous service to payment for such absence up to .... days in any year, at not less than the appropriate minimum rate of remuneration prescribed by the Orders made under the Wages Councils Act 1959, less any payments of Social Security benefits in respect of the absence receivable by him [her] provided that no such deductions shall be made in computing payment or the first three days of such absence in any year.

   (b) The foregoing provisions of this clause shall not entitle an employee to any payment during absence arising out of an accident for which damages are awarded at Common Law, or of any accident arising out of or in the course of following another occupation under a contract of service with another employer.

(c) For the purposes of this clause:

"day" means weekday, and the daily rate of sickness pay shall be one-sixth of the weekly rate;

"year" means a period of twelve months starting from . . . . . . .

5. *Pensions*

There is no pension scheme applicable to you *or*

You [may be required] or [are entitled] to join our pension scheme full particulars of which are contained in a document which you may read during normal working hours in the . . . . . . office or [in the . . . . . . department] at your place of employment.

[There is [not] a contracting-out certificate in force in respect of your employment][6]

6. *Notice to terminate employment*[7]

(a) The notice to be given by us [me] to terminate your contract of employment except when your conduct merits summary dismissal is as follows:

(i) One weeks notice if your period of continuous employment is less than two years.

(ii) One weeks notice for each year of continuous employment if your period of continuous employment is two years or more but less than twelve years.

(iii) twelve weeks notice if your period of continuous employment is twelve years or more.

(b) The notice to be given by you to terminate your contract of employment with us [me] is one week.

7. NOTE:

(i) If you are dissatisfied with any disciplinary decision relating to you, application can be made to the Works Manager.

(ii) You can apply to your foreman to seek redress of any grievance relating to your employment.

(iii) Further steps to be taken in connection with such applications are set out in the Rules relating to disciplinary and grievance procedures, copies of which are available in the Wages Office and Staff Room.

8. *Changes in particulars given in a document*[8]

Future changes in the relevant particulars in the following documents referred to in this statement will not be notified to you but the documents will be amended and maintained up to date within one month of any change and may be read during normal working hours in the Wages Office and Staff Room at your place of employment. The documents are:

The prescribed notices under the Wages Councils Act and orders pursuant to that Act.

Pension Scheme.

Disciplinary and Grievance Procedures.

Dated ...... 197 .

Received a statement of which the above is a duplicate the ...... day of ...... 197 .

Signature of employee ......

[1] In view of the additional powers conferred on Wages Councils by the Employment Protection Act 1975 their orders will have wider coverage than the former "wage regulation orders".

[2] If there are no particulars to be entered under any head state "none".

[3] This date must not be more than one week before the statement is given.

[4] If this clause is adapted by the person filling it in care must be taken to ensure that the scale or rate of remuneration, or the method of calculating remuneration, is clearly set out. The remuneration must be not less than the statutory minimum (including guaranteed weekly remuneration) in the orders pursuant to the Wages Councils Act 1959.

[5] The second alternative is to be used only when overtime is paid at a higher rate than that provided by the orders pursuant to the Wages Councils Act 1959.

[6] It is expected that the amendment introduced by the Social Security Pensions Act 1975 will come into force on 6th April 1978.

[7] The length of notice in this clause is the minimum obligatory under Contracts of Employment Act 1972, s. 1 (1) to terminate the contract of an employee who has been continuously employed for four weeks or more.

[8] Any change in particulars given in the original statement by reference to another document must be recorded *within one month* after the change is made. This can be done by amending the document which is kept available under clauses 1, 3, 5 and 7, of this statement. If this is correctly done, no written statement of this type of change need be given to an individual employee.

Changes in particulars which are not dealt with in the original statement by reference to another document must be notified personally to the employee. See Form 8, at p. 465, below.

FORM 5

## Statement of Written Particulars of Terms of Employment suitable for Employees who are employed subject to a Collective Agreement

From: [*name and address of employer*]
To: [*name and address of employee*]
Your employment began on ...... [*insert date*]. Your period of continuous employment starting on       197  with X Ltd. your present employers predecessors counts as part of your period of continuous employment with your present employer.
The title of your job is .......
The following are the particulars[1] of the terms of your employment as at ...... [*insert date*][2].

1. *Remuneration*[3]
(a) Remuneration for normal working hours is at a rate of .... an hour payable in arrear on the .... day in each week.
(b) Overtime is calculated in accordance with the ...... Agreement as amended, a copy of which may be read during normal working hours in the ...... office or [in the ...... department] at your place of employment. *or*[4]
    Overtime is payable on the following basis .......
(c) Bonus is payable to you on the following basis .......
(d) Any other emoluments to which you are entitled may be ascertained by reference to the ...... Agreement for the ...... Trade as amended, a copy of which may be read during normal working hours in the ...... office or [in the ...... department] at your place of employment.
(e) For particulars of holiday remuneration see Clause 3 of this form.

2. *Hours of work*
   Your normal working hours are as follows:

Monday       .. a.m. to .. p.m.       Thursday   .. a.m. to .. p.m.
Tuesday      .. a.m. to .. p.m.       Friday     .. a.m. to .. p.m.
Wednesday    .. a.m. to .. p.m.       Saturday   .. a.m. to .. p.m.
You are entitled to the following breaks .......

3. *Holidays and holiday pay*
   The terms and conditions relating to annual holidays, public holidays and holiday pay are those contained in the ...... Agreement as amended, a copy of which may be read during normal

working hours in the ...... office or [in the ...... department] at your place of employment.

4. *Absence due to sickness or injury*

There are no terms or conditions relating to incapacity for work due to sickness or injury nor any terms or conditions regarding sick pay. No payment is made when you are absent from work.

5. *Pensions*

There is no pension scheme applicable to you, *or*

You may be required or [are entitled] to join our pension scheme full particulars of which are contained in a document which may be read during normal working hours in the ...... office or [in the ...... department] at your place of employment. [There is [not] a contracting-out certificate in force in respect of your employment.]

6. *Notice to terminate employment*[5]

(a) The notice to be given by us [me] to terminate your contract of employment is:

   (i) One weeks notice if your period of continuous employment is less than two years.

   (ii) One weeks notice for each year of continuous employment if your period of continuous employment is two years or more but less than twelve years.

   (iii) Twelve weeks notice if your period of continuous employment is twelve weeks or more.

(b) The notice to be given by you to terminate your contract of employment with us [me] is one week.

7. NOTE

   (i) If you are dissatisfied with any disciplinary decision relating to you, application may be made to the Works Manager.

   (ii) You can apply to your foreman to seek redress of any grievance relating to your employment.

   (iii) Further steps to be taken in connection with such applications are set out in the Rules relating to disciplinary and grievance procedures copies of which are available in the Wages Office and Staff Room.

8. *Changes in particulars given in a document*[8]

Future changes in the relevant particulars in the following documents referred to in this statement will not be notified to you but the document will be amended and maintained up to date within one month of any change and may be read during normal working hours in the ...... office or [in the ...... department] at your place of employment.

The documents are:

The                    Agreement.

Pension Scheme.

Rules of Disciplinary and Grievance Procedures.

Dated ...... 197 .

Signed for and on behalf of the employer[s]. ...............

Received a statement of which the above is a duplicate and which correctly sets out the terms therein the ...... day of ...... 197

Signature of employee ......

[1] If there are no particulars to be entered under any head state "none".

[2] This date must not be more than one week before the statement is given.

[3] Care must be taken to ensure that not less than the basic rate in the collective agreement is paid and correctly inserted here.

[4] The second alternative is to be used only when overtime is paid at a higher rate than that provided by the collective agreement.

[5] The length of notice in this clause is the minimum obligatory notice under Contracts of Employment Act 1972, s. 1 (1) to terminate the contract of employment of an employee who has been continuously employed for four weeks or more.

[6] The collective agreement together with all amendments in existence at the date when this form is given to the employee must be kept in the office or department designated. For future changes see note to Form 9, p. 467, below. The Pension Scheme Rules must also be kept in the same place, unless there is no pension scheme applicable, together with other documents referred to.

FORM 6

## Particulars of Fixed Term Contract to be included in Statement of Particulars when appropriate

The date on which your employment began is 8th July 197 for a term certain expiring on 2nd August, 197 .[1]

[1] For the position in connection with fixed term contracts see p. 100, above.

FORM 7

## Notification of Change in Terms of Employment[1]

To ...... [*name and address of employee*]

This statement is given[2] to you pursuant to the Contracts of Employment Act 1972.

The following changes in the terms of your employment, as previously notified to you on the ...... day of ...... 197.., pursuant to the above-mentioned Act, have taken place by mutual agreement:

(1) Your remuneration is paid monthly instead of weekly from the ...... day of ...... 197...

(2) A pension scheme has been inaugurated, full particulars whereof are attached hereto. [A contracting-out certificate is now in force in respect of your employment.][3]

Signed [signature of employer or duly authorised agent]

[1] The employee should be informed of the nature of the change not more than one month after the change. See the detailed provisions of Contracts of Employment Act 1972, s. 5 at p. 105, above. The form may be varied as appropriate in the circumstances.

[2] The safest course is to give the statement to the employee and obtain a receipt. See p. 107, above.

[3] The provision introduced by the Social Security Pensions Act 1975 is expected to come into effect on 6th April, 1978.

FORM 8

## Notice of Changes in Particulars of Terms of Employment for Employees who are subject to Orders made pursuant to Wages Councils Act 1959, section 11 and who have already received Form 4 to be given to the Employee within not more than one month after the change[1]

From: [*name and address of employer*]

To: [*name and address of employee*]

Pursuant to the Contracts of Employment Act 1972, (as amended) you are hereby notified of the following changes in the

terms of your employment as previously notified to you on ......
have taken place:
1. *Title of your job*
   Date of Change ......
   The title now is ......
2. *Remuneration*
   Date of changes .......
   Your remuneration for normal working hours is now at the
rate of .... a day [week] [month].
   Overtime is now .......
   Commission is now .......
   You are now paid in arrear on .......
3. *Hours of work*
   Date of changes .......
   Your normal working hours have been altered as follows:
.......
4. *Absence due to sickness or injury*
   Date of changes .......
   The following changes in the terms or conditions relating to
incapacity for work due to sickness or injury and in the provisions
for sick pay have taken place .......
5. *Holiday*
   Date of changes .......
   Your holiday entitlement has been altered as follows .......
6. *Pensions*[2]
   Date of change .......
   There is now a Pension Scheme which you are at liberty or
[required] to join. A copy of the Scheme may be read during
normal working hours in the ...... office or [in the ......
department] at your place of employment. Future changes will
not be notified to you but the copy of the Scheme will be
amended and maintained up to date within one month of any
change. A contracting-out certificate is now in force in respect of
your employment.
7. *Notice to terminate employment*[3]
   Date of change .......
(a) The notice to be given by us [me] to terminate your employment has been varied as follows: .......
(b) The notice to be given by you to terminate your employment
   has been varied as follows: .......
   Dated ...... 197 .

Signed for and on behalf of the employer[s] .......

Received a statement of which the above is a duplicate and which correctly sets out the terms therein the ...... day of ...... 197 .

Signature of employee ..............

[1] This form must be used when there is a change in any of the particulars included in or referred to in Form 4 except those particulars which are designated in Form 4 by a reference to the relevant orders pursuant to the Wages Councils Act 1959, or other documents referred to, changes in which are covered by clause 8 of Form 4. This form must be given to the employee within one month of the change.

[2] Clause 6 of this form is to be used when a pension scheme which did not exist or was not appropriate to the particular employee when Form 4 was used now has to be mentioned as a change in the terms of his employment. The copy of the pension scheme must be maintained up to date by recording in it any future change not more than one month after the change is made, see p. 105, above.

[3] In no circumstances must the length of notice be reduced below that required by s. 1 (1) and (2) of the Act.

FORM 9

## Notice of Changes in Particulars of Terms of Employment relevant to Form 5, i.e., for Employees who are employed subject to a Collective Agreement and who have already received Form 5[1]

From: [*name and address of employer*]
To: [*name and address of employee*]
Pursuant to the Contracts of Employment Act 1972 (as amended) you are hereby notified of the following changes in the terms of your employment as previously notified to you on ...... which have now taken place.

1. *Title of your job*
   Date of change .......
   The title now is .......
2. *Remuneration*[2]
   Date of changes .......

Your remuneration for normal working hours is now at the rate of .... an hour.

Overtime is now .......

Bonus is now .......

You are now paid in arrear on .......

3. *Hours of work*

Date of changes .......

Your normal working hours have been altered as follows:
.......

4. *Absence due to sickness or injury*

Date of changes .......

The following terms or conditions relating to incapacity for work due to sickness or injury and sick pay have been agreed
.......

5. *Holidays*

Date of changes .......

Your holidays have been altered as follows .......

6. *Pensions*[3]

Date of change .......

There is now a Pension Scheme which you are at liberty [required] to join. A copy of the Scheme may be read during normal working hours in the ...... office [in the ...... department] at your place of employment. Future changes will not be notified to you but the copy of the Scheme will be amended and maintained up to date within one month of any change. [A contracting out certificate is now in force in respect of your employment.][4]

7. *Notice to terminate employment*[5]

Date of changes .......

(a) The notice to be given by us [me] to terminate your employment has been varied as follows: .......

(b) The notice to be given by you to terminate your employment has been varied as follows: .......

Signed for and on behalf of the employer[s] .......

Dated ........ 197 .

Received a statement of which the above is a duplicate and correctly sets out the terms therein the ........ day of ........ 197 .

Signature of employee ........

[1] This form must be used when there is a change in any of the particulars

included in or referred to in Form 5, p. 462, above except those particulars which are designated in Form 5 by reference to the Collective Agreement, as amended, and other documents referred to, changes in which are covered by clause 8 of Form 5. This form must be given to the employee within one month of the change.

2 All changes in the scale or rate of remuneration or the method of calculating remuneration must be notified personally by means of this form, except those covered by clause 1 (d) or (e) of Form 5.

3 Clause 6 of this form is to be used when a pension scheme which did not exist or was not appropriate to the particular employee when Form 5 was used now has to be mentioned as a change in the terms of his employment. The copy of the rules of the pension scheme must be maintained up to date by recording in it any future change not more than one month after the change is made.

4 See p. 461, note 6, above.

5 In no circumstances must the length of notice be reduced below that required by s. 1 (1) and (2) of the Act.

# Appendix 4

## RULES AS TO ABSENCE DUE TO SICKNESS AND INJURY, HOLIDAYS AND DISCIPLINARY AND GRIEVANCE PROCEDURES

FORM 1

### Specimen Rules as to Absence due to Sickness and Injury

1. An employee absent from work as a result of sickness or injury should notify the Company of the reason for his absence as soon as possible.

2. A Medical Certificate as to the reason for the absence must be sent to the Company if the employee is absent for any period of three or more consecutive working days, or three working days in one working week.

3. (a) No payment will be made in respect of periods of absence through sickness or injury to an employee with less than three months continuous service with the Company immediately prior to the first day of the absence.

(b) For those continuously employed for a period of three months or more immediately preceeding the first day of the absence payment will be made at the normal basic rate (less any benefits from the Department of Health and Social Security or other state benefits receivable by the employee) for up to a maximum of five weeks' absence in any 12-month period. The employee must notify the Company as to benefit payable by the Department of Health and Social Security and other benefits receivable by him.

FORM 2

### Specimen Rules relating to Holidays and Holiday Pay

1. Employees shall be entitled to the following customary holidays with pay:

New Year       —New Year Day
Easter         —Easter Monday and Tuesday
May            —May Day
Spring         —Spring Bank Holiday Monday
Summer/Autumn  —Late Summer Bank Holiday Monday
Christmas      —Christmas day and Boxing day (or in appro-
                priate years two working days appointed by
                the employer).

2. Annual holidays are to be taken in such periods and at such times as may be agreed with the employer.

3. The holidays of employees engaged, or re-engaged, during a holiday year will be agreed at the time of engagement, or re-engagement, as the case may be.

4. Subject as below, employees employed on the 1st January in each holiday year and throughout that year are entitled to three weeks annual holiday with pay.

5. Employees who have been employed for a continuous period of five years or more, prior to the 1st January each year and are employed throughout that year are entitled to four weeks annual holiday with pay.

6. The holiday year begins on the first day of January in each year, and ends on the last day of December of that year. Holiday which has not been taken in respect of a holiday year cannot be carried forward and no payment will be made in lieu thereof to continuing employees.

7. Employees leaving the Company's employment during a holiday year who have not taken accrued holidays are entitled to payment in lieu of untaken holiday. For these purposes holidays of all employees shall be deemed to accrue at the rate of one and one half days for each complete and continuous month of employment during the holiday year, to a maximum of 15 days in the case of employees to whom rule 4 applies, and 18 days for employees to whom rule 5 applies. In the calculation of any payment due, a day's pay will be one-fifth of the normal weekly basic payment. No other payment for holiday entitlements will be made.

FORM 3

## Specimen Grievance Procedure[1]

1. An employee having a grievance relating to his employment should raise the matter initially with his foreman or immediate superior to ascertain whether it is possible for the difficulty to be resolved informally.

2. If the foreman is not able to deal with the grievance at the time he should within the next three working days look into the matter and give the results of the investigation to the employee.

3. If the grievance is not satisfactorily resolved at that time the employee should hand brief written details of the grievance in at the Works Office.

4. Within three days the Works Manager will arrange a meeting between himself or his deputy, the aggrieved employee and his Shop Steward or any other employee he wishes to attend with him, and the foreman or immediate superior. At that meeting the employee will have the right to explain the grievance.

5. After the meeting the Works Manager, or his deputy, will give his decision on the matter within five working days.

6. Should the grievance not be resolved then the Works Manager will arrange for a written report of the meeting to be prepared for an Appeals Committee which will consist of the Personnel Director of the Company or some other person nominated by him, and the Senior Shop Steward of the trade union of which the employee is a member or, a person nominated by the Senior Shop Steward. If the employee is not a member of a trade union, the second member of the Appeals Committee will be the Chairman of the Works Committee, or a person nominated by him.

7. The Appeals Committee will consider:
(1) The outline of the grievance prepared by the employee.
(2) The report of the meeting with the Works Manager or his deputy prepared by the Works Manager or his deputy.
(3) Further written comments made by or on behalf of the employee; and
(4) Written comments made by or on behalf of the foreman or immediate superior.

There will then be a meeting of the Appeals Committee at which the employee and his representative will attend and make such further comments as they wish and the foreman (or immediate superior) and Works Manager may do likewise.

8. The decision of the Appeals Committee will be final and if the two members do not agree then the Personnel Director or his representative will have a casting vote. A short note of the reasons for the decision of the Appeals Committee will be given to the employee.

¹ See Code of Practice, paras. 120–125, issued pursuant to the Industrial Relations Act 1971 and continued in effect by the Employment Protection Act 1975, Sch. 17, para. 4. The procedure should be established with employee representatives or trade unions concerned except in very small establishments where there is close personal contact between the employer and his employees, The Industrial Relations Code of Practice is in force on 1st August 1976 although there is power for the Advisory, Conciliation and Arbitration Service to issue Codes of Practice pursuant to Employment Protection Act 1975, s. 6.

### Form 4

**Specimen Disciplinary Procedure** (this should be agreed with Employee Representatives or Trade Unions concerned)¹

1. The Company reserves the right in its discretion to suspend or dismiss employees guilty of gross misconduct, such as theft or dishonesty, without the necessity of instituting the following procedure.

2. The rights of suspension given by these rules may be exercised by the Company so that the suspension is with, or without, pay as it shall determine.

3. (a) Except in cases of gross misconduct after a first breach of contract, disciplinary rules or other obligations of the employee, the employee will be given an oral warning, or in the case of more serious misconduct, a written warning, setting out the circumstances giving rise to the complaint. Details of the warning will be recorded in the Company's records relating to the employee.

(b) As is set out above in cases of gross misconduct the Company may suspend or dismiss the employee without warning. If suspension or dismissal is exercised the employee will be given a written statement of the reasons.

(c) If in a case where a warning has been given the conduct of the employee complained of is repeated, or continues, a further warning in writing will be given where the first warning was oral. This warning will set out the circumstances in which it is given and will be recorded in the Company's records relating to the employee.

(d) If after a written warning has been given the conduct complained of, is repeated or continues, a final warning in writing will be given. This will be recorded in the Company's records relating to the employee.

(e) If notwithstanding the final written warning the conduct complained of, continues, or is repeated, the Company may exercise the right of suspension or dismissal. If a decision is taken to suspend or dismiss the employee notification in writing will be given to the employee and, if he requests, to his Shop Steward or representative on the Works Committee.

4. (a) Warnings, other than a final warning, may be given by the employee's immediate superior.

(b) The decision to exercise the right of suspension may be taken by the immediate superior (i.e. foreman) after consulting the Works Manager and the Chief Shop Steward for the Section in which the employee works.

(c) The decision to exercise the right of dismissal may be taken by the Works Manager after consulting with the Chief Shop Steward and the employee's immediate superior.

5. If it is proposed to suspend or dismiss the employee he will be given a written notice informing him of the Company's reasons and will be given an opportunity to explain his conduct to the Works Manager. If the employee so wishes his Shop Steward or another employee may be present at the meeting.

6. If the employee is dissatisfied with the decision he can indicate in writing that he wishes to appeal, when the matter will be considered by the Personnel Manager, or a deputy appointed by him, who will arrange to see the employee and his representative at a meeting to be held as soon as convenient.

7. Should the employee still not be satisfied after that meeting then the Personnel Manager will arrange for a written report of the meeting to be prepared for an Appeals Committee which will consist of a Director of the Company, or some other person nominated by the Board of Directors of the Company, and the Senior Shop Steward of the trade union of which the employee is a member, or a person nominated by the Senior Shop Steward. If the employee is not a member of a trade union the second

member of the Appeals Committee will be the Chairman of the Works Committee, or a person nominated by him.

8. The Appeals Committee will consider:

(1) The statement of reasons given to the employee.
(2) Any written representations which the employee may care to make, or which are made on his behalf.
(3) The report prepared by the Personnel Manager on the matter.
(4) Any further comments made by or on behalf of the employee.

There will be a meeting of the Appeals Committee at which the employee and his representative may attend and make such further comments which they may wish and the foreman and Works Manager may do likewise.

9. The decision of the Appeals Committee will be final and if the two members do not agree then the representative of the Company will have a casting vote. A short note of their reasons will to be given to the employee.

10. If possible steps will be taken to ensure that in the case of an employee given notice of dismissal the above procedure will be implemented and the decision of the Appeals Committee given before the notice takes effect. In cases which appear to him to be suitable the Personnel Manager has power to extend the notice period to enable this to be done.

[1] See Code of Practice, paras. 130–133, issued pursuant to the Industrial Relations Act 1971 and continued in effect by the Employment Protection Act 1975, Sch. 17, para. 4 and also effect on unfair dismissal claims, p. 328, above. The procedures should be agreed with employee representatives or trade unions. There should be a formal procedure except in very small establishments where there is close personal contact between the employer and the employees; Code of Practice, para. 130.

The Advisory, Conciliation and Arbitration Service have produced a draft Code of Practice relating to Disciplinary Practice and Procedures and it is intended that a new Code based on this should replace paras. 130 to 133. Disciplinary rules should be carefully drafted to ensure that they suit the particular circumstances of the case and follow the Code of Practice for the time being in force.

# Appendix 5

# FORMS RELATING TO RIGHT TO RETURN TO WORK AFTER ABSENCE BECAUSE OF PREGNANCY OR CONFINEMENT

## Form 1

### Notification by Employee that she intends to return to work after absence because of pregnancy or confinement[1]

Dear

I hereby inform you that as from the
I expect to be absent from work in consequence of pregnancy.
After my child is born I intend to return to work with you and in accordance with the Employment Protection Act 1975, section 35 (2), notify you of such intention.

Yours faithfully,

---

[1] See Employment Protection Act 1975, s. 35 (2), and p. 75, above. The notification need only be given in writing if the employer so requests. The notification should be at least three weeks before the absence begins, or if that is not reasonably practicable, as soon as is reasonably practicable.

## Form 2

### Notice on the Exercise of Right to return to Work— Employment Protection Act 1975, section 49 (1)[1]

I HEREBY NOTIFY you in pursuance of Employment Protection Act 1975, section 49 (1) that I propose to return to work

following my pregnancy and confinement on the        day of
19  .

[1] See p. 81, above. Notice can be to the original employer or a successor of that employer. The notification which need not be in writing should be given at least one week before the day on which the employee proposes to return.

## FORM 3

### Notice to postpone Employee's Return to Work pursuant to the Employment Protection Act 1975, section 49 (2).[1]

Dear        ,
          Thank you for notifying us of your proposal to return to work following your pregnancy and confinement on the        day of        . Unfortunately, because [of difficulties involved on our recent move of office] it will not be convenient for you to return on that day. Would you postpone your return until the following Monday the        1977, when we look forward to seeing you.

Yours faithfully,

[1] See p. 82, above. The employer may postpone the return to work until a date not more than four weeks after the notified day of return. The reasons for the postponement should be given. There is no requirement that the notification should be in writing.

## FORM 4

### Postponement of Return to Work from Notified Day of Return[1]

Dear        ,
          I have to notify you that I will not be able to return to work on the        day of        as I previously notified you because I am suffering from        . I now propose to return to work on the        day of        19  . I enclose a

certificate from my registered medical practitioner.

Yours faithfully,

---

[1] See Employment Protection Act 1975, s. 49(3), and p. 82, above. The medical certificate should be given to the employer before the notified day of return. All that is required by statute is that the employee gives the employer a certificate from a registered medical practitioner stating that by reason of disease or bodily or mental disablement she will be incapable of work on the notified day of return. The right of postponement may be exercised once only, section 49(4). See p. 82, above.

## Form 5

### Postponement of Return when no Day of Return notified[1]

Dear          ,

    I write to inform you that I am not able to return to work before the end of the period of 29 weeks beginning with the week in which my baby was born because I am suffering from
Accordingly, I propose to work on the          day of
19    . I enclose a certificate from my registered medical practitioner.

Yours faithfully,

---

[1] Employment Protection Act 1975, s. 49(3), see p. 82, above. See note to Form 4, above. The medical certificate should be given to the employer before the expiration of the 29 week period. The right of postponement may be exercised once only, s. 49(4). See p. 82, above.

## Form 6

### Dismissal of Replacement for Person absent by Reason of Pregnancy or Confinement
### Notice under the Employment Protection Act 1975, section 51[1]

YOU ARE INFORMED that your employment will be

terminated on the return to work of                   who
is [will be] absent wholly or partly because of pregnancy or
confinement and you will be dismissed in order to make it
possible to provide work for her on her return.

Date...............               Signed................................

                      [By or on behalf of the Employer]

[On Duplicate]
To [Employer]

I confirm that on my engagement by you I received the notice
of which the above is a copy which I fully understand.

Dated ......................            Signed .............................[2]

                          [Employee]

---

[1] See p. 83, above. The notice must be in writing and given to the
employee on engagement.

[2] There is no requirement that a copy should be signed by the employee
but it is obviously good practice to obtain such an acknowledgement.

# Appendix 6

# DISMISSAL OR REPLACEMENT FOR PERSON SUSPENDED ON MEDICAL GROUNDS

## Notice under Employment Protection Act 1975, section 33[1]

YOU ARE HEREBY INFORMED that your employment is temporary only[2] and will be terminated on the ending of suspension of                    on medical grounds as is referred to in Section 29 (1) of the Employment Protection Act 1975 and that you will be dismissed in order to make it possible to allow him to resume work when he is able to do so.

Dated................                    Signed...................................
                                        [By or on behalf of the Employer]
[On Duplicate]
To [Employer]

I confirm that on my engagement by you I received the notice of which the above is a copy and which I fully understand.

Dated ....................                    Signed .........................3
                                              [Employer]

---

[1] See p. 63, above. The notice must be in writing and be given to the employee on engagement.

[2] There is no requirement for the word "temporary" to appear. However, it makes it clear that the employee should have fully understood the meaning of the notice.

[3] There is no requirement that a copy should be signed by the employee but it is obviously good practice to obtain such an acknowledgement.

# Appendix 7

# FORMS APPLICABLE IN CIRCUMSTANCES OF REDUNDANCY

FORM 1

### Notice by Employer of Intention to Contest Redundancy Payment given under the Redundancy Payments Act 1965, section 4 (3)

[ *To be delivered to the employee, or left for him at his usual or last-known place of residence, or sent by post addressed to him at that place; see Redundancy Payments Act 1965, section 53 (1) and p. 273, above.*]

To.............................................. [*Name and address of employee*]

Take notice that you are required to withdraw your notice dated ........................... terminating your contract of employment and to continue in our employment until the date on which our notice dated ........................... expires, namely [........................... insert date]. If you fail to do so we shall contest your liability to pay you a redundancy payment in respect of the termination of your contract of employment, see section 4 (3) of the Redundancy Payments Act 1965.

*Signed*...........................................

*Date*...........................................

FORM 2

### Offer[1] of New Contract made by Employer to Redundant Employee under Redundancy Payments Act 1965, section 2 (3) (as amended)

The following are the particulars of the employment which I, ...........
........................... [*Name and address of employer*], am offering you, ...........
........................... [*Name and address of employee*], to begin on ...........................

1. Brief description of employment ...........................................
2. Place of employment ...........................................
3. Scale or rate of remuneration or method of calculating remuneration ...........................................
4. Intervals at which remuneration is paid ...........................................
5. Normal hours of work and any other terms and conditions relating to hours of work ...........................................
6. Holidays and holiday pay ...........................................
7. Terms and conditions relating to incapacity for work due to sickness or injury and particulars of any sick pay ...........................................
8. There is no pension scheme applicable to you *or* particulars of pension scheme ...........................................
9. Amount of notice[2] to terminate contract to be given by:
   (1) employee ...........................................
   (2) employer ...........................................
10. All other terms and conditions of employment will remain as set out on the Statement dated ........................... 197..... given to you pursuant to the Contracts of Employment Act 1972 (as amended).

$$\begin{array}{ll} \textit{Signed} & \text{.....................................} \\ \textit{Date} & \text{.....................................} \end{array}$$

[1] The offer must be made to the employee while still employed by the employer, and must take effect either immediately on the ending of that employment or after an interval of not more than four weeks; Redundancy Payments Act 1965, s. 2(3). See p. 209, above. See s. 2(6) and p. 210, above, when the contract ends on a Friday, Saturday or Sunday. It is no longer a requirement that the offer should be in writing but as a matter of evidence is better if it is.

[2] If the contract is for a fixed term the date of expiry should be given.

FORM 3

### Agreement to extend Trial Period pursuant to Redundancy Payments Act 1965, section 3 (6) (as amended)[1]

This Agreement is made the       day of       197
between       ("the
Employer") and
("the Employee").
WHEREBY it is agreed as follows:
1. That upon the determination of the Employee's present

employment by reason of redundancy he will undergo a period of retraining for the post of

2. That for the purposes of Section 3 (6), Redundancy Payments Act 1965 (as amended), the trial period therein mentioned will commence on the 197 and continue until the 197 .

3. Both during the training period and thereafter the Employee's terms and conditions of employment will be as set out on the attached Statement.[2]

Signed by the Employee.................................................................................................

Signed on behalf of the Employer ...............................................................

[1] See p. 198, above.

[2] Attach statement setting out the terms and conditions of employment. As there will have been a change in the terms of employment the notification under the Contracts of Employment Act 1972, s. 5, could serve this purpose.

FORM 4

## Notice by Employee requiring Employer to give a Written Statement under Redundancy Payments Act 1965, section 18, indicating how the amount of a Redundancy Payment has been Calculated[1]

[*Unless a redundancy payment is made as a result of the decision of a tribunal the employer must on making a payment give the employee a written statement indicating how the amount has been calculated. This statement will be an arithmetical calculation made in accordance with Schedule 1 to the Redundancy Payments Act. Failure to give such a statement without reasonable excuse amounts to an offence (under section 18 (2)) carrying a maximum fine of £20, but after notice by an employee (under section 18 (3)) there is a maximum fine of £100 for a second or subsequent offence.*

*This notice must be served on the employer in accordance with section 53 (2) of the Act, see p. 273, above.*]

To ..................................................    [*Name and address of employer*]

This notice is given to you under section 18 (3) of the

Redundancy Payments Act 1965, and requires you to give to me not later than ........................................[1] a written statement indicating how the amount of the redundancy payment received by me on ............. ................................................ has been calculated.

........................................ [*Signature of employee*]

Date ........................................

[1] The minimum period is not less than one week beginning with the day on which the notice is given; see s. 18 (3), p. 250, above. "Not less than" means a clear or whole week; see *McQueen* v. *Jackson*, [1903] 2 K.B. 163 and *Re Hector Whaling, Ltd.*, [1936] Ch. 208; [1935] All E.R. Rep. 302.

FORM 5

## "Notice of Extension" to be given by Employer under the Redundancy Payments Act 1965, section 40[1]

[*Form A and Form B below are variants of the "notice of extension" to be given under Redundancy Payments Act 1965. section 40. Form A is applicable when the notice is not served until the participation of the employee in the strike has concluded and the number of working days lost is thus ascertainable. Under section 40 (1) (b), ibid., the employer may, however, serve a "notice of extension" as soon as the employee "begins to take part in a strike of employees of the employer". Form B is thus applicable when the "notice of extension" is served during the period of participation in the strike.*

*The "notice of extension" must be delivered to the employee or left for him at his usual or last-known place of residence, or sent by post addressed to him at that place (see section 53 (1)).*]

FORM A

To ........................................ [*Name and address of employee*]

This notice is served on you in accordance with section 40 of the Redundancy Payments Act 1965.

You are requested to agree to extend your contract of employment beyond the time of expiry, i.e.[2] ........................................ by an additional period of[3] ........................................

484

We make this request because you took part in a strike of our employees from ........................................ to ........................................
Unless you comply with this request or we are satisfied that, in consequence of sickness, injury or otherwise, you are unable to comply with it or that (notwithstanding that you are able to comply with it) in the circumstances it is reasonable for you not to do so, we shall contest any liability to pay you a redundancy payment in respect of your dismissal.

........................................ [*Signature of employer*]

*Date* ........................................

[1] For the effect of the Redundancy Payments Act 1965, s. 40, see p. 205, above. "Strikes during notice of termination".
[2] Here insert the date of expiry of the employer's notice of termination (see the Redundancy Payments Act 1965, s. 40 (9)).
[3] Here insert the number of working days lost by striking (see the Redundancy Payments Act 1965, s. 40 (8) and (9)).

## FORM B

To ........................................ [*Name and address of employee*]

This notice is served on you in accordance with section 40 of the Redundancy Payments Act 1965. You are requested to agree to extend your contract of employment beyond the time of expiry, i.e.[1] ........................................ by an additional period comprising as many available days as the number of working days lost by striking[2] which period is not yet ascertainable. We make this request because you began to take part in a strike of our employees on ........................................
........................................ Unless you comply this request or we are satisfied that, in consequence of sickness, injury or otherwise, you are unable to comply with it or that (notwithstanding that you are able to comply with it) in the circumstances it is reasonable for you not to do so, we shall contest any liability to pay you a redundancy payment in respect of your dismissal.

........................................ [*Signature of employer*]

*Date* ........................................

[1] See Redundancy Payments Act 1965, s. 40 (9).
[2] See Redundancy Payments Act 1965, s. 40 (8) and (9).

485

FORM 6

## Prior Notice of Expected Redundancy under the Redundancy Payments Act 1965, section 30 (4)[1]

[*To enable the Secretary of State for Employment to attempt to place redundant employees, prior notice of redundancies giving rise to a claim for a rebate from the Fund must be given by employers to the "local office", usually the local employment exchange. This procedure is governed by the Redundancy Payments Rebates Regulations 1965 (S.I. 1965 No. 1893) as amended by S.I. 1965 No. 2067. In the case of ten or more employees, the notice required is not less than 21 days; otherwise it is not less than 14 days.*

*When the particulars required are not known or not completely known, that fact must be stated in the notice (see S.I. 1965 No. 1893, reg. 4 (1)). If the information required under item (h) in the form below involves a calculation which it is not practicable to make in time for it to be included in the notice, an intimation that it will follow later should be included (see S.I. 1965 No. 1893, reg. 4 (2)). Every employer who gives prior notice of a claim for a rebate must provide information including documentary information in support (see S.I. 1965 No. 1893, reg. 6 (1)).*]

To the local office of the Department of Employment [*give address*]

........................................................................................................................................

    D. & Co., Ltd. [*give address*] hereby give you prior notice in accordance with the Redundancy Payments Rebates Regulations 1965, that a claim for a rebate may arise in consequence of the termination by them of the contracts of employment of the following employees:

    [*Alternative form for use where appropriate:* ............................... in consequence of the expiration of the contracts of employment for a fixed term of the following employees]:

(a) Name and sex: ...............................................................................
(b) National Insurance number: ......................................................
(c) Income tax reference number: .................................................
(d) Date of birth: ................................................................................
(e) Date on which employee commenced his current period of continuous employment: ...........................................................
(f) Date on which employment is expected to terminate: ..............

(g) Reason for the expected termination of employment: ..............

.....................................................................................................................

(h) Amount of week's pay calculated in accordance with Employment Protection Act 1975, Schedule 4, Part II : ................................

.....................................................................................................................

..................................................................... [*Signature of employer*]

[*Date*]...........................................................................................

¹ This is a form of notice of intention to claim rebate from the
Redundancy Fund. It differs, and is separate, from the form satisfying the
requirement to notify the Secretary of State for Employment in certain
circumstances pursuant to the Employment Protection Act 1975, s. 100. See
p. 267, above, and Form 12, below.


FORM 7

**Notice by Employee of Intention to Claim
Redundancy Payment in respect of Lay-off or
Short-time, combined with Notice Terminating
Contract, given under the Redundancy Payments Act
1965, s. 6**

[*The Act specifically covers some informality of wording by the
use in section 6 (1) of the words " ... notice in writing to his
employer indicating (in whatsoever terms) his intention to claim a
redundancy payment ..." The wording of the following form is thus not
in any way essential, but whatever words are used the terms of the Act
must be accurately complied with; see p. 273, above.*]

I, ................................. of .........................................,
hereby give you as my employer notice under section 6 of the
Redundancy Payments Act 1965, that I intend to claim a
redundancy payment in respect of lay-off [*or in respect of short-time*]
having been laid off [*or kept on short-time*] for the period of ..............
consecutive weeks ended on ................................. [*or
having been paid off* (or kept on short-time) *for a series of six or
more weeks within the meaning of section 6 (1) (b) of the Redundancy
Payments Act 1965, the last of such weeks having ended on the* ..............
.................................*, and I further¹ give you one
week's² notice to terminate my employment by you on the
..................... day of ..................... 197......

Signed ................................................      [*Signature of employee*]

To [*name and address of employer*]

    This notice was served[3] ................................................................

by ................................................................................................

[1] Redundancy Payments Act 1965, s. 6(3), and p. 223, above.

[2] One week is the minimum, see the Redundancy Payments Act 1965, s. 6 (3) (*a*), and proviso.

[3] Here insert date and means of service. See the Redundancy Payments Act 1965, s. 53, and p. 273, above, as to methods of service and p. 223, above, as to relevance of date of service.

FORM 8

8a

### Counter-notice[1] by Employer of Intention to Contest Liability given under Redundancy Payments Act 1965, section 6 (5), in reply to Employee's Notice of Intention to Claim

To ................................................      [*Name and address of employee*]

    In reply to your notice of intention to claim served on the ........................................ please take notice pursuant to section 6 (5) of the Redundancy Payments Act 1965, that I intend to contest any liability to pay you a redundancy payment in pursuance of your said notice.

Signed ................................................................................

    [*Signature of employer or duly authorised agent*]

    This notice was served on[3] ........................................ by

................................................................................................

[1] Within seven days after service of notice of intention to claim.

[2] When the employer is a limited company the contract must be signed by a person acting under its authority, see also Companies Act 1948, ss. 32 (1) and 36.

[3] Here insert date and means of service. See p. 273, above, as to methods of service.

8b

## Notice of Withdrawal of Counter-notice given by Employer under Redundancy Payments Act 1965, section 7 (4)

To ............................................... [*Name and address of employee*]

I hereby give you notice under section 7 (4) of the Redundancy Payments Act 1965, that I withdraw my counter-notice served upon you on (*date of service of counter-notice*).

*Date*............................................

Signed[1] ............................................................................
[*Signature of employer or duly authorised agent*]

This notice was served on[2] ......................................... by
............................................................................

---

[1] When the employer is a limited company the contract must be signed by a person acting under its authority. See also Companies Act 1948, ss. 32 (1) and 36.

[2] Here insert date and means of service. See the Redundancy Payments Act 1965, s. 53. See p. 273, above.

## FORM 9

## Agreement[1] by Employee under a Fixed-term Contract: Redundancy Payments Act 1965, section 15 (2)

To ............................................... [*Name and address of employer*]

I, [*Name and address of employee*] .........................................
being employed by you under a contract of employment for a fixed term of[2] ......................... years commencing on .........................
hereby agree that I am not entitled to a redundancy payment under the Redundancy Payments Act 1965, in respect of the expiry of that term without its being renewed.

*Date* ............................................

Signed [*Signature of employee*] .........................................

[1] This may be contained either in the contract itself or in a separate agreement. "Agreement" appears to be used in the sense of unilateral consent; Redundancy Payments Act 1965, s. 15 (3). See p. 164, above. See also Appendix 2, Form 3 above.

[2] Two years or more.

## FORM 10

### Specimen letter inviting Consultation pursuant to Employment Protection Act 1975, section 99[1]

To: The Senior Shop Steward of Registered Independent Trade Union[2]

Dear Sir,

I have to inform you that as a result of financial difficulties which have been occasioned to this Company by the current economic situation, resulting in a substantial decline in sales, it has been decided to reorganise our production facilities. Unfortunately this will result in the complete closure of the            Works during the present financial year. It is proposed that the reorganisation will have the following effects:

1. 350 manual workers and 50 office workers will be made redundant out of a total of 400 manual workers and 65 office workers at            Works.

2. It is proposed to select the number to be made redundant on a "last in, first out" basis. The employees remaining will assist in closing down plant and offices and will then be offered work at our            Works in

3. It is anticipated that the dismissals will take place over a period of three months. We propose that approximately one third of those redundant should be dismissed at the end of            , another third at the end of the following month and the remainder on the last day of            The selection for order of dismissal will also be made on a "last in, first out" basis.

The Board of Directors very much regret having to take this action and I will be pleased to discuss the matter with you and your colleagues.

Yours faithfully,

[1] For discussion of the obligations under the Employment Protection Act 1975, s. 99, see p. 262, above. It is to be noted that the obligation is on the employer to consult with the recognised independent trade union however small the number of employees to be made redundant and whether or not such employee or employees have been employed for the qualifying period to be entitled to a redundancy payment or redundancy payments. For minimum periods of consultation in certain cases, see p. 264, above.

[2] For "recognised independent trade union", see p. 264, above.

FORM 11

## Specimen letter to Representatives of Trade Union after Negotiations with and Consideration of Representations made by the Trade Union[1]

Dear Sir,

I am obliged to you for your assistance in the consideration of proposed redundancies at our                    Works.
We have noted and carefully considered the representations which you have made and the other points raised both in writing and at our several meetings.

My Board appreciates that it will be easier for the redundant employees if the dismissals are all postponed for one month so that none take effect during the holiday period, and I can confirm that this will be done. Accordingly, the first redundancies will not now take place until

Unfortunately, your suggestion that redundancies would not be necessary if our other plants all went on short time, is not acceptable, nor are the Board able to implement the other representations which you made. The financial position of the Company is such that unless the action which we propose is taken and carried out very quickly, serious damage will be caused to the remainder of our business and other jobs will be endangered.

Yours faithfully,

[1] See Employment Protection Act 1975, s. 99 (7), discussed at p. 264, above.

FORM 12

## Specimen letter of Notification to be addressed to the Secretary of State for Employment[1]

To: The Secretary of State for Employment [at the Regional Office of the Department of Employment]

Dear Sir,

I have to inform you that as a result of financial difficulties which have been occasioned to this Company by the current economic situation, resulting in a substantial decline in sales, it has been decided to re-organise our production facilities. Unfortunately, this will result in a complete closure of the
works during the present financial year. It is proposed that the reorganisation will have the following effects:

1. 350 manual workers and 50 office workers will be made redundant out of a total of 400 manual workers and 65 office workers at                     Works.

2. Of the 350 manual workers 38 are apprentices under the age of 20. 15 of the office workers are under the age of 20 but none of them is apprenticed.

3. It is proposed to select the number to be made redundant on a "last in, first out" basis. The employees remaining will assist in closing down plant and offices and will then be offered work at our                     Works in

4. It is anticipated that the dismissals will take place over a period of three months. We propose that approximately one-third of those redundant should be dismissed at the end of                     ,
another third at the end of the following month and the remainder on the last day of                     . The selection for order of dismissal will also be made on a "last in, first out" basis.

5. On the                     of                     197     consultation was begun with the                     union which is the recognised independent trade union relating to the manual workers and on the same day consultation began with the
                    union the recognised independent trade union in respect of the office workers. At present agreement has not been reached with either of the unions but negotiations are proceeding.

The Board of Directors regret having to take this action and will do all in their power to assist with the placement of the redundant employees. If I can provide further information please let me know.

Yours faithfully,

[1] As required in certain circumstances by the Employment Protection Act 1975, s. 100. For a discussion of these provisions, see p. 267, above. Where the notice relates to employees of any description in respect of which the employer recognises an independent trade union a copy of the notice should be given to the representatives of that union.

# Appendix 8

# NOTICE REQUIRING REINSTATEMENT OR RE-ENGAGEMENT

**Notice to Employer that dismissed Employee wishes to be reinstated or re-engaged pursuant to Employment Protection Act 1975, s. 71[1]**

TO: (Employer)

Dear Sir,

I write to inform you that I am applying to an industrial tribunal claiming that my dismissal was unfair, and to notify you that it is my wish that I be reinstated or re-engaged.

Yours faithfully,

[Employee]

---

[1] There is no requirement that notice should be given to the employer. However, if the employer has engaged a permanent replacement for the dismissed employee the industrial tribunal may take that fact into account if the employer can show that he engaged the replacement after the lapse of a reasonable period without having heard from the dismissed employee that he wished to be reinstated or re-engaged and that it was no longer reasonable for him to arrange for the dismissed employee's work to be done except by a permanent replacement. See p. 348, above.

# Appendix 9

# NOTICES TO TERMINATE EMPLOYMENT

## Form 1

### Specimen Letter of Notice by Employer terminating employment[1]

Dear

Unfortunately, despite the oral and written warnings given to you on the         ,          , and          it is regretted that your conduct has continued to deteriorate and you have again been found fighting in the Works. I have discussed the position with the Personnel Manager and in the circumstances have no alternative but to give you          weeks notice to terminate your employment on the          day of          197 . Would you attend at the Wages Office on that day to collect your final wages.

I have to inform you that there is a disciplinary procedure applicable to your employment and the Rules are available for your inspection during the normal working hours in the Wages Office.[2]

[Further take note that your employer would by reason of your conduct be entitled to terminate your contract without notice and this statement is given to you pursuant to section 2 (2) (c) of the Redundancy Payments Act 1965.][3]

Yours faithfully,

[The letter should be signed by a senior member of management.]

---

[1] This should not be given until the employer's check-list of dismissal, p. 438, above, has been considered. All the matters mentioned there must be taken into account. The form of notice may be used in evidence and it is essential that it is carefully prepared.

[2] There is no obligation to draw attention to disciplinary rules at this stage but to do so may assist the employer in contending that he acted fairly.

[3] If there is a redundancy situation yet the employee is dismissed for misconduct, Redundancy Payments Act 1965, s. 2 (2) should be considered, see p. 177, above.

## FORM 2

## Notice by Employee Terminating Employment

I hereby give you one week's notice[1] in accordance with section 1 (2) of the Contracts of Employment Act 1972, to terminate my employment by [*name of company*] or [*name of firm*] or, [*in the case of an individual,*] [*you*] on the ...... day of ...... 197 .

Dated the .... day of ........ 197..

Signed [*Signature of employee*]

[1] This period notice which may be incorporated in a letter must be given by every employee who has been continuously employed for four weeks or more and one clear week's notice must be given. It may be provided by contract that more than one week's notice is required and it can also be given if desired. Written notice though not obligatory is desirable.

## FORM 3

## Request for Written Statement of Reasons for Dismissal[1]

TO: [Employer]

Pursuant to section 70, Employment Protection Act 1975, I request that within 14 days you provide me with a written statement giving particulars of the reasons for my dismissal.

Date .......                                    Signature .......

[1] See Employment Protection Act 1975, s. 70 discussed at p. 152, above, If no written statement of reasons for the dismissal has been given it should be requested as soon as possible after the dismissal. An employer is only entitled to the statement if at the effective date of termination he has been, or will be, continuously employed for a period of 26 weeks ending with the last complete week before that date. There is no requirement that the request should be in writing.

## FORM 4

## Written Statement of Reasons for Dismissal[1]

TO: [Employee][2]

In response to your request we set out below particulars of the reasons for your dismissal. You were dismissed because:

The dismissal was carried out after the disciplinary procedure was invoked and after your representations had been considered.

Date . . . . . . . .                                    Signature . . . . . . . .

[1] See the Employment Protection Act 1975, s. 70 discussed at p. 152, above.
[2] The written statement should be provided within 14 days of the request. See p. 152 for the position where there is default. Since the statement is admissible in evidence in any proceedings great care should be exercised in its preparation.

# Appendix 10

# APPEALS TO THE EMPLOYMENT APPEAL TRIBUNAL

## (Forms Reproduced from the Employment Appeal Tribunal Rules 1976)[1]

[1] S.I. 1976 No. 322. The two forms applicable in circumstances relevant to the topics covered by this work are shown here since they will not be readily available from offices of the Department of Employment. For requirements as to service see p. 426, above.

## FORM 1

### Notice of Appeal from Decision of Industrial Tribunal

1. The appellant is (*name and address of appellant*).

2. Any communication relating to this appeal may be sent to the appellant at (*appellant's address for service, including telephone number if any*).

3. The appellant appeals from
(*here give particulars of the decision of the industrial tribunal from which the appeal is brought*)
on the following question of law:
(*here set out the question of law on which the appeal is brought*).

4. The parties to the proceedings before the industrial tribunal, other than the appellant, were (*names and addresses of other parties to the proceedings resulting in decision appealed from*).

5. The appellant's grounds of appeal are:
(*here state the grounds of appeal*).

6. A copy of the industrial tribunal's decision is attached to this notice.

Date                    Signed

FORM 3

## Respondent's Answer

1. The respondent is (*name and address of respondent*).

2. Any communication relating to this appeal may be sent to the respondent at (*respondent's address for service, including telephone number if any*).

3. The respondent intends to resist the appeal of (*here give name of appellant*). The grounds on which the respondent will rely are [the grounds relied upon by the industrial tribunal/Certification Officer for making the decision or order appealed from] [and] [the following grounds]:
(*here set out any grounds which differ from those relied upon by the industrial tribunal or Certification Officer, as the case may be*).

4. The respondent cross-appeals from:
(*here give particulars of the decision appealed from*).

5. The respondent's grounds of appeal are:
(*here state the grounds of appeal*).

Date          Signed

# Appendix 11

# RACIAL DISCRIMINATION

It was intended to discuss the statutory control of discrimination on the grounds of colour, race, nationality or ethnic or national origin in that part of Chapter 1 dealing with anti-discrimination legislation. However on 17th February 1976 the House of Commons ordered a Race Relations Bill to be printed and it was expected that this would receive the Royal Assent prior to the summer recess. Thus discussion of such discrimination has been postponed to this Appendix. The Race Relations Bill had not passed all its stages when Parliament rose but it still appears likely that it will be enacted prior to the ending of the current Parliamentary session.

The Race Relations Act 1968, which is in force on 1st August 1976, makes it unlawful to discriminate against employees and prospective employees on the grounds of colour, race, or ethnic or national origin:—

(*a*) by refusing or deliberately omitting to employ a person seeking employment on work of any description which is available and for which he is qualified,

(*b*) by refusing or deliberately omitting to afford or offer an employee like terms of employment conditions of work and opportunities for training and promotion as the employer makes available for persons of like qualifications and in like circumstances, and

(*c*) by dismissing an employee in circumstances in which other persons employed on work of that description by the employer are not, or would not be, dismissed.[1]

It is unlawful to publish or display, or cause to be published or displayed an advertisement or notice which indicates, or could be reasonably understood as indicating, an intent to discriminate even if it is not unlawful by virtue of the Act.[2]

[1] Race Relations Act 1968, s. 3.
[2] *Ibid.*, s. 6(1). See also *ibid.*, s. 6(2).

The Act does not make unlawful acts done for the purpose

of safe-guarding national security and the usual rule: making certificates that acts were done for such purpose, conclusive evidence of that fact, applies.[1] It is not unlawful to discriminate against any person with respect to the engagement or employment in, or selection for work within an undertaking, or part of an undertaking, if the act is done in good faith for the purpose of securing or preserving a reasonable balance of persons of different racial groups employed in the undertaking, or that part of the undertaking.[2] In determining whether a balance is reasonable regard should be had to all the circumstances and in particular to the proportion of persons employed in those groups in the undertaking or part of the undertaking as the case may be, and the extent, if any, to which the employer engages, with respect to employment in the undertaking, or part of the undertaking, as the case may be, in unlawful discrimination.[3] An employer wishing to rely on this exception is best advised to consult the Race Relations Board before doing so, to ensure that the criteria which he intends to apply are acceptable. The provisions of the Race Relations Act 1968 do not apply to the employment of any person for the purpose of a private household,[4] or to any employment which is, or application, for employment which is to be, wholly or mainly outside Great Britain, wholly on a British ship or aircraft outside Great Britain, or wholly or mainly on a ship or aircraft outside Great Britain, other than a British ship or aircraft.[5] The provisions do not apply to employment, or an application for employment, of a person on a ship or aircraft if the person employed or seeking employment was engaged, or applied for the employment, outside Great Britain. A person brought to Great Britain with a view to his entering into an agreement, in Great Britain, to be employed on any ship or aircraft is treated as engaged for, or seeking, the employment outside Great Britain. It is not unlawful to discriminate against any person in respect of employment on a ship, if compliance with the requirements in that respect would result in persons of different colour, race or ethnic or national origins being compelled to share sleeping, or mess, rooms or sanitary accommodation.[6] In addition, it is not unlawful to select a person of a particular nationality or particular descent for employment requiring attributes especially possessed by persons of that nationality or descent,[7] such as an Italian cook for an Italian restaurant.

[1] Race Relations Act 1968, s. 10.

[2] *Ibid.*, s. 8(2). "Racial group" means a group of persons defined by reference to colour, race, or ethnic or national origins and for the purposes of the sub-section, persons wholly or mainly educated in Great Britain are treated as members of the same racial group: *ibid.*, s. 8(4).

[3] *Ibid.*, s. 8 (3).

[4] *Ibid.*, s. 8 (6).

[5] *Ibid.*, s. 8 (7).

[6] *Ibid.*, s. 8 (10).

[7] *Ibid.*, s. 8 (11).

A person who considers that he has been unlawfully discriminated against may make a complaint to the Race Relations Board, a Conciliation Committee or the Secretary of State for Employment, and if after investigation the complaint is substantiated an attempt at conciliation will be made.[1] If this attempt fails, or any assurance given is broken, the Race Relations Board may institute proceedings in accordance with the provisions of the Race Relations Act 1968.

[1] Race Relations Act 1968, s. 16 and Sch. 2.

When under the Race Relations Act 1968 a complaint is made to the Secretary of State or the Race Relations Board[1] that an act has been done which is unlawful by virtue of section 3 (1) of that Act, or a matter falling to be investigated by that Board raises the question of whether any such act has been done, then if it appears to the Secretary of State, or the Board, that the act is one in respect of which a complaint of unfair dismissal has been presented to an industrial tribunal, or in respect of which a complaint could be so presented (or could have been so presented if the requirements of industrial tribunal regulations relating to it has been complied with), and that a complaint so presented to an industrial tribunal has not been dismissed by virtue of any provision contained in or made under paragraphs 9 to 13 of the First Schedule to the Trade Union and Labour Relations Act 1974 or (as the case may be) would not fall, or have fallen, to be so dismissed, the Secretary of State, or the Board, will not proceed any further under the Race Relations Act 1968 in relation to that act,[2] except that if on determining a complaint of unfair dismissal an industrial tribunal has recorded a finding that the dismissal was unfair and also that the reason or one of the reasons for the dismissal was the complainant's colour, race or ethnic or national origins, then the

Secretary of State, or the Race Relations Board, may proceed for
the purpose of securing a written assurance against a repetition of
that action, or may proceed under that Act in consequence of
forming an opinion, or receiving a report, that a written assurance
so secured has been broken.[3]

[1] In this paragraph references to the "Race Relations Board" are constituted as including any conciliation committee constituted under the Race
Relations Act 1968 and any other body of persons to whom a matter could
be referred for investigation under Schs. 2 and 3 to that Act. Trade Union
and Labour Relations Act 1974, Sch. 1, para. 28 (4).

[2] Trade Union and Labour Relations Act 1974, Sch. 1, para. 28 (1).

[3] *Ibid.*, Sch. 1, para. 28 (2). The Secretary of State and the Board may so
proceed notwithstanding any limitation imposed by the Race Relations Act
1968 as to the time within which anything may be done under that Act;
*ibid.*, Sch. 1, para 28 (3).

The Race Relations Bill which, if enacted is intended to
repeal the Race Relations Act 1968, follows the form of, and
where possible is framed in similar terms to, the Sex Discrimination
Act 1975.[1]

[1] The Bill is discussed in the form in which it was brought from the
House of Commons on 9th July 1976. See p.    , above for a discussion of the
Sex Discrimination Act 1975. The machinery proposed by the Bill is very similar
to that set up by the 1975 statute.

Discrimination for the purpose of the Bill is defined in Clause I
in like form to that used in section 1 of the Sex Discrimination
Act 1975. Such discrimination takes place if on racial grounds a
person treats another less favourably than he treats or would treat
other persons, or he applies to that other a requirement or condition which he applies or would apply equally to persons not
of the same racial group as that other, but which is such that the
proportion of persons of the same racial group as that other who
can comply with it is considerably smaller than the proportion of
persons not of that racial group who can comply with it, and
which he cannot show to be justifiable irrespective of the colour,
race, nationality or ethnic or national origins of the person to
whom it is applied and which is to the detriment of that other
because he cannot comply with it.[1] Segregating a person from
other persons on racial grounds is treating him less favourably
than they are treated for this purpose.[2] "Racial grounds" means
any of the following grounds, namely colour, race, nationality or

ethnic or national origins and "racial group" means a group of
persons defined by reference to colour, race, nationality or ethnic
or national origins and references to a person's racial group refer
to any racial group into which he falls.[3] There are special provisions
relating to discrimination by way of victimisation[4] and Part II of
the Bill relates to discrimination in the employment field rather like
Part II of the Sex Discrimination Act 1975. Discrimination by
employers is defined in appropriate terms[5] and there are a small
number of exceptions for genuine occupational qualifications.[6]
There are similar provisions to those in the Sex Discrimination
Act 1975 relating to discrimination against contract workers,[7]
partnership,[8] trade unions,[9] qualifying bodies,[10] vocational training bodies,[11] employment agencies[12] and the police.[13] For obvious
reasons there are differing stipulations relating to an exception for
employment intended to provide training in skills to be exercised
outside Great Britain[14] and seamen recruited abroad.[15]

[1] Race Relations Bill, Cl. 1 (2).
[2] *Ibid.*, cl. 1 (2).
[3] *Ibid.*, cl. 3 (1).
[4] *Ibid.*, cl. 2 (1).
[5] *Ibid.*, cl. 4.
[6] *Ibid.*, cl. 5.
[7] *Ibid.*, cl. 7.
[8] *Ibid.*, cl. 10.
[9] *Ibid.*, cl. 11.
[10] *Ibid.*, cl. 12.
[11] *Ibid.*, cl. 13.
[12] *Ibid.*, cl. 14.
[13] *Ibid.*, cl. 16.
[14] *Ibid.*, cl. 6.
[15] *Ibid.*, cl. 9.

There are clauses dealing with discriminatory practices,[1]
instructions to discriminate,[2] pressure to discriminate,[3] the liability
of employers and principals[4] and aiding unlawful acts,[15] which
are similar in form to those in the Sex Discrimination Act 1975,
amended as appropriate.[6] Exceptions relate to charities,[7] the special
needs of racial groups with regard to education, training and
welfare[8] and the provision of education or training for persons
not ordinarily resident in Great Britain.[9] Other exceptions concern
discriminatory training by certain bodies,[10] sports and com-
petitions,[11] indirect access to benefits,[12] acts done under statutory
authority[13] and the Bill would not render unlawful acts done for

the purpose of safeguarding national security.[14]

1 Race Relations Bill, cl. 28.
2 *Ibid.*, cl. 30.
3 *Ibid.*, cl. 31.
4 *Ibid.*, cl. 32.
5 *Ibid.*, cl. 33.
6 *Ibid.*, cl. 29 relating to discriminatory advertisements differs more markedly in form from the provisions of its precursor in the Sex Discrimination Act 1975 although it is likely to be similar in effect.
7 Race Relations Bill, cl. 34.
8 *Ibid.*, cl. 35.
9 *Ibid.*, cl. 36.
10 *Ibid.*, cl. 37.
11 *Ibid.*, cl. 39.
12 *Ibid.*, cl. 40.
13 *Ibid.*, cl. 41.
14 *Ibid.*, cl. 42.

The Bill if enacted will give statutory authority to the Commission for Racial Equality which has features much like those of the Equal Opportunities Commission.[1]

1 Race Relations Bill, cl. 43.

A person who claims that another has committed an act of discrimination against him which is unlawful by virtue of Part II of the Bill is able to present a complaint to an industrial tribunal.[1] If the tribunal finds that the complaint is well founded it should make such of, an order declaring the rights of the complainant and respondent, an order requiring the respondent to pay compensation and a recommendation that the respondent takes, within a specified period, action appearing to the tribunal to be practicable for the purpose of obviating or reducing the adverse effect on the complainant or any act discrimination to which the complaint relates, as it considers just and equitable.[2] The provision as to compensation is very like that of the Sex Discrimination Act 1975.[3] The award is subject to the limit imposed by paragraph 20 of the First Schedule to the Trade Union and Labour Relations Act 1974[4] and the same limit applies where compensation falls to be awarded in respect of any act under both the Sex Discrimination Act 1975 and the provisions of the Bill.[5]

1 Race Relations Bill, cl. 54.
2 *Ibid.*, cl. 56 (1).

[3] *Ibid.*, cl. 56 (1) (*b*) and cl. 57.
[4] *Ibid.*, cl. 56 (2).
[5] *Ibid.*, cl. 56 (3).

The Commission for Racial Equality has powers of investigation[1] and may issue non-discrimination notices.[2] Help for aggrieved persons is provided for[3] and in certain cases the Commission may assist persons in connection with a complaint or prospective complaint.[4] There is a question and reply procedure similar to that in the Sex Discrimination Act 1975.[5]

[1] Race Relations Bill, cl. 48. It is also empowered to issue Codes of Practice. Such a Code is admissible in evidence before an industrial tribunal and if any of its provisions appear to the tribunal to be relevant to any question arising in the proceedings it should be taken into account by the tribunal, *ibid.*, cl. 47.
[2] *Ibid.*, cl. 58.
[3] *Ibid.*, cl. 65.
[4] *Ibid.*, cl. 66.
[5] *Ibid.*, cl. 65.

If enacted in its present form, the Bill will amend the Employment Protection Act 1975, section 72,[1] which deals with dismissals in respect of which there may be a higher additional award of compensation, so that the reference to a dismissal which is an unlawful act of discrimination by virtue of section 3 (1) of the Race Relations Act 1968 is replaced by reference to a dismissal which is an act of discrimination within the meaning of the new Act, which is unlawful by virtue of that Act. A new section 77 of the Employment Protection Act 1975 will be substituted which in effect provides that matters will be taken into account only once when compensation is awarded under the Employment Protection Act 1975 and in addition under either, or both, the Sex Discrimination Act 1975, or the new act.[2] An appeal will lie to the Employment Appeal Tribunal on a question of law arising from any decision of, or in any proceedings before, an industrial tribunal under, or by virtue of, the new act, in addition to the statutes specified in section 88 (1) of the Employment Protection Act 1975.[3]

[1] Race Relations Bill, Sch. 3. For Employment Protection Act 1975, s. 72 (3), see p. 350, above.
[2] *Ibid.*, Sch. 3, para. 1 (3). See pp. 355 and 371, above.
[3] *Ibid.*, Sch. 3, para. 1 (4). See p. 420, above.

## Appendix 11 Racial discrimination

Some dismissals which were acts of racial discrimination have been dealt with under the unfair dismissal provisions since their introduction and the most likely effect of the Bill, if it is enacted, so far as industrial tribunals are concerned, is to bring before them cases of racial discrimination not amounting to dismissal and of discrimination on appointment and recruitment of employees.

# INDEX

509

# Index

BREACH—*cont.*
damages, remedy of, 143, 153–157, 388
equitable remedies, 157–159

BUILDING CONTRACTORS,
contract of service, 5–6

BUSINESS,
change of ownership of,
continuity of employment and, 217, 220, 240–241
Crown servant, transfer of functions to, 223
effect of, 221–223
meaning of, 217–221, 240
redundancy payments where, 217, 218, 219, 240
re-engagement or renewal, offer of, 212–213, 221–223
definition of, 178
sale or closure of, payments on, 375


CENTRAL ARBITRATION COMMITTEE,
reference to, under Equal Pay Act, 27
terms and conditions, award as to, 54, 272

CHECK-LIST,
dismissal, on,
employee, for, 439
employer, for, 438
engagement, on, 435
service agreement, on preparation of, 436

CIVIL SERVANTS. *See also* CROWN
Contracts of Employment Act, not subject to, 95, 138

CODE OF PRACTICE,
appeals procedure, 330, 331
Disciplinary Practice and Procedures, on, 329, 475*n.*
evidence before tribunal, admissible as, 328, 329, 330, 389
failure to observe provisions of, 328, 329
grievance procedure, 331, 473*n.*
time off work, as to, 85, 87
unfair dismissal, as to, 312, 324, 327, 328–334
warnings, 330, 332–334

COLLECTIVE AGREEMENTS,
collective bargaining, 386
guarantee payment scheme,
exclusion from, where, 71

COLLECTIVE AGREEMENTS—*cont.*
incorporation of, into contract of employment, 53–54
legally enforceable, whether, 53
statement of written particulars, form of, 462
changes, notice of, 467

COMMISSION,
clause providing for, by reference to turnover, 449
secret, employee to account for, 110

COMPANY. *See also* CORPORATIONS
capital transfer tax, 377
contract of employment, form of, 6
corporation tax, 375–377
director, 15–16
receiver, appointment of, 151, 205, 262
shares, transfer of, of former employee, 376
winding up of, 151, 203, 205, 262, 380*n.*

COMPENSATION,
basic award,
calculation of, 351–354
reduction of, 351, 354
two weeks' pay, 351, 354
benefits, recoupment of, 365
compensatory award,
benefits, loss of expected, 354, 362
expenses incurred, 354, 361, 362
losses taken into account, 354–362
manner of dismissal, 357
mitigation of loss, 355, 363
payments taken into account, 362
pension schemes, losses in respect of, 358–361
reduction of, 355, 362–363, 364
review of decision, 364
wages, loss of, 356, 357, 370
wrongful dismissal, damages for, effect on, 370, 371
composite claims, 40*n.*, 355, 365, 368–373
Equal Pay Act, under, 26
loss of office, for, 362, 377–379
racial discrimination, where, 505, 506
reasons for dismissal, where no statement of, 152
Redundancy Payments Statutory Compensation Regulations, 1965, 246
re-engagement or reinstatement, where no, 349–350, 366
Sex Discrimination Act, under, 39–40, 350, 370

# Index

HOUSE OF COMMONS,
staff, unfair dismissal provisions applicable to, 285

HUSBAND,
employer, of,
redundancy payments not made to, 166
unfair dismissal provisions not applicable, 275
written particulars of terms not required, 92, 98

IMMIGRATION ACT 1971,
restrictions on entry of non-patrials, 18

IMPLIED TERM,
contract of employment, in, 2
notice of termination, as to, 133
sickness, for payment during, 72–73

INDEPENDENT CONTRACTORS,
contract for services, with, 17, 27

INDEX OF RETAIL PRICES,
salary, variation of, by reference to, 450

INDUSTRIAL ACTION. *See* LOCK-OUT, STRIKE
pressure on employer to dismiss unfairly, 45, 337–338, 355
unfair dismissal in connection with, 316–318

INDUSTRIAL RELATIONS ACT 1971,
Code of Practice, 328, 329
repeal of, 274

INDUSTRIAL TRIBUNAL,
appeal from, 413, 420–434, 498. *See also* APPEAL
appearance, notice of, 396–397
application, originating, 390–395. *See also* APPLICATION
award by, 411, 412
chairman of, 388, 402, 408
Code of Practice admissible in evidence before, 328, 329, 330, 389
complaint to,
consult as to redundancies, failure to, 265–267
Equal Pay Act, under, 26
guarantee payments, of non-payment of, 71
insolvency, where failure to make .payments on, 383
maternity pay, of non-payment of, 77, 78, 80

INDUSTRIAL TRIBUNAL—*cont.*
racial discrimination, of, 505
reasons for dismissal, where no statement of, 152
rebate of maternity pay, of non-payment of, 80
Sex Discrimination Act, under, 39
suspension on medical grounds, where non-payment for, 63
time off work refused, where, 87, 89, 90, 271, 272
trade union membership and activities, as to, 44
unfair dismissal, of, 274, 338–346, 391, 410
exclusion of right, 283–204
composition of, 388
conciliation officers,
communications, privileged, to, 387, 406–407
copy of complaints to, 386, 396
no proceedings in, where action by, 387
continuation of contract of employment, order for, 344–346
costs, award of, 409
death of party, 256, 411–412
decision of, 413
review of, 364, 413, 414–419, 423
revocation or variation of, 414
execution of decisions of, 390
hearing, 403–409. *See also* PROCEDURE
interim relief, application for, to, 343–344, 389
interlocutory matters, 397–402. *See also* PROCEDURE
jurisdiction, scope of, 388, 395*n*.
legal aid and advice, 390
members of, 388
prerogative orders, 423
procedure. *See* PROCEDURE
protective award, 265–267, 379, 380, 412
redundancy payments,
claim relating to, 161, 172, 251–252
rebate from Redundancy Fund, 257, 259, 263, 268
re-engagement, order for, 344, 346, 347–350
reference to,
pay statement, as regards itemised, 55–56
written statement of particulars, as to, 108–109
reinstatement, order for, 344, 346, 347–350
representation at hearing, 404, 405, 411

517

527

Printed by Thomson Litho Ltd, East Kilbride, Scotland